Handbook of
20th Century
Quotations

Handbook of
20th Century
Quotations

Compiled and edited by Frank S Pepper

Sphere Study Aids

Sphere Books Ltd.
30–32 Gray's Inn Road
London WC1X 8JL

First published 1984
Copyright © Frank S. Pepper 1984

Reproduced, printed and bound in Great Britain by
Hazell Watson & Viney Ltd., Aylesbury, Bucks

Phototypeset in Great Britain by
C. Leggett & Son Ltd, Mill Green Road, Mitcham, Surrey

This book is sold subject to the condition that it shall not, by way of trade or
otherwise, be lent, re-sold, hired out, or otherwise circulated without the
publisher's prior consent in any form of binding or cover other than that in which it
is published and without a similar condition including this condition being imposed
on the subsequent purchaser.

Preface

In 1922, when I was twelve, I made my first attempt át writing for money. I sent a paragraph to the *Daily News* and they paid me half-a-crown for it, which was a lot of money in those days, especially to a schoolboy. Obviously I had struck a goldmine. From that time on I was hooked. I was going to be a writer and make a fortune. It didn't quite work out. Nobody told me about beginner's luck. It was four years before I earned my next half-a-crown.

After Matriculation my parents wanted me to go to university, but hearing that Arthur Mee, editor of *Children's Newspaper* and *Children's Encyclopedia*, needed an office boy, I got myself the job, in the firm belief, which future experience did nothing to change, that a few years with Arthur Mee would teach me more about becoming a professional journalist than any university.

I stayed with Arthur Mee for five years, learning my craft. Of all the many things I learnt from my experience on that side of the editorial fence I think the single most valuable lesson was that 'writer' and 'author' are not synonyms. Anyone with a feel for words can be taught to write well enough to get into print. But it's what you write about that counts. A talent for writing is about 10% of the craft. What one is in business to sell is not writing, but ideas.

By 1930 I felt that I knew enough about the trade of giving editors what they wanted and turned freelance. Since then, until semi-retirement a few years ago, I averaged a weekly output of 20,000 words, fact and fiction, for dozens of journals and magazines, under ten pen names [see 131:12, my only claim to fame (being sent up by *Punch* I mean)]. Wrote four non-fiction hardbacks for Nelson's. Was finishing the fifth, on the then new topic of television, when there came that bit of bother with the person Winston Churchill called "that bloodthirsty little guttersnipe". Alexandra Palace shut down abruptly in the middle of a Mickey Mouse film and we all went off to war. I tied a portable typewriter to my kitbag, and managed to knock out a short story every couple of weeks or so.

In 1938 I suggested to Reg Eves, editor of a boys' paper called *Champion*, a series of stories about a fighter pilot called *Rockfist*

Rogan. He said he couldn't see much future in it, but commissioned 13 instalments. It ran in weekly episodes for 22 years.

When the paper shortage ended a few years after the war was over American imports had created a market for picture-strip stories. Eves was instructed to produce a rival to *Eagle*. He called me in to devise a character to match *Dan Dare* saying "We've got to have science fiction on the cover. I know nothing about it and am not in the least interested in it. You've got a free hand to do whatever you like – so long as it's successful". I came up with a character called *Captain Condor*. He ran for 12 years.

Two years later Eves launched a picture-strip paper called *Tiger*. It was to specialise in sport. This time my briefing from Reg Eves was "I need a football story for the front page. I want something that will run for years". I produced a character called *Roy of the Rovers*, who is running to this day, although it is now some years since I did a weekly stint on him.

Because I have been, as a writer, so many different people, turning out so many different kinds of work, I have needed to amass a huge quantity of reference material – so much, in fact, that it is now housed in a barn.

It was always my ambition, one day, when I had the time, to use this collection as a source from which to compile some entertaining anthologies. The *Handbook of Twentieth-Century Quotations* is the first of them.

Frank S. Pepper
February 1984

Foreword

All of us come across, what we ourselves at least, consider to be potential quotations. Our minds filter out snippets of curious or preposterous conversation (which, because of the nature of life, often remain unresolved and seemingly unresolvable), or we start at printed lines that seem particularly apposite or profound. These and many other phrases we have every intention of preserving and may even record on scraps of paper or in obscure parts of current diaries – never to be found again. – What discipline, then, is needed to maintain a catalogued collection of contemporary quotations over a period of fifty years! Mr. Pepper has collected some 20,000 quotations during that time and this book of over 6,000 has been taken from that collection.

On the whole these are not quotations that will be found in other quotation books on the market. Many are now too familiar to bear further repetition and of others, it's too early to tell if they'll survive. Potential survival indeed is not even a prerequisite for inclusion here: this is meant to be a kaleidoscope of impressions from our recent past through which we hope you will make your own trails, aided by the subject alphabeticalisation – which is intended to make browsing more illuminating. The juxtaposition of similar quotations by very different sorts of people or of quotations that directly contradict each other, where they would have stood unchallenged on their own, are thrown into a harsher light.

The more usual index by keyword would not have the value it attains in the 'classical' quotation dictionaries, but an index of names at the end of the book allows reference by both quoter and quoted. From here too one can be led to bizarrerie: "I got the blues" comes strange from D. H. Lawrence – and stranger the cure – making marmalade. Or try Nancy Reagan's "A woman is like a tea bag" (see 347:5 to find out why). Who do you suppose looked "as if he had been weaned on a pickle"? (His "really notable talent" was that "he slept more than any other President", and when Dorothy Parker was told of his death remarked, famously, "Why I never even knew that he was alive.") (79:18–20). Clement Attlee also attracted barbed insults, there are many here, but the best is "An empty taxi drew up outside No. 10

and out got Clem Attlee.'' Trying to outwit Noël Coward may seem like foolishness but Edna Ferber did very well (81:23). And Kenneth Tynan is not to be put upon by anyone either (8:9). You might instead, like to use the book as a compendium of useful advice. Go straight to 40:9 if you want to find out how to read in bed without getting cold. And if you *are* reading in bed why not try wearing a colander (40:12)? Lord Carrington, too, (91:15) offers a personal tip that might prove useful in a crisis.

But quotations do not have to be amusing or insulting to be successful – in the hands of master writers only a few words are needed to instil the emotion they aim for (163:1, 244:6, 319:11).
Editor
Sphere Study Aids
February 1984

Contents

Handbook of
20th Century
Quotations

A

ABDICATION

1 God grant him peace and happiness but never understanding of what he has lost.
Stanley Baldwin of Edward VIII's abdication.

2 I have found it impossible to carry the heavy burden of responsibility and to discharge my duties as King as I would wish to do, without the help and support of the woman I love.
Edward VIII. Abdication speech 11 Dec 1936.

3 Are they going to chop off Uncle David's head?
Princess Margaret, on hearing of the abdication. Quoted Marion Crawford, THE LITTLE PRINCESSES

4 68 is no age to give up your job.
Queen Mary on hearing of the abdication of Queen Wilhelmina of Holland. Quoted Peter Lane, OUR FUTURE KING

ABILITY

5 The finest plans have always been spoiled by the littleness of them that should carry them out. Even emperors can't do it all by themselves.
Bertolt Brecht, MOTHER COURAGE AND HER CHILDREN 1939

6 Time goes by: reputation increases, ability declines.
Dag Hammarskjöld, MARKINGS 1964

7 And skill's a joy to any man.
John Masefield, THE EVERLASTING MERCY 1911

8 Intelligence is quickness to apprehend as distinct from ability, which is capacity to act wisely on the thing apprehended.
A. N. Whitehead, DIALOGUES

ABNORMALITY

9 If it weren't for the fact that all of us are slightly abnormal there wouldn't be any point in giving each person a separate name.
Ugo Betti, THE FUGITIVE 1953

10 *Abnormal, adj.* Not conforming to standard. In matters of thought and conduct, to be independent is to be abnormal, to be abnormal is to be detested.
Ambrose Bierce, THE DEVIL'S DICTIONARY 1906

11 Life is an abnormal business.
Eugene Ionesco, RHINOCEROS 1959

12 She cut off her nipples with garden shears. You call that normal?
Elizabeth Taylor. Line spoken to Marlon Brando in REFLECTIONS IN A GOLDEN EYE (film)

ABORTION

13 Abortion leads to an appalling trivialisation of the act of procreation.
Dr. Donald Coggan, when Archbishop of York. Speech to Shaftesbury Society 2 Oct 1973

14 You ought to be ashamed, I said, to look so antique / (And her only Thirty-one). / I can't help it she said, pulling a long face / It's them pills I took to bring it off, she said / (She's had five already, and nearly died of young George) / The chemist said it would be all right, but I've never been the same / You're a proper fool, I said.
T. S. Eliot, THE WASTE LAND, A Game of Chess 1922

15 Abortion is a step beyond contraception. They both control or interfere with birth. I don't see how anyone who favours contraception or considers it permissible can object to abortion.
Dr. Oscar Fasker. Quoted Edward F. Murphy, MACMILLAN TREASURY OF RELEVANT QUOTATIONS

16 We cannot treat the human embryo as cheap and worthless without passing

judgment on all human life, including our own.
Monica Furlong, CHRISTIAN UNCERTAINTIES

1 If men could get pregnant, abortion would be a sacrament.
Florynce Kennedy. Quoted Barbara Rowe, THE BOOK OF QUOTES

2 Sadie said: "How does she manage it?" and Aunt Emily said: "Skiing or hunting, or just jumping off the kitchen table."
Nancy Mitford, THE PURSUIT OF LOVE 1945

3 It serves me right for putting all my eggs in one bastard.
Dorothy Parker, on having an abortion

4 The greatest destroyer of peace is abortion because if a mother can kill her own child what is left for me to kill you and you to kill me? There is nothing between.
Mother Teresa, Nobel Peace Prize Lecture 1979

5 As one priest gloomily admitted, if they really accepted the conception argument, then they ought to spend their time baptising the menstrual flow.
Katharine Whitehorn, Observer, *Our bodies, Ourselves and Them* 15 Jul 1979

6 Abortion is the worst approach to the problem of birth control because it puts all the responsibility on women.
Shirley Williams, interviewed by Miriam Gross, Observer 22 Mar 1981

ABSENCE

7 I was courtmartialled in my absence, and sentenced to death in my absence, so I said they could shoot me in my absence.
Brendan Behan, THE HOSTAGE 1959

8 Absence blots people out. We really have no absent friends.
Elizabeth Bowen, DEATH OF THE HEART 1938

9 Absence and letters are the forcing ground of love. What renews it and confirms it is presence and bed.
Gerald Brenan, THOUGHTS IN A DRY SEASON 1979

10 That which you love most in him (a friend) may be clearer in his absence.
Kahil Gibran, THE PROPHET 1923

11 Where you used to be there is a hole in the world which I find myself constantly walking round in the daytime and falling into at night. I miss you like hell.
Edna St. Vincent Millay, LETTERS 1952

12 But when he's gone / Me and them lonesome blues collide / The bed's too big / The frying pan's too wide.
Joni Mitchell, MY OLD MAN (*song*)

13 A cry of Absence, Absence in the heart / And in the wood the furious winter blowing.
John Crowe Ransome, SELECTED POEMS, *Winter Remembered* 1945

ABSENTMINDEDNESS

14 That Greek one then is my hero, who watched the bath water / Rise above his navel and rushed out naked. "I found it / I found it" into the street in all his shining, and forgot / That others would only stare at his genitals.
Dannie Abse, WALKING UNDER WATER, *Letter to Alex Comfort*

15 I liked the store detective who said he'd seen a lot of people who were so confused that they'd stolen things, but never one so confused that they'd paid twice.
Baroness Phillips, Sunday Telegraph 14 Aug 1977

16 The Reverend Eli Jenkins finds a rhyme and dips a pen in his cocoa.
Dylan Thomas, UNDER MILK WOOD 1954

ABSOLUTE

17 In this unbelievable universe in which we live there are no absolutes. Even parallel lines, reaching into infinity, meet somewhere yonder.
Pearl S. Buck, A BRIDGE FOR PASSING 1962

ABSTINENCE

18 One reason I don't drink is that I want to know when I am having a good time.
Nancy Astor

19 When a reformed drunkard gives advice you don't just hear it, you see it.
Dr. Seldon Bacon, Chairman Connecticut Commission on Alcoholism. Quoted News Review 24 Jun 1948

20 *Abstainer:* a weak person who yields to the temptation of denying himself a pleasure.
Ambrose Bierce, THE DEVIL'S DICTIONARY 1906

1 *Total abstainer:* one who abstains from everything but abstention, and especially from inactivity in the affairs of others.
Id.

2 Half the vices which the world condemns most loudly have seeds of good in them and require moderate use rather than total abstinence.
Samuel Butler, THE WAY OF ALL FLESH 1903

3 Teetotallers lack the sympathy and generosity of men that drink.
W. H. Davies, Introduction to SHORTER LYRICS OF THE 20TH CENTURY

4 My stories written when sober are stupid.
F. Scott Fitzgerald

5 Abstinence is the thin edge of the pledge.
Graffito. Quoted Nigel Rees, GRAFFITI RULES O.K. 1979

6 He drank like a fish, if drinking nothing but water could be so described.
A. E. Housman

7 Abstemiousness can be a form of self-indulgence.
Malcolm Muggeridge, CHRONICLES OF WASTED TIME, *The Infernal Grove* 1972

8 An abstainer is the sort of man you wouldn't want to drink with even if he did.
George Jean Nathan

9 It ought to give pause to the most fanatical teetotaller that the only humans worth saving in the Flood were a family of vintners.
Dr. Bernard Rudofsky, NOW I LAY ME DOWN TO EAT

10 The people who are regarded as moral luminaries are those who forgo ordinary pleasures themselves and find compensation in interfering with the pleasures of others.
Bertrand Russell, SCEPTICAL ESSAYS

11 Self denial is not a virtue, it is only the effect of prudence on rascality.
George Bernard Shaw, MAN AND SUPERMAN 1905

12 He'll probably never write a good play again.
George Bernard Shaw of Eugene O'Neill on hearing he was giving up drinking. Quoted Arthur and Barbara Gelb, O'NEILL

13 A lady temperance candidate concluded her passionate oration "I would rather commit adultery than take a glass of beer." Whereupon a clear voice from the audience asked "Who wouldn't?"
Adlai Stevenson

ABSTRACT

14 The utmost abstractions are the true weapons with which to control our thought of concrete fact.
A. N. Whitehead, SCIENCE AND THE MODERN WORLD 1925

ABSURD

15 I have a fine sense of the ridiculous, but no sense of humour.
Edward Albee, WHO'S AFRAID OF VIRGINIA WOOLF? 1962

16 There is always something absurd about the past.
Max Beerbohm, AND EVEN NOW

17 The absurd has meaning only in so far as it is not agreed to.
Albert Camus, THE MYTH OF SISYPHUS 1942

18 As an absurdity it was so colossal that it took on the air of a great truth.
William Cooper, SCENES FROM PROVINCIAL LIFE

19 As a man is so's his God; this word / Explains why God's so often absurd.
Giles and Melville Harcourt, SHORT PRAYERS FOR THE LONG DAY 1978

20 The world is so overflowing with absurdity that it is difficult for the humorist to compete.
Malcolm Muggeridge on becoming editor of Punch

21 What I try to do in my plays is to get this recognisable reality of the absurdity of what we do and how we behave and how we speak.
Harold Pinter. Quoted Martin Esslin, THE THEATRE OF THE ABSURD

22 Life is full of infinite absurdities, which strangely enough, do not even need to appear plausible, since they are true.
Luigi Pirandello, SIX CHARACTERS IN SEARCH OF AN AUTHOR 1921

23 The more absurd life is, the more insupportable death is.
Jean-Paul Sartre, THE WORDS

ABUSE

1 To hell with you. Offensive letter follows.
Anonymous telegram sent to Sir Alec Douglas-Home

2 I very rarely indulge in abusive epithets, and when I used the word stupidity I meant what I said.
Stanley Baldwin, House of Commons 25 Oct 1926

3 Go on, abuse me — your own husband that took you off the streets on a Sunday morning when there wasn't a pub open in the city.
Brendan Behan, THE HOSTAGE 1958

4 To abuse a man is a lover-like thing and gives him rights.
Joyce Cary, HERSELF SURPRISED 1941

5 Abuse is in order, but it is best if it is supported by argument.
Robin Day as chairman of Election Call, BBC Radio 13 *Apr* 1979

6 No one can be as calculatedly rude as the British, which amazes Americans, who do not understand studied insult and can only offer abuse as a substitute.
Paul Gallico, New York Times 14 *Jan* 1962

7 Among the working classes one of the unforgivable words of abuse is 'bastard' — because they take bastardy seriously.
Robert Graves, OCCUPATION: WRITER

8 Had your father spent more of your mother's immoral earnings on your education you would not even then have been a gentleman.
Seymour Hicks, VINTAGE YEARS

9 It is not for nothing that, in the English language alone, to accuse someone of trying to be funny is highly abusive.
Malcolm Muggeridge, TREAD SOFTLY FOR YOU TREAD ON MY JOKES 1966

10 A. E. Housman kept a little notebook in which he jotted down hurtful and disparaging phrases as they occurred to him. He applied the phrases later when suitable enemies presented themselves.
Quoted Frank Muir, THE FRANK MUIR BOOK

11 When political ammunition runs low, inevitably the rusty artillery of abuse is always wheeled into action.
Adlai Stevenson. Speech, New York 22 *Sep* 1952

12 "He called me a muddle-headed old ass" he said. "Well you are a muddle-headed old ass," I pointed out, quick as a flash, and he seemed to see the justice of this.
P. G. Wodehouse, PIGS HAVE WINGS 1952

ACCENT

13 My mother came from Nashville, Tennessee, and try as she might she couldn't obliterate her accent. Just like Margaret Thatcher. Just like Ted Heath.
Lord Hailsham. Quoted Observer 18 *Oct* 1981

ACCEPTANCE

14 Ah, when to the heart of man / Was it ever less than a treason / To go with the drift of things / To yield with a grace to reason / And bow and accept at the end / Of a love or season.
Robert Frost, RELUCTANCE 1913

ACCIDENT

15 An act of God was defined as something which no reasonable man could have expected.
A. P. Herbert, UNCOMMON LAW 1935

16 "I knew a rent collector that fell down in a pub and stabbed himself in the heart with his own pencil" says Dagswood.
Gerald Kersh, THE NINE LIVES OF BILL NELSON 1941

17 so unlucky / that he runs into accidents / which started out to happen / to somebody else.
Don Marquis, ARCHY'S LIFE OF MEHITABEL 1933

18 A hole is nothing at all, but you can break your neck in it.
Austin O'Malley

19 It is the overtakers who keep the undertakers busy.
William Pitts. Quoted Observer 27 *Dec* 1963

ACCLAIM

20 It took him twenty years to become an overnight sensation.
Milton Berle of Phil Silvers in the show TOP BANANAS

21 I have myself a constitutional dislike to limelight, which often disfigures that which

it is intended to adorn.
Viscount Harcourt. Speech, Corona Club
18 Jun 1912

1 Glory is largely a theatrical concept. There is no striving for glory without a vivid awareness of an audience.
Eric Hoffer, THE TRUE BELIEVER 1951

2 They gave me star treatment because I was making a lot of money. But I was just as good when I was poor.
Bob Marley, Radio Times 18 Sep 1981

ACCOMPLISHMENT

3 It is all very well to be able to write books, but can you waggle your ears?
J. M. Barrie, who could, to H. G. Wells, who couldn't. Quoted J. A. Hamerton,
BARRIE: THE STORY OF A GENIUS 1929

4 I know a girl who can tie a knot in the stalk of a cherry with her tongue.
A. A. Milne, NOT THAT IT MATTERS, *Golden Fruit* 1919

5 I used to have a cousin who could open a beer bottle with his teeth. That was his only accomplishment, all he could do — he was just a human bottle-opener. And then one day, at a wedding party, he broke his front teeth off!
Tennessee Williams, A STREETCAR NAMED DESIRE 1947

6 One of his [Sir R. Baden-Powell's] accomplishments is to draw a picture with his left hand and shade it at the same time with his right hand.
Marcus Woodward, John o'London's Weekly 1929

ACHIEVEMENT

7 Achievement is the end of endeavour and the beginning of disgust.
Ambrose Bierce

8 The lizard that essayed to become a crocodile burst at the moment of attainment.
Ernest Bramah, KAI LUNG UNROLLS HIS MAT 1928

9 If there are obstacles, the shortest line between two points may be the crooked one.
Bertolt Brecht, GALILEO 1938

10 To reach completion is to return to one's starting point. My instinctive bent, which

takes pleasure in curves and spheres and circles.
Colette, reputed last words 1954

11 Few who reach the summit can be acquitted of vanity or conceit.
Sir John Colville, THE CHURCHILLIANS 1982

12 Happiness is in the imagination. What we perform, is always inferior to what we imagine.
Cyril Connolly, THE UNQUIET GRAVE 1948

13 People love chopping wood. In this activity one immediately sees results.
Albert Einstein. Quoted Carl Seelig,
ALBERT EINSTEIN

14 Only the mediocre are always at their best.
Graffito. Quoted BBC Radio 4, *Quote Unquote* 29 May 1980

15 To stretch the octave twixt the dream and deed. Ah, that's the thrill.
Richard le Gullienne, THE DECADENT TO HIS SOUL

16 Those who believe that they are exclusively in the right are generally those who achieve something.
Aldous Huxley, PROPER STUDIES 1927

17 The achievements which society rewards are won at the cost of diminution of personality.
Carl Jung, PSYCHOLOGICAL REFLECTIONS 1951

18 All struggle has for its end relief or repose.
(Percy) Wyndham Lewis, THE ART OF BEING RULED 1926

19 You can do anything in this world if you are prepared to take the consequences.
W. Somerset Maugham, THE CIRCLE 1921

20 In the past things that men could do were very limited. Bad men, even with the very worst intentions, could do only a very finite amount of harm. Good men, with the very best intentions, could do only a very limited amount of good. But with every increase in knowledge there has been an increase in what men can achieve.
Bertrand Russell, Saturday Evening Post, *The Expanding Mental Universe* 18 Jul 1959

21 Who are the men that do things? The husbands of the shrew and the drunkard, the men with the thorn in the flesh.
George Bernard Shaw, HEARTBREAK HOUSE 1920

1 There are two things to aim at in life; first to get what you want, and, after that, to enjoy it. Only the wisest of mankind achieve the second.
Logan Pearsall Smith, ALL TRIVIA, *Afterthoughts* 1931

2 I am an American and I have lived half my life in Paris, not the half which made me, but the half in which I made what I made.
Gertrude Stein, AN AMERICAN AND FRANCE 1930

3 There are no gains without pains.
Adlai Stevenson, Democratic Convention acceptance speech 26 *Jul* 1952

4 Looking back at the age of eighty-eight I see clearly that I achieved practically nothing. The world today and the history of the human anthill during the last fifty-seven years would be exactly the same if I had played ping pong instead of sitting on committees and writing books and memoranda . . . I must have in a long life ground through between a hundred and fifty thousand and two hundred thousand hours of perfectly useless work.
Leonard Woolf, THE JOURNEY NOT THE ARRIVAL MATTERS

ACQUAINTANCE

5 *Acquaintance:* a degree of friendship called slight when the object is poor or obscure, and intimate when he is rich or famous.
Ambrose Bierce, THE DEVIL'S DICTIONARY 1906

6 It was possible to be acquainted with him [Lord Birkenhead] and to dislike him intensely; it was impossible to know him and not to love him.
Sir Austen Chamberlain. Quoted 2nd Earl of Birkenhead, LIFE OF LORD BIRKENHEAD VOL 2

7 The art of life is to keep down acquaintances. One's friends one can manage but one's acquaintances can be the devil.
E. V. Lucas, OVER BEMERTON'S 1908

8 The intimacy of shipboard, which is due to propinquity rather than any community of taste.
W. Somerset Maugham, RAIN 1921

9 The mere process of growing old together will make the slightest acquaintance seem a bosom friend.
Logan Pearsall Smith, ALL TRIVIA 1931

10 Acquaintanceship stands in the same relation to friendship that a flirtation does to a love affair — exciting but unsatisfying.
Alec Waugh, ON DOING WHAT ONE LIKES

ACTING

11 A year or two ago Ralph Richardson had the habit of acting all his parts with his buttocks. I cured him of this and his Henry V had no backside at all, though it reappeared, and rightly, in his next comic part.
James Agate, EGO I 1935

12 Mr. Ainley played the old codger (Prospero) like a toastmaster celebrating his golden wedding.
James Agate, Sunday Times 1 *Aug* 1934

13 Julie Andrews is like a nun with a switchblade.
Anon. Quoted Leslie Halliwell, FILMGOER'S BOOK OF QUOTES 1973

14 There are lots of methods. Mine involves a lot of talent, a glass, and some cracked ice.
John Barrymore. Quoted Leslie Halliwell, FILMGOER'S BOOK OF QUOTES 1973

15 In *Casablanca* there was often nothing in my face. But the audience put into my face what they thought I was giving.
Ingrid Bergman, MY STORY

16 An actor is a guy who, if you aren't talking about him, isn't listening.
Marlon Brando. Quoted Observer, *Jan* 1956

17 On a fine December day in 1924, as I walked down Hollywood Boulevard towards nowhere in particular, I was down to that essential starting place for all actors. I was broke.
Gary Cooper, Saturday Evening Post, *Well, It Was This Way* 7 *Apr* 1956

18 The general consensus seems to be that I don't act at all.
Id.

19 Acting is not a matter of being somebody else, it's a matter of seeming to be somebody else. — I'd have been a murderess, a suicide and a drunkard if I'd lived all my parts. You've got to stay outside what you're doing.
Gladys Cooper. Quoted Sheridan Morley, Sunday Times 15 *Dec* 1968

1 I've always thought I'd be particularly good in Romeo — as the nurse.
Noël Coward. Quoted William Marchant, THE PLEASURE OF HIS COMPANY

2 Gertie has an astounding sense of the complete reality of the moment and her moments, dictated by the extreme variability of her moods, change so swiftly that it is frequently difficult to discover what, apart from eating, sleeping and acting, is true of her at all.
Noël Coward of Gertrude Lawrence, PRESENT INDICATIVE 1931

3 Why make the effort to learn long and exquisitely written speeches by good authors when "I love you, damn you", and "What about a drink?" succeeded even better among the public and took less time to say?
Daphne Du Maurier, GERALD 1934

4 What are known as 'straight' parts are the most difficult as one has to try to be natural, which is only possible in the bathroom.
Gerald Du Maurier, in a letter to Reginald Pound. Quoted, THEIR MOODS AND MINE 1935

5 The question actors most often get asked is how they can bear saying the same things over and over again, night after night, but God knows what the answer to *that* is, don't we all *anyway*; might as well get paid for it.
Elaine Dundy, THE DUD AVOCADO 1958

6 I may never have been very pretty but I was jolly larky and that's what counts in the theatre. That and being able to act, of course. Nowadays, you know, it's all done by lights and machinery, but I always tell them in film studios that they're not to try to make me look young any more — I just want to look nice.
Dame Edith Evans at 89 in TV Times

7 You spend your life doing something they put people in asylums for.
Jane Fonda. Quoted Leslie Halliwell, FILMGOER'S BOOK OF QUOTES 1973

8 All actors are darlings backstage.
Bamber Gascoigne, FROM FRINGE TO FLYING CIRCUS, *Preface*

9 Work it out in front of the bedroom mirror and astonish us in the morning.
Tyrone Guthrie, advice to an actor at rehearsal

10 Actors and burglars work better at night.
Sir Cedric Hardwicke

11 Julie Andrews has the wonderful British strength that makes you wonder why they lost India.
Moss Hart

12 It is best in the theatre to act with confidence no matter how little right you have to it.
Lillian Hellman, PENTIMENTO

13 Acting isn't a very high class way of making a living, is it?
Katherine Hepburn. Quoted Observer 26 *Jan* 1979

14 He [Rudolf Valentino] had the acting talents of the average wardrobe.
Clyde Jeavons and Jeremy Pascall, A PICTORIAL HISTORY OF SEX IN THE MOVIES

15 Life as an actor is a constant series of equations. You've got to balance your work with how you want to live . . . It's no use playing all the great roles and ending up late in life living in a poky bedsit in Notting Hill Gate with your wife having left you.
Freddie Jones, Radio Times 24 *Mar* 1979

16 The necessary qualifications for a successful actress are, the face of Venus, the figure of Juno, the brains of Minerva, the memory of Macaulay, the chastity of Diana, the grace of Terpsichore, but above and beyond all the *hide* of a rhinoceros.
Dame Madge Kendal, AUTOBIOGRAPHY

17 Joan Crawford is the only actress to read the whole script. Most actresses just read their own lines to find out what clothes they're going to wear.
Anita Loos. Quoted Leslie Halliwell, FILMGOER'S BOOK OF QUOTES 1973

18 All acting is illusion and the last reward therefore disillusion.
J.P. McEvoy, Stage, *Jun* 1941

19 It's extraordinary how they keep young. Actresses I mean. I think it's because they are always playing different parts.
W. Somerset Maugham, THE CIRCLE 1921

20 I played the part of the mad king in *Beau Brummell* exactly the same way as I played Louis XVI in *Marie Antoinette*, but no one noticed. You see, I wore a different wig.
Robert Morley. Quoted Margaret Morley, LARGER THAN LIFE

21 Can you imagine being wonderfully overpaid for dressing up and playing games?
David Niven, in an interview

1 When I cry do you want the tears to run all the way, or shall I stop them half way down?
Margaret O'Brien, child actress, to her director. Quoted Leslie Halliwell, FILMGOER'S BOOK OF QUOTES 1973

2 Acting is not a profession for adults.
Laurence Olivier

3 She ran the whole gamut of the emotions from A to B.
Dorothy Parker of Katherine Hepburn in a Broadway play

4 Alfred Hitchcock was once reported as saying that "actors are like cattle" but he denied this. "What I said was, 'actors should be *treated* like cattle.' "
Nigel Rees, BBC Radio 4, *Quote Unquote*

5 The most precious things in speech are the pauses.
Advice given by Ralph Richardson in an interview

6 Mr. Novello plays the King with all the assurance of a man who has gauged public taste down to the last emotional millimetre.
Milton Shulman, Evening Standard, *reviewing King's Rhapsody* 1949

7 Some of my best leading men have been dogs and horses.
Elizabeth Taylor in an interview with John Higgins, The Times 18 *Feb* 1981

8 Last night Cleopatra barged up the Nile and sank.
Frank Thring, Argus (*Melbourne*)

9 I am quite a good enough critic to know that my performance is not "quite dreadful"; it is, in fact, only slightly less than mediocre. I do not actually exit through the scenery, or wave to my friends in the audience.
Kenneth Tynan, replying to criticism from Beverley Baxter in the Evening Standard of his performance as the Player King in Alex Guinness's production of Hamlet 1949

10 The actor doesn't mind screaming and crying on the stage, but would sooner not do it on the street.
John Updike. Quoted John Heilpern, Observer 25 *Mar* 1979

11 I grew a beard for Nero, in *Quo Vadis*, but Metro-Goldwyn-Mayer thought it didn't look real, so I had to wear a false one.
Peter Ustinov, DEAR ME 1977

12 The only emotion excited was a horrible sort of pity . . . for all the people who live by this terrible compulsion to act, to be applauded, living alone in their bed-sitters, knowing nothing and nobody.
Auberon Waugh of Richard Huggett's one-man show A Talent to Abuse, about Evelyn Waugh, The Times 1 *Aug* 1981

13 Nobody likes my acting except the public.
John Wayne. Quoted obituary, Daily Telegraph 13 *Jun* 1979

14 I learned two things at RADA: first that I couldn't act; second that it didn't matter.
Wilfred Hyde White. Quoted Richard Murdoch, BBC1 TV, *The Old Boy Network* 8 *Oct* 1981

15 Every now and then when you're on the stage, you hear the best sound that a player can hear. It is a sound you can't get in movies or in television. It is the sound of a wonderful deep silence that means you've hit them where they live.
Shelley Winters, Theatre Arts, *Jun* 1956

16 The scenery was beautiful, but the actors got in front of it.
Alexander Woollcott, New Yorker

ACTION

17 Action springs not from thought, but from a readiness for responsibility.
Dietrich Bonhoeffer, LETTERS AND PAPERS FROM PRISON

18 The world can only be grasped by action not by contemplation. The hand is more important than the eye.
Jacob Bronowski, THE ASCENT OF MAN 1973

19 Action is the only reality; not only reality but morality as well.
Abbie Hoffman. Quoted Barbara Rowe, THE BOOK OF QUOTES

20 No action is in itself good or bad, but only such according to convention.
W. Somerset Maugham, A WRITER'S NOTEBOOK 1949

21 Trust the man who hesitates in his speech and is quick and steady in action, but beware of long arguments and long beards.
George Santayana, SOLILOQUIES IN ENGLAND 1922

22 Nothing is ever done in this world until men are prepared to kill one another if it is not done.
George Bernard Shaw, MAJOR BARBARA 1905

1 From the moment of birth we are immersed in action, and can only fitfully guide it by taking thought.
A. N. Whitehead, SCIENCE AND THE MODERN WORLD 1925

2 It does not matter what men say in words, so long as their activities are controlled by settled instincts.
Id.

ACTIVITY

3 You've been a busy bugger, haven't you?
George V to Capt. Billy Bishop V C, air ace of World War 1

4 Men rushing around the office with their paper cups of coffee, like conscripts carrying their urine samples.
Malcolm Glask, Punch, *Portrait of New York* 18 *Aug* 1976

5 I got the blues thinking of the future, so I left off and made some marmalade. It's amazing how it cheers one up to shred oranges.
D. H. Lawrence, LETTERS 1932

6 He had given, for a time, a tremendously effective impression, which turned out on closer inspection to be only activity.
Bernard Levin, of Harold Wilson, THE PENDULUM YEARS 1976

ADAPTATION

7 Human creatures have a marvellous power of adapting themselves to necessity.
George Gissing, THE PRIVATE PAPERS OF HENRY RYECROFT 1903

8 Remember that cartoon of a couple watching a sticky kiss on the silver screen and the man saying wistfully "in the book he hits her with an axe".
Katherine Whitehorn, Observer, *In Praise of Shorter Books* 11 *Oct* 1981

ADDICTION

9 It was a shock to discover that Ivor Novello was addicted to Nescafé.
Gabriele Annan, Times Literary Supplement, *review of Sandy Wilson's Ivor* 19 *Dec* 1975

10 All sins tend to be addictive, and the terminal point of addiction is what is called damnation.
W. H. Auden, A CERTAIN WORLD

11 Cocaine isn't habit-forming. I should know. I've been using it for years.
Tallulah Bankhead. Quoted Leslie Halliwell, FILMGOER'S BOOK OF QUOTES 1973

12 I always keep a supply of stimulant handy in case I see a snake — which I also keep handy.
W. C. Fields. Quoted Carey Ford, THE TUNE OF LAUGHTER

13 First you take a drink. Then the drink takes a drink, then the drink takes you.
F. Scott Fitzgerald. Quoted Jules Feiffer, ACKROYD

14 Jack London was corporally mature, innerly a child. He mastered the outward circumstances of life and then played with toys. He preferred to live in a nursery and blamed his excess drinking on the fact that no nurse was there to keep the liquor from his lips.
Waldo Frank. Quoted Joan London, JACK LONDON

15 Blow your mind — smoke dynamite.
Graffiti. Quoted Nigel Rees, GRAFFITI LIVES — O.K.

16 Every form of addiction is bad, no matter whether the narcotic be alcohol or morphine or idealism.
Carl Jung, MEMORIES, DREAMS, REFLECTIONS

17 Is marijuana addictive? Yes in the sense that most of the really pleasant things in life are worth endlessly repeating.
Richard Neville, PLAYPOWER

18 The Koala bears feed, I understand, on leaves so potent they spend half their time stoned out of their fur.
Katherine Whitehorn, Observer 25 *Mar* 1979

ADMINISTRATION

19 He thinks that to say something is to do something, which is an imperfect view of administration.
Henry Cabot Lodge, of William Jennings Bryant in a letter to Sturgis Bigelow 28 *May* 1913

20 He becomes fussy about filing, keen on seeing that pencils are sharpened, eager to ensure that the windows are open (or shut) and apt to use two or three different-coloured inks.
C. Northcote Parkinson, PARKINSON'S LAW 1957

1 We have so many forms to fill in and the excessive time spent on paper work means there is less time for prayer.
Abbot Leo Smith, of Buckfast Abbey.
Quoted Observer 22 *Apr* 1979

ADMIRATION

2 *Admiration:* our polite recognition of another man's resemblance to ourselves.
Ambrose Bierce, THE DEVIL'S DICTIONARY 1906

3 When we admire somebody we like to hear him praised by others — but not too much.
Gerald Brenan, THOUGHTS IN A DRY SEASON 1979

4 The worst tragedy for a poet is to be admired through being misunderstood.
Jean Cocteau, LE RAPPEL À L'ORDRE

5 No one can make us hate ourselves like an admirer.
Cyril Connolly, ENEMIES OF PROMISE 1938

6 I have been the recipient of excessive admiration and reverence from my fellow beings through no fault and no merit of my own.
Albert Einstein, IDEAS AND OPINIONS

7 Let us feel that we are still alive, instead of constantly going around in deedless admiration for the conventional.
Carl Nielsen, MY CHILDHOOD

8 Melba's voice stirs me to almost passionate admiration, but admiration isn't joy; admiration doesn't satisfy; there is no ecstasy in admiration.
Selwyn Rider, Triad 10 *Mar* 1919

ADOLESCENCE

9 Were I to deduce any system from my feelings on leaving Eton, it might be called The Theory of Permanent Adolescence.
Cyril Connolly, ENEMIES OF PROMISE 1938

10 Too chaste an adolescence makes for a dissolute old age.
André Gide, JOURNALS 1939–1950

11 The whole National Youth Movement is being weakened by the failure of those in charge of girls to understand that the natural characteristics of adolescent boys are not the same as those of adolescent girls.
Basil Henriques. Quoted News Review 10 *Apr* 1947

12 So much adolescence is an ill-defined dying, / An intolerable waiting, / A longing for another place and time, / Another condition.
Theodore Roethke, COLLECTED VERSE, *I'm Here* 1961

13 As a result of all his education, from everything he sees and hears around him, the child absorbs such a lot of lies and foolish nonsense, mixed in with essential truths, that the first duty of the adolescent who wants to be a healthy man is to disgorge it all.
Romain Rolland, JEAN CHRISTOPHE 1912

14 It is the highest creatures who take the longest to mature, and are the most helpless during their immaturity.
George Bernard Shaw, BACK TO METHUSELAH 1922

15 First love is only a little foolishness and a lot of curiosity.
George Bernard Shaw, JOHN BULL'S OTHER ISLAND 1904

16 That toil of growing up. / The ignominy of boyhood: the distress / Of boyhood changing into man: / The unfinished man and his pain.
W. B. Yeats, THE WINDING STAIR AND OTHER POEMS 1929

ADORATION

17 I am a true adorer of life, and if I can't reach the face of it I plant my kiss somewhere lower down.
Saul Bellow, HENDERSON THE RAIN KING 1959

18 I hope you have lost your good looks for while they last any fool can adore you, and the adoration of fools is bad for the soul. No, give me a ruined complexion and a lost figure and sixteen chins on a farmyard of crow's feet and an obvious wig. Then you shall see me come out strong.
George Bernard Shaw, letter to Mrs Pat Campbell

ADULATION

19 That layer of blubber which encases an English peer, the sediment of permanent adulation.
Cyril Connolly, ENEMIES OF PROMISE 1938

20 There is no such thing as a great man or a great woman. People believe in them, just as they used to believe in unicorns and

dragons. The greatest man or woman is 99 per cent just like yourself.
George Bernard Shaw, BBC Radio 11 *Jul* 1932

1 Adulation is all right if you don't inhale.
Adlai Stevenson

ADULT

2 If this was adulthood the only improvement she could detect in her situation was that she could now eat dessert without eating her vegetables.
Lisa Alther, KINFLICKS 1976

3 Grown up, and that is a terribly hard thing to do. It is much easier to skip it and go from one childhood to another.
F. Scott Fitzgerald, THE CRACK-UP 1936

4 One of the most obvious facts about grown-ups to a child is that they have forgotten what it is like to be a child.
Randall Jarrell, THIRD BOOK OF CRITICISM 1969

5 The process of maturing is an art to be learned, an effort to be sustained. By the age of fifty you have made yourself what you are and if it is good it is better than your youth.
Marya Mannes, MORE IN ANGER 1958

6 Adults are obsolete children.
Dr. Seuss

ADULTERY

7 At her confirmation classes they had worked through the Commandments. At the seventh an evening had been devoted to impure curiosity.
Elizabeth Bowen, TO THE NORTH 1932

8 Sara could commit adultery at one end and weep for her sins at the other, and enjoy both operations at once.
Joyce Cary, THE HORSE'S MOUTH 1944

9 Throughout history frail women have fascinated men, have confessed their adultery to them, and have been forgiven.
Judge Fraser Harrison. Quoted News Review 10 *Jul* 1947

10 There are few who would not rather be taken in adultery than in provincialism.
Aldous Huxley, ANTIC HAY 1923

11 Time's up for Sir John and for little Lady Jane. Put thy shimmy on, Lady Chatterley.
D. H. Lawrence, LADY CHATTERLEY'S LOVER 1928

12 Accursed from their birth they be / Who seek to find monogamy. / Pursuing it from bed to bed — / I think they would be better dead.
Dorothy Parker, REUBEN'S CHILDREN

13 On a sofa upholstered in human skin / Mona did researches in original sin.
William Plomer, MEWS FLAT MONA

14 The psychology of adultery has been falsified by conventional morals, which assume, in monogamous countries, that attraction to one person cannot coexist with affection for another. Everybody knows that this is untrue.
Bertrand Russell, MARRIAGES AND MORALS 1929

ADVENTURE

15 Adventure is the vitalising element in histories, both individual and social.
William Bolitho, TWELVE AGAINST THE GODS 1929

16 One does not discover new lands without consenting to lose sight of the shore for a very long time.
André Gide, THE COUNTERFEITERS 1926

17 How narrow is the line which separates an adventure from an ordeal.
Harold Nicolson, SMALL TALK

18 Anything, everything, little or big becomes an adventure when the right person shares it. Nothing, nothing, nothing is worthwhile when we have to do it alone.
Katherine Norris, HANDS FULL OF LIVING

19 Had we lived I should have had a tale to tell of the hardihood, endurance and courage of my companions which would have stirred the heart of every Englishman. These rough notes and our dead bodies must tell the tale.
Capt. Robert Falcon Scott, last message 1912

20 Adventure is the result of poor planning.
Col. Blatchford Snell

21 Without adventure civilisation is in full decay.
A. N. Whitehead, ADVENTURES OF IDEAS 1933

ADVERSITY

1 Adversity, if a man is set down to it by degrees, is more supportable with equanimity by most people than any great prosperity arrived at in a single lifetime.
Samuel Butler, THE WAY OF ALL FLESH 1903

2 I'll say this for adversity — people seem to be able to stand it, and that's more'n I kin say fer prosperity.
Kim Hubbard, ABE MARTIN'S BROADCAST

ADVERTISING

3 Parenthesis-proud, bracket-bold, happiest with hyphens / The writers stagger intoxicated by terms, adjective-unsteadied / Describing in graceless phrase fizzling soda-syphon / All things crisp, crunchy, malted, tangy, sugared and shredded.
Anthony Brode, BREAKFAST WITH GERARD MANLEY HOPKINS

4 He [John Snagge] had been against commercial broadcasting ever since he heard a Toscanini radio concert in New York interrupted by the sponsor's slogan "It may be December outside, ladies; but it is always August under your armpits."
Evening Standard. *Quoted* News Review 13 *Nov* 1947

5 The case cannot stand if it is the process of satisfying the wants that creates the wants.
J. K. Galbraith, THE AFFLUENT SOCIETY 1958

6 In a well-to-do community we cannot be much concerned to buy. The marginal utility of money is low; were it otherwise, people would not be open to persuasion.
J. K. Galbraith, ECONOMICS, PEACE AND LAUGHTER

7 There is little that can be said about most economic goods. A toothbrush does little but clean teeth. Aspirin does little but dull pain. Alcohol is important mostly for making people more or less drunk . . . There being so little to be said, much to be invented.
Id.

8 We live surrounded by a systematic appeal to a dream world which all mature, scientific people readily would reject. We quite literally advertise our commitment to immaturity, mendacity and profound gullibility. It is the hallmark of the culture.
Id.

9 How can you ever forgive yourself?
Greta Garbo to one who admitted composing for the film NINOTCHKA *the rubric* 'Garbo laughs'

10 With regard to anything that is likely to obsess a society, it is important not to give it too much advertisement.
(Percy) Wyndham Lewis, TIME AND WESTERN MAN 1927

11 Who are these advertising men kidding? Between the tired, sad, gentle faces of the subway riders and the grinning Holy Families of the Ad-Mass, there exists no possibility of even a wishful identification.
Mary McCarthy, ON THE CONTRARY 1961

12 Ads push the principle of noise all the way to the plateau of percussion. They are quite in accord with the procedures of brainwashing.
Marshall McLuhan, UNDERSTANDING MEDIA 1964

13 It isn't advertising *anything*, dammit.
Father to a small boy looking at a rainbow. Caption to a cartoon by Charles H. Martin, in the New Yorker

14 I think that I shall never see / A billboard lovely as a tree / Indeed unless the billboards fall / I'll never see a tree at all.
Ogden Nash, HAPPY DAYS, *The Song of the Open Road*

15 The Hidden Persuaders.
Vance Packard. Book title

16 Living in an age of advertisement we are perpetually disillusioned. The perfect life is spread before us every day but it changes and withers at a touch.
J. B. Priestley, ALL ABOUT OURSELVES

17 Those who prefer their English sloppy have only themselves to thank if the advertising writer uses his mastery of vocabulary and syntax to mislead their minds.
Dorothy L. Sayers, Spectator 19 *Nov* 1937

18 I will not permit, while I live, a teleview of 'The Man Born To Be King' punctuated by advertisements. Though, of course, it offers scope: the episode of the Feeding of the Five Thousand presented by Hovis bread and MacFisheries for instance, would be very suitable.
Dorothy L. Sayers. Quoted Janet Hitchman, SUCH A STRANGE LADY

19 Lloyd George said to me that once one had assured oneself of food and shelter, which

meant security, the next thing that mattered was advertisement.
A. J. Sylvester, DIARY 27 *Apr* 1933

1 I must say we really enjoy all the commercials in our household, but I always get a tense feeling in case anyone picks the wrong pile of washing in that detergent advertisement.
Letter to TV Times

2 Like! Like! Like! The babble of this subculture is drowning me.
Gore Vidal, MYRA BRECKINRIDGE 1968

3 Half the money I spend on advertising is wasted, and the trouble is, I don't know which half.
John Wanamaker. Quoted David Ogilvy, CONFESSIONS OF AN ADVERTISING MAN

ADVICE

4 To consult is to seek another's advice on a course already decided upon.
Ambrose Bierce, THE DEVIL'S DICTIONARY 1906

5 As a grown man you should know better than to go round advising people.
The Cook to the Chaplain in Bertolt Brecht's MOTHER COURAGE AND HER CHILDREN 1939

6 Friendship will not stand the strain of very much good advice for very long.
Robert Lynd, A PEAL OF BELLS

7 England is, and always has been, a country infested with people who love to tell us what to do, but who very rarely seem to know what's going on.
Colin MacInnes, ENGLAND, HALF ENGLISH

8 A good man giving bad advice is more dangerous than a nasty man giving bad advice.
Conor Cruise O'Brien, Observer, *The Pope and the Unwanted Child* 2 *Oct* 1979

9 I hope, for his own sake, that he has younger people than me at his disposal if he wishes to ask for bad advice, especially if he means to follow it.
Marcel Proust, REMEMBRANCE OF THINGS PAST 1913–27

10 Ann will do just exactly what she likes. And what's more, she'll force us to advise her to do it; and she'll put the blame on us if it turns out badly.
George Bernard Shaw, MAN AND SUPERMAN 1905

11 Don't tell your friends their social faults; they will cure the fault and never forgive you.
Logan Pearsall Smith, ALL TRIVIA, *Afterthoughts* 1931

12 No one wants advice—only corroboration.
John Steinbeck, THE WINTER OF OUR DISCONTENT 1961

13 I have found the best way to give advice to your children is to find out what they want and then advise them to do it.
Harry S Truman, TV interview 27 *May* 1955

AFFECTION

14 I do not know how it comes about, but if you sit opposite a man every day and you are engaged in fighting him, you cannot help getting a liking for him whether he deserves it or not.
A. J. Balfour. Quoted by his niece, Blanche E. Dugdale, Daily Telegraph 16 *Apr* 1936

15 A mixture of admiration and pity is one of the surest recipes for affection.
André Maurois, ARIEL 1923

16 You can have an affection for a murderer or a sodomite, but you cannot have an affection for a man whose breath stinks — habitually stinks, I mean.
George Orwell, THE ROAD TO WIGAN PIER 1937

17 Human nature is so constructed that it gives affection most readily to those who least demand it.
Bertrand Russell, THE CONQUEST OF HAPPINESS 1930

AFFLUENCE

18 Why not? Isn't God a millionaire?
Frank Buchman, founder of Moral Re-Armament, on being challenged to explain how he could afford to live in the best hotels

19 With increasing well-being all people become aware, sooner or later, that they have something to protect.
J. K. Galbraith, THE AFFLUENT SOCIETY 1958

20 Increase of material comforts, it may be generally laid down, does not in any way whatsoever conduce to moral growth.
Mahatma Gandhi. Quoted obituary, News Chronicle 31 *Jan* 1948

1 The affluent society has made everyone dislike work, and come to think of idleness as the happiest life.
Sir Geoffrey Keynes. Quoted Robert Chesshyre, Observer 25 *Oct* 1981

2 I don't know how much money I've got . . . I did ask the accountant how much it came to. I wrote it down on a bit of paper. But I've lost the bit of paper.
John Lennon. Quoted Hunter Davies, THE BEATLES

3 Most of our people have never had it so good. Go around the country, go to the industrial towns, go to the farms — and you will see a state of prosperity such as we have never had in my lifetime, or indeed ever in the history of this country.
Harold Macmillan. Speech, Bradford 20 *Jul* 1951

4 When I am a rich man with my own bicycle and can have beer for breakfast I shall give up writing poetry altogether and just be absolutely disgusting.
Dylan Thomas and John Davenport, THE DEATH OF THE KING'S CANARY

AFRICAN

5 We have the happiest Africans in the world.
Ian Smith. Quoted Observer, *Sayings of the Week* 28 *Nov* 1971

AGE

6 Age has its compensations. It is less apt to be brow-beaten by discretion.
Charlie Chaplin, MY AUTOBIOGRAPHY 1962

7 A very old twelve.
Noël Coward's reply when asked how old a certain society lady looked after her most recent facelift

8 My age is 39 plus tax.
Liberace in his TV show

9 Paradoxical as it may seem, to believe in youth is to look backward; to look forward we must believe in age.
Dorothy L. Sayers, STRONG MEAT

10 I'd like to go on being 35 for a long time.
Margaret Thatcher, in 1961

11 He was either a man of about a hundred and fifty who was rather young for his years, or a man of about a hundred and ten who had been aged by trouble.
P. G. Wodehouse

12 If I'd known how old I was going to be I'd have taken better care of myself.
Adolph Zukor, founder of Paramount Pictures, on the approach of his hundredth birthday. Quoted Benny Green, Radio Times 17 *Feb* 1979

AGENT

13 My agent gets ten per cent of everything I get, except my blinding headaches.
Fred Allen, American radio comedian

14 Pimps who . . . don't do anything, don't make anything — they just stand there and take their cut.
Jean Giraudoux, THE MADWOMAN OF CHAILLOT 1945

AGGRESSION

15 Pale Ebenezer thought it wrong to fight / But Roaring Bill (who killed him) thought it right.
Hilaire Belloc, EPIGRAMS

16 One of his minor purposes is to disembowel his enemies who are numerous for the simple reason that he wants them to be numerous. He would be less tiresome if he were more urbane.
Arnold Bennett of (Percy) Wyndham Lewis, Evening Standard 28 *Apr* 1927

17 A literary aphorism makes a poor defence against a well-propelled battleaxe.
Ernest Bramah, KAI LUNG UNROLLS HIS MAT 1928

18 Fighting is essentially a masculine idea; a woman's weapon is her tongue.
Hermione Gingold. Quoted Barbara Rowe, BOOK OF QUOTES

19 Guns before butter. Guns will make us powerful; butter will only make us fat.
Hermann Goering, German broadcast 1936

20 Nobody ever forgets where he buried the hatchet.
Kim Hubbard, ABE MARTIN'S BROADCAST

21 No doubt there are other important things in life besides conflict but there are not many other things so inevitably interesting. The very saints interest us most when we think of them in conflict with the Devil.
Robert Lynd, THE BLUE LION

22 It is no use speaking in soft, gentle tones if everyone else is shouting.
J. B. Priestley, THOUGHTS IN THE WILDERNESS

1 Of the four wars in my lifetime none came about because the United States was too strong.
Ronald Reagan, Presidential campaign speech 9 *Jun* 1980

2 Do not hit at all if it can be avoided, but never hit softly.
Theodore Roosevelt, AUTOBIOGRAPHY 1913

3 To knock a thing down, especially if it is cocked up at an arrogant angle, is a deep delight to the blood.
George Santayana, THE LIFE OF REASON, *Reason in Society* 1906

AGNOSTIC

4 John Grubby, who was short and stout / And troubled with religious doubt / Refused about the age of three / To sit upon the curate's knee.
G. K. Chesterton, THE NEW FREETHINKER

5 Those who deny Thee could not deny, if Thou didst not exist; and their denial is never complete, for if it were so, they would not exist.
T. S. Eliot, MURDER IN THE CATHEDRAL 1935

6 The sheer babyhood of the human race against the background of incalculable time makes anything but a questing agnosticism absurdly presumptuous.
L. E. Jones, I FORGOT TO TELL YOU

7 The question most commonly asked by the agnostic is not "Do you believe in the authenticity of the Holy House at Loreto?" or "Do you think an individual can justly inherit a right to the labour of another?" but "Do you believe in Hell?"
Evelyn Waugh, Commonweal 16 *Jul* 1948

AGREEMENT

8 When you accept our views we shall be in full agreement with you.
Moshe Dayan to Cyrus Vance 10 *Aug* 1977

ALCOHOL

9 Mona Lisa cocktail — two of them and you can't get the silly grin off your face.
Anon.

10 Reality is a delusion created by an alcohol deficiency.
Anon. Quoted BBC Radio 4 *Quote Unquote* 7 *Jun* 1979

11 Always remember, I have taken more out of alcohol than alcohol has taken out of me.
Winston Churchill. Quoted Quentin Reynolds, BY QUENTIN REYNOLDS

12 It smells like gangrene starting in a mildewed silo, it tastes like the wrath to come, and when you absorb a deep swig of it you have all the sensations of having swallowed a lighted kerosene lamp.
Irvin S. Cobb, defining corn liquor for the Distillers' Code Authority

13 Maybe alcohol picks you up a little bit, but it sure lets you down in a hurry.
Betty Ford, wife of President Ford, on admitting to being an alcoholic

14 The sway of alcohol over mankind is unquestionably due to its power to stimulate the mystic faculties of human nature, usually crushed to earth by the cold facts and dry criticisms of the sober hour.
William James. Quoted New York Times 29 *Feb* 1948

15 Crazy folks shouldn't drink — it's like throwing gasoline on a banked fire.
Donald Newlove, THOSE DRINKING DAYS

16 There is an unbroken testimony of all history that alcoholic liquors have been used by the strongest, wisest, handsomest and in every way best races of all times.
George Saintsbury, NOTES ON A CELLAR BOOK

17 When I do come to town, bang go my plans in a horrid alcohol explosion that scatters all my good intentions like bits of limbs and clothes over the doorsteps and into the saloon bars of the tawdriest pubs in London.
Dylan Thomas in a letter to a friend 1936

18 It was my Uncle George who discovered that alcohol was a food well in advance of modern medical thought.
P. G. Wodehouse, THE INIMITABLE JEEVES

19 Alcohol sobers me. After a few swallows of brandy I no longer think of you.
Margaret Yourcenar, FIRES

ALIMONY

20 You never realise how short a month is until you pay alimony.
John Barrymore, in an interview.

21 The wages of sin is alimony.
Carolyn Wells

15

1 Judges, as a class, display, in the matter of arranging alimony, that reckless generosity that is found only in men who are giving away somebody else's cash.
P. G. Wodehouse, LOUDER AND FUNNIER

ALTERNATIVE

2 Alternatives, and particularly desirable alternatives, grow only on imaginary trees.
Saul Bellow, DANGLING MAN 1944

3 The weak are always forced to decide between alternatives they have not chosen themselves.
Dietrich Bonhoeffer, LETTERS AND PAPERS FROM PRISON

4 "I have decided that the office cannot continue to hold both you and me. One of us must go. Which shall it be?"
"Well, Mr Wrackham, your name is painted on the door, so I suppose it would be simpler if you stayed."
F. Scott Fitzgerald, THE CRACK-UP 1936

5 Germany will either be a world power or will not be.
Adolf Hitler, MEIN KAMPF 1924

6 I cannot see who is ahead — it is either Oxford or Cambridge.
John Snagge, commentary on 1949 *boat race*.

AMATEUR

7 Professionals built the *Titanic* — amateurs the ark.
Anon. Quoted BBC Radio 4, *The News Quiz* 27 Oct 1979

AMBIGUITY

8 One of the questions was "Do you think contraceptives are 100 per cent reliable?" Unfortunately the word 'contraceptive' was not always understood so when the answer was "I don't know" it was not clear if the answer referred to the reliability of contraceptives or merely that the question was not understood.
M. Schofield, THE SEXUAL BEHAVIOUR OF YOUNG PEOPLE

AMBITION

9 A desire is real when the possibility of satisfaction exists for the individual who entertains it — a desire for a Cadillac which may be real for a prosperous American businessman would be fantastic for a Chinese peasant.
W. H. Auden, THE DYER'S HAND 1962

10 I have been absolutely hag-ridden with ambition. If I could wish to have anything in the world it would be to be free of ambition.
Tallulah Bankhead. Quoted Lee Israel, MISS TALLULAH BANKHEAD

11 I have decided to be the stationmaster at Blake Hall on the Ongar branch of the Central Line. There's a lovely wooden Saxon church near there. I'll be able to walk over the fields this springtime to Ongar where 'Twinkle, twinkle little star' was written.
Sir John Betjeman, Observer Magazine 1 *Apr* 1979

12 I want to earn an honest living.
Ronald Biggs, Observer, *Saying of the Week* 12 *May* 1974

13 I've always had a secret ambition to be the master of a tideway tug, either on the Thames or on the Solent, and I'm finally going to try it. Every day you can deal bossily and skilfully with ships of all sizes in every sort of wind and tide. The bridge is easy: the scenery is varied; it's never very rough, and you get home at night.
Sir Hugh Casson, Observer Magazine 1 *Apr* 1979

14 His childhood ambition had been to be a taxidermist, and for a year or two he toddled around in a cloud of formaldehyde.
Alistair Cooke, of Theodore Roosevelt, AMERICA

15 I should like to be a horse.
Queen Elizabeth II, *when a child*

16 My ambition is to live in a hot country and watch someone throw stones in the sea.
Gracie Fields, News Chronicle 9 *Jan* 1932

17 Modern man lives under the illusion that he knows what he wants, while he actually wants what he is supposed to want.
Erich Fromm, ESCAPE FROM FREEDOM 1941

18 If you start acting when you're five there isn't a lot of point in finding something else to do when you're 84 . . . I'd like to go have a look at Saturn now that they seem to have got cameras up there.
Lillian Gish, The Times 19 *Nov* 1980

1 The average girl's ambition is to make some man a good husband.
Chal Herry, Saturday Evening Post 20 *Nov* 1948

2 I can conceive no better fortune when the time comes than to cultivate private rather than public aspirations, to live, love, garden and die deep in the English countryside.
Douglas Jay, CHANGE AND FORTUNE

3 We all want to be famous people, and the moment we want to *be* something we are no longer free.
Krishnamurti, THE PENGUIN KRISHNA-MURTI READER

4 Vocational Guide for the Truly Ambitious, or — So You Want to be the Pope.
Fran Lebowitz. Essay title

5 All I want is a room somewhere / Far away from the cold night air / With one enormous chair. / Ooh, wouldn't it be lov-er-ly.
Alan Jay Lerner, MY FAIR LADY 1956

6 The trouble is that really wanting things is so rare. It's a lukewarm world.
E. V. Lucas, 365 DAYS AND ONE MORE

7 You've got a goal. I've got a goal. Now all we need is a football team.
Groucho Marx, A NIGHT AT THE OPERA

8 Men do not heed the rungs by which they climb.
John Masefield, AUTOBIOGRAPHY

9 If men could regard the events of their own lives with more open minds they would frequently discover that they did not really desire the things they failed to obtain.
André Maurois, THE ART OF LIVING

10 [The average man] is always waiting for something to happen to him instead of setting to work to make it happen. For one person who dreams of making fifty thousand pounds a hundred people dream of being left fifty thousand pounds.
A. A. Milne, IF I MAY

11 The end of ambition comes as a great relief.
Malcolm Muggeridge at 78 to John Mortimer, Sunday Times 19 *Apr* 1981

12 If I had not been born Perón I would have liked to be Perón.
President Juan Perón. Quoted Observer, Sayings of the Week 21 *Feb* 1960

13 Ambition is the grand enemy of all peace.
John Cowper Powys, THE MEANING OF CULTURE 1930

14 The Palmer family of Camden Town have failed in their great war-time ambition — to breed a red, white and blue mouse before World War II came to an end.
Reynolds News. *Quoted Michael Bateman*, THIS ENGLAND

15 I want to be another Emma Hamilton. I'm looking for another Lord Nelson, only taller.
Mandy Rice-Davies, at the time of the Profumo scandal 1963

16 The young have aspirations that never come to pass, the old have reminiscences of what never happened.
Saki, REGINALD AT THE CARLTON 1904

17 The indefatigable pursuit of an unattainable perfection, even though it consist in nothing more than in the pounding of an old piano, is what alone gives meaning to our life on this unavailing star.
Logan Pearsall Smith, ALL TRIVIA, *Afterthoughts* 1931

18 Dan Jones was going to compose the most prodigious symphony, Fred James paint the most miraculously meretricious picture, Charles Fisher catch the poshest trout, Vernon Watkins and Young Thomas write the most boiling poems, how they would ring the bells of London and paint it like a tart.
Dylan Thomas, THE RETURN JOURNEY

19 A Spanish writer who was described as the best writer in Spain became angry because he wanted to be told he was the best in the world. I must confess I recognise something of myself in that.
John Updike. Quoted John Heilpern, Observer 25 *Mar* 1979

20 There are few *Vogue* readers who have never harboured a slinking desire to be thrown across the saddle of a plunging white stallion, galloped to a palmy oasis and stuffed with dates in a striped prison by swarthy warriors.
Vogue

21 We think that what we are doing is for reasons of idealism but people's ambition begins to grow as they feel the attraction of power.
Shirley Williams. Interviewed by Miriam Gross, Observer 22 *Mar* 1981

22 Caged birds accept each other but flight is what they long for.
Tennessee Williams, CAMINO REAL 1953

1 I would like to be the head of an advertising agency.
The Duchess of Windsor

IDI AMIN

2 I remember Amin as being a typical, good warrant officer type. He was a big, bluff, cheerful soldier who always had a great beaming smile on his face. I never thought he had any great intellect. He was just a good, rough, tough soldier and a bustling Rugby forward.
Gen. Sir Richard Goodwin. Quoted Alexander Mitchell and Russell Miller, Sunday Times, *Amin — the Untold Story* 29 Oct 1972

3 His is a clown's face, all the more terrible for its drollery masking in Mr. Smith's words "the solitary conductor of an orchestra of devils"; Satan as buffoon.
Tony Samstag, The Times *2 Oct* 1980

AMOEBA

4 Amoebas at the start / Were not complex; / They tore themselves apart / And started sex.
Arthur Guiterman, SEX

ANALOGY

5 Though analogy is often misleading it is the least misleading thing we have.
Samuel Butler, NOTEBOOKS, *Music, Pictures and Books* 1912

6 Analogies prove nothing, that is quite true, but they can make one feel more at home.
Sigmund Freud, NEW INTRODUCTORY LECTURES ON PSYCHOANALYSIS

ANARCHY

7 I am a Tory Anarchist. I should like everyone to go about doing just as he pleased — short of altering any of the things to which I have grown accustomed.
Max Beerbohm

8 To a real anarchist a poke in the eye is better than a bunch of flowers. It makes him see stars.
Joyce Cary, THE HORSE'S MOUTH 1944

9 Anarchism is a game at which the Police can beat you.
George Bernard Shaw, MISALLIANCE 1910. *Epigraph to Joe Orton's* LOOT 1967

10 My political opinions lean more and more towards anarchy . . . The most improper job of any man, even saints, is bossing other men.
J. R. R. Tolkien, LETTERS

ANATOMY

11 We tolerate shapes in human beings that would horrify us if we saw them in a horse.
W. R. Inge (Dean of St. Pauls), NOTEBOOKS

12 A human being: an ingenious assembly of portable plumbing.
Christopher Morley, HUMAN BEING

13 He [man] is proud that he has the biggest brain of all the primates, but attempts to conceal that he also has the biggest penis.
Desmond Morris, THE NAKED APE

ANCESTRY

14 Genealogy is an account of one's descent from a man who did not particularly care to trace his own.
Ambrose Bierce, THE DEVIL'S DICTIONARY 1906

15 Somewhere back along your pedigree a bitch got over the wall.
Robert Bolt, A MAN FOR ALL SEASONS 1960

16 We all of us may have kings' blood in our veins . . . We tell ourselves that Shakespeare was the son of a wool-peddler and Napoleon of a farmer and Luther of a peasant, and we hold up our hands at the marvel. But who knows what kings and prophets they had in their ancestry.
John Buchan, THE PATH OF THE KING

17 Henry I is in lots of family trees. He was very good at it. He had twenty illegitimate children before he was married and nobody counted them afterwards.
Will Cuppy, THE DECLINE AND FALL OF PRACTICALLY EVERYBODY

18 A study of family portraits is enough to convert a man to the theory of reincarnation.
Sir Arthur Conan Doyle, THE HOUND OF THE BASKERVILLES 1902

19 There is no king who has not had a slave among his ancestors, and no slave who has not had a king among his.
Helen Keller, STORY OF MY LIFE 1947

1 Family trees are often like St. Pancras station, the incongruous fruits of the Gothic revival.
Harold Kurtz, Daily Telegraph 18 Aug 1966

2 [Ezra] Pound has spent his life trying to live down a family scandal — he's Longfellow's grand-nephew.
D. H. Lawrence in a letter to Robert Graves

3 i have often noticed that / ancestors never boast / of the descendants who boast / of ancestors; i would / rather start a family than / finish one. blood will tell but often / it tells too much.
Don Marquis, A ROACH OF THE TAVERNS

4 To have an ancestor who was hanged for sheep-stealing gives me a certain social standing, don't you think?
Robert Morley, BBC Radio 4, *Start the Week 7 Sep 1981*

5 Our family didn't exactly come from the wrong side of the tracks but we were certainly always within sound of the train whistles.
Ronald Reagan. Quoted Bill Adler, THE REAGAN WIT

6 Of remote ancestors I can discover only one who did not live to a great age, and he died of a disease now rare, namely, having his head cut off.
Bertrand Russell, of Lord William Russell. Quoted Michael Foot, DEBTS OF HONOUR

7 Every president of the US has somehow been found to descend from Edward II.
Gore Vidal. Quoted John Heilpern, Observer 26 Apr 1981

ANGEL

8 Steel engravings of Protestant angels brought up on milk pudding.
Hilaire Belloc in a letter to Mrs. Wansborough 6 Jan 1926

9 God made the angels, to show him splendour.
Robert Bolt, A MAN FOR ALL SEASONS 1960

10 Angels can fly because they take themselves lightly.
G. K. Chesterton, ORTHODOXY 1909

11 An angel whose muscles developed no more power weight for weight than those of an eagle or a pigeon would require a breast projecting for about four feet to house the muscles engaged in working its wings, while to economise in weight, its legs would have to be reduced to mere stilts.
J. B. S. Haldane, POSSIBLE WORLDS 1927

12 If a man is only a little lower than the angels, the angels should reform.
Mary Wilson Little

13 If some angel appeared to me without a carnal body and assured me that it was perfectly happy on prayer and music I should congratulate him, but shouldn't care to emulate him.
George Santayana, LETTERS

14 In heaven, an angel is nobody in particular.
George Bernard Shaw

15 Angels have no private lives.
Stevie Small, Sunday Times 7 Apr 1964

16 There is no reason why good cannot triumph as often as evil. The triumph of anything is a matter of organisation. If there are such things as angels I hope they are organised along the lines of the Mafia.
Kurt Vonnegut, SIRENS OF TITAN

ANGER

17 I was never an Angry Young Man. I am angry only when I hit my thumb with a hammer.
Kingsley Amis, Eton College Chronicle, *Jun 1979*

18 He [Henry Cabot Lodge] could enrage his antagonists by making them feel their own impotence to enrage him.
Anon.

19 Speak when you are angry and you will make the best speech you will ever regret.
Ambrose Bierce, THE DEVIL'S DICTIONARY 1906

20 Few men can afford to be angry.
Augustin Burell, EDMUND BURKE

21 I know of no more disagreeable sensation than being left generally angry without anybody in particular to be angry at.
Frank Moore Colby, THE COLBY ESSAYS 1926

22 "I am beside myself."
"Move over. You're in bad company."
Groucho Marx, A NIGHT AT THE OPERA

23 It is my rule never to lose my temper till it would be detrimental to keep it.
Sean O'Casey, THE PLOUGH AND THE STARS 1926

1 She struck me as being a shade below par, and she spoke with a good deal of animation about skinning you with a blunt knife.
P. G. Wodehouse, PIGS HAVE WINGS 1952

ANGLING

2 The charm of fishing is that it is the pursuit of what is elusive but obtainable, a perpetual series of occasions for hope.
John Buchan, New York Times 15 *Apr* 1951

3 Fishing is undoubtedly a form of madness but, happily for the once-bitten, there is no cure.
Alec Douglas-Home, THE WAY THE WIND BLOWS 1976

4 Someone just back of you while you are fishing is as bad as someong looking over your shoulder while you write a letter to your girl.
Ernest Hemingway. Quoted, BY-LINE ERNEST HEMINGWAY, *edited by William White*

5 I may be wrong, but I don't think there has ever been any anti-blood sports demonstration against angling.
Miles Kington, Punch 22 *Mar* 1972

ANSWER

6 An answer is always a form of death.
John Fowles, THE MAGUS

7 Now I cannot for the life of me pass an Intelligence Test. They ask you questions like this, "Do you know the answer to 2+2?" To such a question I reply "Four". The correct answer is "Yes".
Gerald Kersh, CLEAN BRIGHT AND SLIGHTLY OILED 1940

8 If we can really understand the problem the answer will come out of it, because the answer is not separate from the problem.
Krishnamurti, THE PENGUIN KRISHNAMURTI READER

ANTHOLOGY

9 A well-chosen anthology is a complete dispensary of medicine for the more common mental disorders, and may be used as much for prevention as cure.
Robert Graves, ON ENGLISH POETRY 1962

ANTICIPATION

10 Talk about the joys of the unexpected, can they compare with the joys of the expected, of finding everything delightfully and completely what you knew it was going to be?
Elizabeth Bibesco, BALLOONS

11 The architect smacked his lips in a refined way, like a fox in a henhouse, and went to work.
S. J. Perelman, CRAZY LIKE A FOX 1944

12 The habit of looking to the future and thinking that the whole meaning of the present lies in what it will bring forth is a pernicious one. There can be no value in the whole unless there is value in the parts.
Bertrand Russell, THE CONQUEST OF HAPPINESS 1930

ANTIQUE

13 An antique is something that's been useless st long it's still in pretty good condition.
Franklin P. Jones, Saturday Evening Post 21 *Feb* 1956

APATHY

14 Science may have found a cure for most evils, but it has found no remedy for the worst of them all — the apathy of human beings.
Helen Keller, MY RELIGION 1927

15 Sit on your arse for fifty years and hang your hat on a pension.
Louis MacNeice, BAGPIPE MUSIC

APHORISM

16 We endeavour to stuff the universe into the gullet of an aphorism.
Paul Eldridge, HORNS OF GLASS

17 An aphorism is never exactly truthful. It is either a half-truth or a truth and a half.
Karl Kraus, APHORISMS

APOLOGY

18 To apologise is to lay the foundation for a future offence.
Ambrose Bierce, THE DEVIL'S DICTIONARY 1906

19 It is a good rule in life never to apologise. The right sort of people do not want apologies, and the wrong sort take a mean advantage of them.
P. G. Wodehouse, THE MAN UPSTAIRS

APPEARANCE

1 Lytton Strachey peered at everyone through thick glasses, looking like an owl in daylight. He is immensely tall, and could be even twice his height if he were not as bent as sloppy asparagus.
Cecil Beaton, DIARY 1923

2 She looks like Lady Chatterley above the waist and the gamekeeper below.
Cyril Connolly of Vita Sackville-West

3 Do I look as if I sold Bentleys in Great Portland Street?
Noël Coward, on being mistaken for Rex Harrison

4 He had grey curly hair and a face like a jubilee bonfire.
Lionel Curtis of Cecil Rhodes, WITH MILNER IN SOUTH AFRICA

5 His hair and teeth were both parted in the middle.
Peter De Vries, CONSENTING ADULTS

6 Why not be oneself? That is the whole secret of a successful appearance. If one is a greyhound why try to look like a Pekinese?
Edith Sitwell, WHY I LOOK AS I DO

7 Small, shrivelled chap. Looks like a haddock with lung trouble.
P. G. Wodehouse, THE INIMITABLE JEEVES 1924

8 A tall, drooping man, looking as if he had been stuffed in a hurry by an incompetent taxidermist.
P. G. Wodehouse, THE MATING SEASON

APPEASEMENT

9 An appeaser is one who feeds a crocodile, hoping it will eat him last.
Winston Churchill after Munich 1938

10 If war is so easily averted as all this it does seem a pity no PM has thought of it before . . . Peace without Honour seems to be what we have got. I'm glad. One can't expect *both*.
Rose Macaulay in a letter to Daniel George (Bunting) on the Munich crisis 1938

APPETITE

11 Other people's appetites easily appear excessive when one doesn't share them.
André Gide, THE COUNTERFEITERS 1926

APPLAUSE

12 Applause is the echo of a platitude.
Ambrose Bierce, THE DEVIL'S DICTIONARY 1906

13 When I hear a man applauded by the mob I feel sorry for him. All he has to do to be hissed is to live long enough.
H. L. Mencken, MINORITY REPORT

APPLE

14 The apple was the first fruit of the world, according to Genesis, but it was no Cox's Orange pippin. God gave the crab apple and left the rest to man.
JANE GRIGSON'S FRUIT BOOK

APPRECIATION

15 The power of appreciating is worth any amount of the power of despising.
A. C. Benson, FROM A COLLEGE WINDOW 1906

APPREHENSION

16 Even in slight things the experience of the new is rarely without some stirring of foreboding.
Eric Hoffer, THE ORDEAL OF CHANGE 1964

ARCHITECTURE

17 It has all the earmarks of an eyesore.
American tourist of the Albert Memorial

18 Eh, it would make a grand Co-op.
Anon. Said of All Souls, Oxford

19 Architecture is pre-eminently the art of significant forms in space — that is, forms significant of their functions.
Claud Bragdon, Outlook 27 *May* 1931

20 Architecture is inhabited sculpture.
Constantin Brancusi. Quoted Igor Stravinsky, THEMES AND EPISODES 1966

21 We shape our buildings; thereafter they shape us.
Winston Churchill, Time 12 *Sep* 1960

22 French Classical architecture . . . was the work not of craftsmen but of wonderfully gifted civil servants.
Kenneth, Lord Clark, CIVILISATION 1969

23 Architecture, of all the arts, is the one which acts the most slowly, but the most surely, on the soul.
Ernest Dimnet, WHAT WE LIVE BY

1 A courageous and partly successful attempt to disguise a gasworks as a racquets court.
Peter Fleming, of the Shakespeare Memorial Theatre. Sunday Times 1951

2 Large buildings in London and elsewhere today are too often designed in the lift going down to lunch.
Sir William Holford. Quoted Observer 5 *Jun* 1960

3 A seventeenth-century palace was totally without privacy. Architects had not yet invented the corridor . . . One simply walked through a succession of other people's rooms in which literally anything could be going on.
Aldous Huxley, THEME AND VARIATIONS 1950

4 A hundred and fifty accurate reproductions of Anne Hathaway's cottage each complete with garage and central heating.
Osbert Lancaster, PILLAR TO POST, *Stockbroker's Tudor*

5 The materials of city planning are: sky, space, trees, steel and cement; in that order and that hierarchy.
Le Corbusier

6 There is nothing in which the birds differ more from man than the way they can build and yet leave a landscape as it was before.
Robert Lynd, THE BLUE LION

7 I thought it looked as if it was something that had crawled out of the sea and was up to no good. It reminds me of one of those films where giant ants and things take over.
Beverley Nichols, of the Sydney Opera House. Sydney Sun News Pictorial 5 *Feb* 1968

8 The challenge for the modern architect is the same as the challenge for all of us in our lives, to make out of the ordinary something out-of-the-ordinary.
Patrick Nuttgens, BBC TV, *Architecture for Everyman, Feb* 1979

9 Architecture is the most inescapable of the higher arts.
Anthony Quinton, The Times, *Romantic Crying Wolfe* 25 *Mar* 1982

10 One might regard architecture as history arrested in stone, the movement of time congealed . . . at every point a building expresses the needs, the character of its age.
A. L. Rowse, THE USE OF HISTORY

11 Architecture is the total of everything we have around us, starting from the largest city plan, including the streets we drive on and its telephone poles and signs, down to the building and house we live and work in and does not end until we consider the chair we sit in and the ashtray we dump our pipe in . . . the scope of architecture is man's total physical surroundings outdoors and indoors.
Eero Saarinnen, EERO SAARINEN ON HIS WORK

12 Its shoulders break the clouds apart / A concrete stake in the city's heart.
Richard Usborne, FOUR STAR HOTEL

13 From Tromso to Angora the horrible little architects crept about — curly-headed, horn-spectacled, volubly explaining their 'machines for living'. Villas like sewage farms, mansions like half-submerged Channel steamers, offices like vast beehives or cucumber frames sprang up round their feet, furnished with electric fires that blistered the ankles, windows that blinded the eyes, patent 'sound proof' partitions which resounded with the rattle of a hundred typewriters and the buzzing of a hundred telephones.
Evelyn Waugh, Country Life 20 *Feb* 1936

14 One of the best warehouses I ever saw was the Vatican in Rome.
Arnold Wesker, CHIPS WITH EVERYTHING 1962

15 The modern buildings that you see / Are often most alarming / But I am sure that you'll agree / A ruin / Can be charming.
Sandy Wilson, THE BOY FRIEND

16 One of those mid-Victorian jobs in glazed red brick which always seem to bob up in these olde worlde hamlets and do so much to encourage the drift to the towns.
P. G. Wodehouse, THE MATING SEASON 1949

17 The physician can bury his mistakes, but the architect can only advise his client to plant vines.
Frank Lloyd Wright, New York Times Magazine 4 *Oct* 1953

ARGUMENT

18 Most of the arguments to which I am a party fall somewhat short of being impres-

sive owing to the fact that neither I nor my opponent knows what we are talking about.
Robert Benchley, BENCHLEY — OR ELSE

1 It is no use arguing with a prophet; you can only disbelieve him.
Winston Churchill of Prof. Lindermann. Quoted John Colville, THE CHURCHILLIANS 1981

2 It is only damned fools who argue. Never contradict, never explain, never apologise. These are the secrets of a happy life.
Lord Fisher. Letter to The Times *5 Sep 1919*

3 A disagreement may be the shortest cut between two minds.
Kahil Gibran, SAND AND FOAM 1927

4 A stigma is good enough to beat a dogma with.
Philip Guedella. Speech to Cambridge Union. Quoted H. Montgomery Hyde, PRIVATE PAPERS OF NORMAN BIRKETT

5 By the very act of arguing, you awake the patient's reason; and once it is awake, who can foresee the result.
C. S. Lewis, THE SCREWTAPE LETTERS 1942

6 "Yes, but not in the South" with slight adjustments will do for any argument about any place, if not about any person.
Stephen Potter, LIFEMANSHIP 1950

7 Partisanship is our great curse. We too readily assume that everything has two sides and that it is our duty to be on one or the other.
James Harvey Robinson, THE MIND IN THE MAKING

8 The most savage controversies are those about matters as to which there is no good evidence either way.
Bertrand Russell, UNPOPULAR ESSAYS 1950

ARISTOCRACY

9 The great and very obvious merit of the English aristocracy is that nobody could possibly take it seriously.
G. K. Chesterton, ORTHODOXY 1908

10 The point about the aristocracy is that they all know each other.
Jilly Cooper, CLASS 1980

11 If human beings could be propagated by cutting, like apple trees, aristocracy would be biologically sound.
J. B. S. Haldane, THE INEQUALITY OF MAN

12 A society without an aristocracy, without an élite minority, is not a society.
José Ortega y Gasset, MEDITATIONS ON QUIXOTE 1914

13 The aristocratic rebel, since he has enough to eat, must have other causes of discontent.
Bertrand Russell, HISTORY OF WESTERN PHILOSOPHY 1945

14 Unlike the male codfish, which, suddenly finding itself the parent of three and a half million little codfish, cheerfully resolves to love them all, the British aristocracy is apt to look with a somewhat jaundiced eye on its younger sons.
P. G. Wodehouse, The Listener *30 May 1963*

ARMAMENTS

15 It is not armaments that cause war, but war that causes armaments.
Salvador de Madariaga, MORNING WITHOUT NOON

16 All this about 'the burden of armaments' is rubbish; the cost of the biggest armies at present is not worth counting beside the cost of idle property holding.
George Bernard Shaw. Letter to John Galsworthy 1911. Quoted H.V. Marrot, LIFE AND LETTERS OF JOHN GALSWORTHY

ARMOUR

17 Armour is the kind of clothing worn by a man whose tailor was a blacksmith.
Ambrose Bierce, THE DEVIL'S DICTIONARY 1906

ARMY

18 This is the army, Mr. Jones / No private baths or telephones.
Irving Berlin, THIS IS THE ARMY *(song)*

19 It is characteristic of the military mind that non-human factors are held essential while the human being, his desires and thoughts— in short the psychological factors — are considered unimportant and secondary.
Albert Einstein, OUT OF MY LATER LIFE

20 What is unique about this regiment? It is the only one in which the Colonel is legally married to the Colonel in Chief.
Philip, Duke of Edinburgh, when being entertained to dinner by the Welsh Guards

ARROGANCE

1 A good way to deal with arrogance is simply to allow it to exhaust itself.
Noël Coward. Quoted William Marchant, THE PRIVILEGE OF HIS COMPANY 1980

2 In any imaginable society he [Sinclair Lewis] would be as noticeable as a bashful cyclone. He enters a room with diffident insolence, bracing himself against what lies in wait for him.
Carl Van Doren, SINCLAIR LEWIS

ART

3 Paintings, like people, are prone to diseases. They break out in boils, and crack under the strain of exposure.
Harold Acton, The Times, *Saturday Review* 18 *Sep* 1970

4 Millais once confessed that the only thing he enjoyed about portrait painting was putting the highlights on the boots of his subjects.
James Agate, EGO 1935–48

5 The object of art is to give life shape.
Jean Anouilh, THE REHEARSAL 1950

6 It [art] grows out of me like my toenails. I have to cut it off and then it grows again.
Jean Arp. Quoted The Times 8 *Jun* 1966

7 Klee's pictures seem to me to resemble, not pictures, but a sample book of patterns of linoleum.
The Hon. Sir Cyril Asquith in a letter to Alfred Munnings

8 Art is born of humiliation.
W. H. Auden. Quoted Humphrey Carpenter, AUDEN: A BIOGRAPHY

9 The lower one's vitality, the more sensitive one is to great art.
Max Beerbohm, SEVEN MEN 1919

10 Art and Religion are two roads by which men escape from circumstance to ecstasy.
Clive Bell, ART 1914

11 I mistrust violence in almost any art. It is often an easy way out. It's much more difficult to draw a beautiful face than an ugly one.
Quentin Bell, in an interview with Sarah Howell, Observer Magazine 18 *Mar* 1979

12 Art attempts to find in the universe, in matter as well as in the facts of life, what is fundamental, enduring, essential.
Saul Bellow. Nobel Prize speech 1970

13 I wanted to become a work of art myself, and not an artist.
Bernard Berenson, SUNSET AND TWILIGHT, *Diaries* 1947–58

14 A work of art is no good if it doesn't provoke a furore.
Sir Isaiah Berlin, Observer 2 *Nov* 1980

15 The drawing is on the level of that of an untaught child of seven or eight years old, the sense of colour that of a tea-tray painter, the method that of a schoolboy who wiped his fingers on a slate after spitting on them.
Wilfred Scawen Blunt, on Post Impressionists, MY DIARIES 1920

16 Most of those who call themselves artists are in reality picture dealers, only they make the pictures themselves.
Samuel Butler, NOTEBOOKS 1912

17 Art is what is deposited behind glass in galleries and museums and in the rooms of rich people: but it does not move about live in the streets, it does not twinkle from the handsome cornices of windows, it does not take up its stand at the street corner like a statue.
Karel Čapek, LETTERS FROM ENGLAND

18 Abstract art? A product of the untalented, sold by the unprincipled to the utterly bewildered.
Al Capp, Li'l Abner cartoonist, National Observer 1 *Jul* 1963

19 Remember I'm an artist. And you know what that means in a court of law. Next worse to an actress.
Joyce Cary, THE HORSE'S MOUTH 1944

20 To have an *avant garde* you have to have a *garde*.
Sir Hugh Casson, Daily Telegraph 13 *Jan* 1974

21 What was any art but an effort to make a sheath, a mould, in which to imprison for a moment the shining, elusive element which is life itself.
Willa Cather, THE SONG OF THE LARK 1915

22 In matters of art it is more blessed to respond than to judge.
Lord David Cecil in a radio programme

23 Art is the unceasing effort to compete with the beauty of flowers — and never succeeding.
Marc Chagall 1977

1 The artistic temperament is a disease that afflicts amateurs.
G. K. Chesterton, HERETICS 1905

2 Art is not a pastime, but a priesthood.
Jean Cocteau, New York Times 8 *Sep* 1982

3 That is what the title of artist means; one who perceives more than his fellows, and who records more than he has seen.
Gordon Craig, ON THE ART OF THE THEATRE 1911

4 He made a last desperate coup to persuade the world he was an artist by marrying a model. But this device deceived nobody.
Aleister Crowley, of Sir Gerald Kelly, CONFESSIONS

5 If a cloud is going to support a lady of substantial proportions you must make it fairly solid.
Mr. Justice Darling, Edwards Huntingdon v. Lewis and Simmons, May 1917

6 Artists hate the enlightened amateur unless he buys.
Ernest Dimnet, WHAT WE LIVE BY

7 In our daily lives — eating, dressing, working, or seeking amusement — art, good or bad, is always with us. For most of us, most of the time, it is bad art.
R. L. Duffus, North American Review, *Sep* 1936

8 Every master knows that the material teaches the artist.
Ilya Ehrenburg, Saturday Review 30 *Sep* 1967

9 The more perfect the artist the more completely separate in him will be the man who suffers and the mind which creates.
T. S. Eliot. Quoted Cyril Connolly, THE UNQUIET GRAVE 1945

10 The reputation of the Academy has got to a point where election should be positively distressing to a serious painter.
Evening Standard 22 *Feb* 1961

11 Artists can colour the sky red because they *know* it is blue. Those of us who aren't artists must colour things the way they really are or people might think we were stupid.
Jules Feiffer, CRAWLING ARNOLD

12 Art is significant deformity.
Roger Fry

13 A work of art is part of nature seen through a temperament.
André Gide, PROTESTS

14 I do not think abstract art can ever be as good as the art of a religious age. It stands on a different level of human aspiration.
Sir Ernest Gombrich. Quoted D.A.N. Jones, Radio Times 9 *Feb* 1979

15 The history of art in this century is seen, partly, as a history of revulsion. Artists have tried to *avoid* something, to *not* do something. But in *generic* primitive art they are not trying to *avoid* anything.
Id.

16 All men are creative but few are artists.
Paul Goodman, GROWING UP ABSURD 1960

17 No artist is ahead of his time. He *is* his time; it is just that others are behind the times.
Martha Graham. Quoted John Heilpern, Observer Magazine, *The Amazing Martha* 8 *Jul* 1979

18 It is not puritanism to affirm that the activity of the artist differs from the activity of the sanitary inspector.
Geoffrey Grigson. Quoted News Review 20 *Mar* 1947

19 Great art is the expression of a solution of the conflict between the demands of the world without and that within.
Edith Hamilton, THE GREEK WAY 1930

20 If they [artists] do see fields blue they are deranged, and should go to an asylum. If they only pretend to see them blue, they are criminals and should go to prison.
Adolf Hitler. Speech in Munich

21 The finest works of art are precious, among other reasons, because they make it possible for us to know, if only imperfectly and for a little while, what it actually feels like to think subtly and feel nobly.
Aldous Huxley, ENDS AND MEANS 1937

22 Recognisableness is an artistic quality which most people find profoundly thrilling.
Aldous Huxley, MUSIC AT NIGHT 1931

23 Art is one of the means whereby man seeks to redeem a life which is experienced as chaotic, senseless and largely evil.
Aldous Huxley, THEME AND VARIATIONS 1950

24 The artist, like the God of creation, remains within or behind or beyond or above his handiwork, invisible, refined out of existence, indifferent, paring his fingernails.
James Joyce, A PORTRAIT OF THE ARTIST AS A YOUNG MAN 1916

1 In a free society art is not a weapon.
John F. Kennedy. Speech at dedication of Robert Frost Library, Nov 1962

2 Artists are not engineers of the soul.
Id.

3 Drawing is the art of taking a line for a walk.
Paul Klee

4 Art does not reproduce what we see. It makes us see.
Paul Klee, CREATIVE CREDO

5 Art is art and there is nothing can be done to prevent it, but there is the Mayoress's decency to be considered.
A Lancashire Mayor on the display of nude figures in the Town Hall

6 Art is not a special sauce applied to ordinary cooking; it is the cooking itself if it is good.
W. R. Lethaby, FORM IN CIVILIZATION

7 The goitrous, torpid and squinting husks provided by Matisse in his sculpture are worthless except as tactful decorations for a mental home.
(Percy) Wyndham Lewis, THE ART OF BEING RULED

8 If you want to know what actually is occurring inside, underneath, at the centre, at any given moment, art is a truer guide than politics more often than not.
(Percy) Wyndham Lewis, TIME AND WESTERN MAN 1927

9 In other countries art and literature are left to a lot of shabby bums living in attics and feeding on booze and spaghetti, but in America the successful writer or picture-painter is indistinguishable from any other decent business man.
Sinclair Lewis, BABBITT 1922

10 The poet should believe in art for its own sake, but the draughtsman inevitably moralises. Artists always preach, if it is nothing more than their school of art. Art is pre-eminently didactic.
Vachel Lindsay. Quoted Edgar Lee Masters, VACHEL LINDSAY, A POET IN AMERICA

11 Art enlarges experience by admitting us to the inner life of others.
Walter Lippmann, A PREFACE TO POLITICS, *The Golden Rule and After* 1914

12 Every artist has his own distorting mirror; it is his method of making reality fresh and therefore recognisably real.
Robert Lynd, John o'London's Weekly 10 *Apr* 1930

13 The whole of art is an appeal to a reality which is not without us but in our minds.
Desmond McCarthy, THEATRE 1940

14 A good rocking horse has often more of the true horse about it than an instantaneous photograph of a Derby winner.
Desmond McCarthy, MANET AND HIS CONTEMPORARIES

15 Our feeling for a work of art is rarely independent of the place it occupies in art history.
André Malraux, THE VOICES OF SILENCE 1951

16 All art is a revolt against man's fate.
Id.

17 All works of art are successful because of, not in spite of, the limitations that form places upon them . . . the sense of triumph lies not merely in the humanity of the subject or the story, but also in the skill with which the artist moves freely within his self-imposed limits.
Roger Manvell, FILM

18 It is wrong to try to make art too life-like; it becomes released from its limitations and so loses its sense of form and proportion.
Id.

19 In those days, as a little child, I was living in Paradise and had no need of the arts, which at best are only a shadow of Paradise.
John Masefield, SO LONG TO LEARN

20 The worst sin that can be committed against the artist is to take him at his word, to see in his work a fulfilment instead of a horizon.
Henry Miller, THE COSMOLOGICAL EYE 1939

21 The artist does not tinker with the universe; he re-creates it out of his own experience and understanding of life.
Id.

22 An artist is always alone — if he *is* an artist; the artist needs loneliness.
Henry Miller, TROPIC OF CANCER 1934

23 After Matisse and Picasso there is nothing more to be done.
John Minton to John Moynihan 1957. *Quoted Dan Farson,* OUT OF STEP

24 We are all heirs to the loveliness of the visible world, but only by the process of art can we be inducted into possession of this large estate.
C. E. Montague, A WRITER'S NOTES ON HIS TRADE 1930

1 To be aristocratic in art one must avoid polite society.
George Moore. Quoted Cyril Connolly, ENEMIES OF PROMISE 1938

2 She [Chanel] exemplified the unwelcome truth that a good artist can be a shocking bad lot.
Raymond Mortimer, TRY ANYTHING ONCE

3 People don't learn to enjoy pictures because they seldom look at them; and they seldom look at pictures because they have never learnt to enjoy them.
Id.

4 Communication is the purpose of all art, though a man may write or paint from a desire for self expression. The result does not function as a work of art until somebody receives a communication from it.
Id.

5 The [modern] painter plumes himself upon an independence such as was never dreamed of by Piero della Francesca or Titian or Watteau. To paint the subjects that people relish is, he thinks, below his dignity. In fact it is above his capacity — not because he lacks the accomplishment, but because he lacks the impulse.
Id.

6 A work of art has no importance whatever to society. It is only important to the individual.
Vladimir Nabokov, STRONG OPINIONS

7 Great art is as irrational as great music. It is mad with its own loveliness.
George Jean Nathan, HOUSE OF SATAN

8 Art is a form of catharsis.
Dorothy Parker, ART

9 Painting is a blind man's profession. He paints not what he sees, but what he feels, what he tells himself about what he has seen.
Pablo Picasso. Quoted Jean Cocteau, JOURNALS

10 There are painters who transform the sun into a yellow spot, but there are others who, with the help of their art and their intelligence, transform a yellow spot into the sun.
Attributed to Pablo Picasso by Edith Sitwell, RHYMES AND REASON

11 If your man says of some picture "Yes but what does it mean?" ask him and keep on asking him, what his carpet means, or the circular patterns on his rubber shoe-soles. Make him lift up his foot to look at them.
Stephen Potter, ONE-UPMANSHIP 1952

12 Thanks to art, instead of seeing a single world, our own, we see it multiply until we have before us as many worlds as there are original artists.
Marcel Proust, MAXIMS 1948

13 Artistic genius in its reactions is like those extremely high temperatures which have the power to disintegrate combinations of atoms which they proceed to combine afresh in a diametrically opposite order.
Marcel Proust, REMEMBRANCE OF THINGS PAST 1913–27

14 Right now we're into creative groups. That's where taxidermy turns into an art form.
Jonathan Raban, OLD GLORY

15 Half of art is knowing when to stop.
Arthur William Radford

16 A work of art is good if it has sprung from necessity.
Rainer Maria Rilke, LETTER TO A YOUNG POET 1903

17 We walk in the dark — we do what we can — we give what we have. Our doubt is our passion and our passion is our task. The rest is the madness of art.
Philip Roth, THE GHOST WRITER

18 What garlic is to salad, insanity is to art.
Augustus Saint-Gandens, REMINISCENCES 1913

19 Nothing is so poor and melancholy as art that is interested in itself and not in its subject.
George Santayana, THE LIFE OF REASON, *Reason in Art* 1905

20 If it is art it is not for all, and if it is for all it is not art.
Arnold Schoenberg. Quoted Nat Shapiro, ENCYCLOPEDIA OF QUOTATIONS ABOUT MUSIC

21 The true artist will let his wife starve, his children go barefoot, his mother drudge for her living at seventy, sooner than work at anything but his art.
George Bernard Shaw, MAN AND SUPERMAN 1905

22 The artist, like the idiot or clown, sits on the edge of the world, and a push may send him over it.
Sir Osbert Sitwell, THE SCARLET TREE 1945

1 The vitality of a new movement in art or letters can be pretty accurately gauged by the fury it arouses.
Logan Pearsall Smith, of Impressionism, ALL TRIVIA, *Afterthoughts* 1931

2 A portrait is a picture in which there is something wrong with the mouth.
Eugene Speicher. Quoted Frank Muir, THE FRANK MUIR BOOK

3 The naked truth about me is to the naked truth about Salvador Dali as an old ukulele in the attic is to a piano in a tree, and I mean a piano with breasts.
James Thurber, THE THURBER MERRY-GO-ROUND 1945

4 The arts are an even better barometer of what is happening in our world than the stock market or debates in Congress.
Henrik Willem Van Loon, THE ARTS

5 I was so desirous of getting it [a picture] right that I did it with my shoes off.
G. F. Watts. Quoted Christopher Hassall, EDWARD MARSH

6 I took Art at College as my second subject one semester. I'd have taken it as my first subject only Dad lost his money in religion so I had to learn a trade.
Evelyn Waugh, THE LOVED ONE 1948

7 A work of art has an author and yet, when it is perfect, it has something which is anonymous about it.
Simone Weil, GRAVITY AND GRACE 1927

8 He [Sinclair Lewis] is a master of that species of art to which belong glass flowers, imitation fruit, Mme Tussaud's waxworks, and barnyard symphonies which aims at deceiving the spectator into thinking that the work in question is not an artificial product but the real thing.
T. K. Whipple, SPOKESMAN

9 Art flourishes where there is a sense of adventure, a sense of nothing having been done before.
A. N. Whitehead, DIALOGUES 1953

10 Art is the imposing of a pattern on experience, and our aesthetic enjoyment in recognition of the pattern.
Id.

11 Art for art's sake is a philosophy of the well-fed.
Cao Yu, Chinese playwright, Observer 13 *Apr* 1980

ASPIRATE

12 J. H. Thomas: I've got an 'orrible 'eadache.
Birkenhead: Why not try a couple of aspirates?
Quoted 2nd Earl Birkenhead in his biography of his father

HERBERT HENRY ASQUITH

13 He brought to Cabinet meetings the cool calculation that he displayed at the bridge table.
Robert Cecil, LIFE IN EDWARDIAN ENGLAND 1969

14 Arthur [Balfour] is wicked and moral. Asquith is good and immoral.
Winston Churchill. Quoted Ernest Raymond, MR BALFOUR

15 His mind opened and shut smoothly and exactly, like the breech of a gun.
Winston Churchill, GREAT CONTEMPORARIES 1937

16 Asquith worries too much about small points. If you were buying a large mansion he would come to you and say "Have you thought there is no accommodation for the cat?"
David Lloyd George. Letter to Lord Riddell 1915

MARGOT ASQUITH

17 A *café chantant* attached to a cathedral.
Anon.

18 That gifted entertainer, the Countess of Oxford and Asquith, author of The Autobiography of Margot Asquith (four volumes, ready boxed, suitable for throwing purposes).
Dorothy Parker, (Constant Reader) New Yorker, *Re-enter Margot Asquith, A Masterpiece from the French* 22 *Oct* 1927

19 I think it must be pleasanter to be Margot Asquith than to be any other living human being . . . Her perfect confidence in herself is a thing to which monuments should be erected . . . The affair between Margot Asquith and Margot Asquith will live as one of the prettiest love stories in all literature.
Id.

20 Her face, except her forehead, is wrinkled past makeup; she uses a vivid orange

lipstick not perhaps as an expression of her vitality but as a gesture to it. Her voice is the unfaltering instrument of moods that still seem to be as varying as a debutante's.
Reginald Pound, THEIR MOODS AND MINE 1937

ASSASSINATION

1 Assassination — an accident of my trade.
Alfonso XIII of Spain, after the attempt on his life on his wedding day 31 *May* 1906

2 If someone is going to shoot you there is nothing much you can do about it. If you're going to start worrying about it, it's time to give up.
Prince Charles, on Australian TV 1974

3 Assassination should be used as the vote should ideally be used, that is, bearing in mind only the public good and regardless of personal interest.
Edward Hyams, KILLING NO MURDER

4 If someone wants to shoot me from a window with a rifle, nobody can stop it, so why worry about it?
John F. Kennedy to his wife Jacqueline, before starting for Dallas the day he was assassinated 22 *Nov* 1963

5 I live each day under a threat of death. I know that I can meet a violent end.
Martin Luther King, in an interview with Gerald Priestland, broadcast by the BBC the day he was shot 4 *Apr* 1968

6 But how did you enjoy the *play* Mrs. Lincoln?
Tom Lehrer

7 He was a liar, and he was nothing but a damned demagogue. It didn't surprise me when they shot him. These demagogues, the ones that live by demagoguery, they all end up the same way.
Harry S Truman, of Huey Long. Quoted Merle Miller, PLAIN SPEAKING

ASSURANCE

8 . . . on whom assurance sits / As a silk hat on a Bradford millionaire.
T. S. Eliot, THE WASTE LAND 1922

FRED ASTAIRE

9 He is the nearest we are ever likely to get to a human Mickey Mouse.
Graham Greene. Quoted Leslie Halliwell, FILMGOER'S BOOK OF QUOTES 1973

10 The audience meets Mr. Astaire and the film at their best when he is adjusting his cravat to an elaborate dance routine or saying delicious things with his flashing feet that a lyricist would have difficulty putting into words.
André Sennwald reviewing The Gay Divorce

ASTONISHMENT

11 I could not be more astonished if you told me there were fleas at the Ritz.
Ronald Firbank, THE FLOWER BENEATH THE FOOT 1923

LORD ASTOR

12 He would, wouldn't he?
Mandy Rice-Davies, at the trial of Stephen Ward 29 *Jun* 1963, *when told that Lord Astor had denied her allegations*

NANCY ASTOR

13 Nobody wants me as a Cabinet Minister and they are perfectly right. I am an agitator, not an administrator.
Nancy Astor. Speech 1929

14 When you come into the Debating Chamber, Nancy, I feel as though you had come into my bathroom and I had only a sponge to cover myself with.
Winston Churchill to Lady Astor. Quoted John Beavers, Sunday Referee 19 *Feb* 1939

15 Her uncompromising Protestantism was tenuous but unyielding, like a strand of barbed wire in a hedge.
Walter Eliot. Quoted Christopher Sykes, NANCY

16 Viscount Waldorf Astor owned Britain's two most influential newspapers, *The Times* and the *Observer,* but his American wife, Nancy, had a wider circulation than both papers put together.
Emery Kelen, PEACE IN THEIR TIME

17 Nancy was a devout Christian Scientist, but not a good one. She kept confusing herself with God. She didn't know when to step aside and give God a chance.
Mrs Gordon Smith. Quoted Elizabeth Langhorne, NANCY ASTOR AND HER FRIENDS

ASTROLOGY

18 If Leo your own birthday marks / You will lust until forty, when starts / A new

29

pleasure in stamps / Boy Scouts and their camps / And fondling nude statues in parks.
Anon. Quoted Frank Muir, FRANK MUIR GOES INTO SUPERSTITION 1981

1 If you had been born two days later you would have been kind, generous and witty.
Cartoon caption by Hoest

2 As soon as man began to realise his own insignificance astrology died an instant, natural and inevitable death.
Sir James Jeans. Quoted The People

ASTRONOMY

3 *Observatory:* A place where astronomers conjecture among the guesses of their predecessors.
Ambrose Bierce, THE DEVIL'S DICTIONARY 1906

4 A thousand million years before you were born a parcel of light was sent off from a distant star. Yesterday it was delivered at Mount Palomar in California.
Ritchie Calder, News Chronicle 8 *Mar* 1948

5 I have loved the stars too fondly to be fearful of the night.
Epitaph of unknown astronomer; epigraph to Len Deighton's TWINKLE, TWINKLE, LITTLE SPY 1976

6 Astronomy teaches the correct use of the sun and the planets.
Stephen Leacock, LITERARY LAPSES 1910

ATHEIST

7 Man without God risks his life for impure causes and cannot avoid doing so . . . Atheist-humanism can define itself only by accepting the limits of human existence.
Raymond Aron, SELECTED ESSAYS

8 I am an atheist still, thank God.
Luis Buñuel. Quoted Ado Kyrou, LUIS BUÑUEL: AN INTRODUCTION

9 An atheist is a man with no visible means of support.
H. E. Fosdick. Attributed by Jonathan Hunt, DICTIONARY OF QUOTATIONS. *Also attributed to John Buchan,* MEMORY HOLD THE DOOR 1940

10 There seems to be a terrible misunderstanding on the part of a great many people to the effect that when you cease to believe you may cease to behave.

Louis Kronenberger, COMPANY MANNERS, *The Spirit of the Age* 1954

11 She calls herself an atheist, though she has a somewhat inconsistent regard for Quakers.
Observer, *Profile of Pat Arrowsmith* 13 *May* 1982

12 The sort of atheist who does not so much disbelieve in God as personally dislike Him.
George Orwell, DOWN AND OUT IN PARIS AND LONDON 1933

13 God can stand being told by Professor Ayer and Marghanita Laski that he doesn't exist.
J. B. Priestley, THE BBC'S DUTY TO SOCIETY

14 The highest praise of God consists in the denial of Him by the atheist, who finds creation so perfect that he can dispense with a creator.
Marcel Proust, REMEMBRANCE OF THINGS PAST 1913–27

15 I was told that the Chinese said they would bury me by the Western Lake and build a shrine to my memory. I have some slight regret that this did not happen as I might have become a god, which would have been very *chic* for an atheist.
Bertrand Russell, AUTOBIOGRAPHY 1967

16 My atheism, like Spinoza's, is true piety towards the universe and denies only gods made by men in their own image to be servants of their human interests.
George Santayana, SOLILOQUIES IN ENGLAND 1927

17 When the atheist is confronted with one of the natural outrages against the dignity and decency of life he is tempted to act for the moment as if God existed simply in order to have something on which to unloose his outraged feelings.
Philip Toynbee, Observer, *Death of a Mother* 17 *Apr* 1968

18 The worst moment for an atheist is when he feels grateful and doesn't know who to thank.
Wendy Ward. Attributed by P and J Holton, QUOTE AND UNQUOTE

ATHLETICS

19 The popular belief in athletics is grounded upon the theory that violent exercise makes for bodily health and that bodily health is

necessary to mental vigour. Both halves of this theory are highly dubious. Athletes, as a class, are not above the normal in health, but below it.
H. L Mencken, American Mercury, *Jun* 1951

ATOM

1 We have grasped the mystery of the atom and rejected the Sermon on the Mount.
Gen. Omar Bradley. Speech 11 *Nov* 1948

2 That is how the atom is split. But what does it mean? To us who think in terms of practical use it means — Nothing!
Ritchie Calder, Daily Herald, 27 *Jun* 1932

3 It was in 1909 at the Cavendish laboratory, Cambridge, that they drank a toast "to the electron. May it never be of use to anybody."
Cyril Connolly, Observer, *Turned to Dust and Ashes* 2 *Oct* 1977

4 One of the things which distinguishes ours from all earlier generations is this, that we have seen our atoms.
Karl Kelchner Darrow, THE RENAISSANCE OF PHYSICS

5 There is no evil in the atom — only in men's souls.
Adlai Stevenson. Speech, Harvard 18 *Sep* 1952

ATOM BOMB

6 And the criminal, multi-coloured flash / Of an H-bomb is no more beautiful / Than an autopsy when the belly's opened / To show cathedral windows never opened.
Dannie Abse, POEMS, GOLDER'S GREEN, *Pathology of Colours*

7 Let us not deceive ourselves; we must elect world peace or world destruction.
Bernard Baruch. Address to UN Atomic Energy Commission 14 *Jun* 1946

8 Atomic energy might be as good as our present day explosives but it is unlikely to produce anything much more dangerous.
Winston Churchill in 1939. *Quoted Chris Morgan and David Langford*, FACTS AND FALLACIES

9 No country without an atom bomb could properly consider itself independent.
Charles de Gaulle. Quoted New York Times Magazine 12 *May* 1968

10 We've got to take the atom bomb seriously. It's dynamite.
Sam Goldwyn. Quoted Alva Johnson, THE GREAT GOLDWYN

11 My God! It worked.
M. Griesen, observer at first test

12 The bomb that fell on Hiroshima fell on America, too.
Hermann Hagedorn, THE BOMB THAT FELL ON AMERICA

13 Aside from being tremendous it was one of the most aesthetically beautiful things I have ever seen.
Donald Hornig, THE DECISION TO DROP THE BOMB

14 The atom bomb will never go off, and I speak as an expert on explosives.
Admiral William Leahy to President Truman 1943. *Quoted Chris Morgan and David Langford*, FACTS AND FALLACIES

15 Surely if all the human race is obliterated the Creator will look rather foolish. But to whom?
George Lyttelton

16 The atom bomb is a paper tiger with which the Americans try to frighten people.
Mao Tse Tung. Speech 1946

17 And all because mankind would persist in tinkering with atoms.
George F. Morrell, This and That 2 *Aug* 1930

18 I am become Death, the shaker of worlds.
Dr. Robert Oppenheimer, quoting a Hindu poem, after the Los Alamos test explosion 16 *July* 1945

19 The genius of Einstein leads to Hiroshima.
Pablo Picasso. Quoted Francoise Gilot and Carlton Lake, LIFE WITH PICASSO

ATOMIC ENERGY

20 The release of atomic power has changed everything except our way of thinking and thus we are being driven unarmed towards a catastrophe.
Albert Einstein. Quoted Carl Seilig's biography of him

21 We cannot control atomic energy to an extent which would be of any value commercially, and I believe we are not likely ever to be able to do so.
Prof. Ernest Rutherford. Speech to British Association for the Advancement of Science 1933

1 The terror of the atom age is not the violence of the new power but the speed of man's adjustment to it — the speed of his acceptance.
E. B. White, THE SECOND TREE FROM THE CORNER, *Notes On Our Time* 1953

ATROCITY

2 The greatest horrors in our world, from the executions in Iran to the brutalities of the IRA, are committed by people who are totally sincere.
John Mortimer. Quoted Observer 5 *Aug* 1979

ATTENTION

3 I have always suffered from the diverted attention of the two distinct general compartments of my mind. The one into which the sun most rarely shines is the one reserved for soul-stirring impressions. If a monkey and a minaret were competing for my attention, the monkey would always win.
Stella Benson, THE LITTLE WORLD 1925

CLEMENT ATTLEE

4 An empty taxi drew up outside No. 10 and out got Clem Attlee.
Anon.

5 He seems determined to make a trumpet sound like a tin whistle.
Aneurin Bevan, writing in Tribune 1945

6 He brings to the fierce struggle of politics the tepid enthusiasm of a lazy summer afternoon at a cricket match.
Id.

7 He is a sheep in sheep's clothing.
Winston Churchill

8 He is a modest little man with much to be modest about.
Id.

9 Mr. Attlee combines a limited outlook with strong qualities of resistance.
Winston Churchill. Speech 27 *Apr* 1951

10 Mr. Attlee touches nothing that he does not dehydrate.
The Economist 16 *Aug* 1947

11 He is a bourgeois who is strangling the British bourgeoisie out of existence with a smile.
Peter Howard, Daily Mail 28 *May* 1947

12 His capacity for saying nothing was absolutely pre-eminent and he avoided all the traps which other people fell into. We used to say he would never use one syllable where none would do.
Douglas Jay, Thames TV, *The Day Before Yesterday* 1970

13 Charisma? He did not recognise the word, except as a clue in his beloved *Times* crossword.
James Margach, THE ABUSE OF POWER 1981

14 He succeeded in presiding over the biggest social, political and economic revolutions of the century. He never lost a single by-election and after five years of ceaseless press harassment he polled the highest popular vote at any election before or since.
Id.

15 He was a man who tucked his personality behind a pipe and left colleagues and public to make what they could of the smoke signals.
Frederick Newman, in the Daily Sketch. *Quoted James Margach*, THE ABUSE OF POWER 1981

16 Attlee is a charming man, but as a public speaker he is, compared to Winston, like a village fiddler after Paganini.
Harold Nicolson, DIARIES 10 *Nov* 1947

17 He reminds me of nothing so much as a dead fish before it has had time to stiffen.
George Orwell

18 He must have been pretty shrewd because he managed to escape from three conspiracies to throw him out.
Lord Shinwell, Thames TV, *The Day Before Yesterday* 1970

ATTRACTION

19 Men of every age flocked around her like gulls round a council tip.
John Carey, of Diana Cooper. Sunday Times 20 *Sep* 1981

20 They became, and remained, lovers for over 10 years. He said he was attracted to her 'hard mind'. She said she was was attracted to him because he smelt of walnut.
Of Rebecca West and H. G. Wells, Guardian *obituary* 16 *Mar* 1983

ATTRIBUTION

1 I had far far rather that people should attribute my verses to you than yours to me.
A. E. Housman, to his brother Laurence. LETTERS *(edited by Henry Maas)*

W. H. AUDEN

2 We have one poet of genius in Auden who is able to write prolifically, carelessly and exquisitely, nor does he seem to have to pay any price for his inspiration. It is as if he worked under the influence of some mysterious drug, which presents him with a private vision, a mastery of form and vocabulary.
Cyril Connolly, ENEMIES OF PROMISE 1938

3 Auden is something of an intellectual jackdaw, picking up bright pebbles of ideas so as to fit them into exciting conceptual patterns.
Richard Hoggart, W. H. AUDEN 1951

4 One never steps twice into the same Auden.
Randall Jarrell, THE THIRD BOOK OF CRITICISM 1969

5 An engaging, bookish, American talent, too verbose to be memorable and too intellectual to be moving.
Philip Larkin. Quoted George T. Wright, W. H. AUDEN

6 He is all ice and woodenfaced acrobatics.
(Percy) Wyndham Lewis, BLASTING AND BOMBARDIERING 1937

7 The high watermark, so to speak, of Socialist literature is W. H. Auden, a sort of gutless Kipling.
George Orwell, THE ROAD TO WIGAN PIER 1937

AUDIENCE

8 Long experience has taught me that in England nobody goes to the theatre unless he or she has bronchitis.
James Agate, EGO 1935

9 Of the type of audience at a chamber-music concert an Oxford don once remarked "They look like the sort of people who go to the English Church abroad".
W. H. Auden, A CERTAIN WORLD

10 To go back to *Punch and Judy* — what acting could add anything to that tremendous drama? What a relief to think that the audience standing there in the Tottenham Court Road did not go away saying: "She was very good, but that's not my idea of Judy".
Maurice Baring. Quoted Dame Ethel Smyth, MAURICE BARING

11 Ladies and gentlemen. We will now play you the work you think you have just heard.
Sir Thomas Beecham. Quoted C. R. Rees, Radio Times 12 *Jul* 1946

12 You look as if you have lived on grass for three years, like the King in the Bible. On the whole I would prefer to conduct for people in deepest Africa who beat tom-toms and live on nuts.
Sir Thomas Beecham. Quoted Charles Reid, THOMAS BEECHAM

13 Audiences don't know anybody writes a picture. They think the actors make it up as they go along.
William Holden. Lines from film, SUNSET BOULEVARD

14 Those in the cheaper seats, clap; the rest of you rattle your jewellery.
John Lennon, at Royal Command Performance, Nov 1963

15 If one talks to more than four people it is an audience, and one cannot really exchange thoughts with an audience.
Anne Morrow Lindbergh, NORTH TO THE ORIENT 1935

16 The audience is not the least important actor in the play and if it will not do its allotted share the play falls to pieces.
W. Somerset Maugham, THE SUMMING UP 1938

17 If all the world's a stage, and all the men and women merely players, where do all the audiences come from?
Denis Norden, BBC Radio 4, *My Word* 30 *Feb* 1977

18 I never fully understood the need for a 'live' audience. My music, because of its extreme quietude, would be happiest with a dead one.
Igor Stravinsky, London Magazine, *Mar* 1967

19 There have been more complaints about our inaudible actors. Perhaps they do not wish to interrupt the conversation in the stalls and boxes.
Sunday Express 5 *Nov* 1933

20 In England they cough all the time and they don't know they're doing it. In America all

you see is a sea of disappearing backs as they rush out, and in Australia they're always so hungry that they eat right through the performance.
Googie Withers at a Foyles Literary Lunch 12 Jun 1979

1 The audience strummed their catarrhs.
Alexander Woollcott, WHILE ROME BURNS 1934

AUNT

2 *Everyone* has an aunt in Tunbridge Wells.
Brian Johnston, BBC Radio 4, *Down Your Way* 24 Mar 1981

3 Why is it that the sudden mention of an aunt is so deflating to a poem?
Edward Marsh, AMBROSIA AND SMALL BEER

4 By the time one has educated them to an appreciation of the fact that one does not wear red woollen mittens in the West End, they die, or quarrel with the family, or do something equally inconsiderate.
Saki, REGINALD ON CHRISTMAS PRESENTS

5 Aunt Agatha . . . the Pest of Pont Street, the human snapping turtle.
P. G. Wodehouse, CARRY ON JEEVES 1925

6 It is no use telling me there are bad aunts and good aunts. At the core they are all alike. Sooner or later, out pops the cloven hoof.
P. G. Wodehouse, THE CODE OF THE WOOSTERS 1938

7 Aunt Agatha, who eats broken bottles and wears barbed wire next the skin.
Id.

8 Aunt Agatha's demeanour was now rather like that of one who, picking daisies on the railway, has just caught the down express in the small of the back.
P. G. Wodehouse, THE INIMITABLE JEEVES 1924

9 In this life it is not aunts that matter, but the courage one brings to them.
P. G. Wodehouse, THE MATING SEASON 1949

AUSTRALIA

10 Australia got me over my shyness.
Charles, Prince of Wales. Quoted Noël St. George, ROYAL QUOTES

11 I couldn't imagine a better place for making a film on the end of the world.
Attr. Ava Gardner, of Melbourne. Quoted Keith Dunstan, KNOCKERS

12 It was deathly still. Even the few birds seemed to be swamped in silence. Waiting — waiting — the bush seemed to be warily waiting. And he could not penetrate into its secret. He couldn't get at it. Nobody could get at it. What was it waiting for?
D. H. Lawrence, KANGAROO 1923

13 It's so empty and featureless, like a newspaper that has been entirely censored. We used to drive for miles, always expecting that round the next corner there would be something to look at, and there never was. That's the charm of Australia.
Robert Morley, RESPONSIBLE GENTLEMAN

AUTHOR

14 Is the bedroom door open or shut?
Ruby M. Ayres, asking for editorial instructions on being commissioned to write a serial

15 When I decided to write I didn't have any of the background or equipment that was considered necessary then. I thought all authors were Englishmen.
Rex Beach. Quoted in his obituary notice, Reuters 8 Dec 1949

16 When I am dead I hope it may be said / "His sins were scarlet, but his books were read."
Hilaire Belloc, EPIGRAMS

17 Bad authors are those who write with reference to an inner context which the reader cannot know.
Albert Camus, NOTEBOOKS 1935–1942

18 Coleridge was a drug addict. Poe was an alcoholic. Marlowe was killed by a man whom he was treacherously trying to stab. Pope took money to keep a woman's name out of a satire then wrote a piece so that she could still be recognised anyhow. Chatterton killed himself. Byron was accused of incest. *Do you still want to be a writer — and if so, why?*
Bennett Cerf, SHAKE WELL BEFORE USING 1948

19 Yes, I am exactly like the characters in my books. I am very tough and have been known to break a Vienna roll with my bare hands. I am very handsome, have a power-

ful physique and change my shirt every Monday.
Raymond Chandler, RAYMOND CHANDLER SPEAKING

1 A good novel tells us the truth about its hero; but a bad novel tells us the truth about its author.
G. K. Chesterton, HERETICS 1905

2 An author arrives at a good style when his language performs what is required of it without shyness.
Cyril Connolly, ENEMIES OF PROMISE 1938

3 Authors are sometimes like tomcats: they distrust all the other toms but they are kind to kittens.
Malcolm Cowley, WRITERS AT WORK 1958

4 I killed myself off at the end of my book because it seemed high time.
Bruce Frederic Cummings (W. N. P. Barbellian) writing of his JOURNAL OF A DISAPPOINTED MAN

5 An author ought to write for the youth of his own generation, the critics of the next, and schoolmasters of ever after.
F. Scott Fitzgerald. Quoted the Guardian *13 Nov 1964*

6 It does seem to me very bad to spend months writing a book and then months constantly being asked what you meant by it.
Sir John Gielgud at a Foyles Literary Lunch 8 Feb 1979

7 Authors are easy enough to get on with — if you are fond of children.
Michael Joseph. Quoted Observer *29 May 1949*

8 Being a novelist I consider myself superior to the saint, the scientist, the philosopher and the poet, who are all great masters of different bits of life but never get the whole hog.
D. H. Lawrence, PHOENIX 1936

9 Authors and uncaptured criminals are the only people free from routine.
Eric Linklater, POET'S PUB 1925

10 I write for no other purpose than to add to the beauty that now belongs to me. I write a book for no other reason than to add three or four hundred acres to my magnificent estate.
Jack London. Quoted Charles Child Walcutt, JACK LONDON

11 Almost anyone can be an author; the business is to collect money and fame from this state of being.
A. A. Milne, NOT THAT IT MATTERS 1919

12 I am the kind of writer that people think other people are reading.
V. S. Naipaul, Radio Times *24 Mar 1979*

13 In this country it is rare for anyone, let alone a publisher, to take writers seriously.
Anthony Powell, Daily Telegraph *8 Feb 1979*

14 Any man who becomes a novelist forfeits all the rights to scholarship.
Anthony Powell, BBC Radio 3 *6 Oct 1980*

15 Real men do things. They don't just write about them.
Frederic Raphael, Sunday Times *8 Oct 1978*

16 Writing is not a profession, but a vocation of unhappiness
Georges Simenon. Quoted John Heilpern, Observer *25 Mar 1979*

17 I would never read a book if it were possible to talk for half an hour with the man who wrote it.
President Woodrow Wilson in a speech to students at Princeton University 1910

AUTHORITY

18 Anything you make a mistake about, I will get you out of, and anything you do well, I will take credit for.
Ernest Bevin to a subordinate. Quoted Alan Bullock, LIFE AND TIMES OF ERNEST BEVIN

19 There is one thing about being a president — nobody can tell you when to sit down.
President Dwight Eisenhower to an interviewer, Jul 1953

AUTOBIOGRAPHY

20 Autobiography is now as common as adultery and hardly less reprehensible.
Lord Altrincham. Quoted Leon Harris, THE FINE ART OF POLITICAL WIT

21 Autobiography is the outcome of a struggle in the author's brain between the desire to be truthful and the desire to be interesting.
Vernon Bartlett, I KNOW WHAT I LIKED

22 Autobiography, to be any good, must be largely untrue.
Patricia Beer, The Listener

1 Just as there is nothing between the admirable omelette and the intolerable, so with autobiography.
Hilaire Belloc, A CONVERSATION WITH A CAT

2 One learns little more about a man from the feats of his literary memory than from the feats of his alimentary canal.
F. M. Colby. Quoted C. Fadiman, READING I HAVE LIKED

3 An autobiography is an obituary in serial form with the last instalment missing.
Quentin Crisp, THE NAKED CIVIL SERVANT

4 Twenty-five seems to me the latest age at which anybody should write an autobiography. It has an air of finality about it, as though one had clambered to the summit of a great hill, and were waving goodbye to some distant country which can never be revisited.
Beverley Nichols, TWENTY-FIVE 1925

5 I have a certain hesitation in starting my biography too soon for fear of something important having not yet happened. Suppose I should end my days as President of Mexico; the biography would seem incomplete if it did not mention this fact.
Bertrand Russell. Letter to Stanley Unwin, Nov 1930

6 You'll want to know . . . all that David Copperfield type of crap. But I don't feel like going into it.
J. D. Salinger, CATCHER IN THE RYE 1951

7 Autobiographies ought to begin with Chapter Two.
Ellery Sedgwick, THE HAPPY PROFESSION

AUTOGRAPH

8 He seemed such a nice old gentleman I thought I would give him my autograph as a souvenir.
Adolf Hitler, of Austen Chamberlain after Munich

AUTUMN

9 Fallen leaves lying on the grass in November bring more happiness than daffodils.
Cyril Connolly, THE UNQUIET GRAVE 1945

10 Now it is autumn and the falling fruit / And the long journey to oblivion. / The apples falling like great drops of dew / To bruise themselves an exit from themselves.
D. H. Lawrence, THE SHIPS OF DEATH 1932

AVARICE

11 The trouble is, Mr. Goldwyn, that you are only interested in art, and I am only interested in money.
George Bernard Shaw. Quoted Alva Johnson, THE GREAT GOLDWYN

AVERAGE

12 Most people are such fools that it is really no great compliment to say that a man is above the average.
W. Somerset Maugham, A WRITER'S NOTEBOOK 1949

AVIATION

13 It felt as if angels were pushing.
Adolf Galland, on flying a jet aircraft, THE FIRST AND THE LAST

14 The aeroplane will never fly.
Lord Haldane, Secretary for War 1907. Quoted Chris Morgan and David Langford, FACTS AND FALLACIES

15 I don't know how old the plane was, but Lindbergh's lunch was still on the seat. The path to the washroom was outside.
Bob Hope, I OWE RUSSIA 1200 DOLLARS 1963

16 Concorde is great. It gives you three extra hours to find your luggage.
Bob Hope, to reporters at Heathrow

17 In the space age, man will be able to go around the world in two hours — one hour for the flying and the other to get to the airport.
Neil McElroy, Look Magazine 18 *Feb* 1958

18 The aeroplane has unveiled for us the true face of the earth.
Antoine de Saint-Exupéry, WIND, SAND AND STARS 1939

B

BABY

1 A baby is an alimentary canal with a loud voice at one end and no responsibility at the other.
E. Adamson

2 Save trouble and tiredness. Put the baby in a D-Baby Cot which folds up flat in a second and can be carried like an attaché case.
Advertisement in Kent newspaper

3 There is no finer investment for any community than putting milk into babies.
Winston Churchill in a radio broadcast 21 *Mar* 1943

4 When Baby's cries grew harder to bear / I popped him in the Frigidaire / I never would have done so if / I'd known he'd be frozen stiff. / My wife said "George I'm so unhappy / Our darling's now completely frappé".
Harry Graham, MORE RUTHLESS RHYMES

5 We all of us wanted babies — but did we want children?
Eda J. Leshan. Quoted Katharine Whitehorn, HOW TO SURVIVE CHILDREN

6 A bit of talcum / Is always walcum.
Ogden Nash, REFLECTIONS ON BABIES

7 I can see that it is a very homely baby, indeed. Still I never see many babies that I consider rose geraniums for looks, anyway.
Damon Runyon, GUYS AND DOLLS 1932

8 How to fold a diaper depends on the size of the baby and the diaper.
Dr. Benjamin Spock, BABY AND CHILD CARE 1941

9 There was in his possession a photograph of himself at the same early age, in which he, too, looked like a homicidal fried egg.
P. G. Wodehouse, SONNY BOY

BALDNESS

10 The only thing that can stop hair falling is the floor.
Will Rogers, AUTOBIOGRAPHY 1949

STANLEY BALDWIN

11 It is medicine man talk . . . Murmurs of admiration break out as this second-rate orator trails his tawdry wisps of mist over the parliamentary scene.
Aneurin Bevan, Tribune 1947

12 The candle in that great turnip has gone out.
Winston Churchill, on Baldwin's retirement. Quoted Harold Nicolson, DIARIES 17 *Aug* 1950

13 At times I could have murdered S.B. but I would always have voted him a state funeral.
Colin R. Coote, Daily Telegraph, *A New Judgment on Baldwin* 15 *Nov* 1973

14 Not even a public figure. A man of no experience. And of the utmost insignificance.
Lord Curzon, when passed over in favour of Baldwin as Prime Minister. Quoted Harold Nicolson, CURZON, THE LAST PHASE

15 Baldwin was never quite sure that anybody was right, especially himself.
Harold Macmillan, THE PAST MASTERS

16 As a man he was unattractive, with unpleasant habits, always scratching himself.
Diana Mosley, THE DUCHESS OF WINDSOR

17 Stanley Baldwin always hits the nail on the head, but it doesn't go in any further.
G. M. Young. Quoted G. W. Lyttelton, THE LYTTELTON HART-DAVIS LETTERS 2 *May* 1951

A. J. BALFOUR

18 He played politics in the same spirit as he played golf.
Robert Cecil, LIFE IN EDWARDIAN ENGLAND 1969

19 A lay priest seeking a secular goal.
Winston Churchill, GREAT CONTEMPORARIES 1937

1 A powerful, graceful cat, walking delicately and unsoiled across a rather muddy street.
Id.

2 When Arthur Balfour launched his scheme for peopling Palestine with Jewish immigrants, I am credibly informed that he did not know there were Arabs in the country.
W. R. Inge (Dean of St. Pauls), The Evening Standard

BANK

3 Banks lend you money as people lend you an umbrella when the sun is shining and want it back when it starts to rain.
Sir Edward Beddington-Behrens, LOOK BACK — LOOK FORWARD

TALLULAH BANKHEAD

4 Tallulah is always skating on thin ice. Everyone wants to be there when it breaks.
Mrs. Patrick Campbell, The Times *obituary* 13 *Dec* 1968

J. M. BARRIE

5 When I began writing novels people said they were not real novels. When I began writing plays folk said they were not real plays. I expect they are going about now saying I am not a real baronet.
J. M. Barrie on receiving a knighthood. Quoted J. A. Hammerton, BARRIE: THE STORY OF A GENIUS

6 Like all sentimentalists he took refuge at times in ferocious cynicism.
Hamilton Fyfe, John o'London's Weekly 2 *Jul* 1937

7 The cheerful clatter of Sir James Barrie's cans as he went round with the milk of human kindness.
Philip Guedella, SOME CRITICS

BATH

8 Whenever I have a bath I make a list of the things I am going to need and check it carefully before entering the water.
Patrick Campbell, Sunday Times

9 If you don't lock the bathroom some people are taking baths every day.
J. Glenton, speaking to Morecombe Hotels and Caterers' Association. Reported Morecombe Guardian

10 I test my bath before I sit / And I'm always moved to wonderment / That what chills the finger not a bit / Is so frigid upon the fundament.
Ogden Nash, SAMSON AGONISTES

11 I have had a good many more uplifting thoughts, creative and expansive visions, while soaking in comfortable baths or drying myself after bracing showers in well-equipped American bathrooms than I have ever had in any cathedral.
Edmund Wilson, A PIECE OF MY MIND 1956

BEARD

12 He had a thin vague beard, or rather he had a chin on which large numbers of hairs weakly curled and clustered to cover its retreat.
Max Beerbohm. Quoted S. C. Roberts, THE INCOMPARABLE MAX

13 Shaw's wife . . . implored Nancy [Astor] to look after him and make him wash his beard. These instructions Nancy carried out faithfully, to the point of washing Shaw's beard personally, in the Metropole Hotel, Moscow, watched by the fascinated hotel staff.
Geoffrey Bocca, Sunday Express, *The Lady and the Commisar 5 Feb* 1956

14 It always seemed to me that men wore their beards like they wore their neckties, for show.
D. H. Lawrence, ST. MAWR 1925

15 An irregular greying beard was a decoration to a face which badly needed assistance.
Edgar Wallace, AGAIN SAUNDERS 1931

THE BEATLES

16 Q. How do you rate your music?
A. We're good musicians. Just adequate.
Q. Then why are you so popular?
A. Maybe people like adequate music.
The Beatles, in an interview. Quoted Nat Shapiro, ENCYCLOPEDIA OF QUOTATIONS ABOUT MUSIC

17 Lots of people who complained about us receiving the M.B.E. received theirs for heroism in war — for killing people. We received ours for entertaining other people. I'd say we deserve ours more.
John Lennon, BEATLES ILLUSTRATED LYRICS

1 Do you remember when everyone began analysing Beatle songs? I don't think I understood what some of them were supposed to be about.
Ringo Starr. Quoted Nat Shapiro, ENCY-CLOPEDIA OF QUOTATIONS ABOUT MUSIC

BEAUTY

2 She looked very beautiful with some red roses in her hat and the dainty red rouge in her cheeks looking quite the thing.
Daisy Ashford (aged 9), THE YOUNG VISITERS 1919

3 Her beauty sweetens her wit like honey on the tip of a dagger.
Raymond Asquith of Lady Diana Manners, LIFE AND LETTERS

4 Only in romantic novels are the beautiful guaranteed happiness.
Lady Cynthia Asquith, DIARIES

5 Incredibly, inordinately, devastatingly, immortally, calamitously, hearteningly, adorably beautiful.
Rupert Brooke of the actress Cathleen Nesbitt

6 It is hard, if not impossible, to snub a beautiful woman — they remain beautiful and the snub recoils.
Winston Churchill

7 Beauty often starts small and becomes immense.
Jean Cocteau in an interview with Derek Prouse, Sunday Times 20 *Oct* 1963

8 Beautiful women must think about their beauty as capitalists think about their investments or politicians about their majorities; it is all they have to ensure their places in the world.
Cyril Connolly, Sunday Times 21 *Apr* 1968

9 She was often underrated because she was so beautiful.
George Cukor, of Vivien Leigh. Quoted Gavin Lambert, ON CUKOR

10 Only with beauty wake wild memories — / Sorrow for where you are, for where you would be.
Walter De La Mare, THE CAGE

11 After a certain degree of prettiness, one pretty girl is as pretty as another.
F. Scott Fitzgerald, THE CRACK-UP 1936

12 Nonsense and beauty have close connections.
E. M. Forster, THE LONGEST JOURNEY 1907

13 Think of all the beauty still left around you and be happy.
Anne Frank, DIARY OF A YOUNG GIRL 1952

14 Beauty is intrinsically edifying.
Aldous Huxley, TIME MUST HAVE A STOP 1944

15 I'm tired of all this nonsense about beauty only being skin deep. That's deep enough. What do you want — an adorable pancreas?
Jean Kerr, THE SNAKE HAS ALL THE LINES

16 Beauty is an *experience*, nothing else. It is not a fixed pattern or an arrangement of features. It is something *felt*.
D. H. Lawrence, ESSAYS

17 Beauty you lifted up my sleeping eye / And filled my heart with longing with a look.
John Masefield, SONNETS

18 Beauty is perfect, and perfection (such is human nature) holds our attention for but a little while . . . Let us face it, beauty is a bit of a bore.
W. Somerset Maugham, CAKES AND ALE 1930

19 The beautiful should be defined as that of which the admiring contemplation is good in itself.
G. E. Moore, PRINCIPIA ETHICA 1903

20 Beauty is everlasting / And dust is for a time.
Marianne Moore, IN DISTRUST OF MERITS 1951

21 Beauty is a sequence of hypotheses which ugliness cuts short when it bars the way that we could already see opening into the unknown.
Marcel Proust, REMEMBRANCE OF THINGS PAST 1913–1927

22 Beauty is all very well at first, but who ever looks at it when it has been in the house three days.
George Bernard Shaw, MAN AND SUPERMAN 1905

23 All ugliness passes and beauty endures; except of the skin.
Edith Sitwell, LETTERS

24 Use harms and even destroys beauty. The noblest function of an object is to be contemplated.
Miguel de Unamuno, MIST

1 The beauty of the world has two edges, one of laughter, one of anguish, cutting the heart asunder.
Virginia Woolf, A ROOM OF ONE'S OWN 1929

LORD BEAVERBROOK

2 Beaverbrook is so pleased to be in the Government that he is like the town tart who has finally married the Mayor.
Beverley Baxter. Quoted Henry Channon, DIARY 12 *Jun* 1940

3 The Beaver is not a bad man; he is a bad boy.
John Buchan. Quoted Observer 29 *May* 1949

4 David Lloyd George called at Chertley Court near Leatherhead where Beaverbrook lived, to consult his friend about a current political conspiracy.
"Is the lord at home?" he asked the butler.
"No sir, the lord is out walking."
"Ah", said Lloyd George. "On the water, I presume."
Hugh Cudlipp, WALKING ON THE WATER

SAMUEL BECKETT

5 You either like Samuel Beckett's plays or you think they are a heap of twaddle. They remind me of something Sir John Betjeman might do if you filled him up with benzedrine and then force-fed him Guinness intravenously.
Tom Davis, Observer 17 *Jun* 1979

6 He believed in this kind of literature being a kind of murmur, out of which sense gradually should emerge.
Martin Esslin on Samuel Beckett's radio work, The Listener 25 *Nov* 82

BED

7 The cool kindness of sheets that soon smooth away trouble; and the rough male kiss of blankets.
Rupert Brooke, THE GREAT LOVER

8 Personally I am a great believer in bed, in constantly keeping horizontal. The heart and everything else goes slower and the whole system is refreshed.
Sir Henry Campbell-Bannerman. Letter to Mrs. Whiteley 11 *Sep* 1900

9 I am surprised that none of your correspondents has proposed the obvious solution [to reading in bed] — the provision of a series of slits in the bedclothes through which the hands may be projected in the manner of the old-fashioned Turkish bath box. When not in use the slits may be closed by zips or buttons.
H. Malcolm Carter. Letter to The Times 10 *Jan* 1962

10 No civilised person ever goes to bed the same day he gets up.
Richard Harding Davis, GALLAGHER

11 Dr. Marie Stopes could not and would not sleep unless her bed was aligned north to south. If unable to move it she would lie across it slantwise, correctly orientated.
Mary Eden and Richard Carrington, THE PHILOSOPHY OF THE BED

12 When my husband reads in bed on warm nights he puts a colander over his head. He says it keeps off the flies, shades his eyes from the light, and lets in air at the same time.
Letter to Good Shopping. *Quoted* New Statesman

13 No human being believes that any other human being has a right to be in bed when he himself is up.
Robert Lynd, RAIN, RAIN GO TO SPAIN

14 I forget who it was that recommended men for their souls' sake to do each day two things they disliked. It is a precept that I have followed scrupulously; for every day I have got up and I have gone to bed.
W. Somerset Maugham, THE MOON AND SIXPENCE 1919

15 It was such a lovely day I thought it was a pity to get up.
W. Somerset Maugham, OUR BETTERS 1923

16 He really is a hero for his bed. I have known him often being *tired* of laying in bed, get up to have a rest, and after he had rested get back into bed again like a martyr.
Henry Moat. Quoted Sir Osbert Sitwell, THE SCARLET TREE 1945

17 So we switched on the emotion heater and went to bed.
Overheard. Quoted Mary Malcolm, BBC Radio, *Quote Unquote* 4 *Feb* 1981

18 To prevent bedtime from becoming monotonous my husband gets into bed at the right side on Mondays and Tuesdays, the left side on Wednesdays and Thursdays, and

climbs the footboard on Fridays, Saturdays and Sundays.
Letter to Reveille. *Quoted* New Statesman.

1 Rose is a wonderful hand for making up beds, although several times, when she is in a hurry to get off, I hear she makes up beds with guests still in them.
Damon Runyon, MORE THAN SOMEWHAT 1937

BEE

2 And bees will stand / Upon their hands in fragrant deeps.
W. H. Davies, COMPLETE POEMS, *Days Too Short* 1943

3 Forget not bees in winter though they sleep.
Vita Sackville-West, THE LAND 1926

4 A German general claims that bees can now be enrolled as spies. They have strong homing instincts and can carry messages by means of varying colours painted on their backs.
Titbits 14 *Mar* 1936

5 According to the theory of dynamics and as may be readily demonstrated through wind-tunnel experiments, the bumble-bee is unable to fly. This is because the size, weight and shape of his body in relation to the total wingspread makes flying impossible. But the bumble bee, being ignorant of these scientific facts, goes ahead and flies anyway — and makes a little honey every day.
War-time sign in General Motors factory

6 A dark Assyrian beard began to grow on one of the topmost twigs of the elm. The bees were clustering about the new queen.
Henry Williamson, LIFE IN A DEVON VILLAGE 1935

SIR THOMAS BEECHAM

7 I was always touched by the friendliness and humility beneath the brilliant exterior. Remember he always bowed first to the *orchestra* and only secondly to the audience.
Richard Arnell, BEECHAM REMEMBERED *(edited by Humphrey Proctor-Gregg)*

8 There was a break in the recording session of an opera in the Kingsway Hall. Sir Thomas was alone when some recording engineers entered and one asked how things were progressing.
"Reasonably well," said Sir Thomas, "But I sometimes long for the days of the old castrati. You knew where you were with them."
Harold Atkins and Archie Norman, BEECHAM STORIES

9 Beecham was deeply rooted in provincial England. In this respect he resembled Arnold Bennett. One from Lancashire, one from the Potteries. Both enjoyed being thought of as 'cards' which indeed they were.
Lord Boothby, MY YESTERDAY, YOUR TOMORROW 1962

10 A complex character — Falstaff, Puck and Malvolio all mixed up, each likely to overwhelm the others. Witty, then waggish, supercilious, then genial, kindly and sometimes cruel, an artist in affectation, yet somehow always himself. Lancashire in his bones, yet a man of the world.
Neville Cardus, SIR THOMAS BEECHAM

BEGGING

11 Once I built a railroad, now its done / Brother can you spare a dime.
Edgar Y. Harburg (song) 1932

BEGINNING

12 With the possible exception of the equator, everything begins somewhere.
Peter Fleming, ONE'S COMPANY

13 You're searching, Joe / For things that don't exist. I mean beginnings. / Ends and beginnings — there are no such things / There are only middles.
Robert Frost, IN THE HOME STRETCH

BEHAVIOUR

14 He neither drank, smoked, nor rode a bicycle. Living frugally, saving his money, he died early, surrounded by greedy relatives. It was a great lesson to me.
John Barrymore. Quoted J. P. McEvoy, Stage, *Jan* 1941

15 There is no surer way of calling the worst out of anyone than that of taking their worst as being their true selves; no surer way of bringing out the best than by only accepting that as being true of them.
E. F. Benson, REX

1 You must never do that! That's what little French boys do.
Sir Hugh Casson and Joyce Grenfell, NANNY SAYS 1972

2 Sit up straight at the table so there's room for a mouse at the front and a cat at the back.
Id.

3 Shoddy table manners have broken up many a happy bond.
Colette, GIGI 1945

4 I like to eat with nice people, drink with nice people, and sleep with a clear conscience.
Lord Denning, Observer, *Sayings of the Week* 18 *Jul* 1982

5 A man's ethical behaviour should be based effectually on sympathy, education and social ties and needs; no religious basis is necessary. Man would indeed be in a poor way if he had to be restrained by fear of punishment and hope of reward after death.
Albert Einstein, New York Times Magazine, *Religion and Science* 9 *Nov* 1930

6 Many things — such as loving, going to sleep or behaving unaffectedly — are done worst when we try hardest to do them.
C. S. Lewis, STUDIES IN MEDIEVAL AND RENAISSANCE LITERATURE

7 He is Harrow and Oxford, and often behaves like Borstal and Parkhurst.
Reginald Pound of Beachcomber (J.B. Morton), THEIR MOODS AND MINE 1935

8 If people behaved in the way nations do they would all be put into straitjackets.
Tennessee Williams on BBC Radio

BEHAVIOURISM

9 Behaviourism has substituted for the erstwhile anthropomorphic view of the rat a ratomorphic view of man.
Arthur Koestler, THE GHOST IN THE MACHINE

10 Behaviourism is a kind of flat-earth view of the mind.
Id.

11 If 'mind' acts on body, then all physical laws are invalid.
John Broadus Watson, BEHAVIOURISM

BELIEF

12 What matters to me is not whether it is true or not but that I believe it to be true, or rather not that I *believe* it, but that *I* believe it — I trust I make myself obscure?
Robert Bolt, A MAN FOR ALL SEASONS 1960

13 If people stop believing in religion they don't then believe in nothing, they believe in everything.
G. K. Chesterton. Quoted Katherine Whitehorn, Observer 16 *Sep* 1979

14 The majority of people live below the level of belief or doubt. It takes application and a kind of genius to believe anything.
T. S. Eliot, THE ENEMY

15 A man must not swallow more beliefs than he can digest.
Havelock Ellis, THE DANCE OF LIFE 1923

16 My dear child, you must believe in God in spite of what the clergy tell you.
Dr. Benjamin Jowett on his death bed. Quoted Margot Asquith, AUTOBIOGRAPHY 1936

17 The constant assertion of belief is an indication of fear.
Krishnamurti, THE PENGUIN KRISHNAMURTI READER

18 No amount of manifest absurdity could deter those who wanted to believe from believing.
Bernard Levin, THE PENDULUM YEARS 1976

19 The world goes on because a few men in each generation believe in it utterly, accept it unquestioningly, they underwrite it with their lives.
Henry Miller, THE AIR-CONDITIONED NIGHTMARE 1945

20 You're not free / Until you have been made captive by / Supreme belief.
Marianne Moore, COLLECTED POEMS, *Spencer's Ireland* 1951

21 In view of the widespread silliness of the majority of mankind a widespread belief is more likely to be foolish than sensible.
Bertrand Russell, MARRIAGE AND MORALS 1929

22 The brute necessity of believing something so long as life lasts does not justify any belief in particular.
George Santayana, SCEPTICISM AND ANIMAL FAITH 1923

1 I confused things with their names. That is belief.
Jean-Paul Sartre, WORDS

2 When Cardinal Newman was a child he "wished he could believe the Arabian Nights were true". When he came to be a man his wish seems to have been granted.
Lytton Strachey, EMINENT VICTORIANS 1918

3 To believe in God is to yearn for His existence and furthermore, it is to act as if He did exist.
Miguel de Unamuno, THE TRAGIC SENSE OF LIFE 1913

BELLS

4 I heard the church bells hollowing out the sky, / Deep beyond deep, like never-ending stars, / And turned to Archibald, my safe old bear, / Whose woollen eyes looked sad or glad at me.
Sir John Betjeman, SUMMONED BY BELLS 1960

TONY BENN

5 He is the Bertie Wooster of Marxism.
Reported by Malcolm Bradbury in BBC Radio 4, *Quote Unquote* 13 *Sep* 1979

6 He led the left, not through any rigorous approach, but through dazzling rhetoric and an instinctive popularism, owing much of his appeal to his ability to always appear thoroughly English, reasonable and Christian.
Anthony Sampson, THE CHANGING ANATOMY OF BRITAIN 1982

7 I have always said about Tony that he immatures with age.
Sir Harold Wilson, THE CHARIOT OF ISRAEL

ARNOLD BENNETT

8 Arnold Bennett was assuredly the super-realist of his age.
Lilian Arnold

9 He was avuncular to the Sitwells and Aldous Huxley, a talent-spotter and friend to the young. He was neither so grand as Shaw, nor so philistine as Wells, so aloof as Galsworthy, so critical as Eliot, so envious as Wyndham Lewis, so feline as Gosse.
Dudley Barker, WRITER BY TRADE, *A View of Arnold Bennett*

10 Bennett — a sort of pig in clover.
D. H. Lawrence, letter to Aldous Huxley 27 *Mar* 1928

11 He never outgrew the provincialism that made the Savoy Hotel in his eyes the Earthly Paradise.
S. P. B. Mais, ALL THE DAYS OF MY LIFE

12 Arnold Bennett knew his eggs. Whatever his interest in good writing, he never showed his public anything but his avarice. Consequently they adored him.
Ezra Pound, Criterion magazine 1937

13 Is Dickens of no value to the world any more because Mr. Arnold Bennett has found it impossible to finish one of his novels?
Hugh Walpole, T.P's and Cassell's Weekly, *Literary Dogmatists* 6 *Aug* 1927

14 As a novelist Arnold Bennett was more interested in human beings than in human nature, and in human backgrounds than human hopes. I see him more as a great registrar of life than as a great interpreter. It was as though he had abundant material on which to form conclusions about life, but did not form them.
Wilfred Whitten, John o'London's Weekly 28 *May* 1932

BEREAVEMENT

15 She revealed such a depth and intensity of suffering as made me feel one could never be happy while she was alive. She regards the remainder of her life as a bad debt to be discharged.
Lady Cynthia Asquith of her widowed sister-in-law, DIARIES 1915

16 Not the least hard thing to bear when they go away from us, these quiet friends [dogs] is that they carry away with them so many years of our own lives.
John Galsworthy, MEMOIRS

17 It was sea and islands now. Atlantis had sunk.
C. S. Lewis on the death of his mother, SURPRISED BY JOY, *The Shape of My Early Life* 1965

18 Passionate grief does not link us with the dead but cuts us off from them.
C. S. Lewis, A GRIEF OBSERVED

19 I am not resigned to the shuttering away of loving hearts in the hard ground. / So it is, and so it will be, for so it has been, time out of mind. / Into the darkness they go, the

wise and the lovely. Crowned / With lilies and with laurel they go; but I am not resigned.
Edna St. Vincent Millay, DIRGE WITHOUT MUSIC 1928

SIR JOHN BETJEMAN

1 He has a passion for Victoriana / Nostalgia flows like lava from his quill / How lovely the remembered dreams of Cornwall! / How long the golden days of Muswell Hill.
Roger Woddis, Radio Times, *Far more than freckled girls* 12 *Feb* 1983

BETRAYAL

2 All a man can betray is his conscience.
Joseph Conrad, UNDER WESTERN EYES 1911

3 If I had to choose between betraying my country and betraying my friend I hope I should have the guts to betray my country.
E. M. Forster, WHAT I BELIEVE

4 Greater love hath no man than this, that he lay down his friends for his life.
Jeremy Thorpe, of Selwyn Lloyd's dismissal as Chancellor of the Exchequer by Harold Macmillan 13 *Jul* 1962

ANEURIN BEVAN

5 That squalid nuisance and Welsh soapbox buccaneer.
James Robertson Armstrong, founder of the Vermin Club. Quoted News Review 19 *Aug* 1948

6 If thy Nye offend thee, pluck it out.
Clement Attlee to Labour NEC, Mar 1955

7 He will be as great a curse to this country in peace as he was a squalid nuisance in time of war.
Winston Churchill. Quoted Robert Lewis Taylor, THE AMAZING MR. CHURCHILL

8 A merchant of discourtesy.
Winston Churchill. Quoted Michael Foot, ANEURIN BEVAN, VOL. I

9 Nye wasn't cut out to be a leader. He was cut out to be a prophet. It's no joke being leader of the Labour Party, and Nye didn't want the bother; he just wanted to have it all led for him.
Richard Crossman, Thames TV, *The Day Before Yesterday* 1970

10 He was like a fire in a room on a cold day.
Constance Cummings. Quoted Michael Foot, ANEURIN BEVAN 1897–1945

11 Repent, for the kingdom of Bevan is Nye.
Election slogan, Northampton 1959

12 He should have been a poet, political parties only chain such spirits.
Michael Foot, ANEURIN BEVAN 1945–1960

13 Aneurin Bevan was a true orator in the sense that even on quite important issues he did not know what he was going to say until he had said it.
Paul Johnson, Daily Telegraph, *Searching for a Phrase* 27 *Jul* 1979

14 He could boil blood with the evidence of misery, split sides with his jests, and make spirits soar with his visions.
Neil Kinnock, The Times 3 *May* 1982

15 Nye was born old and died young.
Jennie Lee. Quoted Michael Foot, ANEURIN BEVAN 1897–1945

16 An ideal Welsh type, the Prophet Aneurin; fatal charm, magic voice, exquisite sensitiveness to beauty, and a liability to break loose at any moment and create 15 different kinds of roaring hell.
Timothy Shy, News Chronicle 1946

ERNEST BEVIN

17 A speech from Ernest Bevin on a major occasion had all the horrific fascination of a public execution. If the mind was left immune, eyes and ears and emotions were riveted.
Michael Foot, ANEURIN BEVAN

18 Bevin always treated the Soviet Union as if it were a breakaway faction of the Transport and General Workers Union.
Kingsley Martin, HAROLD LASKI

19 He objected to ideas only when others had them.
A. J. P. Taylor, ENGLISH HISTORY 1914–1945

20 Bevin thought he was Palmerston wearing Keir Hardie's cloth cap, whereas he was really the Foreign Office's Charlie McCarthy.
Konni Zilliacus. Quoted Kingsley Martin, HAROLD LASKI

BIBLE

21 Had the Bible been in clear straightforward language, had the ambiguities and contra-

dictions been edited out, and had the language been constantly modernised to accord with contemporary taste it would almost certainly have been, or become, a work of lesser influence.
J. K. Galbraith, ECONOMICS, PEACE AND LAUGHTER

1 The number one book of the ages was written by a committee, and it was called the Bible.
Louis B. Mayer. Quoted Leslie Halliwell, FILMGOER'S BOOK OF QUOTATIONS 1973

2 A lady's husband seeks compensation by reading the lessons in church with great gusto, particularly such passages as deal with fornication.
Douglas Sutherland, THE ENGLISH GENTLEMAN'S WIFE 1979

BIGAMY

3 Sometimes people commit bigamy to please the landlady.
Sir Gerald Dodson. Quoted Observer, Sayings of the Week 18 *Oct* 1942

4 "That's bigamy."
"Yes and its big of me, too. It's big of all of us. I'm sick of these conventional marriages. One woman and one man was good enough for your grandmother, but who wants to marry your grandmother? Nobody, not even your grandfather."
Groucho Marx, ANIMAL CRACKERS

5 The plural of spouse is spice.
Robert Morley

6 My wife is going to be very nervous when she hears about this. My wife is very strict with me. My wife does not allow me to go around marrying people.
Damon Runyon, MORE THAN SOMEWHAT 1937

BIGOTRY

7 We call a man a bigot or a slave of dogma because he is a thinker who has thought thoroughly and to a definite end.
G. K. Chesterton, ALL THINGS CONSIDERED 1908

8 The more you are right, the more natural that everyone else should be bullied into thinking likewise.
George Orwell, SELECTED ESSAYS 1968

9 How it infuriates a bigot when he is forced to drag into the light his dark convictions.
Logan Pearsall Smith, ALL TRIVIA, *Afterthoughts* 1931

10 Bigotry tries to keep truth safe in its hand with a grip that kills it.
Rabindranath Tagore, FIREFLIES 1928

11 Human beings are perhaps never more frightening than when they are convinced beyond doubt that they are right.
Laurens Van Der Post, THE LOST WORLD OF THE KALAHARI 1958

BIOGRAPHY

12 Biography should be written by an acute enemy.
A. J. Balfour. Quoted S. K. Ratcliffe, Observer 30 *Jan* 1927

13 The art of Biography / Is different from Geography / Geography is about maps / Biography is about chaps.
E. C. Bentley, BIOGRAPHY FOR BEGINNERS

14 I enjoy reading biographies because I want to know about the people who messed up the world.
Marie Dressler, Passing Show 3 *Feb* 1934

15 Not all the secrets of the human heart are known to official biographers.
Lord Francis-Williams, A PATTERN OF RULERS

16 Biography, like big-game hunting, is one of the recognised forms of sport, and it is as unfair as only sport can be.
Philip Guedella, SUPERS AND SUPERMAN

17 It simplifies even while seeking to enrich.
Henry James. Quoted Leon Edel, HENRY JAMES THE MASTER 1901–1916

18 It is by no means true that the major figures of history are the most interesting. Indeed, in a sense, the opposite is the case. Those who take the leading roles in the world of action are so obvious that there is really nothing to say about them, and vice versa.
Malcolm Muggeridge, TREAD SOFTLY FOR YOU TREAD ON MY JOKES 1966

19 Biography, if it is to enhance understanding, add to history or interpret character, must be constructive and not destructive.
Harold Nicolson, The Times 20 *Mar* 1949

20 It is perhaps as difficult to write a good life as to live one.
Lytton Strachey. Quoted as epigraph to

John Gunther's ROOSEVELT IN RETRO-
SPECT

1 After you have traced a man down to the
last munched bath bun you are still left with
the whole mystery of 'the madness of art'.
Tony Tanner, reviewing Leon Edel's,
HENRY JAMES, THE MASTER 1901–1916,
The Times *3 Aug 1972*

2 The primary duty of a serious biographer is
to illuminate his subject's life work, not to
play the spy in his bedroom.
*Philip Toynbee, reviewing Vincent
Broome's* HAVELOCK ELLIS, PHILOSOPHER
OF SEX, Observer *18 Mar 1979*

3 The best sort of book to start with is
biography. If you want to make a success of
it, choose as a subject someone very
famous who has had plenty of books
written about him quite recently. Many
young writers make the mistake of choosing some forgotten Caroline clergyman or
eighteenth-century traveller.
Evelyn Waugh, Passing Show, *The Way to
Fame 2 Feb 1929*

4 There is so little information about Marshal
Louis Nicolas Davout, one of the leaders of
Napoleon's army, that a Huddersfield man
is writing his biography.
Yorkshire Post. *Quoted* Punch *23 Feb 1972*

BIRD

5 And hear the pleasant cuckoo loud and
long / The simple bird that thinks two notes
a song.
W. H. Davies, APRIL CHARMS

6 All thrushes (not only those in this neck of
the Glyndebourne woods) sooner or later
sing the tune of the first subject of Mozart's
G Minor Symphony (K. 550) — and what's
more phrase it a sight better than most
conductors. The tempo is always dead right
and there is no suggestion of an unauthor-
ised accent on the ninth note of the phrase.
Spike Hughes, letter to The Times *15 Jun
1962*

7 Cuckoos, like noise falling in drops off
leaves.
D. H. Lawrence, FANTASIA OF THE
UNCONSCIOUS *1922*

8 A fly can't bird, but a bird can fly.
A. A. Milne, WINNIE THE POOH *1926*

LORD BIRKENHEAD
(F. E. SMITH)

9 Lord Birkenhead is very clever but sometimes his brains go to his head.
Margot Asquith, AUTOBIOGRAPHY *1936*

10 "Who is this Effie Smith?" asked an old
lady when the country was ringing with his
maiden speech. "She can't be a modest girl
to be talked about so much".
2nd Earl of Birkenhead, F.E. THE LIFE OF
F.E. SMITH, FIRST EARL OF BIRKENHEAD

11 He was an orator in an age of mutterers.
Id.

BIRTH

12 When Lady Louise Moncrieff's last [six-
teenth] child was born her sister, Lady
Elizabeth Arthur was present and called
out, "It's all right, Louise, and you have
got another little boy!" And the reply of the
poor tired lady was: "My dear, I really
don't care if it is a parrot."
Lord Ormathwaite, WHEN I WAS AT COURT

13 Congratulations. We all knew you had it in
you.
*Dorothy Parker, telegram to a friend who
had just become a mother. Quoted Alexander Woollcott,* WHILE ROME BURNS, *Our
Mrs. Parker 1934*

14 I was born because it was a habit in those
days. People didn't know any different.
Will Rogers, AUTOBIOGRAPHY *1949*

15 He is always breaking the law. He broke
the law when he was born. His parents
were not married.
George Bernard Shaw, MAJOR BARBARA
1905

16 What a perfect escape the return to the
womb was. Better by far than Religion or
Art or the South Sea Islands. It was so snug
and warm there, and the feeding was
automatic. Everything perfect in that hotel.
No wonder the memory of those accom-
modations lingered in the blood and nerves
of everyone. It was dark, yes, but what a
warm, rich darkness. The grave wasn't in
it. No wonder one fought so desperately
against being evicted when the nine
months' lease was up.
Nathanael West, THE DAY OF THE
LOCUST *1939*

BIRTHDAY

17 It's strange how I seem to spend my
birthdays away from home. I must subcon-

sciously arrange these trips so the dagger of time pierces an empty bed.
John Updike. Quoted John Heilpern, Observer 25 Mar 1979

BIRTH-RATE

1 Despite the efforts of Mussolini and the Pope, the birthrate of Italy is declining.
Nancy Astor. Quoted John Beevers, Sunday Referee 19 Feb 1939

OTTO VON BISMARCK

2 If the sole duty of a statesman is to do the best he can for his country, then Bismarck did his duty. If, between nations, honour and justice count for anything, then Bismarck was a bandit.
Kenneth Bell, Teacher's World, The Iron Chancellor, Sep 1929

3 If he was never foolish enough to say "power transcends right" that, nevertheless, was his belief.
Emil Ludwig, BISMARCK, THE STORY OF A FIGHTER

BLAME

4 Her whole life was governed by her desire not to be blamed, so she never did anything, and got blamed for that.
Gerald Brenan, THOUGHTS IN A DRY SEASON 1979

BLASPHEMY

5 Blasphemy itself could not survive religion; if anyone doubts that let him try to blaspheme Odin.
G. K. Chesterton, Daily News 25 Jun 1904

6 Beware of the community in which blasphemy does not exist; underneath, atheism runs rampant.
Antonio Machado, JUAN DE MAIRENA 1943

BLINDNESS

7 A picture gallery is a dull place for a blind man.
George Bernard Shaw, MAN AND SUPERMAN 1905

BLOOMSBURY

8 An article in *Harper's* by Duncan Grant's granddaughter explained how he'd taught her to roast an egg in a bonfire.
Frances Donnelly, The Listener, Bloomsbury Boom 5 Aug 1982

BOASTFULNESS

9 Christianity will go. We're more popular than Jesus now.
John Lennon 1966

10 A boaster is not always a liar.
Eric Partridge, John o'London's Weekly 7 Oct 1938

BOAT

11 Believe me my young friend there is nothing — absolutely nothing — half so much worth doing as simply messing about in boats.
Kenneth Grahame, WIND IN THE WILLOWS 1908

BOGNOR

12 Bugger Bognor!
Reputedly George V's last words (he had recently been there for his health and it was suggested he might return)

BOOK

13 This book tells more about penguins than I am interested in knowing.
Attr. to unknown schoolchild's essay

14 A best-seller is a book which somehow sells well because it is selling well.
Daniel Boorstin, THE IMAGE 1962

15 Books most of all resemble us in their precarious hold on life.
Joseph Conrad, NOTES ON LIFE AND LETTERS 1921

16 A book is not harmless merely because no one is consciously offended by it.
T. S. Eliot, RELIGION AND LITERATURE

17 One always tends to overpraise a long book because one has got through it.
E. M. Forster, ASPECTS OF THE NOVEL 1927

18 I know every book of mine by its scent, and I have but to put my nose between its pages to be reminded of all sorts of things.
George Gissing, THE PRIVATE PAPERS OF HENRY RYECROFT 1903

1 Even bad books are books and therefore sacred.
Günther Grass, THE TIN DRUM 1962

2 Books of poems lying around are handy /
For killing persistent irritating flies.
Geoffrey Grigson, HISTORY OF HIM 1951

3 All good books are alike in that they are truer than if they really happened and after you are finished reading one you will feel that all that happened to you, and afterwards it all belongs to you.
Ernest Hemingway

4 The mortality of all inanimate things is terrible to me, but that of books most of all.
William Dean Howells. Letter to Charles Eliot Norton 6 Apr 1903

5 The proper study of mankind is books.
Aldous Huxley, CROME YELLOW 1921

6 The librarian gave Geordie 'Mother Goose's Nursery Rhymes'. Geordie read it from cover to cover, and when I asked him how he liked it he said "It's nowt but a pack of lies."
Gerald Kersh, THE NINE LIVES OF BILL NELSON 1941

7 Few books today are forgivable.
R. D. Laing, THE POLITICS OF EXPERIENCE

8 Books are a load of crap.
Philip Larkin, A STUDY OF READING HABITS

9 My books are not scandalous, not sexy, and the story waves about from place to place — and yet, much to my surprise, they are still in print.
Laurie Lee in an interview with Philip Radcliffe, Observer 8 *Jan* 1979

10 Book — the noblest sound that man has yet uttered.
Bernard Levin, TAKING SIDES

11 It's not a dirty book, it's an earthy book, which is a very different thing.
Librarian to borrower. Cartoon caption in the New Yorker

12 Books have no value in themselves. They are valuable because they make more real, more interesting, more effective the other things that readers are doing, thinking, feeling and enjoying.
Lionel McColvin, THE PERSONAL LIBRARY

13 Many of those who make insufficient use of books neglect them because they mistakenly regard books as something separate and apart from life; because they think of 'books' as synonymous with literature.
Id.

14 In the main there are two sorts of books; those that no one reads, and those that no one ought to read.
H. L. Mencken, PREJUDICES 1919

15 If good books did good, the world would have been converted long ago.
George Moore, HAIL AND FAREWELL 1914

16 There are some books which cannot be adequately reviewed for twenty or thirty years after they come out.
John Morley, RECOLLECTIONS 1917

17 Booksellers' returns and the computer have freed the modern bookbuyer from the agonies of decision making. Once a book has been declared a bestseller, its sales accelerate — like the freshwater polyp, the best seller breeds from itself — and the book-buyer can happily accept the judgment of the great majority.
Frank Muir, THE FRANK MUIR BOOK 1976

18 An anthologist is a lazy fellow who likes to spend a quiet evening at home raiding good books.
Dorothy Parker

19 This is not a novel to be tossed aside lightly. It should be thrown with great force.
Id.

20 Surely there's enough happiness in life without having to go to books for it.
Id.

21 At last, an unprintable book that is readable.
Ezra Pound of Henry Miller's TROPIC OF CANCER

22 You might think the least important thing about a book is its title. Surely what matters is the content. And yet one fusses over the title for hours, as if, like the figurehead of some romantic merchantman, it conferred magic properties on the ship and all who sailed in her.
Gerald Priestland, PRIESTLAND'S PROGRESS 1982

23 We all know that books burn — yet we have the greater knowledge that books cannot be killed by fire. People die, but books never die.
Franklin D. Roosevelt, to American Booksellers Association 23 Apr 1942

1 A best seller is the guilded tomb of a mediocre talent.
Logan Pearsall Smith, ALL TRIVIA, *Afterthoughts* 1931

2 Give me a bed and a book and I am happy.
Id.

3 Much is written of the power of the Press, a power which may last but a day; by comparison little is heard of the power of books, which may endure for generations.
Sir Stanley Unwin, THE TRUTH ABOUT PUBLISHING

4 Books, I don't know what you see in them . . . I can understand a person reading them, but I can't for the life of me see why people have to write them.
Peter Ustinov, PHOTO-FINISH

5 One book's very like another — after all what is it? Something to read and done with. It's not a thing that matters like print dresses and serviettes — where you either like 'em or don't, and people judge you by.
H. G. Wells, KIPPS 1905

BORE

6 For *deliberate* and *intentional* boring you must have a man of some ability to practise it well, as you must practise any art well.
Hilaire Belloc, CONVERSATION WITH A CAT

7 *Bore*: a person who talks when you wish him to listen.
Ambrose Bierce, THE DEVIL'S DICTIONARY 1906

8 The English sent all their bores abroad and acquired the empire as a punishment.
Edward Bond, NARROW ROAD TO THE DEEP NORTH

9 Tony was a first class-bore. He had a habit of choosing a subject and then droning round and round it like an inaccurate bomb-aimer round his target, ever unable to hit.
Nancy Mitford, THE PURSUIT OF LOVE 1945

10 He's an old bore. Even the grave yawns for him.
H. Beerbohm Tree, of Israel Zangwill. Quoted by Hesketh Pearson, BEERBOHM TREE

11 A healthy male adult bore consumes each year one and a half times his own weight in other people's patience.
John Updike, CONFESSIONS OF A WILD BORE

12 Rather inclined to collar the conversation and turn it in the direction of his home town's water supply.
P. G. Wodehouse, MY MAN JEEVES 1919

BOREDOM

13 Millions long for immortality who do not know what to do with themselves on a rainy Sunday afternoon.
Susan Ertz, ANGER IN THE SKY

14 Boredom, which would engulf whole towns in the Middle Ages, and which, because it was a denial of life itself, was made an offence against God by the Church.
Ian Fleming. Quoted John Pearson, LIFE OF IAN FLEMING

15 It is not surprising that boredom — in human beings so often the mask of fear — is a problem in marriage as it is a problem in prayer.
Monica Furlong, CHRISTIAN UNCERTAINTIES

16 No society seems ever to have succumbed to boredom. Man has developed an obvious capacity for surviving the pompous reiteration of the commonplace.
J. K. Galbraith, THE AFFLUENT SOCIETY 1958

17 Living in Coventry is about as interesting as watching a plank warp.
Graffito. Quoted Nigel Rees GRAFFITI 2

18 Boredom seemed to swell like a balloon inside the head; it became a pressure inside the skull; sometimes I feared this balloon would burst and I would lose my reason.
Graham Greene, A SORT OF LIFE

19 The effect of boredom on a large scale in history is underestimated. It is a main cause of revolutions, and would soon bring to an end all the static Utopias and the farmyard civilisation of the Fabians.
W. R. Inge (Dean of St. Pauls), THE END OF AN AGE 1948

20 The average male gets his living by such depressing devices that boredom becomes a sort of natural state to him.
H. L. Mencken, IN DEFENCE OF WOMEN

21 Boredom is a vital problem for the moralist, since half the sins of mankind are caused by the fear of it.
Bertrand Russell, THE CONQUEST OF HAPPINESS 1930

1 One can be bored until boredom becomes a mystical experience.
Logan Pearsall Smith, ALL TRIVIA 1931

2 Somebody's boring me, and I think it's me.
Attr. Dylan Thomas, BBC Radio 4, *Quote Unquote* 21 *Jun* 1980

BOURGEOIS

3 I call bourgeois anyone who says no to himself, who gives up struggle and renounces love in favour of his security. I call bourgeois anyone who places anything above feeling.
Léon-Paul Farque, SOUS LA LAMPE

4 The bourgeois prefers comfort to pleasure, convenience to liberty, and a pleasant temperature to the deathly inner consuming fire.
Hermann Hesse, TREATISE ON THE STEPPENWOLF 1927

5 How beastly the bourgeois is / Especially the male of the species.
D. H. Lawrence, HOW BEASTLY THE BOURGEOIS IS 1929

6 The British Bourgeoise / Is not born / And does not die / But if it is ill / It has a frightened look in its eyes.
Osbert Sitwell, AT THE HOUSE OF MRS. KINFOOT

BOXING

7 He [Muhammad Ali] stings like a bee but lives like a WASP.
Eamonn Andrews, Punch 23 *Feb* 1972

8 There is nothing bellicose about boxing. It is fully in keeping with the principles of the United Nations Organisation.
Field-Marshal Montgomery. Quoted News Review 20 *May* 1948

9 Among the boxing fraternity there is an adage — first the timing goes, then the legs, then the mind and then the friends. That is the history of many people who thought boxing an easy way to riches.
Lord Taylor of Gryfe, introducing the defeated Boxing Bill, House of Lords 26 *Nov* 1981

10 Boxing is glamorised violence.
Id.

BOY SCOUT

11 I have seen thousands of boys and young men, narrow-chested, hunched-up, miserable specimens, smoking endless cigarettes, many of them betting.
Sir Robert Baden-Powell, explaining his reasons for starting the Boy Scout movement 1907

12 The Boer War was obviously a good thing in the end because it was the cause of Boy Scouts and of their remarkable Chief Scout, General Baden Powell (known affectionately as B.O.P.)
W. C. Sellar and R. J. Yeatman, 1066 AND ALL THAT 1930

BRAIN

13 My brain; it's my second favourite organ.
Woody Allen and Marshall Brickman, SLEEPER *(film)*

14 Brain — an apparatus with which we think we think.
Ambrose Bierce, THE DEVIL'S DICTIONARY 1906

15 Never trust men with short legs. Brains too near their bottoms.
Noël Coward. Quoted Nancy McPhee, BOOK OF INSULTS

16 The brain is a wonderful organ; it starts working the moment you get up in the morning, and does not stop until you get to the office.
Robert Frost

17 If the human brain was simple enough for us to understand we'd be so simple we couldn't.
Graffito. Quoted Nigel Rees, GRAFFITI 2

18 So this gentleman said a girl with brains ought to do something with them besides think.
Anita Loos, GENTLEMEN PREFER BLONDES 1925

19 What good are brains to a man? They only unsettle him.
P. G. Wodehouse, ADVENTURES OF SALLY 1920

BRAVERY

20 There is no such thing as bravery; only degrees of fear.
John Wainwright. Quoted Philippa Toomey, The Times 30 *Jul* 1980

BREAD

21 You can travel fifty thousand miles in America without once tasting good bread.

Henry Miller, REMEMBER TO REMEMBER, *The Staff of Life* 1947

1 How important bread is to a nation and how utterly are we betrayed in this country. If Mother's proud she must be the only one.
Robert Morley, MORLEY MARVELS, *Sloshing and Noshing* 1976

2 Bread is an emotive substance. Shortage of it has traditionally been a sign of dangerous irritation among those prone to riot.
Daily Telegraph *leader 9 Nov* 1978

BREAKFAST

3 He was the old buster who, a few years later, came down to breakfast one morning, lifted the first cover he saw, said "Eggs! Eggs! Eggs! Damn all eggs" in an over-wrought sort of voice and instantly legged it for France, never to return to the bosom of his family.
P. G. Wodehouse, JEEVES TAKE CHARGE

4 I hadn't the heart to touch my breakfast. I told Jeeves to drink it himself.
P. G. Wodehouse, MY MAN JEEVES 1919

BERTOLT BRECHT

5 He could make a horse act.
Lotte Lenya, BBC1 TV 24 *May* 1979

6 It [the Days of the Commune] has . . . the eloquence of a conversation between a speak-your-weight machine and a whoopee cushion.
Bernard Levin, Sunday Times 6 *Nov* 1977

BRIBERY

7 When their lordships asked Bacon / How many bribes he had taken / He had at least the grace / To get very red in the face.
Hilaire Belloc, BASELESS BIOGRAPHY

BRITISH EMPIRE

8 Britain is necessarily the world's worst offender as a colonial power. She may be said to be the best of the worst.
Nnamdi Azikiwe, Nigerian politician, News Review 24 *Jul* 1947

9 When we speak of Empire it is in no spirit of flag-wagging. We feel that in this great inheritance of ours, separated as it is by the seas, we have yet one home and one people.
Stanley Baldwin. Speech 5 *Dec* 1924

10 The British Empire has done so much harm to so many nations and peoples that it deserves to perish.
William Scawen Blunt, MY DIARIES 1889–1914

11 Learn to think imperially.
Joseph Chamberlain. Speech, London Guildhall 19 *Jan* 1904

12 I have not become the King's First Minister in order to preside over the liquidation of the British Empire.
Winston Churchill, Lord Mayor's Banquet 10 *Nov* 1942

13 It may well be that Britain will be more honoured by the historian for the way in which she disposed of an empire than for the way she acquired it.
Sir David Ormsby Gore. Press interview 28 *Oct* 1962

14 A great Empire will be destroyed which it was never my intention to destroy or even to harm.
Adolf Hitler. Speech 19 *Jul* 1940

15 Britain was led by adventurers when she built her empire. Today she is ruled merely by incompetents.
Adolf Hitler. Quoted Alan Bullock, HITLER

16 It took God longer to write the Bible than it has taken him to build the British Empire.
William C. MacDonald, MODERN EVANGELISM

17 Providence is on the side of the British Empire after all.
Lord Northcliffe, on hearing how Kitchener had drowned when HMS Hampshire was sunk by a mine. Quoted A. J. P. Taylor, ENGLISH HISTORY 1914–1945

18 The so-called British Empire is in reality an *English* empire, of which Ireland, Scotland and Wales formed the original colonies.
F. A. Ridley, Socialist Leader, *Feb* 1948

19 The British Empire is one of the greatest enslavers of human beings in the world.
Paul Robeson. Quoted News Review 3 *Oct* 1946

20 Gentlemen like to hoard relics of the great days of the British Empire — assegais from the Matabele campaign, daggers from China and a solar topee with a hole in the brim where great-uncle George tried to shoot himself in Pondicherry and missed.
Douglas Sutherland, THE ENGLISH GENTLEMAN 1978

1 From the day it broke away from the British Empire the United States has been living in large measure under the protection of that Empire, and in particular of the British Fleet.
President Harry S Truman. Quoted News Review 20 *Mar* 1947

2 Other nations use 'force'; we Britons alone use 'might'.
Evelyn Waugh, SCOOP 1938

BENJAMIN BRITTEN

3 I may not be the best living composer, but I'm certainly the busiest.
Benjamin Britten of himself to William Plomer, ELECTRIC DELIGHTS

BROADCASTING

4 Of all the things that are broadcast, the thing which gives me the greatest delight and to which I can listen however tired I am, is the sound of Big Ben.
Stanley Baldwin, BBC *dinner* 16 *Dec* 1926

5 *ITMA* is the average man's equivalent of *Finnegan's Wake*
Arthur Calder-Marshall, Tribune

6 If I possessed the power of conveying unlimited sexual attraction through the potency of my voice I would not be reduced to accepting a miserable pittance from the BBC for interviewing a faded female in a damp basement.
Gilbert Harding on being asked to sound more sexy when interviewing Mae West. Quoted in his biography

7 We have got to the stage where, both in radio and television news, agonising over auxiliaries is a prevalent malaise. There is a feeling among newsreaders that they are enhancing their own importance and giving the impression of midden journalistic subtlety by perpetuating the same solecisms. Readers should be taught to discern and stick to the facts and to avoid shaded, argumentative or opinionated inflections.
Alvar Lidell, The Listener 7 *Apr* 1979

8 The BBC to me is like democracy — a good thing that those who run it do their best to spoil.
G. W. Lyttelton, THE LYTTELTON HART-DAVIS LETTERS 30 *Nov* 1955

9 It is a sobering thought that eighty per cent of listeners are doing something else while they are listening to the radio.
Aubrey Singer, director BBC Radio, *at a press interview* 5 *Mar* 1979

BROADMINDEDNESS

10 Human beings never shocked him, never surprised him. He viewed them like the priest in the confessional whose penitent said "I have committed murder" and who merely enquired "How many times?"
Charles Curran MP of Sir Beverley Baxter, The Times 4 *May* 1964

BUCKINGHAM PALACE

11 You've got a smashing house here for a matinee.
Bud Flanagan to the Duke of Edinburgh on being invested with the OBE 1959

12 This isn't ours. It's a tied cottage.
Philip, Duke of Edinburgh. Quoted Noël St. George, ROYAL QUOTES

13 We live in what virtually amounts to a museum — which does not happen to a lot of people.
Id.

BULLFIGHTING

14 Bullfighting is the only art in which the artist is in danger of death and in which the degree of brilliance in the performance is left to the fighter's honour.
Ernest Hemingway, DEATH IN THE AFTERNOON 1932

BUREAUCRACY

15 The perfect bureaucrat everywhere is the man who manages to make no decisions, and escape all responsibility.
Brooks Atkinson, ONCE AROUND THE SUN 1951

16 Some civil servants are neither servants nor civil.
Winston Churchill. Quoted Walter H. Toms in a letter to the Observer 8 *Apr* 1979

17 Though park railings in Manchester are being removed for scrap, the park gates will be retained and locked at night to indicate that the parks are officially shut.
Daily Despatch

18 In the Nuts (unground) (other than groundnuts) Order, the expression nuts will have relevance to such nuts other than groundnuts as would but for this amending order not qualify as nuts (unground) (other than groundnuts) by reason of their being nuts (unground).
Government amendment

1 Official dignity tends to increase in inverse ratio to the importance of the country in which the office is held.
Aldous Huxley, BEYOND THE MEXIQUE BAY 1934

2 A civil servant doesn't make jokes.
Eugene Ionesco, THE KILLER 1958

3 The perfect civil servant is the man who has a valid objection to any possible solution.
A. H. Keates. Speech to Institute of Hospital Management, Connaught Rooms 16 May 1965

4 He picked up a slip of paper and a blue pencil, intending to write the word *Balls*. But the pencil broke and as he sharpened it the gentleman remembered where he was; he compromised, wrote *Round Objects*, inserted the slip and pushed the file aside. Many weeks later the file came back to him with a note from the Director General which said "Who is Mr. Round, and why does he object?"
Gerald Kersh, CLEAN, BRIGHT AND SLIGHTLY OILED 1946

5 For the purpose of this part of the schedule a person over pensionable age, not being an insured person, shall be treated as an employed person if he would be an insured person were he under pensionable age and would be an employed person were he an insured person.
National Insurance Bill, first schedule

6 It will be observed that air travel, considered as a retirement-accelerator, has the advantage of including a fair amount of form-filling.
C. Northcote Parkinson, PARKINSON'S LAW 1957

7 An Edinburgh doctor raised money to get a television set for a disabled patient. He then asked the post office if the man's licence fee could be reduced. "Only," said an official, "if the disabled man was also blind".
Kenneth Robinson, Punch 9 Feb 1972

8 The exercise of power is agreeable, especially when it is an obscure individual who exercises power over a prominent one.
Bertrand Russell, American Mercury, May 1940

9 The working of great institutions is mainly the result of a vast mass of routine, petty malice, self interest, carelessness and sheer mistake. Only a residual fraction is thought.
George Santayana, THE CRIME OF GALILEO

10 There is something about a bureaucrat that does not like a poem.
Gore Vidal, SEX, DEATH AND MONEY *(Preface)*

BURGLAR

11 A burglar who respects his art always takes his time before he takes anything else.
O. Henry, MAKES THE WHOLE WORLD KIN

BUSINESS

12 The gambling known as business looks with austere disfavour on the business known as gambling.
Ambrose Bierce. Quoted H. L. Mencken.

13 A business that makes nothing but money is a poor kind of business.
Henry Ford. Interview 1919

14 Chaplin is no business man — all he knows is that he can't take any less.
Sam Goldwyn. Quoted Charles Chaplin, MY AUTOBIOGRAPHY 1964

15 The aim of all legitimate business is service, for profit, at a risk.
Benjamin C. Leeming, IMAGINATION

16 Few have heard of Fra Luca Parioli, the inventor of double-entry book-keeping; but he has probably had more influence on human life than has Dante or Michelangelo.
Herbert J. Muller, USES OF THE PAST

17 The secret of business is to know something that nobody else knows.
Aristotle Onassis

18 The trouble with senior management, I notice as an outsider, is that there are too many one-ulcer men holding down two-ulcer men's jobs.
Philip, Duke of Edinburgh. Speech 7 May 1963

19 Business only contributes fully to society if it is efficient, successful, profitable and socially responsible.
Lord Sieff, Observer, *Sayings of the Week 30 Aug 1981*

R. A. BUTLER

1 His great failing is that he likes to be a don among politicians and a politician among dons.
Iain Macleod. Quoted Patrick Cosgrave, R. A. BUTLER, AN ENGLISH LIFE

BUTTERFLY

2 The butterfly counts not months but moments, and has time enough.
Rabindranath Tagore, FIREFLIES 1928

C

CALIFORNIA

1 California is a fine place to live in — if you happen to be an orange.
Fred Allen, American Radio Show

2 I met a Californian who would / Talk California — a state so blessed / He said, in climate, none had ever died there / A natural death, and Vigilance Committees / Had had to organise to stock the graveyards / And vindicate the state's humanity.
Robert Frost, NEW HAMPSHIRE 1923

JAMES CALLAGHAN

3 If Hugh Gaitskell's motto was 'fight, fight and fight again' then Jim Callaghan's is 'manœuvre, manœuvre and manœuvre again'.
Ian Bradley, The Times 16 *Oct* 1980

4 He [James Callaghan] is not merely a schemer, he's also got a very nice side to him and I like him because he can't resist talking to me. His feelings about me are very much divided. He's attracted by my ability and probably knows that ultimately I'm not nearly as thrusting and ambitious as he is and that unlike him I am intellectually honest.

So he talks to me in the friendliest way possible and fights me ruthlessly behind my back. It's not an attractive combination but in politics it is sometimes inevitable.
Richard Crossman, DIARIES 21 *Jul* 1968

5 There is nobody in politics I can remember, and no case I can think of in history where a man combined such a powerful political personality with so little intelligence.
Roy Jenkins. Quoted Richard Crossman, DIARIES 5 *Sep* 1969

6 He's inordinately ambitious and inordinately weak. So weak that as Chancellor he used to weep on my shoulder and then go away and intrigue against me. That's a pretty fair analysis.
Harold Wilson. Ibid. 4 *Sep* 1969

7 That fellow is getting above himself. We must teach him a lesson. I'll do so after Cabinet tomorrow.
Id. 29 *May* 1969

8 I'm having to hold his hand. His nerve isn't very good these days.
Harold Wilson of James Callaghan as Chancellor of the Exchequer 1964

CALMNESS

9 He was as cool as an undertaker at a hanging.
H. L. Mencken of Henry Cabot Lodge, Baltimore Evening Sun 15 *Jun* 1920

CAMBRIDGE

10 For Cambridge people rarely smile, / Being urban, squat and packed with guile.
Rupert Brooke, THE OLD VICARAGE, GRANTCHESTER 1912

11 There, much is good because so little is new.
J. K. Galbraith, A LIFE IN OUR TIMES 1982

12 I find Cambridge an asylum, in every sense of the word.
Attr. A. E. Housman

13 Cambridge — the romantic dream of those who never went there.
Malcolm Muggeridge, BBC TV 26 *Feb* 1981

14 Cambridge is the city of perspiring dreams.
Frederic Raphael, THE GLITTERING PRIZES

15 Trinity is like a dead body in a high state of putrefaction. The only interest of it is the worms that come out of it.
Lytton Strachey. Quoted Michael Holroyd, LYTTON STRACHEY

CAMEL

16 The trouble with camels is that they expel foul smells — from both ends at once.
Charles, Prince of Wales, after riding one at Olympia 13 *Dec* 1979

1 Our camels sniff the evening and are glad.
James Elroy Flecker, THE GOLDEN JOUR-
NEY TO SAMARKAND 1913

2 "Humph yourself"
And the camel humphed himself.
Rudyard Kipling, HOW THE CAMEL GOT ITS
HUMP 1902

3 The camel has a single hump / The
dromedary two / Or else the other way
around / I'm never sure. Are you?
Ogden Nash, THE CAMEL

CANADA

4 Canada is a country so square that even the
female impersonators are women.
Richard Benner, OUTRAGEOUS *(film script)*

5 A Canadian is somebody who knows how
to make love in a canoe.
Pierre Berton

6 You have to know a man awfully well in
Canada to know his surname.
John Buchan. Quoted Observer 24 *May*
1950

7 I don't even know what street Canada is
on.
Al Capone

8 When Great Britain dismantled the British
Empire it gave the land back to the original
owners in Africa and Asia. This was not the
case in Canada.
*Chief Noël Starblancket. Speech at a
conference in London* 6 *Jul* 1979

CANARY

9 The song of canaries / Never varies / And
when they're molting / They're revolting.
Ogden Nash, CUSTARD AND CO.

CANDIDATE

10 Any American who is prepared to run for
President should automatically, by defini-
tion, be disqualified from ever doing so.
Gore Vidal

CANNIBAL

11 A cannibal is a guy who goes into a
restaurant and orders the waiter.
Jack Benny, radio script

12 They were inclined to cook their captives
alive, as we do lobsters, to improve their
flavour.
Rose Macaulay, THE TOWERS OF TRE-
BIZOND 1956

13 If cannibals should ever catch me I hope
they will say "We have eaten Dr.
Schweitzer and he was good to the end —
and the end wasn't bad"
Dr. Albert Schweitzer

CAPABILITY

14 I do not think thinking about a situation
does much good. One knows by instinct
what one can do.
A. C. Benson, letter to M.E.A.

CAPITALISM

15 History suggests that capitalism is a neces-
sary condition for political freedom.
Clearly it is not a sufficient condition.
Milton Friedman, CAPITALISM AND FREE-
DOM

16 The system of private property is the most
important guarantee of freedom, not only
for those who own property but scarcely
less for those who do not.
Friedrich August von Hayek, THE ROAD TO
SERFDOM

17 It is the unacceptable face of capitalism but
one should not suggest that the whole of
British industry consists of practices of this
kind.
Edward Heath of the Lonrho Affair 1973

18 The forces of a capitalist society, if left
unchecked, tend to make the rich richer and
the poor poorer.
Jawaharlal Nehru, CREDO

19 Capitalism inevitably and by virtue of the
very logic of its civilisation creates, edu-
cates and subsidises a vested interest in
social unrest.
Joseph Alois Schumpter, CAPITALISM,
SOCIALISM AND DEMOCRACY

20 There is in the capitalist system a tendency
towards self-destruction.
Id.

CAREER

21 A dictionary definition of career is 'A head-
long rush, usually downhill'. Not a bad
description really.
Michael Bentine, THE LONG BANANA SKIN

CARELESSNESS

1 Carelessness about our security is dangerous; carelessness about our freedom is also dangerous.
Adlai Stevenson. Speech, Detroit 7 *Oct* 1952

CARICATURE

2 I seemed to have mislaid my gift for dispraise. Pity crept in. So I gave up caricaturing, except privately.
Max Beerbohm. Quoted S. N. Behrens, CONVERSATION WITH MAX 1960

3 Caricature shows society, sometimes quite literally, the arse of history.
William Feaver, MASTERS OF CARICATURE

4 Caricature shows society, not as it would choose to be shown, but with its breeches down.
George Melly, Observer magazine, *Irreverent Images* 16 *Aug* 1981

JIMMY CARTER

5 He is the only man since my dear husband died, to have the effrontery to kiss me on the lips.
Queen Elizabeth, the Queen Mother. Quoted Peter Hillman, Observer 13 *Feb* 1983

6 I don't know what people have got against Jimmy Carter. He's done nothing.
Bob Hope. Election campaign speech for Ronald Reagan 2 *Nov* 1980

CAT

7 A cat that lives with a good family is used to being talked to all the time.
Lettice Cooper, PARKIN

8 You always ought to have tom cats arranged, you know — it makes 'em more companionable.
Noël Coward, CAT'S CRADLE

9 Within that porch, across the way / I see two naked eyes this night / Two eyes that neither shut nor blink / Searching my face with a green light / But cats to me are strange, so strange / I cannot sleep if one is near; / And though I'm sure I see those eyes / I'm not so sure a body's there!
W. H. Davies, THE CAT

10 What cats most appreciate in a human being is not the ability to produce food which they take for granted but his or her entertainment value.
Geoffrey Household, ROGUE MALE

11 The cat — He walked by himself and all places were alike to him.
Rudyard Kipling, JUST SO STORIES 1902

12 A black cat dropped soundlessly from a high wall, like a spoonful of dark treacle, and melted under a gate.
Elizabeth Lemarchand, ALIBI FOR A CORPSE

13 I would never wound a cat's feelings, no matter how downright aggressive I might be to humans.
A. L. Rowse, THREE CORNISH CATS

14 "We have cats the way other people have mice. (signed) Mrs. C. L. Footloose"
"I see you have. I can't tell from your communication whether you wish advice or are just boasting".
James Thurber, MY LIFE AND HARD TIMES 1933

15 I have just been given a very engaging Persian Kitten . . . and his opinion is that *I* have been given to *him*.
Evelyn Underhill, LETTERS

CATERPILLAR

16 "What's that tickling my back?" said the wall / "Me" said a small / Caterpillar "I'm learning / To crawl."
Ian Serraillier, THE TICKLE RHYME

CATHEDRAL

17 Cathedrals, / Luxury liners laden with souls, / Holding to the east their hulls of stone.
W. H. Auden, ON THIS ISLAND XVII

CAUTION

18 As carefully as an out of work showgirl uses her last good pair of stockings.
Raymond Chandler, THE BIG SLEEP 1939

19 Didn't you hear me keeping still?
Sam Goldwyn. Quoted Alva Johnson, THE GREAT GOLDWYN

20 When one finds oneself in the middle of a minefield it is seldom wise to get up and run.
Michael Howard, reviewing PROTEST AND SURVIVE, *by E. P. Thomson and Dan Smith,* Sunday Times 9 *Nov* 1980

1 Set the foot down with distrust on the crust of the world — it is thin.
Edna St. Vincent Millay, HUNTSMAN, WHAT QUARRY?, *Underground System* 1939

2 If we shake hands with icy fingers it is because we have burnt them so horribly before.
Logan Pearsall Smith, ALL TRIVIA, *Afterthoughts* 1931

3 Closing the door with the delicate caution of one brushing flies off a sleeping Venus, he passed out of my life.
P. G. Wodehouse, VERY GOOD JEEVES, *Jeeves and the Old School Chum*

CELIBACY

4 If every man gave up women in God's name / Where in God's name would be the men / To give up women in a generation's time.
Christopher Fry, CARTMANTLE 1962

5 Celibacy is not an inherited characteristic.
Graffito. Quoted Nigel Rees, GRAFFITI LIVES O.K.

CENSORSHIP

6 What the country wants in its police is that they should be the guardians of law and order and not, as there is a tendency for them now to try to be, censors of public morals.
Lord Balfour of Burleigh on the Savidge Case 1928

7 This film is apparently meaningless, but if it has any meaning it is doubtless objectionable.
British Board of Film Censors, banning Jean Cocteau's THE SEASHELL AND THE CLERGYMAN 1956

8 Lord Longford is against us reading or seeing things that keep our minds below the navel.
William Hardcastle, Punch 1 *Dec* 1972

9 I shall judge films as I would horseflesh or a dog. I shall look for clean lines.
Major Harding de Fontlangue Cox. Quoted Sunday Express

10 The trouble with censors is they worry if a girl has cleavage. They ought to worry if she hasn't any.
Marilyn Monroe. Quoted Leslie Halliwell, FILMGOER'S BOOK OF QUOTES 1973

11 Censors are paid to have dirty minds.
John Trevelyan, British film censor 1970

CEREMONY

12 I am unaccustomed to unveilings busts of any sort, but . . . I now complete the process of helping my father to expose himself.
Prince Charles, unveiling a sculpture of the Duke of Edinburgh at the Royal Thames Yacht Club

13 A lot of time and energy has been spent in arranging for you to listen to me take a long time to declare open a building which everyone knows is open already.
Philip, Duke of Edinburgh. Speech in Chesterfield 21 *Nov* 1958

14 I declare this thing open — whatever it is.
Philip, Duke of Edinburgh, opening an annex to Vancouver City Hall

AUSTEN CHAMBERLAIN

15 He is more loyal to his friends than to his convictions.
Margot Asquith, AUTOBIOGRAPHY 1936

16 He always plays the game, And he always loses it.
Winston Churchill

JOSEPH CHAMBERLAIN

17 Like many successful organisers he has an uninteresting mind.
Margot Asquith, AUTOBIOGRAPHY 1936

NEVILLE CHAMBERLAIN

18 It was like a visit to Woolworths. Everything in its place and nothing over sixpence.
Aneurin Bevan, of a speech by Neville Chamberlain

19 That old town clerk, looking at foreign affairs through the wrong end of a municiple drain pipe.
Attr. Winston Churchill, after Munich, by R. L. Taylor, THE AMAZING MR. CHURCHILL; *but also attr. to David Lloyd George by Leon Harris,* THE FINE ART OF POLITICAL WIT

20 In the depths of that dusty soul there is nothing but abject surrender.
Winston Churchill

21 The people of Birmingham have a specially heavy burden for they have given the world

the curse of the present British Prime Minister.
Sir Stafford Cripps. Speech, Birmingham 18 Mar 1938

1 An unremarkable figure; gaunt, with bushy eyebrows and old-fashioned moustache, but no democratically endearing features.
Robert Graves and Alan Hodge, THE LONG WEEK-END 1940

2 He seemed such a nice old gentleman that I thought I would give him my autograph as a souvenir.
Adolf Hitler after Munich

3 He was a meticulous housemaid, great at tidying up.
A. J. P. Taylor, ENGLISH HISTORY 1916–1945

4 Praise be to God and to Mr. Chamberlain. I find no sacrilege, no bathos, in coupling those two names.
Godfrey Winn, Daily Express, *after Munich*

CHAMBERPOTS

5 Pots, chamber, plain. Pots, chamber, with Admiralty monogram in blue, for hospital. Pots, chamber, fluted, with royal cypher in gold, for flag officers only. Pots, chamber, round, rubber, lunatic.
Classification of chamber pots on an Admiralty stores list

CHANCE

6 Random my bottom! A true miracle say I. / For who is not certain that he was meant to be.
W. H. Auden

7 Who knows how much turns on whether a Prime Minister's pipe is clean or foul, or the head of the Foreign Office has had sufficiency of sleep?
Lord Horder, THE LITTLE GENIUS

CHANGE

8 Most of the change we think we see in life / Is due to truths being in and out of favour.
Robert Frost, THE BLACK COTTAGE 1914

9 Every institution not only carries within it the seeds of its own dissolution but prepares the way for its most hated rival.
W. R. Inge (Dean of St. Pauls), OUTSPOKEN ESSAYS, *The Victorian Age* 1922

10 We do not succeed in changing things according to our desire, but gradually our desire changes.
Marcel Proust, REMEMBRANCE OF THINGS PAST, *The Fugitive* 1925

CHAOS

11 Chaos often breeds life, when order breeds habit.
Henry Brooks Adams, THE EDUCATION OF HENRY ADAMS 1918

12 The whole world's in a state o' chassis.
Sean O'Casey, JUNO AND THE PAYCOCK 1924

CHARLIE CHAPLIN

13 I remain one thing and one thing only, and that is a clown. It places me on a far higher plane than any politician.
Charlie Chaplin, AUTOBIOGRAPHY 1964

14 Chaplin's genius was in comedy. He had no sense of humour.
Lita Grey, ex-wife. Quoted Richard Lamparski, WHATEVER BECAME OF — ? 1983

15 He pitied everything that stumbled or whimpered or wagged a tail, particularly he pitied himself. There has never been a portrait of self pity so vivid or so shocking as Charlie with a rose in his hand.
Robert Hatch, Reporter 25 Nov 1952

16 . . . somehow importing to the peeling of a banana the elegant nonchalance of a duke drawing a monogrammed cigarette from a platinum case.
Alexander Woollcott, WHILE ROME BURNS 1934

CHARACTER

17 He is a very hard guy indeed. In fact I hear the softest thing about him is his front teeth.
Damon Runyon, MORE THAN SOMEWHAT 1937

CHARITY

18 In common with many Christians of the classic type he felt sincerely safer and more at ease when he had given away all he had, like a man passing a ball in a game.
Margery Allingham, TIGER IN THE SMOKE 1957

19 A man who sees another man on the street corner with only a stump for an arm will be

so shocked the first time he'll give him sixpence. But the second time it'll only be a threepenny bit. And if he sees him a third time he'll cold-bloodedly have him handed over to the police.
Bertolt Brecht, THE THREEPENNY OPERA 1928

1 Too many people have decided to do without generosity in order to practise charity.
Albert Camus, THE FALL 1956

2 Philanthropy is commendable, but it must not cause the philanthropist to overlook the circumstances of economic injustice which make philanthropy necessary.
Martin Luther King, STRENGTH TO LOVE 1963

3 Lots of people think they are charitable if they give away their old clothes and things they don't want.
Myrtle Reed, OLD ROSE AND SILVER

4 The dignity of the individual demands that he be not reduced to vassalage by the largesse of others.
Antoine de Saint-Exupéry, FLIGHT TO ARRAS 1942

CHARM

5 [Charm] is a sort of bloom on a woman. If you have it you don't need anything else; and if you don't have it, it doesn't much matter what else you have.
J. M. Barrie, WHAT EVERY WOMAN KNOWS 1908

6 Charm is a way of getting the answer yes, without having asked any clear question.
Albert Camus, THE FALL 1956

7 All charming people have something to conceal, usually their total dependence on the appreciation of others.
Cyril Connolly, ENEMIES OF PROMISE 1938

8 History is bright and fiction dull with homely men who have charmed women.
O. Henry, ROADS OF DESTINY, *Next to Reading Matter* 1909

9 Oozing charm from every pore / He oiled his way across the floor.
Alan Jay Lerner, MY FAIR LADY 1956

10 She whose body's young and cool / Has no need of dancing school.
Dorothy Parker, SALOME'S DANCING LESSON

CHASTITY

11 Chastity; the most unnatural of the sexual perversions.
Aldous Huxley, EYELESS IN GAZA 1936

12 Many citizens claim it is a great shame that such a beautiful doll is wasting her time being good.
Damon Runyon, GUYS AND DOLLS 1932

13 A well-preserved virginity *may* signify a limited capacity for love.
Robert Shields, Observer 13 *Jun* 1965

CHEATING

14 It is almost always worth while to be cheated; people's little frauds have an interest which more than repays what they cost us.
Logan Pearsall Smith, ALL TRIVIA, *Afterthoughts* 1931

CHEESE

15 Ah, Wensleydale! The Mozart of cheeses.
T. S. Eliot. Quoted Roy Perrot, Observer 10 *Jan* 1965

16 Cheese — milk's leap towards immortality.
Clifton Fadiman, ANY NUMBER CAN PLAY 1957

17 How can you have a one-party system in a country that has two hundred varieties of cheese.
General de Gaulle, BBC Radio 4, *Quote Unquote* 18 *Jul* 1979

CHESS

18 Chess — a game in the playing of which there is no element of chance.
Opening words of international rules

G. K. CHESTERTON

19 Remote and ineffectual don / That dared attack my Chesterton.
Hilaire Belloc, LINES TO A DON

CHICAGO

20 Pentonville is joyous to Chicago, Manchester is a paradise to it, Wapping, Whitechapel and Deptford are gardens to it.
John Masefield, in a letter to his wife, Constance 1916

1 Here is the difference between Dante, Milton and me. They wrote about hell and never saw the place. I wrote about Chicago after looking the place over for years and years.
Carl Sandburg. Quoted Harry Golden, CARL SANDBURG

CHILDREN

2 It is no wonder people are so horrible when they start life as children.
Kingsley Amis, ONE FAT ENGLISHMAN 1963

3 "We don't know what to make of him" said his mother (of a badly behaved child).
"How about a nice rug?"
Tallulah Bankhead. Quoted David Frost and Anthony Jay, TO ENGLAND WITH LOVE

4 Childhood is measured out by sounds and smells / And sights before the dark of reason grows.
John Betjeman, SUMMONED BY BELLS 1960

5 Boys do not grow up gradually. They move forward in spurts like the hands of clocks in railway stations.
Cyril Connolly, ENEMIES OF PROMISE 1938

6 The trouble with children is that they are not returnable.
Quentin Crisp, THE NAKED CIVIL SERVANT

7 Anybody who hates children and dogs can't be all bad.
W. C. Fields. Quoted Radio Times 12 *Aug* 1965

8 Nervous breakdowns are hereditary. We get them from our children.
Graffito. Quoted Nigel Rees, GRAFFITI 2

9 There is always one moment in childhood when the door opens and lets in the future.
Graham Greene, THE POWER AND THE GLORY 1940

10 It's a lovely silver star, and you are going to put up your hand and point to it. And what are you going to say when you do that? — No Sidney, he *isn't* going to say "Please may I go to the bathroom".
Joyce Grenfell, GEORGE DON'T DO THAT, *The Nativity Play*

11 Let's put on our thinking caps shall we and think what flowers we are going to be . . . A horse isn't a flower Sidney . . . No a *carrot* isn't a flower Sidney . . . No Sidney

you can't be a super jet — all right you can be a cauliflower, but be it *gently*.
Id., *Flowers*

12 Jenny, when we have paid a visit to the littlest room what do we do? — We pull our knickers up again.
Id., *Going Home Time*

13 Thank you Dicky, for closing the cupboard door for me. — Dicky, is there someone *in* that cupboard? — Well let her out at once.
Id.

14 The business of being a child interests a child not at all. Children very rarely play at being other children.
David Holloway, Daily Telegraph, *As We Grow Up* 15 Dec 1966

15 You Americans do not rear children, you *incite* them, you give them food and shelter and applause.
Randall Jarrell, PICTURES FROM AN INSTITUTION 1954

16 Never have ideas about children — and never have ideas *for* them.
D. H. Lawrence, FANTASIA OF THE UNCONSCIOUS 1922

17 Even when freshly washed and relieved of all obvious confections, children tend to be sticky.
Fran Lebowitz. Quoted Frank Muir, ON CHILDREN

18 This would be a better world for children if parents had to eat the spinach.
Groucho Marx, ANIMAL CRACKERS

19 My mother loved children — she would have given anything if I had been one.
Groucho Marx. Quoted Frank Muir, ON CHILDREN

20 Childhood is the kingdom where no one dies.
Edna St. Vincent Millay, WINE FROM THESE GRAPES 1934

21 A child's spirit is like a child, you can never catch it by running after it; you must stand still, and, for love, it will soon itself come back.
Arthur Miller, THE CRUCIBLE 1953

22 Some people do not make good children. They should spring upon the world fully grown, preferably with a gin and tonic in hand, and conversation in full swing, a

61

camera equipped with sound on the premises to record the event.
Margaret Morley, LARGER THAN LIFE — A BIOGRAPHY OF ROBERT MORLEY

1 Grown-ups never understand anything for themselves, and it is tiresome for children to be always and forever explaining things to them.
Antoine de Saint-Exupéry, THE LITTLE PRINCE 1943

2 Nothing would induce me to go over my childhood days again. I thought I was happy because my mother said I was.
Rev. H. R. L. Sheppard. Quoted Carolyn Scott, DICK SHEPPARD

CHINA

3 Very big, China.
Noël Coward, PRIVATE LIVES 1930

CHOICE

4 Every act is an act of self sacrifice. When you choose anything, you reject everything else.
G. K. Chesterton, ORTHODOXY 1908

5 Man must choose whether to be rich in things or in the freedom to use them.
I. D. Illich, DESCHOOLING SOCIETY

JESUS CHRIST

6 Jesus Christ was not a Conservative.
Eric Heffer, Observer, *Sayings of the Week* 20 Feb 1983

7 He might be described as an under-privileged, colonial, working-class victim of political and religious persecution.
Philip, Duke of Edinburgh, A QUESTION OF BALANCE 1982

8 Whether you think Jesus was God or not, you must admit that he was a first-rate political economist.
George Bernard Shaw, ANDROCLES AND THE LION, *Preface* 1912

CHRISTIANITY

9 *Chapuys*: After all, we are brothers in Christ, you and I.
More: A characteristic we share with the rest of humanity. You live in Cheapside, Signor? To make contact with a brother in Christ you have only to open your window and empty a chamber pot. There is no need to come to Chelsea.
Robert Bolt, A MAN FOR ALL SEASONS 1960

10 The energy of combativeness of Christian nations comes, I suspect, from the doctrine of sin, particularly original sin, and the kind of struggle that must go on for redemption (or for money).
Gerald Brenan, in a letter to Bertrand Russell 1 Jun 1935

11 Christianity flourishes in proportion to the misery and insecurity of life. Prosperity kills it because at its most sincere it is a cry from the depths.
Gerald Brenan, THOUGHTS IN A DRY SEASON 1979

12 It is our business, as readers of literature, to know what we like. It is our business as Christians as *well* as readers of literature, to know what we ought to like. It is our business as honest men not to assume that what we like is what we ought to like.
T. S. Eliot, SELECTED ESSAYS

13 The Gospel is essentially a message of spiritual redemption, not of social reform.
W. R. Inge (Dean of St. Pauls), FREEDOM, LOVE AND TRUTH 1936

14 Christianity is a revolutionary idealism which estranges revolutionaries by its idealism and conservatives by its drastic revaluation of earthly goods.
Id.

15 Christianity promises to make men free; it never promises to make them independent.
W. R. Inge (Dean of St. Pauls), THE PHILOSOPHY OF PLOTINUS 1929

16 I wonder when Christianity will have sufficiently decayed for the fact to be driven out of men's heads that pleasure is not hurtful nor pain beneficial.
W. Somerset Maugham, A WRITER'S NOTEBOOK 1949

17 Christianity is not tied to any ideology.
Dr. Hugh Montefiore (Bishop of Birmingham). Church of England Synod, The Church and the Bomb debate 10 Feb 1983

18 Christianity was not founded by clergymen.
Norman Vincent Peale, FAITH FOR TODAY

19 The worst of the idealistic education most of us have had under Christian authority is that it makes us so ashamed of our real feelings towards human beings that we indulge in a constant process of self deception.
John Cowper Powys, THE MEANING OF CULTURE

1 I submit that Christians ought not to be scared of a moral issue just because someone has stuck a political flag on it.
Gerald Priestland, BBC Radio 4, *Yours Faithfully* 5 *Sep* 1978

2 In the ethic of Christianity it is the relation of the soul to God that is important not the relation of man to his fellow man.
Bertrand Russell, MARRIAGE AND MORALS 1929

3 "The fashion just now is a Roman Catholic frame of mind with an Agnostic conscience: you get the mediaeval picturesqueness of the one with the modern convenience of the other."
The Duchess suppressed a sniff. She was one of those people who regard the Church of England with patronizing affection, as if it were something that had grown up in their kitchen garden.
Saki, REGINALD AT THE THEATRE

4 People may say what they like about the decay of Christianity; the religious system that produced green Chartreuse can never really die.
Saki, REGINALD ON CHRISTMAS PRESENTS

5 Civilisation is perhaps approaching one of those long winters that overtake it from time to time. Romantic Christendom — picturesque, passionate, unhappy episode — may be coming to an end. Such a catastrophe would be no reason for despair.
George Santayana, CHARACTER AND OPINION IN THE UNITED STATES 1920

6 The true Christian is in all countries a pilgrim and a stranger.
George Santayana, WINDS OF DOCTRINE 1913

7 Popular Christianity has for its emblem a gibbet, for its chief sensation a sanguinary execution after torture, for its central mystery an insane vengeance brought off by a trumpery expiation. But there is a nobler and profounder Christianity which affirms the sacred mystery of equality and forbids the glaring futility and folly of vengeance.
George Bernard Shaw, MAJOR BARBARA, *Preface* 1905

8 The nearest he gets to being a Christian is stirring his tea with an apostle spoon.
Peter Spence, BBC TV, *To the Manor Born* 25 *Dec* 1979

9 The Christian believes that he was created to know, love and serve God in this world and to be happy with him in the next. That is the sole reason for his existence.
Evelyn Waugh, Month, Nov 1949

10 Christianity is pre-eminently the religion of slaves, slaves cannot help belonging to it, and I am among them.
Simone Weil, THE NEED FOR ROOTS

CHRISTMAS

11 I'm dreaming of a white Christmas / Just like the ones I used to know.
Irving Berlin, HOLIDAY INN 1942

12 This most tremendous tale of all / Seen in a stained glass window's hue / A baby in an ox's stall.
John Betjeman, CHRISTMAS

13 My mother-in-law has come round to our house at Christmas seven years running. This year we're having a change. We're going to let her in.
Les Dawson, BBC TV, *Pebble Mill* 27 *Dec* 1979

14 A woman who is insidiously ostentatious about the flower-like and impersonal quality of her beauty can be given a hot water bottle or small biscuit-coloured Shetland shawl to wear in bed or a tin of patent food which announces clearly on the front label that it has been specially treated to make it more easily digestible . . . Thrown in with the rest somebody can give her a cheap lipstick, smelling of lard.
Stephen Potter, ONE-UPMANSHIP 1952

15 Poor relations may be maddened by giving them useful [Christmas] presents like scissors, or bradawls.
Id.

16 Fall back on the general suggestion that all this being tremendously nice at Christmas is redolent of somebody covering up a tendency to be tremendously nasty all the rest of the year. Suggest that for you, personally, it makes no difference.
Stephen Potter, SUPERMANSHIP 1952

17 It is good that Christmas comes at the dark dream of the year. / That might wish to sleep for ever.
Anne Ridler, CHRISTMAS AND COMMON BIRTH

18 It always seems such a mixing of this world and the next — but that, after all, is the idea.
Evelyn Underhill, LETTERS

1 Xmas is a good time with all those presents and good food and i hope it will never die out or at any rate not until i am grown up and hav to pay for it.
Geoffrey Willans and Ronald Searle, HOW TO BE TOPP

CHURCH

2 There is little good in filling churches with people who go out just exactly the same as they come in; the call of the Church is not to fill churches but to fill heaven.
Father Andrew, THE WAY OF VICTORY

3 What an amazing capacity for disappointment the Church has.
Nigel Balchin, LORD, I WAS AFRAID

4 The Church's Restoration / In eighteen eighty three / Has left for contemplation / Not what there used to be.
Sir John Betjeman, HYMN

5 The British churchman goes to church as he goes to the bathroom, with the minimum of fuss and no explanation if he can help it.
Ronald Blythe, THE AGE OF ILLUSION

6 The Church of England, that finest flower of our Island genius for compromise; that system, peculiar to these shores, which deflects the currents of religious passion down the canals of moderation.
Robert Bolt, A MAN FOR ALL SEASONS 1960

7 There would never be any stigma attached to a young man going into the Church because the upper classes have to believe in God.
Jilly Cooper, CLASS

8 The hippopotamus's day / Is passed in sleep, at night he hunts. / God works in a mysterious way — / The church can sleep and feed at once.
T. S. Eliot, THE HIPPOPOTAMUS 1920

9 The greatest mistake the bishops make is in thinking they are the Church. The Church is the laity.
Lord Hailsham. Quoted Susan Barnes, BEHIND THE IMAGE

10 People expect the clergy to have the grace of a swan, the friendliness of a sparrow, the strength of an eagle and the night-hours of an owl — and some people expect such a bird to live on the food of a canary.
Rev. Edward Jeffrey. Quoted Observer 14 *Jun* 1964

11 The Church must be reminded that it is not the master or the servant of the state but rather the conscience of the state.
Martin Luther King, STRENGTH TO LOVE 1963

12 There are many who stay away from church these days because you hardly ever mention God any more.
Arthur Miller, THE CRUCIBLE 1953

13 The churches grow old, but do not grow up.
Doris Langley Moore, THE VULGAR HEART

14 He preaches a remarkably good sermon. It is so hard to avoid offending people like us.
Man to Wife, cartoon caption in the New Yorker 1938

15 The Church of England is the perfect church for those who don't go to church.
Gerald Priestland, BBC Radio 4, *Priestland's Progress* 19 *Nov* 1981

16 The Catholic church is a church of sinners in the sense that the Quaker church is a church of saints.
Shirley Williams, interviewed by Miriam Gross, Observer 22 *Mar* 1981

RANDOLPH CHURCHILL

17 Someone, I don't know who, hearing that Randolph Churchill was on the *Queen Mary* with Eden said "I suppose he's the camel to break the straw's back".
Rupert Hart-Davis, THE LYTTELTON HART-DAVIS LETTERS 5 *Mar* 1950

WINSTON CHURCHILL

18 Trouble with Winston; nails his trousers to the mast and can't climb down.
Clement Attlee. Quoted Sir Harold Wilson, A PRIME MINISTER ON PRIME MINISTERS

19 Then comes Winston with his hundred horse-power mind and what can I do?
Stanley Baldwin. Quoted G. M. Young, STANLEY BALDWIN

20 Churchill has the habit of breaking the rungs of any ladder he puts his foot on.
Lord Beaverbrook, letter to Arthur Brisbane 20 *Oct* 1932

21 Churchill, on top of the wave, has in him the stuff of which tyrants are made.
Lord Beaverbrook, POLITICIANS AND THE WAR 1959

22 He never spares himself in conversation. He gives himself so generously that hardly

anybody else is permitted to give anything in his presence.
Aneurin Bevan

1 He always refers to a defeat or a disaster as though it came from God, but to a victory as though it came from himself.
Aneurin Bevan. Quoted Leon Harris, THE FINE ART OF POLITICAL WIT

2 He is a man suffering from petrified adolescence.
Aneurin Bevan. Quoted Vincent Brome, ANEURIN BEVAN

3 [He is] a wholesaler in disaster.
Aneurin Bevan. Quoted Michael Foot, ANEURIN BEVAN VOL. 1

4 Winston has devoted the best years of his life to preparing his impromptu speeches.
Lord Birkenhead

5 Englishman, 25 years old, about five feet eight inches tall, indifferent build, walks with a forward stoop, pale appearance, reddish brown hair, small and hardly noticeable moustache, talks through his nose and cannot pronounce the letter 'S' properly.
Boer description of Churchill after his escape from them

6 Churchill had no objection to us kicking poor old Chamberlain, but he didn't like being hurt himself.
Hugh Cudlipp, WALKING ON THE WATER

7 For a very short period in history Churchill was a necessary shit. He didn't like the upper classes and the upper classes didn't like him. He managed to combine tremendous egalitarianism with being a roaring old snob.
Osbert Lancaster. Quoted Duncan Fallowell, Times Profile 11 *Oct* 1982

8 He has spoilt himself by reading about Napoleon.
David Lloyd George. Quoted Frances Stevenson, DIARIES 19 *May* 1917

9 Winston would go up to his Creator and say that he would very much like to meet His Son, about Whom he had heard a great deal and, if possible, would like to call on the Holy Ghost. Winston *loves* meeting people.
David Lloyd George. Quoted A. J. Sylvester, DIARY 2 *Jan* 1937

10 Churchill's part in World War II reduces the classic figures of Rome and Greece to the relatively inconsequent stature of actors in drama of minor scope.
Mark Sullivan, New York Herald Tribune 11 *May* 1975

11 By his father he is an Englishman, by his mother an American. Behold the perfect man.
Attr. Mark Twain when Churchill was on a lecture tour in the United States

CINEMA

12 Cinema managers are nice and let you pop in to see a film without telling. My mother has seen quite a few films that way recently.
Princess Anne. Quoted Noël St. George, ROYAL QUOTES

13 Movie music is noise. It is even more painful than my sciatica.
Sir Thomas Beecham, Time magazine 24 *Feb* 1958

14 Cecil B. de Mille / Rather against his will / Was persuaded to leave Moses / Out of 'The Wars of the Roses'.
E. C. Bentley, CLERIHEWS

15 The most positive thing in the motion picture business is the negative.
Steve Broidy, President of Monogram Pictures

16 All I need to make a comedy is a park, a policeman and a pretty girl.
Charlie Chaplin, MY AUTOBIOGRAPHY 1964

17 A film is a petrified fountain of thought.
Jean Cocteau, Esquire magazine, *Feb* 1961

18 In Westerns you were permitted to kiss your horse but never your girl.
Gary Cooper, Saturday Evening Post, *Well It was This Way* 17 *Mar* 1958

19 Film music is like a small lamp that you place below the screen to warm it.
Aaron Copland. Quoted Nat Shapiro, AN ENCYCLOPEDIA OF QUOTATIONS ABOUT MUSIC

20 An affair between a mad rockinghorse and a rawhide suitcase.
Noël Coward, of Jeanette MacDonald and Nelson Eddy in Technicolor version of 'Bitter Sweet'

21 Valentino silently acted out the fantasies of women all over the world. Valentino and his world were a dream. A whole generation of females wanted to ride off into a

sandy paradise with him. At thirteen I had been such a female.
Bette Davis, THE LONELY LIFE

1 The cinema has become more and more like the theatre. It's all mumbling and muttering.
Shelagh Delaney, A TASTE OF HONEY 1958

2 A film musician is like a mortician — he can't bring the body back to life, but he is expected to make it look better.
Adolph Deutsch. Quoted Tony Thomas, MUSIC FOR THE MOVIES 1973

3 When I asked her where she had learnt to read so quickly she replied "On the screens at cinemas".
Ronald Firbank, THE FLOWER BENEATH THE FOOT 1923

4 Hollywood is a Jewish holiday, a Gentile tragedy.
F. Scott Fitzgerald. Quoted Matthew J. Bruccoli, SOME SORT OF EPIC GRANDEUR

5 No music has ever saved a bad picture, but a lot of good pictures have saved a lot of bad music.
Jerry Goldsmith. Quoted Irwin Bazedon, KNOWING THE SCORE 1975

6 God makes stars. I just produce them.
Sam Goldwyn. Quoted Paul Holt, Daily Express 16 *May* 1939

7 Who in hell wants to see a picture about a herring?
Sam Goldwyn, on its being suggested that he make a film on the life of Bismarck. Quoted Reginald Pound, THEIR MOODS AND MINE 1937

8 Why should people go out and pay to see bad movies when they can stay at home and see bad television for nothing?
Sam Goldwyn, Observer 9 *Sep* 1956

9 It's greater than a masterpiece — it's mediocre.
Attr. Sam Goldwyn. Quoted Alva Johnson, THE GREAT GOLDWYN

10 Take away the essentials and what have you got?
Sam Goldwyn. Ibid.

11 Every director bites the hand that lays the golden egg.
Id.

12 I want a movie that starts with an earthquake and works up to a climax.
Id.

13 "But Mr. Goldwyn, what is the *message* of this film?"
"I am just planning a movie. I am not interested in messages. Messages are for Western Union."
Sam Goldwyn at a script conference. Ibid.

14 The cinema serves the proletariat as well as the middle classes. So long as we have the cinema and commercialised football the proletariat will give no trouble to their masters in England.
Rev. J. C. Hardwick at the conference of Modern Churchmen, quoted Morning Post

15 There's a lot of nice guys walking around Hollywood but they aren't eating.
Henry Hatheway, producer. Quoted Charles Hamblett, The Times 22 *Mar* 1969

16 The maidens who haunt picture palaces / Know nothing of psycho-analysis / And Sigmund Freud / Would be greatly annoyed / As they cling to their long-standing phalluses.
A. P. Herbert

17 The cinema is not a slice of life but a piece of cake.
Alfred Hitchcock, Sunday Times Magazine 6 *Mar* 1977

18 Folks, you ain't heard nothing yet.
Al Jolson, THE JAZZ SINGER, *Oct* 1927

19 The cinema, like the detective story, makes it possible to experience without danger all the excitement, passion and desirousness which must be repressed in a humanitarian ordering of life.
Carl Jung. Quoted Roger Manvell, FILM

20 God made the fine arts, but man made the film.
Roger Manvell, FILM

21 How I dislike Technicolor, which suffuses everything with stale mustard.
Edward Marsh, AMBROSIA AND SMALL BEER

22 Saddest movie I've ever seen — I cried all the way through. It's sad when you're 82.
Groucho Marx OF LAST TANGO IN PARIS

23 Theda Bara made voluptuousness a common American commodity, as accessible as chewing gum.
Lloyd Morris, NOT SO LONG AGO

24 For a time Henry Luce was on the Board of Directors of Paramount. Hoped to learn something of cinema, heard nothing discussed but banking, resigned sadly.
The New Yorker 28 *Nov* 1936

1 Every film is launched like a squid, in an obscuring cloud of spectacular publicity.
Dudley Nichols, introduction to Lewis Tacobe, ART OF THE MOVIES

2 Hollywood — the city of dreadful day.
S. J. Perelman. Quoted Joe Adamson, GROUCHO, HARPO, CHICO AND SOMETIMES ZEPPO 1973

3 I've done an awful lot of stuff that is a monument to public patience.
Tyrone Power. Quoted David Shipman, THE GREAT MOVIE STARS

4 If you're not very careful I'll play this scene as you want it.
Claude Rains to producer Pascal, during making of JULIUS CAESAR. *Quoted* BBC Radio 4, *Quote Unquote*

5 The cinema in the hands of the Soviet power represents a great and priceless force.
Joseph Stalin. Quoted Roger Manvell, FILM

6 You can seduce a man's wife there [Hollywood], attack his daughter and wipe your hands on his canary, but if you don't like his movie you're dead.
Attr. Joseph von Sternberg

7 Film music should have the same relationship to the film drama that somebody's piano playing in my living room has to the book I am reading.
Igor Stravinsky, Music Digest, Sep 1946

8 The fault in our Hollywood musical credo lies in the simple truth that it is not possible to write real music about an unreal emotion.
Virgil Thomson, New York Herald Tribune 10 Apr 1949

9 I wouldn't say when you've seen one Western you've seen the lot; but when you've seen the lot you get the feeling that you've seen one.
Katherine Whitehorn, SHOUTS AND MURMURS, Decoding the West

10 The way things are going I'd be more interested in seeing Cleopatra play the life of Elizabeth Taylor.
Earl Wilson. Quoted Radio Times, Nov 1962

CITY

11 Cities, like cats, will reveal themselves at night.
Rupert Brooke, LETTERS FROM AMERICA 1916

12 As a remedy to life in society I would suggest the big city. Nowadays it is the only desert within our means.
Albert Camus, NOTEBOOKS 1935–1942

13 No city should be too large for a man to walk out of in a morning.
Cyril Connolly, THE UNQUIET GRAVE 1945

14 A large city cannot be experientially known; its life is too manifold for any individual to be able to participate in it.
Aldous Huxley, BEYOND THE MEXIQUE BAY 1941

15 The city is not a concrete jungle. It is a human zoo.
Desmond Morris, THE HUMAN ZOO

CIVILISATION

16 Civilised people can talk about anything. For them no subject is taboo.
Clive Bell, CIVILISATION, AN ESSAY 1928

17 All great civilisations, in their early stages, are based on success in war.
Kenneth, Lord Clark, CIVILISATION 1969

18 Civilisation is an active deposit which is formed by the combustion of the present and the past.
Cyril Connolly, ENEMIES OF PROMISE 1938

19 No man who is in a hurry is quite civilised.
Will Durant, WHAT IS CIVILISATION?

20 Civilised men arrived in the Pacific, armed with alcohol, syphilis, trousers, and the Bible.
Havelock Ellis, THE DANCE OF LIFE 1923

21 The people of Europe, before they were touched by modern civilisation, had much in common with the people of the East.
Mahatma Gandhi. Quoted obituary, News Chronicle 31 Jan 1948

22 There is precious little in civilisation to appeal to a yeti.
Sir Edmund Hillary. Quoted Observer 3 Jun 1960

23 Compassion is not enough. Civilisation depends upon the cultivation of excellence, and therefore of superiority and inequality.
Philip Howard reviewing John Sparrow's WORDS ON THE AIR

24 Any hopefulness for the future of civilisation is based on the reasonable expectation that humanity is still only beginning its course.
W. R. Inge (Dean of St. Pauls), THE CHURCH AND THE AGE 1911

1 The nineteenth century regarded European civilisation as mature and late, the final expression of the human spirit. We are only now beginning to realise that it is young and childish.
C. E. M. Joad, GUIDE TO MODERN THOUGHT 1933

2 Human history, if you read it right, is the record of the efforts to tame Father . . . the greatest triumph of what we call civilisation was the domestication of the human male.
Max Lerner, THE UNFINISHED COUNTRY, *The Revolt of the American Father* 1959

3 Civilisation — by which I here mean barbarism made strong and luxurious by mechanical power.
C. S. Lewis, A PREFACE TO PARADISE LOST, *being the Ballard Mattheus Lectures, delivered at University College, North Wales* 1941

4 The civilisation of man might be measured by the manner in which he sets about planning and interpreting the flow of sense experiences which constitutes physical life.
Roger Manvell, FILM

5 Teddie: England seems to me full of people doing things they don't want to because other people expect it of them.
Elizabeth: Isn't that what you call a high degree of civilisation?
W. Somerset Maugham, THE CIRCLE 1921

6 Collectivism is the ancient principle of savagery. A savage's whole existence is ruled by tribal leaders. Civilisation is the process of freeing man from men.
Ayn Rand, THE MORAL BASIS OF INDIVIDUALISM

7 All civilised people are in some way what would be thought abnormal, and they suffer because they don't know that really ever so many people are just like them.
Bertrand Russell, letter to Ottoline Morrell. Quoted in his AUTOBIOGRAPHY VOL. II 1967

8 Our laws make law impossible, our liberties destroy all freedom, our property is organised robbery, our morality is an impudent hypocrisy, our wisdom is administered by inexperienced or mal-experienced dupes, our power wielded by cowards and weaklings, and our honour false in all its points. I am an enemy of the existing order for good reasons.
George Bernard Shaw, MAJOR BARBARA, *Preface* 1905

9 Civilisation has made the peasantry a pack animal.
Leon Trotsky, HISTORY OF THE RUSSIAN REVOLUTION 1932

10 Civilisation advances by extending the number of important operations which we can perform without thinking about them.
A. N. Whitehead, AN INTRODUCTION TO MATHEMATICS 1911

11 Civilisation is hooped together, brought / Under a rule, under the semblance of peace / By manifold illusion.
W. B. Yeats, A FULL MOON IN MARCH, *Supernatural Songs, Meru* 1934

CLASS

12 We have barely noticed that the leisured class has been replaced by another and much larger class to which work has none of the old connotations of pain, fatigue, or other mental or physical discomfort.
J. K. Galbraith, THE AFFLUENT SOCIETY 1958

13 The one class you *do* not belong to and are not proud of at all is the lower-middle class. No one ever describes himself as belonging to the lower-middle class.
George Mikes, HOW TO BE INIMITABLE

14 Folkestone was refined, genteel, tidy and, for a child, exciting. The West End . . . was full of PLUs (People Like Us — a phrase used by the gentry of the period to distinguish the U from the non-U).
Margaret Morley, LARGER THAN LIFE — A BIOGRAPHY OF ROBERT MORLEY

15 I can't help feeling wary when I hear anything said about the masses. First you take their faces from 'em, calling them the masses, and then you accuse 'em of not having any faces.
J. B. Priestley, SATURN OVER THE WATER

16 You can be in the Horseguards and still be common, dear.
Terence Rattigan, SEPARATE TABLES 1954

17 Marx sought to replace natural antagonism by class antagonisms.
H. G. Wells, SHORT HISTORY OF THE WORLD 1922

CLEANLINESS

18 Bath twice a day to be really clean, once a day to be passably clean, once a week to avoid being a public nuisance.
Anthony Burgess, INSIDE MR. ENDERBY 1966

1 Look at your dirty fingernails. Are we in mourning for the cat?
Sir Hugh Casson and Joyce Grenfell, NANNY SAYS 1972

GEORGES CLEMENÇEAU

2 There the old Tiger would be sitting, in his grey gloves and grey skullcap, usually wearing grey slippers, looking like a great grey cat.
Bernard Baruch, THE PUBLIC YEARS

CLERGY

3 The average curate at home was something between a eunuch and a snigger.
Ronald Firbank, THE FLOWER BENEATH THE FOOT 1923

4 He had been a bishop so long that no one knew now what he thought about death, or indeed about anything except the Prayer Book, any change in which he deprecated with determination.
John Galsworthy, MAID IN WAITING

5 Priests are no more necessary to religion than politicians are to patriotism.
John Haynes Holmes, THE SENSIBLE MAN'S VIEW OF RELIGION 1933

6 The clergy should regard themselves as physicians of the soul.
W. R. Inge (Dean of St. Pauls). Quoted Ray Giles, CHRISTIAN HERALD, *Jul* 1941

7 Heaven may be for the laity, but this world is certainly for the clergy.
George Moore, HAIL AND FAREWELL 1914

8 The world would be the poorer without the antics of clergymen.
V. S. Pritchett, IN MY GOOD BOOKS, *The Dean*

9 A parson should light fires in dark rooms and go on lighting them all his life.
Rev. H. R. L. Sheppard. Quoted Carolyn Scott, DICK SHEPPARD

10 There is a species of person called a 'Modern Churchman', who draws the full salary of a beneficed clergyman and need not commit himself to any religious belief.
Evelyn Waugh, DECLINE AND FALL 1928

CLEVERNESS

11 When I have to listen to somebody from one of those American 'think tanks' I cannot help remembering the verdict of Tao Te Ching. "Extreme cleverness is as bad as stupidity".
J. B. Priestley, OUTCRIES AND ASIDES

CLICHÉ

12 Let's have some new clichés.
Sam Goldwyn. Quoted Observer 9 Sep 1956

13 The truths of the past are the clichés of the present.
Ned Rorem, MUSIC FROM INSIDE OUT, *Listening and Hearing* 1967

CLIMATE

14 Let us blame the climate for it; we pass, the climate remains.
John Masefield, SO LONG TO LEARN

15 People get a bad impression of it [the English climate] by continually trying to treat it as if it was a bank clerk, who ought to be on time on Tuesday next, instead of philosophically seeing it as a painter, who may do anything so long as you don't try to predict what.
Katherine Whitehorn, Observer 7 *Aug* 1966

CLOTHES

16 Old age has released me from at least one absurdity — an excessive worry about clothes, which came less from a desire to look smart than from a fear of being conspicuous. More parties have been spoilt for me than for most people because I had on the wrong clothes.
Vernon Bartlett, I KNOW WHAT I LIKED

17 A bit of black material to reduce Old Adam to the Common Man.
Robert Bolt, A MAN FOR ALL SEASONS 1960

18 From the cradle to the coffin, underwear comes first
Bertolt Brecht, THE THREEPENNY OPERA 1928

19 Clothes seem to suffer a sea-change when they get on to me. They look quite promising in the shop, and not entirely without hope when I get them back into my wardrobe. But then, when I put them on they tend to deteriorate with a very strange rapidity and one feels so sorry for them.
Joyce Grenfell, STATELY AS A GALLEON

69

1 You walk into your tailor's and ask for the cheapest suit in the shop, and he says, you're wearing it.
Trevor Griffiths, THE COMEDIANS *(play)*

2 You have got to be a Queen to get away with a hat like that.
Anita Loos, GENTLEMEN PREFER BLONDES 1925

3 Where is the man could ease a heart / Like a satin gown?
Dorothy Parker, ENOUGH ROPE 1926

4 All dress is fancy dress, is it not, except our natural skins.
George Bernard Shaw, SAINT JOAN 1927

5 The trouble with most Englishwomen is that they *will* dress as if they had been a mouse in some previous incarnation.
Edith Sitwell, HOW TO WEAR DRAMATIC CLOTHES

6 The people who have a suit for every day of the week and even, one is reluctantly led to believe, more expansive wardrobes, are parvenus of the worst sort. A gentleman generally has two suits.
Douglas Sutherland, THE ENGLISH GENTLEMAN 1978

7 [A gentleman] always buys his underwear at Marks and Spencer and always tells his friends about it as an indication that he is democratic about clothes. In fact a lot of time is taken up at cocktail parties by gentlemen telling each other where they buy their underwear.
Id.

8 All ladies dress like the Queen, which is much the same as dressing like the Queen Mother. By and large they are at their best dressed for a brisk walk in the rain but they can look awe-inspiring at Hunt Balls and above all at weddings.
Douglas Sutherland, THE ENGLISH GENTLEMAN'S WIFE 1979

9 We still buy cotton frocks in April as a folk magic to bring on summer, forgetting that the golden afternoon of the Edwardian era was due, as much as anything, to the fact that they never (well almost never), abandoned their petticoats and stays and waistcoats.
Katherine Whitehorn, Observer 7 *Aug* 1966

CLOUD

10 Bright towers of silence.
Walter de la Mare, ENGLAND

11 every cloud / has its silver / lining but it is / sometimes a little / difficult to get it to / the mint.
Don Marquis, CERTAIN MAXIMS OF ARCHY 1935

12 . . . carven towers / Stiff sculpted like a heap of marble flowers.
Edward Shanks, CLOUDS

CLUB

13 On his [Sir James Barrie] first visit to the Athenaeum Club he asked an octogenarian biologist the way to the dining room. The biologist burst into tears. He had been a member for fifty years. No one had ever spoken to him before.
Anon.

14 Clubs are places where men spend all their time thinking angrily about nothing.
Viscount Castlerosse. Quoted George Malcolm Thompson, LORD CASTLEROSSE, HIS LIFE AND TIMES

15 Please accept my resignation. I don't want to belong to any club that would accept me as a member.
Attr. Groucho Marx by Bennett Cerf and others

16 Members can amuse themselves by sitting at the window and "watching the demned people getting wet outside".
Douglas Sutherland, THE ENGLISH GENTLEMAN 1978

17 Most clubs have the atmosphere of a Duke's house with the Duke lying dead upstairs.
Id.

COALMINING

18 In other trades there are a thousand diversions to break the monotony of work — the passing traffic, the morning newspaper, above all, the sky, the sunshine, the wind, the rain. The miner has none of these. Every day for eight hours he dies, gives up a slice of life, literally drops out of life and buries himself.
Aneurin Bevan. Quoted Michael Foot, ANEURIN BEVAN 1897–1945

COCOA

19 Half past nine high time for supper / "Cocoa love?" "Of course my dear." / . . . For they've stumbled on the secret / Of a love that never wanes / Rapt beneath the tum-

bled bedclothes / Cocoa coursing through their veins.
Stanley J. Sharpless, CUPID'S NIGHTCAP, New Statesman and Nation 7 *Nov* 1953

COFFEE

1 Coffee in England is just toasted milk.
Christopher Fry, New York Post 29 *Nov* 1962

COINCIDENCE

2 What a marvellous coincidence. You're writing a book and I'm reading one.
Leo Garel. Caption to cartoon of a blonde at a party, Saturday Evening Post 1960

3 Although we talk so much about coincidence we do not really believe in it. In our heart of hearts we think better of the universe, we are secretly convinced that it is not such a slipshod, haphazard affair, that everything in it has meaning.
J. B. Priestley, A COINCIDENCE

COLLECTING

4 One of the silliest questions you can ask a book collector is, "Have you read all these?" Of course he hasn't. Some books are bought to look at, not to read.
Sir John Betjeman, Daily Herald. *Quoted* News Review 28 *Nov* 1946

COLOUR

5 I know the colour rose and it is lovely / but not when it ripens in a tumour / and healing greens, leaves and grass so springlike, / in limbs that fester are not springlike . . . / So in the simple blessing of a rainbow / in the bevelled edge of a sunlit mirror, / I have seen visible, Death's artifact / like a soldier's ribbon on a tunic tacked.
Dannie Abse, GOLDERS GREEN, *Pathology of Colours*

6 Grey is a colour that always seems on the verge of changing to some other colour.
G. K. Chesterton, ALARMS AND DISCURSIONS 1916

7 I don't want the Legion d'honneur — I'd love it if it were pink, but red is vulgar.
Marie Laurencin. Quoted René Gimpel, DIARY OF AN ART DEALER

8 I've been forty years discovering that the queen of all colours is black.
Auguste Pierre Renoir. Quoted Ambrose Vollard, RECOLLECTIONS OF A PICTURE DEALER

COMEDY

9 All comedians are anarchists.
Ken Dodd, Radio Times 24 *Mar* 1979

10 The first thing any comedian does on getting an unscheduled laugh is to verify the state of his buttons; the second is to look around to see if a cat has walked out on the stage.
W. C. Fields. Quoted Robert Lewis Taylor, W. C. FIELDS, ROWDY KING OF COMEDY

11 Comedy is an escape, not from truth but from despair; a narrow escape into faith.
Christopher Fry, Time 22 *Nov* 1950

12 Our comedies are not to be laughed at.
Sam Goldwyn. Quoted Alva Johnson, THE GREAT GOLDWYN

13 Comedy takes place in a world where the mind is always superior to the emotions.
Joseph Wood Krutch, THE MODERN TEMPER 1929

14 The test of a real comedian is whether you laugh at him before he opens his mouth.
George Jean Nathan, American Mercury, Sep 1929

15 Comedy is the last refuge of the nonconformist mind.
Gilbert Seldes, New Republic 20 *Dec* 1954

16 The only rules comedy can tolerate are those of taste, and the only limitations those of libel.
James Thurber, LANTERNS AND LANCES 1961

17 Comedy is the clash of character. Eliminate character from comedy and you get farce.
W. B. Yeats, DRAMATIS PERSONAE

COMFORT

18 Comfort came in with the middle classes.
Clive Bell, CIVILISATION 1928

COMMERCE

19 The myth that holds that the great corporation is the puppet of the market, the powerless servant of the consumer, is in fact, one of the devices by which its power is perpetuated.
J. K. Galbraith, AGE OF UNCERTAINTY 1977

COMMITMENT

1 That this round O of faithfulness / We swear / May never wither to an empty nought / Nor petrify into a square.
W. H. Auden, MODERN CANTERBURY PILGRIMS

2 For I have promises to keep / And many miles to go before I sleep.
Robert Frost, STOPPING BY WOODS ON A SNOWY EVENING 1923

COMMITTEE

3 If Moses had operated through committees the Israelites never would have got across the Red Sea.
Gen. William Booth, Salvation Army founder. Quoted Edward Morello, New York World-Telegram 28 *Jul* 1965

4 A committee is a group of the unwilling, picked from the unfit, to do the unnecessary.
Richard Harkness, New York Herald Tribune 15 *Jun* 1960

5 A committee is an animal with four back legs.
John Le-Carré, TINKER, TAILOR, SOLDIER, SPY

COMMONSENSE

6 Commonsense appears to be only another name for the thoughtlessness of the unthinking. It is made of the prejudices of childhood, the idiosyncrasies of individual character and the opinion of the newspapers.
W. Somerset Maugham, A WRITER'S NOTEBOOK 1949

COMMUNICATION

7 Trying to talk to the government is like trying to hold a conversation with the Talking Clock.
Alan Fisher, TUC Conference 7 Sep 1981

8 In spite of life, in spite of intelligence and intuition and sympathy, one can never really communicate anything to anybody . . . our life is a sentence of perpetual solitary confinement.
Aldous Huxley, COLLECTED ESSAYS 1960

9 The electric age establishes a global network that has much of the character of our central nervous system.
Marshall McLuhan, UNDERSTANDING MEDIA 1964

10 Verbal communication about music is impossible, except among musicians.
Virgil Thomson, THE STATE OF MUSIC 1939

COMMUNISM

11 I would not mind sitting on a platform with a Russian communist, but I would not be seen dead with a British communist.
Lady Astor 1942

12 The Communist Party is not a party, it is a conspiracy.
Aneurin Bevan in an article in Tribune

13 A communist should be tidier, and not make work for the servants.
Caryl Brahms and Ned Sherrin, THE MITFORD GIRLS 1982

14 Communism is the new religion which denies original sin, though seldom do we meet a real communist who seems either complete or happy.
Cyril Connolly, THE UNQUIET GRAVE 1945

15 Communism has never come to power in a country that was not disrupted by war or corruption, or both.
John F. Kennedy. Speech to NATO 3 *Jul* 1963

16 Were I a communist, the type of person whom I should most wish to attack would not be the millionaire or the imperialist, but the soft, reasonable, tolerant, secure, self-satisfied intellectual like Vita and myself.
Harold Nicolson, DIARY 4 *Aug* 1932

17 The Catholic and the Communist are alike in assuming that an opponent cannot be both honest and intelligent.
George Orwell, SELECTED ESSAYS, *The Prevention of Literature* 1968

18 It is one of the weaknesses of Communism, though it has virtues we too often refuse to acknowledge, that it does seem to create a general scene that is altogether too damnably drab.
J. B. Priestley, New Statesman, *Dandy Days*

19 The sturdy young Nazis of Germany (are) Europe's guardians against the Communist danger.
Lord Rothermere, owner of Daily Mirror *and* Mail 1933

20 Communism is the corruption of a dream of justice.
Adlai Stevenson. Speech, Urbana 1951

1 The crusade against Communism was even more imaginary than the spectre of Communism.
A. J. P. Taylor, ORIGINS OF THE SECOND WORLD WAR 1962

COMMUNITY

2 Our most basic common link is that we all inhabit this planet.
John F. Kennedy. Speech 10 Jun 1963

COMPARISON

3 There is no need to worry about mere size. We do not necessarily respect a fat man more than a thin man. Sir Isaac Newton was very much smaller than a hippopotamus, but we do not on that account value him less.
Bertrand Russell, Saturday Evening Post, *The Expanding Mental Universe* 2 Jul 1959

COMPASSION

4 One cannot weep for the entire world, it is beyond human strength. One must choose.
Jean Anouilh, CÉCILE 1949

5 You don't have to be poor to have a heart. Women who have got money are just as interested in the welfare of another as other women.
Lady Astor, House of Commons 1939

6 Billy in one of his nice new sashes / Fell in the fire and was burnt to ashes / Now, although the room grows chilly / I haven't the heart to poke poor Billy.
Harry Graham, RUTHLESS RHYMES

7 Compassion is the albatross of the Liberal.
J. B. Priestley. Quoted Vernon Bartlett, I KNOW WHAT I LIKED

COMPETITION

8 Competitions are for horses, not artists.
Béla Bartók, Saturday Review 25 *Aug* 1962

9 I dislike it [competition] in real life and I do not see why it should be introduced into one's amusements. If it amuses me to do a thing I do not see that it much matters whether I do it better than another person.
A. C. Benson, FROM A COLLEGE WINDOW 1906

COMPLIMENT

10 Nothing is so silly as the expression of a man who is being complimented.
André Gide, JOURNALS 1939–1950

COMPOSING

11 Composing is like driving down a foggy road towards a house. Slowly you see more details of the house — the colour of the slates and bricks, the shape of the windows. The notes are the bricks and mortar of the house.
Benjamin Britten. Quoted Nat Shapiro, AN ENCYCLOPEDIA OF QUOTATIONS ABOUT MUSIC

12 Good music resembles something. It resembles the composer.
Jean Cocteau, COCK AND HARLEQUIN 1918

13 It is a good thing [Sir Hubert] Parry died when he did; otherwise he might have set the whole Bible to music
Frederick Delius. Quoted Philip Heseltine, DELIUS

14 Composers shouldn't think too much — it interferes with their plagiarism.
Howard Dietz. Letter to Goddard Lieberson, Nov 1974

15 Why should I write a fugue or something that won't appeal to anyone, when the people yearn for things that will stir them.
Sir Edward Elgar. Quoted Nat Shapiro, AN ENCYCLOPEDIA OF QUOTATIONS ABOUT MUSIC

16 Things take shape without my knowing it. I am only the lead pencil and cannot foresee.
Sir Edward Elgar. Quoted Basil Maine, ELGAR, HIS LIFE AND WORKS

17 There is music in the air, music all round us: the world is full of it, and you simply take as much as you require.
Id.

18 I have no use at all for those composers who cannot write without being surrounded by stained glass windows for the sake of atmosphere.
Id.

19 I have no opinion of the composer who can think only in terms of the keyboard.
Id.

20 A nation creates music — the composer only arranges it.
Mikhail Glinka, Theatre Arts magazine, *Jun 1958*

1 Never compose anything unless the not composing of it becomes a positive nuisance to you.
Gustav Holst. Letter to W. G. Whittaker 1921

2 The contemporary composer is a gate-crasher trying to push his way into a company to which he has not been invited.
Arthur Honegger, JE SUIS COMPOSITEUR

3 Strauss remembers. Beethoven dreams.
Charles Ives, ESSAYS BEFORE A SONATA 1920

4 A composer is unable to hide anything — by his music you shall know him.
Yehudi Menuhin, THEME AND VARIATIONS 1972

5 With many composers you gradually become aware that they have the defects of their qualities. With [Sir Hubert] Parry the process is reversed; it is only by degrees that you discover him to possess the qualities of his defects.
R. O. Morris, Music and Letters, *Mar* 1920

6 Every great composer, without exception, has been appreciated, admired, applauded and loved in his own time. Even those who died miserably, died famous.
Henry Pleasants, THE AGONY OF MODERN MUSIC 1955

7 If a composer could state in words what being a composer means he would no longer need to be a composer.
Ned Rorem, CRITICAL AFFAIRS 1970

8 The performer may have a responsibility towards the composer, but the composer has none towards the performer beyond the practical one of making his music performable on some terms.
Ned Rorem, THE FINAL DIARY 1974

9 Every composer's music reflects in its subject matter and in its style the source of the money the composer is living on while writing the music.
Virgil Thomson, THE STATE OF MUSIC 1939

COMPREHENSION

10 Thoroughly worldly people never understand even the world: they rely on a few cynical maxims which are not true.
G. K. Chesterton, ORTHODOXY 1908

COMPROMISE

11 The English — or at least those who are in positions of power — like to believe in the efficiency of negotiation, compromise, reconciliation, give-and-take. They would never dream of setting fire to an embassy.
William Davis, Punch 9 *Feb* 1972

12 Compromise is never anything but an ignoble truce between the duty of a man and the terror of a coward.
Reginald Wright Kauffman, THE WAY OF PEACE

13 If one cannot catch a bird of paradise, better take a wet hen.
Nikita Khrushchev. Quoted Time Magazine 1 *Jun* 1958

14 I offer my opponents a bargain; if they will stop telling falsehoods about us, I will stop telling the truth about them.
Adlai Stevenson. Campaign speech 1952

COMPULSION

15 I find I always have to write *something* on a steamed mirror.
Elaine Dundy, THE DUD AVOCADO 1958

COMPUTER

16 To err is human, but to really foul things up requires a computer.
Anon. Quoted BBC Radio 4, *Quote Unquote* 22 *Feb* 1982

17 Man is still the most extraordinary computer of all.
John F. Kennedy. Speech 21 *May* 1963

COMRADESHIP

18 War is too terrible a price to pay even for the advantages of comradeship.
W. H. Nevinson, John o'London's Weekly, *reviewing Edmund Blunden's* UNDERTONES OF WAR 22 *Dec* 1928

CONCEIT

19 Harold [Robbins] could be the best conversationalist in the world — if he ever found anyone he thought worth talking to.
Herbert Alexander. Quoted Alan Whicker in TV interview

20 No poet or novelist wishes he were the only one who ever lived, but most of them wish they were the only one alive, and quite a number fondly believe their wish has been granted.
W. H. Auden, THE DYER'S HAND, *Writing* 1962

1 One of my chief regrets during my years in the theatre is that I couldn't sit in the audience and watch me.
John Barrymore, in an interview

2 Conceit is God's gift to little men.
Bruce Barton, CONCEIT

3 To say that a man is vain means merely that he is pleased with the effect he produces on other people. A conceited man is satisfied with the effect he produces on himself.
Sir Max Beerbohm, AND EVEN NOW, *Quia Imperfectum*

4 I conceived at least one great love in my life, of which I was always the object.
Albert Camus, THE FALL 1956

5 He (Thomas E. Dewey) is just about the nastiest little man I've ever known. He struts sitting down.
Mrs. Dykstra. Quoted J. T. Patterson, MR. REPUBLICAN

6 Try not to despise yourself too much — it is only conceit.
P. J. Kavanagh, A SONG AND DANCE

7 If you think you are not conceited you are very conceited indeed.
C. S. Lewis, MERE CHRISTIANITY

8 He [Arnold Bennett] has described how, when as a young dramatic critic, he went to a Lyceum first night, he would saunter into the stalls and "glancing at the front row of the pit with cold and aloof disdain" would think "don't you wish you were me?"
Robert Lynd. Arnold Bennett obituary, News Chronicle 28 *Mar* 1931

9 Tomorrow every Duchess in London will be wanting to kiss me.
Ramsay MacDonald, on forming the National Government. Quoted Viscount Snowden, AUTOBIOGRAPHY

10 It's about time the piano realised it did not write the concerto.
Joseph L. Mankiewicz, ALL ABOUT EVE *(film)*

11 The affair between Margot Asquith and Margot Asquith will live as one of the prettiest love stories in all literature.
Dorothy Parker, reviewing Margot Asquith's autobiography, New Yorker 1936

12 A lot of men who have accepted — or had imposed upon them in boyhood — the old English public school styles of careful modesty in speech, with much understatement, have behind their masks an appalling and impregnable conceit of themselves. If they do not blow their own trumpets it is because they feel you are not fit to listen to the performance.
J. B. Priestley, OUTCRIES AND ASIDES

13 No person loving or admiring himself is alone.
Theodore Reik, OF LOVE AND LUST 1957

14 If I were a medical man I would prescribe a holiday to any patient who considered his work important.
Bertrand Russell, THE CONQUEST OF HAPPINESS 1930

15 We believe, first and foremost, what makes us feel we are fine fellows.
Bertrand Russell, UNPOPULAR ESSAYS 1950

16 In America everybody is of the opinion that he has no social superiors, but he does not admit that he has no social inferiors.
Id.

17 If I ever felt inclined to be scared going into a room full of people I would say to myself "You're the cleverest member of one of the cleverest families in the cleverest class of the cleverest nation in the world, so what have you got to be frightened of?"
Beatrice Webb. Quoted David A. Shannon, introduction to Beatrice Webb's AMERICAN DIARY

CONCERT

18 Of the type of audience at a chamber music concert an Oxford don once remarked "They look like the sort of people who go to the English Church abroad."
W. H. Auden, A CERTAIN WORLD

19 Even before the music begins there is that bored look in people's faces. A polite form of self-imposed torture, the concert.
Henry Miller, TROPIC OF CANCER 1934

20 A concert is like a bullfight — the moment of truth.
Arthur Rubenstein. Quoted Robert Jacobson, REVERBERATIONS 1974

CONDESCENSION

21 When he greeted one, one always felt like a delicate monkey being put through tricks.
Cyril Connolly of Ian Fleming. Quoted John Pearson, LIFE OF IAN FLEMING 1966

CONDUCTOR

1 There was one respect in which Landon Ronald outshone all other conductors. This was in the gleam of his shirtfront and the gloss of his enormous cuffs, out of which peeped tiny, fastidious fingers. He made music sound as if it, too, had been laundered.
James Agate, EGO 4 1940

2 I spend up to six hours a day waving my arms about and if everyone else did the same they would stay much healthier.
Sir Malcolm Sargent. Quoted Leslie Ayre, The Wit of Music

3 Conductors must give unmistakable and suggestive signals to the orchestra — not choreography to the audience.
George Szell, Newsweek 28 *Jan* 1963

CONFESSION

4 The Roman Catholic Church, by using confession, makes people interested in themselves, and, feeling it right to be interested, it makes everyone form a kind of romantic picture of himself or herself.
A. C. Benson, DIARIES 1920

5 It was reading Rousseau's 'Confessions' that first determined me to write mine and at the same time to have a more satisfactory life to make a record of.
William Scawen Blunt, MY DIARIES 1888–1914

6 We confess our bad qualities to others out of fear of appearing naïve or ridiculous by not being aware of them.
Gerald Brenan, THOUGHTS IN A DRY SEASON 1979

7 There was really no joy in pouring out one's sins while he sat assiduously picking his nose.
Ronald Firbank, VALMOUTH 1919

8 Should we all confess our sins to one another we would all laugh at one another for our lack of originality.
Kahil Gibran, SAND AND FOAM 1927

9 Before confession, be perfectly sure that you do not wish to be forgiven.
Katherine Mansfield. Quoted Anthony Helpen, KATHERINE MANSFIELD

10 Confession may be good for my soul, but it sure plays hell with my reputation.
Mark Twain. Quoted Janet Wells, Observer, *The Diarists* 3 *Jan* 1982

CONFIDENCE

11 I envy people who have the confidence to open and shut train windows without asking if I mind, who can read road maps, or join without inhibition in community singing and applaud themselves afterwards.
Basil Boothroyd, Punch 10 *May* 1972

12 I wasn't lucky. I deserved it.
Margaret Thatcher on receiving school prize, aged 9. Quoted Observer 6 *May* 1979

CONFORMITY

13 For one man who thanks God that he is not as other men there are a few thousand to offer thanks that they are as other men, sufficiently as others to escape attention.
John Dewey, HUMAN NATURE AND CONFLICT

CONFUSION

14 Confusion is a word we have invented for an order which is not understood.
Henry Miller, TROPIC OF CANCER 1934

JOSEPH CONRAD

15 The first mate is a Pole called Conrad, and is a capital chap though queer to look at; he is a man of travel and experience in many parts of the world, and has a fund of yarns on which I draw freely.
John Galsworthy in a letter written at age 26, when travelling home in a clipper from Australia. Quoted Dudley Barker, JOHN GALSWORTHY, MAN OF PRINCIPLE

16 What is Conrad but the wreck of Stevenson floating about in the slip-slop of Henry James.
George Moore. Quoted G. W. Lyttelton, THE LYTTELTON HART-DAVIS LETTERS 8 *Mar* 1950

17 One of the surest signs of his genius is that women dislike his books.
George Orwell, New English Weekly 23 *Jul* 1936

CONSCIENCE

18 You cannot make yourself feel something you do not feel, but you can make yourself do right in spite of your feelings.
Pearl S. Buck, TO MY DAUGHTER, WITH LOVE, *My Neighbour's Son* 1967

1 The wings of a beautiful but ineffectual conscience beating vainly in a vacuum jar.
T. S. Eliot. Quoted J. C. Levenson, THE MIND AND ART OF HENRY ADAMS 1957

2 Conscience is the internal perception of the rejection of a particular wish operating within us.
Sigmund Freud, TOTEM AND TABOO 1918

3 The paradoxical — and tragic — situation of a man is that his conscience is weakest when he needs it most.
Erich Fromm, MAN FOR HIMSELF 1947

4 I cannot and will not cut my conscience to suit this year's fashions.
Lillian Hellman to the Unamerican Activities Committee 1952

5 When one has a conscience it is generally a bad one.
Eugene Ionesco, FRAGMENTS OF A JOURNAL

6 Conscience was the barmaid of the Victorian soul . . . [It] would permit, rather ungraciously perhaps, the indulgence of a number of carefully selected desires. Once the appointed limit was reached conscience would rap on the bar of the soul. "Time's up, gentlemen" she would say.
C. E. M. Joad, UNDER THE FIFTH RIB

7 There is only one way to achieve happiness on this terrestrial ball, / And that is to have a clear conscience, or none at all.
Ogden Nash, I'M A STRANGER HERE MYSELF

CONSEQUENCE

8 In nature there are neither rewards nor punishments — there are consequences.
Robert G. Ingersoll, SOME REASON WHY

CONSERVATION

9 Having to save the old that's worth saving, whether in landscape, houses, manners, institutions or human types, is one of our greatest problems, and the one we bother least about.
John Galsworthy, OVER THE RIVER

10 Save trees — eat a beaver.
Graffito. Quoted Nigel Rees, GRAFFITI LIVES O.K. 1979

11 Such prosperity as we have known up to the present is the consequence of rapidly spending the planet's irreplaceable capital.
Aldous Huxley, THEME AND VARIATIONS 1950

12 We face the question whether a still higher 'standard of living' is worth its cost in things natural, wild and free. For us of the minority, the opportunity to see geese is more important than television.
Aldo Leopold, A SAND COUNTY ALMANAC

13 The Anglo-Saxon conscience does not prevent the Anglo-Saxon from sinning. It merely prevents him from enjoying it.
Salvador de Madariaga. Quoted David Frost and Anthony Jay, TO ENGLAND WITH LOVE 1981

14 People gush and moan too much about the loss of ancient buildings of no special note . . . In towns, as in human bodies, the only state of health is one of rapid wasting and repair.
C. E. Montague, THE RIGHT PLACE

15 To wear the arctic fox / You have to kill it.
Marianne Moore, COLLECTED POEMS, *The Arctic Ox (or Goat)* 1951

16 Here is the Earth, don't spend it all at once.
Barty Phillips, Observer, *Mind Your Planet* 8 *Jul* 1979

17 The nation that destroys its soil destroys itself.
Franklin D. Roosevelt 26 *Feb* 1937

18 Shooting is a great contribution to conservation.
Richard Tracey, British Field Sports Society. Quoted Observer, *Sayings of the Week* 20 *Aug* 81

CONSERVATISM

19 So far as I am concerned the Tory party are lower than vermin.
Aneurin Bevan. Speech, Manchester 4 *Jul* 1949

20 The conservative has little to fear from the man whose reason is the servant of his passions, but let him beware of him in whom reason has become the greatest and most terrible of his passions.
J. B. S. Haldane, DAEDALUS OR SCIENCE AND THE FUTURE

21 The Conservatives know there are books to read, pictures to look at, music to listen to — and grouse to shoot.
Harold Macmillan. Quoted Nigel Nicholson, Thames TV, *The Day Before Yesterday* 1970

CONSISTENCY

1 Consistency is contrary to nature, contrary to life. The only completely consistent people are the dead.
Aldous Huxley, COLLECTED ESSAYS 1960

CONSOLATION

2 Nobody can have the consolation of religion or philosophy unless he has first experienced their desolations.
Aldous Huxley, COLLECTED ESSAYS 1960

CONSUMERISM

3 The first enslaving illusion is the idea that people are born to be consumers and that they can attain any of their goals by purchasing goods and services.
Ivan Illich, DISABLING PROFESSIONS

CONTACT

4 The meeting of two personalities is like the contact of two chemical substances; if there is any reaction both are transformed.
Carl Jung, MODERN MAN IN SEARCH OF A SOUL

CONTENTMENT

5 *Contentment* who had known youth as a child and never seen him since.
Rupert Brooke, THE FUNERAL OF YOUTH

6 Being 'contented' ought to mean in English as it does in French, being pleased. Being content with an attic ought not to mean being unable to move from it and resigned to living in it; it ought to mean appreciating all there is in such a position. For true contentment is a real, even an active virtue — not only affirmative, but creative. It is the power of getting out of a situation all there is in it.
G. K. Chesterton, A MISCELLANY OF MEN 1912

7 A householder, whose lawn needed cutting, saw Mose scuffling along the dusty road and called out "Hey Moses! Want to make a quarter?" Mose paused only long enough to reply, "No, suh. Ah got one."
Alexander Woollcott, WHILE ROME BURNS, *Colossal Bronze* 1934

CONTRACEPTION

8 I would as soon condemn the use of soap as the practice of birth control.
Ernest William Barnes (Bishop of Birmingham), RISE OF CHRISTIANITY

9 He [Pope Paul] could have spared a paragraph in his long encyclical to assist the people who will be left holding the baby.
Lady Antonia Fraser. Quoted Bernard Levin, THE PENDULUM YEARS 1976

10 Most Catholic parents feel that they know more about the practical problems of married life than an elderly bachelor in Rome.
Paul Johnson, New Statesman, *of Pope Paul's encyclical forbidding all artificial forms of contraception*

11 A vast trade is being done in contraceptives. I would like to make a bonfire of them and dance round it.
The Bishop of London, House of Lords

12 Where are the children I might have had? . . . Drowned to the accompaniment of the rattling of a thousand douche bags.
Malcolm Lowry, UNDER THE VOLCANO 1947

13 Contraceptives should be used on all conceivable occasions.
Spike Milligan, THE LAST GOON SHOW OF ALL

14 Birth control would be far more convincing as a scientific argument if it could be guaranteed to improve and not merely thin out our race.
Reginald Pound, THEIR MOODS AND MINE 1935

15 Few will now bother to ask whether the Pope is infallible, they are more concerned with whether the Pill is infallible.
John Robinson (Bishop of Woolwich) of Pope Paul's encyclical forbidding artificial contraception

16 We want far better reasons for having children than not knowing how to prevent them.
Dora Russell, HYPATIA

17 Skullion placed contraceptives in the lower social category of things along with elastic-sided boots and made-up bow ties. Not the sort of attire for a gentleman.
Tom Sharpe, PORTERHOUSE BLUES

CONTRACT

1 A verbal contract isn't worth the paper it is written on.
Sam Goldwyn. Quoted Alva Johnson, THE GREAT GOLDWYN

CONTRAST

2 Active happiness depends to some extent on contrast — a lover's meeting would not be the same without the days of deprivation.
Graham Greene, A SORT OF LIFE

CONVENTION

3 The fact that a convention exists indicates that a way of living has been devised capable of maintaining itself,
George Santayana, PERSONS AND PLACES 1953

CONVERSATION

4 They had no conversation, properly speaking. They made use of the spoken word in much the same way as the guard of a train makes use of his flags or lantern.
Samuel Beckett, MALONE DIES 1951

5 Good talkers, when they have run down, are miserable; they know they have betrayed themselves.
Cyril Connolly, ENEMIES OF PROMISE 1938

6 Apart from theology and sex there is really nothing to talk about.
Harold J. Laski, HOLMES–LASKI LETTERS

7 Good communication is as stimulating as black coffee and just as hard to sleep after.
Anne Lindbergh, GIFT FROM THE SEA 1955

8 Uncle Albert made a list of conversational openings. Among the earliest items was: "Are you aware that the heaviest eater in the zoo is the gnu?"
G. W. Lyttelton, THE LYTTELTON HART-DAVIS LETTERS 15 *Nov* 1955

9 Conversation is one of the greatest pleasures of life. But it wants leisure.
W. Somerset Maugham, THE TREMBLING OF A LEAF 1921

10 Beware of the conversationalist who adds "in other words". He is merely starting afresh.
Robert Morley. Quoted Observer 6 *Dec* 1964

CONVERSION

11 Sudden conversion, a belief which may be right, but which is peculiarly attractive to the half-baked mind.
E. M. Forster, HOWARD'S END 1918

12 Why do born-again people so often make you wish they'd never been born the first time?
Katherine Whitehorn, Observer 20 *May* 1979

CONVICTION

13 At eighteen our convictions are hills from which we look; at forty-five they are caves in which we hide.
F. Scott Fitzgerald, BERNICE BOBS HER HAIR

COOKERY

14 Be content to remember that those who can make omelettes properly can do nothing else.
Hilaire Belloc, A CONVERSATION WITH A CAT

15 The turtle must be put in straw in the cellar and given water every two to three hours. It should be beheaded at night and left hanging neck downwards.
The Cookery Book of Lady Clark of Tillyponce 1909

16 An unwatched pot boils *immediately.*
H. F. Ellis, Punch, *For Men in Aprons*

17 The speed with which boiling milk rises from the bottom of the pan to any point beyond the top is greater than the speed at which the human brain and hand can combine to snatch the wretched thing off.
Id.

CALVIN COOLIDGE

18 He looks as if he had been weaned on a pickle.
Alice Roosevelt Longworth

19 He had one really notable talent. He slept more than any other president.
H. L. Mencken, obituary of Coolidge

20 Why, I never even knew that he was alive.
Dorothy Parker, on being told that ex-President Coolidge had died

CORNWALL

1 O the harbour of Fowey / Is a beautiful
spot / And it's there I enjowey / To sail in a
yot / Or to race in a yacht / round a marker
or buoy / Such a beautiful spacht / Is the
harbour of Fuoy.
Sir Arthur Quiller-Couch

CORRESPONDENCE

2 "Christ Almighty — another letter from my
father" said the Earl of Chesterfield's son.
Caryl Brahms and S. J. Simon, NO
NIGHTINGALES

3 Why it should be such an effort to write to
the people one loves I can't imagine. It's
none at all to write to those who don't really
count.
Katherine Mansfield, JOURNALS 1954

4 An intention to write never turns into a
letter. A letter must happen to one like a
surprise, and one may not know where in
the day there was room for it to come into
being.
Rainer Maria Rilke, LETTERS 1892–1910

5 The letter which merely answers another
letter is no letter at all.
Mark Van Doren. Quoted Clifton Fadiman, ANY NUMBER CAN PLAY 1957

6 His courtesy was somewhat extravagant.
He would write and thank people who
wrote to thank him for wedding presents
and when he encountered anyone as
punctilious as himself the correspondence
ended only with death.
Evelyn Waugh, Life Magazine 8 *Apr* 1946

COSMETICS

7 Most women are not so young as they are
painted.
Max Beerbohm, A DEFENCE OF COSMETICS 1922

8 Waits at the window wearing the face that
she keeps in a jar by the door.
John Lennon and Paul McCartney,
ELEANOR RIGBY *(song)*

9 A girl whose cheeks are covered with
paint / Has an advantage with me over one
whose ain't.
Ogden Nash, BIOLOGICAL REFLECTION

COSMOS

10 The cosmos is about the smallest hole that a
man can hide his head in.
G. K. Chesterton, ORTHODOXY 1908

COUNTRY LIFE

11 The country is laid out in a haphazard,
sloppy fashion, offensive to the tidy,
organised mind.
Alan Brien, Punch 22 *Mar* 1979

12 I have always felt a faint scepticism, a mild
horror about the country. One goes for
quiet and a gang of rooks is at work,
murderously tearing at the furrows.
Fanfarlo (L. M. Storier), SHAVING
THROUGH THE BLITZ

13 No country home is complete without a
surly figure seated in the kitchen like
Rodin's Thinker, wishing she was back in a
hot little room under the Third Avenue
Elevator.
S. J. Perelman, ACHES AND PAINS 1947

14 The pleasure of country life lies really in the
eternally renewed evidences of the will to
live.
Vita Sackville-West, COUNTRY NOTES

15 I'm not a country man; I'd like to believe in
the wide open spaces as the wrapping
around walls, the windy boredom between
house and house . . . man made his house
to keep the world and weather out, making
his own weathery world inside. That's the
trouble with the country; there's too much
public world between the private ones.
Dylan Thomas, letter to Vernon Watkins 2
Apr 1936

16 The average countryman mistrusts trees
and has a fear of anything large and alive,
and not easily tamed or destroyed.
J. R. R. Tolkien, LETTERS

17 A lovely house where an aged colonel plays
wireless music to an obese retriever.
Evelyn Waugh, Country Life 26 *Feb* 1938

COURAGE

18 Until the day of his death, no man can be
sure of his courage.
Jean Anouilh, BECKET 1959

19 The fearless man is his own salvation.
Robert Bridges, THE FIRST SEVEN DIVISIONS

20 Courage is almost a contradiction in terms.
It means a strong desire to live taking the
form of a readiness to die.
G. K. Chesterton, ORTHODOXY 1908

21 The people I respect must behave as if they
were immortal and as if society were eternal.
E. M. Forster, TWO CHEERS FOR DEMOCRACY 1951

1 If the creator had a purpose in equipping us with a neck, he surely meant us to stick it out.
Arthur Koestler, ENCOUNTER 1970

2 One has to be seventy before one is full of courage. The young are always half hearted.
D. H. Lawrence, SELECTED LETTERS 1962

3 It takes a good deal of physical courage to ride a horse. This, however, I have. I get it at about forty cents a flask and take it as required.
Stephen Leacock, LITERARY LAPSES 1910

4 Courage is not simply *one* of the virtues but the form of every virtue at the testing point, which means at the point of highest reality.
C. S. Lewis. Quoted Cyril Connolly, THE UNQUIET GRAVE 1945

5 Life shrinks or expands in proportion to one's courage.
Anaïs Nin, DIARY, *Jun* 1941

6 The man who is courageous in any matter except physical danger is thought ill of.
Bertrand Russell, THE CONQUEST OF HAPPINESS 1930

7 She wasn't courageous, if by courage is meant mastery of fear, for she did not know about fear. She was fearless of physical danger, of criticism, of people.
The Times, *obituary of Nancy, Viscountess Astor* 4 May 1964

COURTESY

8 It is wise to apply the oil of refined politeness to the mechanism of friendship.
Colette, EARTHLY PARADISE

9 There can be no defence like elaborate courtesy.
E. V. Lucas, READING, WRITING AND REMEMBERING

COURTSHIP

10 Let us now bask under the spreading trees said Bernard in a passionate tone.
Oh yes lets said Ethel and she opened her dainty parasole and sank down upon the long grass. She closed her eyes but was far from asleep.
Daisy Ashford (aged 9), THE YOUNG VISITERS 1919

11 And I shall find some girl perhaps / And a better one than you / With eyes as wise, but kinder / And lips as soft, but true / And I daresay she will do.
Rupert Brooke, THE CHILTERNS

12 As soon as I get hold of a hand they sort of disconnect it from the rest of them.
F. Scott Fitzgerald, THIS SIDE OF PARADISE 1920

13 'We might be brother and sister" said Jennie [Lee] the first time they really talked together.
"Aye" said Nye [Aneurin Bevan] with an appraising mischievous grin, "but with a tendency to incest."
Michael Foot, ANEURIN BEVAN 1897–1945

14 No sooner had she decided that she wanted Uncle Tom than she knocked him off his bicycle and told him.
Laurie Lee, CIDER WITH ROSIE 1959

15 Kissing your hand may make you feel very good but a diamond and saffire bracelet lasts forever.
Anita Loos, GENTLEMEN PREFER BLONDES 1929

16 I'm sorry, Sigmund, you frighten me, but that isn't enough for marriage.
Cartoon caption in the New Yorker

17 Men seldom make passes / At girls who wear glasses.
Dorothy Parker, ENOUGH ROPE 1927

18 She will never win him whose / Words showed that she feared to lose.
Dorothy Parker, DEATH AND TAXES 1931

19 Gattling-Fenn was getting bald in a curious way. Yet he was always falling in love with horrifyingly pretty girls of vacant mind.
Stephen Potter, LIFEMANSHIP 1950

20 Throw away your little bedsocks and your Welsh wool knitted jacket. I will warm the sheets like an electric toaster. I will lie by your side like the Sunday roast.
Dylan Thomas, UNDER MILK WOOD 1954

21 . . . watching the moon come up lazily out of the old cemetery in which nine of his daughters were lying, and only two of them were dead.
James Thurber, BATEMAN COMES HOME

COW

22 The cow is of the bovine ilk / One end is moo, the other milk.
Ogden Nash, THE COW

NOËL COWARD

23 Edna Ferber turned up sporting a tailored suit similar to one Noël Coward was wearing. "You look almost like a man"

Coward said. "So" Miss Ferber replied, "do you".
Robert E. Brennan, WIT'S ENDS 1968

1 He was his own greatest invention.
John Osborne. Quoted William Marchant, THE PLEASURE OF HIS COMPANY

2 If his face suggested an old boot it was unquestionably hand made.
Kenneth Tynan, THE SOUND OF TWO HANDS CLAPPING

3 He was once Slightly in Peter Pan, and has been wholly Peter Pan ever since.
Kenneth Tynan. Quoted BBC Radio 4, *Quote Unquote* 13 *Sep* 1979

COWARDICE

4 The last thing a woman will consent to discover in a man whom she loves, or on whom she simply depends, is want of courage.
Joseph Conrad, VICTORY 1915

5 He was just a coward, and that is the worst luck any man can have.
Ernest Hemingway, FOR WHOM THE BELL TOLLS 1940

6 Cowardice, as distinguished from panic, is almost always simply a lack of ability to suspend the functioning of the imagination.
Ernest Hemingway, MEN AT WAR

7 I'm a hero with coward's legs.
Spike Milligan, PUCKOON

8 As an old soldier I admit the cowardice. It's as universal as seasickness and matters just as little.
George Bernard Shaw, MAN AND SUPER-MAN 1905

CREATION

9 The attempt to impose upon man, a creature of growth and capable of sweetness, to ooze juicily at the last round the bearded lips of God, to attempt to impose, I say, laws and conditions appropriate to a mechanical creation, against this I raise my sword-pen.
Anthony Burgess, A CLOCKWORK ORANGE 1962

10 Gabriel: How about cleanin' up de whole mess of 'em and startin' all over ag'n wid some new kind of animal?
God: An' admit I'm licked?
Marc Connelly, THE GREEN PASTURES 1930

11 The presence in Nature of so many phenomena requiring intelligence for their appreciation implied a kindred intelligence to produce them.
Sir Ambrose Fleming, presidential address Victoria Institute 18 *Mar* 1936

12 I can't help feeling sceptical about the Bible's claim that God made man in his own image . . . He could have achieved that simply by creating a couple of mirrors, or a closed-circuit television.
Michael Frayn, CONSTRUCTIONS

13 The universe seems to have been designed by a pure mathematician.
Sir James Jeans, THE MYSTERIOUS UNI-VERSE 1930

14 And God stepped out on space / And he looked around and said / "I'm lonely — / I'll make me a world".
J. W. Johnson, GOD'S TROMBONES 1927

15 God is really only another artist. He invented the giraffe, the elephant and the cat. He has no real style. He just goes on trying other things.
Pablo Picasso. Quoted Françoise Gilot and Carlton Lake, LIFE WITH PICASSO

CREATIVENESS

16 In search of ideas I spent yesterday morning in walking about, and went to the stores and bought things in four departments. A wonderful and delightful way of spending time and money. Better than most theatres . . . I think this sort of activity does stimulate creative ideas.
Arnold Bennett, JOURNALS 1911–1921

17 Every animal leaves traces of what it was; only man leaves traces of what he created.
Jacob Bronowski, THE ASCENT OF MAN 1973

18 "I like," she once confided to me, "to have creative beings around me. I like to live always within the possibility that someone in my house may at this moment be attempting to cut off his ears." She did, however, insist that her violence should be, so to speak, house-trained: screaming and blood on the chair-covers were quite unforgiveable.
William Trevor, A STANDARD OF BEHAVIOUR

CREDIT

1 Never in the history of human credit has so much been owed.
Margaret Thatcher. Quoted Observer, *Sayings of the Week 12 Oct 1975.*

CREDULITY

2 He had been kicked in the head when young and believed everything he read in the Sunday papers.
George Ade, THE SLIM GIRL

CRICKET

3 His off drives are like a white owl flying.
Neville Cardus of Frank Woolley, DAYS IN THE SUN

4 What are the butchers for?
Pauline Chase, an American actress, asking about the umpires at Lords. Quoted Bertie Hollander, BEFORE I FORGET

5 It is not the mere presence of the clergy at Lords that is impressive but rather the twin stamp of English and Anglican which they bear. You can be sure they are cricketers all, and because cricket is of the very soul of England it is in England's Church that they have found their vocation.
The Church Times

6 If Stalin had learned to play cricket the world might now be a better place to live in.
Dr. R. Downey (Bishop of Liverpool), News Review 22 *Apr* 1948

7 My wife had an uncle who could never walk down the nave of his abbey without wondering whether it would take spin.
Lord Home, BBC 1 TV, *The Twentieth Century Revisited* 13 *Jul* 1982

8 The flannelled fool's at the wicket.
Rudyard Kipling, THE ISLANDERS 1902

9 I don't think it at all polite the way bowlers rub the ball all over themselves at cricket.
Letter to the Manchester Evening News

10 Many continentals think life is a game, the English think cricket is a game.
George Mikes, HOW TO BE AN ALIEN 1946

11 I have always looked upon cricket as organised loafing.
William Temple, when Headmaster of Repton, addressing parents

CRIME

12 It is not a fragrant world.
Raymond Chandler. Quoted Colin Watson, Radio Times 21 *Apr* 1979

13 A broad definition of crime in England is that it is any lower-class activity that is displeasing to the upper class.
David Frost and Anthony Jay, TO ENGLAND WITH LOVE

14 Crime doesn't pay, but the hours are good.
Graffito. Quoted Nigel Rees, GRAFFITI 2

15 It was beautiful and simple, as all truly great swindles are.
O. Henry, THE GENTLE GRAFTER 1908

16 A burglar who respects his art always takes his time before taking anything else.
O. Henry, MAKES THE WHOLE WORLD KIN

17 Crime is a logical extension of the sort of behaviour that is often considered perfectly respectable in legitimate business.
Robert Rice, THE BUSINESS OF CRIME 1956

18 Much as he is opposed to law-breaking he is not bigoted about it.
Damon Runyon, MORE THAN SOMEWHAT 1937

19 People who go to prison are not just criminals but, by definition, unsuccessful criminals.
The Times 13 *Apr* 1981

20 Almost all crime is due to the repressed desire for aesthetic expression.
Evelyn Waugh, DECLINE AND FALL 1928

SIR STAFFORD CRIPPS

21 He has a brilliant mind, until he makes it up.
Margot Asquith, AUTOBIOGRAPHY 1936

22 There, but for the grace of God, goes God.
Winston Churchill

23 Sir Stafford has built a high stone wall around his mind, as though it were an intellectual nudist colony.
Tribune. *Quoted* News Review 18 *Mar* 1948

24 No one likes Cripps. He does not allow it.
Alain Verney, Tribune des Nations (*Paris*), *Nov* 1947

CRISIS

25 I felt as if the Suez Canal was flowing through my drawing room.
Lady Eden, recalling the Suez Crisis

1 When written in Chinese the word crisis is composed of two characters. One represents danger and the other represents opportunity.
John F. Kennedy. Speech 12 *Apr* 1959

2 If you can keep your head when all about you are losing theirs, it is just possible that you haven't grasped the situation.
Jean Kerr, PLEASE DON'T EAT THE DAISIES

3 There can't be a crisis next week. My schedule is already full.
Henry Kissinger. Quoted BBC Radio 4, *Quote Unquote* 2 *Feb* 1982

CRITICS

4 Critics always want to put you into pigeon holes, which can be very uncomfortable unless you happen to be a pigeon.
Max Adrian. Quoted Barry Norman, The Times 4 *Jul* 1972

5 The one thing I most emphatically do not ask of a critic is that he tells me what I *ought* to approve or condemn. I have no objection to his telling me what works and authors he likes and dislikes.
W. H. Auden, THE DYER'S HAND 1962

6 Pleasure is by no means an infallible critical guide, but it is the least fallible.
Id.

7 Attacking bad books is not only a waste of time but bad for the character . . . One cannot attack a bad book without showing off.
Id.

8 There is less in this than meets the eye.
Tallulah Bankhead. Quoted Alexander Woolcott, SHOUTS AND MURMURS 1922

9 A critic was a man with a wee foot-rule who measured plays with it, and if it was five by four it was a good play, and if it was no' five by four it was no' a play.
Sir James Barrie. Speech to the Critics' Circle. Quoted Hamilton Fyfe, John o'London's Weekly 2 *Jul* 1937

10 Because a critic is never criticised he passes through the world without knowing what the world thinks of him.
Clifford Bax, John o'London's Weekly, *Mr. Agate keeps egoing on* 2 *Sep* 1940

11 Criticism of the arts in London, taken by and large, ends in a display of suburban omniscience which sees no further than the next door garden.
Sir Thomas Beecham. Quoted Neville Cardus, SIR THOMAS BEECHAM

12 The trouble with music critics is that they so often have the score in their hands and not in their heads.
Sir Thomas Beecham. Quoted Harold Atkins and Archie Newman, BEECHAM STORIES

13 I will try to account for the degree of my aesthetic emotion. That, I conceive, is the function of a critic.
Clive Bell, ART 1914

14 My mother — who was an alertly respectable woman — told me at an early age that I was not to play with critics.
Robert Bolt

15 "They're very noisy at night. You can't sleep . . . because of them."
Mel Brooks interviewed by Maurice Zolotow, New York Times 30 *Mar* 1975

16 In art, rebellion is consummated and perpetuated in the art of real creation, not in criticism or commentary.
Albert Camus, THE REBEL 1951

17 I do not resent criticism, even when, for the sake of emphasis, it parts for the time with reality.
Winston Churchill, House of Commons 22 *Jan* 1941

18 I am the only critic in London who is too small for his boots.
Alan Dent. Quoted James Agate, Ego 4 1939

19 Critics never change; I'm still getting the same notices I used to get as a child. They tell me I play very well for my age.
Mischa Elman, in his seventies. Quoted Anthony Hopkins, MUSIC ALL ROUND ME

20 There is no more absolutely thrilling experience in dramatic criticism than to be absolutely certain that all the others are wrong.
Harold Hobson, INDIRECT JOURNEY

21 The best critic will be the epitome of the best part of any audience, its head, heart and soul.
Philip Hope-Wallace. Quoted The Times obituary 17 *Dec* 1979

22 No critic has ever settled anything.
James Huneker, PATHOS OF DISTANCE

1 The critic should describe and not prescribe.
Eugene Ionesco, IMPROVISATION

2 Never trust the artist. Trust the tale. The
proper function of a critic is to save the tale
from the artist who created it.
D. H. Lawrence, STUDIES IN CLASSIC
AMERICAN LITERATURE

3 The only way to escape misrepresentation
is never to commit oneself to any critical
judgment that makes an impact — that is
never *say* anything.
F. R. Leavis, THE GREAT TRADITION 1948

4 I cried all the way to the bank.
Liberace's retort to adverse criticism

5 People ask you for criticism, but they only
want praise.
W. Somerset Maugham, OF HUMAN BON-
DAGE 1915

6 The savage review is a too easy form of
fun . . . Far too many worthless books are
published every year; why pick out one for
attack, unless it is likely to win more
respect than it deserves.
Raymond Mortimer, REVIEWING

7 Woollcott's reviews resemble either a
gravy bomb, a bursting gladiolus, a palpitating *orissa cantata*, an attack of psychic
hydrophobia, or a Roman denunciation.
George Jean Nathan, SMART SET 1921

8 The greater part of critics are parasites,
who, if nothing had been written, would
find nothing to write.
J. B. Priestley, OUTCRIES AND ASIDES

9 I never read anything concerning my work.
I feel that criticism is a letter to the public
which the author, since it is not directed to
him, does not have to open and read.
Rainer Maria Rilke, LETTERS

10 The golden rule in criticism is for the critic
to be on a level with the author — that is
why the eighteenth-century Dr. Johnson is
still the grandest critic of Shakespeare, and
also why we can ignore 99 per cent of the
production of the critical industry.
A. L. Rowse, PORTRAITS AND VIEWS 1979

11 Pay no attention to what critics say. No
statue has ever been put up to a critic.
Attr. Jean Sibelius

12 I doubt that art needed Ruskin any more
than a moving train needs one of its
passengers to shove it.
Tom Stoppard, Times Literary Supplement 3 *Jun* 1977

13 I had another dream the other day about
music critics. They were small and rodent-
like with padlocked ears, as if they had
stepped out of a painting by Goya.
Igor Stravinsky, Evening Standard 20 *Oct*
1969

14 They criticised Henry James as they might
criticise a cat for not being a dog.
James Thurber, THE WINGS OF HENRY
JAMES

15 A good drama critic is one who perceives
what is happening in the theatre of his time.
A great drama critic is one who perceives
what is not happening.
Kenneth Tynan, TYNAN RIGHT AND LEFT

16 Most writers in the course of their careers,
become thick-skinned and learn to accept
vituperation, which in any other profession
would be unimaginably offensive, as a
healthy counterpoise to unintelligent
praise.
Evelyn Waugh, New York Times
Magazine 30 *Nov* 1952

RICHARD CROSSMAN

17 He is a man of many opinions, most of them
of short duration.
Bessie Braddock, THE BRADDOCKS

CRUELTY

18 The impulse to cruelty is, in many people,
almost as violent as the impulse to sexual
love — almost as violent and much more
mischievous.
Aldous Huxley, BEYOND THE MEXIQUE BAY
1944

19 My mother used to pull my ears and it never
did get that much attention.
*Lyndon B. Johnson, after the protests
caused by a press photograph of him lifting
his dog by the ears.*

20 The infliction of cruelty with a good
conscience is a delight to moralists.
Bertrand Russell, SCEPTICAL ESSAYS 1928

21 Cruelty would be delicious if one could
only find some sort of cruelty that didn't
hurt.
George Bernard Shaw, HEARTBREAK
HOUSE 1920

CRYING

22 Tears were to me what glass beads are to
African traders.
Quentin Crisp, THE NAKED CIVIL SERVANT

1 Many tears are joyful.
Tom Stoppard, JUMPERS

2 Only those who still have hopes can benefit from tears.
Nathanael West, THE DAY OF THE LOCUST 1939

CULTURE

3 Culture is far more dangerous than Philistinism, because it is more intelligent and more pliant; it has a specious air of being on the side of the artist.
Clive Bell, ART 1914

4 And what is culture but palaver and swank. I turn up my nose at culture.
Idris Davies, THE LAY PREACHER PONDERS

5 A man of one idea — that all civilisation was the printed fungus of rottenness. He hated any sign of culture.
D. H. Lawrence, THE WHITE PEACOCK 1911

6 Every man with a belly full of culture is an enemy of the human race.
Henry Miller, TROPIC OF CANCER 1934

7 Culture is not life in its entirety, but just the moment of security, strength and clarity.
José Ortega y Gasset, MEDITATIONS ON QUIXOTE 1914

8 Culture would not be culture if it were not an acquired taste.
John Cowper Powys, THE MEANING OF CULTURE

9 Culture is on the horns of this dilemma; if profound and noble it must remain rare, if common it must become mean.
George Santayana, THE LIFE OF REASON 1906

10 Mrs. Bullinger is one of the ladies who pursue Culture in bands, as though it were dangerous to meet it alone.
Edith Wharton, XINGU

CURIOSITY

11 Curiosity is free-wheeling intelligence.
Alistair Cooke, Vogue, *Jan* 1953

12 The great thing in life is to be simple and the perfectly simple thing is to look through keyholes.
George Bernard Shaw, GREAT CATHERINE 1918

13 He that breaks a thing to find out what it is has left the path of wisdom.
J. R. R. Tolkien, FELLOWSHIP OF THE RING 1956

14 Disinterested intellectual curiosity is the lifeblood of real civilisation.
G. M. Trevelyan, ENGLISH SOCIAL HISTORY, *Preface* 1944

LORD CURZON

15 I met Curzon in Downing Street, from whom I got the sort of greeting a corpse would give to an undertaker.
Stanley Baldwin, after being chosen Prime Minister in preference to Curzon, May 1923

CUSTOM

16 Custom has furnished the only basis which ethics ever had.
J. W. Krutch, THE MODERN TEMPER 1929

CYNIC

17 *Cynic:* a blackguard whose faulty vision sees things as they are, and not as they ought to be.
Ambrose Bierce, THE DEVIL'S DICTIONARY 1906

18 The temptation shared by all forms of intelligence: cynicism.
Albert Camus, NOTEBOOKS 1935–1942

19 Cynicism, that corrosive acid of the spirit.
Reginald Pound, THEIR MOODS AND MINE 1935

D

DANCING

1 Dancing is a perpendicular expression of a horizontal desire.
Anon.

2 I have no desire to prove anything by dancing. I have never used it as an outlet or a means of expressing myself. I just dance.
Fred Astaire. Quoted Leslie Halliwell, FILMGOER'S BOOK OF QUOTES 1973

3 I just put my feet in the air and move them around.
Id.

4 Dancing is the body made poetic.
Ernst Bacon, NOTES ON THE PIANO 1963

5 Wasn't it Nietzsche who said he wouldn't believe in a God who could not dance? Neither could I.
Isadora Duncan. Quoted Lon Tellegan, WOMEN HAVE BEEN KIND

6 Dancing is the loftiest, the most moving and the most beautiful of the arts, because it is no mere translation or abstraction from life, it is life itself.
Havelock Ellis, THE DANCE OF LIFE 1923

7 She clapped me to her bosom like a belladonna plaster.
Richard Gordon, DOCTOR AT SEA

8 It is not important that you should know what a dance means. It is only important that you should be stirred. If you can write the story of your dance, it is a literary thing, but it is not dancing.
Martha Graham. Quoted John Heilpern, Observer Magazine, *The Amazing Martha* 8 Jul 1979

9 I refuse to admit that the dance has limitations that prevent its acceptance and understanding. The reality of the dance is its truth to our inner life. Therein lies its power to move and communicate experience. We are a visually stimulated world today. The eye is not to be denied.
Martha Graham 1930

10 Sometimes I think that dancing, like youth, is wasted on the young.
Max Lerner, THE UNFINISHED COUNTRY 1959

11 I could dance with you till the cows come home. Better still, I'll dance with the cows and *you* come home.
Groucho Marx, DUCK SOUP

12 Fat wet bodies go waddling by / Girded with satin though God knows why / Gripped by satyrs in white and black / With a fat wet hand on a fat wet back.
Alfred Noyes, COLLECTED POEMS, *A Victory Dance* 1947

13 George M. Cohen always dances interestingly; he has sardonic legs.
Gilbert Seldes, THE SEVEN LIVELY ARTS

14 In the next round the first couple will be proper, the second couple improper. Couples will be alternately proper and improper throughout the movement.
Cecil Sharpe, COUNTRY DANCE BOOK

15 Dancing is a very crude attempt to get into the rhythm of life.
George Bernard Shaw, BACK TO METHUSELAH 1922

16 O body swayed to music, O brightening glance / How can we know the dancer from the dance?
W. B. Yeats, THE TOWER, *Among School Children* 1928

DANGER

17 Mortal danger is an effective antidote for fixed ideas.
Field Marshal Erwin Rommel, THE ROMMEL PAPERS

18 Confront a child, a puppy and a kitten with a sudden danger; the child will turn instinctively for assistance, the puppy will grovel in abject submission, the kitten will brace its tiny body for a frantic resistance.
Saki, THE ACHIEVEMENT OF THE CAT

DARKNESS

1 The darkness declares the glory of the light.
T. S. Eliot, MURDER IN THE CATHEDRAL 1935

DAWN

2 The morning breaks like a pomegranate / In a shining crock of red.
D. H. Lawrence, WEDDING MORN

3 An owl flies home past Bethesda, to a chapel in an oak. And the dawn inches up.
Dylan Thomas, UNDER MILK WOOD 1954

4 The town ripples like a lake in the waking haze.
Id.

5 I hate the dawn. The grass always looks as though it has been left out all night.
Clifton Webb, THE DARK CORNER *(film)*

6 For what human ill does not dawn seem to be an alternative?
Thornton Wilder, THE BRIDGE OF SAN LUIS REY 1927

DEATH

7 "Are you sure he is dead?"
"He seemed dead. I did my imitation of Maurice Chevalier and it usually gets a big hand. This time, nothing."
Woody Allen, New Yorker, *The Condemned* 21 *Nov* 1977

8 Life has its appropriate rewards, whereas when you're dead it's hard to find the light switch.
Woody Allen, WITHOUT FEATHERS

9 On the plus side, death is one of the few things that can be done as easily lying down.
Id.

10 It's not that I'm afraid to die. I just don't want to be there when it happens.
Id.

11 My family has always been into death. My father, the Major, used to insist on having an ice pick next to his placemat at meals so that he could perform an emergency tracheotomy when one of us strangled on a piece of meat. Even now, by running my index fingers along my collarbones to the indentation where the bones join, I can locate the optimal site for a tracheal puncture with the same deftness as a junky a vein.
Lisa Alther, KINFLICKS, opening paragraph 1976

12 Death is nature's way of telling you to slow down.
Anon.

13 Death is the only solution to life which has not so far been definitely proved to be the wrong one.
Raymond Asquith, LIFE AND LETTERS

14 To die will be an awfully big adventure.
J. M. Barrie, PETER PAN 1904

15 He has gone to that Bourne from which no Hollingsworth returns.
Beachcomber (J. B. Morton). Quoted Daily Telegraph *obituary* 12 *May* 1979

16 It is time for me to become an apprentice once more.
Lord Beaverbrook in his last public speech

17 Who now dies at home? Who sees death? We sicken and fade in a hospital ward, and dying is for doctors, with a phone call to the family.
Alan Bennett, FORTY YEARS ON

18 She was always very composed. Now she's decomposed.
Ambrose Bierce. Quoted Richard Connor, AMBROSE BIERCE

19 Nought broken save this body, lost but breath; / Nothing to shake the laughing heart's long peace there / But only agony, and that has ending / And the worst friend and enemy is but Death.
Rupert Brooke, PEACE

20 Worn hides that scarcely clothe the soul / They are so rotten, old and thin / Or firm and soft and warm and full / Fellmonger Death gets every skin.
Basil Bunting, VILLON

21 To die is to leave off dying and do the thing once and for all.
Samuel Butler, NOTEBOOKS 1912

22 While other people's deaths are deeply sad, one's own is surely a bit of a joke.
James Cameron, Observer Sayings 17 *Jan* 1982

23 Men are never convinced of your reasons of your sincerity, of the seriousness of your sufferings, except by your death.
Albert Camus, THE FALL 1956

1 I am ready to meet my Maker. Whether my Maker is prepared for the ordeal of meeting me is another matter.
Winston Churchill in an interview on his 75th birthday

2 The problem is not life after death, which I regard as absurd, but life before death. That is urgent, real and earnest.
Hugh Cudlipp, WALKING ON THE WATER

3 When I die I want to decompose in a barrel of porter and have it served in all the pubs in Dublin.
J. P. Donleavy, THE GINGER MAN 1955

4 Phlebas the Phoenician, a fortnight dead / Forget the cry of gulls and the deep sea swell.
T. S. Eliot, THE WASTE LAND 1922

5 Why should the dead be wiser than the living? The dead know only this — that it was better to be alive.
James Elroy Flecker, HASSAN 1923

6 I am afraid to think about my death, / When it shall be and whether, in great pain / I shall rise up and fight the air for breath / Or calmly wait the bursting of my brain.
Id.

7 Our final experience, like our first, is conjectural. We move between two darknesses.
E. M. Forster, ASPECTS OF THE NOVEL 1927

8 The goal of all life is death.
Sigmund Freud. Quoted New York Times Magazine 6 *May* 1966

9 Why fear death? It is the most beautiful adventure in life.
Charles Frohman, last words before going down on the Lusitania 7 *May* 1915

10 The idea of having to die without having lived is unbearable.
Erich Fromm, MAN FOR HIMSELF 1947

11 The nearest friends can go / With anyone to death, comes so far short / They might as well not try to go at all.
Robert Frost, NORTH OF BOSTON, *Home Burial* 1914

12 Death's a new interest in life.
Christopher Fry, A PHOENIX TOO FREQUENT 1949

13 Maintenant elle est comme les autres.
Charles De Gaulle, at the funeral of his handicapped daughter

14 Death is the next step after the pension — it is perpetual retirement without pay.
Jean Giraudoux, THE ENCHANTED 1933

15 As life's span lengthens more time is allowed for the encounter with germs or other accidents. We do not die. We are killed.
George W. Grey, Harper's Magazine, *Feb* 1941

16 I should like to die at the last possible moment not only of old age but even more slowly, for never having had the time to live I should at least like to have time to die. Yes, I ask for a slow death and every possible infirmity. That is essential if I am to go without too much regret.
Sacha Guitry. Quoted Sunday Graphic 13 *Nov* 1933

17 In the last analysis it is our conception of death which decides the answers to all the questions life puts to us.
Dag Hammarskjöld, DIARIES

18 I am not afraid of death. I am afraid of dying. I should be very glad to be dead, but I don't look forward to the actual process of dying.
Gilbert Harding to John Freeman, BBC TV, *Face to Face*

19 Turn up the lights. I don't want to go home in the dark.
O. Henry, last words

20 Death is the only thing we haven't succeeded in completely vulgarising.
Aldous Huxley, EYELESS IN GAZA 1936

21 Ignore death until the last moment; then when it can't be ignored any longer have yourself squirted full of morphia and shuffle off in a corner.
Aldous Huxley, TIME MUST HAVE A STOP 1944

22 Every man his price. Well preserved fat corpse gentleman, epicure, invaluable for fruit garden. A bargain. By carcass of William Wilkinson, auditor and accountant, lately deceased, three pounds thirteen and six. With thanks.
James Joyce, ULYSSES

23 Death is the only pure, beautiful conclusion of a great passion.
D. H. Lawrence, FANTASIA OF THE UNCONSCIOUS 1922

24 I detest life-insurance agents. They always argue that I shall some day die, which is not so.
Stephen Leacock, LITERARY LAPSES 1910

1 When bees swarm in your nostrils / And honey drips from the sockets / Of eyes that today are frantic / With love that is frustrated.
Alun Lewis, TO A COMRADE IN ARMS

2 This is the Black Widow death.
Robert Lowell, MR. EDWARDS AND THE SPIDER

3 The only religious way to think of death is as a part and parcel of life.
Thomas Mann, THE MAGIC MOUNTAIN 1924

4 A man's dying is more the survivor's affair than his own.
Id.

5 Either he's dead or my watch has stopped.
Groucho Marx, A DAY AT THE RACES *(film) script by Robert Pirosh, George Seaton and George Oppenheim* 1937

6 Death opens unknown doors. It is most grand to die.
John Masefield, POMPEY THE GREAT 1910

7 Dying is a very dull dreary affair and my advice to you is to have nothing whatever to do with it.
W. Somerset Maugham, last words

8 Life is a great surprise. I do not see why death should not be an even greater one.
Vladimir Nabokov, PALE FIRE 1962

9 George Gershwin is dead. I don't have to believe it if I don't want to.
John O'Hara. Quoted Alistair Cooke BBC Radio 4, *Letter from America* 31 *May* 1974

10 All victory ends in the defeat of death. That's sure. But does defeat end in the victory of death? That's what I wonder.
Eugene O'Neill, MOURNING BECOMES ELECTRA 1931

11 I don't mind dying; the trouble is you feel so bloody stiff the next day.
Overheard. Quoted George Axlerod, BBC Radio 4, *Quote Unquote* 13 *Sep* 1979

12 In the happy no-time of his sleeping / Death took him by the heart.
Wilfred Owen, POEMS, *Asleep* 1920

13 It costs me never a stab nor squirm / To tread by chance upon a worm / "Aha my little dear", I say / "Your clan will pay me back one day."
Dorothy Parker, SUNSET GUN, *Thought for a Sunshiny Morning* 1928

14 What I look forward to is not a violent death, but dying in the normal way, with my head in the gas oven.
Leo Pavia. Quoted James Agate, Ego 4 9 *Oct* 1938

15 Dying / Is an art, like everything else. / I do it exceptionally well.
Sylvia Plath, ARIEL, *Lady Lazarus*

16 Death is the least we have to fear.
Peter Porter, YOUR ATTENTION PLEASE

17 The people who pretend that dying is rather like strolling into the next room always leave me unconvinced. Death like birth, must be a tremendous event.
J. B. Priestley, OUTCRIES AND ASIDES

18 I have a rendezvous with death / At some disputed barricade.
Alan Seeger, I HAVE A RENDEZVOUS WITH DEATH

19 Life levels all men; death reveals the eminent.
George Bernard Shaw, MAN AND SUPERMAN 1905

20 I was much further out than you thought / And not waving but drowning.
Stevie Smith, NOT WAVING BUT DROWNING

21 If there wasn't death I think you couldn't go on.
Stevie Smith, Observer 9 *Nov* 1969

22 Death is all in the mind, really. Once you're dead you forget all about it.
Jack Trevor Storey, ITV, *Jack on the Box* 19 *Jan* 1979

23 A beautiful death is for people who have lived like animals to die like angels.
Mother Teresa, FOR THE BROTHERHOOD OF MAN

24 And death shall have no dominion / Dead men naked they shall be one / With the man in the wind and the west morn.
Dylan Thomas, AND DEATH SHALL HAVE NO DOMINION 1943

25 Do not go gently into that good night / Old age should burn and rave at close of day / Rage rage against the dying of the light.
Dylan Thomas, DO NOT GO GENTLY INTO THAT GOOD NIGHT 1952

26 After the first death there is no other.
Dylan Thomas, A REFUSAL TO MOURN THE DEATH OF A CHILD 1946

27 Death, the only immortal who treats us all alike, whose peace and whose refuge are

for all. The soiled and the pure, the rich and the poor, the loved and the unloved.
Mark Twain, on his deathbed

1 The great thing about the dead, they make space.
John Updike, RABBIT IS RICH

2 We are secretly more terrified of death now than in medieval times. It is the one aspect of life, so to speak, that civilisation has not improved.
Peter Watson, The Times diary 6 Aug 1981

3 The experiment will be over, the rinsed beaker returned to its shelf, the crystals gone dissolving down the wastepipe; the duster sweeps the bench.
H. G. Wells, FIRST AND LAST THINGS

4 You're old when most people would rather have you dead.
William Wharton, DAD 1981

5 One of us must go.
Oscar Wilde, of himself and the wallpaper in his room. Reputed last words 1900

6 Death is one moment, life is so many of them.
Tennessee Williams, THE MILK TRAIN DOESN'T STOP HERE ANY MORE 1962

DEBT

7 The National Debt is a very Good Thing and it would be dangerous to pay it off for fear of Political Economy.
W. C. Sellar and R. J. Yeatman, 1066 AND ALL THAT 1930

8 In the midst of life we are in debt.
Sunday Express 11 Sep 1932

9 I may be a chump, but it's my boast that I don't owe a penny to a single soul — except tradesmen of course.
P. G. Wodehouse, JEEVES AND THE HARD-BOILED EGG

DECADENCE

10 Youth is fleeting / To the rhythm beating / In your mind / Dance, dance, dance little lady / So obsessed / With second best no rest / You'll ever find.
Noël Coward, THIS YEAR OF GRACE

11 Unlike the alleged Good Woman of the Bible, I'm not above rubies.
Saki, REGINALD ON CHRISTMAS PRESENTS

12 Scythed grass turned as sere as an old man's tea-stained moustaches.
Emma Tennant, WILD NIGHTS

DECEIT

13 O what a tangled web we weave / When first we practise to deceive / But when we've practised quite a while / How vastly we improve our style.
J. R. Pope, A WORD OF ENCOURAGEMENT

DECISIONS

14 Academic staff rather enjoy coming to a conclusion, but they don't like coming to decisions at all.
Lord Annan, Observer 8 Feb 1981

15 I always have one golden rule for such occasions — I ask myself what Nanny would have expected me to do.
Lord Carrington. Quoted Observer, Last of the Tory Grandees 23 Jan 1983

16 Impelled by a state of mind which is destined not to last, we make our irrevocable decisions.
Marcel Proust, REMEMBRANCE OF THINGS PAST 1913–27

DECORUM

17 Their marriage customs when we first settled in the islands were so shocking that I couldn't possibly tell you about them. But I'll tell Mrs. MacPhail and she'll tell you.
W. Somerset Maugham, RAIN 1921

DEDICATION

18 To my daughter Leonora without whose never failing sympathy and encouragement this book would have been finished in half the time.
P. G. Wodehouse

DEFENCE

19 The bomber will always get through. The only defence is an offence, which means you have to kill women and children more quickly than the enemy if you want to save yourselves.
Stanley Baldwin, House of Commons, Nov 1932

DEFERENCE

20 There are only two people you should ever call 'Sir' — God and the King.
Ian Fleming to Philip Brownrigg. Quoted John Pearson, LIFE OF IAN FLEMING 1966

DEFIANCE

1 We shall defend our island whatever the cost may be. We shall fight on the beaches, we shall fight on the landing grounds, we shall fight on the fields and in the streets, we shall fight in the hills; we shall never surrender.
Winston Churchill, House of Commons 4 *Jun* 1940

2 But I, despite expert advice / Keep doing things I think are nice, / And though to good I never come — / Inseparable my nose and thumb.
Dorothy Parker, NEITHER BLOODY NOR UNBOWED

DEFINITION

3 To define a thing is to substitute the definition for the thing itself.
Georges Braque, The Times 12 *May* 1962

DEMOCRACY

4 Democracy means government by discussion, but it is only effective if you can stop people talking.
Clement Attlee, ANATOMY OF BRITAIN

5 The leadership of the privileged has passed away; but it has not been succeeded by that of the eminent. We have entered the region of mass effects.
Winston Churchill, GREAT CONTEMPORARIES 1937

6 What concerns everyone can only be resolved by everyone.
Friedrich Durrenmatt, THE PHYSICISTS, 21 *Points* 1962

7 In every dictatorship wealth is a sacred thing; in democracies it is the *only* sacred thing.
Anatole France, PENGUIN ISLAND 1908

8 Democracy used to be wonderful but now it has got into the wrong hands.
Graffito. Quoted BBC Radio 4, News Quiz 13 *Jan* 1980

9 Even though counting heads is not an ideal way to govern, at least it is better than breaking them.
Judge Learned Hand. Speech to U.S. Federal Bar Association 8 *Mar* 1932

10 I swear to the Lord / I still can't see / Why democracy means / Everybody but me.
Langston Hughes, THE BLACK MAN SPEAKS

11 Democracy is only an experiment in government and it has the obvious disadvantage of merely counting votes instead of weighing them.
W. R. Inge (Dean of St. Pauls), POSSIBLE RECOVERY

12 A democracy is a state which recognises the subjecting of the minority to the majority.
V. I. Lenin, THE STATE AND THE REVOLUTION

13 Democracy which began by liberating man politically has developed a dangerous tendency to enslave him through the tyranny of majorities and the deadly power of their opinion.
Ludwig Lewisohn, THE MODERN DRAMA

14 The democratic movement loves a crowd and fears the individuals who compose it.
Walter Lippmann, A PREFACE TO POLITICS 1914

15 Popular government has not yet been proved to guarantee, always and everywhere, good government.
Walter Lippmann, THE PUBLIC PHILOSOPHY 1955

16 In England it is bad manners to be clear, to assert something confidently. It may be your personal view that two and two make four, but you must not state it in a self-assured way because this is a democratic country and others may be of a different opinion.
George Mikes, HOW TO BE AN ALIEN 1946

17 The blind lead the blind. It's the democratic way.
Henry Miller, THE AIR CONDITIONED NIGHTMARE 1945

18 Man's capacity for justice makes democracy possible, but man's inclination to injustice makes democracy necessary.
Reinhold Niebuhr, THE CHILDREN OF LIGHT AND THE CHILDREN OF DARKNESS 1944

19 Democracy is clearly most appropriate for countries which enjoy an economic surplus and least appropriate where there is an economic insufficiency.
David Morris Potter, PEOPLE OF PLENTY

20 Envy is the basis of democracy.
Bertrand Russell, THE CONQUEST OF HAPPINESS 1930

1 We must be thoroughly democratic and patronise everybody without distinction of class.
George Bernard Shaw, JOHN BULL'S OTHER ISLAND 1904

2 Democracy substitutes election by the incompetent many for appointment by the corrupt few.
George Bernard Shaw, MAN AND SUPERMAN 1905

3 People who want to understand democracy should spend less time in the library with Aristotle and more time on the buses and in the subway.
Simeon Strunsky, NO MEAN CITY

4 There is a limit to the application of democratic methods. You can enquire of all the passengers as to what kind of car they like to ride in, but it is impossible to question them as to whether to apply the brakes when the train is at full speed and an accident threatens.
Leon Trotsky, HISTORY OF THE RUSSIAN REVOLUTION 1932

5 Democracy is supposed to give you the feeling of choice, like Painkiller X and Painkiller Y. But they're both just aspirin.
Gore Vidal. Quoted Martin Amis, Observer 7 Feb 1982

6 The person most to be feared in modern society is the Common Man.
C. V. Wedgwood, VELVET STUDIES

7 Democracy is the recurrent suspicion that more than half of the people are right more than half the time.
E. B. White, THE WILD FLAG 1946

8 That a peasant may become a king does not render the kingdom a democracy.
Woodrow Wilson. Speech, Chattanooga 31 *Aug* 1910

9 The world must be made safe for democracy.
Woodrow Wilson. Speech to U.S. Congress 2 *Apr* 1917

DENTIST

10 The thought of dentists gave him just the same sick horror as the thought of socialism.
H. G. Wells, BEALBY

DEPRESSION

11 It is a bad sign when people are depressed by their own good fortune.
Robert Bolt, A MAN FOR ALL SEASONS 1906

12 In a real dark night of the soul it is always three in the morning, day after day.
F. Scott Fitzgerald, THE CRACK-UP 1931

13 Noble deeds and hot baths are the best cures for depression.
Dodie Smith, I CAPTURE THE CASTLE 1948

DESPAIR

14 I turned to speak to God / About the world in despair / But to make bad matters worse / I found God wasn't there.
Robert Frost, NOT ALL THERE

15 Despair is the price one pays for setting oneself an impossible aim.
Graham Greene, THE HEART OF THE MATTER 1948

16 He who has never hoped can never despair.
George Bernard Shaw, CAESAR AND CLEOPATRA 1906

17 She gave a sort of despairing gesture, like a vicar's daughter who has discovered Erastinism in the village.
P. G. Wodehouse, LAUGHING GAS 1957

DESTINY

18 We are not permitted to choose the frame of our destiny. But what we put into it is ours.
Dag Hammarskjöld, MARKINGS 1964

DESTRUCTION

19 The ridiculous empires break like biscuits.
Roy Fuller, THE MIDDLE OF A WAR

EAMON DE VALERA

20 Lloyd George once remarked that negotiating with De Valera was like picking up mercury with a fork. De Valera replied "Why doesn't he try a spoon?"
Bernard Baruch, THE PUBLIC YEARS

DEVIL

21 An apology for the Devil: It must be remembered that we have only heard one side of the case. God has written all the books.
Samuel Butler, NOTEBOOKS 1912

1 Few people now believe in the devil; but many enjoy behaving as their ancestors behaved when the Fiend was a reality as unquestionable as his opposite number.
Aldous Huxley, THE DEVILS OF LOUDUN 1952

2 The Devil usually speaks a language called Bellsybabble, which he makes up himself as he goes along but when he is very angry he can speak bad French very well though some who have heard him say that he has a strong Dublin accent.
James Joyce, THE CAT AND THE DEVIL

3 It is so stupid of modern civilisation to have given up belief in the devil when he is the only explanation of it.
Ronald Knox, LET DONS DELIGHT

4 It is no use casting out devils. They belong to us, we must accept them and be at peace with them.
D. H. Lawrence, PHOENIX 1936

5 I used to think the Devil hid / In women's smiles and wine's carouse, / I called him Satan, Beelzebub / But now I call him dirty louse.
Isaac Rosenberg, THE IMMORTALS

6 The Devil can quote Shakespeare for his own purpose.
George Bernard Shaw

DIALECT

7 Gag me with a spoon!
The Guardian, *Valspeak: dialect of Valley Girls, San Fernando Valley, California* 26 *Oct* 1982

DIARY

8 Only good girls keep diaries. Bad girls don't have the time.
Attr. Tallulah Bankhead

9 I do not keep a diary. Never have. To write a diary every day is like returning to one's own vomit.
Enoch Powell, Sunday Times 6 *Nov* 1977

10 I always say, keep a diary and one day it will keep you.
Mae West. Quoted Janet Watts, Observer, *The Diarist* 3 *Jan* 1982

11 Nothing has really happened until it has been recorded.
Virginia Woolf. Quoted Harold Nicolson, DIARIES

12 I got out this diary and read, as one always reads one's own writing, with a kind of guilty intensity.
Virginia Woolf, A WRITER'S DIARY 1953

13 Should you wish to make sure that your birthday will be celebrated three hundred years hence, your best course undoubtedly, is to keep a diary.
Virginia Woolf, THE COMMON READER 1925

14 The good diarist writes either for himself alone or for a posterity so distant that it can safely hear every secret and justly weigh every motive.
1d.

DICTATORSHIP

15 Dictators ride to and fro on tigers which they dare not dismount. And the tigers are getting hungry.
Winston Churchill, WHILE ENGLAND SLEPT

16 I suspect that in our loathing of totalitarianism there is infused a good deal of admiration for its efficiency.
T. S. Eliot, THE IDEA OF A CHRISTIAN SOCIETY 1939

17 So long as men worship the Caesars and Napoleons, Caesars and Napoleons will arise to make them miserable.
Aldous Huxley, ENDS AND MEANS 1937

18 The people must be led, but only at a pace with which they can keep up. To lead them we must give a lot of power to a very few men, and the success of such an experiment depends upon the choice of exceptional men.
Dr. Salazar, dictator of Portugal. Quoted Vernon Bartlett, I KNOW WHAT I LIKED

DICTION

19 She is the great lady of the American stage. Her voice is so beautiful that you won't understand a word she says.
Mrs. Pat Campbell of an unnamed actress. Quoted James Agate Ego 3 6 *May* 1937

20 Oh my God. Remember you're in Egypt. The *skay* is only seen in Kensington.
Sir H. Beerbohm Tree, to an actress at rehearsal. Quoted Hesketh Pearson, BEERBOHM TREE

DICTIONARY

1 The responsibility of a dictionary is to record a language, not set its style.
Philip Gove, editor in chief of WEBSTER'S THIRD NEW INTERNATIONAL DICTIONARY, *in a letter to* Life Magazine, 17 *Nov* 1961

DIET

2 The right diet directs sexual energy into the parts that matter.
Barbara Cartland. Quoted Observer 11 *Jan* 1981

3 Don't eat too many almonds. They add weight to the breasts.
Colette, GIGI 1945

4 Unlike Americans, the English do not take their digestions seriously.
Oswald Greene (advertising agent for Colman's Mustard). Quoted Janet Hitchman, SUCH A STRANGE LADY

5 There was only one occasion in my life when I put myself on a strict diet and I can tell you, hand on heart, it was the most miserable afternoon I have ever spent.
Denis Norden, OH, MY WORD

DIFFERENCE

6 "Vot" asked George I courteously, "is the difference between a public nuisance and a public convenience?"
Caryl Brahms and S. J. Simon, NO NIGHTINGALES

DIGNITY

7 It is only people of small stature who need to stand on their dignity.
Arnold Bennett, JOURNALS 1928

8 It is terrifying to see how easily, in certain people, all dignity collapses. Yet when you think about it, this is quite normal since they only maintain this dignity by constantly striving against their own nature.
Albert Camus, NOTEBOOKS 1935–1942

9 The English are, on the whole, much more concerned with dignity than with passion. They resent nothing so much as to be made to look foolish.
William Davies, Punch 9 *Feb* 1972

10 Dignity is something you are born with or without. Too many people confuse dignity with pomposity.
Mary Margaret McBride

DIPLOMACY

11 [John Foster Dulles] invented Brinkmanship, the most popular game since Monopoly.
Richard Armour, IT ALL STARTED WITH COLUMBUS 1961

12 Let us not be deceived — we are today in the midst of a cold war.
Bernard Baruch. Speech South Carolina Legislature 16 *Apr* 1947

13 The ability to get to the verge without getting into the war is the necessary art. If you try to run away from it, if you are scared to go to the brink, you are lost.
John Foster Dulles. Quoted James Shepley, Life Magazine, *How Dulles Avoided War* 16 *Jan* 1956

14 Diplomats never ask. They make representations.
J. K. Galbraith, ECONOMICS, PEACE AND LAUGHTER

15 Diplomacy is to do and say / The nastiest thing in the nicest way.
Isaac Goldberg, THE REFLEX

16 Diplomacy is the art of fishing tranquilly in troubled waters.
J. Christopher Harold, BONAPARTE IN EGYPT

17 Forever poised between a cliché and an indiscretion.
Harold Macmillan. Quoted Newsweek 30 *Apr* 1956

18 Diplomats are just as essential to starting a war as soldiers are to finishing it. You take Diplomacy out of war and the thing would fall flat in a week.
Will Rogers, AUTOBIOGRAPHY 1949

19 A nation does not have to be cruel to be tough.
F. D. Roosevelt. Radio speech 13 *Oct* 1940

20 Speak softly and carry a big stick.
Theodore Roosevelt. Speech 2 *Sep* 1901

21 One of the defects of the summit meeting is that if it doesn't come off there's nowhere else to go.
Lord Sheffield, Thames Television, *The Day Before Yesterday* 1970

22 Brinkmanship — the art of bringing us to the edge of the nuclear abyss.
Adlai Stevenson. Speech 25 *Feb* 1952

1 A diplomat is a person who can tell you to go to hell in such a way that you actually look forward to the trip.
Caskie Stinnet, OUT OF THE RED

2 A diplomat these days is nothing but a head waiter who's allowed to sit down occasionally.
Peter Ustinov, ROMANOFF AND JULIET

3 Moral power is probably best when it is not used. The less you use it the more you have.
Andrew Young in an interview with Jonathan Power, Observer 8 Sep 1979

DISAGREEMENT

4 The history of scholarship is a history of disagreements.
Charles Evans Hughes. Speech to American Law Institute 7 May 1936

DISAPPROVAL

5 Disapproval from persons whose approval is as weightless as a man in space, is no worse than bouquets from them.
William Plomer, London Magazine, *Oct 1963*

DISARMAMENT

6 We are discussing the end of the world — or how to delay it.
Stuart Blanche (Archbishop of York), Church of England Synod, The Church and the Bomb debate 10 Feb 1983

DISBELIEF

7 If faith can move mountains, disbelief can deny them existence and faith is impotent against such importance.
Arnold Schoenberg, preface to Anton Webern's SIX BAGATELLES FOR STRING QUARTET 1908

DISCIPLINE

8 Historically, those people that did not discipline themselves had discipline thrust upon them from the outside.
Alistair Cooke, AMERICA

DISCOMFORT

9 How did the Greeks stand marble benches in their theatres?
Aldous Huxley, ANTIC HAY 1923

DISCONTENT

10 Sir Humphry Davy / Detested gravy / He died in the odium / Of having discovered sodium.
E. C. Bentley, BIOGRAPHY FOR BEGINNERS 1921

11 While not exactly disgruntled, he was far from feeling gruntled.
P. G. Wodehouse, CODE OF THE WOOSTERS 1938

DISCRETION

12 Drawing on my fine command of language, I said nothing.
Robert Benchley, CHIPS OFF THE OLD BENCHLEY 1949

13 If you don't say anything you won't be called on to repeat it.
Calvin Coolidge

DISGUST

14 I had something of the feeling that one has when one looks into a sink without holding one's nose.
John Galsworthy of serving on a Grand Jury, MEMORIES

DISILLUSION

15 The coach has turned into a pumpkin and the mice have all run away.
Lady Bird Johnson on leaving the White House on the election of Richard Nixon. Quoted Lyndon B. Johnson, THE VANTAGE POINT

16 There aren't any big, brave causes left.
John Osborne, LOOK BACK IN ANGER 1957

17 Nothing can be more deeply wounding than the disillusionments of a child or adolescent, but the disillusionments of an old man are old scars, slowly formed over the wounds of a long lifetime.
William Plomer, BBC broadcast on Leonard Woolf 14 Dec 1969

DISLIKE

18 You really have to get to know Dewey to dislike him.
James T. Patterson, MR. REPUBLICAN, A BIOGRAPHY OF ROBERT A. TAFT

WALT DISNEY

1 Soft little faces turned stony when I dealt out books by such counterfeit authors as Barrie, Collodi or Salten. Was I really too dumb, their withering looks asked plainly, to know that Walt Disney had written 'Peter Pan' and 'Pinocchio' and 'Bambi'?
Wanda Burgan, Punch, *Librarian* 12 *Sep* 1962

2 I love Mickey Mouse more than any woman I've every known.
Walt Disney. Quoted Walter Wagner, YOU MUST REMEMBER THIS

3 He can make an endlessly amusing operetta out of some old razor blades, a needle and thread, and perhaps a few soft-shelled crabs.
Otis Ferguson, THE FILM CRITICISM OF OTIS FERGUSON

4 Disney . . . an artist who uses his brains, the most significant figure in graphic art since Leonardo.
David Low. Quoted R. Schickel, WALT DISNEY

DISPARAGEMENT

5 Lord Montague of Beaulieu . . . has a splendid motor museum. My husband refers cattily to him and his collection as "Edward and his Garage".
Duchess of Bedford, NICOLE NOBODY

DISRESPECT

6 I suggest that speakers in 'Children's Hour' should not use the word 'Hello' when addressing children. Country children now invariably greet their elders with this word, spoken in anything but a respectful tone.
Letter to Radio Times

DIVERSITY

7 Every divergence deserves to be cherished, simply because it widens the bounds of life. Let us be united by everything that divides us.
Karel Capek, LETTERS FROM SPAIN

DIVORCE

8 Divorce of one's parents is said to be disturbing, but I don't know that I want sympathy. I might otherwise have been a factory hand in Leeds.
Paul Ableman in an interview, The Times 11 *Jul* 1970

9 She blamed me for cruelty and flagrant infidelity. I spent a whole weekend in Brighton with a lady called Vera Williams. She had the nastiest-looking hair brush I have ever seen.
Noël Coward, PRIVATE LIVES 1930

10 Divorce is America's great contribution to marriage.
Edmund Fawcett and Tony Thomas, AMERICA, AMERICANS 1983

11 You never really know a man until you have divorced him.
Zsa-Zsa Gabor

12 The trouble is, Jane is still young enough to think one man may be better than another.
Jennie Lee. Quoted Jill Craigie, The Times 13 *Nov* 1980

DOCTOR

13 My dear old friend George V always told me he would never have died but for that vile doctor [Dawson of Penn].
Margot Asquith, AUTOBIOGRAPHY 1936

14 Physicians of the utmost fame / Were called at once; but when they came / They answered as they took their fees, / "There is no cure for this disease?"
Hilaire Belloc, CAUTIONARY TALES 1907

15 They leave it to Nature to cure in her own time, but they take the credit. As well as very fat fees.
Anthony Burgess, NOTHING LIKE THE SUN 1964

16 I went to my doctor and asked for something for persistent wind. He gave me a kite.
Les Dawson, BBC TV, *The Good Old Days* 24 *Apr* 1979

17 The doctor was puzzled by the fact that it wasn't quite jaundice. If it became jaundice they could treat it. If it didn't become jaundice and went away they could discharge him. But this just being short of jaundice all the time confused them.
Joseph Heller, CATCH 22 1961

18 Medicine's real triumphs lie in improving the quality of life for everyone not in death-defying heroics that benefit or torment a few.
New York Times, *on the first artificial heart implant* 16 *Dec* 1982

19 When treating a cold a Doctor can go rather mechanically through a list of prescriptions, remedies and a routine which the

patient "must" follow and then say "I've got just the same sort of cold myself. They're about everywhere. What do I do about it? Well personally I do nothing whatever. Absolutely nothing — I'm sorry to say. Just go on as if nothing has happened. What? Bed — that is my order to you."
Stephen Potter, ONE-UPMANSHIP 1952

1 If Patient turns out to be really ill after all, it is always possible to look grave at the same time and say "You realise, I suppose, that twenty-five years ago you'd have been dead"
Id.

2 Doctors really must get typewriters. This lady is suffering from something unreadable.
Judge Tudor Rees, Brentford County Court. Quoted News Review 27 Nov 1947

3 Let no one suppose that the words doctor and patient can disguise from the parties the fact that they are employer and employee.
George Bernard Shaw, DOCTOR'S DILEMMA, preface 1906

DOG

4 The woman who is really kind to dogs is always one who has failed to inspire sympathy in men.
Max Beerbohm, ZULEIKA DOBSON 1911

5 The great pleasure of a dog is that you may make a fool of yourself with him and not only will he not scold you, he will make a fool of himself too.
Samuel Butler, NOTEBOOKS 1912

6 It's a rough-haired canary.
Mrs. Pat Campbell, to a customs officer who found her pet pekinese smuggled in her muff

7 The dog is the public enemy of a large and increasing proportion of men. What dear Fido does when he goes out for his constitutional seems to be quite out of the realm of ordinary jurisprudence.
Dr. O. P. Clark, Medical World, Mar 1947

8 Anybody who hates children and dogs can't be all bad.
W. C. Fields. Quoted Robert Lewis Taylor, W. C. FIELDS, ROWDY KING OF COMEDY

9 To his dog, every man is Napoleon, hence the constant popularity of dogs.
Aldous Huxley

10 If you go out for a walk with a friend, don't say a word for hours; if you go out for a walk with your dog, keep chatting to him.
George Mikes, HOW TO BE AN ALIEN 1946

11 The censure of a dog is something no man can stand.
Christopher Morley, THE HAUNTED BOOKSHOP 1919

12 A dog gladly admits the superiority of his master over himself, accepts his judgment as final, but, contrary to what many dog-lovers believe, he does not consider himself as a slave. His submission is voluntary, and he expects his own small rights to be respected.
Axel Munthe, THE STORY OF SAN MICHELE

13 A door is what a dog is always on the wrong side of.
Ogden Nash, THE PRIVATE DINING ROOM, A Dog's Best Friend is His Illiteracy 1953

14 Dogs display reluctance and wrath / If you try to give them a bath / They bury bones in hideaways / And half the time they trot sideways.
Ogden Nash, I'M A STRANGER HERE MYSELF, An Introduction to Dogs 1938

15 The dogs had eaten the upholstery of a Packard convertible that afternoon, and were consequently somewhat subdued.
S. J. Perelman, THE LAST LAUGH

16 In the case of the gentleman the worship of his dogs reaches its apotheosis when they are so old and cantankerous that they are deaf and blind and smell of blocked drains. Then they enjoy the best chair in the drawing room, from which point of vantage they enjoy their last remaining pleasure of biting anyone who comes near them.
Douglas Sutherland, THE ENGLISH GENTLEMAN 1978

17 He was always sorry, mother said, after he bit someone, but we could not understand how she figured this out. He didn't act sorry.
James Thurber, THE DOG THAT BIT PEOPLE

18 It is a terrible thing for an old lady to outlive her dogs.
Tennessee Williams, CAMINO REAL 1953

19 I can train any dog in five minutes. It's training the owner that takes longer.
Barbara Woodhouse

20 The poor dog had a distressing malady. Mrs. (Dorothy) Parker issued bulletins about his health. Confidential bulletins,

tinged with scepticism. "He *said* he got it from a lamp post."
Alexander Woollcott, WHILE ROME BURNS, *Our Mrs. Parker* 1935

DOGMATISM

1 When people are least sure, they are often the most dogmatic.
J. K. Galbraith, THE GREAT CRASH 1955

2 The greater the ignorance the greater the dogmatism.
Sir William Osler, Montreal Medical Journal 1902

DOUBT

3 Your doubt may be a good quality if you *train it*.
Rainer Maria Rilke, LETTERS TO A YOUNG POET 1903

4 The trouble with the world is that the stupid are cocksure and the intelligent full of doubt.
Bertrand Russell, AUTOBIOGRAPHY 1969

5 Doubt is part of all religion. All the religious thinkers were doubters.
Isaac Bashevis Singer. Quoted Richard Burgen, New York Times Magazine 3 *Dec* 1978

DRAMA

6 Drama is a synthetic and not an analytical art. Very few novelists grasp the fact that a tone of voice and a slight change of facial expression may suggest more than pages of analysis and description.
E. A. Baughan, John o'London's Weekly, *Galsworthy: The Plays* 8 *Dec* 1928

7 A play should give you something to think about. When I see a play and understand it the first time, then I know it can't be much good.
T. S. Eliot, New York Post 22 *Sep* 1963

8 In my plays I want to look at life — at the commonplace of existence — as if we had just turned a corner and run into it for the first time.
Christopher Fry, Time 20 *Nov* 1952

9 The theatre, so called, can flourish on barbarism, but any *drama* worth speaking of can develop but in the air of civilisation.
Henry James, letter to C. E. Wheeler 2 *Apr* 1911

10 All playwrights should be dead for three hundred years.
Joseph L. Mankiewicz, ALL ABOUT EVE (film)

11 The drama is make-believe. It does not deal with truth but with effect.
W. Somerset Maugham, THE SUMMING UP 1938

12 The structure of a play is always the story of how the birds came home to roost.
Arthur Miller, Harper's, *Aug* 1958

13 Drama — what literature does at night.
George Jean Nathan, TESTAMENT OF A CRITIC

14 Drama is action, sir, action and not confounded philosophy.
Luigi Pirandello, SIX CHARACTERS IN SEARCH OF AN AUTHOR 1921

15 A play isn't a text. It's an event.
Tom Stoppard. Quoted Pendennis, Observer 30 *Aug* 1981

16 The unencumbered stage encourages the truth operative in everyone. The less seen, the more heard. The eye is the enemy of the ear in real drama.
Thornton Wilder, New York Times 6 *Nov* 1961

DREAM

17 Last night I dreamt I went to Manderley again.
Daphne du Maurier, REBECCA, *opening words* 1938

18 I'm one of those people given to dreaming about the Queen. In one, I remember, I was just getting on very well with the Queen when Prince Charles came in, dressed in Boy Scout uniform.
Graham Greene, in an interview with J. W. Lambert, Sunday Times 5 *Mar* 1978

19 To say that, when you dream, you are not conscious is to speak loosely; one is only conscious, only lucid in dreams.
Eugene Ionesco, FRAGMENTS OF A JOURNAL

20 I was never able to agree with Freud that the dream is a 'façade' behind which its meaning was hidden — a meaning already known but maliciously, so to speak, withheld from consciousness. To me dreams are a part of nature, which harbours no intention to deceive but expresses something

as best it can, just as a plant grows or an animal seeks its food as best it can.
Carl Jung, MEMORIES, DREAMS, REFLECTIONS

1 It is on the whole probable that we continually dream, but that consciousness makes such a noise that we do not hear it.
Carl Jung. Quoted Charles Rycroft, THE INNOCENCE OF DREAMS

2 If you can dream, and not make dream your master.
Rudyard Kipling, IF 1910

3 All men dream; but not equally. Those who dream by night in the dusty recesses of their minds wake in the day to find it was vanity; but the dreamers of the day are dangerous men, for they may act their dream with open eyes, to make it possible.
T. E. Lawrence, SEVEN PILLARS OF WISDOM 1926

4 The boys are dreaming wicked or of the bucking ranches of the night and the jollyrodgered sea.
Dylan Thomas, UNDER MILK WOOD 1954

5 One can write, think and pray exclusively of others; dreams are all egocentric.
Evelyn Waugh, DIARIES 5 *Oct* 1962

6 I have spread my dreams under your feet; / Tread softly because you tread on my dreams.
W. B. Yeats, HE WISHES FOR THE CLOTHS OF HEAVEN 1950

DRESS

7 It was necessary to abolish the fez, which sat on the heads of our nation as an emblem of ignorance, negligence, fanaticism and hatred of progress and civilisation; to accept in its place the hat, the headgear worn by all the civilised world.
Kemal Ataturk, addressing the Turkish Assembly, Oct 1927

8 I prefer the clothes I wear in Worcestershire to those I wear in London.
Stanley Baldwin. Speech 5 May 1925

9 There is invariably something odd about women who wear ankle socks.
Alan Bennett, THE OLD COUNTRY

10 One cannot say she was dressed. She was clothed. And so uncertainly that it was unsure she would remain even that.
Ivy Compton-Burnett. Quoted Julian Mitchell, BBC Radio 4, *Quote Unquote* 5 *Feb* 1982

11 Edith Sitwell, in that great Risorgimento cape of hers, looks as if she were covering a teapot, or a telephone,
Noël Coward. Quoted William Merchant, THE PRIVILEGE OF HIS COMPANY 1980

12 His clothes were pressed, like pretty leaves, when they / Are found in Bibles closed for many a day.
W. H. Davies, ONE POET VISITS ANOTHER

13 An overcoat of a plaid so loud that when it was removed and shut in a closet a hush seemed to fall over the house.
Peter De Vries, CONSENTING ADULTS

14 Contrary to popular belief, English women do not wear tweed nightgowns.
Hermione Gingold, Saturday Review 10 *Apr* 1955

15 The pull-over, of subfusc colouring and worn by daring young men over a soft-collared shirt, with a coloured tie and no tie-pin . . . was the first garment that could be used interchangeably by men and women.
Robert Graves and Alan Hodge, THE LONG WEEKEND 1940

16 When I was a boy they were so covered up that I thought all women were solid down to the ankles, where they branched out into a pair of feet.
C. E. M. Joad. Quoted News Review 16 *Jan* 1947

17 He [Marlon Brando] dressed himself up so nattily for his first audition that none of the people there took him for an actor. "From that time on I determined to become the messiest dresser of them all" he says. Thus was the torn T-shirt launched.
Roderick Mann, Sunday Express 16 *Jul* 1961

18 There was a young belle of old Natchez / Whose garments were always in patchez / When comment arose / On the state of her clothes / She drawled; When Ah itchez Ah scratchez.
Ogden Nash, I'M A STRANGER HERE MYSELF, *Requiem* 1938

19 His socks compelled one's attention without losing one's respect.
Saki, MINISTERS OF GRACE

20 We cannot congratulate Mr. Churchill on his wedding outfit. It was not a success. The sleeves were too short and too backward hanging, and consequently creased badly when the arms were brought

forward. It was too long and heavy for a morning coat, and too skimpy for a 'frock'.
Tailor and Cutter 1908

1 Gloves have always been in some sense a symbol of gentility.
The Times. *Quoted* News Review 24 *Jul* 1947

DRINK

2 The point about white Burgundies is that I hate them myself. They so closely resemble a blend of cold chalk soup and alum cordial with an additive or two to bring it to the colour of children's pee.
Kingsley Amis, THE GREEN MAN 1969

3 Some years ago a couple of friends of mine stopped drinking suddenly and died in agony. I swore then that such a thing should never happen to me.
John Barrymore. Quoted J. P. McEvoy, Stage, Jan 1941

4 "Do you realise that those martinis you keep drinking are slow poison?"
"I'm in no hurry."
Retort, variously attributed but believed originated by Robert Benchley at a party

5 Note in the barracks: "Drink drives out the man and brings out the beast". Which makes men understand why they like it.
Albert Camus, NOTEBOOKS 1935–1942

6 Lord Carson: Do you drink?
Witness: That's my business.
Carson: Any other?
Lord Carson. Quoted Edward Bell, THESE MEDDLESOME ATTORNEYS

7 By the end of five days I had completely overcome my repugnance for the taste of whisky.
Winston Churchill, MY EARLY LIFE 1930

8 Swill champagne but sip claret.
Winston Churchill. Quoted John Boyd Carpenter, WAY OF LIFE 1982

9 You can no more keep a martini in the refrigerator than you can keep a kiss there. The proper union of gin and vermouth . . . is one of the happiest marriages on earth and one of the shortest lived.
Bernard De Voto, THE HOUR 1951

10 When he buys his ties he has to ask if gin will make them run.
F. Scott Fitzgerald, NOTEBOOKS

11 Never have a small glass of port, my lad. It just goes wambling around looking for damage to do. Have a large glass. It settles down and does you good.
Attr. Lord Goddard, advising a young member at his club

12 I'd rather have a full bottle in front of me than a full-frontal lobotomy.
Grafitto. Quoted BBC Radio 4, Quote Unquote

13 You might make that a double.
Neville Heath, when offered a drink by the prison governor before being executed for a double murder, Oct 1946

14 Champagne is the right drink for politics. It stimulates at the time and does not deaden afterwards. In the nineteenth century it was prized for its medicinal qualities. It is a pity that most twentieth-century politicians have abandoned champagne for other drinks which are heavier and just as expensive.
Douglas Hurd, AN END TO PROMISES: A SKETCH OF GOVERNMENT 1970–74

15 Champagne has the taste of an apple peeled with a steel knife.
Aldous Huxley, TIME MUST HAVE A STOP 1944

16 The Spanish wine, my God it is foul, catpiss is champagne compared, this is the sulphurous urination of some aged horse.
D. H. Lawrence. Letter to Rhys Davis 25 Apr 1929

17 Pubs make you as drunk as they can, as soon as they can, and turn nasty when they succeed.
Colin MacInnes, ENGLAND HALF-ENGLISH

18 Two inches to the north-west is written a word full of meaning — the most purposeful word that can be written on a map — "Inn".
A. A. Milne, IF I MAY

19 Three highballs and I think I'm St. Francis of Assisi.
Dorothy Parker, JUST A LITTLE ONE

20 Champagne and orange juice is a great drink. The orange improves the champagne. The champagne definitely improves the orange.
Philip, Duke of Edinburgh. Quoted Noël St. George, ROYAL QUOTES

21 Beer drinking don't do half the harm of lovemaking.
Eden Philpotts, THE FARMER'S WIFE

22 I can't drink Guinness out of a thick mug. I only like it out of a thin glass.
Harold Pinter, THE CARETAKER 1959

1 A good general rule is to say the bouquet is better than the taste, and vice versa.
Stephen Potter, ONE-UPMANSHIP 1952

2 I am only a beer teetotaller, not a champagne teetotaller.
George Bernard Shaw, CANDIDA 1904

3 I think I am the only one of His Majesty's Ministers who has drunk a Soviet Minister under the table.
Harold Wilson, when President of the Board of Trade. Quoted News Review 13 May 1948

4 I must get out of these wet clothes and into a dry martini.
Alexander Woollcott. Quoted Howard Techmann, SMART ALEC 1976

DRUNKENNESS

5 . . . a drunken, ridiculous air, like solemn men in paper hats.
J. G. Farrell, TROUBLES

6 You are not drunk if you can lie on the floor without holding on.
Dean Martin. Quoted Peter Dickson, THE OFFICIAL RULES

7 I am as drunk as a lord, but then, I am one, so what does it matter?
Bertrand Russell. Quoted Ralph Schoenmann, BERTRAND RUSSELL, PHILOSOPHER OF THE CENTURY

DUKE

8 The advantages of being a Duke may be completely undeserved, but they are numerous and enormous.
Duke of Bedford, BOOK OF SNOBS

9 I am the rock-and-roll version of Pomp and Circumstance.
Duke of Bedford. Quoted David MacDonald, Saturday Evening Post 11 *Jul* 1959

10 Lord Lucky, by a curious fluke / Became a most important duke / From living in a vile hotel / A long way east of Camberwell / He rose in less than half an hour / To riches, dignity and power.
Hilaire Belloc, MORE PEERS

11 A fully equipped duke costs as much to keep up as two dreadnoughts. They are just as great a terror, and last longer.
David Lloyd George at Newcastle upon Tyne 1909

12 Of course, in these days, Russian Dukes are about as useful as dandruff.
Damon Runyon, MORE THAN SOMEWHAT, *Broadway Financier* 1937

DUTY

13 There are a lot of things in life which need doing which you may not like the idea of doing. This is the whole idea of duty.
Charles, Prince of Wales. Quoted Time Magazine

14 Let us therefore brace ourselves to our duties, and so bear ourselves that, if the British Empire and its Commonwealth last for a thousand years, men will say "This was their finest hour."
Winston Churchill, House of Commons 18 *Jun* 1940

15 When a duty ceases to be a pleasure then it ceases to exist.
Norman Douglas, GOODBYE TO WESTERN CULTURE

16 Duty largely consists of pretending that the trivial is critical.
John Fowles, THE MAGUS 1965

17 The dull, leaden, soul-depressing sensation known as the sense of duty.
O. Henry, NO STORY

18 Do your duty. Fear God. Honour the King.
Lord Kitchener. Message in soldier's paybooks 1914–18 war

19 If we believe a thing to be bad, and if we have a right to prevent it, it is our duty to try to prevent it, and damn the consequences.
Alfred, Lord Milner. Speech, Glasgow 26 *Nov* 1909

20 O Duty / Why has thou not the visage of a sweetie or a cutie? / Why glitter thy spectacles so ominously? / Why art thou clad so abominously? / Why art thou so different from Venus? / And why do you and I have so few interests in common between us?
Ogden Nash, KIND OF AN ODE TO DUTY

21 A sense of duty is useful in work, but offensive in personal relations. People wish to be liked, not endured with patient resignation.
Bertrand Russell, THE CONQUEST OF HAPPINESS 1930

1 When a stupid man is doing something he is ashamed of, he always declares that it is his duty.

George Bernard Shaw, CAESAR AND CLEO-PATRA 1906

2 The worst of doing one's duty was that it apparently unfitted one for doing anything else.

Edith Wharton, THE AGE OF INNOCENCE 1920

E

EAR

1 Miss Penny laughed and rattled the minia-
ture gallows of her ears.
Aldous Huxley, MORTAL COILS 1922

EAST

2 The mysterious East, perfumed like a
flower, silent like death, dark like a grave.
Joseph Conrad, YOUTH 1902

EATING

3 The last man in the world whose opinion I
would take on what to eat would be a
doctor. It is far safer to consult a waiter,
and not a bit more expensive.
Robert Lynd, SOLOMON IN ALL HIS GLORY

4 On the Continent people use a fork as
though a fork were a shovel: in England
they turn it upside down and push everything — including peas — on top of it.
George Mikes, HOW TO BE AN ALIEN 1946

5 In England — whether the meal is divine or
foul — you eat it as if you did not notice the
difference.
Id.

6 The man in evening clothes dining with the
napkin in his lap will eat only half as much
food as a diner in evening clothes with his
napkin in his collar. The former will not
only be worrying about spotting his shirt
bosom but about the remarks his wife will
make if he does.
Damon Runyon, MORE THAN SOMEWHAT
1937

7 I eat merely to put food out of my mind.
N. F. Simpson, THE HOLE

8 The Russians in the late war were enormously impressed by Churchill at the table.
His appetite for caviar and vodka convinced them that they were fighting on the
right side.
Robert Lewis Taylor, THE AMAZING MR.
CHURCHILL

9 "If you don't mind" said Colonel Blount,
"I prefer not to talk at meals." He popped a
morocco-bound volume of *Punch* before
his plate against a vast silver urn from
which grew a small castor-oil plant.
"Give Mr. Symes a book," he said.
Mrs. Florin put another volume of *Punch*
beside Adam.
"If you come across anything really funny,
read it to me," said Colonel Blount.
Then they had luncheon.
Evelyn Waugh, VILE BODIES 1930

ECCENTRICITY

10 She used to eat chops in the small hours and
sleep in a hat. Once she arrived home at
seven a.m. carrying a gate. Who am I to say
there was anything wrong with her?
Alan Coren, THE SANITY INSPECTOR 1974

11 I am not going to be quite as reclusive as I
have been because it has apparently
attracted so much attention that I have just
got to live a somewhat modified life in order
not to be an oddity.
Howard Hughes, last public statement
1972

ECONOMICS

12 Man will never be enslaved by machinery *if*
the man tending the machine be paid
enough.
*Karel Čapek. Quoted in obituary by Guy
Ramsay*, News Chronicle 27 *Dec* 1938

13 Economics, whether you like it or not, are
here to stay.
Charles, Prince of Wales, BBC Radio
London 14 *Nov* 1980

14 There is no such thing as a free lunch.
*Economists' aphorism. Quoted Richard
Rose and Gay Peters*, CAN GOVERNMENTS
GO BANKRUPT?

15 Economics as a positive science is a body of
tentatively accepted generalisations about
economic phenomena that can be used to

predict the consequences of changes in circumstances.
Milton Friedman, ESSAYS ON POSITIVE ECONOMICS

1 Just as there must be balance in what a community produces, so there must also be a balance in what the community consumes.
J. K. Galbraith, THE AFFLUENT SOCIETY 1958

2 Economists are economical, among other things, of ideas. They make those they acquire as graduate students do for a lifetime. Changes in economics come only with changing generations.
J. K. Galbraith, AGE OF UNCERTAINTY 1977

3 What is wholly mysterious in economics is not likely to be important.
J. K. Galbraith, ECONOMICS, PEACE AND LAUGHTER

4 Economists have vanities of expression and an accomplished practitioner can often get the words parameter, stochastic and aggregation into a single sentence.
Id.

5 The individual serves the industrial system not by supplying it with savings and the resulting capital; he serves it by consuming its products.
J. K. Galbraith, THE NEW INDUSTRIAL STATE 1967

6 The economists who are most highly regarded in their own time have almost always been those who confined themselves to abstract speculation unmarred by social purpose.
J. K. Galbraith, A LIFE IN OUR TIMES 1982

7 There is little point in producing more food if the hungry cannot afford to buy it.
Geoffrey Lean, Observer 20 *Aug* 1978

8 There are in the field of economic events no constant relations, and consequently no measurement is possible.
Ludwig Elder von Mises, HUMAN ACTION

9 Recession is when your neighbour loses his job; depression is when you lose yours.
Ronald Reagan, Presidential campaign speech, Oct 1980

10 The government is paying peanuts and getting monkeys.
Richard Wainwright MP, BBC Radio 4, *The Week in Westminster* 10 *Jul* 1982

11 One man's pay rise is another man's price increase.
Sir Harold Wilson

ECONOMY

12 Everyone is always in favour of general economy and specific expenditure.
Sir Anthony Eden. Quoted Observer 17 *Jun* 1958

ECSTASY

13 The ecstasy of religion, the ecstasy of art and the ecstasy of love are the only things worth thinking about and experiencing.
Don Marquis, THE ALMOST PERFECT STATE

ANTHONY EDEN

14 He is more pathetic than sinister. Beneath the sophistication of his appearance and manner he has all the unplumbable stupidities and unawareness of his class and type.
Aneurin Bevan, Tribune 15 *Jan* 1943

15 The charming milksop who became the blood-lusting monster.
Brendan Bracken. Quoted David Carlton, ANTHONY EDEN 1981

16 That's Anthony for you — half mad baronet, half beautiful woman.
R. A. Butler. Ibid.

17 ... his unfortunate propensity to offer clichés and platitudes on a scale unusual even for a politician.
David Carlton, ANTHONY EDEN 1981

18 He is an overripe banana, yellow outside, squishy in.
Reginald Paget

19 He will be the worst prime minister since Lord North.
Lord Swinton to Winston Churchill. Quoted J. A. Cross, LORD SWINTON 1983

20 The best advertisement the Fifty Shilling Tailors ever had.
Bonar Thompson. Quoted Michael Foot, DEBTS OF HONOUR 1981

EDINBURGH

21 ... a dignified spinster with syphilis.
Charles Higham, THE ADVENTURES OF CONAN DOYLE

EDUCATION

1 "Whom are you?" he said, for he had been to night school.
George Ade, BANG! BANG!, *The Steel Box*

2 More will mean worse.
Kingsley Amis, Encounter

3 My degree was a kind of inoculation. I got just enough education to make me immune from it for the rest of my life.
Alan Bennett, FORTY YEARS ON

4 Education bewildered me with knowledge and facts in which I was only mildly interested.
Charles Chaplin, MY AUTOBIOGRAPHY 1964

5 I learn the way the monkey learns — watching its parents.
Charles, Prince of Wales. Quoted Graham and Heather Fisher, CHARLES: THE MAN AND THE PRINCE

6 The prolonged education indispensable to the progress of society is not natural to mankind.
Winston Churchill, MY EARLY LIFE 1930

7 She has set herself an extremely low standard, which she has failed to maintain.
Quoted from her school report by Jilly Cooper, Sunday Times 16 *Jul* 1978

8 The one real object of education is to leave a man in the condition of continually asking questions.
Bishop Creighton. Quoted C. A. Alington, THINGS ANCIENT AND MODERN

9 It is nothing short of a miracle that modern methods of instruction have not yet strangled the holy curiosity of enquiry.
Albert Einstein, AUTOBIOGRAPHY

10 Discussion in all higher education, is the vacuum which is used to fill a vacuum.
J. K. Galbraith, A LIFE IN OUR TIMES 1981

11 Yesterday I couldn't spell engineer. Now I are one.
Graffito. Quoted Nigel Rees Graffiti 2

12 Until all teachers are geniuses and enthusiasts, nobody will learn anything, except what they teach themselves.
Aldous Huxley, ANTIC HAY 1923

13 The urge to do something for the young is strong only in parents, and in them only for the few years during which their children are at school.
Aldous Huxley, THE DOORS OF PERCEPTION 1954

14 The aim of education is the knowledge not of facts, but of values.
W. R. Inge (Dean of St. Pauls), THE CHURCH IN THE WORLD

15 Ruth's grandchildren are at that fashionable school in Dorset, and can already change wheels, top batteries and milk cows. They are going to learn to read next year you say. At ten and twelve? Isn't that a little soon?
Rose Macaulay, PERSONAL PLEASURES

16 Education must have an end in view, for it is not an end in itself.
Sybil Marshall, AN EXPERIMENT IN EDUCATION

17 Today nearly everyone can read, but only a few people can think.
Cardinal Alfredo Ottaviani. Speech 1956

18 Barnsley Grammar School did for education what myxamatosis did for rabbits.
Michael Parkinson, BBC TV 31 *Jan* 1981

19 Learning against a background of no experience means that there is no way of assessing the importance or the relevance of what is being taught.
Philip, Duke of Edinburgh, A QUESTION OF BALANCE 1982

20 The so-called method of co-education is false in theory and harmful to Christian training.
Pope Pius XI, Divini illius magistri 31 *Dec* 1929

21 Real education must ultimately be limited to one who really insists on knowing; the rest is merely sheep-herding.
Ezra Pound, ABC OF READING 1934

22 A man who has never gone to school may steal from a freight car, but if he has a university education he may steal the whole railroad.
Franklin D. Roosevelt

23 We are faced with the paradox that education has become one of the chief obstacles to intelligence and freedom of thought.
Bertrand Russell, SCEPTICAL ESSAYS 1928

24 Children with Hyacinth's temperament don't know better as they grow older, they merely know more.
Saki, THE JOYS OF PEACE

25 *Educ:* during the holidays from Eton.
Sir Osbert Sitwell, entry in WHO'S WHO

1 Education is what survives when what has been learnt has been forgotten.
B. F. Skinner, New Scientist 21 *May* 1964

2 Socrates gave no diplomas or degrees and would have subjected any disciple who demanded one to a disconcerting catechism on the nature of true knowledge.
G. M. Trevelyan, HISTORY OF ENGLAND 1926

3 Education has produced a vast population able to read, but unable to distinguish what is worth reading.
Id.

4 I always tell students that it is what you learn after you know it all that counts.
Harry S Truman

5 The overthrow of the public school system would be most welcome as it would put more money in the pockets of middle-class parents.
Auberon Waugh, IN THE LION'S DEN

6 By introducing a uniform system of education and by seeking to make it universal and compulsory the State is attempting to minimise natural superiorities. The precocious child is regarded as a problem and his development is, when possible, stunted.
Evelyn Waugh, commentary to T. A. MacInery's THE PRIVATE MAN

7 Human history becomes more and more a race between education and catastrophe.
H. G. Wells, THE OUTLINE OF HISTORY 1920

EDWARD VII

8 The leader writer on a great Northern Daily said on the morning after King Edward died that if he had not been a king he would have been the best type of sporting publican.
James Agate, Ego 1 1935

9 I wouldn't know the King from the Knave.
Nancy Astor, declining an invitation to play bridge with Edward VII. Quoted Geoffrey Bocca, NANCY, THE INCREDIBLE ASTOR, Sunday Express 8 *Jan* 1956

10 A capable, amiable, but very crafty man, with a remarkably sinister look in his eyes — not our friend.
Prince Eulenberg, to Kaiser Wilhelm II. Quoted Dr. Johannes Haller, PRINCE EULENBERG, THE KAISER'S FRIEND

11 He wasn't clever, but he always did the right thing, which is better than brains.
Lord Fisher. Letter to Reginald McKenna 14 *May* 1910

12 He had many romantic occupations. He went betting and visited Paris and was sometimes late for dinner; in addition he was merry with actresses and kind to gipsies.
W. C. Sellar and R. J. Yeatman, 1066 AND ALL THAT 1930

13 Edward VII smoked cigars and was addicted to entente cordials, married a Sea King's daughter and invented appendicitis.
Id.

14 Edward VII, who was not quite a gentleman, but let that pass, was among the first to spread around the rumour that the young ladies of Paris threw off their clothes more readily than their English sisters and the French named a boulevard after him in recognition of his researches on that subject.
Douglas Sutherland, THE ENGLISH GENTLEMAN 1978

15 We shall not pretend that there is nothing in his long career which those who respect and admire him would wish otherwise.
The Times, *leader on Edward* VII's *accession* 23 *Jan* 1901

16 You cannot imagine what a Satan he is.
Kaiser Wilhelm II. Quoted Robert Cecil, LIFE IN EDWARDIAN ENGLAND 1969

EDWARD VIII

17 As a prince, as a King, as a man, he was at his best only when the going was good.
Alistair Cooke, SIX MEN

18 He was born to be a salesman. He would be an admirable representative of Rolls Royce. But an ex-King cannot start selling motor cars.
Duchess of Windsor. Quoted Harold Nicolson, DIARIES 28 *May* 1947

EFFICIENCY

19 Efficiency . . . should possess a sweeping gesture — even if that gesture may at moments sweep the ornaments off the mantelpiece.
Harold Nicolson, SMALL TALK

20 There are only two qualities in the world, efficiency and inefficiency; and only

two sorts of people, the efficient and the inefficient.
George Bernard Shaw, JOHN BULL'S OTHER ISLAND 1904

EFFORT

1 All struggle has for its end relief and repose.
(Percy) Wyndham Lewis, THE ART OF BEING RULED 1926

2 The world is an oyster but you don't crack it open on a mattress.
Arthur Miller, DEATH OF A SALESMAN 1949

EGG

3 It was obvious that the egg had come first. There was something dignified about a silent passive egg, whereas Aunt Irene found it difficult to envisage an angel bearing a hen — which despite its undoubted merits, was a foolish and largely intractable bird.
Alice Thomas Ellis, THE 27TH KINGDOM 1982

EGO

4 One may understand the cosmos, but never the ego; the self is more distant than any star.
G. K. Chesterton, ORTHODOXY 1908

EGOTISM

5 Only the insane take themselves seriously.
Max Beerbohm. Quoted S. N. Behren, CONVERSATIONS WITH MAX

6 *Egotist:* a person of low taste, more interested in himself than me.
Ambrose Bierce, THE DEVIL'S DICTIONARY 1906

7 Egotism is the anaesthetic that dulls the pain of stupidity.
Frank Leary, Look Magazine 10 *Jan* 1955

8 No egotism is so insufferable as that of the Christian with regard to his soul.
W. Somerset Maugham, A WRITER'S NOTEBOOK 1969

9 He fell in love with himself at first sight and it is a passion to which he has always remained faithful. Self-love seems so often unrequited.
Anthony Powell, THE ACCEPTANCE WORLD 1955

10 The man who loves only himself cannot, it is true, be accused of promiscuity in his affections, but he is bound in the end to suffer intolerable boredom from the inevitable sameness of his affections.
Bertrand Russell, AUTOBIOGRAPHY 1967

11 Interest in oneself leads to no activity of a progressive kind. It may lead to the keeping of a diary, to getting psycho-analysed, or perhaps to becoming a monk.
Bertrand Russell, THE CONQUEST OF HAPPINESS 1930

EGYPT

12 I dare say you can't judge Egypt by Aida.
Ronald Firbank, THE ECCENTRICITIES OF CARDINAL PIRELLI 1926

ALBERT EINSTEIN

13 If my theory of relativity is proved successful Germany will claim me as a German and France will declare I am a citizen of the whole world. Should my theory prove untrue, France will say I'm a German and Germany will say I am a Jew.
Albert Einstein. Quoted News Review 8 *May* 1947

14 Einstein — the greatest Jew since Christ.
J. B. S. Haldane, DAEDALUS OR SCIENCE AND THE FUTURE

DWIGHT D. EISENHOWER

15 The best clerk I ever fired.
General MacArthur. Quoted Marquis Childs, EISENHOWER, CAPTIVE HERO

ELECTION

16 Elections are won by men and women chiefly because most people vote against somebody rather than for somebody.
Franklin P. Adams, NODS AND BECKS 1944

17 The labour candidate represents the shirking classes but I represent the working classes.
Lady Astor. Election speech 1919

18 Minorities are valuable people, and on the whole those who are opposed to you are more likely to vote than those who support you.
Richard Crossman, DIARIES 5 *Feb* 1970

1 No matter who you vote for, the Government always gets in.
Graffito. Quoted, BBC South West 30 *Apr* 1979

2 Anyone who votes labour ought to be locked up.
Field Marshal Montgomery. Speech at Woodford, Essex 1959

3 Many immigrants vote Labour because they think the labour exchanges at which they sign on belong to the Labour Party.
Frank Muir, BBC Radio 22 *Apr* 1979

ELECTRICITY

4 Electrical force is defined as something which causes motion of electrical charge; an electrical charge is something which exerts electrical force.
Sir Arthur Eddington, THE NATURE OF THE PHYSICAL WORLD

5 Pylons, those pillars / Bare like nude giant girls that have no secret.
Stephen Spender, THE PYLONS

ELECTRONICS

6 The new electronics interdependence re-creates the world in the image of a global village.
Marshall McLuhan, THE MEDIUM IS THE MESSAGE 1967

ELEGANCE

7 To achieve harmony in bad taste is the height of elegance.
Jean Genet, THE THIEF'S JOURNAL 1949

8 Tom [Mix] was as elegant on a horse as Fred Astaire on a dance floor, and that's the elegantest there is.
Adela Rogers St. Johns, THE HONEYCOMB

ELEPHANT

9 "Where are elephants found?"
"Elephants are so large that they are rarely lost."
Anonymous schoolchild. Quoted Cecil Hunt, HOWLERS

10 Elephants in the circus / Have aeons of weariness round their eyes / Yet they sit up / And show vast bellies to the children.
D. H. Lawrence, COLLECTED POEMS 1928

11 Did I ever tell you how I shot a wild elephant in my pyjamas? How he got into my pyjamas I'll never know. Getting his tusks off was quite a problem. In Alabama the Tuscaloosa.
Groucho Marx, ANIMAL CRACKERS *(film)*

EDWARD ELGAR

12 Elgar's A flat symphony is the musical equivalent of St. Pancras Station.
Sir Thomas Beecham. Quoted Neville Cardus, SIR THOMAS BEECHAM

13 Elgar's *Gerontius* has been rightly described by George Moore as holy water in a German beer barrel.
Sir Thomas Beecham. Quoted Lord Boothby, MY YESTERDAY, YOUR TOMORROW

T. S. ELIOT

14 As a poet Eliot could more easily achieve intensity than extension, and the same thing was true of his prose writing.
Bernard Bergonzi, T. S. ELIOT

15 How unpleasant to meet Mr. Eliot / With his features of clerical cut / And his brow so grim / And his mouth so prim / And his conversation so nicely / Restricted to What Precisely / And If and Perhaps and But.
T. S. Eliot, SELF PORTRAIT

16 Smell . . . was Eliot's special sense, his special delicacy.
Geoffrey Grigson, THE PRIVATE ART

QUEEN ELIZABETH II

17 It always frightens me that people should love her so much.
Queen Elizabeth the Queen Mother, of her daughter as a child

18 The Queen is a very pleasant middle to upper-class type of lady, with a talkative, retired Navy husband.
Malcolm Muggeridge, Saturday Evening Post

EMOTION

19 Lord Lundy from his earliest years / Was far too easily moved to tears.
Hilaire Belloc, CAUTIONARY TALES 1907

20 Amanda: I sort of melted like snow in the sunlight.
Elyot: That must have been an edifying spectacle.
Noël Coward, PRIVATE LIVES 1930

1 An intimate friend and a hated enemy have always been indispensable to my emotional life.
Sigmund Freud. Quoted Helen Walker Pinner, FREUD, HIS LIFE AND HIS MIND

2 What we feel and think and are is to a great extent determined by the state of our ductless glands and viscera.
Aldous Huxley, MUSIC AT NIGHT, *Meditation on El Greco* 1931

3 One of the effects of a safe and civilised life is an immense oversensitiveness which makes all the primary emotions seem somewhat disgusting.
George Orwell, COLLECTED ESSAYS 1968

4 She ran the gamut of the emotions from A to B.
Dorothy Parker, Life Magazine, *of Katherine Hepburn in* THE LAKE

5 Intellect is to emotion as our clothes are to our bodies; we could not very well have civilised life without clothes, but we would be in a poor way if we had only clothes without bodies.
A. N. Whitehead, DIALOGUES

6 He groaned slightly and winced, like Prometheus watching his vulture dropping in for lunch.
P. G. Wodehouse. Quoted R. Usborne, WODEHOUSE AT WORK 1961

7 It is so many years before one can believe enough in what one feels even to know what that feeling is.
W. B. Yeats, AUTOBIOGRAPHIES 1955

EMPIRE

8 The day of small nations has long passed away. The day of Empires has come.
Joseph Chamberlain. Speech, Birmingham 12 *May* 1904

9 The empires of the future are empires of the mind.
Winston Churchill. Address, Harvard University 1945

ENCOURAGEMENT

10 It is always pleasant to be urged to do something on the ground that one can do it well.
George Santayana, LETTERS

ENDEAVOUR

11 In such a heart as Robert Falcon Scott's it was human endeavour that mattered, not mere ambition to achieve.
Herbert G. Pouting, THE GREAT WHITE SOUTH

ENDURANCE

12 The manner in which one endures what must be endured is more important than the thing that must be endured.
Dean Acheson. Quoted Merle Miller, PLAIN SPEAKING: AN ORAL BIOGRAPHY OF HARRY S TRUMAN

ENEMY

13 If I have enemies — perhaps to have enemies is as great an honour as my friendships.
Stanley Baldwin. Speech at Unionist Conference 11 *Feb* 1924

14 You shall judge of a man by his foes as well as by his friends.
Joseph Conrad, LORD JIM 1900

15 One loves him for the enemies he has made.
Bernard Crick of A. J. P. Taylor, Sunday Times 9 *Nov* 1980

16 All enemies, except those fighting for the strictly limited food supply of a given territory, may be described as artificial enemies.
Aldous Huxley, BEYOND THE MEXIQUE BAY 1944

17 There is nothing ignoble in loving one's enemies; but much that is dangerous.
Bernard Levin, THE PENDULUM YEARS 1976

ENGLISH

18 That typically English characteristic for which there is no English name — *esprit de corps*.
Sir Frank Adcock

19 Think of what our nation stands for / Books from Boots and country lanes. / Free speech, free passes, class distinction, / Democracy and proper drains.
Sir John Betjeman, IN WESTMINSTER ABBEY 1940

20 Ever since Sherloc Holmes most Englishmen have been born with a detective novel attached to their umbilical cords.
Tristan Bisch, SECRET SERVICE UNMASKED

1 The English sent all their bores abroad and acquired the empire as a punishment.
Edward Bond, NARROW ROAD TO THE DEEP NORTH

2 No Englishman could pass for an American.
Heywood Brown, PIECES OF HATE 1922

3 It seems to me that you can go sauntering along for a certain period telling the English some interesting things about themselves, and then all at once it feels as if you have stepped on the prongs of a rake.
Patrick Campbell, LIFE IN THIN SLICES

4 The English never draw a line without blurring it.
Winston Churchill, House of Commons 16 *Nov* 1948

5 At twelve noon / The natives swoon / And no further work is done / But mad dogs and Englishmen / Go out in the noonday sun.
Noël Coward, MAD DOGS AND ENGLISHMEN

6 I have never met an Englishman who did not speak of his countrymen as if he was quite unlike them.
Pierre Daninos, MAJOR THOMPSON AND I

7 England is the single country where patriotism does not represent a threat or challenge to the rest of the world.
Wilhelm Dibelius, ENGLAND

8 It is said, I believe, that to behold the Englishman at his best one should watch him play tip and run.
Ronald Firbank, THE FLOWER BENEATH THE FOOT 1923

9 [An Englishman] must not express great joy or sorrow, or even open his mouth too wide when he talks — his pipe might fall out if he did.
E. M. Forster, ABINGER HARVEST 1936

10 The Englishman is unable to like anyone who cannot knock him down.
E. M. Forster. Quoted Raymond Mortimer, TRY ANYTHING ONCE

11 René Gimpel's definition of an English gentleman — a man with a passion for horses, playing with a ball, probably many a broken bone in his body and in his pocket a letter to *The Times*.
Gimpel fils, letter to The Times 31 *Jan* 1970

12 The Englishman never enjoys himself except for a noble purpose.
A. P. Herbert, UNCOMMON LAW 1935

13 The place was so English I wouldn't be surprised if the mice wore monocles.
Bob Hope, I OWE RUSSIA 1200 DOLLARS

14 This man looked English! . . . He *is* an Englishman, she decided with queer mounting excitement, for only an Englishman would have ridden so spirited a mount without the help of spurs.
Elizabeth Hoy, TO WIN A PARADISE

15 If it is good to have one foot in England it is still better, or at least as good, to have the other out of it.
Henry James. Quoted F. O. Mattheissen, THE JAMES FAMILY 1946

16 It will be said of this generation that it found England a land of beauty and left it a land of beauty spots.
C. E. M. Joad. Quoted Observer 31 *May* 1953

17 An Englishman's way of speaking absolutely classifies him. The moment he talks he makes some other Englishman despise him.
Alan Jay Lerner, MY FAIR LADY *(film)* 1956

18 England is only a little island where one cannot go far out of one's way.
Eric Linklater, POET'S PUB 1929

19 Here is one of the points about the planet which should be remembered; into every penetrable corner of it, and into most of the impenetrable corners, the English will penetrate.
Rose Macaulay, CREWE TRAIN 1926

20 The Englishman is naturally wasteful, especially of public money. It is a question of a blunted sense of life, a dullness towards a bright design, an apathy. Let us blame the climate for it; we pass, the climate remains.
John Masefield, SO LONG TO LEARN 1952

21 Be on your guard against an Englishman who speaks French perfectly; he is very likely to be a card-sharper or an attaché in the diplomatic service.
W. Somerset Maugham, THE SUMMING UP 1936

22 An Englishman, even if he is alone, forms an orderly queue of one.
George Mikes, HOW TO BE AN ALIEN 1946

23 When people say England, they sometimes mean Great Britain, sometimes the United Kingdom, sometimes the British Isles, — but never England.
George Mikes, HOW TO BE AN ALIEN 1946

1 Continental people have a sex life, the English have hot water bottles.
Id.

2 Englishmen know instinctively that what the world needs most is whatever is best for Great Britain.
Ogden Nash, ENGLAND EXPECTS

3 I always suspect Englishmen who admire Arabs, and who put on fancy dress when entertaining parties in Sussex.
Harold Nicolson. Reviewing WILFRED SCAWEN BLUNT, *by the Earl of Lytton*, Observer 11 *Jun* 1961

4 Remember that you are an Englishman and have consequently won first prize in the lottery of life.
Cecil Rhodes. Quoted Peter Ustinov, DEAR ME 1977

5 The English react to things slowly. This produces an effect of self-mastery or strength in repose. Their unhurried habit gives them time to stoke up the fire of decision.
Ranjee Shahani, Illustrated Weekly of India. *Quoted* News Review 23 *Oct* 1947

6 Do you think the laws of God will be suspended in favour of England because you were born in it?
George Bernard Shaw, HEARTBREAK HOUSE 1920

7 An Englishman thinks he is moral when he is only uncomfortable.
George Bernard Shaw, MAN AND SUPERMAN 1905

8 The Englishman's games have made him less fatalistic and as a result of the discipline of sport he will keep struggling even though his intellect would indicate his cause to be lost.
John R. Tunis, DEMOCRACY AND SPORT

9 You English are an extraordinary people. You think war is a joke. Yet you take this [*Chu Chin Chow*] seriously.
Unknown French Lady. Quoted Richard Prentis, John o'London's Weekly 4 *Apr* 1936

10 You never find an Englishman among the underdogs — except in England of course.
Evelyn Waugh, THE LOVED ONE 1948

ENJOYMENT

11 I'm all for rational enjoyment, and so forth, but I think a fellow makes himself conspicuous when he throws soft-boiled eggs at the electric fan.
P. G. Wodehouse, JEEVES AND THE UNBIDDEN GUEST

ENTERPRISE

12 Buying and selling securities on the Stock Exchange do not start new industries. Big business never starts anything new. It merely absorbs, consolidates and profits at the expense of others.
Franklin D. Roosevelt. Quoted Harold L. Ickes, MY TWELVE YEARS WITH F. D. R.

ENTERTAINMENT

13 What the mass media offer is not popular art, but entertainment which is intended to be consumed like food, forgotten, and replaced by a new dish.
W. H. Auden, THE DYER'S HAND 1962

14 Give the public what they want. Most people don't want works of art. They want cups of tea and donkey rides.
Duke of Bedford. Quoted David MacDonald, Saturday Evening Post 11 *Jul* 1959

15 [David N. Martin] received a telegram stating "Show stopped by flying ants." He is supposed to have replied by cable: "Book them for a further week."
Michael Bentine, THE LONG BANANA SKIN

16 There's no business like show business.
Irving Berlin, ANNIE GET YOUR GUN *(film)* 1946

17 Night clubs are places where the tables are reserved and the guests aren't.
Frank Caspar, American radio comedian 1942

18 I am interested in everything so long as it is well done. I would rather see a good juggler than a bad Hamlet.
C. B. Cochran, SECRETS OF A SHOWMAN

19 Comedy, like sodomy, is an unnatural act.
Marty Feldman, The Times 9 *Jun* 1969

20 We're an institution. And our staunchest supporters are the intellectuals — like the Queen Mother and Princess Margaret.
Bud Flanagan. Quoted in his obituary, Daily Express 21 *Oct* 1968

21 All my shows are great. Some of them are bad. But they are all great.
Sir Lew Grade. Quoted George Brook and Tony Lyons, Observer 6 *Sep* 1981

1 I've always felt England was a great place to work in. It's an island and the audience can't run very far.
Bob Hope, I OWE RUSSIA 1200 DOLLARS

2 To the music of Rimsky-Korsakoff / I could never take my corset off / And where are the sailors who would pay / To see me strip to Massenet.
Gypsy Rose Lee. Quoted N. Shapiro, AN ENCYCLOPEDIA OF QUOTATIONS ABOUT MUSIC

3 We are more popular than Jesus.
John Lennon, of the Beatles, in an interview in 1966

4 What else is the tale of Dick Whittington but a glorification of private enterprise and bourgeois ideals?
Observer. Quoted News Review 23 *Jan* 1947

5 The interval can be filled by a ballet *Six Who Pass While the Concrete Boils* in which half a dozen stocky Bryn Mawr girls in grey jerseys stride compulsively from one end of the stage to the other tugging at a veil. This symbolises the forces of water, sand and Portland cement at first refusing to work harmoniously, then uniting for the common good.
S. J. Perelman, CRAZY LIKE A FOX 1944

6 So Silk becomes a Ziegfeld dancer and she is quite a sensation with the dramatic critics on the night she opens because she dances with all her clothes on which is considered a very big novelty indeed.
Damon Runyon, MORE THAN SOMEWHAT, *Broadway Financier* 1937

7 A unique evening! I wouldn't have left a turn unstoned.
A. Wimperis. Quoted E. Short, FIFTY YEARS OF VAUDEVILLE

ENTHUSIASM

8 Enthusiasm without imagination tends to make a man a crank.
Benjamin C. Leeming, IMAGINATION

ENVIRONMENT

9 We are the children of our landscape; it dictates behaviour and even thought, in the measure to which we are responsive to it.
Lawrence Durrell, JUSTINE 1957

10 Dr. Karl Pearson has said that the influence of environment is "possibly not one tenth that of heredity". This is an absurdity. Shakespeare, born among the Esquimaux, could not have written ninety per cent of *Hamlet*.
G. A. Studdart-Kennedy, ENVIRONMENT 1928

ENVY

11 I go about looking at horses and cattle. They eat grass, make love, work when they have to, bear their young. I am sick with envy of them.
Sherwood Anderson, LETTERS 1953

12 Envy is everywhere / Who is without envy? And most people / Are unaware or unashamed of being envious.
T. S. Eliot, THE ELDER STATESMAN

13 There is a strong disposition in youth, from which some individuals never escape, to suppose that everyone else is having a more enjoyable time than we are ourselves.
Anthony Powell, A BUYER'S MARKET 1952

14 Beggars do not envy millionaires, though of course they will envy other beggars who are more successful.
Bertrand Russell, THE CONQUEST OF HAPPINESS 1930

15 The man with toothache thinks everyone happy whose teeth are sound.
George Bernard Shaw, MAN AND SUPERMAN 1905

EPIDEMIC

16 The Black Death started under the armpits and spread all over Europe.
Schoolboy howler. Quoted Christopher Matthews, BBC Radio 4, *Quote Unquote* 17 *Jul* 1980

EPIGRAM

17 An epigram is only another word for a platitude on its night out.
Philip Guedella, speech to Cambridge Union.

18 *Epigram:* a wisecrack that played Carnegie Hall.
Oscar Levant, Coronet magazine, *Sep* 1968

19 Anyone can tell the truth but only very few of us can make epigrams.
W. Somerset Maugham, A WRITER'S NOTEBOOK 1949

1 Such is epigram, requiring / Wit, occasion, and good luck.
Christopher Morley, The Epigram

EPITAPH

2 Let us honour if we can / The vertical man / Though we value none / But the horizontal one.
W. H. Auden, EPIGRAPH FOR POEMS 1930

3 I've played everything but the harp.
Lionel Barrymore on being asked what words he would like on his tombstone

4 "What would you like your epitaph to be?" "I'll be right back."
Johnny Carson at a press conference. Quoted Kenneth Tynan, New Yorker 20 Feb 1978

5 The best you can expect is a few daffodils in a jam-jar and a rough-hewn stone bearing the legend "He came and he went."
Tony Hancock, BBC Radio, *Hancock's Half Hour* 1964

6 At last God caught his eye.
Harry Secombe, Punch, *epitaph for a head waiter* 17 May 1962

JACOB EPSTEIN

7 They are a form of statuary which no careful father would wish his daughter, or no discerning young man his fiancée, to see.
Evening Standard and St. James Gazette 1908

8 The Epstein . . . makes me feel physically sick. The wretched woman has two sets of breasts and a hip joint like a merrythought.
John Galsworthy

EQUALITY

9 From the point of view of sexual morality the aeroplane is valuable in war in that it destroys men and women in equal numbers.
Ernest William Barnes (Bishop of Birmingham), RISE OF CHRISTIANITY

10 The social process requires the standardisation of man, and this standardisation is called equality.
Erich Fromm, THE ART OF LOVING 1956

11 Equality is a mortuary word.
Christopher Fry, VENUS OBSERVED 1950

12 We clamour for equality chiefly in matters in which we ourselves cannot hope to obtain excellence.
Eric Hoffer, THE PASSIONATE STATE OF MIND 1954

13 That all men are equal is a proposition to which, in ordinary times, no sane individual has ever given his assent.
Aldous Huxley, PROPER STUDIES 1927

14 Be careful that mindless clichés about élitism and the cult of personality are not back to front ways of attacking excellence.
Prof. J. Jones in a lecture at Oxford 19 Feb 1979

15 All men are created equal — until they prove otherwise.
Ben Kuroki, New York Herald Tribune 4 Nov 1945

16 No man who says "I am as good as you" believes it. The St. Bernard never says it to the toy dog, nor the scholar to the dunce, nor the employable to the bum, nor the pretty woman to the plain. The claim to equality is made only by those who feel themselves to be in some way inferior.
C. S. Lewis, SCREWTAPE PROPOSES A TOAST

17 All animals are equal, but some animals are more equal than others.
George Orwell, ANIMAL FARM 1945

18 The idea of taking away property from other people has much more appeal if one has none of one's own.
Philip, Duke of Edinburgh, A QUESTION OF BALANCE 1982

19 True education makes for inequality; the inequality of individuality, the inequality of success; the glorious inequality of talent, of genius; for inequality, not mediocrity, individual superiority, not standardisation, is the measure of progress in the world.
Felix E. Schelling, PEDAGOGICALLY SPEAKING

EROTICISM

20 — the rather refined young man who preferred sex dreams to visiting brothels because he met a much nicer type of girl that way.
Vivian Mercier, PERSPECTIVES ON PORNOGRAPHY

ESCAPE

1 We don't even talk of an escape from Bristol prison. The word is dematerialisation.
Lord Mancroft. Quoted Observer 5 *Aug* 1956

ETERNITY

2 We have no guarantee that the afterlife will be any less exasperating than this one, have we?
Noël Coward, BLITHE SPIRIT 1941

3 Eternity is not something that begins after you are dead. It is going on all the time. We are in it now.
Charlotte P. Gilman, THE FORERUNNER

4 Eternity's a terrible thought. I mean, where's it going to end?
Tom Stoppard, ROSENCRANTZ AND GUILDENSTERN ARE DEAD 1967

ETHICS

5 The inescapable though often dodged fact is that anything, absolutely anything, which may be used to do good may be used to do harm, or worse.
J. W. Lambert, Sunday Times 26 *Feb* 1978

6 I can only say that while my own opinions as to ethics do not satisfy me, other people's satisfy me still less.
Bertrand Russell, REPLY TO MY CRITICS

7 The first step in the evolution of ethics is a sense of solidarity with other human beings.
Albert Schweitzer, THE TEACHING OF REVERENCE FOR LIFE

ETIQUETTE

8 Whatever your Uncle Bob's failures were, he never tucked his serviette into his dickie.
Noël Coward, THE CAFÉ DE LA PAIX

9 Etiquette can be at the same time a means of approaching people and of staying clear of them.
David Riesman, THE LONELY CROWD 1950

10 Never speak loudly unless the house is on fire.
H. W. Thompson, BODY, BOOTS AND BREECHES

11 He found that a fork in his inexperienced hand was an instrument of chase rather than capture.
H. G. Wells, KIPPS 1905

12 When a girl lit up a cigarette after the soup her hostess said icily "We seem to have finished" and led the entire party from the room. That was the end of the dinner.
Katherine Whitehorn, Observer 27 *Jul* 1980

EUPHEMISM

13 You must not use the word 'poor'. They are described as 'the lower income group'.
Winston Churchill. Speech, Cardiff 8 *Feb* 1950

14 Those extraordinary Australian euphemisms for vomiting — parking the tiger, yodelling on the lawn, the technicolor yawn, the liquid laugh.
Barry Humphries. Quoted FROM FRINGE TO FLYING CIRCUS 1981

15 Any euphemism ceases to be euphemistic after a time and the true meaning begins to show through. It is a losing game but we keep on trying.
Joseph Wood Krutch, IF YOU DON'T MIND MY SAYING SO 1964

EUTHANASIA

16 It is easier to accept the principle of euthanasia than to devise satisfactory plans for putting it into operation.
Lord Devlin. Quoted Observer 23 *Aug* 1981

EVENING

17 It is in this unearthly first hour of twilight that earth's almost agonised livingness is felt. This hour is so dreadful to some people that they hurry indoors and turn on the lights.
Elizabeth Bowen, THE DEATH OF THE HEART 1938

18 An evening hush, broken by humming wings.
Rupert Brooke, THE BUSY HEART

19 When the evening is spread out against the sky / Like a patient etherised upon a table.
T. S. Eliot, LOVE SONG OF J. ALFRED PRUFROCK 1915

20 Homeward, and brings the sailor home from sea / The typist home at teatime.
T. S. Eliot, THE WASTE LAND 1922

EVENT

21 People to whom nothing has ever happened / Cannot understand the unimportance of words.
T. S. Eliot, THE FAMILY RENUNION 1939

EVIL

1 Good can imagine Evil; but Evil cannot
imagine Good
W. H. Auden, A CERTAIN WORLD

2 Evil is unspectacular and always human /
And shares our bed and eats at our own
table.
W. H. Auden, HERMAN MELVILLE

3 A belief in a supernatural source of evil is not
necessary; men alone are quite capable of
every sort of wickedness.
Joseph Conrad, UNDER WESTERN EYES
1911

4 He who passively accepts evil is as much
involved in it as he who helps to perpetrate
it.
Martin Luther King, STRIDE TOWARDS
FREEDOM 1958

5 Theologists are always bothering about the
origin of evil, but evil is just natural
behaviour; it's the origin of human goodness that is really so extraordinary and
inexplicable.
Kingsley Martin

6 There is no explanation for evil. It must be
looked upon as a necessary part of the order
of the universe. To ignore it is childish, to
bewail it senseless.
W. Somerset Maugham, THE SUMMING UP
1938

7 Between two evils I always pick the one I
have never tried before.
Mae West, KLONDIKE ANNIE *(film)*

EVOLUTION

8 Does Nature care in the least whether we
evolve or not? Her instincts are for the
gratification of hunger and sex, the destruction of rivals and the protection of offspring. What monster first slipped in the
idea of progress?
Cyril Connolly, THE UNQUIET GRAVE 1945

9 It isn't easy to see how the first stages in the
development of certain organs could be of
survival value. Evolution remains a
hypothesis.
*J. N. Hawthorne (Professor of Biochemis-
try, Nottingham),* QUESTIONS OF SCIENCE
AND FAITH

10 Even without the aid of artificial gadgetry
human beings are able to survive and
flourish in forests and in deserts, in the
tropics and the Arctic . . . no other natural
species has this kind of flexibility. So if man
evolved from his predecessors by natural
selection associated with adaptation to a
specialised environment, what kind of
environment was that?
*Sir Edmund Leach, address to British
Association* 2 *Sep* 1981

11 The death of the failure. This is the path by
which the beast rose to manhood, by which
man goes on to higher things.
H. G. Wells, THE SLEEPER WAKES 1911

12 Descended from the apes? My dear, we
will hope it is not true. But if it is, let us pray
that it may not become generally known.
*Wife of a canon of Worcester Cathedral, on
hearing the theory of evolution. Quoted F.
Ashley Montagu,* MAN'S MOST DANGEROUS
MYTH, *The Fallacy of Race*

13 We are all of us guinea-pigs in the
laboratory of God. Humanity is just a work
in progress.
Tennessee Williams, CAMINO REAL 1953

EXAGGERATION

14 An exaggeration is a truth that has lost its
temper.
Kahil Gibran, THOUGHTS AND MEDITAT-
IONS 1961

EXAMINATION

15 I am surprised that in my later life I should
have become so experienced in taking
degrees when as a schoolboy I was so bad
at passing examinations. In fact one might
almost say that no one ever passed so few
examinations and received so many
degrees.
Winston Churchill. Quoted Colin Coote, A
CHURCHILL READER

16 Examinations — nature's laxative.
*Graffito, City of London Polytechnic.
Quoted Nigel Rees,* GRAFFITI 2

17 Examinations are harmless when the
examinee is indifferent to their result, but
as soon as they matter they begin to distort
his attitude to education and to conceal its
purpose.
Sir Richard Livingstone, ON EDUCATION

18 The defect in the intelligence test is that
high marks are gained by those who
subsequently prove to be practically illiterate. So much time has been spent in
studying the art of being tested that the

candidate has rarely had time for anything else.
C. Northcote Parkinson, PARKINSON'S LAW 1957

1 Do not on any account attempt to write on both sides of the paper at once.
W. C. Sellar and R. J. Yeatman, 1066 AND ALL THAT 1930

2 Examinations, thought by the progressives of the last century to be a defence against privilege, are now denounced in the consultations of school-teachers as introducing an unhealthy spirit of competition into education.
Evelyn Waugh, commentary for T. A. MacInerys, THE PRIVATE MAN

EXAMPLE

3 Example moves the world more than doctrine.
Henry Miller, THE COSMOLOGICAL EYE 1934

EXCESS

4 A poet always has too many words in his vocabulary, a painter too many colours in his palette, a musician too many notes on his keyboard.
Jean Cocteau. Quoted Nat Shapiro, ENCYCLOPEDIA OF QUOTATIONS ABOUT MUSIC

5 It would be possible to rob even a healthy beast of prey of its voraciousness if it were possible, with the aid of a whip, to force the beast to devour continuously, even when it was not hungry.
Albert Einstein, AUTOBIOGRAPHY

6 An unrestricted satisfaction of every need presents itself as the most enticing method of conducting one's life, but it means putting enjoyment before caution, and soon brings its own punishment.
Sigmund Freud, CIVILISATION AND ITS DISCONTENTS 1930

7 Excess on occasion is exhilarating. It prevents moderation from acquiring the deadening effect of habit.
W. Somerset Maugham, THE SUMMING UP 1938

EXCUSE

8 I was bold enough to decline an invitation to *Hamlet* on the grounds that I already knew who won.
Quentin Crisp, THE NAKED CIVIL SERVANT

9 Several excuses are always less convincing than one.
Aldous Huxley, POINT COUNTER POINT 1934

10 I'm sorry I'm late. Someone stole my hoop so I had to walk here.
Ted Kavanagh, BBC Radio, *ITMA*

11 A Shakespearian exit. (I go to look upon a hedge.)
E. Arnot Robertson, FOUR FRIGHTENED PEOPLE 1931

EXERCISE

12 Exercise is bunk. If you are healthy you don't need it, if you are sick you shouldn't take it.
Henry Ford

13 It was Gloria Bristol [Hollywood beauty specialist] who put the Duchess of Windsor wise to the benefits of standing on her head.
Sheila Graham. Quoted News Review 16 *Jan* 1947

14 Little good can come of regular exercise which reduces life to a monotonous machine.
E. V. Knox, GORGEOUS TIMES

15 I have always said that exercise is a short cut to the cemetery.
John Mortimer, RUMPOLE OF THE BAILEY 1978

16 The beneficent effects of the regular quarter-hour's exercise before breakfast is more than offset by the mental wear-and-tear in getting out of bed fifteen minutes earlier than one otherwise would.
Simeon Strunsky, THE PATIENT OBSERVER

EXISTENCE

17 Common sense tells us that our existence is but a brief crack of light between two eternities of darkness.
Vladimir Nabokov, SPEAK, MEMORY 1967

EXPEDIENCY

18 No man is justified in doing evil on the ground of expediency.
Theodore Roosevelt, THE STRENUOUS LIFE 1900

EXPENDITURE

19 Expenditure rises to meet income. Individual expenditure not only rises to meet income but tends to surpass it.
C. Northcote Parkinson, THE LAW AND THE PROFITS

EXPERIENCE

1 One should try everything once, except folk dancing and incest.
Arnold Bax, FAREWELL TO MY YOUTH

2 You will think me lamentably crude; my experience of life has been drawn from life itself.
Max Beerbohm, ZULEIKA DOBSON 1911

3 There is no unique image of our whole world of experience.
Niels Bohr

4 You cannot acquire experience by making experiments. You cannot create experience. You must undergo it.
Albert Camus, NOTEBOOKS 1935–1942

5 You have not had thirty years of experience. You have had one year's experience thirty times.
J. L. Carr, THE HARPOLE REPORT

6 No one over thirty-five is worth meeting who has not something to teach us, something more than we could learn for ourselves, from a book.
Cyril Connolly, THE UNQUIET GRAVE 1945

7 What one has not experienced one will never understand in print.
Isadora Duncan, MY LIFE 1927

8 We had the experience but missed the meaning / And approach to the meaning restores the experience / In a different form, beyond any meaning / We can assign to happiness.
T. S. Eliot, FOUR QUARTETS 1942

9 What a man knows he has by experience / But what a man is precedes experience.
Christopher Fry, CURTMANTLE 1961

10 The most important lesson is to understand life, not to make *a priori* judgments about it.
David Garnett, GREAT FRIENDS

11 We cannot afford to forget any experiences even the most painful.
Dag Hammarskjöld, MARKINGS 1964

12 Experience is never limited, and it is never complete; it is an immense sensibility, a kind of huge spider-web of the finest silk threads suspended in the chamber of consciousness, and catching every airborne particle in its tissue.
Henry James, THE ART OF FICTION 1934

13 Welcome, O life! I go to encounter for the millionth time the reality of experience and to forge in the smithy of my soul the uncreated conscience of my race.
James Joyce, A PORTRAIT OF THE ARTIST AS A YOUNG MAN 1916

14 Mythology, religion and philosophy are alike in that each has as its function the interpretation of experience in terms which have human value.
Joseph Wood Krutch, THE MODERN TEMPER 1929

15 Judgement comes from experience — and experience comes from bad judgement.
Brig. Gen. J. W. Lang

16 How different the new order would be if we could consult the veteran instead of the politician.
Henry Miller, THE WISDOM OF THE HEART 1941

17 Experience is a fruit-tree fruitless / Experience is a shoe-tree bootless. / For sterile wearience and drearience / Depend, my boy, upon experience.
Ogden Nash, EXPERIENCE TO LET

18 When I was young I was told "You'll see when you are fifty". I am fifty and I haven't seen a thing.
Erik Satie. Quoted Pierre-Daniel Templier, ERIK SATIE

19 Men are wise in proportion, not to their experience, but to their capacity for experience.
George Bernard Shaw, MAN AND SUPERMAN 1905

20 Experience is the comb life brings you after you have lost your hair.
Judith Stern. Quoted BBC Radio 4, *Quote Unquote*

21 What a man knows at 50 which he didn't know at 20 is, for the most part, incommunicable.
Adlai Stevenson

22 We live in reference to past experience and not to future events, however inevitable.
H. G. Wells, MIND AT THE END OF ITS TETHER 1946

EXPERIMENT

23 One disadvantage of being a hog is that at any moment some blundering fool may try to make a silk purse out of your wife's ear.
Beachcomber (J. B. Morton), Daily Express, *By the Way*

1 There is always more chance of hitting upon something valuable when you aren't too sure what you want to hit upon.
A. N. Whitehead, DIALOGUES

EXPERT

2 An expert is a man who has made all the mistakes that can be made in a very narrow field.
Niels Bohr. Quoted A. L. Mackay, THE HARVEST OF A QUIET EYE

3 An expert is one who knows more and more about less and less.
Nicholas Murray Butler

4 An expert is someone who knows some of the worst mistakes that can be made in his subject, and how to avoid them.
Werner Heisenberg, PHYSICS AND BEYOND

5 [Experts are] pundits of the technological age who can't put a fresh ribbon in their typewriters, and resounding authorities on the problems of the farmer who has never grown a geranium in a pot.
Westbrook Pegler. Quoted Alistair Cooke, BBC Radio 4, *Letter from America* 29 *Jun* 1969

6 Even when all the experts agree, they may well be mistaken.
Bertrand Russell, AUTOBIOGRAPHY 1967

EXPLANATION

7 A little inaccuracy sometimes saves tons of explanation.
Saki, THE SQUARE EGG

EXPLOITATION

8 When you are skinning your customers you should leave some skin on to grow, so that you can skin them again.
Nikita Khrushchev. Speech to British Industrialists, May 1961

9 Round all the Arts there is a vast exploitation fringe.
J. B. Priestley. Quoted News Review 12 *Dec* 1946

EXPLORATION

10 Polar exploration is at once the cleanest and most isolated way of having a bad time which has been devised.
Apsley Cherry-Gerard, THE WORST JOURNEY IN THE WORLD

EXPRESSION

11 Ethel pulled her hair and looked very sneery.
Daisy Ashford (aged 9), THE YOUNG VISITERS 1919

12 A short man with a hard red face like a book of rules.
Anthony Carson, New Statesman 22 *Nov* 1964

13 She looks at other women as though she would inhale them.
Ronald Firbank, THE FLOWER BENEATH THE FOOT 1923

14 I do not think I have ever seen a nastier looking man. Under the black hat, when I had first seen them, the eyes were those of an unsuccessful rapist.
Ernest Hemingway of (Percy) Wyndham Lewis, A MOVEABLE FEAST 1964

15 When I look into a girl's eyes I can tell just what she thinks of me. It's pretty depressing.
Bob Hope, MY FAVOURITE SPY (*film*)

16 He hung his mouth open as though he were an animal in a zoo inviting buns.
(Percy) Wyndham Lewis of Ford Maddox Ford, RUDE ASSIGNMENT 1950

EXTRAVAGANCE

17 He [Lord Birkenhead] had no idea of the value of money. He refused to attend to his income tax returns and incurred an enormous overdraft. When remonstrated with he would buy another car or a new motor launch.
2nd Earl of Birkenhead, LIFE OF LORD BIRKENHEAD

18 A policy of buying a biscuit early in the morning and walking about all day looking for a dog to give it to.
Winston Churchill, House of Commons, Budget debate 1929

19 We're too poor to economise. Economy is a luxury: our only salvation is extravagance.
F. Scott Fitzgerald. Quoted Paul Sann, THE LAWLESS DECADE

20 She not only worships the Golden Calf, she barbecues it for lunch.
Oscar Levant, of Zsa-Zsa Gabor

21 My candle burns at both ends; / It will not last the night / But oh my foes, and oh my friends / It gives a lovely light.
Edna St. Vincent Millay, A FEW FIGS FROM THISTLES 1923

1 Tories as well as Socialists should question the wisdom of granting to the three-year old Prince Charles an income of £10,000. It is never good for a small boy to have too much money to spend.
Daily Telegraph

2 It takes only one gramme of explosive to kill a man, so why waste five tons.
Solly Zuckerman, FROM APES TO WARLORDS

EYE

3 Eyes the colour of a poison bottle.
Dannie Abse, GOLDERS GREEN, *The French Master*

4 Your eyes are like bluebells dipped in hot brilliantine.
Vivian Ellis and Clifford Gray, MR. CINDERS *(musical)* 1929

5 Her eyes are like I do not know what, except that they are one hundred per cent eyes in every respect.
Damon Runyon, GUYS AND DOLLS 1932

6 Her eyes are big, and as black as doughnuts, and she has a look in them that somehow makes me think she may know more than she lets on, which I afterwards find out is very true indeed.
Id.

F

FACE

1 I do not say that I was ever what is called 'plain' but I have the sort of face that bores me when I see it on other people.
Margot Asquith, Countess of Oxford, Lilliput 1938

2 My face looks like a wedding cake that has been left out in the rain.
W. H. Auden. Quoted Humphrey Carpenter, AUDEN, A BIOGRAPHY

3 After a certain age every man is responsible for his face.
Albert Camus, THE FALL 1956

4 A blank helpless sort of face, rather like a rose just before you drench it with DDT.
John Carey, of a photograph of Diana Cooper, Sunday Times 20 *Sep* 1981

5 Her face returned to childhood because it wore that expression of inhuman innocence, of angelic hardness which ennobles children's faces.
Colette, THE OTHER ONE

6 What will this face be like twenty years from now? At the moment it isn't so much a face as a pre-face.
Noël Coward, of a photograph of Truman Capote. Quoted William Marchant, THE PRIVILEGE OF HIS COMPANY 1980

7 . . . that half-melted vanilla face.
Brad Darrack, of Elvis Presley, Life 1974

8 Glenda Jackson has a face to launch a thousand dredgers.
Jack De Manio. Quoted Diana Rigg, NO TURN UNSTONED 1982

9 Not so much a face as part of her person that she happened to leave uncovered so that her friends might recognise her.
E. V. Lucas, THE OLDEST JOKE

10 Faces like buildings, are very much the product of their times. Prewar faces don't look like postwar faces.
David Mendel, Observer 21 *Jan* 1979

11 He had a face, even in his twenties, which looked as though he had rented it on a long lease and had lived in it so long he didn't want to move out.
David Niven, of George Sanders, BRING ON THE EMPTY HORSES

12 At fifty everyone has the face he deserves.
George Orwell, last entry in his notebook

13 He had a queer, puckered, grimacing face as if he had been born in blazing sunshine and had never got over it.
Reginald Pound, THEIR MOODS AND MINE 1935

14 She had one of those faces to which distance . . . gives form and outline and which, seen close at hand, dissolve back into dust.
Marcel Proust, REMEMBRANCE OF THINGS PAST 1913–1927

15 The human face is indeed like the faces of the God of some oriental theogony, a whole cluster of faces, crowded together but on different surfaces so that one does not see them all at once.
Id.

16 A woman whose face looked as if it had been made of sugar and someone had licked it.
George Bernard Shaw of Isadora Duncan. Quoted Hesketh Pearson, BERNARD SHAW 1961

17 He had a face that faintly resembled a large wad of cotton wool.
Joseph von Sternberg of Charles Laughton

18 He has features that always look slightly (if he will forgive me) as though he had been photographed through a fish-eye lens.
Paul Vaughan of Dr. Jonathan Miller, Radio Times 17 *Feb* 1979

19 A face like a carving abandoned as altogether too unpromising for completion.
H. G. Wells, FOOD OF THE GODS 1904

20 Time had removed the hair from the top of his head and distributed a small dividend of

plunder in little bunches carelessly and impartially over the rest of his features.
H. G. Wells, HISTORY OF MR. POLLY 1910

1 He had the face of a saint but he had rendered this generally acceptable by growing side-whiskers.
H. G. Wells, THE LAST TRUMP

FACT

2 Realities are less dangerous than fancies. Fact-finding is more important than fault-finding.
Carl Lotus Becker, PROGRESS AND POWER

3 The trouble with facts is that there are so many of them.
Samuel McChord Crothers, THE GENTLE READER

4 Facts are only the material of thought.
Ernest Dimnet, THE ART OF THINKING 1928

5 You can't alter facts by filming them over with dead romances.
John Drinkwater, MARY STUART 1921

6 Facts do not cease to exist because they are ignored.
Aldous Huxley, A NOTE ON DOGMA

7 Facts are ventriloquists' dummies. Sitting on a wise man's knee they may be made to utter words of wisdom; elsewhere they say nothing or talk nonsense.
Aldous Huxley, TIME MUST HAVE A STOP 1944

FAILURE

8 The worst of failure of this kind is that it spoils the market for more competent performers.
James Agate, of the bungled attempt to assassinate Hitler, EGO 7 21 *Jul* 1944

9 In a game, just losing is almost as satisfying — in life the loser's score is always zero.
W. H. Auden, THE DYER'S HAND 1962

10 I find failure endearing, don't you?
Max Beerbohm. Quoted S. N. Behren, CONVERSATIONS WITH MAX 1960

11 There is much to be said for failure. It is more interesting than success.
Max Beerbohm, MAINLY ON THE AIR 1946

12 Meet success like a gentleman and disaster like a man.
Lord Birkenhead

13 He was totally used to failure and he did not easily resign himself to a change of regime.
Jorge Louis Borges, FICCIONES

14 The world is made up of people who never quite get into the first team and who just miss the prizes at the flower show.
Jacob Bronowski, THE FACE OF VIOLENCE

15 Everything works out for the best. Even failure.
Gp Captain Leonard Cheshire, THE FACE OF VICTORY

16 If the failures of this world could realise how desperate half the present-day geniuses once felt, they would take heart and try again.
Fay Compton, MEMOIRS

17 I'm a connoisseur of failure. I can smell it, roll it round my mouth, tell you the vintage and the side of the hill that grew it.
Giles Cooper, UNMAN, WITTERING AND ZIGO (*radio play*)

18 Failure must be but a challenge to others.
Amelia Earhart, LAST FIGHT

19 He was a self-made man who owed his lack of success to nobody.
Joseph Heller, CATCH 22 1961

20 Failure is always more attractive than success.
Anthony Howard, Observer, *Labour's Lost Leader* 21 *Oct* 1979

21 His failures are priceless experiences in that they not only open up the way to a deeper truth, but force him to change his views and methods.
Carl Jung, MODERN MAN IN SEARCH OF HIS SOUL 1933

22 There is something distinguished about even his [Eugene O'Neill] failures; they sink not trivially but with a certain air of majesty, like a great ship, its flags flying, full of holes.
George Jean Nathan, AMERICAN DRAMA AND ITS CRITICS (*edited Alan S. Downs*)

23 A living failure is better than a dead masterpiece.
George Bernard Shaw, THE ADVENTURES OF THE BLACK GIRL IN HER SEARCH FOR GOD

24 He [Senator W. E. Borah] was always winding himself up, but never struck twelve.
John Chalmers Vinson, WILLIAM E. BORAH AND THE OUTLAWING OF WAR

FAITH

1 I do not pretend to see light, but I do see gleams and I know I am right to follow those gleams.
Father Andrew, LIFE AND LETTERS

2 I am one of those who would rather sink with faith than swim without it.
Stanley Baldwin. Speech, Leeds 12 Oct 1923

3 Faith is belief without evidence in what is told by one who speaks without knowledge of things without parallel.
Ambrose Bierce, THE DEVIL'S DICTIONARY 1906

4 It has been said that faith can move mountains, but no one has seen it done, save by the faith that man has in himself, in the steam shovels and the dynamite he has invented in the face of a hostile Nature.
Louis Bromfield, THE STRANGE CASE OF MISS ANNIE SPRAGG 1928

5 One may not doubt that, somehow, good / Shall come of water and of mud. / And, sure, the reverent eye must see / A purpose in liquidity.
Rupert Brooke, HEAVEN 1913

6 You can do very little with faith, but you can do nothing without it.
Samuel Butler, NOTEBOOKS 1912

7 We derive our inspiration from God, but we are grateful to *The Times* for the strengthening of our convictions.
Bishop of Carlisle. Speech to a diocesan conference

8 Faith has need of the whole truth.
Pierre Teilhard de Chardin, THE APPEARANCE OF MAN

9 No faith is our own that we have not arduously won.
Havelock Ellis, THE DANCE OF LIFE 1923

10 The contradictions of the Old Testament mean that with a little effort anyone can find a faith that accords with his preferences and a moral code that is agreeable to his tastes, even if fairly depraved.
J. K. Galbraith, ECONOMICS PEACE AND LAUGHTER

11 In spite of his faith in one medicine for many unseen and unknown diseases he (the Englishman) cannot accept miracles; he burks at the infallibility of the Pope but unquestioningly accepts the infallibility of the pill "just as much as will fit on a threepenny piece" instead of as many angels as will stand on the point of a needle.
Oliver St. John Gogarty, AS I WAS GOING DOWN SACKVILLE STREET 1937

12 If you have abandoned one faith, do not abandon all faith. There is always an alternative to the faith we lose. Or is it the same faith under another mask?
Graham Greene, THE COMEDIANS 1966

13 Where there is the necessary technical skill to move mountains there is no need for the faith that moves mountains.
Eric Hoffer, THE PASSIONATE STATE OF MIND 1954

14 Faith in a holy cause is to a considerable extent a substitute for the lost faith in ourselves.
Eric Hoffer, THE TRUE BELIEVER 1951

15 A faith cannot be a faith against but *for*.
Archibald MacLeish, Survey Graphic, *Feb* 1941

16 . . . an illogical belief in the occurrence of the improbable.
H. L. Mencken, PREJUDICES 1922

17 I respect faith, but doubt is what gets you an education.
Wilson Mizner

18 Nothing true or beautiful or good makes complete sense in any immediate context of history; therefore we must be saved by faith.
Reinhold Niebuhr, THE IRONY OF AMERICAN HISTORY 1952

19 Faith is a quality which the scientist cannot dispense with.
Max Planck, WHERE IS SCIENCE GOING? 1932

20 It is at night that faith in light is admirable.
Edmond Rostand, CHANTICLEER 1907

21 Faith, even when profound, is never complete.
Jean-Paul Sartre, WORDS 1964

22 I do not believe I know anything about faith. Jesus is my God. I don't think I have any faith but that. But I have a love for men; somewhere in me I have love. I hang on to that.
Rev. H. R. L. Sheppard, IMPATIENCE OF A PARSON 1929

23 Faith which does not doubt is dead faith.
Miguel de Unamuno, THE AGONY OF CHRISTIANITY

1 People are going mad and talking balls to psychiatrists not because of accidents to the chamberpot in the nursery but because there is no logical structure to their beliefs.
Evelyn Waugh, letter to John Betjeman 22 *Dec* 1946

2 Such lapses from knowledge to faith are perhaps necessary that human heroism may be possible.
H. G. Wells, MR. BRITLING SEES IT THROUGH 1946

3 I am more harassed by doubt, insecurity, ambivalence and rebelliousness than ever, and to be once more in St. Peter's boat is to be subject to such violent seasickness that every few months I am tempted to throw myself overboard.
Antonia White, THE HOUND AND THE FALCON

FALSENESS

4 That which has been believed by everyone, always and everywhere, has every chance of being false.
Paul Valéry, TELQUEL 1943

FAME

5 There is no future in being an ordinary person.
Susan Mary Alsop on BBC Radio 4

6 I find in London I am getting known by sight. I saw two very rough-looking men on the pavement the other day and one said to the other "That's the old bloke".
Stanley Baldwin. Speech, Worcester 10 *Aug* 1926

7 A friend of mine once said to me "Everybody is famous for something, and you are famous for living opposite Bernard Shaw."
J. M. Barrie, Presidential address to the Society of Authors 28 *Nov* 1928

8 Fame always brings loneliness. Success is as ice cold and lonely as the north pole.
Vicki Baum, GRAND HOTEL

9 It took me fifteen years to discover I had no talent for writing but I couldn't give it up because by that time I was too famous.
Robert Benchley, CHIPS OFF THE OLD BENCHLEY 1949

10 The celebrity is a person who is known for his well-knownness.
Daniel Boorstin, THE IMAGE 1962

11 A sign of a celebrity is often that his name is worth more than his services.
Id.

12 There is a lot to be said for not being known to the readers of the *Daily Mirror*.
Anthony Burgess, INSIDE MR. ENDERBY 1966

13 Fame is being asked to sign your autograph on the back of a cigarette packet.
Billy Connolly

14 We like to appear in the newspapers, so long as we are in the right column.
T. S. Eliot, THE FAMILY REUNION 1939

15 Once you're dead you're made for life.
Jimmy Hendricks

16 Fame is delightful, but as collateral it does not rank high.
Elbert Hubbard, EPIGRAMS 1915

17 Those who are created by publicity will eventually be destroyed by it.
Bernard Levin, THE PENDULUM YEARS 1976

18 Fame, like a drunkard, consumes the house of the soul.
Malcolm Lowry, of the reception given to UNDER THE VOLCANO 1947

19 It is strange how the memory of a man may float to posterity on what he would have himself regarded as the most trifling of his works.
Sir William Osler, APHORISMS

20 In opera, as with any performing art, to be in great demand and to command high fees you must be good of course, but you must also be famous. The two are different things.
Luciano Pavarotti, AUTOBIOGRAPHY

21 The transient nature of television fame was well illustrated when I was buying a ticket for the Motor Show. The ticket-seller looked at me closely and said: "Aren't you what's 'is name?". "Yes," I said. "I thought you were." she said.
Michael Pertwee, NAME DROPPING

22 There is no second money in the hall of fame. Take the case of Methuselah's grandpa, Jared. He lived to be 962 years old — only seven years younger than his illustrious grandson. That wasn't good enough; he remains to this day unknown, unhonoured and unsung.
M. Pitkin

23 If I was in life for fame and fortune I'd be in the movies or as Whistler said, jump off

Westminster Bridge with fireworks in my pockets.
John Romer, BBC 2 TV, *Romer's Egypt* 4 Sep 1981

1 In the future, everyone will be famous for 15 minutes.
Andy Warhol

FAMILIARITY

2 There is probably nothing like living together for blending people to each other.
Ivy Compton-Burnett, MOTHER AND SON 1955

3 Familiar things happen, and mankind does not bother about them. It requires a very unusual mind to undertake the analysis of the obvious.
A. N. Whitehead, SCIENCE AND THE MODERN WORLD 1925

FAMILY

4 I was the seventh of nine children. When you come from that far down you have to struggle to survive.
Robert F. Kennedy. Quoted B. G. Clinch, THE KENNEDY NEUROSIS

5 Far from being the basis of the good society, the family, with its narrow privacy and tawdry secrets, is the source of all our discontents.
Sir Edmund Leach, BBC Reith Lectures 1967

6 However much you dislike a relation, and whatever ill you may yourself say of him, you do not like others to say anything which shows him in a ridiculous or objectionable light; since the discredit thrown on your relation reflects upon yourself and wounds your vanity.
W. Somerset Maugham, A WRITER'S NOTEBOOK 1949

7 Every man sees in his relations, and especially in his cousins, a series of grotesque caricatures of himself.
H. L. Mencken, PREJUDICES 1919

8 The secret of neurosis is to be found in the family battle of wills to see who can refuse longest to help wash the dishes. The sink is the great symbol of the bloodiness of family life. All life is bad but family life is worse.
Julian Mitchell, AS FAR AS YOU CAN GO

9 Every generation revolts against its fathers and makes friends with its grandfathers.
Lewis Mumford, THE BROWN DECADE 1931

10 One would be in less danger / From the wiles of the stranger / If one's own kin and kith / Were more fun to be with.
Ogden Nash, FAMILY COURT

11 The best way to keep children home is to make the home atmosphere pleasant — and let the air out of the tyres.
Dorothy Parker. Quoted Frank Muir, ON CHILDREN

12 When our relatives are at home we have to think of all their good points or it would be impossible to endure them.
George Bernard Shaw, HEARTBREAK HOUSE 1920

13 That dear octopus from whose tentacles we never quite escape, nor in our innermost hearts never quite wish to.
Dodie Smith, DEAR OCTOPUS 1938

FANATIC

14 A fanatic is one who can't change his mind and won't change the subject.
Winston Churchill. Attributed by John Bartlett, FAMILIAR QUOTATIONS

15 A fanatic is a man that does what he thinks the Lord would do, if He knew the facts of the case.
Finley Peter Dunne, MR. DOOLEY'S OPINIONS, *Casual Observations* 1900

16 Defined in psychological terms, a fanatic is a man who consciously over-compensates a secret doubt.
Aldous Huxley, PROPER STUDIES 1927

17 The evil is not what they [extremists] say about their cause, but what they say about their opponents.
Robert F. Kennedy, THE PURSUIT OF JUSTICE 1964

18 It is characteristic of all movements and crusades that the psychopathic elements rises to the top.
Robert Linder, MUST YOU CONFORM? 1956

19 The more you are in the right the more natural that everyone else should be bullied into thinking likewise.
George Orwell, THE ROAD TO WIGAN PIER 1937

1 Fanaticism consists in redoubling your effort when you have forgotten your aim.
George Santayana, THE LIFE OF REASON, *Reason in Commonsense* 1906

2 There is nobody as enslaved as the fanatic, the person in whom one impulse, one value, has assumed ascendency over all others.
Milton B. Saperstein, PARADOXES OF EVERYDAY LIFE 1955

FANTASY

3 All fantasy should have a solid base in reality.
Max Beerbohm, ZULEIKA DOBSON, *note to 1946 edition*

4 . . . dreams of her lover, tall as the town clock tower, Samson-syrup-gold maned, whacking thighed and piping hot, thunderbolt-bassed and barnacle-breasted, flailing up the cockles with his eyes like blowlamps and scooping low over her lonely loving hotwaterbottled body.
Dylan Thomas, UNDER MILK WOOD 1954

5 The poet is in command of his fantasy, while it is exactly the mark of the neurotic that he is possessed by his fantasy.
Lionel Trilling, THE LIBERAL IMAGINATION, *Freud and Literature* 1950

FARMING

6 I have just read an article complaining that there will be a serious shortage of scientists for agriculture after the war. This is terrible. We may have to use farmers again.
Beachcomber (J.B. Morton), HERE AND NOW

7 The field and wood all bone-fed loam / Shot up a roaring harvest home.
Edmund Blunden, SELECTED POEMS, *Rural Economy* 1957

8 "If you put a bull in a field with a herd of cows you wouldn't expect to see a lot of calves the next morning."
"No. But you'd expect to see a lot of contented faces."
James Callaghan, retort to James Prior, Minister of Agriculture

9 Lately, I have taken to farming in a modest way . . . If I had heard about it when I was young I probably should never have gone into politics at all.
Winston Churchill. Speech at Kent Agricultural Show, Maidstone. Quoted News Review 29 *Jul* 1948

10 But it's useless to argue the why and the wherefore / When a crop is so thin / There's nothing to do but set the teeth / And plough it in.
Cecil Day Lewis, A FAILURE

11 Farming looks mighty easy when your plough is a pencil and you're a thousand miles from the cornfield.
Dwight D. Eisenhower. Speech, Peoria 25 *Sep* 1956

12 A good farmer needs a strong back and a weak mind.
J. K. Galbraith, A LIFE IN OUR TIMES 1982

13 No one can understand farmers unless it is known that, the rarest exceptions apart, they are afflicted with a serious sense of inferiority . . . Working farmers are always struggling with the thought that they are hicks.
Id.

14 No one hates his job so heartily as a farmer.
H.L. Mencken, American Mercury, *What is Going On In the World? Nov* 1933

15 To expect an average farmer to be not only a sower and a reaper, but an agricultural chemist, an accountant, a meteorologist, a veterinary expert, a merchant, a financier and a resident housekeeper all united in a single Admirable Crichton is ridiculous; yet this is our practice.
George Bernard Shaw. Quoted News Review 10 *Apr* 1947

16 A farmer was asked what sort of year he had just had. "Medium," came the reply. "What do you mean by 'medium'?" "Worse than last year but better than next."
Peter Walker. Speech at Royal Horticultural Society 21 *May* 1979

FASCINATION

17 You fascinated me; but I loved you; so it was heaven. This sister of yours fascinates me; but I hate her; so it is hell.
George Bernard Shaw, HEARTBREAK HOUSE 1920

FASCISM

18 But for the bold experiment of Fascism the decade has not been fruitful in constructive statesmanship.
John Buchan, Morning Post, *Dec* 1929

19 Fascism was little more than terrorist rule by corrupt gangsters. Mussolini was not

corrupt himself but he did nothing except to rage impotently.
A. J. P. Taylor, Observer, *The Cardboard Lion* 28 Feb 1982

FASHION

1 [Clothes] play such an intimate part in the delicate business of getting oneself across that it seems impossible to discuss them, for long, objectively.
Elizabeth Bowen, COLLECTED IMPRESSIONS 1950

2 Don't ever wear artistic jewellery. It wrecks a woman's reputation.
Colette, GIGI 1945

3 Most of the change we think we see in life / Is due to truths being in and out of favour.
Robert Frost, NORTH OF BOSTON

4 In the [1914–18] war the shortage of sugar and butter and the popularisation of hockey and tennis, greatly reduced women's weight and when they were freed of their tight corsets the popular 'hour-glass' figure gave place to the neatly cylindrical.
Robert Graves and Alan Hodge, THE LONG WEEK-END 1940

5 I find I am not as closely in touch with modern life as I once was; I no longer seem to meet ladies in antique shops who are besotted about antlers.
Joyce Grenfell at 60

6 Brought up in an epoch when ladies apparently rolled along on wheels, Mr. Quarles was peculiarly susceptible to calves.
Aldous Huxley, POINT COUNTER POINT 1934

7 The surest way to be out of fashion tomorrow is to be in the forefront of it today.
Derek Marlowe, A DANDY IN ASPIC 1966

8 The reason for all this feminine adornment is that women are indulged just because they are in an alien (male) society. They are like girls in a mining camp being rewarded with gold nuggets. Because they are out of place they must be given a treat.
J.B. Priestley, THOUGHTS IN THE WILDERNESS

9 Her frocks are built in Paris, but she wears them with a strong English accent.
Saki, REGINALD ON WOMEN 1904

10 Fashions, after all, are only induced epidemics.
George Bernard Shaw, DOCTOR'S DILEMMA, *Preface* 1906

11 To call a fashion wearable is the kiss of death. No new fashion worth its salt is ever wearable.
Eugenia Sheppard, New York Herald Tribune 13 *Jan* 1960

12 You cannot be both fashionable and first rate.
Logan Pearsall Smith, ALL TRIVIA, *Afterthoughts* 1931

13 If Botticelli were alive today he'd be working for *Vogue*.
Peter Ustinov. Quoted Observer, *Sayings of the Week* 21 *Oct* 1968

14 And if you feel exotic and extravagant you *could* have some tiny jewelled nose clips.
Woman and Beauty

15 If a woman wishes to be really smart this winter she must wear a coloured ring on the small toe of her left foot to match the colour of the nail varnish she uses on her fingers.
Yorkshire Telegraph and Star

FATALISM

16 I go the way that Providence dictates with the assurance of a sleepwalker.
Adolf Hitler. Speech, Munich 26 *Sep* 1938

17 One would think we must needs all complete our destinies, merely by the process of living out our lives to the end.
Rose Macaulay, A CASUAL COMMENTARY

18 Death is a warm cloak and an old friend. I regard death as something that comes up on a roulette wheel once in a while.
Gram Papons, rock musician, on being warned that his drug addiction could prove fatal

FATE

19 There is no return game between a man and his stars.
Samuel Beckett, MURPHY 1938

20 The dead leaf on the highlands / The old tramp on the mill drove / Each whirls on nor understands / God's freezing love.
Edmund Blunden, POEMS 1911–1930

21 Only the fool, fixed in his folly, may think he can turn the wheel on which he turns.
T. S. Eliot, MURDER IN THE CATHEDRAL 1935

1 Human reason needs only to will more strongly than fate, and she *is* fate.
Thomas Mann, THE MAGIC MOUNTAIN 1924

2 Fate is the gunman that all gunmen dread. / Fate stings the stinger for his roll of green; / Fate, Strong-Arm-Worker, on the bean / Of strong-arm-workers bumps his pipe of lead.
Don Marquis, PROVERBS

3 However much we dawdle in the sun / We have to hurry at the touch of Fate.
John Masefield, THE WIDOW IN THE BY STREET 1912

4 Listen son, don't fight your custard.
S. J. Perelman

FATHER

5 The night my father got me / His mind was not on me; / He did not plague his fancy / To muse if I should be / The son you see.
A. E. Housman, LAST POEMS 1922

6 It is easier for a father to have children than for children to have a real father.
Pope John XXIII

7 Happy is the child whose father acquits himself with credit in the presence of his friends.
Robert Lynd, THE BLUE LION

8 The fundamental defect of fathers is that they want their children to be a credit to them.
Bertrand Russell, AUTOBIOGRAPHY 1967

9 The time not to become a father is eighteen years before a world war.
E. B. White, THE SECOND TREE FROM THE CORNER 1954

10 A father should know how to flirt with a small daughter without making his wife feel like an old discarded bedsock.
Katherine Whitehorn, HOW TO SURVIVE CHILDREN

FATHER-IN-LAW

11 Well, Betjeman, if you're going to be my son-in-law you needn't go on calling me 'Sir'. Call me 'Field Marshal'.
Field Marshal Lord Chetwode to John Betjeman. Quoted Observer 8 *Feb* 1959

FAULT

12 There is absolutely nothing wrong with Oscar Levant that a miracle can't fix.
Alexander Woollcott. Quoted Margaret Case Harriman, THE VICIOUS CIRCLE 1951

FAVOUR

13 Never claim as a right what you can accept as a favour.
Churton Collins, APHORISMS

FEAR

14 The wild hound, Fear, black ravenous and gaunt.
Lascelles Abercrombie, COLLECTED POEMS, *Marriage Shy* 1930

15 Fears wide as the night.
Laurence Binyon, WESTWARD

16 Doesn't know how to be frightened? Why then, he never put his hand in a candle.
Robert Bolt, A MAN FOR ALL SEASONS 1960

17 Fear tastes like a rusty knife and do not let her into your house.
John Cheever, THE WAPSHOT CHRONICLE 1957

18 I have seen the moment of my greatness flicker / And I have seen the eternal Footman hold my coat and snicker / And, in short, I was afraid.
T. S. Eliot, THE LOVE STORY OF J. ALFRED PRUFROCK 1915

19 I will show you fear in a handful of dust.
T. S. Eliot, THE WASTE LAND 1922

20 Fear is an indispensable element in the human make-up. Even in its simpler forms we cannot dispense with it. On the streets of a modern city a fearless man, if the phrase be taken literally, would probably be dead before nightfall.
H. E. Fosdick, ON BEING A REAL PERSON

21 Fear born of ignorance is worse than fear born of knowledge.
Dr. Charles Hill. Address to Hunterian Society. Quoted News Review 2 *Dec* 1948

22 I'm a stranger and afraid / In a world I never made.
A. E. Housman, LAST POEMS 1922

23 The one permanent emotion of the inferior man, as of all the simple mammals, is fear — fear of the unknown, the complex, the

inexplicable. What he wants beyond everything else is safety.
H. L. Mencken, The Yale Review, *Jun 1920*

1 When you ask her how she felt inside the cement mixer, she thinks it over and says "Frightened".
Observer, *profile of Pat Arrowsmith* 13 *May 1962*

2 Modern man is aggressive because he is fearful. Almost all propaganda is designed to create fear. Heads of governments and other officials know that a frightened people is easier to govern, will forfeit rights it would otherwise defend, is less likely to demand a better life, and will agree to millions and millions being spent on 'Defence'.
J. B. Priestley, OUTCRIES AND ASIDES

3 Let me assert my firm belief that the only thing we have to fear is fear itself.
Franklin D. Roosevelt. Speech 2 *Jul* 1932

4 Fear is the main source of superstition and one of the main sources of cruelty. To conquer fear is the beginning of wisdom.
Bertrand Russell, AN OUTLINE OF INTELLECTUAL RUBBISH 1950

5 Fear will drive men to any extreme; and the fear inspired by a superior being is a mystery which cannot be reasoned away.
George Bernard Shaw, ST. JOAN, *Preface* 1927

6 Everybody is afraid for himself, and everybody thinks his neighbours' fears are ridiculous, as they generally are.
J. A. Spender, THE COMMENTS OF BAGSHOT

FEAST

7 Feasts must be solemn and rare, or else they cease to be feasts.
Aldous Huxley, DO WHAT YOU WILL

FEATURES

8 Her features did not seem to know the value of team work.
George Ade

9 She has a Siamese forehead and a mouth like a galosh.
Mrs. Pat Campbell of an un-named actress. Quoted James Agate, EGO 3, 6 *May* 1937

FEET

10 He is a big guy . . . with very funny feet which is why he is called Feet. These feet are extra large feet even for a big guy and Dave the Dude says he wears violin cases for shoes. Of course this is not true, because Feet cannot get either of his feet into a violin case, unless it is a case for a very large violin, such as a cello.
Damon Runyon, GUYS AND DOLLS 1932

FEMINISM

11 The suffragettes were triumphant. Woman's place was in the gaol.
Caryl Brahms and S. J. Simon, NO NIGHTINGALES

12 Nothing would induce me to vote for giving women the franchise. I am not going to be henpecked into a question of such importance.
Winston Churchill. Quoted Robert Lewis Taylor, THE AMAZING MR. CHURCHILL

13 The all-male religions have produced no religious imagery . . . The great religious art of the world is deeply involved with the female principle.
Kenneth, Lord Clark, CIVILISATION 1969

14 When a woman behaves like a man, why can't she behave like a nice man?
Dame Edith Evans. Quoted Observer, *Sayings of the Week* 30 *Sep* 1957

15 Women fail to understand how much men hate them.
Germaine Greer, THE FEMALE EUNUCH

16 Field Marshal Montgomery: Lady Astor, I must tell you that I do not approve of female politicians.
Lady Astor: That's all right. The only General I approve of is Evangeline Booth.
Quoted John Grigg, NANCY ASTOR, PORTRAIT OF A PIONEER

17 In the eighteenth century, when logic and science were the fashion, women tried to talk like men. The twentieth century has reversed the process.
Aldous Huxley, TWO OR THREE GRACES

18 The homo is the legitimate child of the suffragette.
(Percy) Wyndham Lewis, THE ART OF BEING RULED 1926

19 You cannot trust the interests of one class entirely to another class, and you cannot

trust the interests of one sex entirely to another sex.
David Lloyd George. Speech on Suffrage 1911

1 This frenzied search for female identity, this *me, me*, what am *I*, what do *I* want, is the kind of self-preoccupation that can send anyone down the path to complete isolation — which is not a path the wife and mother can follow.
Joyce Lubold, THIS HALF OF THE APPLE IS MINE

2 Women these days do not find it difficult to behave like men; but they often find it extremely difficult to behave like gentlemen.
Compton Mackenzie, ON MORAL COURAGE

3 Women's Liberation is just a lot of foolishness. It's the men who are discriminated against. They can't bear children. And no one's likely to do anything about that.
Golda Meir

4 I just hope other women see me as one of them. My main hope as Prime Minister would be to give women more confidence.
Margaret Thatcher. Quoted Observer, *Sayings of the Week* 6 *May* 1979

5 People call me a feminist whenever I express sentiments that differentiate me from a doormat or a prostitute.
Rebecca West 1913

6 Whatever women do they must do twice as well as men to be thought half as good. Luckily this is not difficult.
Charlotte Whitton on becoming mayor of Ottawa

7 The Catholic Church has never really come to terms with women. What I object to is being treated either as Madonnas or Mary Magdalenes.
Shirley Williams. Interview with Miriam Gross, Observer 22 *Mar* 1981

FICTION

8 A novel is balanced between a few true impressions and the multitude of false ones that make up most of what we call life.
Saul Bellow, Nobel Prize speech 1976

9 Every fine story must leave in the mind of the sensitive reader an intangible residuum of pleasure, a cadence, a quality of voice that is exclusively the writer's own, individual, unique.
Willa Cather, NOT UNDER FORTY, *Miss Jewett* 1936

10 There are only two or three human stories, and they go on repeating themselves as fiercely as if they had never happened before.
Willa Cather, O PIONEER 1913

11 When the plot flags, bring in a man with a gun.
Raymond Chandler, giving advice to an interviewer. Quoted RAYMOND CHANDLER SPEAKING

12 What greater prestige can a man like me (not too greatly gifted, but very understanding) have than to have taken a cheap, shoddy and utterly lost kind of writing, and have made of it something that intellectuals claw each other about?
Id.

13 Mr. Faulkner, of course, is interested in making your mind rather than your flesh creep.
Clifton Fadiman, New Yorker 21 *Apr* 1934

14 The novel . . . supplies pictures and evidence from which each reader may take that food which best suits her growth. It is the great fertiliser, the quiet fertiliser of people's imagination.
John Galsworthy, LIFE AND LETTERS 1935

15 The novel supplies revelation . . . browsed upon, brooded over, soaked up into the fibre of the mind and conscience.
Id.

16 The novel . . . changes the currents of judgment in a man's mind before he even suspects there is a change going on. The more unaware he is, the more surely he is undermined, for he has no means of mobilising his defences.
Id.

17 Cynics have claimed there are only six basic plots. Frankenstein and My Fair Lady are really the same story.
Leslie Halliwell, FILMGOER'S BOOK OF QUOTES 1973

18 Do you abominate detective stories? I read two a week in bed at night; can't concentrate on much else then. To me they are a

great solace, a sort of mental knitting where it doesn't matter if you drop a stitch.
Rupert Hart-Davis, THE LYTTELTON HART-DAVIS LETTERS 30 *Oct* 1955

1 When writing a novel a writer should create living people; people, not characters. A *character* is a caricature.
Ernest Hemingway, DEATH IN THE AFTERNOON 1932

2 All good books are alike in that they are truer than if they really happened. After you are finished reading one you will feel that all that happened to you, and afterwards it all belongs to you.
Ernest Hemingway, Esquire, *An Old Newsman Writes, Dec* 1934

3 Do your bit to save humanity from lapsing back into barbarity by reading all the novels you can.
Richard Hughes. Speech at a Foyle's Library Lunch, to mark his 75th birthday 1975

4 She rode the trash-horse hell-for-leather.
Rose Macaulay of Ethel M. Dell

5 Casting my mind's eye over the whole of fiction, the only absolutely original creation I can think of is Don Quixote.
W. Somerset Maugham, NOVELS AND THEIR AUTHORS 1955

6 An autobiography can distort; facts can be realigned. But fiction never lies, it reveals the writer totally,
V. S. Naipaul. Quoted Janet Hitchman, SUCH A STRANGE LADY

7 Mr. [John] O'Hara's world is populated by the cheap, vulgar, debased and self-destroyed. His reaction to it is a mixture of sardonic scorn, savage contempt and romantic wonder.
Orville Prescott, IN MY OPINION

8 A short story is always a disclosure, frequently an evocation . . . frequently a celebration of a character at bursting point.
V. S. Pritchett, OXFORD BOOK OF SHORT STORIES, *Introduction*

9 The principle of procrastinated rape is said to be the ruling one in all the great bestsellers.
V. S. Pritchett, THE LIVING NOVEL 1946

10 The central theme of the novel is that they were glad to see each other.
Gertrude Stein. Quoted John Malcolm Brinnin, THE THIRD ROSE

11 My brother-in-law wrote an unusual murder story. The victim got killed by a man from another book.
Robert Sylvester

12 Rockfist was born in the mind of Mr. Frank Pepper and he first appeared in the pages of *The Champion*, a boy's comic, in October 1938. He finally left the scene some 1000 chapters and five million words later on May 6, 1961. And considering that Leo Tolstoy used 700,000 words in *War and Peace* that must put Rockfist among the all-time greats of fiction.
Tiverton Gazette. *Quoted* Punch 22 *Mar* 1972

13 Religion and immorality are the only things that sell books nowadays. I am going to start a middle course and give them crime and blood and three murders to a chapter; such is the insanity of the age that I do not doubt for one moment the success of the venture.
Edgar Wallace, in a letter to his wife 1905

14 Nothing is more insulting to a novelist than to assume that he is incapable of anything except the mere transcription of what he observes.
Evelyn Waugh, Daily Mail 31 *May* 1930

15 Dialogue in fiction should be reserved for the culminating moments and regarded as the spray into which the great wave of narrative breaks in curving towards the watcher on the shore.
Edith Wharton, THE WRITING OF FICTION 1925

16 In any really good subject one has only to probe deep enough to come to tears.
Id.

17 Fiction is like a spider's web, attached ever so slightly perhaps, but still attached, to life at all four corners.
Virginia Woolf, A ROOM OF ONE'S OWN 1929

FIDELITY

18 Faithful women are all alike. They think only of their fidelity and not of their husbands.
Jean Giraudoux, AMPHITRYON 38, 1929

19 For he was a man of unwearied and prolific conjugal fidelity.
Blasco Ibanez, BLOOD AND SAND 1908

FINANCE

1 A man accustomed to think in millions — other people's millions.
Arnold Bennett, JOURNALS 1933

2 First payments is what made us think we were prosperous and the other nineteen is what showed us we were broke.
Will Rogers, AUTOBIOGRAPHY 1949

3 I go to the bank every morning and when I say "No" I return home at night without worry. But when I say "Yes" it's like putting your finger into a machine — the whirring wheels may drag your whole body in after the finger.
Sir Nathan Meyer Rothschild. Quoted Virginia Cowles, THE ROTHSCHILDS: A FAMILY OF FORTUNE

4 The faults of the burglar are the qualities of the financier.
George Bernard Shaw, MAJOR BARBARA, *Preface* 1905

FIRE

5 The fire rose in two branched flames like the golden antlers of some enchanted stag.
Katherine Mansfield, JOURNALS 1954

6 The garnered fervours of forgotten Junes / Flare forth again and waste away.
Don Marquis, AN OPEN FIRE

7 The fire was furry as a bear.
Edith Sitwell, DARK SONG

FISH

8 Fish in the unruffled lakes / The swarming colours wear.
W. H. Auden, FISH IN THE UNRUFFLED LAKES 1936

9 And nigh the toppling reed, still as death / The great pike lies, the murderous patriarch.
Edmund Blunden, THE PIKE

10 Fish say they have their stream and pond / But is there anything beyond?
Rupert Brooke, HEAVEN

11 Fish die belly upwards and rise to the surface. It is their way of falling.
André Gide, JOURNALS 1939–1950

12 The tiny fish enjoy themselves in the sea / Quick little splinters of life / Their little lives are fun to them in the sea.
D. H. Lawrence, COLLECTED POEMS, *Little Fish* 1928

13 The Herring is a lucky fish / From all disease inured / Should he be ill while caught at sea; / *Immediately* — he's cured /
Spike Milligan, SILLY VERSES FOR KIDS

FISHING

14 A canny young fisher named Fisher / Once fished on the edge of a fissure / A fish with a grin / Pulled the fisherman in — Now they're fishing the fissure for Fisher.
Anon.

15 1st Woman: Look at that Nogood Boyo now.
2nd Woman: Too lazy to wipe his snout.
3rd Woman: And going out fishing every day and all he ever brought back was a Mrs. Samuels.
1st Woman: Been in the water a week.
Dylan Thomas, UNDER MILK WOOD 1954

F. SCOTT FITZGERALD

16 Mr. Fitzgerald is a novelist. Mrs. Fitzgerald is a novelty.
Ring Landner, THE OTHER SIDE

17 Of good social standing and addicted to strong liquor, he had neither the stamina of a Hemingway nor the peasant goodness of a Faulkner to withstand the corrupting influences attendant on success in the materialistic U.S.A. He wasted his energies on the glossier magazines, wrote rubbishy film scripts, and died in his forties, a bitter exhausted man.
News Review, reviewing THIS SIDE OF PARADISE 9 *Dec* 1948

FLATTERY

18 You must not stop in front of a painting and say "That must have cost you a fortune!" But you may stop, nod, examine it carefully and ask if it is an early Rembrandt.
George Mikes, HOW TO BE AN ALIEN 1946

19 Tell me all my faults as man to man. I can stand anything but flattery.
George Bernard Shaw, JOHN BULL'S OTHER ISLAND 1904

20 What really flatters a man is that you think him worth flattering.
Id.

21 Flattery is all right so long as you don't inhale.
Adlai Stevenson. Speech 1 *Feb* 1961.
Quoted Roy Jenkins, ADLAI STEVENSON

1 The only man who wasn't spoiled by being lionized was Daniel.
Sir H. Beerbohm Tree. Quoted Hesketh Pearson, BEERBOHM TREE

FLEA

2 The fleas that tease in the High Pyrenees.
Hilaire Belloc, TARANTELLA

3 And I have more power / To upset the world / Than the elephant. / When I think of that / I could die of laughing.
Carmen de Bernos Gazztold, THE BEASTS' CHOIR

FLIRTATION

4 Men want a woman whom they can turn on and off like a light switch.
Ian Fleming

5 The trouble with Ian [Fleming] is that he gets off with women because he can't get on with them.
Rosamond Lehmann. Quoted John Pearson, THE LIFE OF IAN FLEMING 1966

6 Flirtation is merely an expression of considered desire coupled with an admission of its impracticability.
Marya Mannes, BUT WILL IT SELL? 1964

FLOGGING

7 I am all for bringing back the birch but only between consenting adults.
Gore Vidal in a television interview with David Frost

FLOWER

8 The fairest thing in nature, a flower, still has its roots in earth and manure.
D. H. Lawrence. SELECTED LITERARY CRITICISM *(edited Anthony Beal)* 1956

9 People from a planet without flowers would think we must be mad with joy the whole time to have such things about us.
Iris Murdoch, A FAIRLY HONOURABLE DEFEAT

FLY

10 God in his wisdom made the fly / And then forgot to tell us why.
Ogden Nash, GOOD INTENTIONS

FLYING

11 Today we hear so much musical sound all the time, in trains, in aeroplanes, in restaurants, that we are becoming deadened to it. We are able to turn off television or walk out of a bad motion picture or poor concert. You can't walk out of an aeroplane.
Leopold Stokowski. Quoted Nat Shapiro, ENCYCLOPEDIA OF QUOTATIONS ABOUT MUSIC

12 Success. Four flights. Thursday morning. All against twenty-one-mile wind.
Wilbur and Orville Wright, telegram from Kitty Hawk 17 Dec 1903

FLYING SAUCER

13 Some people say these objects are due to the excessive consumption in the United States of Scotch whisky. But it is not so. They are due to a Soviet athlete, a discus-thrower, practising for the Olympic Games and quite unconscious of his own strength.
Andrei Gromyko, Soviet Foreign Minister. Quoted Lord Glendurgan, House of Lords 17 Jan 1979

FOG

14 The yellow fog that rubs its back upon the window panes.
T. S. Eliot, LOVE SONG OF J. ALFRED PRUFROCK 1915

15 The fog is in the bones of the drowned.
Norman Nicholson, CAEDMON

FOLLY

16 The follies which a man regrets the most in his life, are those which he didn't commit when he had the opportunity.
Helen Rowland, A GUIDE TO MEN

17 He [Jack London] made many mistakes and committed innumerable follies, but at least he had the satisfaction of knowing that they had been big ones.
Irving Stone, SAILOR ON HORSEBACK: *The Biography of Jack London*

FOOD

18 They eat and drank deeply of the charming viands ending up with merangs and chocolates.
Daisy Ashford (aged 9), THE YOUNG VISITERS 1919

1 There is no such thing as a little garlic.
Arthur Baer. Quoted, THE FRANK MUIR BOOK

2 Rightly thought of there is poetry in peaches, even when they are canned.
Granville Barker, THE MADRAS HOUSE 1910

3 It would appear that the Ministry of Food base their standards of our bodily requirements of food on calories alone. Surely this is incorrect? After all there are calories in hay, but how many calories can be absorbed by man?
Dr. J. M. Bellamy. letter to Daily Telegraph

4 Birds in their little nests agree / With Chinamen but not with me.
Hilaire Belloc, ON FOOD

5 Huntley and Palmer / Grew calmer and calmer. / When either felt restive / He ate a digestive.
E. C. Bentley, CLERIHEWS

6 I like sandwiches.
Ernest Bevin when asked his choice of menu for dinner. Potsdam Conference, Aug 1945

7 *Edible. Adj.* good to eat and wholesome to digest, as a worm to a toad, a toad to a snake, a snake to a pig, a pig to a man, and a man to a worm.
Ambrose Bierce, THE DEVIL'S DICTIONARY 1906

8 Once at dinner when the menu announced Roast Duck and the scouts [at Merton] brought Roast Lamb, "La Malade Imaginaire" he [Hugh Dyson] said.
Humphrey Carpenter, THE INKLINGS 1980

9 The turkey has practically no taste except a dry fibrous flavour reminiscent of a mixture of warmed-up plaster of Paris and horsehair. The texture is like wet sawdust and the whole vast feathered swindle has the piquancy of a boiled mattress.
Cassandra (William Connor), Daily Mirror 24 *Dec* 1953

10 Always get up from the table feeling as if you could still eat a penny bun.
Sir Hugh Casson and Joyce Grenfell, NANNY SAYS 1972

11 Take this pudding away. It has no theme.
Winston Churchill to a waiter at the Savoy Hotel. Quoted Lord Butler, Thames TV, *The Day Before Yesterday*

12 I poke my braised welly with a fork . . . the food is indescribably dire. Malta is the only place in the world where the local delicacy is the bread.
Alan Coren, Punch 12 *Jan* 1972

13 The food was so abominable that I used to cross myself before I took a mouthful. I used to say "Ian, it tastes like armpits."
Noël Coward, of Ian Fleming's hospitality. Quoted John Pearson, THE LIFE OF IAN FLEMING 1966

14 I found out what that white stuff was we had in Taipan — it was rice.
Overheard by Noël Coward from a tourist in Raffles Hotel, Singapore

15 It's a very odd thing / As odd as can be, / That whatever Miss T. eats / Turns into Miss T.
Walter De La Mare, MISS T

16 Bouillabaise is only good because cooked by the French, who, if they cared to try, could produce an excellent and nutritious substitute out of cigar stumps and empty matchboxes.
Norman Douglas, SIREN LANDS 1911

17 With packaging materials in short supply people may have to eat fresh food.
The Economist

18 Luckily for him the average Englishman has no culinary sense at all. His palate is burned by tobacco, cocktails and whisky, and cannot appreciate fine savoury sauces.
L'Epoque (Paris). Quoted News Review 3 *Jul* 1947

19 The French cook: we open tins.
John Galsworthy

20 "Waiter, I found this in my food. It's a cockroach."
"Listen. With paella, ingredients vary from place to place."
Malcolm Gluck, Punch, *A Portrait of New York* 18 *Aug* 1976

21 Food is the most primitive form of comfort.
Sheila Graham, A STATE OF HEAT

22 Give me a little ham and egg / And let me be alone I beg / Give me my tea, hot, sweet and weak, / Bring me *The Times* and do not speak.
A. P. Herbert, A BOOK OF BALLADS, *Breakfast*

23 Bring porridge, bring sausage, bring fish for a start, / Bring kidneys and mushrooms and

partridge's legs. / But let the foundation be bacon and eggs.
Id.

1 To know how to order and enjoy good food is part of a civilised education.
Lady Blanche Hozier, mother of Clementine Churchill. Quoted Mary Soames, CLEMENTINE CHURCHILL 1981

2 What was one day a sheep's hind leg and a handful of spinach was the next part of the hand that wrote, the brain that conceived the slow movement of the Jupiter Symphony.
Aldous Huxley, POINT COUNTER POINT 1928

3 It requires a certain kind of mind to see beauty in a hamburger bun.
Ray Kroc, chairman of McDonalds

4 I am very fond of mushrooms. Often I go out into the country and gather a whole basketful. I carry them part of the way home; then I throw them away.
Stephen Leacock, FOOD FOR THOUGHT

5 Cold soup is a very tricky thing and it is a rare hostess who can carry it off. More often than not the dinner guest is left with the impression that had he only come a little earlier he could have gotten it while it was still hot.
Fran Lebowitz, METROPOLITAN LIFE

6 "What on earth is this?"
"A piece of cod, sir"
"The piece of cod which passeth all understanding."
Attr. Sir Edwin Lutyens, to a waiter at Brooks'

7 Coffee and rolls took on the nature of an orgy. We positively scintillated. Anecdotes of the High Born were poured out, sweetened and sipped: we gorged on scandals of High Birth generously buttered.
Katherine Mansfield, IN A GERMAN PENSION, *The Sisters of the Baroness*

8 We asked for a square meal and they offered us dog biscuits.
John Marshall, SERGEANT DUNN'S FIGHTING SPORTSMEN 1935

9 To eat well in England you should have breakfast three times a day.
W. Somerset Maugham. Quoted David St. John Thomas, THE BREAKFAST BOOK 1981

10 On the continent people have good food; in England people have good table manners.
George Mikes, HOW TO BE AN ALIEN 1946

11 Americans can eat garbage provided you sprinkle it liberally with ketchup.
Henry Miller, REMEMBER TO REMEMBER 1947

12 What is the matter with Mary Jane? / She's perfectly well and she hasn't a pain, / And it's lovely rice pudding for dinner again, / What is the matter with Mary Jane?
A. A. Milne, RICE PUDDING

13 It is impossible to have a failure with chutney; there's nothing to set and no ingredient barred.
Robert Morley, MORLEY MARVELS, *Accustomed as I am to Public Speaking*

14 When Captain Cook first arrived in the South Seas the islanders were amazed that his sailors chose to take their meals in public and make love in private; to those simple natives it seemed far more seemly to do things the other way round.
John Mortimer, Observer Magazine, *How to Avoid Bad Restaurants* 16 Jul 1978

15 Restaurants have this in common with ladies: the best are often not the most enjoyable, nor the grandest the most friendly, and the pleasures of the evening are frequently spoiled by the final writing of an exorbitant cheque.
Id.

16 Avoid any restaurant where a waiter arrives with a handful of knives and forks just as you reach the punch-line of your best story and says "Which of you is having the fish?"
Id.

17 The golden rule when reading the menu in a restaurant is, if you can't pronounce it, you can't afford it.
Frank Muir, ENGLISH DIGEST

18 Some breakfast food manufacturer hit upon the simple notion of emptying out the leavings of carthorse nosebags, adding a few other things like unconsumed portions of chicken layer's mash, and the sweepings of racing stables, packing the mixture in little bags and selling them in health food shops.
Frank Muir, OH, MY WORD

19 Parsley / Is gharshley.
Ogden Nash, FURTHER REFLECTIONS

20 I never see any home cooking. All I get is fancy stuff.
Philip, Duke of Edinburgh in a speech. Quoted Observer, *Dec* 1962

1 The effect of eating too much lettuce is 'soporific'.
Beatrix Potter, FLOPSY BUNNIES 1902

2 If one were to set up a series of electrodes in a field and pass a current from one electrode to another all the worms would come to the surface and be harvested for food. An average acre contains a ton of worms. There's nothing wrong with worms as food. Fish eat them every day.
Magnus Pyke, BUTTER SIDE UP

3 He orders a Bismarck herring with sliced onions to come along, which is a dish that is considered most invigorating.
Damon Runyon, MORE THAN SOMEWHAT 1937

4 There is no love sincerer than the love of food.
George Bernard Shaw, MAN AND SUPERMAN 1905

5 Sheppards Pie peppered with genuine sheppard on top.
Stephen Sondheim, SWEENEY TODD *(musical)*

6 We are, literally, what we eat.
Terence Stamp

7 Gentlemen do not like food that has been 'messed about with'. Continental cookery gives them diarrhoea.
Douglas Sutherland, THE ENGLISH GENTLEMAN 1978

8 I always have smoked salmon and cheese when I eat at the National Liberal Club because they don't have to cook anything.
Jeremy Thorpe

9 Cider and tinned salmon are the staple diet of the agricultural classes.
Evelyn Waugh, SCOOP 1938

10 "Turbot, sir" said the waiter, placing before me two fishbones, two eyeballs on a bit of wet mackintosh.
Thomas Earle Welby, THE DINNER KNELL

11 You breed babies and you eat chips with everything.
Arnold Wesker, CHIPS WITH EVERYTHING 1962

12 A food is not necessarily essential just because your child hates it.
Katherine Whitehorn, HOW TO SURVIVE CHILDREN

13 One cannot think well, love well, sleep well, unless one has dined well.
Virginia Woolf, A ROOM OF ONE'S OWN 1929

FOOL

14 Why is it that fools always have the instinct to hunt out the unpleasant secrets of life, and the hardiness to mention them?
Emily Eder, THE SEMI-ATTACHED COUPLE

MICHAEL FOOT

15 A good man fallen among politicians.
Daily Mirror, *leader* 20 *Feb* 1983

FOOTBALL

16 Like sex, the movements in football are limited and predictable.
Peter Ackroyd, The Times, *Football Fantasy* 21 *Jun* 1982

17 . . . miry gladiators whose sole purpose in life is to position a surrogate human head between two poles.
Elizabeth Hogg, Daily Telegraph, *The Games People Play* 7 *Sep* 1979

18 I loathed the game . . . it was very difficult for me to show courage at it. Football, it seemed to me, is not really played for the pleasure of kicking a ball about, but is a species of fighting.
George Orwell, SUCH, SUCH WERE THE JOYS

19 I am convinced that the greatest contribution Britain has made to the national life of Uruguay was teaching the people football.
Philip, Duke of Edinburgh, on a visit to Montevideo

20 Soccer has elements of both ballet and chess.
Vidal Sassoon, Observer 10 *Aug* 1979

21 Association football is no longer considered a gentlemanly game. The practice of footballers kissing each other after a goal is scored has lowered the tone. Kissing in public, even between consenting gentlemen, is not considered the done thing.
Douglas Sutherland, THE ENGLISH GENTLEMAN 1978

GERALD FORD

22 Jerry Ford is so dumb that he can't fart and chew gum at the same time.
Lyndon B. Johnson

FOREIGNER

23 "Frogs," he would say, "are slightly better than Huns or Wops, but abroad is unutterably bloody and foreigners are fiends."
Nancy Mitford, THE PURSUIT OF LOVE 1945

FORESIGHT

1 If you do not think about the future you cannot have one.
John Galsworthy, SWAN SONG 1928

2 Nothing is harder than to make people think about what they are going to *do*.
André Malraux, MAN'S FATE 1933

FORGETFULNESS

3 Not the power to remember, but its very opposite, the power to forget is a necessary condition for our existence.
Sholem Asch, THE NAZARENE 1939

FORGIVENESS

4 I have looked on a lot of women with lust. I've committed adultery in my heart many times. God recognises I will do this and forgives me.
Jimmy Carter during American Presidential campaign 1976

5 Forgive, O Lord, my little jokes on Thee / And I'll forgive Thy great big one on me.
Robert Frost, FROM IN THE CLEARING 1962

6 If you forgive people enough you belong to them, and they to you, whether either person likes it or not — squatters' rights of the heart.
James Hilton, TIME AND TIME AGAIN 1953

7 Forgiveness needs to be accepted, as well as offered, before it is complete.
C. S. Lewis, THE PROBLEM OF PAIN 1940

8 A woman can forgive a man the harm he does her; but she can never forgive him for the sacrifices he makes on her account.
W. Somerset Maugham, THE MOON AND SIXPENCE 1919

9 It is by forgiving that one is forgiven.
Mother Teresa, FOR THE BROTHERHOOD OF MAN 1980

E. M. FORSTER

10 Leonard [Woolf] said he thought *Passage to India* much the best of Morgan Forster's books, but remarked that on re-reading it he had been struck anew by the oppressively feminine influences under which M. had grown up. I said if one grew up with a lot of old women it must do a good deal to one's outlook. "But Morgan *is* an old woman," he said. "He always has been."
William Plomer, ELECTRIC DELIGHTS

FRANCE

11 France may be the only country in the world where the rich are sometimes brilliant.
Lillian Hellman, AN UNFINISHED WOMAN 1969

12 The French never allow a distinguished son of France to lack a statue.
E. V. Lucas, WANDERINGS AND DIVERSIONS 1926

13 France is a country where the money falls apart and you can't tear the toilet paper.
Billy Wilder. Quoted Leslie Halliwell, THE FILMGOER'S BOOK OF QUOTES 1973

GENERAL FRANCO

14 We met General Franco. I think he is a very nice man. He is a keen golfer with a handicap of two. He is received with great enthusiasm whenever he appears.
P. Dunne, MP for Stalybridge and Hyde, reported Sunday Despatch

FRAUD

15 There are no new forms of financial fraud; in the last several hundred years there have only been small variations on a few classical designs.
J. K. Galbraith

FREEDOM

16 None who have always been free can understand the terrible fascinating power of the hope of freedom on those who are not free.
Pearl S. Buck, WHAT AMERICA MEANS TO ME 1943

17 I do not believe in freedom in the philosophical sense. Everybody acts not only under external compulsion but also in accordance with inner necessity.
Albert Einstein, IDEAS AND OPINIONS

18 Freedom does not guarantee masterpieces.
E. M. Forster, CULTURE AND FREEDOM, BBC *broadcast* 1940

19 I ought to feel free, yet I cannot keep my hat on in church, even if no one is looking.
E. M. Forster. Quoted Raymond Mortimer, TRY ANYTHING ONCE

20 A society in which men recognise no check upon their freedom soon becomes a society

where freedom is a possession of only a savage few.
Judge Learned Hand, Life Magazine 1 *Jul* 1944

1 What good is freedom if you've not got the money for it? It's all very fine to go on about Nora's escape at the end of *A Doll's House* but just how was she planning to eat that night?
Lillian Hellman

2 Unless a man has the talents to make something of himself, freedom is an unknown burden.
Eric Hoffer, THE TRUE BELIEVER 1951

3 There can be no freedom without the freedom to fail.
Eric Hoffer, THE ORDEAL OF CHANGE 1963

4 Sexual freedom? It's an 'orrible 'ideous slavery. That's what it is.
Aldous Huxley, ANTIC HAY 1923

5 Christianity promises to make men free; it never promises to make them independent.
W. R. Inge (Dean of St. Pauls), THE PHILOSOPHY OF PLOTINUS 1929

6 It is often safer to be in chains than to be free.
Franz Kafka, THE CASTLE 1926

7 The free way of life proposes ends, but it does not prescribe means.
Robert F. Kennedy, THE PURSUIT OF JUSTICE 1964

8 All free men, wherever they may live, are citizens of Berlin. And therefore, as a free man, I take pride in the words *Ich bin ein Berliner.*
John F. Kennedy. Speech at City Hall, West Berlin 26 *Jun* 1963

9 Freedom is never voluntarily given by the oppressor; it must be demanded by the oppressed.
Martin Luther King, WHY WE CAN'T WAIT 1964

10 Men are freest when they are most unconscious of freedom.
D. H. Lawrence, STUDIES IN CLASSIC AMERICAN LITERATURE 1923

11 People should be compelled to be freer and more individualistic than they naturally desire to be.
(Percy) Wyndham Lewis, TIME AND WESTERN MAN 1927

12 Freedom is the right to tell people what they do not want to hear.
George Orwell, THE ROAD TO WIGAN PIER 1937

13 Freedom cannot be bestowed. It must be achieved.
Franklin D. Roosevelt. Speech 16 *Sep* 1936

14 In the future days, which we seek to make secure, we look forward to a world founded on four essential freedoms. The first is freedom of speech and expression — everywhere in the world. The second is freedom of every person to worship God in his own way — everywhere in the world. The third is freedom from want. The fourth is freedom from fear.
Franklin D. Roosevelt. Message to Congress 6 *Jan* 1941

15 Englishmen never will be slaves; they are free to do whatever the Government and public opinion allows them to do.
George Bernard Shaw, MAN AND SUPERMAN 1905

16 You took my freedom away a long time ago and you can't give it back because you haven't got it yourself.
Alexander Solzhenitsyn, THE FIRST CIRCLE 1964

17 The dangers of freedom are appalling.
Lytton Strachey, letter to Duncan Grant 12 *Apr* 1907

18 Freedom does not always win. This is one of the bitterest lessons of history.
A. J. P. Taylor

19 I blame Rousseau, myself. 'Man is born free', indeed! Man is *not* born free, he is born attached to his mother by a cord and is incapable of looking after himself for at least seven years, (seventy in some cases).
Katherine Whitehorn, HOW TO SURVIVE CHILDREN

20 Freedom exists only where people take care of the government.
Woodrow Wilson. Speech, New York 22 *Sep* 1912

FREE SPEECH

21 Everybody favours free speech in the slack moments when no axes are being ground.
Heywood Brown, COLLECTED WORKS 1941

1 The right to be heard does not automatically include the right to be taken seriously.
Hubert H. Humphrey. Speech, National Student Association, Wisconsin 22 Aug 1965

2 Freedom of speech does not include freedom to cry 'Fire' in a crowded theatre.
William Rusher, American TV commentary 10 Dec 1979

FREE-WILL

3 Only two possibilities exist; either one must believe in determinism and regard free-will as a subjective illusion, or one must become a mystic, and regard the discovery of natural laws as a meaningless intellectual game.
Max Born, Bulletin of the Atomic Scientists, Jun 1957

4 The human will is free *only* within the bounds of a determined cosmic system.
Albert Einstein, THE WORLD AS I SEE IT 1934

5 We have to believe in free-will. We've got no choice.
Isaac Bashevis Singer. Quoted Times Diary 21 *Jun* 1982

SIGMUND FREUD

6 Our rational voice is dumb; over a grave / The household of Impulse mourns one dearly loved / Sad is Eros, builder of cities / And weeping anarchic Aphrodite.
W. H. Auden, IN MEMORY OF SIGMUND FREUD 1940

7 Tranquillity comes with years, and that horrid thing which Freud calls sex is expunged.
E. F. Benson, MAPP AND LUCIA 1935

8 "Why are you looking like that?" asked Kyril.
"I was wondering why people put ferrets in their trousers," said Aunt Irene.
"*Thanatos*," said Kyril. "An illustration of the death wish."
"What I wish," said Aunt Irene, "is that you'd never read Freud. It's had a very leaden effect on your conversation."
Alice Thomas Ellis, THE 27TH KINGDOM 1982

9 He has shown us all how awful we really are, for ever nursing grudges we felt in childhood.
Rebecca West. Quoted Jill Craigie, The Times 6 *Dec* 1982

FRIEND

10 One friend in a lifetime is much, two are many, three are hardly possible.
Henry Brooks Adams, THE EDUCATION OF HENRY ADAMS 1916

11 A friend in power is a friend lost.
Id.

12 I have the best friends any man ever had. If I have any enemies — perhaps to have enemies is as great an honour to me as the friendships of these men.
Stanley Baldwin, Unionist conference 11 *Feb* 1924

13 Old friends are generally the refuge of unsociable persons.
Max Beerbohm. Quoted C. S. Roberts, THE INCOMPARABLE MAX

14 When friendship disappears then there is a space left open to that awful loneliness of the outside world which is like the cold space between the planets. It is an air in which men perish utterly.
Hilaire Belloc, THE FOUR MEN 1912

15 In love one has need of being believed; in friendship of being understood.
Abel Bonnard, THE ART OF FRIENDSHIP

16 He was a man who liked his friends, yet whenever one of them was mentioned he said something disparaging about him.
Gerald Brenan, THOUGHTS IN A DRY SEASON 1979

17 A good friend can tell you what is the matter with you in a minute. He may not seem such a good friend after the telling.
Arthur Brisbane, THE BOOK OF TODAY

18 Churchill's devotion to Beaverbrook always puzzled him [Ernest Bevin]. In the end he decided that Churchill was "like a man who's married to a whore; he knows she's a whore but he loves her just the same."
Alan Bullock, LIFE AND TIMES OF ERNEST BEVIN

19 A man's friendships are, like his will, invalidated by his marriage — but they are no less invalidated by the marriages of his friends.
Samuel Butler, THE WAY OF ALL FLESH 1903

20 The friendships which last are those wherein each friend respects the other's dignity to the point of not really wanting anything from him.
Cyril Connolly, THE UNQUIET GRAVE 1945

1 The tragedy of war is that the sense of fellowship it engenders seems to be unable to survive the coming of peace.
Harold Dearden, THE WIND OF CIRCUMSTANCE

2 It is in the thirties that we want friends. In the forties we know they won't save us any more than love did.
F. Scott Fitzgerald, NOTE-BOOKS 1945

3 Never apologise for your terrible friends. We are all *somebody's* terrible friends.
J. Gallagher, Dean of Trinity

4 Friendship needs no words — it is solitude delivered from the anguish of loneliness.
Dag Hammarskjöld, MARKINGS 1964

5 I have no trouble with my enemies — but my goddam friends, they are the ones that keep me walking the floor at night.
Warren Harding to William A. White

6 Friends are God's apology for relations.
Hugh Kingsmill. Quoted Michael Holroyd, THE BEST OF KINGSMILL

7 If you want to make a dangerous man your friend let him do you a favour.
Lewis E. Lawes (warden of Sing-Sing prison), 20,000 YEARS IN SING-SING

8 [Friendship] has no survival value; rather it is one of the things that gives value to survival.
C. S. Lewis, THE FOUR LOVES

9 Many a person has held close, throughout their entire lives, two friends to him that always remained strange to each other, because one of them was attracted by virtue of similarity and the other by virtue of difference.
Emil Ludwig, OF LIFE AND LOVE

10 I always felt that the great high privilege, relief and comfort of friendship was that one had to explain nothing.
Katherine Mansfield. Quoted Antony Alpen, KATHERINE MANSFIELD 1954

11 I am treating you as my friend, asking you to share my present *minuses* in the hope that I can ask you to share my future *pluses*.
Katherine Mansfield, MEMORIES

12 She's been my greatest friend for fifteen years. I know her through and through and I tell you that she hasn't got a single redeeming quality.
W. Somerset Maugham, OUR BETTERS 1923

13 I know a woman who, whenever one of her intimates is attacked in her presence, merely states: "She is my friend" and refuses to say more.
André Maurois, THE ART OF LIVING

14 One of the most mawkish of human delusions is the notion that friendship should be lifelong. The fact is that a man of resilient mind outwears his friendships just as certainly as he outwears his love affairs and his politics.
H. L. Mencken, SELECTED PREJUDICES

15 The golden period when I had not a single friend.
Henry Miller, TROPIC OF CANCER 1934

16 Money can't buy friends, but you can get a better class of enemy.
Spike Milligan, PUCKOON

17 Two buttocks of one bum.
T. Sturge Moore, of Hilaire Belloc and G. K. Chesterton

18 Soustelle, who had just returned from a visit to Algeria, remarked that all his friends there were bitterly opposed to the General's present policy. "Alors mon vieux," de Gaulle said, "Changez vos amis."
Malcolm Muggeridge, TREAD SOFTLY FOR YOU TREAD ON MY JOKES 1966

19 Each friend represents a world in us, a world possibly not born until they arrive, and it is only by this meeting that a new world is born.
Anaïs Nin, DIARY, *Mar* 1937

20 The sacrifices of friendship were beautiful in her eyes so long as she was not asked to make them.
Saki, BEASTS AND SUPERBEASTS

21 To win a friend is success, but if you can snatch the friend of a friend, then blow your trumpet.
Logan Pearsall Smith, ALL TRIVIA, *Afterthoughts* 1931

22 I do not believe that friends are necessarily the people you like best; they are merely the people who got there first.
Peter Ustinov, DEAR ME 1977

23 Whenever a friend succeeds a little something in me dies.
Gore Vidal. Quoted Susan Barnes, BEHIND THE IMAGE

24 There was a definite process by which one made people into friends, and it involved

talking to them and listening to them for hours at a time.
Rebecca West, THE THINKING REED 1936

1 Comprehension must be the soil in which grow all the fruits of friendship.
Woodrow Wilson. Speech, Mobile Alabama 1913

2 I have lost friends, some by death — others by sheer inability to cross the street.
Virginia Woolf, THE WAVES 1931

FRIGIDITY

3 She [Maureen O'Hara] looks as though butter wouldn't melt in her mouth — or anywhere else.
Elsa Lanchester. Quoted Leslie Halliwell,
THE FILMGOER'S BOOK OF QUOTES 1973

FRONTIER

4 When you think about the defence of England you no longer think of the chalk cliffs of Dover. You think of the Rhine. That is where our frontier is today.
Stanley Baldwin, House of Commons 30 *Jul* 1934

FROST

5 The frost stings sweetly with a burning breath / As ultimate as love, as cold as death; / Their lips, whereon delicious tremors hiss, / Fume with the ghostly pollen of their breath.
Roy Campbell, THE SISTERS

ROBERT FROST

6 If it were thought that anything I wrote was influenced by Robert Frost I would take that particular work of mine, shred it and flush it down the toilet, hoping not to clog the pipes.
James Dickey, WRITERS AT WORK *(Fifth Series)*

7 He worked very hard at his own reputation even when he had no need to.
Archibald MacLeish, Ibid.

FULFILMENT

8 I drive along the lanes in my Rolls and I pass some old bloke out walking his dog, and I wonder which of us has got it right.
Paul McCartney, Observer 24 *Jun* 1972

FUNERAL

9 In the city a funeral is just an interruption of traffic. In the country it is a form of entertainment.
George Ade, Cosmopolitan magazine, *Feb* 1928

10 Her funeral sermon (which was long / And followed by a sacred song) / Mentioned her virtues it is true / But dwelt upon her vices too.
Hilaire Belloc, CAUTIONARY TALES, Rebecca 1907

11 To those left behind memorial services serve as a sort of surrogate encounter with death.
Hugh Casson, DIARY 1981

12 If you don't go to other people's funerals they won't come to yours.
Clarence Day, LIFE WITH FATHER 1935

13 I remember Sarah Bernhardt's funeral perfectly. I have never had to wait so long to cross the street.
Eric Dunston. Quoted James Agate, Ego 9 14 *Oct* 1946

14 Friends make pretence of following to the grave / But before one is in it, their minds are turned / And making the best of their way back to life / And living people and things they understand.
Robert Frost, HOME BURIAL 1914

15 It is a pity they should have chosen the day of the Eton and Harrow match for the funeral.
Aldous Huxley, THE GIOCONDA SMILE

16 And all around the path to the cemetery / The round dark heads of men crowded silently / And black-scarved heads of women, wistfully / Watch at the banner of death, and the mystery.
D. H. Lawrence, GIORNI DE MORTI

17 A mortician's life is full of flowers, flowers and beauty.
Eric Linklater, JUAN IN AMERICA 1931

18 There is no sign of depression among us morticians. Our parlours, I'm happy to say, are never empty.
Id.

19 One of the crying needs of the time is for a suitable Burial Service for the admittedly damned.
H. L. Mencken, PREJUDICES 1927

1 I have nothing against undertakers personally. It's just that I wouldn't want one to bury my sister.
Jessica Mitford, Saturday Review 1 *Feb* 1968

2 I can't think of a more wonderful thanksgiving for the life I have had than that everyone should be jolly at my funeral.
Lord Mountbatten in a TV interview shown after his death

3 It gives me a kind of trespassin' joy.
Sean O'Casey at his son's funeral. Quoted Eileen O'Casey, SEAN

4 It only goes to prove that the public will still come if you give them what they want.
Onlooker at funeral of Harry Cohn, head of Columbia Pictures. Quoted Benny Green, Radio Times 17 *Feb* 1979

5 I wants to arrive up there so grand that the Almighty just won't have the heart to turn me back.
John Quigley, TO REMEMBER WITH TEARS

6 I want Bach's Toccata and Fugue in D played at my funeral. If it isn't I shall jolly well want to know why.
Dame Sybil Thorndike. Quoted English Digest, *Mar* 1965

7 The best undertaker in Brooklyn respected, esteemed. He knew all the best people well — knew them well enough even before they died.
Thornton Wilder, THE MATCHMAKER 1955

8 You just came home in time for the funerals, Stella. And funerals are pretty compared to deaths.
Tennessee Williams, A STREETCAR NAMED DESIRE 1947

FURNITURE

9 Lady Kitty: I think it's a beautiful chair. Hepplewhite?
Arnold: No, Sheraton.
Lady Kitty: Oh I know. *The School for Scandal*.
W. Somerset Maugham, THE CIRCLE 1921

10 Gentlemen do not buy furniture. They inherit it. The last time any furniture was bought by any gentlemanly family was in the Victorian era with the result that their drawing-rooms are still filled with understuffed sofas, high-backed chairs, and little tables which fall over when you put anything on them.
Douglas Sutherland, THE ENGLISH GENTLEMAN 1978

11 The chair was upholstered in one of those flagrant chintzes, designed, apparently, by the art editor of a seed catalogue.
Alexander Woollcott, WHILE ROME BURNS 1934

FUTILITY

12 Getting the costumes right in *The Cleopatras* [a TV series] was like polishing the fish-knives on the *Titanic*.
Julian Barnes, Observer, *Quite Beggaring All Description* 13 *Mar* 1983

13 If you board the wrong train it is no good running along the corridor in the other direction.
Dietrich Bonhoeffer, THE WAY TO FREEDOM

14 A man might as well chain himself to the railings of St. Thomas's Hospital and say he wouldn't move until he has a baby.
Winston Churchill. Quoted Robert Lewis Taylor, THE AMAZING MR. CHURCHILL

15 A man who has pedalled twenty-five thousand miles on a stationary bicycle has not circled the globe. He has only garnered weariness.
Paul Eldridge, HORNS OF GLASS

16 Only the fool, fixed in his folly, may think / He can turn the wheel on which he turns.
T. S. Eliot, MURDER IN THE CATHEDRAL 1935

17 Carrying bricks to Babel is neither a duty nor a privilege; it seems to be a necessity built into the chromosomes of our species.
Arthur Koestler, BRICKS TO BABEL, Epilogue 1983

18 Figure it out. Work a lifetime to pay off a house. You finally own it, and there's no one to live in it.
Arthur Miller, DEATH OF A SALESMAN 1949

19 At last the ultimate in television party political broadcasts. The programmes no one wants, are to be shown on Channel 4, the channel no one watches. There hasn't been such a brilliant idea since the *Daily Express* offered a trip to the Antarctica as the prize in a competition and only three readers entered for it.
Daily Mirror, *leader* 16 *Feb* 1983

FUTURE

20 The energies of our system will decay, the glory of the sun will be dimmed, and the

earth, tideless and inert, will no longer tolerate the race which has for a moment disturbed its solitude. Man will go down into the pit, and his thoughts will perish.
A. J. Balfour, THE FOUNDATIONS OF BELIEF

1 The composer of the future may well be a combination physicist–mathematician, architect–electronic-engineer–musician.
Irwin Bazelon, KNOWING THE SCORE

2 I never think of the future. It comes soon enough.
Albert Einstein, in an interview, Dec 1930

3 When even lovers find their peace at last / And Earth is but a star that once had shone.
James Elroy Flecker, THE GOLDEN JOURNEY TO SAMARKAND 1913

4 I go to school in youth to learn the future.
Robert Frost, WEST RUNNING BROOK, *What Fifty Said 1928*

5 The future is not what it was.
Bernard Levin, The Sunday Times 22 *May 1977*

6 The future is something which everyone reaches at the rate of sixty minutes an hour, whatever he does, whoever he is.
C. S. Lewis, SCREWTAPE LETTERS 1941

7 To most of us the future seems unsure; but then it always has been; and we who have seen great changes must have great hopes.
John Masefield, GRACE BEFORE PLOUGHING

8 We cannot always build the future for our youth, but we can build our youth for the future.
Franklin D. Roosevelt. Speech, University of Pennsylvania 20 Sep 1940

9 Time enough to think of the future when you haven't any future to think of.
George Bernard Shaw, PYGMALION 1913

10 Time and space — time to be alone, space to move about — these may well become the greatest scarcities of tomorrow.
Edwin Way Teale, AUTUMN ACROSS AMERICA 1956

11 Human history becomes more and more a race between education and catastrophe.
H. G. Wells, OUTLINE OF HISTORY 1919

12 The future is the most expensive luxury in the world.
Thornton Wilder, THE MATCHMAKER 1955

G

GAIN

1 There are no gains without pains.
Adlai Stevenson. Speech, Chicago 26 *Jul* 1952

HUGH GAITSKELL

2 That desiccated calculating machine.
Aneurin Bevan. Quoted Philip M. William, HUGH GAITSKELL: A POLITICAL BIOGRAPHY

3 Gaitskell has a Wykehamistical voice and manner and a 13th century face.
Henry Channon, DIARY 10 *Apr* 1951

4 An intellectual highbrow who is naturally anxious to impress British labour with the fact that he learnt Latin at Winchester.
Winston Churchill

5 Morally, he was the bravest of all categories; he flinched, but he always went on.
Roy Jenkins. Quoted W.T. Rodgers, HUGH GAITSKELL

JOHN GALSWORTHY

6 Among literary reputations Galsworthy is a corpse that will not lie down.
Cyril Connolly, Sunday Times 27 *Jan* 1963

7 He has the gift of becoming, as it were, a statesman of literature.
Robert Lynd, John o'London's Weekly 8 *Dec* 1928

8 Galsworthy began as a critic of the Edwardian upper middle classes. He endures as their chronicler.
Robert Pitman, Sunday Express 27 *Jan* 1963

9 The author of the *Forsyte Saga* must be the most widely read Harrovian since Byron.
David Williams, Daily Telegraph 4 *Oct* 1968

GAMBLING

10 The gambling known as business looks with austere disfavour upon the business known as gambling.
Ambrose Bierce. Quoted H.L. Mencken

11 He who can predict winnning numbers has no need to let off fire-crackers.
Ernest Bramah, KAI LUNG UNROLLS HIS MAT 1928

12 No wife can endure a gambling husband unless he is a steady winner.
Lord Dewar. Speech

13 The strength of Monaco is the weakness of the world.
H. A. Gibbons, RIVIERA TOWNS: MONTE CARLO

14 It is a serious indictment of society if gambling is the only way to raise money for certain good causes.
Rev. Dr. Stanley Heavenor

15 Lose as if you like it; win as if you were used to it.
Jonas Hitchcock's advice to his son Tommy Hitchcock Jr. Quoted Newsweek

16 Gambling is a disease of barbarians, superficially civilised.
W. R. Inge (Dean of St. Pauls), OUT-SPOKEN ESSAYS 1919

17 If you can make one heap of all your winnings / And risk it on one turn of pitch-and-toss / And lose, and start again at your beginnings / And never breathe a word about your loss.
Rudyard Kipling, REWARDS AND FAIRIES, *If —* 1910

18 ... the apparent desire to accept the certainty of losing money in the long run in return for the remote possibility of winning it in the short.
Bernard Levin, THE PENDULUM YEARS 1976

1 The race is not always to the swift, nor the battle to the strong — but that's the way to bet.
Damon Runyon, MORE THAN SOMEWHAT 1937

2 The reason he is called Sky is because he goes so high when it comes to betting on any proposition whatever. He will bet all he has, and nobody can bet any more than that.
Damon Runyon, GUYS AND DOLLS 1932

3 Time spent in a casino is time given to death, a foretaste of the hour when one's flesh will be diverted to the purposes of the worm and not the will.
Rebecca West. Quoted Peter Wolfe, REBECCA WEST: ARTIST AND THINKER

4 Britain's strength, freedom and solvency apparently depend on the proceeds of a squalid raffle.
Harold Wilson on the introduction of Premium Bonds

GAMEKEEPER

5 Ever since (and possibly before) D. H. Lawrence immortalised the gamekeeper, ladies have liked them a lot . . . As a result many gentlemen say that if they were not gentlemen they would have liked to be gamekeepers.
Douglas Sutherland, THE ENGLISH GENTLEMAN'S WIFE 1979

GAMES

6 There is a vast difference between games and play. Play is played for fun, but games are deadly serious and you do not play them to enjoy yourself.
Maurice Baring, THE PUPPET SHOW OF MEMORY 1922

7 There's something wrong with a young chap who doesn't play games. Not even snooker.
Bernard Hollowood, SCOWLE IN THE SIXTIES

8 Almost any game with any ball is a good game.
Robert Lynd, THE PEAL OF BELLS

9 It is only children who are irresponsible and ill-educated enough to make a game of games.
Stephen Potter, SENSE OF HUMOUR 1954

10 Games always cover something deep and intense, else there would be no excitement in them, no pleasure, no power to stir us.
Antoine de Saint-Exupéry, AIRMAN'S ODYSSEY

11 Proficiency at billiards is proof of a misspent youth.
Herbert Spencer to a young member of the Athaeneum

INDIRA GANDHI

12 Extraordinarily imaginative, and self-centred or subjective, remarkably selfish, she lives in a world of dreams and vagaries and floats about on imaginary clouds full probably of all manner of brave fancies.
Pandit Nehru (her father). Quoted Observer, PROFILE, *The Last Empress of India* 21 *Mar* 1982

13 A woman who has mastered the art of adapting her demeanour to the occasion, but whose true self is rigorously concealed, and whose look, if you happen to catch her unawares, is often one of cold disdain.
Observer, PROFILE, *The Last Empress of India* 21 *Mar* 1982

14 It is a measure of her iron will that private grief has never been allowed to mar her public appearances except, perhaps, when tears could be expected to yield a dividend.
Id.

MAHATMA GANDHI

15 . . . a dear old man, with his bald pate and spectacles, beaky nose and bird-like lips and benign but somewhat toothless smile.
Rodney Bennett, Teacher's World 7 *May* 1930

16 It is . . . nauseating to see Mr. Gandhi, a seditious Middle Temple lawyer, now posing as a fakir of a type well known in the East, striding half naked up the steps of the Viceregal Palace, while he is still organising and conducting a defiant campaign of civil disobedience, to parley on equal terms with the representative of the King Emperor.
Winston Churchill. Speech, Epping 23 *Feb* 1931

17 Behind the simplicity and mischievous smile was a very complex man whose conception of life and death was different from those of lesser mortals. He had learned that non-violence provoked violence.

He perhaps knew that he would be murdered by a religious fanatic.
Louis Heren, The Times 4 Dec 1982

1 You've no idea what it costs to keep the old man in poverty.
Lord Mountbatten. Quoting a colleague, BBC 1 TV, Lord Mountbatten Remembers 12 Nov 1980

2 It costs a great deal of money to keep Gandhi in poverty.
Sarojini Naidu, Indian poetess. Quoted Woodrow Wyatt, Sunday Times 27 Nov 1977

3 The greatest Indian since Buddha.
Edward Thompson, Gandhi's obituary, News Chronicle 31 Jan 1948

4 Gandhi was very keen on sex. He renounced it when he was 36, so therefore it was never very far from his thoughts.
Woodrow Wyatt, Sunday Times, Homage to India's Strange Saint 27 Nov 1977

GRETA GARBO

5 There is no doubt she can act, if by acting is meant the power to suggest that she is feeling emotion and giving it out again in terms of her own personality.
James Agate of Greta Garbo, AROUND CINEMAS

6 People who know that we both appeared in *Grand Hotel* ask me "Is Garbo as strange a person as the newspapers say she is?" To which I answer "I don't know. I've never seen her. Though I have been on the same lot with her for four years I have never met her. She goes between her dressing room and her seat in a car, or closely guarded and in disguise. She never visits other actors or allows them to visit her."
Wallace Beery, MY UGLY MUG

7 What, when drunk, one sees in other women, one sees in Garbo sober.
Kenneth Tynan, Sunday Times 25 Aug 1963

GARDEN

8 After his death the gardener does not become a butterfly, intoxicated by flowers, but a garden worm tasting all the dark nitrogenous and spicy delights of the soil.
Karel Capek, THE GARDENER'S YEAR

9 The more help a man has in his garden, the less it belongs to him.
W. H. Davies

10 Oh Adam was a gardener and God who made him sees / That half a proper gardener's work is done upon his knees.
Rudyard Kipling, THE GLORY OF THE GARDEN 1911

11 Observing the ancient housekeeper wrestling with the plantlife in the garden, I occasionally point out a weed, and encourage her from the deck chair.
Arthur Marshall, Radio Times 23 Jul 1977

12 You must not praise the elegance of an Englishman's house — though you may always be impressed by the garden.
George Mikes, HOW TO BE AN ALIEN 1946

13 My garden will never make me famous / I'm a horticultural ignoramus / I can't tell a stringbean from a soy bean / Or even a girl bean from a boy bean.
Ogden Nash, HE DIGS, HE DUG, HE HAS DUG

14 It is not the business of the botanist to eradicate the weeds. Enough for him if he can just tell us how fast they grow.
C. Northcote Parkinson, PARKINSON'S LAW 1957

15 We have descended into the garden and caught 300 slugs. How I love the mixture of the beautiful and the squalid in gardening. It makes it so lifelike.
Evelyn Underhill, LETTERS

GENERAL DE GAULLE

16 I have every sympathy with General de Gaulle and his violent tantrums but let us conquer some of his country before we start squabbling about how it is to be governed. Yes, let's give him a bit of land to govern first.
Winston Churchill at an invasion conference

17 Intelligent — brilliant — resourceful, he spoils his undoubted talents by his excessive assurance, his contempt for other people's point of view, and his attitude of a king in exile.
Report of French War College 1922

GENEROSITY

18 We cannot win the weak by sharing our wealth with them. They feel our generosity as oppression.
Eric Hoffer, THE ORDEAL OF CHANGE 1962

1 The overpaying instinct is a generous one; better than the underpaying instinct, and not so common.
George Bernard Shaw, CANDIDA 1903

2 Generosity is a two-edged virtue for an artist — it nourishes his imagination but has a fatal effect on his routine.
Alexander Solzhenitsyn, THE FIRST CIRCLE 1964

GENIUS

3 We will always admire, but can never emulate, Genius; and though there is much that can be done with talent there is little you can do with Genius. In essence Genius is not a degree of kind, but a variation in type, and to how few can we apply that word?
Margot Asquith, obituary of Lord Birkenhead, News Chronicle 1 *Oct* 1930

4 Genius takes many shapes and colours. You have genius of one sort in Jerome Kern. Why deny it?
John Barbirolli, Observer 6 *Jul* 1947

5 Genius does what it must and talent does what it can.
Maurice Baring

6 I have known no man of genius who had not to pay in some affliction or defect, either physical or spiritual, for what the gods had given him.
Max Beerbohm, NO. 2 THE PINES

7 Genius-worship is the inevitable sign of an uncreative age.
Clive Bell, ART 1914

8 We define genius as the capacity for productive reaction against one's training.
Bernard Berenson, THE DECLINE OF ART

9 Where a human being has contributed something of genius to human thought and human art he is entitled to claim that the generations which follow shall extirpate from their minds recollections, however grave and painful, of any human infirmity which may have disfigured his career. For art is one thing and morals are quite another.
Lord Birkenhead addressing Scott Society, Edinburgh

10 The most vulgar of art's temptations; to be a genius.
Jorge Luis Borges, FICCIONES 1945

11 There are dancing motes or elements in genius which are impossible to pin down. One can only note their action, marvel at what they leave behind.
Elizabeth Bowen, COLLECTED IMPRESSIONS 1950

12 His genius has open arms.
George Brandes, of Björnstjerne Björnson. Quoted Oliver Edwards, The Times 4 *Aug* 1966

13 It might be more fitly described as a supreme capacity for getting its possessors into trouble of all kinds and keeping them therein so long as the genius remains.
Samuel Butler, NOTEBOOKS 1912

14 Genius, meaning by that an original creative power, is both much more common than we suppose and much more fragile. It is certainly more fragile than talent. For talent belongs to the capable and intelligent who understand their own powers and know how to manage them. Genius is sensitive and impressionable.
Joyce Cary, ART AND REALITY

15 In the presence of a masterpiece something of the artist's intention seems to pass into one's possession.
Hugh Casson, DIARY 1981

16 A genius she may be, but talent she hasn't got.
Mike Curtis, on viewing a screen test. Quoted Jan Peerce (singer)

17 But the genius, as with the birds, discovers within himself that which never need be sought. "I do not seek, I find" Picasso says, and before him, Cézanne spoke "I am the primitive of my way."
Louis Danz, DYNAMIC DISSONANCE

18 Mediocrity knows nothing higher than itself, but talent instantly recognises genius.
Sir Arthur Conan Doyle, THE VALLEY OF FEAR

19 It keeps repeating itself / In this world so fine and honest / The parson alarms the populace / The genius is executed.
Albert Einstein, of the campaign against Bertrand Russell in America 1940

20 In every man of genius a new strange force is brought into the world.
Havelock Ellis, SELECTED ESSAYS

21 It is a sign of real genius that it remains unspoiled by success.
Martin Esslin, THE THEATRE OF THE ABSURD

1 Simply because I have no seniors / The literati will raise the cry / Ewart's a genius.
Gavin Ewart. THE COLLECTED EWART

2 You can see how good things are done, but about the great you can only wonder how the devil he did it.
Charles Fisher, apropos Keats' La Belle Dame Sans Merci. *Quoted G. W. Lyttelton,* THE LYTTELTON HART-DAVIS LETTERS *30 Nov 1959*

3 The most gifted members of the human species are at their creative best when they cannot have their own way.
Eric Hoffer, THE ORDEAL OF CHANGE *1963*

4 Some men come by the name of genius in the same way as an insect comes by the name of centipede — not because it has a hundred feet but because most people can't count above fourteen.
George Lichtenberg

5 Genius is talent provided with ideals.
W. Somerset Maugham, A WRITER'S NOTEBOOK *1949*

6 Genius is an African who dreams up snow.
Vladimir Nabokov, THE GIFT *1963*

7 The heart and soul of genius may be mad, but the mind of true genius is ever as clear as the heavens seen through pine trees.
George Jean Nathan, MATERIA CRITICA

8 One of the surest signs of his [Joseph Conrad's] genius is that women dislike his books.
George Orwell, New English Weekly *23 Jul 1936*

9 Before I was a genius I was a drudge.
Paderewski

10 To the question "Do you think genius is hereditary?" he [James McNeil Whistler] replied, "I can't tell you; heaven has granted me no offspring."
Hesketh Pearson, LIVES OF THE WITS

11 The genius of Einstein leads to Hiroshima.
Pablo Picasso. Quoted Françoise Gilot and Carlton Lake, LIFE WITH PICASSO

12 The concept of genius as akin to madness has been carefully fostered by the inferiority complex of the public.
Ezra Pound, THE ABC OF READING *1934*

13 Genius is the capacity to see ten things where the ordinary man sees one, and where the man of talent sees two or three, *plus* the ability to register that multiple perception in the material of his art.
Ezra Pound, JEFFERSON AND/OR MUSSOLINI

14 Everything great in the world is done by neurotics; they alone founded our religions and created our masterpieces.
Marcel Proust, REMEMBRANCE OF THINGS PAST *1913–1927*

15 The man of genius, to shelter himself from the ignorant contempt of the world, may say to himself that since one's contemporaries are incapable of the necessary detachment, works written for posterity should be read by posterity alone, like certain pictures which one cannot appreciate when one stands too close to them.
Id.

16 Genius doesn't necessarily wear a beard and have neurotic love affairs, but may be found in a Kensington churchwarden who discusses cheese with the scholarly taste of a connoisseur.
James Reeves, T. S. ELIOT: A SYMPOSIUM

17 Addicts of nonsense haven't the sense to see that men and women of genius educate themselves.
A. L. Rowse, PORTRAITS AND VIEWS, *Jane Austen as Social Realist 1979*

18 All the men of genius that we have ever heard of have triumphed over adverse circumstances, but there is no reason for supposing that there were not innumerable others who succumbed in youth.
Bertrand Russell, THE CONQUEST OF HAPPINESS *1930*

19 The essential definition of a genius, I think, is that he is a man who not only knows the laws of things, but experiences them in himself with self-evident certainty. This experience of pure being transcends even love.
Oswald Schwartz, THE PSYCHOLOGY OF SEX

20 There is a certain characteristic common to all those whom we call geniuses. Each of them has a consciousness of being a man apart.
Miguel de Unamuno, ESSAYS AND SOLILOQUIES *1924*

21 He is the only genius with an IQ of 60.
Gore Vidal, ANDY WARHOL

22 Genius is in the planet's blood / You are either a poet or a Lilliputian.
Andrei Voznesensky, WHO ARE WE? *1960*

1 The man's a genius. From the collar upwards he stands alone.
P. G. Wodehouse, JEEVES TAKES CHARGE

2 When a country produces a man of genius he never is what it wants or believes it wants; he is always unlike its idea of itself.
W. B. Yeats, AUTOBIOGRAPHY 1955

GENTILITY

3 I keep picturing poor dear Nancy Mitford as a house guest in some baronial estate in Wiltshire or Norfolk, having been shown all the blue-ribbon cattle and praising them later to her hostess, unable to use the taboo word "cows" for fear of causing offence and opting instead for "the bulls and their wives".
Noël Coward. Quoted William Marchant, THE PRIVILEGE OF HIS COMPANY 1980

4 I don't want to talk grammar. I want to talk like a lady.
George Bernard Shaw, PYGMALION 1913

GENTLEMAN

5 He [Evelyn Waugh] was very conscious of what a gentleman should or should not do; no gentleman looks out of a window; no gentleman wears a brown suit.
Cecil Beaton, THE STRENUOUS YEARS

6 Jim thought that doing nothing meant being a gentleman.
Louis Bromfield, THE STRANGE CASE OF MISS ANNIE SPRAGG 1928

7 To be born a gentleman is an accident, to die one is an achievement.
Bob Goddard, St. Louis Globe-Democrat

8 We are all esquires now, and none of us are gentlemen any more.
Sir Ernest Gowers, Introduction to the revised edition of FOWLERS MODERN ENGLISH USAGE

9 This is the final test of a gentleman: his respect for those who can be of no possible service to him.
William Lyon Helps

10 I was brought up to believe that a gentleman appears in the papers three times: when he is born, when he gets married, and when he dies. With good behaviour — and a little bit of luck — that can be managed even today.
Michael Hogg, Daily Telegraph 2 *Dec* 1978

11 The criterion of a gentleman is that however poor he may be he still refuses to do useful work.
George Mikes, HOW TO BE AN ALIEN 1946

12 A gentleman does not utter everything he thinks.
Nigel Nicholson, ALEX: THE LIFE OF FIELD MARSHAL EARL ALEXANDER OF TUNIS

13 A gentleman never heard a story before.
Austin O'Malley, KEYSTONES OF THOUGHT

14 Anyone can be heroic from time to time, but a gentleman is something you have to be all the time.
Luigi Pirandello, THE PLEASURE OF HONESTY 1917

15 A gentleman never eats. He breakfasts, he lunches, he dines — but he never eats.
Cole Porter, quoting advice given by his tutor

16 Of course Miss Missouri Martin is not in a position to argue about gentlemen, because she meets so very few.
Damon Runyon, MORE THAN SOMEWHAT

17 A gentleman is a man whose grandfather earned more than £1000 a year.
Bertrand Russell. Quoted Rupert Crawshay-Williams, RUSSELL REMEMBERED

18 The concept of the gentleman was invented by the aristocrats to keep the middle classes in order.
Id.

19 I am a gentleman. I live by robbing the poor.
George Bernard Shaw, MAN AND SUPERMAN 1905

20 A gentleman is someone who gets out of the bath to go to the toilet.
Freddie Trueman. Quoted Jilly Cooper, CLASS

21 A gentleman is a man whose principal ideas are not connected with his personal needs and his personal services.
W. B. Yeats, AUTOBIOGRAPHY 1955

GEOGRAPHY

22 Geography is everywhere.
Graffito. Nigel Rees, GRAFFITI 2

GEORGE V

23 The 700 pages [of Eden's memoirs] contain only one joke — by King George V apropos Sir Samuel Hoare's resignation. "No more

coals to Newcastle; no more Hoares to Paris."
Malcolm Muggeridge, TREAD SOFTLY FOR YOU TREAD ON MY JOKES 1966

1 He had a gruff, blue-water approach to all human problems.
Duke of Windsor, A KING'S STORY

GEORGE VI

2 Constant tact from others had the effect of making him far too modest and he had quite lost sight of his own merits, if he ever knew them. He was, in fact, ideally suited for the British Throne.
Ronald Blythe, THE AGE OF ILLUSION

3 George VI in the conventional parlance was a Good King who sacrificed his life to his sense of duty. If we are to have monarchs it would be hard to find a better one.
A. J. P. Taylor, Observer, *A Dutiful Monarch* 24 Oct 1982

4 I am sure it will in no way detract from the prestige of my kingly brother when I say that when we were young I could always manage him.
Duke of Windsor. Quoted News Review 11 Dec 1947

GERIATRICS

5 Most treatment of the old requiring professional intervention not only tends to heighten their pain but, if successful, also protracts it.
Ivan D. Illich, MEDICAL NEMESIS

GERMANY

6 The German mind has a talent for making no mistakes except the very greatest.
Clifton Fadiman

7 In 1914 Europe had arrived at a point in which every country except Germany was afraid of the present and Germany was afraid of the future.
Viscount Grey of Fallodon, House of Lords 24 Jul 1924

8 As goes Germany, so goes Europe.
V. Holston, Moscow conference 1947

9 Germany is a machine for producing geniuses. Its crowning product was the German Jew which in suitably dramatic style it then tried to destroy.
Michel Tournier. Quoted Theodore Zeldin, Observer, *The Prophet of Unisex* 30 Jan 1983

GESTICULATION

10 *Gesticulation*: Any movement made by a foreigner.
Beachcomber (J. B. Morton)

GESTURE

11 Watch it, old son! That last gesture you made was untheatrical, unnecessary, and in your case, downright suspicious.
Robert Atkins to an effeminate actor. Quoted Michael Bentine, THE LONG BANANA SKIN

12 The gesture is the thing truly expressive of the individual — as we think so will we act.
Martha Graham. Quoted John Heilpern, Observer Magazine, *The Amazing Martha* 8 Jul 1979

13 She plucked from my lapel the invisible strand of lint — the universal act of woman to proclaim ownership.
O. Henry, STRICTLY BUSINESS, *A Ramble in Aphasia*

PAUL GETTY

14 ... who had always been vastly, immeasurably wealthy, and yet went about looking like a man who cannot quite remember whether he remembered to turn the gas off before leaving home.
Bernard Levin, THE PENDULUM YEARS 1976

GHOST

15 O lost, and by the wind grieved, ghost, come back again.
Thomas Wolfe, LOOK HOMEWARD ANGEL 1929

GIVING

16 You never want to give a man a present when he's feeling good. You want to do it when he's down.
Lyndon B. Johnson. Quoted Doris Kearns, LYNDON JOHNSON AND THE AMAZING DREAM

17 In choosing presents people should remember that the whole point of a present is that it is an extra.
E. V. Lucas, READING, WRITING AND REMEMBERING

18 One should, I think, always give children money, for they will spend it for themselves

far more profitably than we can ever spend it for them.
Rose Macaulay, A CASUAL COMMENTARY

1 The selection of presents for children is never easy, because in order to extract real pleasure from the purchase it is necessary to find something that excites the donor as much as it is likely to excite the recipient.
Compton Mackenzie, POOR RELATIONS

2 Send two dozen roses to Room 424 and put "Emily I love you" on the back of the bill.
Groucho Marx, A NIGHT IN CASABLANCA

3 If somebody gives you one of those de luxe editions of Jane Austen in a stand-up cardboard case, immediately buy any old nineteenth-century copy of a George Eliot novel and tell the Jane Austen giver that you have hunted for years for this example "of the Bristol edition" (you call it a Bristol First) and that when you found it six months ago you knew he would be the person to appreciate it.
Stephen Potter, ONE-UPMANSHIP 1952

4 The first rule in buying Christmas presents is to select something shiny . . . the wariest person will often mistake shininess for expensiveness.
P. G. Wodehouse, LOUDER AND FUNNIER

GLAMOUR

5 It was a sumpshous place all done up in gold with plenty of looking glases.
Dairy Ashford (aged 9), THE YOUNG VISITERS 1919

6 My grandfather Frank Lloyd Wright wore a red sash on his wedding night. That is glamour.
Anne Baxter, Time Magazine 5 *May* 1952

7 It was a blonde. A blonde to make a bishop kick a hole in a stained glass window.
Raymond Chandler, FAREWELL MY LOVELY 1940

8 Glamour is when a man knows a woman is a woman.
Gina Lollobrigida. Quoted Observer 15 *Jul* 1956

GLUTTONY

9 My boy you are not an MP, you are a gastronomic pimp.
Aneurin Bevan, to a colleague he accused of attending too many public dinners. Quoted Michael Foot, ANEURIN BEVAN 1897–1945

10 Gluttony is an emotional escape, a sign that something is eating us.
Peter De Vries, COMFORT ME WITH APPLES 1956

11 "What I like about gluttony" a bishop I once knew used to say, "is that it doesn't hurt anyone else."
Monica Furlong, CHRISTIAN UNCERTAINTIES

12 Only men in rags / And gluttons old in sin / Mistake themselves for carpet bags / And tumble victuals in.
Sir Walter Raleigh, LAUGHTER FROM A CLOUD

13 There is no love sincerer than the love of food.
George Bernard Shaw, MAN AND SUPERMAN 1905

14 The sin comes in with the determination to refuse food and the self-disgust that follows having, on the contrary, just eaten a whole bar of chocolate all by yourself in the middle of the afternoon. It's worse than going to the pictures in the morning.
Katherine Whitehorn, Punch 10 *May* 1972

ELINOR GLYN

15 Would you like to sin / With Elinor Glyn / On a tiger skin / Or would you prefer / To err with her / On some other fur?
Anon.

16 Elinor Glyn, fortified with coffee and brandy, took to her bed to write a 90,000 word novel in three weeks, and did it in 18 days.
Laurence Wright, WARM AND SNUG

GOD

17 Every man thinks God is on his side. The rich and powerful know he is.
Jean Anouilh, THE LARK 1953

18 Does God ever judge us by appearances? I suspect that he does.
W. H. Auden. Quoted New Yorker 21 *Nov* 1977

19 What is the prose for God?
H. Granville Barker, WASTE

20 I cannot be angry at God, in whom I do not believe.
Simone de Beauvoir. Quoted Observer 7 *Jan* 1979

1 To my mind the most poignant mystical exhortation ever written is "Be Still and know that I am God."
Arnold Bennett, JOURNALS, *Dec* 1929

2 A God who let us prove his existence would be an idol.
Dietrich Bonhoeffer, NO RUSTY SWORDS

3 Immense, of fishy form and mind / Squamous, omnipotent and kind; / And under that Almighty Fin / The little fish may enter in.
Rupert Brooke, HEAVEN 1913

4 An honest God: the noblest work of man.
Samuel Butler, NOTEBOOKS 1912

5 God is love — I dare say. But what a mischievous devil Love is.
Id.

6 The Lord will provide, dear, but you must give him some help.
Sir Hugh Casson and Joyce Grenfell, NANNY SAYS 1972

7 When God shuts a door he opens a window.
Id.

8 There can only be fairy godmothers because there are godmothers, and there can only be godmothers because there is God.
G. K. Chesterton, AUTOBIOGRAPHY

9 I took it completely for granted that God had never spoken anything but the most dignified English.
Clarence Day, LIFE WITH FATHER 1935

10 It is the final proof of God's omnipotence that He need not exist in order to save us.
Peter De Vries, THE MACKEREL PLAZA 1958

11 God does not play dice.
Albert Einstein, a favourite axiom, frequently used

12 God is subtle, but he is not malicious.
Albert Einstein

13 God is an unutterable sign in the Human Heart, said the old German mystic. And therewith said the last word.
Havelock Ellis, IMPRESSIONS AND COMMENTS

14 At bottom God is nothing more than an exalted father.
Sigmund Freud, TOTEM AND TABOO 1918

15 I turned to speak to God / About the world's despair; / But to make bad matters worse / I found God wasn't there.
Robert Frost, COLLECTED POEMS, *Not All There* 1951

16 God is a verb / Not a noun.
R. Buckminster Fuller, NO MORE SECOND-HAND GOD 1963

17 The Mister God Light inside us is so's we can see the Mister God Light outside us and the Mister God Light outside us is so we can see the Mister God Light inside us.
Fynn, MISTER GOD, THIS IS ANNA 1974

18 Mister God ain't got no bum.
Id.

19 God has no religion.
Mahatma Gandhi

20 God depends on us. It is through us that God is achieved.
André Gide, JOURNALS 1939–1950

21 God is alive and well but considering a less ambitious project.
Graffito. Quoted Patrick Moore, Observer 18 *Mar* 1979

22 How much reverence can you have for a Supreme Being who finds it necessary to include such phenomena as phlegm and tooth decay in this divine system of creation?
Joseph Heller, CATCH 22 1961

23 The change in our conception of God necessitates the stressing of religious experience as such, as against belief in particular dogma, or in the efficacy of special ritual.
Julian Huxley, ESSAYS OF A BIOLOGIST 1933

24 Operationally, God is beginning to resemble not a ruler but the last fading smile of a cosmic Cheshire cat.
Julian Huxley, RELIGION WITHOUT REVOLUTION

25 The God whom science recognises must be a God of universal laws exclusively . . . He cannot accommodate his processes to the convenience of individuals.
William James, THE VARIETIES OF RELIGIOUS EXPERIENCE 1902

26 One cannot expect to be conscious of God's presence when one has only a bowing acquaintance with Him.
Mme. Chiang Kai-shek, I CONFESS MY FAITH

27 The only God that is of use is a being who is personal, supreme and good, and whose existence is as certain as that two and two make four.
W. Somerset Maugham, THE SUMMING UP 1938

1 When men make gods there is no God.
Eugene O'Neill, LAZARUS LAUGHED 1927

2 God is really only another artist. He invented the giraffe, the elephant and the cat. He has no real style. He just goes on trying other things.
Pablo Picasso. Quoted Françoise Gilot and Carlton Lake, LIFE WITH PICASSO

3 Polite Society believed in God so that it need not talk of Him.
Jean-Paul Sartre, WORDS

4 God ain't said nothing for years, He ain't.
Johnny Speight, BBC 1 TV, *Till Death Us Do Part*

5 Her [Florence Nightingale] conception of God was certainly not orthodox. She felt towards him as she might have felt towards a glorified sanitary engineer; and in some of her speculations she seems hardly to distinguish between the Deity and the Drains.
Lytton Strachey, EMINENT VICTORIANS 1918

6 By and large gentlemen believe in God because, by and large, they are confident God believes in them.
Douglas Sutherland, THE ENGLISH GENTLEMAN 1978

7 It is a mistake to suppose that God is only, or even chiefly, concerned with religion.
William Temple (Archbishop of Canterbury). Quoted R.V.C. Bodley, IN SEARCH OF SERENITY

8 God in his whirlwind silence save, who marks the sparrow's hail / For their souls' song.
Dylan Thomas, OVER ST. JOHN'S HILL

9 Thou canst see all the time, O God, man, you're like a bloody cat.
Dylan Thomas, THE PREACHER

10 God is a sort of burglar. As a young man you knock him down; as an old man you try to conciliate him, because he may knock you down.
Sir H. Beerbohm Tree. Quoted Hesketh Pearson, BEERBOHM-TREE

11 "Let God do it all," someone will say; but if man folds his arms, God will go to sleep.
Miguel de Unamuno, TRAGIC SENSE OF LIFE 1913

12 I don't care what other people say about God. He has been very sweet to me.
Godfrey Winn. Quoted Cyril Fletcher, NICE ONE CYRIL

HERMANN GOERING

13 He may be a blackguard, but he is not a dirty blackguard.
Sir Neville Henderson. Speech, Sleaford, Lancs

GOLDEN AGE

14 The Golden Age comes to men when they have, if only for a moment, forgotten gold.
G. K. Chesterton, New York Times Magazine 3 *May* 1931

GOLDFISH

15 He pasted picture postcards around goldfish bowls to make the goldfish think they were going places.
Fred Allen, American radio comedian

SAM GOLDWYN

16 You always knew where you were with Goldwyn — nowhere.
F. Scott Fitzgerald. Quoted Matthew J. Bruccoli, SOME SORT OF EPIC GRANDEUR

GOLF

17 Met her [Celia Johnson's] uncle on the first tee of a golf course recently. He said "Is my niece as good as you say she is?" I said "No", drove off and walked away. I will *not* be talked to about the theatre when I am playing golf.
James Agate, EGO 1 1935

18 Golf seems to me an arduous way to go for a walk. I prefer to take the dogs out.
Princess Anne. Quoted Noël St. George, ROYAL QUOTES

19 "What do you go round in, Miss Champion?" enquired one of the men. "My ordinary clothes." replied Jane.
Florence L. Barclay, THE ROSARY 1909

20 Golf is a game whose aim is to hit a very small ball into an even smaller hole, with weapons singularly ill-designed for the purpose.
Winston Churchill. Quoted Alistair Cooke, BBC Radio 4 27 *Dec* 1974

21 Golf has given me an understanding of the futility of human effort.
Ebra Eban. Quoted Milton Gross, EIGHTEEN HOLES IN MY HEAD

22 Golf always makes me so damned angry.
George V. Quoted Peter Ross, Sunday Referee 28 *Dec* 1938

1 I find it more satisfying to be a bad player at golf. The worse you play, the better you remember the occasional good shot.
Nubar Gulbenkian. Quoted in his obituary, Daily Telegraph 12 *Jan* 1972

2 Golf may be played on Sunday, not being a game within the view of the law, but being a form of moral effort.
Stephen Leacock, OTHER FANCIES, *Why I Refuse to Play Golf*

3 I do much of my creative thinking while golfing. If people know you are working at home they think nothing of walking in for a cup of coffee. But they wouldn't dream of interrupting you on the golf course.
Harper Lee, author of TO KILL A MOCKING BIRD. *Quoted Bruce and Mark Fowler*, WRITER'S DIGEST

4 Few people are sensible about holidays. Many play golf, and one odd effect of that pursuit is that they return to work *manifestly* stupider than they were. It is, I think, the company of other golfers.
G. W. Lyttelton, THE LYTTELTON HART-DAVIS LETTERS 18 *May* 1956

5 The uglier a man's legs are, the better he plays golf. It is almost a law.
H. G. Wells, BEALBY 1915

GOODNESS

6 Goodness is easier to recognise than to define.
W. H. Auden

7 Good is that which makes for unity. Evil is that which makes for separateness.
Aldous Huxley, ENDS AND MEANS 1937

8 When I'm good I'm very very good, but when I'm bad I'm better.
Mae West, I'M NO ANGEL *(film)*

9 "Goodness, what beautiful diamonds."
"Goodness had nothing to do with it."
Mae West, NIGHT AFTER NIGHT *(film)*

GOSSIP

10 There are many who dare not kill themselves for fear of what the neighbours will say.
Cyril Connolly, THE UNQUIET GRAVE 1945

11 I'd love to stay chatting all day, but you know what it's like.
Diana, Princess of Wales, during an Australian walkabout 26 *Mar* 1983

12 To tell me he doesn't like gossip is like someone telling me he doesn't like Queen's Pudding. I simply cannot understand it, nor do I approve.
Robert Morley, MORLEY MARVELS 1976

13 And what she did *next* summer was even worse. I'll tell you when the music starts.
Overheard at Festival Hall, London. Quoted Pendennis, Observer 26 *Apr* 1959

14 Miss Missouri Martin tells everything she knows as soon as she knows it, which is often before it happens.
Damon Runyon, MORE THAN SOMEWHAT 1937

GOURMET

15 A gourmet is just a glutton with brains.
Philip W. Haberman, Jr., Vogue 1 *May* 1961

GOVERNMENT

16 Attended Cabinet — I forget what about.
Leo Amery, DIARIES

17 If the King asks you to form a government you say "Yes" or "No" not "I'll let you know later."
Clement Attlee. Quoted Kenneth Harris, ATTLEE

18 A statesman wants courage and a statesman wants vision; but believe me, after six months' experience, he wants first, second, third and all the time — patience.
Stanley Baldwin. Speech, Plymouth 26 *Oct* 1923

19 This island is almost made of coal and surrounded by fish. Only an organising genius could produce a shortage of both in Great Britain at the same time.
Aneurin Bevan. Quoted Vincent Broome, ANEURIN BEVAN

20 The object of government in peace and in war is not the glory of rulers or of races, but the happiness of the common man.
William, Lord Beveridge, SOCIAL INSURANCE

21 The only good government is a bad one in the hell of a fright.
Joyce Cary, THE HORSE'S MOUTH 1944

22 I've never regretted being in the government. I love responsibility and I don't mind unpopularity.
Barbara Castle. Quoted Peter Dunn, Sunday Times 2 *Jul* 1967

1 All governments are pretty much alike, with a tendency on the part of the last to be the worst.
Austen Chamberlain, House of Commons 1919

2 Democracy means government by the uneducated, while aristocracy means government by the badly educated.
G. K. Chesterton, New York Times 1 Feb 1931

3 Few things are more mischievous to good government and to "domestic tranquillity" than splendid rhetoric that doesn't pay off.
Alistair Cooke, AMERICA

4 Everything goes wrong for a government which is going wrong.
Richard Crossman, DIARIES 1 Dec 1968

5 A Royal Commission is a broody hen sitting on a china egg.
Michael Foot

6 Governments never learn. Only people learn.
Milton Friedman. Quoted Observer 30 Mar 1980

7 A government that is big enough to give you all you want is big enough to take it all away.
Barry Goldwater. Speech, Westchester 21 Oct 1964

8 Mr. Callaghan blamed them on strikes and the weather, implying that a government was in varying degrees powerless against both. Strikes, he presumably felt, were acts of God, although a government might one day be able to do something about the weather.
Frank Johnson, Daily Telegraph 16 Mar 1979

9 Amendments are (a) The afterthoughts of law-makers, (b) A method of defeating a resolution by improvement.
Emery Kelen, Christian Science Monitor. Quoted News Review 27 May 1948

10 When we got into office the thing that surprised me most was to find that things were just as bad as we'd been saying they were.
John F. Kennedy. Quoted Barbara Rowe, BOOK OF QUOTES

11 The title [A Distant Mirror, by Barbara W. Tuchman] suggests that the fourteenth and twentieth centuries are directly comparable. I doubt it. Governments now understand their problems even if they cannot cure them.
John Kenyon, Observer, Death of Chivalry 4 Mar 1979

12 The first thing [for a government] to do in a crisis is to set up a committee.
Bernard Levin, THE PENDULUM YEARS 1976

13 In a free society the state does not administer the affairs of men. It administers justice among men who conduct their own affairs.
Walter Lippmann, AN ENQUIRY INTO THE PRINCIPLES OF A GOOD SOCIETY

14 The paradox of British politics; the moment one appropriates power one becomes impotent.
Ramsay MacDonald, to Charles Chaplin. Quoted MY AUTOBIOGRAPHY 1964

15 It is the duty of H.M. Government neither to flap nor falter.
Harold Macmillan. The remark made when Prime Minister which earned him the epithet 'unflappable'

16 After a few months learning geography, now I've got to learn arithmetic.
Harold Macmillan, on moving from the Foreign Office to the Treasury, to Harold Wilson. Quoted, A PRIME MINISTER ON PRIME MINISTERS 1977

17 The worst government is the most moral. One composed of cynics is often very tolerant and humane. But when fanatics are on top there is no limit to oppression.
H. L. Mencken, NOTEBOOKS

18 All government, in its essence, is a conspiracy against the superior man.
H. L. Mencken, SMART SET, Dec 1919

19 It is much easier being Prime Minister than Lord President of the Council. All you have to do is delegate the work to somebody else.
Herbert Morrison. Quoted News Review, 19 Aug 1948

20 The government of England is a limited mockery.
Extract from child's essay. Quoted, THE NELSONIAN

21 I like to operate like a submarine or sonar. When I am picking up noise from both the left and the right I know my course is correct.
President Ordaz of Mexico. Inaugural speech

1 It is said that every people has the government it deserves. It is more to the point that every Government has the electorate it deserves; for the orators of the front bench can edify or debauch an ignorant electorate at will.
George Bernard Shaw, HEARTBREAK HOUSE, *Preface* 1920

2 Down with government by the grey-haired.
George Bernard Shaw, MAN AND SUPERMAN 1905

3 The art of government is the organisation of idolatry.
Id. *Maxims for Revolutionists.*

4 It would be desirable if every government, when it comes to power, should have its old speeches burnt.
Philip Snowden. Quoted in the biography of him by C. E. Bechofer Roberts (Ephesian)

5 Any woman who understands the problems of running a home will be nearer to understanding the problems of running a country.
Margaret Thatcher. Quoted Observer 8 May 1979

6 In the whole course of history there's been no government that could alter the laws of nature.
E. Temple Thurston, MR. BOTTLEBY DOES SOMETHING

7 To govern is to choose how the revenue from taxes is to be spent.
Gore Vidal, HOMAGE TO DANIEL SHAYS

8 Theoretically there is a vast difference between the United States and the United Kingdom. My country is not a democracy. It is a monarchy, aided by two houses of parliament, one of which, of lesser importance, is predominantly hereditary and therefore richly representative of the 'private man' in all his idiosyncrasies.
Evelyn Waugh, commentary for T. A. MacInery's THE PRIVATE MAN

9 My reading of history convinces me that most bad government has grown out of too much government.
John Sharp Williams, THOMAS JEFFERSON

10 I was not going to play every position myself, administer to the wounded, and bring on the lemon at half time, but would be a deep-lying centre half, concentrating on defence, distributing the ball and moving upfield only for set-piece occasions.
Harold Wilson, FINAL TERM: THE LABOUR GOVERNMENT 1974–1976

11 No man ever saw a government. I live in the midst of the Government of the United States but I never saw the Government of the United States.
Woodrow Wilson. Speech, Pittsburgh 29 Jan 1916

GRAFFITO

12 Popular education was bringing the graffito lower on the walls.
Oliver St. John Gogarty, AS I WAS GOING DOWN SACKVILLE STREET 1937

13 If God had not meant us to write on walls he would never have set us an example.
Graffito. Quoted Nigel Rees, GRAFFITO 2 1980

14 Poster advertising had, of course, long had an erotic content which disturbed many people and many of them found relief from the impulses thus stirred by writing or drawing on the advertisements in an obscene manner and perhaps finding relief in this pictorial masturbation from the desires which tormented them.
Bernard Levin, THE PENDULUM YEARS 1976

15 He [Ernest Thesiger] was in Moscow on a theatrical tour. He went into one of the public conveniences and finding himself alone, wrote on the wall 'Burgess loves Maclean.'
Michael Pertwee, NAME DROPPING

GRANDMOTHER

16 Everyone should try to have a granny, especially those who have no TV. Grannies are the only grown-ups who always have time.
Child quoted by Annejet Campbell, LISTEN TO THE CHILDREN

17 They can answer questions like "Why do dogs hate cats?" and "Why isn't God married?" They never mind reading the same story over and over again.
Id.

18 They are usually fat but not too fat to tie your shoelaces. They wear glasses and sometimes they can take their teeth out.
Id.

GRATITUDE

1 The obligation of gratitude may easily become a trap, and the young are often caught and maimed in it.
Eric Gill, AUTOBIOGRAPHY

2 Gratitude is a sickness suffered by dogs.
Joseph Stalin. Quoted Nikolai Tolstoy, STALIN'S SECRET WAR

GRAVE

3 For rain it hath a friendly sound / To one who's six feet underground; / And scarce the friendly voice or face; / A grave is such a quiet place.
Edna St. Vincent Millay, RENASCENCE 1912

4 All roads end at the grave, which is the gate to nothingness.
George Bernard Shaw, A BLACK GIRL IN HER SEARCH FOR GOD

GRAVITY

5 Gravity was discovered by Isaac Walton. It is chiefly noticed in the autumn when the apples are falling off the trees.
Extract from child's essay, reported by correspondent to Teacher's World 1931

GREATNESS

6 You don't have to be a good man to be a great man.
Marquis of Bath in an interview with Tim Heald, Daily Express 4 *Apr* 1968

7 There is a great man who makes every man feel small. But the really great man is the man who makes every man feel great.
G. K. Chesterton, CHARLES DICKENS 1906

8 Mrs. Asquith remarked indiscreetly that if Kitchener was not a great man, he was, at least, a great poster.
Sir Philip Magnus, KITCHENER: PORTRAIT OF AN IMPERIALIST 1958

GREECE

9 The most un-Greek thing we can do is copy the Greeks. For emphatically they were not copyists.
A. N. Whitehead, ADVENTURES OF IDEAS 1933

GREED

10 We take what we want and God sends the bill.
Dr. Rhodes Boyson MP, Daily Telegraph 20 *Feb* 1979

11 Greed, like the love of comfort, is a kind of fear.
Cyril Connolly, THE UNQUIET GRAVE 1945

12 There is enough for the needy but not for the greedy.
Mahatma Gandhi

13 Believe me, of all the people in the world, those who want the most are those who have the most.
David Grayson, THE FRIENDLY ROAD

14 The instinct of acquisitiveness has more perverts, I believe, than the instinct of sex. At any rate people seem to me to be odder about money than about even their amours.
Aldous Huxley, POINT COUNTER POINT 1934

15 Something better than Freedom from Want is Freedom from Wanting
J. P. McEvoy, Travel Magazine, *Jun* 1946

GRAHAM GREENE

16 He has created a climate of crack-brained confusion between vices and virtues — a climate in which the traitor flourishes.
Rebecca West. Quoted J. W. Lambert, Sunday Times, *The Private World of Graham Greene* 5 *Mar* 1978

GREETING

17 I step over to his table and give him a medium hello, and he looks up and gives me a medium hello right back for, to tell the truth, Maury and I are never bosom friends.
Damon Runyon, MORE THAN SOMEWHAT 1937

18 He [John Cartwright MP] seized the newcomers by the hand. Either he was pleased to see them or they owed him money.
Michael White, Guardian, *reporting SDP Conference at Bradford* 8 *Oct* 1981

GRIEF

19 Happiness is beneficial for the body but it is grief that develops the powers of the mind.
Marcel Proust, REMEMBRANCE OF THINGS PAST, *Time Regained* 1927

GRIEVANCE

1 To have a grievance is to have a purpose in life.
Eric Hoffer, THE PASSIONATE STATE OF MIND 1954

GUARANTEE

2 Behold the guarantee — the bold print giveth, and the fine print taketh away.
Anon. Farmer's Digest

GUEST

3 First impressions mean a lot so always have good luggage.
Sir Hugh Casson and Joyce Grenfell, NANNY SAYS 1972

4 I entertained on a cruising trip that was such fun that I had to sink my yacht to make my guests go home.
F. Scott Fitzgerald, NOTEBOOKS

5 Some people can stay longer in an hour than others can in a week.
William Dean Howells. Quoted John Bartlett, FAMILIAR QUOTATIONS

6 Go — and never darken my towels again.
Groucho Marx, DUCK SOUP

7 My father used to say "Superior people never make long visits".
Marianne Moore, BLACK EARTH

GUILT

8 I too am a reluctant puritan, feel uneasy / Sometimes as if I travelled without a ticket. / Yet here I am in England, way out in the centre.
Dannie Abse, WAY OUT IN THE CENTRE

9 All those saints covered in blood and the harping on guilt. It's macabre and futile.
Federico Fellini, Observer, *Profile 26 Aug* 1963

10 True guilt is guilt at the obligation one owes to oneself to be oneself.
R. D. Laing, SELF AND OTHERS

GUITAR

11 Electric guitars are an abomination. Whoever heard of an electric violin? Or for that matter an electric singer?
Andres Segovia, THE BEATLES, WORDS WITHOUT MUSIC 1968

12 The turning point in the history of western civilisation was reached with the invention of the electric guitar.
Leni Sinclair. Quoted John Sinclair, GUITAR ARMY 1972

H

HABIT

1 Violet Trefusis always has a delightfully insouciant way of putting her cigarette out in a pat of butter.
Cecil Beaton. Caption to drawing in Eileen Hope's collection, Salisbury.

2 Habit is a great deadener.
Samuel Beckett, WAITING FOR GODOT 1952

3 "Music" she said dreamily, and such is the force of habit that "I don't" she added, "know anything about music really, but I know what I like."
Max Beerbohm, ZULEIKA DOBSON 1911

4 I take a decided pleasure in forming habits and re-forming old ones . . . The pleasure of doing the same thing in the same way at the same time each day should be noted.
Arnold Bennett, JOURNALS 1911–1921

5 Widget takes a nicotine-stained forefinger out of his nostril which he had been exploring with perseverance worthy of a better object.
Gerald Kersh, CLEAN, BRIGHT AND SLIGHTLY OILED 1946

6 I've grown accustomed to the trace / Of something in the air, / Accustomed to her face.
Alan Jay Lerner, MY FAIR LADY 1956

7 Every afternoon at 4.30 for the past five months I had fallen into an exact routine. First off, I'd tap the dottle from my pipe by knocking it against the hob. I never smoke a pipe, but I like to keep one with a little dottle in it and an inexpensive hob to tap it against. When you're in the writing game these are the little accessories you need.
S. J. Perelman, CRAZY LIKE A FOX 1944

8 To fall into a habit is to begin to cease to be.
Miguel de Unamuno, TRAGIC SENSE OF LIFE 1913

9 She stamped Kipps so deeply with the hat-raising habit that he would uncover if he found himself in the same railway ticket office with a lady, and so stand ceremoniously until the difficulties of change drove him to an apologetic provisional oblique resumption of his headgear.
H. G. Wells, KIPPS 1905

DOUGLAS, EARL HAIG

10 With the publication of his Private Papers in 1952, he committed suicide 25 years after his death.
Lord Beaverbrook, MEN AND POWER

LORD HAILSHAM

11 When self indulgence has reduced a man to the shape of Lord Hailsham, sexual continence involves no more than a sense of the ridiculous.
Reginald Paget MP, House of Commons 16 Jun 1963

HAND

12 Old hands soil, it seems, whatever they caress, but they too have their beauty when they are joined in prayer. Young hands were made for caresses and the sheathing of love. It is a pity to make them join too soon.
André Gide, JOURNALS 21 Jan 1929

13 The hand that signed the paper felled a city / Five sovereign fingers taxed the breath / Doubled the globe of dead and halved a country / These five kings did a king to death.
Dylan Thomas, THE HAND THAT SIGNED THE PAPER 1930

HANDICAP

14 It is, of course, a bit of a drawback that science was invented after I left school.
Lord Carrington. Quoted Observer, *Last of the Tory Grandees 23 Jan 1983*

HANGOVER

15 His mouth has been used as a latrine by some small animal of the night.
Kingsley Amis, LUCKY JIM 1954

1 A mouth like the inside of a zoo-keeper's welly.
Peter Watson, The Times Diary 27 *Nov* 1981

HAPPINESS

2 Only in romantic novels are the beautiful guaranteed happiness.
Lady Cynthia Asquith, DIARIES

3 One should never let one's happiness depend on other people.
H. Granville Barker, THE VOYSEY INHERITANCE 1905

4 Happy people are failures because they are on such good terms with themselves that they don't give a damn.
Agatha Christie, SPARKLING CYANIDE

5 What we call happiness in the strictest sense of the word comes from the (preferably sudden) satisfaction of needs which have been dammed up to a high degree.
Sigmund Freud, CIVILISATION AND ITS DISCONTENTS

6 Happiness makes up in height what it lacks in length.
Robert Frost, title of poem 1942

7 Nothing is more fatal to happiness than the remembrance of happiness.
André Gide, THE IMMORALIST 1902

8 Happiness is the sublime moment when you get out of your corsets at night.
Joyce Grenfell, in a luncheon club speech

9 It's pretty hard to tell what does bring happiness; poverty and wealth have both failed.
Kim Hubbard, ABE MARTIN 1930

10 There is something curiously boring about somebody else's happiness.
Aldous Huxley, LIMBO, *Cynthia*

11 Happiness is like coke — something you get as a by-product in the process of making something else.
Aldous Huxley, POINT COUNTER POINT 1928

12 Many persons have a wrong idea of what constitutes true happiness. It is not obtained through self-gratification, but through fidelity to a worthy purpose.
Helen Keller, JOURNAL 1938

13 "Did you have a happy childhood?" is a false question. As a child I did not know what happiness was, and whether I was happy or not. I was too busy *being*.
Alistair Reid, THE WORLD OF CHILDREN

14 Really high-minded people are indifferent to happiness, especially other people's.
Bertrand Russell, THE CONQUEST OF HAPPINESS 1930

15 If you wish to be happy yourself you must resign yourself to seeing others happy.
Id.

16 To be without some of the things you want is an indispensable part of happiness.
Id.

17 A happy life must be to a great extent a quiet life, for it is only in an atmosphere of quiet that true joy dare live.
Id.

18 I do not believe that science *per se* is an adequate source of happiness, nor do I think my own scientific outlook has contributed very greatly to my own happiness which I attribute to defecating twice a day with unfailing regularity.
Bertrand Russell, letter to W. W. Norton 27 *Jan* 1931

19 Happiness is not best achieved by those who seek it directly.
Bertrand Russell, MYSTICISM AND LOGIC 1918

20 Happiness is the only sanction of life; where happiness fails, existence remains a mad and lamentable experiment.
George Santayana, THE LIFE OF REASON, *Reason in Commonsense* 1906

21 We have no more right to consume happiness without producing it than to consume wealth without producing it.
George Bernard Shaw, CANDIDA 1903

22 A man is happy so long as he chooses to be happy and nothing can stop him.
Alexander Solzhenitsyn, CANCER WARD

23 It is not swinish to be happy unless one is happy in swinish ways.
Susan Stebbing, IDEALS AND ILLUSIONS

24 Happiness is an imaginary condition formerly often attributed by the living to the dead, now normally attributed by adults to children, and by children to adults.
Thomas Szasz, THE SECOND SIN, *Emotions*

25 Who never knew the price of happiness will not be happy.
Yevgeny Yevtushenko, BABI YAR 1961

PRESIDENT HARDING

26 He has a bungalow mind.
Woodrow Wilson. Quoted C. W. Thompson, PRESIDENTS I HAVE KNOWN

HARPSICHORD

1 The sound of a harpsichord: two skeletons copulating on a tin roof.
Sir Thomas Beecham. Quoted Nat Shapiro, ENCYCLOPEDIA OF QUOTATIONS ABOUT MUSIC 1978

HAT

2 Eleanor Roosevelt's hats had the look of having been found under the bed.
Joseph Alsop, FDR 1882/1945: THE LIFE AND TIMES OF FRANKLIN D. ROOSEVELT

3 That's a hat to go to a concert half an hour late in.
Margot Asquith. Quoted Arnold Bennett, JOURNALS 1932

4 He can't think without his hat.
Samuel Beckett, WAITING FOR GODOT 1952

5 The bowler of Mr. Jerome K. Jerome is a perfect preface to all his works.
Max Beerbohm, DANDIES AND DANDIES

6 The top hat [at Eton] was the most useful of items, being a splendid place to keep ice-cream in summer, and white mice in winter.
Michael Bentine, THE LONG BANANA SKIN

7 He is known to often carry a gun in his pants pocket and to shoot people down as dead as doornails with it if he does not like the way they wear their hats — and Rusty Charlie is very critical of hats.
Damon Runyon, MORE THAN SOMEWHAT 1937

HATE

8 One of the reasons people cling to their hates so stubbornly is because they seem to sense, once hate is gone, that they will be forced to deal with pain.
James Baldwin, NOTES OF A NATIVE SON 1955

9 Hatred rarely does any harm to its object. It is the hater who suffers. His soul is warped and his life poisoned by dwelling on past injuries or projecting schemes of revenge. Rancour in the bosom is the foe of personal happiness.
Lord Beaverbrook, THE DIVINE PROPAGANDIST

10 It does not matter much what a man hates, provided he hates something.
Samuel Butler, NOTEBOOKS 1912

11 I tell you there is such a thing as creative hate.
Willa Cather, THE SONG OF THE LARK 1915

12 I hate nobody except Hitler — and that's professional.
Winston Churchill, to John Colville. Quoted, THE CHURCHILLIANS

13 Hate has what lust entirely lacks — persistence and continuity; the persistence and continuity of purposive spirit.
Aldous Huxley, BEYOND THE MEXIQUE BAY

14 We must hate — hatred is the basis of Communism. Children must be taught to hate their parents if they are not Communists.
V. I. Lenin. Speech to the Commissars of Education, Moscow 1923

15 We never will forgo our hate / We have all but a single hate / We love as one, we hate as one / We have one foe and one alone / England.
Ernst Lissaner, SONG OF HATE 1914

16 Any kiddie in school can love like a fool / But hating, my boy, is an art.
Ogden Nash, PLEAS FOR LESS MALICE TOWARDS NONE

17 Enemies are not those who hate us, but rather those whom we hate.
Dagobert Runes, A DICTIONARY OF THOUGHT

18 Few people can be happy unless they hate some other person, nation or creed.
Bertrand Russell, AUTOBIOGRAPHY 1961

19 Hatred is the coward's revenge for being intimidated.
George Bernard Shaw, MAJOR BARBARA 1905

20 Love for the same thing never makes allies. It's always hate for the same thing.
Howard Spring, MY SON, MY SON 1938

21 To be choked with hate / May well be of all evil chances chief.
W. B. Yeats, COLLECTED POEMS, *A Prayer for My Daughter* 1933

22 An intellectual hatred is the worst.
Id.

HEALTH

23 Every day and in every way I am getting better and better.
Emile Coué, AUTOSUGGESTION

1 Many Britons a hundred years ago were bursting with good health, and the remarkable thing was that they knew nothing of vitamins.
Lord Horder, THE LITTLE GENIUS

2 Get your room full of good fresh air. Then shut up the windows and keep it in. It will keep for years. Anyway, don't keep using your lungs all the time. Let them rest.
Stephen Leacock, LITERARY LAPSES 1910

3 What is the thing called health? Simply the state in which the individual happens transiently to be perfectly adapted to his environment. Obviously such states cannot be common, for the environment is in constant flux.
H. L. Mencken, American Mercury, *Mar* 1930

4 There is no human activity, eating, sleeping, drinking or sex which some doctor somewhere won't discover leads directly to cardiac arrest.
John Mortimer, Observer 20 *Aug* 1978

5 Too much health is unhealthy.
Leo Rosten, HOORAY FOR YIDDISH 1983

6 Use your health, even to the point of wearing it out.
George Bernard Shaw, DOCTOR'S DILEMMA, *Preface* 1908

7 *Mens sana in corpore sano* is a foolish saying. The sound body is a product of a sound mind.
George Bernard Shaw, MAN AND SUPERMAN 1905

WILLIAM RANDOLPH HEARST

8 Upon my honour, I saw a Madonna / Hanging within a niche / Above the door of the private whore / Of the world's worst son of a bitch.
Dorothy Parker, of a picture given by William Randolph Hearst to his mistress. Quoted Joseph Alsop, THE RARE ART TRADITIONS 1983

HEAT

9 When you're hot, anything can happen.
Jimmy Connors. Quoted Observer, Sayings of the Week 27 *Jun* 1976

EDWARD HEATH

10 If only he had lost his temper in public the way he does in private he would have become a more commanding and successful national leader.
William Davis. Quoted James Margach THE ABUSE OF POWER 1981

11 Edward Heath was once news editor of the *Church Times*. It was a part of his career that he kept in the background. As Prime Minister . . . he never expected a good Press and was always wary of journalists.
James Margach, THE ABUSE OF POWER 1981

12 We must kick Ted in the groin. We must be rough with him.
Harold Wilson. Quoted Richard Crossman, DIARIES 20 *Oct* 1969

HEATHEN

13 *Heathen, n.* A benighted creature who has the folly to worship something he can see and feel.
Ambrose Bierce, THE DEVIL'S DICTIONARY 1906

HEAVEN

14 Hell is paved with good intentions, but heaven goes in for something more dependable. Solid gold.
Joyce Cary, THE HORSE'S MOUTH 1944

15 *Heaven:* the Coney Island of the Christian imagination.
Elbert Hubbard. Quoted Evan Esar, TREASURY OF HUMOROUS QUOTATIONS

16 People who believe they are going there often wonder what they will do with themselves in Heaven. They make the mistake of assuming that the place will be all complete, finished to the last bit of gilding, when they get there. But of course it won't.
J. B. Priestley, DELIGHTS

17 If you go to Heaven without being naturally qualified for it you will not enjoy yourself there.
George Bernard Shaw, MAN AND SUPERMAN 1905

18 The human mind is inspired enough when it comes to inventing horrors; it is when it tries to invent a Heaven that it shows itself cloddish.
Evelyn Waugh, PUT OUT MORE FLAGS 1942

19 "It is a curious thing," he thought "that every creed promises a paradise which will be absolutely uninhabitable for anyone of civilised taste."
Id.

HELL

1 That's what Hell must be like, small chat to the babbling of Lethe about the good old days when we wished we were dead.
Samuel Beckett, EMBERS 1960

2 They order things so damnably in Hell.
Hilaire Belloc, TO DIVES

3 The religion of Hell is patriotism and the government is an enlightened democracy.
J. B. Cabell, JURGEN 1919

4 What is Hell? Hell is oneself / Hell is alone, the other figures in it / Merely projections.
T. S. Eliot, THE COCKTAIL PARTY 1949

5 The fear of hell is hell itself.
Kahil Gibran, SPIRITUAL SAYINGS 1963

6 If hell is paved with good intentions, it is, among other reasons, because of the impossibility of calculating consequences.
Aldous Huxley, AFTER MANY A SUMMER 1939

7 His brain was simmering and bubbling within the cracking tenement of the skull. Flames burst forth from his skull like a corolla, shrieking like voices: — Hell! Hell! Hell! Hell! Hell!
James Joyce, A PORTRAIT OF THE ARTIST AS A YOUNG MAN

8 There is wishful thinking in Hell as well as on earth.
C. S. Lewis, SCREWTAPE LETTERS 1942

9 It is idle to believe that a stirrup-pump can extinguish hell.
Henry Reed, A MAP OF VERONA 1946

10 The infliction of cruelty with a good conscience is a delight to moralists. That is why they invented Hell.
Bertrand Russell, SCEPTICAL ESSAYS 1928

11 To work hard, to live hard, to die hard, and then go to hell after all would be too damned hard.
Carl Sandburg, THE PEOPLE, YES 1936

12 Hell is full of musical amateurs.
George Bernard Shaw, MAN AND SUPERMAN 1905

13 There is plenty of humbug in Hell.
Id.

HELP

14 You can only help one of your luckless brothers / By trampling down a dozen others.
Bertolt Brecht, THE GOOD WOMAN OF SETZUAN 1938

15 If you see anybody fallen by the wayside and lying in the ditch, it isn't much good climbing into the ditch and lying by his side.
Rev. H. R. L. Sheppard. Quoted Carolyn Scott, DICK SHEPPARD

16 I've already had medical attention — a dog licked me when I was on the ground.
Neil Simon, IT HURTS ONLY WHEN I LAUGH

HEREDITY

17 No one has ever proved that a human being, through his descent from a certain group of people, must of necessity have certain mental characteristics.
Franz Bons, RACE AND DEMOCRATIC SOCIETY

18 Purity of race does not exist. Europe is a continent of energetic mongrels.
H. A. L. Fisher, A HISTORY OF EUROPE

HERESY

19 I did try to find a heresy of my own; and when I had put the last touches to it, I discovered that it was orthodoxy.
G. K. Chesterton, ORTHODOXY 1908

20 Heresy is but the bridge between two orthodoxies.
Francis Hackett, HENRY VIII

21 Collective wisdom is no adequate substitute for the intelligence of individuals. Individuals who opposed received opinion have been the source of all progress. Socrates, Christ and Galileo all equally incurred the censure of the orthodox.
Bertrand Russell, American Mercury

22 How can what an Englishman says be heresy? It is a contradiction in terms.
George Bernard Shaw, ST. JOAN 1923

23 Heresy is the lifeblood of religions. It is faith that begets heretics. There are no heresies in a dead religion.
André Suarès, PÉGNY 1912

HERO

24 Heroes exterminate each other for the benefit of people who are not heroes.
Havelock Ellis. Quoted Evan Esar, TREASURY OF HUMOROUS QUOTATIONS

25 As you get older it is harder to have heroes, but it is sort of necessary.
Ernest Hemingway. Quoted Lillian Ross, PORTRAIT OF HEMINGWAY 1961

1 Too much has been said of the heroes of history — the strong men, the troublesome men; too little of the amiable, the kindly, the tolerant.
Stephen Leacock, ESSAYS AND LITERARY STUDIES

2 What is our task? To make Britain a fit country for heroes to live in.
David Lloyd George. Speech 22 *Nov* 1918

3 A hero is a man who would argue with the Gods and awakens devils to contest his vision.
Norman Mailer, PRESIDENTIAL PAPERS 1963

4 I'm a hero with coward's legs. I'm a hero from the waist up.
Spike Milligan, PUCKOON

5 To be a hero, one must give an order to oneself.
Simone Weil, NOTEBOOKS

6 Lapses from knowledge to faith are perhaps necessary that human heroism may be possible.
H. G. Wells, MR. BRITLING SEES IT THROUGH 1916

HESITATION

7 It is all right to hesitate if you then go ahead.
Bertolt Brecht, THE GOOD WOMAN OF SETZUAN 1938

8 He who hesitates is sometimes saved.
James Thurber, THE THURBER CARNIVAL, *The Glass in the Field* 1945

HINDSIGHT

9 We have constantly to check ourselves in reading history with the remembrance that, to the actors in the drama, events appeared very different from the way they appear to us. We know what they were doing far better than they knew themselves.
Randolph Bourne, YOUTH AND LIFE

HIRE-PURCHASE

10 A judge has said that all his experience had been spent on sorting out the difficulties of people who, upon the recommendation of people they did not know, signed documents they did not read, to buy goods they did not need, with money they had not got.
Gilbert Harding on TV

HISTORY

11 You don't have to be a Marxist to see that history repeats itself, first as tragedy then as farce.
Anon.

12 History does not repeat itself. Historians repeat each other.
A. J. Balfour. Quoted by his biographer Kenneth Young

13 The ideal thing is for the historian to write his history and then to have a gang of trained slaves who can go through the proofs for various aspects. That is why, taking it all in all, gentlemen have made the best historians.
Hilaire Belloc, letter to Arthur Pollen. Quoted Robert Speight, LIFE OF HILAIRE BELLOC

14 It is always curious to read as 'history' what one has experienced oneself.
Max Beloff, Daily Telegraph 5 *Apr* 1979

15 History must not be written with bias, both sides should be given, even if there is only one side.
John Betjeman, FIRST AND LAST LOVES

16 To walk into history is to be free at once, to be at large among people.
Elizabeth Bowen, THE HOUSE IN PARIS 1935

17 It has been said that though God cannot alter the past, historians can; it is perhaps because they can be useful to Him in this respect that He tolerates their existence.
Samuel Butler, EREWHON REVISITED 1901

18 History will record it. I know it will because I shall write it myself.
Winston Churchill. Quoted John Boyd Carpenter, WAY OF LIFE

19 History creates confusion, even in its own time.
Jean Cocteau in an interview with Derek Prouse, Sunday Times 20 *Oct* 1963

20 History has many cunning passages, contrived corridors and issues.
T. S. Eliot, GERONTION 1920

21 A people without history / Is not redeemed for time, for history is a pattern / Of timeless moments. So while the light fails / On a winter's afternoon, in a secluded chapel / History is now and England.
T. S. Eliot, FOUR QUARTETS, *Little Gidding* 1942

1 The historical sense involves a perception, not only of the pastness of the past, but of its presence.
T. S. Eliot, TRADITION AND THE INDIVIDUAL TALENT 1919

2 The future is dark, the present burdensome. Only the past, dead and buried, bears contemplation.
G. R. Ellin, THE PRACTICE OF HISTORY

3 Men wiser and more learned than I have discovered in history a plot, a rhythm, a predetermined pattern. These harmonies are concealed from me. I can see only one emergency following upon another, wave on wave.
H. A. L. Fisher, HISTORY OF EUROPE 1934

4 History is bunk.
Henry Ford, as a witness in his libel suit against Chicago Tribune, Jul 1914

5 We want to live in the present and the only history that is worth a tinker's damn is the history we make today.
Henry Ford, Chicago Tribune 25 *May* 1916

6 The historian must have some conception of how men who are not historians behave. Otherwise he will move in a world of the dead.
E. M. Forster, ABINGER HARVEST 1936

7 History is attractive to the more timid of us [because] we can recover self-confidence by snubbing the dead.
Id.

8 History never looks like history when you are living through it. It always looks confusing and messy, and it always feels uncomfortable.
John W. Gardner, NO EASY VICTORIES 1968

9 My argument is that War makes rattling good history, but Peace is poor reading.
Thomas Hardy, THE DYNASTS 1903

10 It is not the neutrals or the lukewarm who make history.
Adolf Hitler. Speech, Berlin 23 *Apr* 1933

11 The writing of history may be as creative as the making of it. Both are an interpretation of life.
Philip Hope-Wallace. Quoted The Times, obituary 17 *Dec* 1979

12 Historians have a responsibility to make some sense of the past and not simply to chronicle it.
Michael Howard. Reviewing Herbert But-

terfield, THE ORIGIN OF HISTORY, Times Literary Supplement 7 *Aug* 1981

13 There is no such thing as a neutral or purely objective historian. Without an opinion a historian would be simply a ticking clock, and unreadable besides.
Philip Howard, The Times, *review of Barbara Tuchman's* PRACTISING HISTORY 4 *Feb* 1982

14 Events in the past may roughly be divided into those which probably never happened and those which do not matter.
W. R. Inge (Dean of St. Pauls), ASSESSMENTS AND ANTICIPATIONS 1929

15 Our chief interest in the past is as a guide to the future.
Id.

16 History is a relentless master. It has no present, only the past rushing into the future. To try to hold fast is to be swept aside.
John F. Kennedy. Quoted Barbara Rowe, A BOOK OF QUOTES

17 The lessons of history . . . teach the consequences of certain actions, but they cannot force a recognition of comparable situations.
Henry Kissinger, A WORLD RESTORED 1957

18 We cannot afford to make the world our fellow citizens live in historically unintelligible.
Prof. W. H. MacNeil, A DEFENCE OF WORLD HISTORY, *Royal Historical Society Lecture* 1981

19 The history of the world is the history of the privileged few.
Henry Miller, THE SUNDAY AFTER THE WAR 1944

20 History is seldom tidy.
Simon Nowell-Smith, EDWARDIAN ENGLAND

21 History is not a department of *belles lettres* [not] just an elegant, instructive amusing narrative, but a brand of science.
York Powell, Regius Professor at Oxford. Quoted A. L. Rowse, THE USE OF HISTORY

22 A man without a bias cannot write interesting history — if indeed such a man exists.
Bertrand Russell, AUTOBIOGRAPHY VOL II 1967

23 The memories of men are too frail a thread to hang history on.
John Still, THE JUNGLE TIDE

1 It is not the historian's business to be complimentary; it is his business to lay bare the facts of the case, and he understands them . . . dispassionately, impartially and without ulterior motives.
Lytton Strachey, EMINENT VICTORIANS, *Preface 1918*

2 When I write I have no loyalty except to historical truth as I see it and care no more about British achievements and mistakes than any other.
A. J. P. Taylor, POLITICIANS, SOCIALISM, AND HISTORIANS *1980*

3 The task of history is to explain the past, neither to justify nor condemn it.
Id.

4 Historians are like deaf people who go on answering questions that no one has asked them.
Leo Tolstoy. Quoted Manning Clark, A DISCOVERY OF AUSTRALIA

5 Perhaps one of the most prolific sources of error in contemporary thinking rises precisely from the popular habit of lifting history out of its proper context and bending it to the values of another age and day. In this way history is never allowed to be itself.
Laurens Van Der Post, THE LOST WORLD OF THE KALAHARI *1958*

6 The history of the world is the record of a man in quest of his daily bread and butter.
H. W. Van Loon, THE STORY OF MANKIND *1921*

7 Human history becomes more and more a race between education and catastrophe.
H. G. Wells, OUTLINE OF HISTORY *1920*

8 History, especially Church History, is always written to justify the survivors.
Morris West, THE CLOWNS OF GOD

9 The real history does not get written, because it is not in people's brains but in their nerves and vitals.
A. N. Whitehead, DIALOGUES *1953*

ADOLF HITLER

10 Hitler talks platitudes, but he believes them. The Duce [Mussolini] controls the crowd. Hitler *is* the crowd. Everything it feels, he feels.
Vernon Bartlett, THIS IS MY LIFE *1937*

11 It was impossible to converse with him in any normal way . . . he suddenly started shouting . . . I imagine that a man in a trance would behave in much the same way, and while he was shouting I am convinced that I could have walked out of the room and he would not have noticed my departure.
Id.

12 I, and many others who had interviews with him, were at first impressed by his sincerity, and later realised that he was sincere only in his belief that he was destined to rule the world.
Vernon Bartlett, I KNOW WHAT I LIKED

13 Mind you, like Churchill he was a very bad artist. Neither of them were any bloody good at it.
Marquis of Bath, of Hitler paintings bought for Longleat, Daily Express 4 *Apr* 1968

14 The moustache of Hitler, / Could hardly be littler / Was the thought that kept recurring / To Field Marshal Goering.
E. C. Bentley, CLERIHEWS

15 Hitler showed surprising loyalty to Mussolini, but it never extended to trusting him.
Alan Bullock, HITLER

16 Hitler has missed the bus.
Neville Chamberlain, of the invasion of Norway, House of Commons 4 *Apr* 1940

17 The German dictator, instead of snatching the victuals from the table, has been content to have them served to him course by course.
Winston Churchill, House of Commons. Speech after Munich 5 *Oct* 1938

18 This wicked man Hitler, the repository and embodiment of many forms of soul-destroying hatred, this monstrous product of former wrongs and shame.
Winston Churchill, BBC *broadcast* 11 *Sep* 1940

19 That bloodthirsty guttersnipe.
Winston Churchill, House of Commons

20 I have only one purpose, the destruction of Hitler and my life is much simplified thereby. If Hitler invaded Hell I would make at least a favourable reference to the Devil in the House of Commons.
Winston Churchill, THE GRAND ALLIANCE

21 To reject the world the most effective way is to act in such a manner as to force the world to spew one out — in which case

Hitler came 'nearer to God' than St. Joan, St. Theresa or St. Vincent de Paul.
Richard Coe, THE VISION OF JEAN GENET

1 I could not bear it if I ever had to despair of this man. This man has everything needed to be king.
Paul Joseph Goebbels, DIARIES

2 German history does not end with Hitler. Anyone believing that it does, and possibly even rejoicing in it, does not realise just how much he is thereby fulfilling Hitler's last will and testament.
Sebastian Haffner, THE MEANING OF HITLER

3 He disapproved of Adolf Hitler who had done such a great job combatting unAmerican activities in Germany.
Joseph Heller, CATCH 22 1962

4 If Hitler had put his energies into promoting nuclear physics instead of persecuting the Jews, the history of the world might have been very different. The first atom bomb could well have exploded over London instead of Hiroshima.
David Irving, THE VIRUS HOUSE

5 I tell you, as one who has studied the whole situation I don't think Hitler is a fool — he is not going to challenge the British Empire.
David Lloyd George. Speech 1937

6 It would have been better for the rest of us if, instead of German Führer, he had been editor of *The Times* or Director General of the BBC or Moderator of the Church of Scotland, or compère of a late-night television show, but so far as he personally was concerned it would not have made any appreciable difference.
Malcolm Muggeridge, TREAD SOFTLY FOR YOU TREAD ON MY JOKES 1966

7 Herr Hitler has one of the endearing characteristics of Ferdinand the Bull. Just when the crowds expect him to be most violent he stops and smells the flowers.
Beverley Nichols, Sunday Graphic

8 Hitler was a profoundly *uneducated* man of genius; there could be nothing more dangerous, with such a criminal mentality in a position of power.
A. L. Rowse, THE USE OF HISTORY

9 I wouldn't believe Hitler was dead, even if he told me so himself.
Hjalmar Schacht 3 *May* 1945

10 A racing tipster who only reached Hitler's level of accuracy would not do well for his clients.
A. J. P. Taylor, ORIGINS OF THE SECOND WORLD WAR 1961

11 Hitler, a bilious ascetic, drank next to nothing and picked at his food like an anxious raccoon.
Robert Lewis Taylor, THE AMAZING MR. CHURCHILL

12 The most pathetic thing about Adolf Hitler was his passionate desire to be approved of by English gentlemen.
Daily Telegraph. *Quoted Michael Bateman*, THIS ENGLAND

13 There is nothing yet to show that the new Chancellor intends to be immoderate in his foreign policy.
The Times, *leader* 1933

14 The machine is running away with *him* as it ran away with *me*.
Kaiser Wilhelm II, to Sir Robert Bruce Lockhart at Doorne 27 *Aug* 1939

HOBBY

15 Ornithology used to be an arcane hobby for embittered schoolmasters, dotty spinsters and lonely little boys but now it is as normal a weekend occupation as rug-making or wife-swapping.
Kyril Bonfiglioli, DON'T POINT THAT THING AT ME

HOLIDAY

16 We've never had a holiday. A week or two at Balmoral, or ten days at Sandringham, is the nearest we get.
Princess Anne. Quoted Noël St. George, ROYAL QUOTES

17 I'm not wild about holidays. They always seem a ludicrously expensive way of proving there's no place like home.
Jilly Cooper, Sunday Times 16 *Nov* 1977

18 A period of activity so intense that it can only be undertaken three or four weeks in the year.
Miles Kington. The Times, *A Guide to Real Meanings* 7 *Feb* 1983

19 I don't mind doing the bracing British beach bit, anoraks and gumboots and soggy fish fingers in the Sun-'n'-Sands Cafe, so long as no one suggests I am supposed to enjoy it.
Katherine Whitehorn, HOW TO SURVIVE CHILDREN

HOLLAND

1 Apart from cheese and tulips, the main product of the country is advocaat, a drink made from lawyers.
Alan Coren, THE SANITY INSPECTOR 1974

HOLLYWOOD

2 Hollywood is too much publicised. There are too many people here. Some of them should go back on a slow train.
Sam Goldwyn. Quoted News Review 11 *Dec* 1947

3 Hollywood is a locality where people without reputation try to live up to it.
Tom Jenk. Quoted Dick Richards, GINGER, SALUTE TO A STAR

4 Strip the phoney tinsel off Hollywood and you'll find the real tinsel underneath.
Oscar Levant. Quoted Leslie Halliwell, THE FILMGOER'S BOOK OF QUOTES 1973

5 Back to the mink-lined rut.
Anita Loos, on returning to writing film scripts. Quoted Stanley Reynolds, in his obituary of her, The Guardian 20 *Aug* 1981

6 A trip through a sewer in a glass-bottomed boat.
Wilson Mizner. Quoted A. Johnson, LEGEND OF A SPORT

7 Hollywood is a sewer with service from the Ritz Carlton.
Wilson Mizner

8 Hollywood is a combination of Heaven, Hell and a lunatic asylum.
Salvation Army Gen. Albert William Thomas Osborn. Quoted News Review 28 *Nov* 1946

9 We just got here — you can't judge a place so fast. Besides it's raining. It's probably beautiful when the sun comes out.
S. J. Perelman, THE LAST LAUGH 1981

10 In Europe an actor is an artist. In Hollywood, if he isn't acting, he's a bum.
Anthony Quinn. Quoted Leslie Halliwell, THE FILMGOER'S BOOK OF QUOTES 1973

11 In Hollywood if you don't have happiness you send out for it.
Rex Reed. Quoted J. R. Colombo, HOLLYWOOD THE BAD

12 They know only one word of more than one syllable here, and that is fillum.
Louis Sherwin

HOME

13 Home is the place where, when you have to go there / They have to take you in.
Robert Frost, THE DEATH OF THE HIRED MAN 1914

14 The best / Thing we can do is to make wherever we are lost in / Look as much like home as we can.
Christopher Fry, THE LADY'S NOT FOR BURNING 1950

15 It was a typical old English country house, fifty-six rooms and a bath. It was a strange kind of bath — it went all round the place. It was called a moat.
Bob Hope, I OWE RUSSIA 1200 DOLLARS

16 I want a house that has got over all its troubles; I don't want to spend the rest of my life bringing up a young and inexperienced house.
Jerome K. Jerome, THEY AND I

17 A real English home it is, just like yours or mine or Mr. Anthony Eden's, with a Great Dane on the hearthrug, yards of mullion round the windows and Miss Marlene Dietrich sleeping in the best bedroom.
C. A. Lejeune, Observer *review of the film* ANGEL 1936

18 There was but one thing wrong with the Babbitt house, it was not a home.
Sinclair Lewis, BABBITT 1922

19 Home is the girl's prison and the woman's workhouse.
George Bernard Shaw, MAN AND SUPERMAN 1905

LORD HOME

20 I had to see that Master Alex didn't talk to the servants and that he didn't leave our part of the house.
Mrs. Florence Hill, (Alec Douglas-Home's nurse). Quoted Evening Standard

21 I suppose when you come to think of it, Mr. Wilson is the 14th Mr. Wilson.
Lord Home, BBC TV 21 *Aug* 1963

22 The only real and distinctive achievement of the fourteenth Earl was to have been born the heir of the thirteenth.
Sunday Express 1960

23 The whole process [of democracy[has ground to a halt with a 14th Earl.
Harold Wilson, Labour Party Conference 1 *Aug* 1963

HOMESICKNESS

1 Dear People, I am at present in Bethlehem where Jesus Christ was born. I wish to Christ I was in Wigan where I was born.
Soldier writing home in 1917. Quoted Lord Esher, JOURNALS AND LETTERS

HOMOSEXUALITY

2 Buggery is spiritually valuable because of its difficulties and torments.
W. H. Auden. Quoted Humphrey Carpenter, AUDEN, A BIOGRAPHY

3 Everything is controlled by the sods. The country is riddled with homosexuals who are teaching the world how to behave — a spectacle of revolting hypocrisy.
Sir Thomas Beecham. Quoted Charles Reed, BEECHAM, AN INDEPENDENT BIOGRAPHY

4 We're here because we're queer / Because we're queer because we're here.
Brendan Behan, THE HOSTAGE 1958

5 If God had meant to have homosexuals he would have created Adam and Bruce.
Anita Bryant. Quoted Barbara Rowe, A BOOK OF QUOTES

6 Tchaikovsky thought of committing suicide for fear of being discovered as a homosexual, but today, if you are a composer and *not* homosexual you might as well put a bullet through your head.
Sergei Diaghilev. Quoted Vernon Duke, LISTEN HERE!

7 Nature's attempt to get rid of the soft boys by sterilising them.
F. Scott Fitzgerald, THE CRACK-UP 1936

8 It is a perfectly ordinary little case of a man charged with indecency with four or five guardsmen.
Mervyn Griffiths-Jones, prosecuting counsel. Reported in the Guardian. *Quoted Michael Bateman*, THIS ENGLAND

9 "Fundamentally, unconsciously, I believe he's a homosexualist." "Perhaps," said Irene gravely. She knew her Havelock Ellis.
Aldous Huxley, BARREN LEAVES 1925

10 There is probably no sensitive heterosexual alive who is not preoccupied with his latent homosexuality.
Norman Mailer, ADVERTISEMENTS FOR MYSELF 1959

11 This sort of thing may be tolerated by the French — but we are British, thank God.
Viscount Montgomery, House of Lords 26 *May* 1965

12 It is a hard fate to love the untouchable.
David Newsome, A. C. BENSON, DIARIST

13 "I am not your fader but your moder," quoth he. "Your father was a rich merchant in Stamboul."
Ezra Pound, CANTOS 1925

14 . . . the woman whom a mistake on the part of nature had enshrined in the body of M. de Charles.
Marcel Proust, REMEMBRANCE OF THINGS PAST, *Cities of the Plain* 1921–2

15 The middle age of buggers is not to be contemplated without horror.
Virginia Woolf

HONESTY

16 I will have no locked cupboards in my life.
Gertrude Bell. Quoted Janet E. Courtney, AN OXFORD PORTRAIT GALLERY

17 Honesty is incompatible with amassing a large fortune.
Mahatma Gandhi, NON-VIOLENCE IN PEACE AND WAR 1948

18 I am afraid we must make the world honest before we can honestly say to our children that honesty is the best policy.
George Bernard Shaw, BBC Radio 11 *Jul* 1932

HONEYMOON

19 Honeymoons do not seldom end worse than they began and to recover from them may take quite a long time.
Arnold Bennett, HOW TO MAKE THE BEST OF LIFE

20 You mustn't be blasé about honeymoons just because this is your second.
Noël Coward, PRIVATE LIVES 1930

21 Here we are on the first night of our honeymoon, with the moon coming up and the music playing, and all you can do is talk about my first husband. It's downright sacrilegious.
Id.

22 Honeymooning is a very overrated occupation.
Id.

1 The honeymoon wasn't such a ghastly experience really; it was afterwards that was so awful.
Id.

HONOURS

2 Literature is always a good card to play for Honours. It makes people think that Cabinet Ministers are educated.
Arnold Bennett, THE TITLE 1918

3 Why should I accept the Garter from His Majesty when his people have just given me the boot?
Winston Churchill after losing the 1945 *election*

4 Members rise from C.M.G. (known sometimes in Whitehall as Call Me God) to K.C.M.G. (Kindly Call Me God) to G.C.M.G. (God calls me God.)
Anthony Sampson, ANATOMY OF BRITAIN 1962

5 M. Ravel refuses the Legion of Honour, but all his music accepts it.
Erik Satie. Quoted Nat Shapiro, ENCYCLOPEDIA OF QUOTATIONS ABOUT MUSIC

6 Titles distinguish the mediocre, embarrass the superior and are disgraced by the inferior.
George Bernard Shaw, MAN AND SUPERMAN 1905

7 I have been offered titles, but I think they get one into bad company.
George Bernard Shaw, at 90, *on becoming a freeman of Dublin*, News Review 5 *Sep* 1946

8 What harm did I ever do the Labour party?
R. H. Tawney on being offered a peerage by Ramsay MacDonald.

9 How justly we can refer to the Tories as the party of dreadful knights.
Jeremy Thorpe, Liberal assembly 1963

HOPE

10 Hope is a risk that must be run.
Georges Bernanos, LAST ESSAYS 1955

11 There is some comfort in the thought that in the universe we are not alone, but surrounded by our elders and betters.
Arthur Koestler, BRICKS TO BABEL, *Epilogue* 1983

12 There are no hopeless situations; there are only men who have grown hopeless about them.
Clare Boothe Luce, EUROPE IN THE SPRING

13 To face life without hope can mean to live without despair.
Terence Rattigan, THE DEEP BLUE SEA 1952

14 He who has never hoped can never despair.
George Bernard Shaw, CAESAR AND CLEOPATRA 1906

HORSE

15 Did you know horses lead to divorces? You've no idea how sexually promiscuous they are in the shires. It's all that jumping up and down on horses that does it. They get over-stimulated.
Lord Arran, Sunday Times 15 *Jan* 1967

16 I saw him riding in the Row, clinging to his horse like a string of onions.
Margot Asquith of Lord Hugh Cecil, AUTOBIOGRAPHY 1936

17 It's awfully bad luck on Diana / Her ponies have swallowed their bits; / She fished down their throats with a spanner / And frightened them all into fits.
Sir John Betjeman

18 *J. M. Astbury K.C.*: Mr. Bottomley, why did you tell me that you never kept racehorses?
Horatio Bottomley: I gave you a correct answer. I never kept racehorses. They kept me.
Horatio Bottomley at his examination for bankruptcy. Quoted Alan Hyman, THE RISE AND FALL OF HORATIO BOTTOMLEY

19 I say to parents, especially wealthy parents, "Don't give your son money. As far as you can afford it, give him horses."
Winston Churchill, MY EARLY LIFE 1930

20 A horse is dangerous at both ends and uncomfortable in the middle.
Ian Fleming. Quoted Sunday Times 9 *Oct* 1966

21 The horse, the horse! The symbol of surging potency and power of movement, of action, in man.
D. H. Lawrence, APOCALYPSE 1931

1 You may have my husband but not my horse . . . I'll preserve one last male thing in the museum of this world if I can.
D. H. Lawrence, KANGAROO 1923

2 There are no handles to a horse.
Stephen Leacock, LITERARY LAPSES 1910

3 It takes a good deal of physical courage to ride a horse. This, however, I have. I get it at about forty cents a flask and take it as required.
Id.

4 He flung himself on his horse and rode off madly in all directions.
Stephen Leacock, NONSENSE NOVELS 1911

5 The outside of a horse is good for the inside of a man.
Lt. Col. Harry Llewellyn, Sunday Express 25 *Jun* 1956

6 I'd horsewhip you — if I had a horse.
Groucho Marx, ANIMAL CRACKERS

7 Nobody has any right to go around looking like a horse and behaving as if it was all right. You don't catch horses going around looking like people, do you?
Dorothy Parker, HORSIE

8 You'll have to hope that all the horses don't pee at the same time.
Philip, Duke of Edinburgh, commenting on the shortage of drains for the Moscow Equestrian Olympics 7 *Mar* 1979

9 I don't even like *old* cars . . . I'd rather have a goddam horse. A horse is at least *human,* for God's sake.
J. D. Salinger, THE CATCHER IN THE RYE 1951

10 Horseback Hall, consisting of a prison for horses with an annexe for the ladies and gentlemen who rode them, hunted them, talked about them, bought them and sold them, and gave nine tenths of their lives to them.
George Bernard Shaw, HEARTBREAK HOUSE, *Preface* 1920

11 There are only two classes in good society in England, the equestrian classes and the neurotic classes.
Id.

12 Go anywhere in England where there are natural, wholesome, contented and really nice English people, and what do you always find? That the stables are the real centre of the household.
Id.

13 The men of the Golden Horde were almost as kind to children as to horses — though naturally they regarded them with less reverence.
Sir Osbert Sitwell, THE SCARLET TREE 1945

14 We attended stables, as we attended church, in our best clothes, thereby no doubt showing the degree of respect due to horses, as to the deity.
Id.

HORSE RACING

15 How amusing racing would be if it were not for the horses. They take people's minds off conversation.
Viscount Castlerosse, Sunday Express, *Londoner's Log*

16 I'm getting to be so big on the turf they are calling me the Aga Cohen.
Bud Flanagan. Quoted in his obituary, Daily Express 21 *Oct* 1968

17 My horse was in the lead, coming down the home stretch, but the caddie fell off.
Sam Goldwyn. Quoted Alva Johnson, THE GREAT GOLDWYN

18 I have no intention of watching undersized Englishmen perched on horses with matchstick legs race along courses planned to amuse Nell Gwynne.
Gilbert Harding. Quoted Wynford Vaughan Thomas, GILBERT HARDING BY HIS FRIENDS

19 I was a passenger on a very good horse. It was an easy ride.
Walter Swinburn to reporters, on winning the Derby on Shergar 3 *Jun* 1981

HORSE-RIDING

20 That the world is out of balance and lop-sided we know without being reminded of it by the side-saddle.
Lord Brabazon of Tara. Quoted News Review 19 *Jun* 1947

HOSPITAL

21 One of the most difficult things to contend with in a hospital is the assumption on the part of the staff that because you have lost your gall bladder you have also lost your mind.
Jean Kerr, PLEASE DON'T EAT THE DAISIES

1 To be ill, or to undergo an operation is to be initiated into the mystery of nursing and to learn the comforts and discomforts of an invalid's life; the unearthly fragrance of tea at daybreak; the disappointment of rice-pudding when you thought it was going to be orange jelly; and the behaviour of every constituent part of the bedclothes.
Stephen Paget, CONFESSIO MEDICI

HOSPITALITY

2 To mankind in general Macbeth and Lady Macbeth stand out as the supreme type of all that a host and hostess should not be.
Max Beerbohm

3 Hospitality is a wonderful thing. If people really want you they'll have you even if the cook has just died in the house with smallpox.
F. Scott Fitzgerald, NOTEBOOKS

4 Only ask those people to stay with you or to dine with you, who can ask you in return.
W. Somerset Maugham, A WRITER'S NOTEBOOK 1949

5 There's a sort of person who rushes out of his house to shake hands with you in order not to have to take you inside.
Frederick Raphael. Quoted Janet Watts, Observer 15 *Jul* 1979

HOST

6 Nor was he insincere in saying "Make my house your inn." Inns are not residences.
Marianne Moore, BLACK EARTH

HOTEL

7 Airport hotels are so alike that the only way you can make sure of where you are is by looking at the book matches in the ashtray beside your bed.
William Hardcastle, Punch

8 A whiskered cove who looked like a bandit, as no doubt he was, being the proprietor of the hotel.
P. G. Wodehouse, AUNT AGATHA TAKES THE COUNT

HOUSEWIFE

9 I would rather lie on a sofa than sweep beneath it.
Shirley Conran, SUPERWOMAN 1975

HOWARD HUGHES

10 It is a tragedy that Hughes had to die to prove that he was alive.
Walter Kane. Quoted Barbara Rowe, A BOOK OF QUOTES

HUMAN BEING

11 Not philosophers but fret-sawyers and stamp collectors compose the backbone of society.
Aldous Huxley, BRAVE NEW WORLD 1932

12 He is a human being and terrible things are happening to him. So attention must be paid.
Arthur Miller, DEATH OF A SALESMAN 1945

13 A human being is an ingenious assembly of portable plumbing.
Robert Morley, HUMAN BEING

14 We are Borrowers — like you're a — a Human Bean, or whatever it's called.
Mary Norton, THE BORROWERS

15 Human beings are the only animals of which I am thoroughly and cravenly afraid.
George Bernard Shaw

HUMANISM

16 If you can't believe in God, Humanism is the next best thing.
Lord Longford, DIARY OF A YEAR

HUMANITY

17 The human race, to which so many of my readers belong.
G. K. Chesterton, THE NAPOLEON OF NOTTING HILL 1904

18 People are only human, but it really doesn't seem much for them to be.
Ivy Compton-Burnett, A FAMILY AND A FORTUNE 1939

19 It is an unproved assumption that the domination of this planet by our own species is a desirable thing, which must give satisfaction to its creator.
W. R. Inge (Dean of St. Pauls), OUTSPOKEN ESSAYS 1919

20 It is not the belief in God, but the belief in man that has been shattered; and it is amid the ruins not of Christianity, but of humanitarianism, that we English live today.
Douglas Jerrold, GEORGIAN ADVENTURE 1938

1 There are one hundred and ninety-three living species of monkeys and apes. One hundred and ninety-two of them are covered in hair. The exception is the naked ape self-named *homo sapiens*.
Desmond Morris, THE NAKED APE

2 Fortunate are those who find some good cause in which they can act as a man for other men. Their own humanity will be enriched.
Albert Schweitzer, THE TEACHING OF REVERENCE FOR LIFE

3 I can think of no more stirring symbol of man's humanity to man than a fire engine.
Kurt Vonnegut, THE SIRENS OF TITAN 1959

HUMBUG

4 He was a man after my own heart — the greatest humbug I have ever known.
Horatio Bottomley to Arnold Bennett, of Dr. Parker of City Temple

HUMILIATION

5 The one thing to do is to do nothing. Wait . . . You will find that you survive humiliation and that's an experience of incalculable value.
T. S. Eliot, THE COCKTAIL PARTY 1949

HUMILITY

6 It is difficult to be humble. Even if you aim at humility there is no guarantee that when you have attained the state you will not be proud of the feat.
Boname Dobrée, JOHN WESLEY 1933

7 The only wisdom we can hope to acquire / Is the wisdom of humility, humility is endless.
T.S. Eliot, FOUR QUARTETS, *East Coker* 1940

8 Humility is the most difficult of all virtues to achieve, nothing dies harder than the desire to think well of oneself.
T. S. Eliot, SHAKESPEARE AND THE STOICISM OF SENECA

9 The virtue of pride, which was once the beauty of mankind, has given place to that fount of all ugliness, Christian humility.
Max Ernst. Quoted John Russell, MAX ERNST, HIS LIFE AND WORK

10 Turning the other cheek is a kind of moral ju-jitsu.
Gerald Stanley Lee, CROWDS

11 Archbishop Ullathorne, lecturing on humility was asked by a student, "Your Grace, what is the best book on humility?" He replied, "There is only one. I wrote it myself."
Lord Longford, HUMILITY

12 Humiliation has nothing to do with humility.
Clifford Longley, The Times 2 *Jun* 1980

13 Christian humility is preached by the clergy, but practised only by the lower classes.
Bertrand Russell, AUTOBIOGRAPHY 1967

14 To expect us to feel humble in the presence of astronomical dimensions merely because they are big is a sort of cosmic snobbery. What is significant is mind.
Lord Samuel, BELIEF AND ACTION

15 The Church must learn humility, as well as teach it.
George Bernard Shaw, ST. JOAN, *Preface* 1923

16 I detest the humility I should have, and am angry when I am humble. I appreciate the social arrogance I have in the face of my humility.
Dylan Thomas. Quoted Andrew Sinclair, DYLAN THOMAS, POET OF HIS PEOPLE

17 In the intellectual order, the virtue of humility is nothing more nor less than the power of attention.
Simone Weil, GRAVITY AND GRACE 1947

HUMOUR

18 I have a fine sense of the ridiculous but no sense of humour.
Edward Albee, WHO'S AFRAID OF VIRGINIA WOOLF 1962

19 Though the English pride themselves on their sense of humour, they distrust humorous men.
Lord Annan, Observer 2 *Nov* 1980

20 When Nehru invaded Goa I called him a Goa Constrictor! Wasn't that funny? I find all my jokes funny. They're so good. But I only expect one out of six to go down well.
Earl of Arran, Sunday Times 15 *Jan* 1967

21 The marvellous thing about a joke with a double meaning is that it can only mean one thing.
Ronnie Barker, SAUCE

22 Humour undiluted is the most depressing of all phenomena. Humour must have its

background of seriousness. Without this contrast there comes none of that incongruity which is the mainspring of laughter.
Max Beerbohm, AROUND THEATRES

1 It is a good deed to forget a poor joke.
Brendan Bracken. Quoted Observer 17 *Oct* 1943

2 To appreciate nonsense requires a serious interest in life.
Gelert Burgess, THE ROMANCE OF THE COMMONPLACE 1916

3 Humorists are not happy men. Like Beachcomber and Saki and Thurber, they burn while Rome fiddles.
Cyril Connolly, ENEMIES OF PROMISE 1938

4 A joke isn't a joke until someone laughs.
Michael Crawford to Alex Coleman in an interview, TV Times 29 *Mar* 1979

5 When you say a friend has a sense of humour do you mean that he makes you laugh, or that he can make you laugh?
Max Frisch, SKETCHBOOK 1966–1971

6 In considering economic behaviour, humour is especially important for, needless to say, much of that behaviour is infinitely ridiculous.
J. K. Galbraith, ECONOMICS, PEACE AND LAUGHTER

7 The essence of humour is surprise; that is why you laugh when you see a joke in *Punch*.
A. P. Herbert. Speech Foyle's Literary Lunch, Dec 1948

8 I have never understood why it should be considered derogatory to the Creator to suppose that He has a sense of humour.
W. R. Inge (Dean of St. Pauls)

9 It has been discovered experimentally that you can draw laughter from an audience anywhere in the world, of any class or race, simply by walking on to a stage and uttering the words "I am a married man".
Ted Kavanagh, News Review 10 *Jul* 1947

10 Fun is fun but no girl wants to laugh all of the time.
Anita Loos, GENTLEMEN PREFER BLONDES 1925

11 One matter Englishmen don't think in the least funny is their happy consciousness of possessing a deep sense of humour.
Marshall McLuhan, THE MECHANICAL BRIDE 1951

12 Impropriety is the soul of wit.
W. Somerset Maugham, THE MOON AND SIXPENCE 1919

13 Humour must be a by-product of either profound or vivid interest in persons and events, however much this interest be clothed in levity. The impression is made that Miss Macaulay is amused by, but not deeply interested in, people.
New Statesman. *Reviewing Rose Macaulay's* THEY WERE DEFEATED

14 Instead of doing "I say, I say, my mother-in-law" you could do "I say, I say, Harold Macmillan" and it could be the same joke — and very often *was* the same joke.
Bill Oddie, of BBC TV's *That Was The Week That Was. Quoted* FROM FRINGE TO FLYING CIRCUS 1980

15 There is no more dangerous literary symptom than a temptation to write a book about wit and humour. It indicates the total loss of both.
George Bernard Shaw. Quoted Neville Hilditch, IN PRAISE OF HUMOUR

16 Mark Twain and I are very much in the same position. We have to put things in such a way as to make people, who would otherwise hang us, believe that we are joking.
George Bernard Shaw. Quoted Justin Wintle and Richard Kenin, DICTIONARY OF BIOGRAPHICAL QUOTATIONS

17 There has never been a book on humour written by a funny man. George Meredith's essay on comedy was so dreary I don't think anybody but the proof reader ever got through it all.
Arthur Sheekman, script-writer to the Marx Brothers

18 If a person desires to be a humorist it is necessary that the people around him shall be at least as wise as he is, otherwise his humour will not be comprehended.
James Stephens, THE DEMI-GODS 1914

19 Humour is a serious thing. I like to think of it as one of our greatest and earliest national resources which must be preserved at all costs.
James Thurber, CBS *television* 4 *Mar* 1956

20 Humour is emotional chaos remembered in tranquillity.
James Thurber, New York Post 29 *Feb* 1960

1 The difficulty with humorists is that they will mix what they believe with what they don't; whichever seems likelier to win an effect.
John Updike, RABBIT, RUN 1960

HUNGER

2 A man with money to pay for a meal can talk about hunger without demeaning himself. But for a man with no money hunger is a disgrace.
Vicki Baum, MARTIN'S SUMMER

3 Nobody wants to kiss when they are hungry.
Dorothy Dix. Quoted Burton Stevenson,
BOOK OF QUOTATIONS

4 An empty stomach is not a good political adviser.
Albert Einstein, COSMIC RELIGION

5 A hungry man is not a free man.
Adlai Stevenson. Speech 6 Sep 1952

6 No one can worship God or love his neighbour on an empty stomach.
Woodrow Wilson. Speech 23 May 1912

7 We sprang at the black pudding like wolves at a Russian peasant.
P. G. Wodehouse, PERFORMING FLEA 1953

HUNTING

8 Without foxes there would be no fox-hunting and without fox-hunting many would find it impossible to live through an English winter.
Anon. Horse and Hound

9 Hi! Handsome hunting man / Fire your little gun. / Bang! / Now the animal / Is dead and dumb and done / Nevermore to peep again, creep again, leap again / Eat or sleep or drink again, oh what fun.
Walter De La Mare, THE HUNTSMAN

10 I am alarmed to learn from your leading article today that the Duke of Beaufort rides in a car bearing the registration number MFH 1. At these works we travel in FOX 1. May I be assured that, should we happen to meet his Grace on the road, no unseemly incident will occur?
H. P. Forder. Samuel Fox & Co. Ltd., letter to The Times

11 If there is one word in the English language I hate, it is 'game'. It seems to imply that other creatures are about for our sport.
William Holden. Quoted Robert Ottaway,
TV Times 24 *Aug* 1972

12 I have known a fox that was absolutely devoted to fox hunting . . . after we had hunted him many seasons I regret to say we killed him.
Col. Sir Lancelot Rolleston DSO, Daily Mail. *Quoted Michael Bateman*, THIS ENGLAND

13 If foxes, like women, had a vote I think they would vote unanimously for the keeping up of fox hunting.
Id.

14 It isn't mere convention. Everyone can see that the people who hunt are the right people and the people who don't are the wrong ones.
George Bernard Shaw, HEARTBREAK HOUSE 1920

15 The gentleman must realise that once he is in the saddle he must be as rude as possible to anyone who crosses his path.
Douglas Sutherland, THE ENGLISH GENTLEMAN 1978

HUSBAND

16 I never married because there was no need. I have three pets at home which answer the same purpose as a husband. I have a dog which growls every morning, a parrot which swears all the afternoon and a cat that comes home late at night.
Marie Corelli. Quoted James Crichton-Browne, WHAT THE DOCTOR THOUGHT

17 A husband is a man who two minutes after his head / Touches the pillow is snoring like an overloaded / Omnibus.
Ogden Nash, MARRIAGE LINES

18 A husband is what is left of the lover after the nerve has been extracted.
Helen Rowland, A GUIDE TO MEN

19 A man ought to be able to be fond of his wife without making a fool of himself about her.
George Bernard Shaw, CANDIDA 1903

20 Chumps always make the best husbands. When you marry, Sally, grab a chump. Tap his head first, and if it rings solid, don't hesitate.
P. G. Wodehouse, ADVENTURES OF SALLY 1920

HYGIENE

21 Clean-shaven, with that mien of scrupulously shampooed and almost medical

cleanliness and freshness which is so typical of the hygienic American.
Harold Begby, describing Frank Buchman in LIFE CHANGERS

1 Sybil: I feel smirched and unclean, as if slimy things have been crawling all over me.
Edgar: Maybe they have. That's a very old sofa.
Noël Coward, PRIVATE LIVES 1930

2 I've never had a great many baths and . . . it does not make a great difference to health . . . As for appearance, most of that is underneath and nobody sees it.
Hugh Gaitskell, Minister for Fuel and Power, speaking at an economy drive in 1947, which drew from Winston Churchill in the Commons — When a Minister advocates the policy of fewer baths, is it surprising that the Government gets into increasingly bad odour?

3 Henry IV's feet and armpits enjoyed an international reputation.
Aldous Huxley, THE DEVILS OF LOUDUN 1952

4 With many people, women especially, bacilli have taken the place of spirits. Microbes for them are the personification of evil. They live in terror of germs.
Aldous Huxley, PROPER STUDIES, *The Substitute for Religion* 1927

5 "I see an article where it says mice cause fevers" says somebody else. "Don't be silly", says Monk. "They don't get near enough to you to breathe on you or anything."
Gerald Kersh, CLEAN, BRIGHT AND SLIGHTLY OILED 1946

6 Of nothing are you allowed to get the real odour or savour. Everything is sterilized and wrapped in cellophane. The only odour which is recognised and admitted as an odour is halitosis and of this all Americans live in mortal dread.
Henry Miller, THE AIR-CONDITIONED NIGHTMARE 1942

7 On the day there was a full chamber pot under the breakfast table I decided to leave.
George Orwell, THE ROAD TO WIGAN PIER 1937

8 Epstein is a great sculptor. I wish he would wash, but I understand Michelangelo *never* did, so I suppose it is part of the tradition.
Ezra Pound. Quoted Charles Norman, EZRA POUND

9 Gentlemen sleep in unheated bedrooms with the windows wide open, for they are very healthy in early life. In later years, of course, they become crippled with rheumatism.
Douglas Sutherland, THE ENGLISH GENTLEMAN 1978

10 There were never more bathrooms in England than there are today and never so many dirty necks and fingernails. Countless (girls) should be sent to bed supperless.
Evelyn Waugh, Daily Mail 1961

11 If men cannot live on bread alone, still less can they do so on disinfectant.
A. N. Whitehead. Quoted Peter Viereck. THE UNADJUSTED MAN

HYPOCHONDRIA

12 The man who wants to subject himself to regular examination is the equivalent of the fussy owner-driver, who wants to take excessive care of his car and is perpetually taking the engine down to discover the origin of some supposed abnormality or even to reassure himself all is well.
Dr. Adolphe Abrahams, THE HUMAN MACHINE, *lecture to Guild of Public Pharmacists* 22 Jan 1930

13 None of my patients are hypochondriacs but you should see some of the owners.
Anonymous veterinary surgeon, Saturday Evening Post, *I've Never Lost an Owner* 10 Jul 1948

14 — and he *baffled* the surgeons. They had Mr. Venables look at him — he's one of the top people — he looked at Ulford's stomach and he said "Well, it could go either way" — Frankly, I think it's *nerves*.
Alan Bennett. Quoted Roger Wilmut, FROM FRINGE TO FLYING CIRCUS 1981

15 She says her blood is nothing but rosewater.
Ronald Firbank, VALMOUTH 1918

16 Everyone has a body and many, revelling in its disorders, really enjoy bad health. There are those who divide their lives into two parts — "before my operation" and "since my operation".
Lord Hill of Luton (The Radio Doctor), BOTH SIDES OF THE HILL

17 All interest in disease and death is only another expression of interest in life.
Thomas Mann, THE MAGIC MOUNTAIN 1934

1 Some people can act as Boswell to their own bowels.
Dr. Jonathan Miller, THE BODY IN QUESTION

2 The desire to take medicine is perhaps the greatest feature which distinguishes man from animals.
Sir William Osler, SCIENCE AND IMMORTALITY

3 Neurotic subjects are perhaps less addicted than any, despite the time-honoured phrase, to 'listen to their insides'. They can hear so many things going on inside themselves by which they realise later that they did wrong to let themselves be alarmed, that they end by paying no attention to any of them.
Marcel Proust, REMEMBRANCE OF THINGS PAST 1913–1927

4 He complained about his ribs and told him [the doctor] that they seemed to be giving him claustrophobia.
N. F. Simpson, THE HOLE

HYPOCRISY

5 No man is a hypocrite in his pleasures.
Albert Camus, THE FALL 1956

6 We ought to see far enough into a hypocrite to see even his sincerity.
G. K. Chesterton, HERETICS 1905

7 Other nations may sneer at the hypocritical English but only we can carry it off in the grand manner.
Daily Sketch. Quoted Michael Bateman, THIS ENGLAND

8 There is always a type of man who says he loves his fellow men and expects to make a living at it.
Edgar Watson Howe, VENTURES IN COMMON SENSE

9 The most grave and awful denunciations of obscenity in literature are to be found precisely in those periodicials whose directors are most notoriously alcoholic.
Aldous Huxley, BARREN LEAVES 1925

10 Hypocrisy is the most difficult and nerve-racking vice that a man can pursue; it needs an increasing vigilance and a rare detachment of spirit. It cannot, like adultery or gluttony, be practised at spare moments; it is a whole-time job.
W. Somerset Maugham, CAKES AND ALE 1930

11 Hypocrisy is the homage paid by vice to virtue. It is the conscious assumption of virtue by the unvirtuous.
Gustav Renier, THE ENGLISH — ARE THEY HUMAN?

12 If there is one thing hypocrites hate, it's hypocrisy.
Jack Rosenthal, DEAR ANYONE *(radio play)*

13 Our morality is an impudent hypocrisy.
George Bernard Shaw, MAJOR BARBARA, *Preface* 1905

14 In my day there were things that were done, and things that were not done, and there was even a way of doing things that were not done.
Peter Ustinov, PHOTO-FINISH

15 Like many another he deliberately stooped for success and then, having achieved it, slowly put on garments of righteousness.
Oswald Garrison Villard, of Joseph Pulitzer, SOME NEWSPAPERS AND NEWSPAPER-MEN

HYSTERIA

16 Hysteria, a snake whose scales are tiny mirrors in which the dead world takes on a semblance of life.
Nathanael West, MISS LONELY HEARTS 1933

17 Hysteria is a natural phenomenon, the common denominator of the female nature. It's the big feminine weapon, and the test of a man is his ability to cope with it.
Tennessee Williams, THE NIGHT OF THE IGUANA 1961

I

IDEA

1 At first it is difficult to recognise an idea as original. Nearly any notion, whether old, banal, spurious, novel or brilliant may pop up with a flutter of excitement. How is one to distinguish? Notice, after three days, whether it still quivers.
Kenneth Fisher, THE GURU THERAPIST'S NOTEBOOK

2 Very simple ideas lie within the reach only of complex minds.
Rémy de Gourmont. Quoted Evan Esar, TREASURY OF HUMOROUS QUOTATIONS

3 Men die but an idea does not.
Alan Jay Lerner, THE STREET WHERE I LIVE 1978

4 A man must let his ideas grow, not be continually rooting them up to see how they are getting on.
William McFee, HARBOURS OF MEMORY 1921

5 An idea isn't responsible for the people who believe in it.
Don Marquis, ARCHY DOES HIS PART 1935

6 A powerful idea communicates some of its strength to him who challenges it.
Marcel Proust, REMEMBRANCE OF THINGS PAST 1913–1927

7 Ideas that enter the mind under fire remain there securely and for ever.
Leon Trotsky, MY LIFE 1930

8 He had ideas about everything. He could no more help having ideas about everything than a dog can resist smelling at your heels.
H. G. Wells, MR. BRITLING SEES IT THROUGH 1916

9 Ideas won't keep. Something must be done about them. When the idea is new its custodians have fervour, live for it, and, if need be, die for it.
A. N. Whitehead, DIALOGUES 1953

10 Whenever I hear, as I sometimes do, one of my colleagues say that there are no ideas which cannot be expressed clearly in simple language, I think "Then your ideas must be very superficial."
Id.

11 I pressed down the mental accelerator. The old lemon throbbed fiercely. I got an idea.
P. G. Wodehouse, JEEVES TAKES CHARGE

IDEALISM

12 Idealism may be defined as well as in any other way, by calling it that spirit which impels an individual or group of individuals to a loftier standard of conduct than that which ordinarily prevails around him or them.
Lord Birkenhead, Rectorial address, Glasgow University, on Idealism in International Politics

13 Man is ready to die for an idea, provided that idea is not quite clear to him.
Paul Eldridge, HORNS OF GLASS

14 Positive ideals are becoming a curse, for they can seldom be achieved without someone being killed or maimed or interned.
E. M. Forster, TWO CHEERS FOR DEMOCRACY 1941

15 Idealism is the noble toga that political gentlemen drape over their will to power.
Aldous Huxley, New York Herald Tribune 25 Nov 1963

16 A man has no right to live until he has found something to die for.
Martin Luther King. Quoted BBC Radio 4 26 Jul 1981

17 Away with all ideals. Let each individual act spontaneously from the for ever incalculable prompting of the creative well-head from within him. There is no universal law.
D. H. Lawrence, PHOENIX 1936

18 'Dying for an idea' sounds well enough, but why not let the idea die instead of you?
(Percy) Wyndham Lewis, THE ART OF BEING RULED 1926

1 Few people are so terrible as frustrated idealists, who begin to despise or hate ordinary human nature because it insists upon behaving like ordinary human nature.
J. B. Priestley, OUTCRIES AND ASIDES

2 Idealism, even subjective idealism, did not prevent great philosophers from still having hearty appetites or from presenting themselves with untiring perseverance for election to the Academy.
Marcel Proust, REMEMBRANCE OF THINGS PAST 1913–1927

3 I am an idealist. I don't know where I'm going, but I'm on my way.
Carl Sandburg. Quoted Laurence J. Peter, PETER'S QUOTATIONS

4 This creature man, who in his own selfish affairs is a coward to the backbone, will fight for an idea like a hero.
George Bernard Shaw, MAN AND SUPERMAN 1905

IDLENESS

5 Idleness, that is the curse of other men, is the muse of poets.
D'Arcy Cresswell, THE POET'S PROGRESS

6 You can tell a British workman by his hands. They are always in his pockets.
Graffito reported on BBC Radio 4, *Quote Unquote* 26 Jun 1980

IDOLATRY

7 He who slays a king and he who dies for him are alike idolaters.
George Bernard Shaw, MAN AND SUPERMAN 1905

8 The savage bows down to idols of wood and stone; the civilised man to idols of flesh and blood.
Id.

IGNORANCE

9 'Tis ignorance makes the child sublime.
George Barlow, POETRY AND SCIENCE

10 The full area of ignorance is not yet mapped. We are at present only exploring its fringes.
J. D. Bernal, THE PERPETUAL PESSIMIST

11 *Ignoramus, n.* A person unacquainted with certain kinds of knowledge familiar to yourself, and having certain other kinds that you know nothing about.
Ambrose Bierce, THE DEVIL'S DICTIONARY 1906

12 The evil that is in the world almost always comes of ignorance, and good intentions may do as much harm as malevolence if they lack understanding.
Albert Camus, THE PLAGUE 1947

13 The most incorrigible vice being that of an ignorance which fancies it knows everything.
Id.

14 It is the tragedy of the world that no one knows what he doesn't know — and the less a man knows, the more sure he is that he knows everything.
Joyce Cary, ART AND REALITY

15 all ignorance toboggans into know / and trudges up to ignorance again.
e. e. cummings, ONE TIMES ONE 1944

16 The pleasures of ignorance are as great, in their way, as the pleasures of knowledge.
Aldous Huxley, COLLECTED ESSAYS 1960

17 The greater our knowledge increases the more our ignorance unfolds.
John F. Kennedy. Address, Rice University 12 Sep 1962

18 It is surprising how few of one's friends are really sure where Carinthia is.
Philip Lewis, THE LADY, *Summer in Carinthia* 24 Jun 1953

19 In expanding the field of knowledge we but increase the horizon of ignorance.
Henry Miller, THE WISDOM OF THE HEART 1941

20 His ignorance was an Empire State Building of ignorance. You had to admire it for its size.
Dorothy Parker, of Harold Ross

21 Our knowledge can only be finite while our ignorance must necessarily be infinite.
Sir Karl Popper, CONJECTURES AND REFUTATIONS

22 Everybody is ignorant, only on different subjects.
Will Rogers, AUTOBIOGRAPHY 1949

23 Somebody else's ignorance is bliss.
Jack Vance, STAR KING

24 Ignorance is not bliss — it is oblivion.
Philip Wylie, GENERATION OF VIPERS 1942

ILLEGITIMACY

1 There are no illegitimate children — only illegitimate parents.
Judge Leon R. Yankwich, decisions in Californian court, Jun 1978

ILLNESS

2 "Ye can call it influenza if ye like," said Mrs. Machin "there was no illness in my young days. We called a cold a cold."
Arnold Bennett, THE CARD 1911

3 My father invented a cure for which there was no disease and unfortunately my mother caught it and died of it.
Victor Borge, IN CONCERT

4 Ill health from early youth brings advantages in its train; it disciplines the human spirit and economises its resources.
Lord Curzon. Quoted Edward Marjoribanks, LIFE OF LORD CURZON

5 Men make use of their illnesses at least as much as they are made use of by them.
Aldous Huxley, COLLECTED ESSAYS 1960

6 Illness is not something a person *has*; it's another way of *being*.
Dr. Jonathan Miller, THE BODY IN QUESTION

7 I have Bright's disease and he has mine.
S. J. Perelman. Quoted Bennet Cerf, SHAKE WELL BEFORE USING 1948

8 Illness is the doctor to whom we pay most heed; to kindness, to knowledge, we make promise only; pain we obey.
Marcel Proust, REMEMBRANCE OF THINGS PAST 1913–1927

9 When you were ill you behaved like a true philosopher; every time that you came to yourself you made a joke.
Bertrand Russell, quoting his doctor, AUTOBIOGRAPHY 1967

10 I enjoy convalescence. It is the part that makes illness worth while.
George Bernard Shaw, BACK TO METHUSELAH 1922

ILLUSION

11 Every age is fed on illusions, lest men should renounce life early and the human race come to an end.
Joseph Conrad, VICTORY 1915

12 It is characteristic of the illusion that it derives from men's wishes . . . It need not necessarily be false, that is to say, unrealisable or incompatible with reality.
Sigmund Freud, THE FUTURE OF AN ILLUSION 1928

13 An illusion is not the same as an error . . . Aristotle's belief that vermin are evolved out of dung was an error . . . it was an illusion on the part of Columbus that he had discovered a new sea route to India.
Id.

14 If only we can give them faith that mountains can be moved they will accept the illusion that mountains are moveable, and thus an illusion may become a reality.
Benito Mussolini. Quoted Denis Mack Smith, MUSSOLINI

IMAGINATION

15 Imagination is dependent for its activity on the quantity and quality of its available material. There is nothing in imagination that has not been in sensation.
Montgomery Belgian, READING FOR PROFIT

16 To treat your facts with imagination is one thing, to imagine your facts is another.
John Burroughs, THE HEART OF BURROUGHS' JOURNALS

17 The most imaginative people are the most credulous, for to them everything is possible.
Alexander Chase, PERSPECTIVES 1966

18 Only in men's imagination does every truth find an effective and undeniable existence. Imagination, not invention, is the supreme master of art as of life.
Joseph Conrad, SOME REMINISCENCES 1912

19 Imagination is more important than knowledge.
Albert Einstein, ON SCIENCE

20 There is no better way of exercising the imagination than studying law.
Jean Giraudoux, TIGER AT THE GATES 1935

21 [Man] does not see the real world. The real world is hidden from him by the wall of imagination.
George Gurdjieff. Quoted P. D. Ouspensky, IN SEARCH OF THE MIRACULOUS

22 Imagination grows by exercise and contrary to common belief is more powerful in the mature than in the young.
W. Somerset Maugham, THE SUMMING UP 1938

1 A rock pile ceases to be a rock pile the moment a single man contemplates it, bearing within him the image of a cathedral.
Antoine de Saint-Exupéry, FLIGHT TO ARRAS 1942

2 It is the spirit of the age to believe that any fact, however suspect, is superior to any imaginative exercise, no matter how true.
Gore Vidal, Encounter, *Dec* 1967

3 Imagination and fiction make up more than three quarters of our real life.
Simone Weil, GRAVITY AND GROUSE 1947

IMITATION

4 What gives the artist real prestige is his imitators.
Igor Stravinsky, London Magazine, *Mar* 1967

IMMIGRANT

5 The immigrant, no matter how illiterate or ignorant he may be, always learns too soon.
Henry Frick (partner of Andrew Carnegie). Quoted Alistair Cooke, AMERICA

6 America is not to be made a polyglot boarding house for money-hunters of twenty different nationalities who have changed their former countries for this country only as farmyard beasts change one feeding trough for another.
Theodore Roosevelt. Speech, Bridgeport, Connecticut

7 Some Americans need hyphens in their names because only half of them has come over.
Woodrow Wilson. Speech, Washington 16 *May* 1914

IMMORALITY

8 The only immorality is not to do what one has to do when one has to do it.
Jean Anouilh, BECKET 1959

IMMORTALITY

9 I don't want to achieve immortality through my work, I want to achieve it through not dying.
Woody Allen. Quoted E. Lax, WOODY ALLEN AND HIS COMEDY

10 We are not made to rest in this world. It is not our true native land.
Father Andrew, IN THE SILENCE

11 One cannot live for ever by ignoring the price of coffins.
Ernest Bramah, KAI LUNG UNROLLS HIS MAT 1928

12 The belief in immortality rests not very much on the hope of going on. Few of us want to do that, but we would like very much to begin again.
Heywood Brown, PIECES OF HATE

13 Man is the only animal that contemplates death, and also the only animal that shows any sign of doubt of its finality.
William Ernest Hocking, THE MEANING OF IMMORTALITY IN HUMAN EXPERIENCE 1957

14 God needs imortality to vindicate his ways to man.
W. Somerset Maugham, THE SUMMING UP 1938

15 Either the soul is immortal and we shall not die, or it perishes with the flesh, and we shall not know that we are dead. Live, then, as if you were eternal.
André Maurois. Quoted W. J. Durant, ON THE MEANING OF LIFE

16 I am a temporary enclosure for a temporary purpose; that served, my skull and teeth, my idiosyncrasy and desire, will disperse, I believe, like the timbers of a booth after a fair.
H. G. Wells, FIRST AND LAST THINGS

IMPARTIALITY

17 You must not miss Whitehall. At one end you will find a statue of one of our kings who was beheaded; at the other the monument to the man who did it. This is just an example of our attempts to be fair to everybody.
Sir Edward Appleton. Speech, Stockholm. Quoted News Review 1 *Jan* 1948

18 I decline utterly to be impartial as between the Fire Brigade and the Fire.
Winston Churchill when editing the British Gazette during the General Strike of 1926

IMPERFECTION

19 We are always glad when a great man reassures us of his humanity by possessing a few peculiarities.
André Maurois, THE ART OF LIVING

IMPERMANENCE

1 There is nothing at all that remains, nor any house; nor any castle; however strong; nor any love, no matter how tender and sound; nor any comradeship among men, however hardy.
Hilaire Belloc, THE FOUR MEN

2 Anything that calls itself new is doomed to a short life.
Tom Wolfe, IN OUR TIMES

IMPOSSIBILITY

3 You can't make soufflé rise twice.
Alice Roosevelt Longworth. Quoted James T. Patterson, MR. REPUBLICAN, *a biography of Robert A. Taft*

IMPROPRIETY

4 Impropriety is the soul of wit.
W. Somerset Maugham, THE MOON AND SIXPENCE 1919

IMPULSE

5 The most decisive actions of our life — I mean those that are most likely to decide the whole course of our future — are more often than not, unconsidered.
André Gide, THE COUNTERFEITERS 1926

6 Most of us stifle enough good impulses during the course of a day to change the current of our lives . . . The mistakes of inaction, flanked by heavy reasoning, are likely to be worse than the mistakes of genuine impulse.
William Moulton Martin in a CBS *broadcast* 18 *Mar* 1941

7 Impulse has more effect than conscious purpose in moulding men's lives.
Bertrand Russell, AUTOBIOGRAPHY 1967

IMPULSIVENESS

8 You are always taking the bull between your teeth.
Sam Goldwyn. Quoted Alva Johnson, THE GREAT GOLDWYN

9 When a prisoner sees the door of his dungeon open he dashes for it without stopping to think where he shall get his dinner.
George Bernard Shaw, BACK TO METH-USELAH, *Preface* 1922

INADEQUACY

10 Who ever is adequate? We all create situations each other can't live up to, then break our hearts at them because they don't.
Elizabeth Bowen, THE DEATH OF THE HEART 1938

11 Our accepting what we are must always inhibit our being what we ought to be.
John Fowles, THE MAGUS 1965

12 Like Brighton pier, all right as far as it goes, but inadequate for getting to France.
Neil Kinnock. Speech, House of Commons 2 *Feb* 1981

INATTENTION

13 Organ Morgan, you haven't been listening to a word I said. It's organ, organ all the time with you.
Dylan Thomas, UNDER MILK WOOD 1954

INCENTIVE

14 If there hadn't been women we'd still be squatting in a cave eating raw meat because we made civilisation in order to impress our girlfriends.
Orson Welles. Quoted Barbara Rowe, A BOOK OF QUOTES

INCOME TAX

15 The hardest thing in the world to understand is income tax.
Albert Einstein. Quoted Barbara Rowe, A BOOK OF QUOTES

16 I decided to turn myself into a company. In those days it was a fashionable tax ploy. It didn't work of course; no tax ploy ever really works. If it did it would mean the end of chartered accountants.
Robert Morley, MORLEY MARVELS 1976

INCOMPETENCE

17 Henry, who can't even strike a match.
Margot Asquith of her husband. Quoted J. A. Spender and Cyril Asquith, LIFE OF LORD OXFORD AND ASQUITH

18 I was dressed by a man who evidently had read his instructions in Braille.
Bette Davis, of her first screen test in THE LONELY LIFE

INCOMPREHENSIBILITY

1 The advantage of the imcomprehensible is that it never loses its freshness.
John Weightman. Quoting Paul Varley, Observer 5 *Aug* 1979

INDECENCY

2 You have left your hero and heroine tied up in a cavern for a week, and they are not married.
G. K. Chesterton quoting, in his autobiography, an editor's complaint to his sister-in-law, Mrs. Cecil Chesterton, about a serial story

INDECISION

3 The Right Honourable Gentleman [Sir John Simon] has sat so long on the fence that the iron has entered his soul.
David Lloyd George, House of Commons 1931

4 Like King Solomon, when confronted by an enterprising buyer who showed him 271 new wives in a new harem, he knew perfectly well what was expected of him but did not quite know where to begin. I am in the same position.
Lord Mancroft. Speech, Buyers Benevolent Association, Grosvenor House, London 9 Mar 1954

5 Nothing is so exhausting as indecision, and nothing is so futile.
Bertrand Russell, THE CONQUEST OF HAPPINESS 1930

INDEPENDENCE

6 It's the man who dares to take, who is independent, not he who gives.
D. H. Lawrence, SELECTED LETTERS 1962

INDIA

7 There was so much sculpture that I should certainly have missed the indecencies if Major Poonby hadn't been considerate enough to point them out.
J. R. Ackerley, HINDOO HOLIDAY

8 If the British had not been in India that woman Mrs. Pandit would have been burnt on her husband's funeral pyre.
Nancy Astor. Quoted John Grigg, NANCY ASTOR: PORTRAIT OF A PIONEER

9 India is a geographical term. It is no more a united nation than the Equator.
Winston Churchill. Speech, Royal Albert Hall 18 *May* 1931

INDIGNATION

10 Hate is a kind of passive suffering, but indignation is a kind of joy.
W. B. Yeats, LETTERS 1954

INDISCRETION

11 Dentopedology is the science of opening your mouth and putting your foot in it. I've been practising it for years.
Philip, Duke of Edinburgh

INDOLENCE

12 It behoves you for your own well-being not to suffer the grass to grow around your tardy ankles in the matter.
Ernest Bramah, KAI LUNG UNROLLS HIS MAT 1928

13 Alas! The hours we waste in work / And similar inconsequence, / Friends, I beg you do not shirk / Your daily task of indolence.
Don Marquis, THE ALMOST PERFECT STATE

14 Loafing needs no explanation and is its own excuse.
Christopher Morley, MINCE PIE 1919

15 The right to laziness is one of the rights that sensible humanity will learn to consider as something self-evident.
Dr. Wilhelm Stekel, THE DEPTHS OF THE SOUL

16 There is a case, and a strong case, for that particular form of indolence that allows us to move through life knowing only what immediately concerns us.
Alec Waugh, ON DOING WHAT ONE LIKES

INDULGENCE

17 Unrestrained indulgence kills not merely passion, but, in the end, even amusement.
Aldous Huxley, COLLECTED ESSAYS 1960

INDUSTRIOUSNESS

18 By working faithfully eight hours a day you may eventually get to be a boss and work twelve hours a day.
Robert Frost. Quoted Barbara Rowe, A BOOK OF QUOTES

INDUSTRY

1 I tell you, the only safeguard of order and discipline in the modern world is a standardised worker with interchangeable parts. That would solve the entire problem of management.
Jean Giraudoux, THE MADWOMAN OF CHAILLOT

2 The God of Industry supplies his worshippers with objects and can only exist on condition that his gifts are gratefully accepted.
Aldous Huxley, BRIEF CANDLES

INEQUALITY

3 We all live under the same sky, but we don't all have the same horizons.
Konrad Adenauer. Quoted Barbara Rowe, A BOOK OF QUOTES

4 The only inequalities that matter begin in the mind. It is not income levels but differences in mental equipment that keep people apart, breed feelings of inferiority.
Jacquetta Hawkes, New Statesman, *Jan* 1957

5 We need inequality in order to eliminate poverty.
Sir Keith Joseph. Quoted Audrey Hillar, THIS ENGLAND

6 There is always inequality in life. Some men are killed in a war and some men are wounded and some men never leave the country — Life is unfair.
John F. Kennedy, at a press conference 21 *Mar* 1962

INEVITABILITY

7 Nothing is inevitable until it happens.
A. J. P. Taylor. Quoted George Hutchinson, Daily Telegraph 7 *Jan* 1980

8 The inevitability of gradualness.
Sidney Webb. Presidential address to the annual conference of the Labour Party 1920

INEXPERIENCE

9 She had to confess to inexperience: her personality was still too much for her, like a punt pole.
Elizabeth Bowen, FRIENDS AND RELATIONS 1931

10 I did not yet know the meaning of life, although I was now 26.
Ilya Ehrenburg, FIRST YEARS OF REVOLUTION

11 Inexperience is what makes a young man do what an older man says is impossible.
Herbert V. Prochow, Saturday Evening Post 4 *Dec* 1948

INFERIORITY

12 No one can make you feel inferior without your consent.
Eleanor Roosevelt. Quoted Don Peretz Elkins, GLAD TO BE ME

INFIDELITY

13 Marriage without love means love without marriage.
Kenneth, Lord Clark, CIVILISATION 1969

14 It is the fear of middle age in the young, and of old age in the middle-aged, which is the prime cause of infidelity, Man's infallible rejuvenator.
Cyril Connolly, THE UNQUIET GRAVE 1945

15 Husbands are chiefly good lovers when they are betraying their wives.
Marilyn Monroe. Quoted Barbara Rowe, A BOOK OF QUOTES

16 One man's folly is another man's wife.
Helen Rowland, A GUIDE TO MEN

INFINITY

17 All finite things reveal infinitude.
Theodore Roethke, THE FAR FIELD

INFLATION

18 Nothing so weakens governments as persistent inflation.
J. K. Galbraith, THE AFFLUENT SOCIETY 1958

19 I don't think one can spend oneself rich.
George Humphrey. Quoted Rhoda Thomas Tripp, INTERNATIONAL THESAURUS OF QUOTATIONS

20 Governments are the chief culprit in inflation because, wishing to avoid unpopularity, they spend too much and tax too little.
Prof. Lord Kaldar, MEMORANDA ON MONETARY POLICY 17 *Aug* 1980

21 The best way to destroy the capitalist system is to debauch the currency. By a continuing process of inflation governments can confiscate, secretly and unobserved, an important part of the wealth of their citizens.
J. M. Keynes, ESSAYS IN PERSUASION 1931

1 Inflation is like sin; every government denounces it and every government practises it.
Sir Frederick Leith-Ross, Observer 30 *Jun* 1957

2 Inflation is bringing us true democracy. For the first time in history luxuries and necessities are selling at the same price.
Robert Orben. Quoted Barbara Rowe, A BOOK OF QUOTES

3 Just about the time you think you can make both ends meet, somebody moves the ends.
Pansy Penner. Quoted Reader's Digest, Dec 1944

4 Inflation sooner or later makes more extensive unemployment inevitable . . . by drawing more and more workers into kinds of jobs which depend on continuing or even accelerating inflation.
F. A. Von Hagek, New York Times 15 *Nov* 1974

5 The disease is painless; it's the cure that hurts.
Katherine Whitehorn, Observer, *Deckchair Economics* 21 *Aug* 1966

6 From now on the pound abroad is worth 14% or so less in terms of other currencies. It does not mean, of course, that the pound here in Britain, in your pocket, or purse, or in your bank, has been devalued.
Harold Wilson, broadcast 18 *Nov* 1967

INFLUENCE

7 One of the things a man has to fight most bitterly is the influence of those who love him.
Sherwood Anderson, LETTERS 1953

8 Influence is neither good nor bad in an absolute manner, but only in relation to the one who experiences it.
André Gide, PRETEXTS 1903

INFORMALITY

9 He watched her [Lady Astor] fan herself with a dinner plate and push back her tiara like an old hat.
Ernesta Barlow. Quoted Christopher Sykes, NANCY

INFORMATION

10 Information is not culture. In the mind of a truly educated man, facts are organised and they make up a living world in the image of the world of reality.
André Maurois, THE ART OF LIVING

INGRATITUDE

11 Somebody who puts 10p in a blind beggar's tray and gets thanked for it thinks no more about it; but if the beggar spits in his eye he'll probably remember it for the rest of his life. Gratitude, you see, is a pleasant thing, but unexciting; it is *ingratitude* which fascinates us.
Christopher Mayhew, Punch 16 *May* 1973

INHUMANITY

12 A man can only live by absolutely / Forgetting he's a man like other folk.
Bertolt Brecht, THE THREEPENNY OPERA 1928

INJUSTICE

13 Injustice anywhere is a threat to justice everywhere.
Martin Luther King, Atlantic Monthly, *Aug* 1963

INNOCENCE

14 Innocence with ignorance is not worth having.
Lucilla Andrews, HIGHLAND INTERLUDE

15 'Tis e'er the lot of the innocent in the world to fly to the wolf for succour from the lion.
John Barth, THE SOT-WEED FACTOR 1960

16 Your innocence is on at such a rakish angle / It gives you quite an air of iniquity.
Christopher Fry, THE LADY'S NOT FOR BURNING 1949

17 Innocence is like a dumb leper who has lost his bell, wandering the world, meaning no harm.
Graham Greene, THE QUIET AMERICAN 1955

18 She [Ellen Terry] was an extremely beautiful girl and as innocent as a rose. When Watts kissed her she took it for granted that she was going to have a baby.
George Bernard Shaw. Quoted Stephen Winston, DAYS WITH BERNARD SHAW

INNOVATION

1 Any new thing must find a new shape, then afterwards one can call it art.
Frieda Lawrence, letter to Edward Garnett 1912

INQUISITIVENESS

2 My advice to you is not to inquire why or whether, but just enjoy your ice cream while it is on your plate — that's my philosophy.
Thornton Wilder, THE SKIN OF OUR TEETH 1942

INSIGHT

3 Insight — the titillating knack for hurting!
Colette, EARTHLY PARADISE, *The Pure and Impure* 1966

4 All men enjoy flashes of insight beyond meanings already established in etymology and grammar.
A. N. Whitehead, ADVENTURES OF IDEAS 1933

INSOMNIA

5 I ain't sleeping. I'm just taking a good look at the insides of my eyelids.
Jonathan Raban, OLD GLORY

INSPIRATION

6 My sole inspiration is a telephone call from a director.
Cole Porter in a press interview 8 *Feb* 1955

7 Inspiration could be called inhaling the memory of an act never experienced.
Ned Rorem, MUSIC FROM INSIDE OUT 1967

8 Work brings inspiration, if inspiration is not discernible at the beginning.
Igor Stravinsky, CHRONICLES OF MY LIFE 1935

9 When I was writing *The Shadow of the Glen* I got more aid than any learning could have given me from a chink in the floor of the old Wicklow House where I was staying, that let me hear what was being said by the servant girls in the kitchen.
J. M. Synge, PLAYBOY OF THE WESTERN WORLD, *Preface* 1907

INSULT

10 Duplicitous bastard. European fiends — just plain cowardly. British, lying through their teeth.
Alexander Haig of Lord Carrington 1982

11 [James Whitcomb Riley] the unctuous, over-cheerful, word-mouthing, flabby-faced citizen who condescendingly tells Providence, in flowery and well-rounded periods, where to get off.
Hewlett Howland. Quoted Richard Crowder, THOSE INNOCENT YEARS

12 He [Drew Pearson] is not a sunnavbitch. He is only a filthy brain child, conceived in ruthlessness and dedicated to the proposition that Judas Iscariot was a piker.
Senator William Jenner of Indiana. Quoted Morris A. Beale, ALL AMERICAN LOUSE

13 . . . has all the depth and glitter of a worn dime.
Dorothy Parker, of Margot Asquith's LAY SERMONS

14 Westbrook Pegler, a guttersnipe, is a gentleman compared to you. You can take that as more of an insult than a reflection of your ancestry.
Harry S Truman, protesting against a criticism of his daughter Margaret's singing by Paul Hume of the Washington Post

15 She missed the last Lobby briefing, I hear. At the vet's with hard pad, no doubt.
Harold Wilson, of a woman journalist he disliked. Quoted James Margach, THE ABUSE OF POWER 1981

INSURANCE

16 If it were not for the insurance companies there would be little litigation of any sort today.
A. P. Herbert, MORE MISLEADING CASES

INTEGRITY

17 I never truckled; I never took off the hat to Fashion and held it out for pennies. By God, I told them the truth.
Frank Norris, THE RESPONSIBILITIES OF A NOVELIST 1903

INTELLECT

18 Since it is seldom clear whether intellectual activity denotes a superior mode of being or a vital deficiency, opinion swings between

considering intellect a privilege and seeing it as a handicap.
Jacques Barzun, THE HOUSE OF INTELLECT 1959

1 Intellect has nothing to do with equality except to respect it as a sublime convention.
Id.

2 We should take care not to make the intellect our god; it has, of course, powerful muscles, but no personality.
Albert Einstein, OUT OF MY LATER LIFE 1950

3 Little minds are interested in the extraordinary; great minds in the commonplace.
Elbert Hubbard

4 His mind was like a soup dish, wide and shallow; it could hold a small amount of nearly everything, but the slightest jarring spilt the soup into somebody's lap.
Irving Stone of William Jennings Bryant, THE ALSO RAN

5 I rank the wide thinker far above the ready writer. Goethe knew twice as much about the human scene as Shakespeare but could not put it on paper half as well.
Wilfred Whitten, John o' London's Weekly, *A Priest of Thought* 21 *Jul* 1939

6 The grinding of the intellect is for most people as painful as a dentist's drill.
Leonard Woolf, Observer 28 *Jun* 1959

INTELLECTUAL

7 An intellectual is a man who doesn't know how to park a bike.
Spiro Agnew

8 To the man-in-the-street who I'm sorry to say / Is a keen observer of life / 'Intellectual' suggests straight away / A man who's untrue to his wife.
W. H. Auden, NEW YEAR LETTER

9 The intellectuals' chief cause of anguish are one another's works.
Jacques Barzun, THE HOUSE OF INTELLECT 1959

10 Intellectuals are people who believe that ideas are of more importance than values. That is to say, their own ideas and other people's values.
Gerald Brenan, THOUGHTS IN A DRY SEASON 1979

11 An intellectual is someone whose mind watches itself. I am happy to be both halves, the watcher and the watched.
Albert Camus, NOTEBOOKS 1935–1942

12 Berenson said to Bauer, the antique dealer "A man as scholarly as yourself shouldn't be a dealer. It is horrible to be a dealer." To which Bauer replied "Between you and me there is no great difference; I am an intellectual dealer and you're a dealing intellectual." Berenson never forgave him.
René Gimpel, DIARY OF AN ART DEALER

13 Intellectuals can tell themselves anything, sell themselves any bill of goods, which is why they are so often patsies for the ruling classes in nineteenth-century France and England, or twentieth-century Russia and America.
Lillian Hellman, AN UNFINISHED WOMAN 1969

14 A highbrow is the kind of person who looks at a sausage and thinks of Picasso.
A. P. Herbert, THE HIGHBROW

15 A highbrow is a person educated beyond his intelligence.
Attr. Brander Matthews, STEVENSON'S BOOK OF QUOTATIONS

16 Every man with a bellyful of the classics is an enemy of the human race.
Henry Miller, TROPIC OF CANCER 1934

17 I do not know a single person whose intellect I respect deeply who enjoys good health.
Sir Peter Chalmers Mitchell, MY FILL OF DAYS

18 Intellectuals incline to be individualists, or even independents, are not team conscious and tend to regard obedience as a surrender of personality.
Harold Nicolson, Observer 12 *Oct* 1958

19 Intellectuals have the same problems as other people. But they do not bear their sufferings so nobly.
Rev. D. Edward Norman, REITH LECTURES 1978

20 Annabel was accounted a beauty and intellectually gifted; she never played herring, and was reputed to have read Maeterlinck's *Life of the Bee*. If you abstain from tennis *and* read Maeterlinck in a small country village, you are of necessity intellectual.
Saki, REGINALD AT THE THEATRE

1 The trouble with me is, I belong to a vanishing race. I'm one of the intellectuals.
Robert E. Sherwood, THE PETRIFIED FOREST 1935

2 A highbrow is a man who has found something more interesting than women.
Edgar Wallace to a Hollywood reporter, Dec 1931

3 A man or woman of thoroughbred intelligence galloping across country in pursuit of an idea.
Virginia Woolf. Quoted Kenneth Tynan, CURTAINS

INTELLIGENCE

4 The intelligent are to the intelligentsia what a man is to a gent.
Stanley Baldwin. Quoted his biographer, G. M. Young

5 Intelligence is the faculty of making artificial objects, especially tools, to make tools.
Henri Bergson, CREATIVE EVOLUTION 1907

6 Intelligence is not to make no mistakes / But quickly to see how to make them good.
Bertolt Brecht, THE MEASURES TAKEN 1930

7 An intelligent man on one plane can be a fool on others.
Albert Camus, NOTEBOOKS 1935–42

8 There may be an optimum level of intelligence and perhaps we have already exceeded it. Our brains may be too big — dooming us as Triceratops was doomed by his armour.
Arthur C. Clarke, THE LOST WORLDS OF 2001

9 The greatest intelligence is precisely the one that suffers most from its own limitations.
André Gide, THE COUNTERFEITERS 1926

10 Military Intelligence is a contradiction in terms.
Graffito on Ministry of Defence building. Quoted Nigel Rees, GRAFFITI RULES O.K.

11 It takes brains not to make money. Any fool can make money. But what about people with talent and brains.
Joseph Heller, CATCH 22 1961

12 A child of five would understand this. Send somebody to fetch a child of five.
Groucho Marx, DUCK SOUP

13 Simplicity of character is no hindrance to subtlety of intellect.
John Morley, LIFE OF GLADSTONE 1963

14 There are three kinds of intelligence — the intelligence of man, the intelligence of animals, and the intelligence of the military, in that order.
Gottfried Reinhardt. Quoted Lillian Ross, PICTURE

INTEREST

15 There is no such thing on earth as an uninteresting subject; the only thing that can exist is an uninterested person.
G. K. Chesterton, HERETICS 1905

INTERVIEW

16 I'm notorious for giving a bad interview. I'm an actor and I can't help but feel I'm boring when I'm on as myself.
Rock Hudson. Quoted Alan Martin, TV Times 19 Oct 1972

17 "Mr. Coward, have you anything to say to the Sun?" a lady interviewer once asked him. "Shine." Noël said pleasantly.
William Marchant, THE PRIVILEGE OF HIS COMPANY 1980

INTOLERANCE

18 What is objectionable, what is dangerous about extremists is not that they are extreme but that they are intolerant.
Robert F. Kennedy, THE PURSUIT OF JUSTICE

19 Intolerance itself is a form of egoism and to condemn egoism intolerantly is to share it.
George Santayana, WORDS OF DOCTRINE

INTRUSION

20 Bloody hell, Ma'am, what's he doing here?
Elizabeth Andrew, the Queen's Chambermaid, faced with Michael Fagan, intruder in the Queen's bedroom 1982

21 Miss Twye was soaping her breasts in the bath / When she heard behind her a meaning laugh / And to her amazement she discovered / A wicked man in the bathroom cupboard.
Gavin Ewart, THE COLLECTED EWART

INTUITION

22 Whereas the mind works in possibilities, the intuitions work in actualities, and what

you *intuitively* desire, that is possible to you.
D. H. Lawrence, SELECTED ESSAYS

1 Some of the finest moral intuitions come to quite humble people. The visiting of lofty ideas doesn't depend on formal schooling. Think of those Galilean peasants.
A. N. Whitehead, DIALOGUES

INVECTIVE

2 He [Aneurin Bevan] was the only man I knew who could make a curse sound like a caress.
Michael Foot, ANEURIN BEVAN 1897–1945

INVENTION

3 The Doctor is said to have invented an extraordinary weapon which will make war less brutal. It is described as a very powerful liquid which rots braces at a distance of a mile.
Beachcomber (J. B. Morton), Daily Express, *By The Way*

4 I don't think necessity is the mother of invention — invention, in my opinion, arises directly from idleness, possibly also from laziness. To save oneself trouble.
Agatha Christie, AUTOBIOGRAPHY

5 The English are not an inventive people; they don't eat enough pie.
Thomas A. Edison, GOLDEN BOOK, *Apr* 1931

6 Inventions that are not made, like babies that are not born, are not missed.
J. K. Galbraith, THE AFFLUENT SOCIETY 1958

7 The means by which we live have outdistanced the ends for which we live.
Martin Luther King, STRENGTH TO LOVE

8 His absent-minded scientist, Dr. Strabismus (whom God Preserve) of Utrecht, had to his credit a list of inventions that included 'a leather grape', 'a revolving wheelbarrow', 'a hollow glass walking stick for keeping very small flannel shirts in', 'waterproof onions', 'a bottle with its neck in the middle', 'false teeth for swordfish', and 'a foghorn sharpener'.
Bernard Levin, obituary of J. B. Morton (Beachcomber), Observer 13 *May* 1979

9 We live in a time when a man believes himself fabulously capable of creation, but he does not know what to create.
José Ortega y Gasset, THE REVOLT OF THE MASSES 1930

10 Innovation depends on invention and inventors should be treated as the pop stars of industry.
Philip, Duke of Edinburgh. Quoted Noël St. George, ROYAL QUOTES

11 In the acts of life man invents nothing; but in the acts of death he outdoes Nature herself, and produces by chemistry and machinery all the slaughter of plague, pestilence and famine.
George Bernard Shaw, MAN AND SUPERMAN 1905

12 At Elm he [Sir George Sitwell] invented a musical toothbrush which played 'Annie Laurie' as you brushed your teeth, and a small revolver for killing wasps.
Sir Osbert Sitwell, THE SCARLET TREE 1945

IRELAND

13 It is a geographical accident that Ireland is surrounded by sea. This should not be ignored.
A. J. Balfour. Quoted Thomas Jones, WHITEHALL DIARIES VOL. III, IRELAND 1918–25

14 Anyone who isn't confused here doesn't really understand what is going on.
Belfast man 1970. Quoted Nigel Rees, QUOTE UNQUOTE

15 Stone-walled cabin thatched with reeds / Where a Stone Age people breeds / The last of Europe's stone-age race.
Sir John Betjeman, IRELAND WITH EMILY

16 It is not necessary to climb the painful stairs of Irish history, that treadmill of a nation whose labours are as vain for her own uplifting as the convict's are for his own redemption.
Roger Casement, at the end of his trial for high treason

17 In so far as Lloyd George can link his political misfortunes with this Irish story, he may be content. In falling through Irish difficulties he may fall with Essex and with Strafford, with Pitt and with Gladstone; and with a line of sovereigns and statesmen, great or small, spread across the English history books of seven hundred years.
Winston Churchill, THE WORLD CRISIS, *Aftermath* 1929

1 By yesterday morning British troops were patrolling the streets of Belfast. I fear that once Catholics and Protestants get used to our presence they will hate us more than they hate each other.
Richard Crossman, DIARIES 17 *Aug* 1969

2 I never met anyone in Ireland who understood the Irish question, except one Englishman who had only been there a week.
Sir K. Fraser MP, House of Commons, May 1919

3 Ireland is the old sow that eats her farrow.
James Joyce, A PORTRAIT OF THE ARTIST AS A YOUNG MAN 1914

4 The Irish don't know what they want and are prepared to fight to the death to get it.
Sir Sidney Littlewood, President of the Law Society. Speech 13 *Apr* 1961

5 I am troubled, I'm dissatisfied. I'm Irish.
Marianne Moore, SPENSER'S IRELAND 1941

6 The Irish do not want anyone to wish them well; they want them to wish their enemies ill.
Harold Nicolson, SMALL TALK

7 Dublin is a city where you can see a sparrow fall to the ground and God watching it.
Conor Cruise O'Brien

8 The English should give Ireland home rule — and reserve the motion picture rights.
Will Rogers, AUTOBIOGRAPHY 1949

9 An Irishman's heart is nothing but his imagination.
George Bernard Shaw, JOHN BULL'S OTHER ISLAND 1904

IRON CURTAIN

10 From Stettin in the Baltic to Trieste in the Adriatic, an iron curtain has descended across the continent.
Winston Churchill. Speech, Fulton, Missouri, Mar 1946

ISOLATION

11 We're all of us sentenced to solitary confinement inside our own skins.
Tennessee Williams, ORPHEUS DESCENDING 1956

ISOLATIONISM

12 Personally I can't see that foreign stories are ever news — not real news.
Evelyn Waugh, SCOOP 1938

ITALY

13 Venice is like eating an entire box of chocolate liqueurs at one go.
Truman Capote. Quoted Observer 26 *Nov* 1961

14 Italy is a poor country full of rich people.
Richard Gardner, ex-U.S. Ambassador in Rome. Quoted Observer 16 *Aug* 1981

15 She said that all the sights in Rome were called after London cinemas.
Nancy Mitford, PIGEON PIE 1940

J

HENRY JAMES

1 Henry James was one of the nicest old ladies I ever met.
William Faulkner

2 Many readers cannot get interested in James. They cannot grant his premise, which is that most of human life has to disappear before he can do us a novel.
E. M. Forster, ASPECTS OF THE NOVEL 1927

3 Sargent's portrait of Henry James is nearly finished, and I hear is a masterpiece. There is a plaid waistcoat in it, like a sea in a storm, which is said to be prodigious.
Edmund Gosse, letter to Thomas Hardy 1913

4 The work of Henry James has always seemed divisible by a simple dynastic arrangement into three reigns: James I, James II and the Old Pretender.
Philip Guedella, MEN OF LETTERS

5 He was a great American writer who came to Venice and looked out of the window and smoked his cigar and thought.
Ernest Hemingway, SELECTED LETTERS 1917–1961

6 Mr. James' cosmopolitanism is, after all, limited; to be really cosmopolitan, a man must be at home even in his own country.
Thomas Wentworth Higginson, SHORT STUDIES OF AMERICAN AUTHORS

7 He did not live, he observed life from a window, and too often was inclined to content himself with no more than what his friends told him they saw when *they* looked out of a window.
W. Somerset Maugham, A WRITER'S NOTE-BOOK 1949

8 Leviathan retrieving pebbles . . . a magnificent but painful hippopotamus resolved at any cost, even at the cost of its dignity, upon picking up a pea.
H. G. Wells, BOOR

JAPAN

9 The Japs have done nothing for thousands of years but write the wrong way round and paint unrecognisable pictures of red mullet on bits of scented paper.
Raymond Asquith, LIFE AND LETTERS

10 While we spend energy and imagination on inventing new ways of cleaning the floors of our houses, the Japanese solve the problem by not dirtying them in the first place.
Bernard Rudofsky, THE KIMONO HIND

11 The Japanese have perfected good manners and made them indistinguishable from rudeness.
Paul Theroux, THE GREAT RAILWAY BAZAAR

JAZZ

12 Down South where I come from you don't go around hitting too many white keys.
Eubie Blake, centenarian Negro pianist and composer, on being asked on TV why his compositions contained so many sharps and flats 1983

13 Jazz is the only music in which the same note can be played night after night but differently each time.
Ornette Coleman. Quoted Wilfred Mellars, MUSIC IN A NEW FOUND LAND 1964

14 Playing 'bop' is like playing Scrabble with all the vowels missing.
Duke Ellington, Look magazine 10 *Aug* 1954

15 Jazz without the beat is a telephone yanked from the wall; it just can't communicate.
Leonare Feather, Show magazine, *Jan* 1962

16 A jazz musician is a juggler who uses harmonics instead of oranges.
Benny Green, THE RELUCTANT ART

17 It was the first time that I had ever clearly seen a jazz band. The spectacle was positively terrifying.
Aldous Huxley, DO WHAT YOU WILL 1929

1 Jazz is playin' from the heart, you don't lie.
William Geary (Bunk) Johnson. Quoted Nat Shapiro, ENCYCLOPEDIA OF QUOTATIONS ABOUT MUSIC

2 Jazz has never existed in Africa, and it doesn't exist there today.
Max Kaminsky, MY LIFE IN JAZZ 1963

3 If you're in jazz, and more than ten people like you, you're labelled commercial.
Herbie Mann. Quoted Henry Pleasante, SERIOUS MUSIC—AND ALL THAT JAZZ 1919

4 I want to hear screaming and hollering and kicking and biting. That's what the world's about today . . . Life is a bit chaotic, and I think jazzmen should express something of the way life is lived.
Charlie Mariano, DOWNBEAT YEARBOOK 1967

5 During the early years of the century jazz became fortuitously identified with brothels.
Frank Muir, THE FRANK MUIR BOOK 1976

6 What a terrible revenge by the culture of the Negroes on that of the whites.
Ignacy Paderewski. Quoted Nat Shapiro, ENCYCLOPEDIA OF QUOTATIONS ABOUT MUSIC

7 The basic difference between classical music and jazz is that in the former the music is always greater than its performance — whereas the way jazz is performed is always more important than what is being played.
André Previn. Quoted Miles Kington, The Times 1967

8 Jazz is either a thrilling communication with the primitive soul, or an ear-splitting bore.
Winthrop Sargent. Quoted Nat Shapiro, ENCYCLOPEDIA OF QUOTATIONS ABOUT MUSIC

9 Jazz will endure just as long as people hear it through their feet instead of their brains.
John Philip Sousa. Ibid.

JEALOUSY

10 Jealousy is no more than feeling alone among smiling enemies.
Elizabeth Bowen, THE HOUSE IN PARIS 1935

11 It is not love that is blind, but jealousy.
Lawrence Durrell, JUSTINE 1957

12 Jealousy, that dragon which slays love under the pretence of keeping it alive.
Havelock Ellis, ON LIFE AND SEX

13 To jealousy, nothing is more frightful than laughter.
Françoise Sagan, LA CHAMADEN 1966

JEW

14 It's their own silly fault — they ought to have left God alone.
Hilaire Belloc. Quoted Robert Speight, LIFE OF HILAIRE BELLOC

15 The pursuit of knowledge for its own sake, an almost fanatical love of justice and the desire for personal independence — these are the features of the Jewish tradition which make me thank my stars that I belong to it.
Albert Einstein, THE WORLD AS I SEE IT

16 How odd / Of God / To choose / The Jews.
William Norman Ewer, HOW ODD

17 You call me a damned Jew. My race was old when you were all savages. I am proud to be a Jew.
John Galsworthy, LOYALTIES 1922

18 Pessimism is a luxury that a Jew never can allow himself.
Golda Meir. Quoted Observer 29 *Dec* 1974

19 A Jewish man with parents alive is a fifteen year old boy, and will remain a fifteen year old boy until they die.
Philip Roth, PORTNOY'S COMPLAINT 1969

20 If a Jew is fascinated by Christians it is not because of their virtues, which he values little, but because they represent anonymity, humanity without race.
Jean-Paul Sartre, ANTI-SEMITE AND JEW

21 The Jews generally give good value. They make you pay; but they deliver the goods. In my experience the men who want something for nothing are invariably Christians.
George Bernard Shaw, ST. JOAN 1923

JEWELLERY

22 Have you ever noticed that many jewels make women either incredibly fat or incredibly thin.
J. M. Barrie, THE TWELVE POUND LOOK 1912

LYNDON B. JOHNSON

1 Let's face it, Mr. President, you're not a very likeable man.
Dean Acheson, when Johnson asked why he wasn't popular. Quoted Robert A. Caro, THE YEARS OF LYNDON JOHNSON: THE PATH TO POWER 1983

JOKE

2 Readers of *Punch* have much the same attitude to their jokes as port-drinkers have to port. They like them laid down in a cellar to mature. Then, on special occasions they can bring them up, encrusted with cobwebs and savour again their rich, familiar bouquet.
Malcolm Muggeridge, TREAD SOFTLY FOR YOU TREAD ON MY JOKES 1966

JOURNALISM

3 The world really isn't any worse. It's just that the news coverage is so much better.
Anon. English Digest, *Mar* 1965

4 "The fact is, Mr. Balfour, all the faults of the age come from Christianity and journalism."
"Christianity, of course. But why journalism?"
Conversation between A. J. Balfour and Frank Harris. Quoted, AUTOBIOGRAPHY OF MARGOT ASQUITH

5 What the proprietorship of these newspapers is aiming at is power, and power without responsibility, the privilege of the harlot throughout the ages.
Stanley Baldwin at a by-election meeting 1931

6 I run the *Daily Express* purely for propaganda and for no other purpose.
Lord Beaverbrook to the Royal Commission on the Press 1948

7 If you want to make mischief come and work on my papers.
Lord Beaverbrook inviting Anthony Howard to join his staff. Quoted Radio Times 27 *Jun* 1981

8 Journalists say a thing that they know isn't true, in the hope that if they keep on saying it long enough it *will* be true.
Arnold Bennett, THE TITLE 1918

9 I can write about anything, from gee-gees to Jesus.
Horatio Bottomley. Quoted Alan Hyman, THE RISE AND FALL OF HORATIO BOTTOMLEY

10 Journalism is the only job that requires no degrees, no diplomas and no specialised knowledge of any kind.
Patrick Campbell, MY LIFE AND EASY TIMES

11 A free press can, of course, be good or bad, but, most certainly, without freedom it will never be anything but bad.
Albert Camus, RESISTANCE, REBELLION AND DEATH 1961

12 Journalism largely consists of saying 'Lord Jones is dead' to people who never knew Lord Jones was alive.
G. K. Chesterton

13 *The Times* is speechless, and takes three columns to express its speechlessness.
Winston Churchill. Speech on Irish Home Rule, Dundee, 14 May 1908

14 The journalist is partly in the entertainment business and partly in the advertising business.
Claud Cockburn, IN TIME OF TROUBLE

15 Literature is the art of writing something that will be read twice and journalism what will be grasped at once.
Cyril Connolly, ENEMIES OF PROMISE 1938

16 Media is a word that has come to mean bad journalism.
Graham Greene, WAYS OF ESCAPE

17 He put words into my mouth which I had to look up in the dictionary.
Graham Greene of Anthony Burgess interviewing him in the Observer 28 *Nov* 1982

18 Good taste is, of course, an utterly dispensable part of any journalist's equipment.
Michael Hogg, Daily Telegraph 2 *Dec* 1978

19 My motto is publish and be sued.
Richard Ingrams, editor of Private Eye, BBC Radio 4, 4 *May* 1977

20 The secret of successful journalism is to make your readers so angry that they will write half your paper for you.
C. E. M. Joad. Quoted News Review 17 *Apr* 1947

21 An editor is a man who takes a French poodle, and clips him into the shape of a lion.
Emery Kelen, American cartoonist. *Quoted* News Review 27 *May* 1948

22 The best headlines never fi
Bernard Levin, The Times 5 Jul 1980

1 A good newspaper, I suppose, is a nation talking to itself.
Arthur Miller. Quoted Observer 26 *Nov* 1961

2 It is *hard* news that catches readers. Features hold them.
Lord Northcliffe. Quoted Tom Clarke, THE NORTHCLIFFE DIARY

3 I operate by a sense of smell. If something smells wrong, I go to work.
Drew Pearson. Quoted Oliver Pilat, DREW PEARSON

4 In America journalism is apt to be regarded as an extension of history, in Britain as an extension of conversation.
Anthony Sampson, ANATOMY OF BRITAIN 1962

5 Comment is free but facts are sacred.
Charles Prestwich Scott, Manchester Guardian 6 *May* 1921

6 [Journalists are] nameless men and women whose scandalously low payment is a guarantee of their ignorance and their servility to the financial department.
George Bernard Shaw, COMMONSENSE ABOUT THE WAR 1914

7 Newspapers are unable, seemingly, to discriminate between a bicycle accident and the collapse of civilisation.
George Bernard Shaw, TOO TRUE TO BE GOOD, *Preface*

8 An editor is one who separates the wheat from the chaff and prints the chaff.
Adlai Stevenson. Quoted Leon Harris, THE FINE ART OF POLITICAL WIT

9 A foreign correspondent is someone who . . . flies around from hotel to hotel and thinks the most interesting thing about any story is the fact that he has arrived to cover it.
Tom Stoppard, NIGHT AND DAY

10 *Punch* — the official journal of dentists' waiting rooms.
The Times 7 *Oct* 1981

11 Their prose was convulsive, they foamed at the headlines.
H. G. Wells, THE WAR IN THE AIR

12 Journalism — an ability to meet the challenge of filling the space.
Rebecca West, New York Herald Tribune 22 *Apr* 1956

JOY

13 Pleasure without joy is as hollow as passion without tenderness.
Alan Jay Lerner, THE STREET WHERE I LIVE 1978

JAMES JOYCE

14 Joyce, in effect, was saying that the depiction of life as it is really lived cannot be achieved in neat, periodic sentences and the puppetry of an author (like Thackeray) smugly in control.
Anthony Burgess, Observer magazine 20 *May* 1979

15 We cannot, I suppose, finally judge *Ulysses* as a work of fiction at all. It is a kind of magical codex of the same order as Dante's *Divine Comedy* (in which hell, heaven and purgatory go on for ever and nothing changes).
Id.

16 *Ulysses* is a dogged attempt to cover the universe with mud.
E. M. Forster, ASPECTS OF THE NOVEL 1927

17 My God, what a clumsy *alla patrida* James Joyce is! Nothing but old fags and cabbage stumps of quotations from the Bible and the rest, stewed in the juice of deliberate, journalistic dirty-mindedness.
D. H. Lawrence in a letter to Aldous Huxley 1928

18 There are passages in *Ulysses* which can be read only in the toilet — if one wants to extract the full flavour of their content.
Henry Miller, BLACK SPRING 1936

19 Joyce has freed us from the superstition of syntax.
Dorothy L. Sayers, CLOUD OF WITNESSES 1926

20 The latest acquisition to her library is *Ulysses*. "It cost me thirty-five shillings, and I got stuck on the first page. I think that's disgusting, don't you? No, not the content. I mean writing a book so that people can't understand it."
Russell Twisk. Quoting Cilla Black, Radio Times 25 *Jan* 1968

JUDGMENT

21 Don't let your opinion sway your judgment.
Sam Goldwyn. Quoted Sidney Skolsky

1 For when the One Great Scorer comes / To write against your name, / He marks — not that you won or lost — / But how you played the game.
Grantland Rice, ALUMNUS FOOTBALL

JUSTICE

2 Justice must not only be seen to be done. It must be seen to be believed.
Beachcomber (J. B. Morton)

3 The price of justice is eternal publicity.
Arnold Bennett, THINGS THAT HAVE INTERESTED ME

4 You can live without kindness; you can't live without justice.
Edward Bond, SUMMER *(play)*

5 Justice is being allowed to do whatever I like. Injustice is whatever prevents my doing it.
Samuel Butler, NOTEBOOKS 1912

6 Absolute freedom mocks at justice. Absolute justice denies freedom.
Albert Camus, THE REBEL 1951

7 Moderation in the pursuit of justice is no virtue.
Senator Barry Goldwater. Acceptance speech, Republican National Convention, San Francisco 16 Jul 1964

8 Justice should not only be done, but be manifestly and undoubtedly be seen to be done.
Lord Hewart, Justius, *Rex v. Sussex 9 Nov 1923*

9 Your justice would freeze beer.
Arthur Miller, THE CRUCIBLE 1953

10 Justice is so subtle a thing, to interpret it one has only need of a heart.
José Garcia Oliver. Quoted Hugh Thornes, THE SPANISH CIVIL WAR

11 I would rather be British than just.
Rev. Ian Paisley. Quoted Desmond Boal, Sunday Times 12 Dec 1971

K

EDWARD KENNEDY

1 Every country needs at least one King
Farouk.
Gore Vidal. Quoted John Heilpern,
Observer 26 *Apr* 1981

NIKITA KHRUSHCHEV

2 Khrushchev's greatest work, outweighing
all his idiocies and major howlers, was his
destruction of the Stalin legend and the
emptying of the labour camps, returning to
their homes millions of survivors and
formally rehabilitating millions who were
dead.
*Edward Crankshaw reviewing Roy Med-
vedev's* KHRUSHCHEV, Observer 9 *Jan* 1983

KINDNESS

3 When kindness has left people, even for a
few moments, we become afraid of them as
if their reason has left them.
Willa Cather, MY MORTAL ENEMY 1926

4 As the car drove in at the gate we struck a
bumpy patch, and I could hear the milk of
human kindness sloshing about inside him.
P. G. Wodehouse, PIGS HAVE WINGS 1947

KING

5 When in the green lanes I muse / Alone and
hear birds sing / Gods pity then, say I, / On
some Poor King.
W.H. Davies, POOR KINGS

6 Scratch a King and find a fool.
Dorothy Parker, SALOME'S DANCING LES-
SON

7 Kings are not born, they are made by mass
hallucination.
George Bernard Shaw, MAN AND SUPER-
MAN 1905

RUDYARD KIPLING

8 One of the greatest literary geniuses of the
Anglo-Saxon race, and when time has

winnowed away all the vulgarity, lack of
taste, jingoism and cocksure brassiness,
the residue will be read and enjoyed
without end.
Rupert Hart-Davis, THE LYTTELTON HART-
DAVIS LETTERS 13 *Nov* 1958

KISS

9 You have to kiss an awful lot of frogs before
you find a prince.
Graffito. Quoted BBC Radio 4, *Quote
Unquote* 7 *Jun* 1979

10 She gave me a sisterly kiss. Older sister.
Norman Mailer, THE DEER PARK 1955

11 Lips that taste of tears, they say / Are the
best for kissing.
Dorothy Parker, THRENODY

12 Blondes have the hottest kisses. Red-heads
are fair-to-middling torrid, and brunettes
are the frigidest of all. It's something to do
with the hormones, no doubt.
Ronald Reagan. Quoted News Review 20
May 1947

13 He gets his kiss, and it is a very large kiss
indeed, with the cut-out open.
Damon Runyon, MORE THAN SOMEWHAT
1937

14 There is always one who kisses and one
who only allows the kiss.
George Bernard Shaw, MAN AND SUPER-
MAN 1905

15 I kissed my first woman and smoked my
first cigarette on the same day. I have never
had time for tobacco since.
Arturo Toscanini. Quoted Evan Esar,
TREASURY OF HUMOROUS QUOTATIONS

LORD KITCHENER

16 He is rather like one of those revolving
lighthouses which radiate momentary
gleams of revealing light far out into the
surrounding gloom, and then relapse into
complete darkness.
David Lloyd George. Quoted John Grigg,
Sunday Times 4 *Sep* 1977

KNOWLEDGE

1 There is no absolute knowledge. Those who claim it . . . Open the door to tragedy. All information is imperfect. We have to treat it with humility.
Jacob Bronowski, THE ASCENT OF MAN 1973

2 Thorstein Veblen made a distinction between esoteric knowledge, which enjoys the greatest academic prestige but is without economic or industrial effect, and esoteric learning, which, in contrast, has negligible academic prestige, but is very useful.
J. K. Galbraith, A LIFE IN OUR TIMES 1981

3 All genuine knowledge originates in direct experience.
Mao Tse-Tung. Address, Tenan, Jul 1937

4 It is a great nuisance that knowledge can be acquired only by hard work.
W. Somerset Maugham, CAKES AND ALE 1930

5 Sin, guilt, neurosis — they are one and the same, the fruit of the tree of knowledge.
Henry Miller, THE WISDOM OF THE HEART, *Creative Death* 1941

6 You can know more and more about one thing but you can never know everything about one thing; it's hopeless.
Vladimir Nabokov, STRONG OPINIONS

7 I am sufficiently proud of my knowing something to be modest about my not knowing it at all.
Vladimir Nabokov, LOLITA 1955

8 Apart from the known and the unknown, what else is there?
Harold Pinter, THE HOMECOMING 1965

9 His had been an intellectual decision founded on his conviction that if a little knowledge was a dangerous thing, a lot was lethal.
Tom Sharpe, PORTERHOUSE BLUES

10 The right to know is like the right to live. It is fundamental and unconditional in its assumption that knowledge, like life, is a desirable thing.
George Bernard Shaw, DOCTOR'S DILEMMA, *Preface* 1906

11 Supreme knowledge of one subject presupposes as supreme an ignorance of others.
Alec Waugh, ON DOING WHAT ONE LIKES

L

LADY

1 I have defined ladies as people who did not do things for themselves.
Gwen Raverat, PERIOD PIECE

LANDLADY

2 The landlady can be reduced to her lowest terms by a series of propositions.
Stephen Leacock, LITERARY LAPSES 1910

LANGUAGE

3 The root function of language is to control the universe by describing it.
James Baldwin, NOTES OF A NATIVE SON 1955

4 A piece dear, a piece; a bit is what goes in a horse's mouth.
Sir Hugh Casson and Joyce Grenfell, NANNY SAYS 1972

5 Language is a uniquely human characteristic. Each person has programmed into his genes a faculty called universal grammar.
Noam Chomsky. Speech to the Royal Society

6 I got into my bones the essential structure of the ordinary British sentence — which is a noble thing.
Winston Churchill, MY EARLY LIFE 1935

7 A physician, at least in the United States, does not tell you that a patient is dying. He says that the prognosis as of this time is without significant areas of encouragement.
J. K. Galbraith, ECONOMICS, PEACE AND LAUGHTER 1971

8 Language always keeps pace with the social development of its users.
John Honey, THE LANGUAGE TRAP 1983

9 The language that can with the greatest ease make the finest and most numerous distinctions of meaning is the best.
C. S. Lewis. Quoted Sir Ernest Gower, MODERN ENGLISH USAGE *(revised)*

10 The sum of human wisdom is not contained in any one language, and no single language is *capable* of expressing all forms and degrees of human comprehension.
Ezra Pound, THE ABC OF READING 1934

11 Learn Greek, it is the language of wisdom.
George Bernard Shaw, THE ADVENTURES OF THE BLACK GIRL IN HER SEARCH FOR GOD

12 I am often told that I look like Winston Churchill and speak English like Charles Boyer. But I wish it were the other way round.
M. Paul-Henri Spaak

13 Perhaps of all the creations of man language is the most astonishing.
Lytton Strachey, WORDS AND POETRY

14 The limits of my language stand for the limits of my world.
Ludwig Wittgenstein. Quoted Harry Zohn, KARL KRAUS

LAUGHTER

15 Of all the countless people who have lived before our time on this planet, not one is known in history or legend as having died of laughter.
Max Beerbohm, LAUGHTER

16 Genuine laughter is the physical effect produced in the rational being by what suddenly strikes his immortal soul as being damned funny.
Hilaire Belloc, A CONVERSATION WITH AN ANGEL

17 He laughed like an irresponsible foetus.
T. S. Eliot, MR. APOLLINX 1917

18 His laughter tinkled among the teacups.
Id.

19 Laugh for the time is brief, a throw the length of a span / Laugh and be proud to belong to the old proud pageant of man.
John Masefield, LAUGH AND BE MERRY

20 The stimulus of a laugh is an intellectual event, yet it quickly goes on to block out all

else. There are only two other phenomena that so completely take over your awareness — the orgasm and the sneeze.
Dr. Howard Pollio. Quoted Observer 24 Dec 1978

1 We are in the world to laugh. In purgatory or hell we shall no longer be able to do so. And in heaven it would not be proper.
Jules Rénard, Journal, *Jun* 1907

2 She has a face the size of a town clock and a laugh so hearty it knocks the whipped cream off an order of strawberry shortcake on a table fifty feet away and arouses the indignation of a customer by the name of Goldstein who is about to consume same.
Damon Runyon, GUYS AND DOLLS 1935

3 The world loved man when he smiled. The world became afraid of him when he laughed.
Rabindranath Tagore, STRAY BIRDS 1916

4 She had a penetrating sort of laugh. Rather like a train going into a tunnel.
P. G. Wodehouse, THE INIMITABLE JEEVES 1924

5 Honoria is one of those robust, dynamic girls with the muscles of a welterweight and a laugh like a squadron of cavalry charging over a tin bridge. A beastly thing to have to face over the breakfast table.
P. G. Wodehouse, THE RUMMY AFFAIR OF OLD BIFFY

6 I haven't laughed so much since my husband died.
Woman complimenting Victor Borge

LAVATORY

7 Here I sit, alone and sixty / Bald and fat and full of sin / Cold the seat and loud the cistern / As I read the Harpic tin.
Alan Bennett

8 "Vot", asked George I courteously "is ze difference between a public nuisance and a public convenience?"
Caryl Brahms and S. J. Simon, NO NIGHTINGALES

9 Though the pipes that supply the bathroom burst / And the lavatory makes you fear the worst / It was used by Charles the First / Quite informally / And later by George the Fourth / On a journey North.
Noël Coward, THE STATELY HOMES OF ENGLAND

10 The water-closet like the harp is essentially a solo instrument.
Graffito. Quoted Robert Reisner, GRAFFITI

11 A place where even the King goes on foot — *enfin*, the toilet cabinet.
Aldous Huxley, TIME MUST HAVE A STOP 1946

12 A very pious man in Prague, a certain K, knew a great deal of the worldly sciences. He had studied them all in the toilet.
Franz Kafka, DIARIES 1914–1923

13 I boast of being the only man in London who has been bombed off a lavatory seat while reading Jane Austen. She went into the bath: I went through the door.
Kingsley Martin, New Statesman 1940

14 And Willy Nilly, rumbling, jockeys out again to the three-seated shack called the House of Commons in the back where the hens weep.
Dylan Thomas, UNDER MILK WOOD 1954

15 When the war broke out she took down the signed photograph of the Kaiser and, with some solemnity, hung it in the servant's lavatory.
Evelyn Waugh, VILE BODIES 1930

LAW

16 Law is merely the expression of the will of the strongest for the time being, and therefore laws have no fixity, but shift from generation to generation.
Henry Brooks Adams, THE LAW OF CIVILISATION AND DECAY 1955

17 Nobody has a more sacred obligation to obey the law than those who make the law.
Jean Anouilh ANTIGONE 1942

18 If a cow with handlebars is a bicycle within the meaning of the Act, then a bicycle with four legs instead of two wheels is a cow.
Beachcomber (J. B. Morton), Daily Express, *By the Way*

19 It is illegal to make liquor privately or water publicly.
Lord Birkett

20 A witness cannot give evidence of his age unless he remembers being born.
Judge Blagden. Quoted Observer 29 Jan 1950

21 The law is a causeway upon which, so long as he keeps to it, the citizen may walk safely.
Robert Bolt, A MAN FOR ALL SEASONS 1960

1 This case bristles with simplicity.
Mr. Justice Comyn, The Old Bailey 11 *Feb* 1980

2 The Law of England is a very strange one: it cannot compel anyone to tell the truth; but what it can do is to give you seven years for not telling the truth.
Lord Darling. Quoted in the biography of him by D. Walker-Smith

3 My husband keeps telling me to go to hell. Have I a legal right to take the children?
Letter to Dorothy Dix. Quoted Denys Parsons, FUNNY AMUSING FUNNY AMAZING

4 Nothing is more destructive of respect for the government and the law of the land than passing laws which cannot be enforced.
Albert Einstein, IDEAS AND OPINIONS

5 A man who applied for a job as gardener at Hampton Court was asked to sign Form E74 in case he gave away information about watering begonias.
Clement Freud, MP for Isle of Ely speaking in support of his bill for repeal of part of the Official Secrets Act, House of Commons 19 *Jan* 1979

6 Public opinion is always in advance of the law.
John Galsworthy, WINDOWS

7 There is no better way of exercising the imagination than the study of law. No poet ever interpreted nature as freely as a lawyer interprets truth.
Jean Giraudoux, TIGER AT THE GATES 1935

8 The language of the law must not be foreign to the ears of those who are to obey it.
Judge Learned Hand. Speech, Washington D.C. 11 *May* 1929

9 The meanest citizen, actuated by the meanest motives, is entitled to insist upon the enforcement of the law. The question is, "What is the law?" a question which frequently arises in our Courts and sometimes receives a satisfactory answer.
A. P. Herbert, MORE MISLEADING CASES

10 The Common Law of England has been laboriously built up about a mythical figure — the figure of 'the reasonable man'.
A. P. Herbert, UNCOMMON LAW 1935

11 I have come to regard the Law Courts not as a cathedral, but as a casino.
Richard Ingrams, The Guardian 30 *Jul* 1977

12 Whenever men take the law into their own hands, the loser is the law. And when law loses, freedom languishes.
Robert Kennedy. Quoted Barbara Rowe, A BOOK OF QUOTES

13 Morality cannot be legislated but behaviour can be regulated. Judicial decrees may not change the heart, but they can restrain the heartless.
Martin Luther King, STRENGTH TO LOVE 1963

14 People starting with the idea that certain things are right and are the law, come to believe that others are right because they are the law.
W. Somerset Maugham, A WRITER'S NOTEBOOK 1949

15 The law is nature. The law is only a word for what has a right to happen.
Arthur Miller, A VIEW FROM THE BRIDGE 1955

16 No brilliance is needed in law. Nothing but common sense and relatively clean finger nails.
John Mortimer, A VOYAGE ROUND MY FATHER

17 A judge is not supposed to know anything about the facts of life until they have been presented in evidence and explained to him at least three times.
Lord Chief Justice Parker, Observer 12 *Mar* 1961

18 Mr. Justice Ridley was known as Mr. Justice Necessity, since necessity knows no law.
Francis Pearson, MEMORIES OF A KC'S CLERK

19 The law must be stable, but it must not stand still.
Roscoe Pound, INTRODUCTION TO THE PHILOSOPHY OF LAW

20 A man's respect for law and order exists in precise relationship to the size of his pay cheque.
Adam Clayton Powell, KEEP THE FAITH BABY

21 No man is above the law and no man is below it; nor do we ask any man's permission when we require him to obey it.
Theodore Roosevelt. Speech, Jan 1905

22 Government can easily exist without law, but law cannot exist without government.
Bertrand Russell, UNPOPULAR ESSAYS 1950

1 It is a very salutary check for a judge to realise that if he does say something silly it is liable to get into the papers.
Mr. Justice Templeman, Observer 20 *Aug* 1978

2 Presumably any person on a bicycle who charges into an old lady is neither parking nor overtaking her but merely striking her and would not be guilty of an offence.
Robin Turton MP on the Countryside Bill

3 There is presumably nothing to prevent someone setting up as a freelance brain surgeon; though the police might well bring a charge of manslaughter if things went awry.
Alan Watkins, Observer 3 *Dec* 1978

ANDREW BONAR LAW

4 It is fitting that we should have buried the Unknown Prime Minister by the side of the Unknown Warrior.
H. H. Asquith after Bonar Law's funeral, Westminster Abbey 5 *Nov* 1923

D. H. LAWRENCE

5 [He is] one of the great denouncers, the great missionaries the English send to themselves to tell them they are crass, gross, lost, dead, mad and addicted to unnatural vices.
Kingsley Amis, WHAT BECAME OF JANE AUSTEN?

6 This pictorial account of the day-to-day life of an English gamekeeper is full of considerable interest to outdoor-minded readers ... Unfortunately one is obliged to wade through many pages of extraneous material ... in this reviewer's opinion, the book cannot take the place of J. R. Miller's *Practical Gamekeeping.*
Anon. Field and Stream, *review of* LADY CHATTERLEY'S LOVER

7 Lawrence seemed to me sometimes to suffer from a delusion similar to the delusion of the sick man who thinks that if a given quantity of medicine will do him good, twice the quantity will do him twice as good.
Arnold Bennett, Evening Standard 12 *Apr* 1930

8 *The Rainbow,* a novel by Mr. D. H. Lawrence, is more hideous than any imaginable reality. The thing is done so coldly, so pompously, so gravely that it is like a savage rite. There is not a gleam of humour in the fog of eloquent lubricity. The thud, thud, thud of hectic phrases is intolerably wearisome.
James Douglas, The Star, *reviewing* THE RAINBOW 22 *Oct* 1915

9 Interesting, but a type I could not get on with. Obsessed with self. Dead eyes and a red beard, long narrow face. A strange bird.
John Galsworthy, LIFE AND LETTERS (*ed. H. V. Marrot*) 1935

10 Is it [*Lady Chatterley's Lover*] a book you would leave lying around your own house? Is it a book that you would wish your wife or even your servant to read?
Mervyn Griffith-Jones, prosecuting in the obscenity case against Penguin Books 1961

11 For Lawrence, existence was one continuous convalescence; it was as though he were newly reborn from a mortal illness every day of his life.
Aldous Huxley, THE OLIVE TREE

12 You mustn't think I advocate perpetual sex. Far from it. Nothing nauseates me more than promiscuous sex in and out of season.
D. H. Lawrence, on LADY CHATTERLEY'S LOVER, *in a letter to Lady Ottoline Morrell* 22 *Dec* 1928

13 I sincerely believe in restoring the phallic consciousness into our lives because it is the source of all real beauty and all real gentleness. And those are the two things, tenderness and beauty which will save us from the horrors.
D. H. Lawrence, letter to Harriet Monroe 15 *Mar* 1928

14 *Lady Chatterley's Lover* is an extremely dull and portentously silly and pretentious book.
G. W. Lyttelton, THE LYTTELTON HART-DAVIS LETTERS 22 *Dec* 1955

15 Capable of an occasional joke in his letters, he is consistently without humour in his books, a failing rarely, if ever, to be found in novelists of the highest class, from Petronius to Proust.
Anthony Powell, THE STRANGERS ARE ALL GONE, VOL. 4, *The Memoirs*

16 No other writer in the twentieth century, except Freud, has been subject to so much abuse from so many otherwise intelligent people.
Philip Rieff, THE TRIUMPH OF THE THERAPEUTIC

1 *Lady Chatterley's Lover* is a book that all Christians might read with profit.
John Robinson (Bishop of Woolwich) speaking for the defence in the obscenity case against Penguin books 1961

2 His descriptive powers were remarkable, but his ideas cannot too soon be forgotten.
Bertrand Russell, AUTOBIOGRAPHY 1967

T. E. LAWRENCE

3 [He was] a bore, a bounder and a prig. He was intoxicated with his own youth and loathed any milieu which he couldn't dominate. Certainly he had none of a gentleman's instincts, strutting about Peace Conferences in Arab dress.
Henry Channon, DIARY 25 *May* 1935

4 There are those who have tried to dismiss his story with a flourish of the Union Jack, a psycho-analytical catchword or a sneer; it should move our deepest admiration and pity. Like Shelley and like Baudelaire, it may be said of him that he suffered, in his own person, the neurotic ills of an entire generation.
Christopher Isherwood, EXHUMATIONS

5 If he hides in a quarry he puts red flags all round.
George Bernard Shaw. Quoted The Guardian 22 *Jan* 1963

6 He had a genius for backing into the limelight.
Lowell Thomas, LAWRENCE OF ARABIA

7 They only got two things right, the camels and the sand.
Lowell Thomas of the film. Quoted The Times, *obituary* 29 *Aug* 1981

LAZINESS

8 He has his law degree and a furnished office. It's just a question now of getting him out of bed.
Cartoon caption by Peter Arno, The New Yorker 1938

9 He throws stones at the wind.
Cypriot saying. Quoted Bernard Newman, MEDITERRANEAN BACKGROUND

LEADER

10 People, like sheep, tend to follow a leader — occasionally in the right direction.
Alexander Chase, PERSPECTIVES 1960

11 To be a leader of men one must turn one's back on men.
Havelock Ellis

12 There is a kind of person who out of the very certainty of his purpose, right or wrong, both assumes leadership and is conceded leadership. No quality so assures public success.
J. K. Galbraith, THE AGE OF UNCERTAINTY 1977

13 All of the great leaders have had one characteristic in common; it was the willingness to confront unequivocally the major anxiety of their people in their time. This, and not much else, is the essence of leadership.
Id.

14 The leader of genius must have the ability to make different opponents appear as if they belonged to one category.
Adolf Hitler, MEIN KAMPF 1924

15 The art of leadership consists in consolidating the attention of the people against a single adversary and taking care that nothing will split that attention.
Id.

16 The English soldiers fight like lions . . . but they are lions led by donkeys.
Max Hoffman. Quoted A. Clark, THE DONKEYS

17 I must follow them, I am their leader.
Andrew Bonar Law. Quoted Ernest Raymond, MR. BALFOUR

18 It is not necessary to have original ideas to be quite a successful leader.
Lord Longford, DIARY OF A YEAR

19 Only one man in a thousand is a leader of men — the other 999 follow women.
Groucho Marx. Quoted News Review 10 *Jul* 1947

20 The most important quality in a leader is to be acknowledged as such. All leaders whose fitness is questioned are clearly lacking in force.
André Maurois, THE ART OF LIVING

21 The real leader has no need to lead — he is content to point the way.
Henry Miller, THE WISDOM OF THE HEART 1941

22 Leadership appears to be the art of getting others to want to do something you are convinced should be done.
Vance Packard, THE HIDDEN PERSUADERS

1 I never came to this through driving personal ambition. A combined opportunity and duty presented itself and I took it.
Margaret Thatcher on becoming leader of the Conservative Party, May 1975

2 No amount of learning will make a man a leader unless he has the natural qualities of one.
Gen. Archibald Wavell, The Times 17 *Feb* 1941

LEARNING

3 They know enough who know how to learn.
Henry Brooks Adams, THE EDUCATION OF HENRY ADAMS 1918

4 I learned just by going around. I know all about Kleenex factories, and all sorts of things.
Princess Anne. Quoted Noël St. George, ROYAL QUOTES

5 I am always ready to learn although I do not always like being taught.
Winston Churchill. Quoted Observer 9 *Nov* 1952

6 In the traditional method the child must say something that he has merely learned. There is all the difference in the world between having something to say, and having to say something.
John Dewey, DEWEY ON EDUCATION

7 It is a very grave mistake to think that the enjoyment of seeing and searching can be promoted by means of coercion and a sense of duty.
Albert Einstein. Quoted George B. Leonard, EDUCATION AND ECSTASY

8 It is the true nature of mankind to learn from mistakes, not from example.
Fred Hoyle, INTO DEEPEST SPACE

9 A learned man is an idler who kills time by study.
George Bernard Shaw, MAN AND SUPERMAN, *Maxims for Revolutionists* 1905

LEISURE

10 We are closer to the ants than to the butterflies. Very few people can endure much leisure.
Gerald Brenan, THOUGHTS IN A DRY SEASON 1979

11 What is this life if full of care / We have no time to stand and stare.
W. H. Davies, LEISURE

12 I am interested in leisure in the way that a poor man is interested in money. I can't get enough of it.
Philip, Duke of Edinburgh. Quoted Noël St. George, ROYAL QUOTES

13 To be able to fill leisure intelligently is the last product of civilisation.
Bertrand Russell, THE CONQUEST OF HAPPINESS 1930

14 Leisure is time at personal risk.
A. M. Sullivan, THE THREE DIMENSIONAL MAN

V. I. LENIN

15 The Germans turned upon Russia the most grisly of all weapons. They transported Lenin in a sealed truck like a plague bacillus from Switzerland into Russia.
Winston Churchill, THE WORLD CRISIS 1929

16 Their [the Russian people's] worst misfortune was his birth; their next worst — his death.
Id.

SINCLAIR LEWIS

17 He was a writer who drank, not, as so many have believed, a drunk who wrote.
James Lundquist, SINCLAIR LEWIS

18 He was one of the worst writers in modern American literature, but without his writing one cannot imagine modern American literature. That is because, without his writing, we can hardly imagine ourselves.
Mark Schorer, SINCLAIR LEWIS, AN AMERICAN LIFE 1961

LIBERALISM

19 If God had been a Liberal there wouldn't have been ten commandments, there would have been ten suggestions.
Malcolm Bradbury and Christopher Bigsby, AFTER DINNER GAME (*TV play*)

20 You Liberals think that goats are just sheep from broken homes.
Id.

21 The theory that one race can be superior to another, but that no race can ever be inferior to another.
Miles Kington, The Times, *A Guide to Real Meanings* 7 *Feb* 1983

22 Liberalism, in one variation or another, the egghead's credo, may be strategically

sound, but it is tactically fallacious, and as such highly misleading as well as highly distinctive. Indeed in my opinion it is *the* destructive force of the age.
Malcolm Muggeridge, TREAD SOFTLY FOR YOU TREAD ON MY JOKES 1966

LIBERTY

1 Freeing oppressed nationalities is perhaps the most dangerous of all philanthropic enterprises.
William Bolitho, TWELVE AGAINST THE GODS 1929

2 Liberty is the way, and the only way, of perfectability. Without liberty, heavy industry can be perfected, but no justice or truth.
Albert Camus, RESISTANCE, REBELLION AND DEATH 1961

3 Liberty is a different kind of pain from prison.
T. S. Eliot, THE FAMILY REUNION 1939

4 Extremism in the defence of liberty is not a vice.
Senator Barry Goldwater. Acceptance speech, Republican National Convention, San Francisco 16 *Jul* 1964

5 Liberty is so much latitude as the powerful choose to accord to the weak.
Judge Learned Hand. Speech, University of Pennsylvania Law School 21 *May* 1944

6 Political liberty's a swindle because a man doesn't spend his time being political. He spends it sleeping, eating, amusing himself a little and working — mostly working.
Aldous Huxley, ANTIC HAY 1923

7 "Liberty, Mr. Gumboil?" he said, "you don't suppose any serious minded person imagines a revolution is going to bring liberty, do you?"
Id.

8 A just society would be one in which liberty for one person is constrained only by the demands created by equal liberty for another.
Ivan Illich, TOOLS FOR CONVIVIALITY

9 The deadliest foe of democracy is not autocracy, but liberty frenzied. Liberty is not fool-proof. For its beneficent working it demands self-restraint.
Otto Kahn, Wisconsin University 14 *Jan* 1918

10 In a state worthy of the name there is no liberty. The people want to exercise power

but what on earth would they do with it if it were given to them?
V. I. Lenin, THE STATE AND REVOLUTION 1917

11 It is true that liberty is precious, so precious that it must be rationed.
Id.

12 There is always a danger that human beings will lose interest in liberty as soon as they have achieved it or — worse still perhaps — use their new-found liberty to destroy the liberty of others.
Robert Lynd, John o'London's Weekly 30 *Jun* 1939

13 What good is an excess of liberty if individuals are afraid to leave their homes or walk the streets.
Sir David McNee, Metropolitan Police Commissioner, Observer 27 *Aug* 1978

14 My government will protect all liberties but one — the liberty to do away with other liberties.
President Ordaz of Mexico, inaugural speech

15 Too little liberty brings stagnation, and too much brings chaos.
Bertrand Russell, AUTHORITY AND THE INDIVIDUAL

16 Liberty means responsibility. That is why most men dread it.
George Bernard Shaw, MAN AND SUPER-MAN, 1905

17 We have confused the free with the free and easy.
Adlai Stevenson, PUTTING FIRST THINGS FIRST

18 Liberty is the hardest test that one can inflict on a people. To know how to be free is not given equally to all men and all nations.
Paul Valéry, REFLECTIONS ON THE WORLD TODAY, *On the Subject of Dictatorship* 1931

19 Liberty does not consist in mere declarations of the rights of man. It consists in the translation of those declarations into definite action.
Woodrow Wilson. Speech 4 *Jul* 1914

LIBRARY

20 I've been drunk for about a week now and I thought it might sober me up to sit in library.
F. Scott Fitzgerald, THE GREAT GATSBY 1925

1 We welcome sleepers here. A sleeping reader is less of a menace to the books than a waking one.
Librarian at Cambridge University. Quoted, The Times

2 A library is thought in cold storage.
Lord Samuel

LIE

3 She tells enough white lies to ice a cake.
Margot Asquith, AUTOBIOGRAPHY 1936

4 Matilda told such Dreadful Lies / It made one Gasp and Stretch one's Eyes.
Hilaire Belloc, CAUTIONARY TALES 1907

5 For every time she shouted "Fire" / They only answered "Little Liar" / And therefore when her Aunt returned / Matilda, and the House, were Burned.
Id.

6 The moment a man talks to his fellows he begins to lie.
Hilaire Belloc, THE SILENCE OF THE SEA

7 Never to lie is to have no lock to your door.
Elizabeth Bowen, THE HOUSE IN PARIS 1935

8 The best liar is he who makes the smallest amount of lying go the longest way.
Samuel Butler, THE WAY OF ALL FLESH 1903

9 I do not mind lying, but I hate inaccuracy.
Samuel Butler, NOTEBOOKS 1912

10 A lie can be half way round the world before the truth gets its boots on.
James Callaghan. Speech 1 Nov 1976

11 It cannot in the opinion of His Majesty's Government be classified as slavery in the extreme acceptance of the word without some risk of terminological inexactitude.
Winston Churchill, House of Commons 22 Feb 1906

12 Without lies humanity would perish of despair and boredom.
Anatole France, THE BLOOM OF LIFE 1922

13 The great masses of the people will more easily fall victims to a great lie than a small one.
Adolf Hitler, MEIN KAMPF 1924

14 A lie goes by the Marconi route, while Truth goes by slow freight and is often ditched at the first water tank.
Elbert Hubbard, EPIGRAMS 1915

15 Nature cannot tell lies, but human beings can and do . . . our ability to tell lies is perhaps our most striking human characteristic.
Sir Edmund Leach. Address to the British Association, York 2 Sep 1981

16 She's too crafty a woman to invent a new lie when an old one will serve.
W. Somerset Maugham, THE CONSTANT WIFE 1926

17 I have never but once succeeded in making him [George Edward Moore] tell a lie and that was by a subterfuge. "More," I said, "Do you *always* tell the truth?" "No", he replied. I believe this to be the only lie he ever told.
Bertrand Russell, AUTOBIOGRAPHY 1967

18 Ellie: But how can you love a liar?
Mrs. Hushabye: I don't know. But you can, fortunately. Otherwise there wouldn't be much love in the world.
George Bernard Shaw, HEARTBREAK HOUSE 1920

19 We are all liars to people we don't care for.
George Bernard Shaw, LETTERS

20 The liar's punishment is not in the least that he is not believed, but that he cannot believe anyone else.
George Bernard Shaw

21 A lie is an abomination unto the Lord and a very present help in trouble.
Adlai Stevenson. Speech, Springfield, Jan 1951

22 He will lie even when it is inconvenient: the sign of the true artist.
Gore Vidal, TWO SISTERS 1970

23 Lies are the mortar that binds the savage individual man into the social masonry.
H. G. Wells, LOVE AND MR. LEWISHAM 1900

LIFE

24 Life is a child playing around your feet, a tool you hold firmly in your grip, a bench you sit down upon in the evening, in your garden.
Jean Anouilh, ANTIGONE 1942

25 If it were possible to talk to the unborn, one could never explain to them how it feels to be alive, for life is washed in the speechless real.
Jacques Barzun, THE HOUSE OF INTELLECT 1959

1 Life is rather like a tin of sardines — we are all looking for the key.
Alan Bennett, BEYOND THE FRINGE

2 Human beings are designed for paradise. How is it our lives are such hell?
Edward Bond, RESTORATION *(play)*

3 To live is like love, all reason is against it, and all healthy instinct for it.
Samuel Butler, NOTEBOOKS 1912

4 Life is a dusty corridor, I say, / Shut at both ends.
Roy Campbell, THE FLAMING TERRAPIN

5 What is life? It is the flash of a firefly in the night. It is a breath of a buffalo in the wintertime. It is as the little shadow that runs across the grass and loses itself in the sunset.
Truman Capote, IN COLD BLOOD 1965

6 Life was a funny thing that occurred on the way to the grave.
Quentin Crisp, THE NAKED CIVIL SERVANT

7 The man who regards his own life and that of his fellow creatures as meaningless is not merely unfortunate but almost disqualified for life.
Albert Einstein, THE WORLD AS I SEE IT 1934

8 I have measured out my life with coffee spoons.
T. S. Eliot, THE LOVE SONG OF J. ALFRED PRUFROCK 1917

9 The most important lesson is to understand life, not to make *a priori* judgement about it.
David Garnett, GREAT FRIENDS

10 Life is made up of sobs, sniffles and smiles, with sniffles predominating.
O. Henry, THE GIFTS OF THE MAGI 1906

11 It is becoming increasingly likely that what distinguishes the matter of living bodies is the presence not of a 'vital force' but of the quite commonplace element, carbon. If this is so, Life exists in the Universe only because the carbon atom possesses certain exceptional properties.
Sir James Jeans, THE MYSTERIOUS UNIVERSE 1930

12 Welcome O Life! I go to encounter for the millionth time the reality of experience and to forge in the smithy of my soul the uncreated conscience of my race.
James Joyce, A PORTRAIT OF THE ARTIST AS A YOUNG MAN *(final words)* 1916

13 Life is something to do when you can't get to sleep.
Fran Lebowitz. Quoted John Heilpern, Observer 21 *Jan* 1979

14 Life is like a sewer. What you get out of it depends on what you put into it.
Tom Lehrer, WE WILL ALL GO TOGETHER WHEN WE GO

15 The four stages of man are infancy, childhood, adolescence and obsolescence.
Art Linklater, A CHILD'S GARDEN OF MISINFORMATION 1965

16 A man's life is made up of a few intense moments, and the time spent in between is just packing and doesn't count.
F. W. Lister, THE WIND THAT BLOWS

17 Life to me is like boarding-house wallpaper. It takes a long time to get used to it, but when you finally do, you never notice that it's there. And then you hear the decorators are arriving.
Derek Marlowe, A DANDY IN ASPIC 1966

18 Life's a long headache in a noisy street.
John Masefield, THE WIDOW IN THE BYE STREET 1912

19 For the complete life, the perfect pattern includes old age as well as youth and maturity.
W. Somerset Maugham, THE SUMMING UP 1938

20 Life is perhaps best regarded as a bad dream between two awakenings.
Eugene O'Neill, MARCO MILLIONS 1928

21 The length of life is generally in inverse proportion to the rate of living — the more rapid the pace the shorter the time that life endures.
Raymond Pearl. Quoted George W. Gray, Harper's magazine, *Feb* 1941

22 Real life is, to most men, a long second-best, a perpetual compromise between the ideal and the possible.
Bertrand Russell, STUDY OF MATHEMATICS

23 When we have found how the nucleus of atoms are built-up we shall have found the greatest secret of all — except life. We shall have found the basis of everything — of the earth we walk on, of the air we breathe, of the sunshine, of our physical body itself, of everything in the world, however great or however small — except life.
Lord Rutherford. Quoted Passing Show 24 *Sep* 1932

1 There is no cure for birth and death save to enjoy the interval.
George Santayana, SOLILOQUIES IN ENGLAND, *War Shrines* 1922

2 Life is not a spectacle or a feast; it is a predicament.
George Santayana, ARTICLES AND ESSAYS

3 Life is a game at which everybody loses.
Leo Sarkadi-Schuller, WITHIN FOUR WALLS

4 Life is a flame that is always burning itself out; but it catches fire again every time a child is born.
George Bernard Shaw, THE ADVENTURES OF THE BLACK GIRL IN HER SEARCH FOR GOD

5 Life is a disease, and the only difference between one man and another is the stage of the disease at which he lives.
George Bernard Shaw, BACK TO METHUSELAH 1922

6 Don't try to live for ever. You will not succeed.
George Bernard Shaw, THE DOCTOR'S DILEMMA, *Preface* 1906

7 Tisn't life that matters! 'Tis the courage you bring to it.
Hugh Walpole, FORTITUDE 1913 (opening sentence)

8 Life is an unanswered question, but let's still believe in the dignity and importance of the question.
Tennessee Williams, CAMINO REAL 1953

9 Most people's lives — what are they but trails of debris, long long trails of debris with nothing to clean it all up but, finally, death.
Tennessee Williams, SUDDENLY, LAST SUMMER 1958

10 If you come to think of it, what a queer thing life is! So unlike anything else, don't you know, if you know what I mean.
P. G. Wodehouse, MY MAN JEEVES 1919

LIGHT

11 The pale, cold light of the winter sunset did not beautify — it was like the light of truth itself.
Willa Cather, MY ANTONIA 1918

LIMITATION

12 Art is limitation; the essence of every picture is the frame!
G. K. Chesterton, ORTHODOXY 1908

LITERACY

13 The ratio of literacy to illiteracy is constant, but nowadays the illiterates can read and write.
Alberto Moravia. Quoted Mary McCarthy, Observer, *A World Out of Joint* 14 Oct 1979

14 Education has produced a vast population able to read but unable to distinguish what is worth reading.
G. M. Trevelyan, ENGLISH SOCIAL HISTORY 1944

LITERATURE

15 Some books are undeservedly forgotten; none are undeservedly remembered.
W. H. Auden, THE DYER'S HAND, *Reading* 1962

16 Of all fatiguing, futile, empty trades, the worst, I suppose, is writing about writing.
Hilaire Belloc, THE SILENCE OF THE SEA

17 Literature is not a parlour game. But neither is it the preserve of a small élite.
John Braine, J. B. PRIESTLEY

18 I've always had enough sense not to try and bite off more than I can chew; in literature no As for effort are awarded.
John Braine, THE QUEEN OF A DISTANT COUNTRY

19 Literature has a way of putting life in a strait-jacket.
Arthur Calder-Marshall, THE TWO DUCHESSES

20 The primary object of a student of literature is to be delighted. His duty is to enjoy himself, his efforts should be directed to developing his faculty of appreciation.
David Cecil, THE FINE ART OF READING 1957

21 He set out seriously to describe the indescribable. That is the whole business of literature and it is a hard row to hoe.
G. K. Chesterton, ALL I SURVEY 1933

22 Literature would be altogether too tense if it were written solely by immortal authors. We must take writers as they are, and not expect them all to last.
Oliver Edwards, The Times 25 Apr 1965

23 Only two classes of books are of universal appeal. The very best and the very worst.
Ford Maddox Ford, JOSEPH CONRAD

1 It is with noble sentiments that bad literature gets written.
André Gide, JOURNAL 2 *Sep* 1940

2 He knew everything about literature except how to enjoy it.
Joseph Heller, CATCH 22 1961

3 That was the chief difference between literature and life. In books, the proportion of exceptional to commonplace people is high; in reality, very low.
Aldous Huxley, EYELESS IN GAZA 1936

4 The fact that many people should be shocked by what he writes practically imposes a duty upon the writer to go on writing.
Aldous Huxley, MUSIC AT NIGHT, *Vulgarity in Literature* 1931

5 There are two literary maladies — writer's cramp and swelled head. The worst of writer's cramp is that it is never cured; the worst of swelled head is that it never kills.
Coulson Kernahan, lecture

6 Our American professors like their literature clear and cold and pure and very dead.
Sinclair Lewis, on receiving the Nobel prize 12 *Dec* 1930

7 Literature is mostly about having sex and not much about having children; life is the other way round.
David Lodge, THE BRITISH MUSEUM IS FALLING DOWN

8 I'm happy the great ones are thriving / But what puzzles my head / Is the thought that they needed reviving / I had never been told they were dead.
Phyllis McGinley, THE PREVALENCE OF LITERARY REVIVAL

9 We have long passed the Victorian Era when asterisks were followed after a certain interval by a baby.
W. Somerset Maugham, THE CONSTANT WIFE 1926

10 Good prose should resemble the conversation of a well-bred man.
W. Somerset Maugham, THE SUMMING UP 1938

11 England produced Shakespeare: the British Empire the six-shilling novel.
George Moore, HAIL AND FAREWELL 1911

12 Books give the kind of comfort one feels when one realises that for all its blunders and boners the inner texture of life is also a matter of inspiration and precision.
Vladimir Nabokov, LECTURES ON LITERATURE

13 Literature is not about something: it is the thing itself, the quiddity.
Id.

14 There is no test of literary merit except survival, which is itself, an index to majority opinion.
George Orwell, SELECTED ESSAYS 1968

15 Great literature is simply language charged with meaning to the utmost possible degree.
Ezra Pound, HOW TO READ 1931

16 Literature is news that *stays* news.
Ezra Pound, ABC OF READING 1931

17 The illusion of art is to make one believe that great literature is very close to life, but exactly the opposite is true. Life is amorphous, literature is formal.
Françoise Sagan, WRITERS AT WORK 1958

18 To turn events into ideas is the function of literature.
George Santayana, LITTLE ESSAYS

19 His [Ronald Firbank's] most rational response to my attempts at drawing him out about literature and art was "I adore italics, don't you?"
Siegfried Sassoon, SIEGFRIED'S JOURNEY 1945

20 For me, Literature with a capital L is rubbish.
Georges Simenon. Quoted Fenton Bresler, THE MYSTERY OF GEORGES SIMENON 1983

21 Few understand the work of cummings / And few James Joyce's mental slummings / And few young Ander's coded chatter / But then it is the few that matter.
Dylan Thomas, letter to Pamela Hansford Johnson

22 No writer before the middle of the 19th century wrote about the working classes other than as grotesques or as pastoral decoration. Then when they were given the vote certain writers began to suck up to them.
Evelyn Waugh, PARIS REVIEW 1963

23 Literature must be an analysis of experience and a synthesis of the finding into a unity.
Rebecca West, ENDING IN EARNEST

1 A man who publishes his letters becomes a nudist — nothing shields him from the world's gaze except his bare skin. A writer, writing away, can always fix himself up to make himself more presentable, but a man who has written a letter is stuck with it for all time.
E. B. White, letter to Corona Macheiner 11 *Jun* 1975

2 Literature is the orchestration of platitudes.
Thornton Wilder, Time Magazine 12 *Jan* 1953

3 A good essay must have this permanent quality about it: it must draw its curtain round us, but it must be a curtain that shuts us in, not out.
Virginia Woolf, THE COMMON READER 1925

4 The poet gives us his essence, but prose takes the mould of the mind and body entire.
Virginia Woolf, THE CAPTAIN'S DEATH BED

LIVERPOOL

5 This god-forsaken city, with a climate so evil that no self-respecting singer would ever set foot in it! It is a catarrhal place that has been the cause through the centuries of the nasal Liverpool accent.
Sir Thomas Beecham. Quoted Harold Atkins and Archie Newman, BEECHAM STORIES

6 Standing on the bridge, staring down at the dirty, rubbish-clogged river, he cried out: "The quality of Mersey is not strained".
Jilly Cooper, THE BRITISH IN LOVE

LIVING

7 If you wish to live, you must first attend your own funeral.
Katherine Mansfield. Quoted Antony Alpers, KATHERINE MANSFIELD 1954

DAVID LLOYD GEORGE

8 Lloyd George could not see a belt without hitting below it.
Margot Asquith, AUTOBIOGRAPHY 1936

9 He [Lloyd George] spent his whole life in plastering together the true and the false and therefrom extracting the plausible.
Stanley Baldwin. Quoted Leon Harris, THE FINE ART OF POLITICAL WIT

10 He did not care in which direction the car was travelling, so long as he remained in the driver's seat.
Lord Beaverbrook, New Statesman 14 *Jun* 1963

11 Mr. Lloyd George spoke for a hundred and seventeen minutes, in which period he was detected only once in the use of an argument.
Arnold Bennett, THINGS THAT HAVE INTERESTED MEN

12 The vehement, contriving, resourceful, nimble-leaping, Lloyd George.
Winston Churchill, GREAT CONTEMPORARIES 1937

13 The Happy Warrior of Squandermania.
Winston Churchill

14 This syren, this goat-footed bard, this half-human visitor to our age from the hag-ridden magic and enchanted woods of Celtic antiquity.
J. M. Keynes. Quoted R. F. Harrod, LIFE OF J. M. KEYNES

15 The rogue elephant among British prime ministers.
Kenneth Morgan, LIFE OF D. LLOYD GEORGE

16 He is without malice of any kind; without prejudices, without morals. He has many enemies and no friends. He does not understand what friendship means . . . and yet he is the best man we have got.
F. S. Oliver, THE ANVIL OF WAR

17 Of the three parties I find them [Labour] the least painful. My objection to the Tories is temperamental and my objection to the Liberals is Lloyd George.
Bertrand Russell in a letter to Maurice Amos MP 16 Jun 1930

18 A master of improvised speech and improvised policies.
A. J. P. Taylor, ENGLISH HISTORY 1914–1945

LOGIC

19 Logic, *n.* The art of thinking and reasoning in strict accordance with the limitations and incapacities of the human understanding.
Ambrose Bierce, THE DEVIL'S DICTIONARY 1906

20 Logic is like the sword — those who appeal to it shall perish by it.
Samuel Butler, NOTEBOOKS 1912

1 The want of logic annoys. Too much logic bores. Life eludes logic, and everything that logic alone constructs remains artificial and forced.
André Gide, JOURNALS 12 *May* 1927

2 Logic is one thing, the human animal another. You can quite easily propose a logical solution to something and at the same time hope in your heart of hearts that it won't work out.
Luigi Pirandello, THE PLEASURE OF HONESTY 1917

3 Pure logic is the ruin of the spirit.
Antoine de Saint-Exupéry, FLIGHT TO ARRAS 1942

4 A mind all logic is like a knife all blade. It makes the hand bleed that uses it.
Rabindranath Tagore, STRAY BIRDS 1916

5 It is no good saying "I don't happen to be logical". Logic is simply the architecture of human reason. If you try to base your life and hopes on logical absurdities *you will go mad.*
Evelyn Waugh, letter to John Betjeman 22 *Dec* 1946

LONDON

6 London is a splendid place to live in for those who can get out of it.
Lord Balfour of Burleigh

7 I don't know what London's coming to — the higher the buildings the lower the morals.
Noël Coward, LAW AND ORDER

8 If I could choose the place where I die it would be London because then the transition from life to death would hardly be noticeable.
Graffito on a wall in Hammersmith. Quoted Nigel Rees, GRAFFITI RULES O.K. 1979

9 Buckingham Palace, the Queen's delightful home in the London suburb of Westminster.
Barry Humphries, DAME EDNA'S COFFEE TABLE BOOK

10 I thought of London spread out in the sun / Its postal districts packed like squares of wheat.
Philip Larkin, THE WHITSUN WEDDINGS

11 London seems to me like some hoary, massive underworld, a hoary ponderous inferno. The traffic flows the rigid grey streets like the rivers of hell through their banks of dry, rocky ash.
D. H. Lawrence, SELECTED LETTERS 1962

12 And London Town, of all the towns I'm glad to leave behind.
John Masefield, LONDON TOWN

13 London is chaos incorporated.
George Mikes, DOWN WITH EVERYBODY

14 London is a town of nice surprises and at any moment you may run into the Queen doing some shopping, or see a swan flying over.
Nursery World. Quoted Michael Bateman, THIS ENGLAND

LONELINESS

15 The work of a Prime Minister is the loneliest job in the world.
Stanley Baldwin. Speech 9 *Jan* 1927

16 I am feeling very lonely. I've been married for fifteen years, and yesterday my wife ran off with the chap next door. I'm going to miss him terribly.
Les Dawson, BBC TV, *Those Were the Days* 24 *Apr* 1979

17 One aged man — one man — can't fill a house.
Robert Frost, AN OLD MAN'S WINTER NIGHT

18 Pray that your loneliness may spur you into finding something to live for, great enough to die for.
Dag Hammarskjöld, DIARIES

19 Lonely people talking to each other can make each other lonelier.
William Hellman, THE AUTUMN GARDEN *(play)* 1951

20 People speak of the sadness of being in a crowd and knowing no one. There is something pleasurable in it too.
Sir Arthur Helps, COMPANIONS OF MY SOLITUDE

21 All the lonely people where do they all come from? / All the lonely people where do they all belong?
John Lennon and Paul McCartney, ELEANOR RIGBY *(song)*

22 We are born helpless. As soon as we are fully conscious we discover loneliness.
C. S. Lewis, THE FOUR LOVES

23 Don't think you can frighten me by telling me I am alone. France is alone; and God is

alone; and what is my loneliness before the loneliness of my country and my God.
George Bernard Shaw, ST. JOAN 1923

1 Loneliness can be conquered only by those who can bear solitude.
Paul Tillich, THE ETERNAL NOW 1963

LONGEVITY

2 Longevity is the revenge of talent upon genius.
Cyril Connolly, Sunday Times 19 *Jun* 1966

ANITA LOOS

3 You are the first American to make sex funny.
Said to her by a friend, on reading
GENTLEMEN PREFER BLONDES

LOVE

4 If I ever really love it will be like Mary Queen of Scots, who said of her Bothwell that she could follow him round the world in her nightie.
J. M. Barrie, WHAT EVERY WOMAN KNOWS *(play)* 1908

5 To fall in love is to create a religion that has a fallible God.
Jorge Luis Borges, OTHER INQUISITIONS 1952

6 It is proverbial that from a hungry tiger and an affectionate woman there is no escape.
Ernest Bramah, KAI LUNG UNROLLS HIS MAT 1928

7 Love is also like a coconut which is good while it is fresh, but you have to spit it out when the juice is gone, what's left tastes bitter.
Bertolt Brecht, BAAL 1926

8 Falling in love is one of the activities forbidden that tiresome person, the consistently reasonable man.
Sir Arthur Eddington, News Chronicle 2 *Mar* 1932

9 Love is the great enemy of Christian morality.
Max Ernst. Quoted John Russell, MAX ERNST, HIS LIFE AND WORK

10 Love is a great force in private life; it is indeed the greatest of all things; but love in public affairs does not work . . . We can only love what we know personally.
E. M. Forster, TWO CHEERS FOR DEMOCRACY, *Tolerance* 1951

11 When one loves somebody everything is clear — where to go, what to do — it all takes care of itself and one doesn't have to ask anybody about anything.
Maxim Gorky, THE ZYKOVS 1914

12 I know nothing about platonic love except that it is not to be found in the works of Plato.
Edgar Jepson. Quoted James Agate, EGO 5, 24 *Aug* 1940

13 The hardships of living together. Forced upon us by strangeness, pity, lust, cowardice, vanity and only deep down, perhaps, a thin little stream worthy of the name of love, impossible to seek out, flashing once in the moment of a moment.
Franz Kafka, DIARIES 1914–23

14 Many a man in love with a dimple makes the mistake of marrying the whole girl.
Stephen Leacock, LITERARY LAPSES 1910

15 So we must say Goodbye, my darling, / and go, as lovers go, for ever; / Tonight remains, to pack and fix on labels / And make an end of lying down together.
Alun Lewis, GOODBYE

16 The only place outside Heaven where you can be safe from all the dangers and perturbations of love is Hell.
C. S. Lewis, THE FOUR LOVES

17 I loved Kirk so much I would have skied down Mount Everest in the nude with a carnation up my nose.
Joyce McKinney, Mormon missionary trial 11 *Dec* 1977

18 Love is simple to understand if you haven't got a mind soft and full of holes. It's a crutch, that's all, and there isn't any one of us that doesn't need a crutch.
Norman Mailer, BARBARY SHORE 1951

19 Love is like quicksilver in the hand. Leave the fingers open and it stays. Clutch it, and it darts away.
Dorothy Parker

20 Here's my strength and weakness gents, / I loved them until they loved me.
Dorothy Parker, BALLADE AT THIRTY FIVE

21 Every love is the love before / In a duller dress.
Dorothy Parker, DEATH AND TAXES 1931

1 Scratch a lover and find a fool.
Dorothy Parker, ENOUGH ROPE 1927

2 By the time you say you're his, / Shivering and sighing / And he vows his passion is / Infinite, undying — / Lady, make a note of this / One of you is lying.
Dorothy Parker, NOT SO DEEP AS A WELL 1936

3 Whose love is given over-well / Shall look on Helen's face in hell / Whilst those whose love is thin and wise / May view John Knox in paradise.
Dorothy Parker, PARTIAL COMFORT

4 Do young men these days still become hopelessly enamoured of married women easily ten years their senior who have mocking, humorous mouths, eyes filled with tender raillery, and indulgent husbands?
S. J. Perelman, KEEP IT CRISP

5 Love is always in the mood of believing in miracles.
John Cowper Powys, THE MEANING OF CULTURE

6 There can be no peace of mind in love since the advantage one has secured is never anything but a fresh starting-point for further desires.
Marcel Proust, REMEMBRANCE OF THINGS PAST 1913–1927

7 A lot of different guys are considered very sensible until they get tangled up with a doll, and maybe loving her, and the first thing anybody knows they hop out of windows, or shoot themselves, or shoot somebody else, and I can see where even a guy like Dave the Dude may go daffy over a doll.
Damon Runyon, MORE THAN SOMEWHAT 1937

8 Of all forms of caution, caution in love is perhaps the most fatal to true happiness.
Bertrand Russell, AUTOBIOGRAPHY 1967

9 To fear love is to fear life, and those who fear life are already three parts dead.
Bertrand Russell, MARRIAGE AND MORALS 1929

10 Loving you is like loving a red hot poker which is a worse bedfellow than even Lytton's Umbrella; every caress brings on agony.
Bertrand Russell, letter to Ottoline Morrell, Jun 1912

11 I did not know I loved you till I heard myself telling you so — for one instant I thought "Good God, what have I said?" and then I knew it was the truth.
Id. *Mar* 1911

12 When we love animals and children too much we love them at the expense of men.
Jean-Paul Sartre, THE WORDS 1964

13 First love is only a little foolishness and a lot of curiosity; no really self-respecting woman would take advantage of it.
George Bernard Shaw, JOHN BULL'S OTHER ISLAND 1904

14 The fickleness of the women I love is only equalled by the infernal constancy of the women who love me.
George Bernard Shaw

15 Love is the only weapon we need.
Rev. H. R. L. Sheppard, THE HUMAN PARSON

16 It is never too late to fall in love.
Sandy Wilson, THE BOY FRIEND

17 "Ah, love, love" he said. "Is there anything like it? Were you ever in love, Beach?"
"Yes, sir, on one occasion, when I was a young under-footman. But it blew over."
P. G. Wodehouse, PIGS HAVE WINGS 1952

18 It is love that I am seeking for / But of a beautiful unheard of kind / That is not in the world.
W. B. Yeats, THE SHADOWY WATERS

LOYALTY

19 He is more loyal to his friends than to his convictions.
Margot Asquith of Austen Chamberlain, AUTOBIOGRAPHY 1936

LUCK

20 I'm told it brings luck whether one believes in it or not.
Niels Bohr on surprise being expressed at his believing in the luck of rabbits' feet. A rabbit's foot was pinned on his laboratory door

21 Some day my boat will come in, and with my luck I'll be at the airport.
Graffito. Quoted Nigel Rees, GRAFFITI 2 1980

1 I am a great believer in luck, and I find the harder I work the more I have of it.
Stephen Leacock, LITERARY LAPSES 1910

LUST

2 Oh whip the dogs away my Lord / That make me ill with lust.
John Betjeman, SENEX

LUXURY

3 The saddest thing I can imagine is to get used to luxury.
Charlie Chaplin, MY AUTOBIOGRAPHY 1964

4 Every luxury was lavished on you — atheism, breast feeding, circumcision.
Joe Orton, LOOT *(play)*

M

RAMSAY MACDONALD

1 He is the greatest living master of falling without hurting himself.
Winston Churchill, House of Commons 21 *Jan* 1921

2 He, more than any other man, has the gift of compressing the largest amount of words into the smallest amount of thought.
Id. 23 *Mar* 1933

3 He dramatizes his position, as always . . . always there is something histrionic and therefore fraudulent about him. I respect and admire him in many ways. But I do see why many people regard him as a complete humbug.
Harold Nicolson, DIARIES 28 *Apr* 1935

4 We travelled up in the train with Ramsay MacDonald, who spent the time telling long stories of pawky Scots humour so dull that it was almost impossible to tell when the point had been reached.
Bertrand Russell, AUTOBIOGRAPHY 1967

5 There are no professions he ever made, no pledges he ever gave to the country, and no humiliation to which he would not submit if they would only allow him still to be called Prime Minister.
Viscount Snowden, House of Lords 3 *Jul* 1934

6 MacDonald owes his pre-eminence largely to the fact that he is the only artist, the only aristocrat by temperament and talent in a party of plebeians and plain men.
Beatrice Webb, DIARY, *May* 1950

MACHINE

7 One cannot walk through a mass production factory and not feel one is in Hell.
W. H. Auden. Quoted Barbara Rowe, A BOOK OF QUOTES

8 When a machine begins to run without human aid it is time to scrap it — whether it be a factory or a government.
Alexander Chase, PERSPECTIVES

9 Machines from the Maxim gun to the computer, are for the most part means by which a minority can keep free men in subjection.
Kenneth, Lord Clark, CIVILISATION 1969

10 Machinery is the sub-conscious mind of the world.
Gerald Stanley Lee, CROWDS

11 You cannot endow even the best machine with initiative. The jolliest steam-roller will not plant flowers.
Walter Lippmann, A PREFACE TO POLITICS 1914

12 It is critical vision alone which can mitigate the unimpeded operation of the automatic.
Marshall McLuhan, THE MECHANICAL BRIDE 1951

13 By his very success in inventing labour-saving devices modern man has manufactured an abyss of boredom that only the privileged classes in earlier civilisations have ever fathomed.
Lewis Mumford, THE CONDUCT OF LIFE 1951

14 Machines are worshipped because they are beautiful and valued because they confer power; they are hated because they are hideous and loathed because they impose slavery.
Bertrand Russell, SCEPTICAL ESSAYS 1928

15 The machine does not isolate man from the great problems of nature but plunges him more deeply into them.
Antoine de Saint-Exupéry, WIND, SAND AND STARS 1939

16 The real problem is not whether machines think, but whether men do.
B. F. Skinner, CONTINGENCIES OF REINFORCEMENT

17 If automation keeps up, man will atrophy all his limbs but the push button finger.
Frank Lloyd Wright, New York Times 27 *Nov* 1955

HAROLD MACMILLAN

1 By far the most radical man I've known in politics wasn't on the labour side at all — Harold Macmillan. If it hadn't been for the war he'd have joined the Labour Party. If that had happened Macmillan would have been Labour Prime Minister, and not me.
Clement Attlee. Quoted James Margach, THE ABUSE OF POWER 1981

2 One can never escape the suspicion with Mr. Macmillan that all his life was a preparation for elder statesmanship.
Frank Johnson, The Times 30 Apr 1981

3 The eyes were *hooded*, they seemed to hover always on the verge of a *wink* at his fantastic good fortune in being set down in the country of the blind, where none could see through him.
Bernard Levin, THE PENDULUM YEARS 1976

4 It was almost impossible to believe that he was anything but a down-at-heel actor resting between engagements at the decrepit theatres of minor provincial towns.
Id.

5 I am MacWonder one moment and Mac-Blunder the next.
Of himself. Quoted Colin R. Coote, Daily Telegraph 15 *Nov* 1973

6 Harold Macmillan always struck me as a parody of a Conservative politician in a novel by Trollope.
Malcolm Muggeridge, CHRONICLES OF WASTED TIME, *The Infernal Grove* 1972

7 Macmillan's role as a poseur was itself a pose.
Harold Wilson, A PRIME MINISTER ON PRIME MINISTERS 1977

MADNESS

8 We are all born mad, and some remain so.
Samuel Beckett, WAITING FOR GODOT 1952

9 Madness alone is entirely free from the commonplace. However terrible or twisted or invalid the visions of sick brains, each is individual and new.
William Bolitho, CAMERA OBSCURA

10 What is madness / To those who only observe, is often wisdom / To those to whom it happens.
Christopher Fry, A PHOENIX TOO FREQUENT 1949

11 Should those about us think us mad it would be difficult to keep faith in one's own sanity.
J. F. Spalding, GLIMPSES OF TRUTH

MAJORITY

12 The one pervading evil of democracy is the tyranny of the majority.
Lord Acton, THE HISTORY OF FREEDOM

13 If it has to choose who is to be crucified the crowd will always save Barabbas.
Jean Cocteau, LE RAPPEL À L'ORDRE 1926

14 One with the law is a majority.
Calvin Coolidge. Speech 27 Jul 1920

15 When great changes occur in history, when great principles are involved, as a rule the majority are wrong.
Eugene V. Debs. Speech 12 Aug 1918

16 The great silent majority.
Richard Nixon. Speech 3 Nov 1969

MALICE

17 I have never killed a man, but I have read many obituaries with a lot of pleasure.
Clarence Darrow, MEDLEY

MAN

18 Men are beasts and even beasts don't behave as they do.
Brigitte Bardot. Quoted Barbara Rowe, A BOOK OF QUOTES

19 Man is an intelligence in servitude to his organs.
Aldous Huxley, THEME AND VARIATIONS 1950

20 Women want mediocre men, and men are working hard to be as mediocre as possible.
Margaret Mead

21 There was, I think, never any reason to believe in any innate superiority of the male, except his superior muscle.
Bertrand Russell, UNPOPULAR ESSAYS 1950

22 A man in the house is worth two in the street.
Mae West, line spoken in film BELLE OF THE NINETIES

MANKIND

1 Mankind is not a tribe of animals to which we owe compassion. Mankind is a club to which we owe our subscription.
G. K. Chesterton, Daily News 10 *Apr* 1906

2 What is man, when you come to think upon him, but a minutely set, ingenious machine for turning, with infinite artfulness, the red wine of Shiraz into urine.
Isak Dinesen, SEVEN GOTHIC TALES, *The Dreamers* 1934

3 Man would be otherwise. That is the essence of the specifically human.
Antonio Machado, JUAN DE MATRENA 1943

4 Man is the measure of all things, and his welfare is the sole and single criterion of truth.
Thomas Mann, THE MAGIC MOUNTAIN 1924

5 Man, unlike any other thing organic or inorganic in the universe, grows beyond his work, walks up the stairs of his concepts, emerges ahead of his accomplishments.
John Steinbeck, THE GRAPES OF WRATH 1939

6 If this is God's world there are no unimportant people.
Rt. Hon. George Thomas, former Speaker of the House of Commons, to Richard Baker, BBC TV 2 *Aug* 1981

MANNERS

7 Phone for the fish knives Norman, / As cook is a trifle unnerved; / You kiddies have crumpled the serviettes / And I must have things daintily served.
Sir John Betjeman, HOW TO GET ON IN SOCIETY

8 Do up your butterflies.
Sir Hugh Casson and Joyce Grenfell, NANNY SAYS 1972

9 The great secret is not having bad manners or good manners or any other particular sort of manners, but having the same manners for all human souls.
George Bernard Shaw, PYGMALION 1933

MARRIAGE

10 You can measure the social caste of a person by the distance between the husband's and wife's apartments.
Alfonso XIII of Spain. Quoted Harold Brooke-Baker, Daily Telegraph 26 *Jul* 1982

11 When I told my mother of my engagement she sank upon the settee, put a handkerchief to her eyes and cried "You might as well marry your groom."
Margot Asquith, AUTOBIOGRAPHY 1936

12 I married beneath me — all women do.
Nancy Astor. Speech, Oldham 1951

13 The state or condition of a community consisting of a master, a mistress and two slaves, making two in all.
Ambrose Bierce, THE DEVIL'S DICTIONARY 1906

14 Marriage is the result of the longing for the deep, deep peace of the double bed after the hurly-burly of the chaise-longue.
Mrs. Pat Campbell

15 The advantage of being married to an archaeologist is that the older one grows the more interested he becomes.
Agatha Christie, MURDER IN MESOPOTAMIA 1936

16 Marriage is a wonderful invention; but then again so is a bicycle repair kit.
Billy Connolly, THE AUTHORISED VERSION

17 The dread of loneliness is greater than the fear of bondage, so we get married.
Cyril Connolly, THE UNQUIET GRAVE 1945

18 Most marriages don't add two people together. They subtract one from the other.
Ian Fleming, DIAMONDS ARE FOR EVER 1956

19 I've had a lot of very good friends. I've always liked them too much to want to marry them.
Lillian Gish, The Times 19 *Nov* 1980

20 The trouble with my wife is that she is a whore in the kitchen and a cook in bed.
Geoffrey Gorer, EXPLORING THE ENGLISH CHARACTER

21 When a woman gets married it is like jumping into a hole in the ice in the middle of winter; you do it once and you remember it the rest of your days.
Maxim Gorky, THE LOWER DEPTHS 1902

22 The concept of two people living together for 25 years without having a cross word suggests a lack of spirit only to be admired in sheep.
A. P. Herbert, News Chronicle 1940

23 The critical period in matrimony is breakfast time.
A. P. Herbert, UNCOMMON LAW 1933

1 One of the difficulties of marriage is not that it ties a man to a woman but that it separates her from all others.
Dr. Charles Hill. Speech to London Chamber of Commerce 4 *Sep* 1956

2 Seldom, or perhaps never does a marriage develop into an individual relationship smoothly and without crises; there is no coming to consciousness without pain.
Carl Jung, CONTRIBUTIONS TO ANALYTICAL PSYCHOLOGY 1928

3 Marrying a man is like buying something you've been admiring for a long time in a shop window. You may love it when you get it home, but it doesn't always go with everything else in the house.
Jean Kerr, THE SNAKE HAS ALL THE LINES

4 He married a woman to stop her getting away / Now she's there all day.
Philip Larkin, SELF'S THE MAN

5 Only the strong of heart can be well married, since they do not turn to marriage to supply what no other human being can ever get from another — a sure sense of the fortress within himself.
Max Lerner, THE UNFINISHED COUNTRY 1929

6 So they were married — to be the more together — / And found they were never again so much together — / Divided by the morning tea, / By the evening paper, / By children and tradesmen's bills.
Louis MacNeice, LES SYLPHIDES

7 If people waited to know each other before they married, the world wouldn't be so overpopulated as it is now.
W. Somerset Maugham, MRS. DOT

8 One doesn't have to get anywhere in a marriage. It's not a public conveyance.
Iris Murdoch, A SEVERED HEAD 1961

9 In every marriage there is a selfish and an unselfish partner. A pattern is set up and soon becomes inflexible, of one person always making the demands and one person always giving way.
Id.

10 Perhaps the saddest lot that can fall mortal man is to be the husband of a lady poet.
George Jean Nathan

11 Marriage is rather a silly habit.
John Osborne. Quoted Observer, *Sayings of the Week* 1 *Jun* 1978

12 A modernist married a fundamentalist wife / And she led him a catechism and dogma life.
Keith Preston, MARITAL TRAGEDY

13 A good marriage is that in which each appoints the other the guardian of his solitude.
Rainer Maria Rilke, LETTERS 1892–1910

14 It takes patience to appreciate domestic bliss, volatile spirits prefer unhappiness.
George Santayana, THE LIFE OF REASON, *Reason in Society* 1906

15 Your aspect is softened. You have been boiled in bread and milk for years and years, like other married men, poor devil!
George Bernard Shaw, HEARTBREAK HOUSE 1920

16 My mother married a very good man . . . and she is not at all keen on my doing the same.
Id.

17 The more a man knows, and the farther he travels, the more likely he is to marry a country girl.
George Bernard Shaw, JOHN BULL'S OTHER ISLAND 1904

18 It is a woman's business to get married as soon as possible; and a man's to keep unmarried as long as he can.
George Bernard Shaw, MAN AND SUPERMAN 1905

19 Those who talk most about the blessings of marriage and the constancy of its vows are the very people who declare that if the chain were broken and the prisoners were left free to choose, the whole social fabric would fly asunder. You can't have the argument both ways.
Id.

20 Marriage is popular because it combines the maximum of temptation with the maximum of opportunity.
Id.

21 What a holler there would be if people had to pay the minister as much to marry them as they have to pay a lawyer to get them a divorce.
Claire Trevor, New York Journal, *American* 12 *Oct* 1960

22 Take it from me, marriage isn't a word — it's a sentence.
From King Vidor's silent film, THE CROWD 1928

1 It isn't silence you can cut with a knife any more, it's interchange of ideas. Intelligent discussion of practically everything is what is breaking up modern marriage.
E. B. White, EVERY DAY IS SATURDAY

2 London is spattered with couples living in sin whose lives are just as dreary as those of the respectably married.
Katherine Whitehorn, Observer 9 *Dec* 1978

3 People who wish to get married should actually have met before deciding to do so.
William Whitelaw, House of Commons 14 *Nov* 1979

4 Marriage is a bribe to make a housekeeper think she's a householder.
Thornton Wilder, THE MATCHMAKER 1955

5 The best part of marriage is the fights. The rest is merely so-so.
Id.

6 All the unhappy marriages came from the husband having brains.
P. G. Wodehouse, ADVENTURES OF SALLY 1920

7 Marriage is the net in which the jade snares the jaded.
P. G. Wodehouse and Guy Bolton, BRING ON THE GIRLS

8 Marriage isn't a process of prolonging the life of love, but of mummifying the corpse.
Id.

9 Don't let your marriage go stale. / Change the bag on the Hoover of life.
Victoria Wood, ITV, *Wood and Walters* 17 *Jan* 1982

MARTYR

10 It is often pleasant to stone a martyr, no matter how much we admire him.
John Barth, THE FLOATING OPERA 1956

11 To die for a religion is easier than to live it absolutely.
Jorge Luis Borges, LABYRINTHES 1962

12 Martyrs, my friend, have to choose between being forgotten, mocked or used. As for being understood — never.
Albert Camus, THE FALL 1956

13 Perhaps there is no happiness in life so perfect as the martyr's.
O. Henry, THE TRIMMED LAMP 1907

14 It is not the least of a martyr's scourges to be canonised by the persons who burned him.
Murray Kempton, PART OF OUR TIME 1955

15 I look on martyrs as mistakes / But still they burned for it at stakes.
John Masefield, THE EVERLASTING MERCY 1911

KARL MARX

16 Karl Marx wasn't a Marxist all the time. He got drunk in the Tottenham Court Road.
Michael Foot. Quoted Susan Barnes, BEHIND THE IMAGE

17 Much of the world's work is done by men who do not feel quite well. Marx is a case in point.
J. K. Galbraith, THE AGE OF UNCERTAINTY 1977

18 He is the apostle of class-hatred, the founder of a Satanic anti-religion, which resembles some religions in its cruelty, fanaticism and irrationality.
W. R. Inge (Dean of St. Pauls), ASSESSMENTS AND ANTICIPATIONS 1929

19 There is not one of his predictions that has not been falsified by events, and there is not one of his theories which has not been riddled by hostile criticism.
Id.

20 Mrs. Karl Marx, at the end of a long and bleak life, remarked "How good it would have been if Karl had made some capital instead of writing so much about it."
Will Rogers. Quoted Leon Harris, THE FINE ART OF POLITICAL WIT

MARXISM

21 The Marxist analysis has got nothing to do with what happened in Stalin's Russia; it's like blaming Jesus Christ for the Inquisition in Spain.
Tony Benn. Quoted Observer 27 *Apr* 1980

22 Marxism is like a classical building that followed the Renaissance; beautiful in its way, but incapable of growth.
Harold Macmillan. Speech to Primrose League 29 *Apr* 1981

23 Marxism is essentially a product of the bourgeois mind.
Joseph Alois Schumpter, CAPITALISM, SOCIALISM AND DEMOCRACY

QUEEN MARY

24 Queen Mary looked life the Jungfrau, white, and sparkling in the sun.
Henry Channon, DIARY 22 *Jun* 1937

JOHN MASEFIELD

1 Masefield's sonnets? Ah yes. Very nice. Pure Shakespeare. Masefield's 'Reynard the Fox'? Very nice, too. Pure Chaucer. Masefield's 'Everlasting Mercy'? H'm. Yes. Pure Masefield.
Robert Bridges. Quoted Beverley Nichols, TWENTY-FIVE

MATHEMATICS

2 What is algebra exactly? Is it those three-cornered things?
J. M. Barrie, QUALITY STREET 1901

3 When we reach the sphere of mathematics we are among processes which seem to some the most inhuman of all human activities and the most remote from poetry. Yet it is here that the artist has fullest scope for his imagination.
Havelock Ellis, THE DANCE OF LIFE 1923

4 The mathematician has reached the highest rung on the ladder of human thought.
Id.

5 One has to be able to count, if only so that at fifty-one doesn't marry a girl of twenty.
Maxim Gorky, THE ZYKOVS 1914

6 Once I had learnt my twelve times table [at the age of three] it was downhill all the way.
Fred Hoyle

7 The only way I can distinguish proper from improper fractions / Is by their actions.
Ogden Nash, ASK DADDY, HE WON'T KNOW

8 The true spirit of delight, the exaltation, the sense of being more than Man, which is the touchstone of the highest excellence, is to be found in mathematics as surely as in poetry.
Bertrand Russell, MYSTICISM AND LOGIC 1917

9 Mathematics, rightly viewed, possesses not only truth but supreme beauty — a beauty cold and austere like that of sculpture.
Id.

10 Mathematics may be defined as the subject in which we never know what we are talking about, nor whether what we are saying is true.
Id.

11 I like mathematics because it is *not* human and has nothing particular to do with this planet or with the whole accidental universe — because, like Spinoza's God, it won't love us in return.
Bertrand Russell, letter to Lady Ottoline Morrell, Mar 1912

12 I knew a mathematician who said "I do not know as much as God. But I know as much as God knew at my age".
Milton Shulman, BBC Radio 4, *Stop The Week* 31 Mar 1979

13 Numbers constitute the only universal language.
Nathanael West, MISS LONELY-HEARTS 1933

14 The science of pure mathematics, in its modern developments, may claim to be the most original creation of the human spirit.
A. N. Whitehead, SCIENCE AND THE MODERN WORLD 1925

15 Mathematics is thought moving in the sphere of complete abstraction from any particular instance of what it is talking about.
Id.

MATRIARCHY

16 In a matriarchy men should be encouraged to take it easy, for most women prefer live husbands to blocks of shares and seats on the board.
J. B. Priestley, THOUGHTS IN THE WILDERNESS

MATURITY

17 The mark of the immature man is that he wants to die nobly for a cause, while the mark of the mature man is that he wants to live humbly for one.
Wilhelm Stekel. Quoted J. D. Salinger, CATCHER IN THE RYE 1951

MAYONNAISE

18 Aunt Irene really inclined to that simplest of all views: the one expressed so cogently in the book of Genesis, which explained everything with appealing clarity. This was the only view that explained, for instance, mayonnaise. It was patently absurd to suppose that mayonnaise had come about through random chance, that anyone could ever have been silly or brilliant enough to predict what would happen if he slowly trickled oil on to egg yolks and then gone ahead and tried it.
Alice Thomas Ellis, THE 27TH KINGDOM 1982

MEANNESS

1 Is Mr. Benny tight? Well a little snug, perhaps. If he can't take it with him, he ain't gonna go.
Eddie Anderson, who played the part of Rochester in Jack Benny's radio programmes. Quoted Irving A. Fein, JACK BENNY

2 I've been in London four days and already I've spent seven pounds. Next time I'll come *alone*.
Jack Benny. Quoted William Marchant, THE PRIVILEGE OF HIS COMPANY

3 Some people have a necessity to be mean, as if they were exercising a faculty which they had to partially neglect since childhood.
F. Scott Fitzgerland, THE CRACK-UP 1936

MEDICINE

4 Stopped at a small chemist's and bought some tablets. Said to Leo "I just can't bear to run short of Acetylmethyldimethyloxamidphenylhydrazine"
James Agate, EGO 3 *9 Apr* 1937

5 A miracle drug is any drug that will do what the label says it will do.
Eric Hodgins, EPISODE

6 When you buy a pill and buy peace with it you get conditioned to cheap solutions instead of deep ones.
Max Lerner, THE UNFINISHED COUNTRY 1959

7 Medicine is a noble profession but a damn bad business.
Sir Humphrey Davy Rolleston, physician to George V. Quoted Lore and Maurice Cowan, THE WIT OF MEDICINE

8 When there's a cure, it was only half a disease.
Leo Rosten, HOORAY FOR YIDDISH 1983

9 There is at bottom only one genuinely scientific treatment for all diseases, and that is to stimulate the phagocytes.
George Bernard Shaw, THE DOCTOR'S DILEMMA 1906

10 Though there are millions of medical men in the world there is only one doctor — nature.
H. de Vere Stacpoole, MEN AND MICE

11 It should be the function of medicine to have people die young as late as possible.
Ernest L. Wynder

MEDIOCRITY

12 Only mediocrity can be trusted to be always at its best.
Max Beerbohm. Quoted S. N. Behrman, CONVERSATIONS WITH MAX 1960

13 Some men are born mediocre, some men achieve mediocrity, and some men have mediocrity thrust upon them.
Joseph Heller, CATCH 22 1961

14 It isn't evil that is ruining the earth, but mediocrity. The crime is not that Nero played while Rome burned, but that he played badly.
Ned Rorem, THE FINAL DIARY 1974

MEDITATION

15 Meditation is not a means to an end. It is both the means and the end.
Krishnamurti, THE PENGUIN KRISHNA-MURTI READER

MEEKNESS

16 We have the highest authority for believing that the meek shall inherit the earth; but I have never found any particular corroboration for this aphorism in the records of Somerset House.
Lord Birkenhead (F. E. Smith). Quoted his son and biographer, 2nd Earl of Birkenhead

17 The meek do inherit the earth, but the modern sceptics are too meek even to claim their inheritance.
G. K. Chesterton, ORTHODOXY 1908

18 The meek shall inherit the earth but not the mineral rights.
Paul Getty

19 The meek shall inherit the earth — if that's all right with you.
Graffito. Quoted Peterborough, Daily Telegraph 12 *Jul* 1979

20 It's going to be fun to watch and see how long the meek can keep the earth when they inherit it.
Kim Hubbard, ABE MARTIN

MEGALOMANIA

21 The megalomaniac differs from the narcissist by the fact that he wishes to be powerful rather than charming and seeks to be feared rather than loved. To his type belong many lunatics and most of the great men of

history.
Bertrand Russell, THE CONQUEST OF HAPPINESS 1930

MELODY

1 The heart of the melody can never be put down on paper.
Pablo Casals, CONVERSATIONS 1956

2 Melody is a form of remembrance. It must have a quality of meritability in our ears.
Gian-Carlo Menotti, Time 1 *May* 1950

MEMORIAL

3 You can keep the things of bronze and stone and give me one man to remember me just once a year.
Damon Runyon, last words

MEMORY

4 Memories are like stones, time and distance crack them like acid.
Ugo Betti, GOAT ISLAND 1946

5 It is all right for beasts to have no memories; but we poor humans have to be compensated.
William Bolitho, CAMERA OBSCURA

6 The charm, one might say the genius, of memory is that it is choosy, chancy and temperamental; it rejects the edifying cathedral and indelibly photographs the small boy outside, chewing a hunk of melon in the dust.
Elizabeth Bowen, Vogue 15 *Sep* 1955

7 Some memories are realities, and are better than anything that can ever happen to one again.
Willa Cather, MY ANTONIA 1918

8 Memory is the thing you forget with.
Alexander Chase, PERSPECTIVES 1960

9 One learns little more about a man from his feats of literary memory than from the feats of his alimentary canal.
Frank Moore Colby, THE COLBY ESSAYS, *Quotation and Allusion* 1926

10 Our memories are card-indexes consulted and then put back in disorder by authorities whom we do not control.
Cyril Connolly, THE UNQUIET GRAVE 1945

11 I have a memory like an elephant. In fact elephants often consult me.
Noël Coward. Quoted J. K. Galbraith, A LIFE IN OUR TIMES 1981

12 We do not know the true value of our moments until they have undergone the test of memory.
Georges Duhamel, THE HEART'S DOMAIN 1919

13 Do not trust your memory, it is a net full of holes; the most beautiful prizes slip through it.
Id.

14 Men live by forgetting — women live on memories.
T. S. Eliot, THE ELDER STATESMAN

15 Midnight shakes the memory as a madman shakes a dead geranium.
T. S. Eliot, RHAPSODY ON A WINDY NIGHT 1917

16 "My name is Eddie Seagoon."
"Gad, what a memory."
The Goon Show, BBC Radio

17 Some women'll stay in a man's memory if they once walked down a street.
Rudyard Kipling, TRAFFICS AND DISCOVERIES 1904

18 Only stay quiet while my mind remembers / The beauty of fire from the beauty of embers.
John Masefield, ON GROWING OLD

19 [My memory is] like a broken goldwasher's pan that often holds the mud and lets through the nuggets.
Raymond Mortimer, TRY ANYTHING ONCE

20 What beastly incidents our memories insist on cherishing — the ugly and disgusting — the beautiful things we have to keep diaries to remember.
Eugene O'Neill, STRANGE INTERLUDE 1928

21 Time, which changes people, does not alter the image we have retained of them.
Marcel Proust, REMEMBRANCE OF THINGS PAST 1913–1927

22 Anything processed by memory is a fiction.
Michael Ratcliffe, reviewing Paul Fussell's ABROAD, The Times 19 *Mar* 1931

23 No man, and no force can abolish memory.
Franklin D. Roosevelt 23 *Apr* 1942

24 The pleasure in music recalled is virtually non-existent. Music must be re-heard to be re-experienced.
Ned Rorem, PURE CONTRAPTION 1974

1 There are three things I always forget. Names, faces and — the third I can't remember.
Italo Svevo

2 The nice thing about having memories is that you can choose.
William Trevor, MATILDA'S ENGLAND, BBC *(play)*

3 In memory everything seems to happen to music.
Tennessee Williams, THE GLASS MENAGERIE 1944

4 Life is all memory, except for the one present moment that goes by you so quick you hardly catch it going.
Tennessee Williams, THE MILK TRAIN DOESN'T STOP HERE ANY MORE 1962

5 All I can recall of the actual poetry is the bit that goes Tum-tum, tum-tum, tum-tumpty-tum
I slew him, tum-tum, tum.
P. G. Wodehouse, JEEVES TAKES CHARGE

6 Memories are like mulligatawny soup in a cheap restaurant. It is best not to stir them.
P. G. Wodehouse and Guy Bolton, BRING ON THE GIRLS

METAPHOR

7 The metaphor is probably the most fertile power possessed by man.
José Ortega y Gasset, THE DEHUMANISATION OF ART

METAPHYSICS

8 The unrest which keeps the never stopping clock of metaphysics going is the thought that the non-existence of the world is just as possible as its existence.
William James, SOME PROBLEMS OF PHILOSOPHY, *The Problem of Being* 1911

MIDDLE-AGE

9 Variously reckoned to suit the reckoner.
Definition as appears in Chambers Dictionary

10 The years between fifty and seventy are the hardest. You are always being asked to do things, and you are not yet decrepit enough to turn them down.
T. S. Eliot, Time 23 *Oct* 1950

11 The long dull monotonous years of middle-aged prosperity or middle-aged adversity are excellent campaigning weather for the Devil.
C. S. Lewis, THE SCREWTAPE LETTERS 1942

12 . . . when a man is always thinking that in a week or two he will feel as good as ever.
Don Marquis, ARCHY AND MEHITABEL 1927

MIDDLE CLASS

13 Who is it that exercises social power today? Who imposes the forms of his own mind on the period? Without a doubt the man of the middle class.
José Ortega y Gassett, THE REVOLT OF THE MASSES, *The Barbarism of Specialisation* 1930

14 A moderately honest man, with a moderately faithful wife, moderate drinkers both, in a moderately healthy house; that is the true middle class unit.
George Bernard Shaw, MAN AND SUPERMAN 1905

15 I have to live for others and not for myself; that's middle class morality.
George Bernard Shaw, PYGMALION 1913

MILLIONAIRE

16 All millionaires love a baked apple.
Ronald Firbank, VAINGLORY 1915

17 I would not say millionaires were mean. They simply have a healthy respect for money. I've noticed that people who don't respect money don't have any.
Paul Getty, interviewed on the TV programme, This Week

A. A. MILNE

18 Tonstant Weader fwowed up.
Constant Reader (Dorothy Parker), of Winnie the Pooh in book review in the New Yorker

MIND

19 His mind was like a Roquefort cheese, so ripe that it was palpably falling to pieces.
Van Wyck Brooks of Ford Maddox Ford. Quoted Douglas Golding, THE LAST PRE-RAPHAELITE

20 I am incurably convinced that the object of opening the mind, as of opening the mouth, is to shut it on something solid.
G. K. Chesterton, AUTOBIOGRAPHY

1 The mind has its own womb to which, baffled by speculation, it longs to return.
Cyril Connolly, THE UNQUIET GRAVE 1945

2 Minds are like parachutes; they only function when open.
Lord Dewar in a speech

3 Experience offers proof on every hand that vigorous mental life may be but one side of a personality, of which the other is moral barbarism.
George Gissing, THE PRIVATE PAPERS OF HENRY RYECROFT 1903

4 It is the mind which creates the world about us, and even though we stand side by side in the same meadow, my eyes will never see what is beheld by yours, my heart will never stir to the emotions with which yours is touched.
Id.

5 The pendulum of the mind oscillates between sense and nonsense, not between right and wrong.
Carl Jung, MEMORIES, DREAMS, REFLECTIONS

6 The mind is like a richly woven tapestry in which the colours are distilled from the experiences of the senses, and the design drawn from the convolutions of the intellect.
Carson McCullers, REFLECTIONS IN A GOLDEN EYE

7 I have never yet met the cultivated mind that has not its shrubbery. I loathe and detest shrubberies.
Katherine Mansfield, JOURNALS 1954

8 Certainly, in our intellectual behaviour we rarely solve a tricky problem by a steady climb to success.
M. Minsky, Steps Towards Artificial Intelligence, Proc. IRE 1961

9 The discovery that the mind can regulate its thoughts, fostering some and dismissing others, is one of the most important stages in the art of self-culture. It is astonishing how little this art is practised among Westerners.
John Cowper Powys, THE MEANING OF CULTURE 1930

10 The mind is a strange machine which can combine the materials offered to it in the most astonishing ways.
Bertrand Russell, THE CONQUEST OF HAPPINESS 1930

11 The Ghost in the Machine.
Gilbert Ryle, CONCEPT OF MIND

12 Hardly anybody, except perhaps the Greeks at their best, has realised the sweetness and glory of being a rational animal.
George Santayana, CHARACTER AND OPINION IN THE UNITED STATES 1921

13 The mind is the expression of the soul, which belongs to God and must be let alone by Government.
Adlai Stevenson. Speech, Salt Lake City 14 Oct 1952

14 The mind is the most capricious of insects — flitting, fluttering.
Virginia Woolf, A WRITER'S DIARY 1953

MINORITY

15 To be in the weakest camp is to be in the strongest school.
G. K. Chesterton, HERETICS 1905

16 Minorities are individuals or groups of individuals especially qualified. The masses are the collection of people not specially qualified.
José Ortega y Gasset, THE REVOLT OF THE MASSES 1930

17 A resolute minority has usually prevailed over an easygoing or wobbly majority whose prime purpose was to be left alone.
James Reston, SKETCHES IN THE SAND 1967

18 The only tyrannies from which men, women and children are suffering in real life are the tyrannies of minorities.
Theodore Roosevelt. Speech 22 *Mar* 1912

MIRACLE

19 True miracles are created by men when they use the courage and intelligence that God gave them.
Jean Anouilh, THE LARK 1955

20 Miracles are laughed at by a nation that reads thirty million newspapers a day and supports Wall Street.
Finley Peter Dunne, MR. DOOLEY'S OPINIONS, *Casual Observations* 1900

21 Everything is miraculous. It is miraculous that one does not melt in one's bath.
Pablo Picasso. Quoted Jean Cocteau

1 Miracles are propitious accidents, the natural causes of which are too complicated to be readily understood.
George Santayana, THE ETHICS OF SPINOZA

2 A miracle is an event which creates faith. Frauds deceive. An event which creates faith does not deceive; therefore it is not a fraud, but a miracle.
George Bernard Shaw, ST. JOAN 1927

MIRROR

3 Mirrors should think longer before they reflect.
Jean Cocteau in an interview with Derek Prouse, Sunday Times 20 Oct 1963

4 Mirrors are the windows of the devil, overlooking nothing but a landscape of lies.
Leon Garfield, THE PRISONERS OF SEPTEMBER

5 The mirror usually reflects only the way others see us, the way we are expected to behave — forecast to behave — hardly ever what we really are.
Luigi Pirandello, THE RULES OF THE GAME 1918

6 Almost always it is the fear of being ourselves that brings us to the mirror.
Antonio Porchia, VOICES 1968

7 The walls of an empty room are mirrors that double and redouble our sense of ourselves.
John Updike, THE CENTAUR 1963

MISANTHROPY

8 The misanthropic idea, as in Byron, is not a truth but it is one of the immortal lies. As long as humanity lies, it can be hated.
G. K. Chesterton, USES OF ADVERSITY 1920

9 I've always been interested in people but I've never liked them.
W. Somerset Maugham. Quoted Observer 28 Aug 1949

10 A young, earnest American brought up the subject of nuclear warfare which, he said, might well destroy the entire human race. "I can't wait" P. G. Wodehouse murmured.
Malcolm Muggeridge, TREAD SOFTLY FOR YOU TREAD ON MY JOKES 1966

MISER

11 The miser puts his gold pieces into a coffer, but as soon as the coffer is closed it is as if it were empty.
André Gide, PRETEXTS, *Concerning Influence in Literature* 1903

MISERY

12 If you feel depressed you shouldn't go out on the street because it will show on your face and you'll give it to others. Misery is a communicable disease.
Martha Graham. Quoted John Heilpern, Observe4 Magazine, *The Amazing Martha* 8 Jul 1979

13 Half the misery in the world is caused by ignorance. The other half is caused by knowledge.
Bonar Thompson, Hyde Park orator, THE BLACK HAT

MISFORTUNE

14 Calamities are of two kinds: Misfortune to ourselves and good fortune to others.
Ambrose Bierce, THE DEVIL'S DICTIONARY 1906

15 Who has not proved the justice of the saying "She who breaks the lid by noon will crack the dish ere nightfall".
Ernest Bramah, KAI LUNG UNROLLS HIS MAT 1928

MISTAKE

16 I see now clearly, / The many, many mistakes I have made / My whole life through, mistake upon mistake / The mistaken attempts to correct mistakes / By methods which proved to be equally mistaken.
T. S. Eliot, THE ELDER STATESMAN

17 For creating a good impression on others there's nothing to beat being totally and catastrophically wrong.
Michael Frayn, SWEET DREAMS

18 The greatest mistake you can make in life is to be continually fearing you will make one.
Elbert Hubbard, THE NOTEBOOK 1927

19 It is a good thing to make mistakes so long as you are found out quickly.
J. M. Keynes

1 To be a victim of one's own mistakes is bad enough, but to be the victim of the other fellow's mistakes as well is too much.
Henry Miller, THE AIR-CONDITIONED NIGHTMARE 1945

2 A life spent in making mistakes is not only more honorable but more useful than a life spent doing nothing.
George Bernard Shaw, DOCTOR'S DILEMMA, *Preface* 1906

3 I have learned throughout my life as a composer chiefly through my mistakes and pursuits of false assumptions, not by my exposure to wisdom and founts of knowledge.
Igor Stravinsky, THEMES AND EPISODES, *Contingencies* 1966

4 If we had more time for discussion we should probably have made a great many more mistakes.
Leon Trotsky, MY LIFE 1930

MISTRUST

5 Everyone likes a kidder, but no one lends him money.
Arthur Miller, DEATH OF A SALESMAN 1957

MISUNDERSTANDING

6 Once he [my husband] thought I remarked that I liked the plays of Mozart. "But Mozart didn't write plays. He was strictly a composer," he said. "Not Mozart," I explained. "Moss Hart."
Duchess of Bedford, NICOLE NOBODY

7 There is no worse lie than a truth misunderstood by those who hear it.
William James, THE VARIETIES OF RELIGIOUS EXPERIENCE 1902

8 It is a misfortune for Anglo-American friendship that the two countries are supposed to have a common language.
Bertrand Russell, Saturday Evening Post 3 *Jun* 1944

9 When a grammar school boy was asked what he knew about VD he replied "Nothing, unless you mean vapour density."
M. Schofield, THE SEXUAL BEHAVIOUR OF YOUNG PEOPLE

NANCY MITFORD

10 Nice cheap girl to take out for the evening. Costs you only eighteen and six for an orangeade in a night club.
Evelyn Waugh of Nancy Mitford. Quoted Maurice Brown, MEMORIES

MODERATION

11 Moderation is a virtue only in those who are thought to have an alternative.
Henry Kissinger, Observer, *Sayings of the Week* 24 *Jan* 1982

12 The reasonable man adapts himself to the world.
George Bernard Shaw, MAN AND SUPERMAN 1905

MODESTY

13 A nun, asked why she wore a chemise in the bath where no one could see her, replied "God sees everything."
Anon.

14 I am not quite a gentleman, but you would hardly notice it.
Daisy Ashford (aged 9), THE YOUNG VISITERS 1919

15 His modesty amounts to a deformity.
Margot Asquith of her husband, H. H. Asquith the Earl of Oxford and Asquith, AUTOBIOGRAPHY 1936

16 I'm a second eleven sort of chap.
J. M. Barrie, THE ADMIRABLE CRICHTON 1902

17 A modest man is usually admired — if people ever hear of him.
Edgar Watson Howe, VENTURES IN COMMON SENSE 1919

18 Reserve is an artificial quality that is developed in most of us as the result of innumerable rebuffs.
W. Somerset Maugham, CAKES AND ALE 1930

19 In some remote regions of Islam it is said, a woman caught unveiled by a stranger will raise her skirt to cover her face.
Raymond Mortimer, COLETTE

20 He was a very modest man, and his most extreme boast was that he did try to have the qualities of his defects.
Bertrand Russell of Prof. A. N. Whitehead, PORTRAITS FROM MEMORY

1 I have often wished I had time to cultivate modesty, but I am too busy thinking about myself.
Edith Sitwell

2 When I pass my name in such huge letters I blush, but at the same time instinctively raise my hat.
Sir H. Beerbohm Tree. Quoted Hesketh Pearson, BEERBOHM TREE

MOLE

3 The houses are blind as moles / (though moles see fine tonight in the snouting, velvet dingles).
Dylan Thomas, UNDER MILK WOOD 1954

MOMENT

4 After all, any given moment has its value; it can be questioned in the light of after-events, but the moment remains.
F. Scott Fitzgerald, THE CRACK-UP 1936

5 In order to be utterly happy the only thing necessary is to refrain from comparing this moment with other moments in the past, which I often did not fully enjoy because I was comparing them with other moments of the future.
André Gide, JOURNALS 1939–1950

6 Florence Farr once said to me, "If we could say to ourselves, with sincerity 'this passing moment is as good as any I shall ever know', we could die upon the instant, and be united with God."
W. B. Yeats, AUTOBIOGRAPHY 1926

MONARCHY

7 We are a middle-class people and we have a middle-class royal family, hard working, with no aristocratic excesses.
Hector Bolitho. Quoted Reginald Pound, THEIR MOODS AND MINE 1935

8 The monarchy is the oldest profession in the world.
Charles, Prince of Wales. Quoted Noël St. George, ROYAL QUOTES

9 On the whole it is wise in human affairs and in the government of men, to separate pomp from power.
Winston Churchill. Speech, Ottawa 1952

10 Life in Buckingham Palace isn't too bad, but too many formal dinners. Yuk!
Diana, Princess of Wales in a letter to former teaching colleague. Quoted Sunday Times Magazine 26 *Jul* 1981

11 There will soon be only five kings left — the Kings of England, Diamonds, Hearts, Spades and Clubs.
King Farouk of Egypt 1951

12 Well, what are you socialists going to do about me?
George V to Ramsay MacDonald when he first presented himself at Buckingham Palace

13 We're not a family; we're a firm.
George VI. Quoted Peter Lane, OUR FUTURE KING

14 The strength of the monarchy does not lie in the power it has, but in the power it denies others.
Anthony Jay. Quoted Anthony Sampson, THE CHANGING ANATOMY OF BRITAIN 1982

15 If you find you are to be presented to the Queen, do not rush up to her. She will eventually be brought around to you like a dessert trolley at a good restaurant.
Los Angeles Times. *Advice given during visit of Queen Elizabeth* II, *Mar* 1983

16 We sometimes forget that monarchs are just normal people trapped by abnormal circumstances.
Michael MacDonald, letter to Daily Telegraph 23 *May* 1979

17 As long as our family can produce nicely brought up young people it will be all right.
Princess Margaret. Quoted Andrew Duncan

18 In this business you can't afford to be a shrinking violet.
Lord Mountbatten's advice to Charles, Prince of Wales. Quoted Anthony Sampson, THE CHANGING ANATOMY OF BRITAIN 1982

19 Monarchy is the gold filling in the mouth of decay.
John Osborne. Quoted Bernard Levin, THE PENDULUM YEARS 1976

20 I am referred to in that splendid language [pidgin English] as Feller-belong-Queen.
Philip, Duke of Edinburgh. Speech, Ottawa 29 *Oct* 1958

21 Royalty puts a human face on the operations of government.
Dr. Runcie (Archbishop of Canterbury), sermon at St. Pauls Cathedral on the occasion of the Queen Mother's 80th birthday 16 *Jul* 1980

1 We have brains enough to know that Kings do not come as small as this little squirt.
Damon Runyon, MORE THAN SOMEWHAT 1937

2 Kings are not born, they are made by artificial hallucination.
George Bernard Shaw, MAN AND SUPERMAN 1905

3 The monarchy is a labour-intensive industry.
Harold Wilson. Quoted Observer 13 Feb 1977

MONEY

4 Old pennies have a picture on the back of a lady riding a bicycle. Her name is Ruby Tanner.
Anonymous schoolgirl

5 A man who has a million dollars is as well off as if he were rich.
J. J. Astor III

6 Money, it turned out, was exactly like sex. You thought of nothing else if you didn't have it and thought of other things if you did.
James Baldwin, NOBODY KNOWS MY NAME, *The Black Boy Looks At the White Boy* 1961

7 My brother down in Texas / Can't even write his name. / He signs his cheques with Xs / But they cash 'em just the same.
Irving Berlin, ANNIE GET YOUR GUN

8 *Money, n.* A blessing that is of no advantage to us excepting when we part with it.
Ambrose Bierce, THE DEVIL'S DICTIONARY 1906

9 One must choose, in life, between making money and spending it.
Edouard Bourdet, LES TEMPS DIFFICILES 1934

10 Life is short and so is money.
Bertolt Brecht, THE THREEPENNY OPERA 1928

11 When you have told anyone you have left them a legacy the only decent thing to do is to die at once.
Samuel Butler. Quoted Festing Jones, SAM BUTLER, A MEMOIR 1917

12 It is a kind of spiritual snobbery that makes people think that they can be happy without money.
Albert Camus, NOTEBOOKS 1935–1942

13 A banker is a man who lends you an umbrella when the sun is shining and wants it back the minute it starts raining.
Bennett Cerf, LAUGHTER UNLIMITED 1951

14 To be clever enough to get all the money one must be stupid enough to want it.
G. K. Chesterton, THE INNOCENCE OF FATHER BROWN 1911

15 All my available funds are completely tied up in ready cash.
W. C. Fields. Quoted Bennett Cerf, TRY AND STOP ME 1947

16 Money is like an arm or leg; use it or lose it.
Henry Ford, New York Times 8 *Nov* 1931

17 One of the evils of money is that it tempts us to look at it rather than at the things that it buys.
E. M. Forster, TWO CHEERS FOR DEMOCRACY 1951

18 Money is a singular thing. It ranks with love as man's greatest source of joy. And with his death as his greatest source of anxiety.
J. K. Galbraith, THE AGE OF UNCERTAINTY 1977

19 Money differs from an automobile, a mistress or cancer in being equally important to those who have it and those who don't.
Id.

20 Maybe money is unreal for most of us, easier to give away than things we want.
Lillian Hellman, AN UNFINISHED WOMAN 1969

21 "To make money", said Mr. Porteous, "one must be really interested in money."
Aldous Huxley, ANTIC HAY 1923

22 The size of sums of money appears to vary in a remarkable way according as they are being paid in or paid out.
Julian Huxley, ESSAYS OF A BIOLOGIST 1923

23 It is extraordinary how many emotional storms one may weather in safety if one is ballasted with ever so little gold.
William McFee, CASUALS OF THE SEA 1916

24 Money doesn't buy friends, but it allows a better class of enemies.
Lord Mancroft, Punch

25 I must say I hate money but it's the lack of it I hate most.
Katherine Mansfield. Quoted Anthony Alpers, KATHERINE MANSFIELD 1954

1 What's a thousand dollars? Mere chicken feed. A poultry matter.
Groucho Marx, COCONUTS

2 Money is like a sixth sense without which you cannot make complete use of the other five.
W. Somerset Maugham, OF HUMAN BONDAGE 1915

3 If one has an income of five thousand a year, four thousand should be considered as pocket money.
Herbert Morgan. Quoted James Agate, EGO 3 27 *Sep* 1936

4 Money is like manure. If you spread it around it does a lot of good. But if you pile it up in one place it stinks like hell.
Clint Murchison Jr. Quoted Time 16 *Jun* 1961

5 Some people's money is merited / And other people's is inherited.
Ogden Nash, THE TERRIBLE PEOPLE

6 I can't take it with me I know / But will it last until I go?
Martha F. Newmeyer, SIMULTANEOUS DEPARTURE

7 Silver money is jolly. It dances and hums. Paper money crackles like dead leaves.
Extract from a child's essay. Quoted New York Times Magazine 8 *Sep* 1940

8 If women didn't exist, all the money in the world would have no meaning.
Aristotle Onassis. Quoted Barbara Rowe, A BOOK OF QUOTES

9 Money is good for bribing your way through the inconveniences of life.
Gottfried Reinhardt. Quoted Lillian Ross, PICTURE

10 Money may not buy happiness. But with it you can rent enough.
Dick Richards, GINGER, SALUTE TO A STAR

11 All decent people live beyond their incomes nowadays, and those who aren't respectable live beyond other people's. A few gifted individuals manage to do both.
Saki, THE MATCH-MAKER

12 The surest way to ruin a man who doesn't know how to handle money is to give him some.
George Bernard Shaw, HEARTBREAK HOUSE 1920

13 Not the least of its virtues is that it destroys base people as certainly as it fortifies and dignifies noble people.
George Bernard Shaw, MAJOR BARBARA, *Preface* 1905

14 The universal regard for money is the one hopeful fact in our civilisation. Money is the most important thing in the world. It represents health, strength, honour, generosity and beauty.
Id.

15 Lack of money is the root of all evil.
George Bernard Shaw, MAN AND SUPERMAN, *Maxims for Revolutionists* 1905

16 There was a time when a fool and his money were soon parted, but now it happens to everybody.
Adlai Stevenson, THE STEVENSON WIT

17 To have subsidised a Bach or Fullbrighted a Beethoven would have done no good at all. Money may kindle but it cannot, by itself for very long, burn.
Igor Stravinsky. Quoted Barbara Rowe, A BOOK OF QUOTES

18 Nine times out of ten money will do the trick required at the moment.
John Wain, Punch 28 *Sep* 1960

19 The easiest way for your children to learn about money is for you not to have any.
Katherine Whitehorn, HOW TO SURVIVE CHILDREN

20 Money should circulate like rainwater.
Thornton Wilder, THE MATCHMAKER 1955

21 I'd give a thousand dollars right now to be a millionaire.
Hal Wilton, DOOMED TO THE BIG HOUSE 1935

22 With money I'll throttle the beast-blind world beneath my fingers. Without it I am strapped, weakened, my life is a curse and a care.
Thomas Wolfe, LETTERS 1956

23 A broker is a man who runs your fortune into a shoestring.
Alexander Woollcott. Quoted Samuel Hopkins Adams, THE WORLD OF A. WOOLLCOTT 1945

MONOGAMY

24 Monogamy is for those who are whole and clear, all in one stroke. But for those whose

stroke is broken into two different directions, then there must be two fulfilments.
D. H. Lawrence, LETTERS 1932

MONOTONY

1 Life is simply one damn thing after another.
Elbert Hubbard, NOTEBOOKS 1927

2 It is not true that life is one damn thing after another — it is one damn thing over and over.
Edna St. Vincent Millay, LETTERS 1952

MARILYN MONROE

3 If she was a victim, she was a victim of friends.
George Cukor. Quoted Gavin Lambert, ON CUKOR

4 She was never permitted to mature into a warm, vibrant woman, or fully use her gifts for comedy, despite the signals and flashes she kept sending up. Instead she was turned into a figure of mockery in the parts she played and to the men she played with.
Molly Haskell, FROM REVERENCE TO RAPE

5 She was good at being inarticulately abstracted for the same reason that midgets are good at being short.
Clive James, AT THE PILLARS OF HERCULES

6 A phenomenon of nature, like Niagara Falls and the Grand Canyon.
Nunnally Johnson. Quoted William Manchester, THE GLORY AND THE DREAM

7 . . . a very Stradivarius of sex, so gorgeous, forgiving, humorous, compliant and tender that even the most mediocre musician would relax his lack of art in the dissolving magic of her violin.
Norman Mailer, MARILYN

8 Marilyn's need to be desired was so great that she could make love to a camera.
William Manchester, THE GLORY AND THE DREAM

9 That she withstood the incredible, unknowable pressures of her public legend as long as she did is evidence of the stamina of the human.
Vogue editorial. Quoted Edward Wagen Knecht, SEVEN DAUGHTERS OF THE THEATRE

FIELD MARSHAL MONTGOMERY

10 In defeat he is unbeatable; in victory unbearable.
Winston Churchill. Quoted Edward Marsh, AMBROSIA AND SMALL BEER

MOON

11 The moon is a different thing to each one of us. It looks like a vast, lonely, forbidding place, an expanse of nothing.
Frank Borman, broadcasting from Apollo VIII 24 *Dec* 1968

12 O the moon shone bright on Mrs. Porter / And on her daughter / They wash their feet in soda water.
T. S. Eliot, THE WASTE LAND 1922

13 The moon is nothing / But a circumambulating aphrodisiac / Divinely subsidized to provoke the world / Into a rising birth-rate.
Christopher Fry, THE LADY'S NOT FOR BURNING 1949

14 The moon was a ghostly galleon tossed upon cloudy seas.
Alfred Noyes, COLLECTED POEMS, *The Highwayman* 1947

HENRY MOORE

15 Sculptor Henry Moore has been asked not to leave any holes in which boys could trap their heads when he carves 'Family Group' for Harlow New Town.
News Chronicle. Quoted Michael Bateman, THIS ENGLAND

MORALITY

16 No morality can be founded on authority, even if the authority were divine.
A. J. Ayer, ESSAY ON HUMANISM

17 I am as pure as the driven slush.
Tallulah Bankhead. Quoted Observer 24 *Feb* 1957

18 Fine feelings are as much a luxury as clean gloves.
Granville Barker, THE VOYSEY INHERITANCE 1905

19 She is the kind of girl who will not go anywhere without her mother. And her mother will go anywhere.
John Barrymore, of his ex-wife Elaine. Quoted J. P. McEvoy, Stage, *Jan* 1941

1 Morality's not practical. Morality's a gesture. A complicated gesture learned from books.
Robert Bolt, A MAN FOR ALL SEASONS 1962

2 It doesn't matter what you do, as long as you don't do it in public and frighten the horses.
Mrs. Pat Campbell

3 What is moral is what you feel good after, and what is immoral is what you feel bad after.
Ernest Hemingway, DEATH IN THE AFTERNOON 1932

4 Half, at least, of all morality is negative and consists in keeping out of mischief.
Aldous Huxley, THE DOORS OF PERCEPTION 1926

5 The quality of moral behaviour varies in inverse ratio to the number of human beings involved.
Aldous Huxley, GREY EMINENCE

6 Morality which is based on ideas, or on an ideal, is an unmitigated evil.
D. H. Lawrence, FANTASIA OF THE UNCONSCIOUS 1922

7 There is nothing so bad but it can masquerade as moral.
Walter Lippmann, A PREFACE TO POLITICS, *Some Necessary Iconoclasm* 1914

8 You can't learn too soon that the most useful thing about a principle is that it can always be sacrificed to expediency.
W. Somerset Maugham, THE CIRCLE 1921

9 As soon as one is unhappy one becomes moral.
Marcel Proust, REMEMBRANCE OF THINGS PAST 1917–1927

10 Morality consists in suspecting other people of not being legally married.
George Bernard Shaw, THE DOCTOR'S DILEMMA 1906

11 I don't believe in morality. I am a disciple of Bernard Shaw.
Id.

12 The so-called new morality is too often the old immorality condoned.
Lord Shawcross, Observer 17 *Nov* 1963

13 Morals are an acquirement — like music, like a foreign language, like piety, poker, paralysis — no man is born with them.
Mark Twain, SEVENTIETH BIRTHDAY 1907

14 As society is now constituted, a literal adherence to the moral precepts scattered throughout the Gospels would mean sudden death.
A. N. Whitehead, ADVENTURES IN IDEAS 1933

15 What is morality in any given time or place? It is what the majority then and there happen to like and immorality is what they dislike.
A. N. Whitehead, DIALOGUES, *recorded by Lucien Price* 1953

J. P. MORGAN

16 J. P. Morgan, it is worth remembering, spent millions on manuscripts and artifacts brought over from the lands of precisely those immigrants who could be bought in job lots for eight cents an hour.
Alistair Cooke, AMERICA

MORNING

17 The principality of the sky lightens now, over our green hill, into spring morning larked and crowed and belling.
Dylan Thomas, UNDER MILK WOOD 1954

WILLIAM MORRIS

18 He [William Morris] is unquestionably an all round man, but the act of walking round him has always tired me.
Max Beerbohm. Quoted S. N. Behrman, CONVERSATIONS WITH MAX 1960

MOTHER

19 Sweet little old lady wishes to correspond with six-foot student with brown eyes and answering to the initials J. D. B. (signed) His Mother.
Advert in a student magazine. Quoted Venture, *Aug* 1980

20 Mother love, particularly in America, is a highly respected and much publicised emotion and when exacerbated by gin and bourbon it can become extremely formidable.
Noël Coward, FUTURE INDEFINITE 1954

21 Mother is the dead heart of the family, spending father's earnings on consumer goods to enhance the environment in which he eats, sleeps and watches television.
Germaine Greer, THE FEMALE EUNUCH

1 My mother was dead five years before I knew that I had loved her very much.
Lillian Hellman, AN UNFINISHED WOMAN 1969

2 Nobody can have the soul of me. My mother has had it, and nobody can have it again. Nobody can come into my very self again, and breathe me like an atmosphere.
D. H. Lawrence, LETTERS 1936

3 Few misfortunes can befall a boy which bring worse consequences than to have a really affectionate mother.
W. Somerset Maugham, A WRITER'S NOTE-BOOK 1949

4 Who has not watched a mother stroke her child's cheek or kiss her child *in a certain way* and felt a nervous shudder at the possessive outrage done to a free solitary human soul?
John Cowper Powys, THE MEANING OF CULTURE 1930

5 There is only one person an English girl hates more than she hates her elder sister; and that is her mother.
George Bernard Shaw, MAN AND SUPER-MAN 1905

MOTHER-IN-LAW

6 The day my mother-in-law called, the mice threw themselves on the traps.
Les Dawson, BBC TV, *Dawson's Watch*

7 Mussolini in knickers.
Les Dawson, BBC TV, *programme title* 18 Oct 1981

8 Nye [Aneurin Bevan] loved telling people that he had to marry Jennie to get his mother-in-law.
Michael Foot, ANEURIN BEVAN 1897–1945

MOTORING

9 A pedestrian is a man who has two cars — one being driven by his wife, the other by one of his children.
Robert Bradbury, New York Times 5 *Sep* 1962

10 We are nourishing at immense cost a monster of great potential destructiveness, and yet we love him dearly.
Prof. Colin Buchanan, INTRODUCTION TO TRAFFIC IN TOWNS 1963

11 Americans are broad-minded people. They'll accept the fact that a person can be an alcoholic, a dope fiend, a wife beater, and even a newspaperman, but if a man doesn't drive, there is something wrong with him.
Art Buchwald, HOW MUCH IS THAT IN DOLLARS? 1961

12 The automobile changed our dress, manners, social customs, vacation habits, the shape of our cities, consumer purchasing, patterns, common tastes and positions of intercourse.
John Ketas, THE INSOLENT CHARIOTS

13 When I caught a glimpse of Rita / Filling in a ticket in her little white book / In a cap she looked much older / And the bag across her shoulder / Made her look a little like a military man / Lovely Rita, Meter Maid.
John Lennon and Paul McCartney, LOVELY RITA *(song)*

14 To George F. Babbitt his motor car was poetry and tragedy, love and heroism. The office was his pirate ship, but the car his perilous journey ashore.
Sinclair Lewis, BABBITT 1922

15 The car has become the carapace, the protective and aggressive shell, of urban and suburban man.
Marshall McLuhan, UNDERSTANDING MEDIA 1964

16 . . . an old bullnosed Morris he called God because it moved in a mysterious way.
Lord Mancroft, Punch

17 Very often a gentleman's wife will have her own car, particularly if she can afford to buy it herself. Anything that is small and uncomfortable will do.
Douglas Sutherland, THE ENGLISH GENTLEMAN 1978

18 The most non-gent car of all is the Rolls Royce. If, however, he happens to have been left one by an eccentric aunt it should be very old and not very clean. Some gentlemen carry this further, keeping old sacks on the back seat and leaving bird messes on the roof where the chickens have roosted.
Id.

MOUSTACHE

19 The huge laughing cockroaches on his top lip.
Osip Mandelstam, POEMS, *Stalin Epigram*

1 He has a moustache like a mosquito's whiskers across his upper lip.
Damon Runyon, MORE THAN SOMEWHAT 1937

2 A kiss without a moustache, they said then, is like an egg without salt. I will add to it. It is like Good without Evil.
Jean-Paul Sartre, WORDS

3 His nicotine, egg yellow, weeping walrus Victorian moustache worn thick and long in memory of Doctor Crippen.
Dylan Thomas, UNDER MILK WOOD 1954

MALCOLM MUGGERIDGE

4 The most wonderful deceitful character — saved by his sense of humour.
Osbert Lancaster. Quoted Duncan Fallowell, Times Profile 11 *Oct* 1982

5 He combines the roles of the voice crying in the wilderness and the voice full of the most worldly relish.
Bernard Levin, THE PENDULUM YEARS 1976

6 Muggeridge found himself in the dire situation of a thief crucified between two Christs.
Anthony Powell, THE STRANGERS ARE ALL GONE, VOL 4, *The Memoirs*

7 He thinks he was knocked off his horse by God, like St. Paul on the road to Damascus. His critics think he simply fell off from old age.
Katherine Whitehorn, Observer 20 *May* 1979

MURDER

8 No actions are bad in themselves — even murder can be justified.
Dietrich Bonhoeffer, NO RUSTY SWORDS

9 Every murderer is probably somebody's old friend.
Agatha Christie, THE MYSTERIOUS AFFAIR AT STYLES 1920

10 Why murder is the greatest of all crimes is not that the life taken may be that of an Abraham Lincoln, but because it might be yours or mine.
F. Tennyson Jesse, COMMENTS ON CAIN

11 He who bears the brand of Cain shall rule the earth.
George Bernard Shaw, BACK TO METHUSELAH 1922

IRIS MURDOCH

12 She is like a character out of Hieronymus Bosch — the very nicest character.
Rachel Billington, Times profile 25 *Apr* 1983

13 A tousled, heelless, ladder-stockinged little lady — crackling with intelligence but nothing at all of a prig.
George Lyttelton, THE LYTTELTON HART-DAVIS LETTERS 1959

MUSIC

14 Delius is all intoxication but it is all the same intoxication. Wagner has a hundred ways of making you tight.
Anon. Quoted James Agate, Ego 7, 17 *Sep* 1944

15 A friend said to Chopin / It would be topin / If only yude / Write an étude.
Anon.

16 There's only two ways to sum up music: either it's good or it's bad. If it's good you don't mess about with it, you just enjoy it.
Louis Armstrong. Quoted Nat Shapiro, AN ENCYCLOPEDIA OF QUOTATIONS ABOUT MUSIC

17 Music is the best means we have of digesting time.
W. H. Auden. Quoted Robert Craft, STRAVINSKY: THE CHRONICLE OF A FRIENDSHIP 1972

18 Music can be made anywhere, is invisible and doesn't smell.
W. H. Auden, IN PRAISE OF LIMESTONE 1941

19 I have played everywhere except in the street. I even played in pantomime at the old Surrey, and I don't regret a minute of it.
John Barbirolli, Observer 6 *Jul* 1947

20 Whether the angels play only Bach praising God I am not quite sure. I am sure however that *en famille* they play Mozart.
Karl Barth. Quoted New York Times *obituary* 11 *Dec* 1968

21 The search for a critical vocabulary in which we may speak of music by strict notations is quite absurd; not even the conventional notes and signs of a score can precisely denote the sounds that we hear.
Jacques Barzun, PLEASURES OF MUSIC 1951

1 All Bach's last movements are like the running of a sewing machine.
Arnold Bax. Quoted Basil Maine, Morning Post 21 *Aug* 1930

2 The English may not like music but they absolutely love the noise it makes.
Sir Thomas Beecham, A MINGLED CHIME 1944

3 Music *per se* means nothing; it is sheer sound and the interpreter can do no more with it than his own capacities, mental and spiritual will allow, and the same applies to the listener.
Id.

4 Music first and last should sound well, should allure and enchant the ear, never mind the inner significance.
Sir Thomas Beecham. Quoted Harold Atkins and Archie Newman, BEECHAM STORIES

5 Even Beethoven thumped the tub; the Ninth Symphony was composed by a sort of Mr. Gladstone of music.
Id.

6 Too much counterpoint — and what is worse, Protestant counterpoint.
Id. *(of Bach)*

7 What can you do with it? It's like a lot of yaks jumping about.
Id. *(of Beethoven's seventh symphony)*

8 If I were a dictator I should make it compulsory for every member of the population between the ages of four and eighty to listen to Mozart for at least a quarter of an hour daily for the coming five years.
Id.

9 In the first movement alone I took notice of six pregnancies and at least four miscarriages.
Id. *(of Bruckner's seventh symphony)*

10 Doctors of Music! That means they have sat on their bottoms for six hours and done a paper on harmony, but they can't play the National Anthem.
Id.

11 Forget about bars. Look at the phrases, please. Remember that bars are only the boxes in which music is packed.
Id.

12 Great music is that which penetrates the ear with facility and quits the memory with difficulty. Magical music never leaves the memory.
Sir Thomas Beecham. Quoted Lord Boothby, MY YESTERDAY, YOUR TOMORROW.

13 Brass bands are all very well in their place — outdoors and several miles away.
Sir Thomas Beecham. Quoted Michael Kennedy, Daily Telegraph 17 *Feb* 1979

14 There are only two things requisite so far as the public is concerned for a good performance. That is for the orchestra to begin together and end together. In between it doesn't matter much.
Sir Thomas Beecham. Quoted Nigel Rees, QUOTE UNQUOTE

15 A musicologist is a person who can read music but can't hear it.
Sir Thomas Beecham. Quoted Harold C. Schonberg, THE GREAT CONDUCTORS 1967

16 A man cannot make the viola agreeable to me. It is the only instrument which women can play supremely well.
Sir Thomas Beecham. Speech at the Savoy. Reported News Review 22 *Aug* 1946

17 *Clarionet, n.* An instrument of torture operated by a person with cotton in his ears. There are two instruments worse than a clarionet — two clarionets.
Ambrose Bierce, THE DEVIL'S DICTIONARY 1906

18 Your true music lover does more than admire the music — he sweats a little in her service.
Catherine Drinker Bowen, FRIENDS AND FIDDLERS 1935

19 Music does not exist until it is performed.
Benjamin Britten. Quoted Timothy Green, BENJAMIN BRITTEN'S WORLD OF MUSIC

20 Almost the only thing music can represent unambiguously is the cuckoo — and that it can't differentiate from a cuckoo clock.
Brigid Brophy, A LITERARY PERSON'S GUIDE TO OPERA 1965

21 Music is edifying, for from time to time it sets the soul in operation.
John Cage, FORERUNNER OF MODERN MUSIC 1949

22 Let no one imagine that in owning a recording he has the muse. The very practice of music is a celebration that we own nothing.
John Cage, SILENCE, *Lecture on Something* 1949

1 To make divine things human, and human things divine; such is Bach, the greatest and purest moment in music of all times.
Pablo Casals. Speech, Prades Bach Festival 1950

2 An oboe is an ill-wind that nobody blows good.
Bennett Cerf, LAUGHING STOCK 1952

3 Strange how potent cheap music is.
Noël Coward, PRIVATE LIVES 1930

4 The Detroit Quartet played Brahms last night. Brahms lost.
Anonymous critic. Quoted Bennett Cerf, TRY AND STOP ME 1943

5 When music sounds, gone is the earth I know. / And all her lovely things lovelier grow.
Walter De La Mare, FARE WELL

6 Music was invented to confirm human loneliness.
Lawrence Durrell, CLEA 1960

7 It is a curious thing that the performances which I have hated and loathed as being a caricature of my thoughts are the very ones held up as patterns.
Sir Edward Elgar. Quoted Basil Maine, ELGAR: HIS LIFE AND WORKS

8 The Third Symphony (of Brahms) is an example at the height of music because the work gives no clue to what it means. It is simply a piece of music.
Id.

9 I believed at this time that the only real composers were dead ones. I saw it as a sort of posthumous award.
Brian Ferneyhough, interviewed in the Observer 8 *Jun* 1978

10 Beethoven's Fifth Symphony is the most sublime noise that has ever penetrated into the ear of man.
E. M. Forster, HOWARDS END 1910

11 Please write music like Wagner, only louder.
Sam Goldwyn, instructing composer for a movie. Quoted Alva Johnson, THE GREAT GOLDWYN

12 This music won't do. There's not enough sarcasm in it.
Sam Goldwyn. Ibid.

13 Music means everything to me when I'm alone. And it's the best way of getting that bloody man Wilson out of my hair.
Edward Heath. Quoted James Margach, THE ABUSE OF POWER 1980

14 I occasionally play works by contemporary composers, and for two reasons. First, to discourage the composer from writing any more, and secondly to remind myself how much I appreciate Beethoven.
Jascha Heifetz, Life magazine 28 *Jul* 1961

15 Music is meaningless noise unless it touches a receiving mind.
Paul Hindemith, A COMPOSER'S WORLD 1961

16 People who make music together cannot be enemies, at least while the music lasts.
Id.

17 Never compose anything unless the not composing of it becomes a positive nuisance to you.
Gustav Holst. Quoted from a letter to W. G. Whittaker, N. Shapiro, ENCYCLOPEDIA OF QUOTATIONS ABOUT MUSIC

18 The public doesn't want new music; the main thing it demands of a composer is that he be dead.
Arthur Honegger. Quoted THE FRANK MUIR BOOK

19 Compare the music of 'the Beggar's Opera' with the music of a contemporary revue. They differ as life in the Garden of Eden differed from life in the artistic quarter of Gomorrah.
Aldous Huxley, ALONG THE ROAD

20 After silence, that which comes nearest to expressing the inexpressible is music.
Aldous Huxley, MUSIC AT NIGHT 1931

21 Humphrey Searle writes music that sounds like the theme from *Star Wars* played backwards through a washing machine.
Clive James, Observer, *The Sorry Serpent* 16 *Mar* 1979

22 All full-time writers, even if they can't tell a tonic solfa from a ton of sulphur should stay in touch with music if they can, if only to remind themselves that compared with musicians they are in a low state of training.
Clive James, Observer 8 *Mar* 1981

23 Of all musicians, flautists are obviously the ones who know something we don't know.
Paul Jennings, JENGUIN PENNINGS

24 Nothing is wrong when done to music.
Jerome Kern. Quoted Nat Shapiro, ENCYCLOPEDIA OF QUOTATIONS ABOUT MUSIC

MYTH

1 Contemporary man has rationalised the myths, but he has not been able to destroy them.
Octavio Paz, THE LABYRINTH OF SOLITUDE 1950

2 A myth is, of course, not a fairy story. It is the presentation of facts belonging to one category in the idioms appropriate to another.
Gilbert Ryle, THE CONCEPT OF MIND

N

NAME

1 The 't' is silent as in Harlow.
Margot Asquith, on her name being mispronounced by Jean Harlow

2 Mr. Ball? How very singular.
Sir Thomas Beecham

3 Don't take action because of a name. A name is an uncertain thing. You can't count on it.
Bertolt Brecht, A MAN'S A MAN 1927

4 Going to call him 'William'? What kind of a name is that? Every Tom, Dick and Harry is called William. Why not call him Bill?
Sam Goldwyn. Quoted Bennett Cerf

5 A self-made man may prefer a self-made name.
Judge Learned Hand, when Samuel Goldwyn changed his name from Goldfish

6 I [Lorelei Lee] was named after a girl who became famous for sitting on a rock in Germany.
Anita Loos, GENTLEMEN PREFER BLONDES 1925

7 The name of a man is a numbing blow from which he never recovers.
Marshall McLuhan, UNDERSTANDING MEDIA 1967

8 Groucho is not my real name. I'm breaking it in for a friend.
Groucho Marx

9 Each planet, each plant, each butterfly, each moth, each beetle, becomes doubly real to you when you know its name. Lucky indeed are those who from their earliest childhood have heard all these things named.
John Cowper Powys, THE MEANING OF CULTURE 1930

10 The medieval saints would scarcely have been pleased if they could have foreseen that their names would be associated nowadays chiefly with racehorses and the cheaper clarets.
Saki, REGINALD AT THE CARLTON 1904

NARROW-MINDEDNESS

11 It is better to be narrow-minded than to have no mind at all, to hold limited and rigid principles than none at all.
Evelyn Waugh, A LITTLE ORDER

NATIONALISM

12 Nationalism is an infantile disease. It is the measles of mankind.
Albert Einstein. Quoted Edwin Muller, EINSTEIN: A STUDY IN SIMPLICITY

NATURE

13 It is an outcome of faith that nature — as she is perceptible to our five senses — takes the character of such a well formulated puzzle.
Albert Einstein, OUT OF MY LATER YEARS 1950

14 How nature loves the incomplete. She knows / If she drew a conclusion it would finish her.
Christopher Fry, VENUS OBSERVED 1950

15 The whole of nature is a conjugation of the verb to eat, in the active and the passive.
W. R. Inge (Dean of St. Pauls), OUTSPOKEN ESSAYS 1919

16 We need for our happiness to feel ourselves part of Nature, as Wordsworth did, although few of us can share his belief that its workings are moral.
Raymond Mortimer, LANDSCAPE

17 A vacuum is a hell of a lot better than some of the stuff that nature replaces it with.
Tennessee Williams, CAT ON A HOT TIN ROOF 1955

NAVY

18 We joined the Navy, to see the world / And what did we see? We saw the sea.
Irving Berlin (song)

19 Don't talk to me of naval tradition. It is all rum, sodomy and the lash.
Winston Churchill, in 1911

NEGRO

1 Only in the case of the Negro has the melting pot failed to bring a minority into the mainstream of American life.
John F. Kennedy, A NATION OF IMMIGRANTS 1958

2 Never forget that two blacks do not make a white.
George Bernard Shaw, THE ADVENTURES OF THE BLACK GIRL IN HER SEARCH FOR GOD

NEIGHBOUR

3 Do not love your neighbour as yourself. If you are on good terms with yourself it is an impertinence; if on bad, an injury.
George Bernard Shaw, MAN AND SUPERMAN 1905

NEUROSIS

4 Modern neurosis began with the discoveries of Copernicus. Science made man feel small by showing him the earth was not at the centre of the universe.
Mary McCarthy, ON THE CONTRARY 1961

5 Neurosis is the way of avoiding non-being by avoiding being.
Paul Tillich, THE COURAGE TO BE 1952

NEUTRALITY

6 The expression 'positive neutrality' is a contradiction in terms. There can be no more positive neutrality than there can be a vegetarian tiger.
V. K. Krishna Menon, New York Times 18 Oct 1960

NEWS

7 I want news of peace. Get me some news of peace.
Lord Beaverbrook, on the eve of the outbreak of World War II. *Quoted Jonah Barrington*, MASTER OF NONE

8 When a dog bites a man that's not news. If a man bites a dog, that's news.
John B. Bogart. Quoted Frank M. O'Brien, THE STORY OF THE NEW YORK SUN

9 Nothing is news until it has appeared in *The Times*.
Ralph Deakin, Foreign News Editor of The Times. *Quoted Claud Cockburn*, COCKBURN SUMS UP

10 News is what a chap who doesn't care much about anything wants to read. And it's only news until he has read it. After that it's dead.
Evelyn Waugh, SCOOP 1938

NEWSPAPER

11 Have you noticed that life, real honest to goodness life, with murders and catastrophes and fabulous inheritances, happens almost exclusively in newspapers?
Jean Anouilh, THE REHEARSAL 1950

12 The occupational disease among newspaper proprietors is megalomania.
Michael Foot, DEBTS OF HONOUR, *The Case for Beelzebub* 1982

13 A good newspaper, I suppose, is a nation talking to itself.
Arthur Miller, Observer 26 *Nov* 1961

14 Produced by office boys for office boys.
Marquis of Salisbury, of the Daily Mail

15 A newspaper, not having to act on its descriptions and reports, but only to sell them to idly curious people, has nothing but honour to lose by inaccuracy and unveracity.
George Bernard Shaw, A DOCTOR'S DILEMMA 1900

16 They were not so much published as carried screaming into the street.
H. G. Wells, WAR IN THE AIR

NEW YORK

17 When an American stays away from New York too long something happens to him. Perhaps he becomes a little provincial, a little dead and afraid.
Sherwood Anderson, LETTERS 1953

18 New York, the hussy, was taken in sin again.
Thomas Beer, THE MAUVE DECADE 1926

19 Long Island represents the American's idea of what God would have done with Nature if he'd had the money.
Peter Fleming in a letter to his brother Rupert 29 *Sep* 1929

20 New York is, after all, a place of business; it is not constructed to be lived in.
(Percy) Wyndham Lewis, AMERICA AND COSMIC MAN

1 New York has a trip-hammer vitality which drives you insane with restlessness, if you have no inner stabiliser.
Henry Miller, THE COLOSSUS OF MAROUSSI 1941

2 I miss the animal buoyancy of New York, the animal vitality. I did not mind that it had no meaning and no depth.
Anaïs Nin, DIARIES VOL 2 1967

3 New York is like a disco, but without the music.
Elaine Stritch. Quoted Observer 17 *Feb* 1980

4 When I leave it I never dare look back lest I turn into a pillar of salt and the conductor throw me over his left shoulder for good luck.
Frank Sullivan

5 New York's a small place when it comes to the part of it that wakes up just as the rest is going to bed.
P. G. Wodehouse, THE AUNT AND THE SLUGGARD

6 One belongs to New York instantly. One belongs to it as much in five minutes as in five years.
Thomas Wolfe, THE WEB AND THE ROCK 1939

NIGHT

7 The teller, Night, through cloudy bars / Into his sack with fingers cold / Counts his scanty change of stars.
Roy Campbell, IN THE TOWN SQUARE

8 Midnight shakes the memory / As a madman shakes a dead geranium.
T. S. Eliot, RHAPSODY ON A WINDY NIGHT

9 In the country the darkness of night is friendly and familiar, but in a city, with its blaze of lights, it is unnatural, hostile and menacing. It is like a monstrous vulture that hovers, biding its time.
W. Somerset Maugham, A WRITER'S NOTEBOOK 1949

10 It is spring, moonless night in the small town, starless and bible-black.
Dylan Thomas, UNDER MILK WOOD 1954

11 It is tonight in Donkey Street, trotting silent, with seaweed on its hooves, along the cockled cobbles, past curtained fernpot, text and trinket, harmonium, holy dresser, watercolours done by hand, china dog and rosy tin teacaddy. It is night neddying among the snuggeries of babies.
Id.

12 The lamps of London uphold the dark as upon the points of a bayonet.
Virginia Woolf, JACOB'S ROOM 1922

NIGHTINGALE

13 The nightingales are singing near / The Convent of the Sacred Heart / And sang within the bloody wood / When Agamemnon cried aloud.
T. S. Eliot, SWEENEY AMONG THE NIGHTINGALES 1920

RICHARD M. NIXON

14 President Nixon's motto was, if two wrongs don't make a right, try three.
Norman Cousins. Quoted Christie Davies, Daily Telegraph 17 *Jul* 1979

15 Nixon is the kind of politician who would cut down a redwood tree, then mount the stump for a conservation speech.
Adlai Stevenson. Quoted Leon Harris, THE FINE ART OF POLITICAL WIT

NOBILITY

16 Godolphin Horne was nobly born: / He held the human race in scorn.
Hilaire Belloc, CAUTIONARY TALES 1901

17 Real nobility is based on scorn, courage, and profound indifference.
Albert Camus, NOTEBOOKS 1935–1942

NOISE

18 Many youngsters are now so accustomed to noise that a quiet room seems sinister and they have to bring a radio or gramophone in.
J. B. Priestley, THOUGHTS IN THE WILDERNESS

NONSENSE

19 It is a far, far better thing to have a firm anchor in nonsense than to put out on troubled seas of thought.
J. K. Galbraith, THE AFFLUENT SOCIETY 1958

20 Even God has been defended with nonsense.
Walter Lippmann, A PREFACE TO POLITICS, *The Golden Rule and After* 1914

LORD NORTHCLIFFE

1 Have you heard? The Prime Minister has resigned and Northcliffe has sent for the King.
A member of Northcliffe's staff. Quoted Hamilton Fyfe, NORTHCLIFFE, AN INTIMATE BIOGRAPHY

2 He aspired to power instead of influence and as a result forfeited both.
A. J. P. Taylor, ENGLISH HISTORY 1914–1945

NOSE

3 Where you get that nose from, Lily? / Got it from my father, silly. / You've got it on upside down! / Oh there's a conk!
Dylan Thomas, UNDER MILK WOOD 1954

NOSTALGIA

4 Nostalgia is like a grammar lesson. You find the present tense and the past perfect.
Anon. New Venture, *Jun* 1981

5 Were we closer to the ground as children, or is the grass emptier now?
Alan Bennett, FORTY YEARS ON

6 Nothing recalls the past so potently as a smell.
Winston Churchill, MY EARLY LIFE 1930

7 Despair abroad can always nurse pleasant thoughts of home.
Christopher Fry, A PHOENIX TOO FREQUENT 1949

8 . . . the glamour / Of childish days is upon me, my manhood is cast / Down in the flood of remembrance, I weep like a child for the past.
D. H. Lawrence, PIANO

9 They spend their time mostly looking forward to the past.
John Osborne, LOOK BACK IN ANGER 1956

10 The earth's about five thousand million years old. Who can afford to live in the past?
Harold Pinter, THE HOMECOMING 1965

NUDITY

11 We cannot return to Eden by the simple expedient of removing our clothes.
Paul Ableman, ANATOMY OF NAKEDNESS

12 What can you give a nudist on his birthday?
Gracie Fields (song title)

13 If we had been meant to go naked there wouldn't be any fig trees.
A speaker on Newstalk BBC 4 *26 May* 1979

14 Nudism is a lot of fuss about nothing.
Piccolo Pete, Pictorial Weekly *3 Sep* 1932

15 As naked as an ash tree in the moon of May.
J. M. Synge, THE PLAYBOY OF THE WESTERN WORLD 1907

16 Modesty is a very odd, subtle thing. Someone, I forget whom, said it is all a matter of beauty. If we were all perfect we should not mind walking about with no clothes at all.
Marie Tempest, letter to The Times *5 Jan* 1935

17 Many people may be depressed by the spectacle of naked humanity. Personally I can't see that an ugly body is any more offensive than an ugly dress.
Evelyn Waugh, Daily Mail *5 Jul 1930*

NUN

18 Monica Baldwin's book 'I leapt over the wall' strengthened my desire not to become a nun.
Noël Coward, DIARIES

O

OBEDIENCE

1 The Englishman walks before the law like a
trained circus-horse. He has the sense of
legality in his bones, in his muscles.
Maxim Gorky, ENEMIES

OBESITY

2 Never get fat, dear child. Fat smothers
anyone's vitality.
Margot Asquith to Anita Loos. Quoted KISS
HOLLYWOOD GOOD-BYE

3 I had to face the facts, I was pear-shaped. I
was a bit depressed because I hate pears.
Charlotte Bingham, CORONET AMONG THE
WEEDS

4 I look like an elderly wasp in an interesting
condition.
Mrs. Pat Campbell. Quoted Alan Dent,
MRS. PATRICK CAMPBELL

5 Obesity is a mental state, a disease brought
on by boredom and disappointment.
Cyril Connolly, THE UNQUIET GRAVE 1945

6 I may be seen any day struggling up Fleet
Street in my worsted bonds like a cocktail
sausage with hernia, in a hail of lethal
buttons that would do credit to a New
Orleans cop.
Alan Coren, THE SANITY INSPECTOR 1974

7 That dark day when a man decides he must
wear his belt under instead of over his
cascading paunch.
Peter De Vries, CONSENTING ADULTS

8 She fitted into my largest armchair as if it
had been built round her by someone who
knew they were wearing armchairs tight
round the hips this season.
P. G. Wodehouse, JEEVES AND THE UN-
BIDDEN GUEST

OBITUARY

9 She [Margot Asquith] had a great taste for
writing obituaries and rarely missed an
opportunity of doing so. Once when she

was staying with Arthur Balfour he was
surprised to find, written in Margot's hand
on a sheet of paper, an unfinished opening:
"So Arthur Balfour is dead–"
*Mark Bonham Carter, Introduction, Mar-
got Asquith's* AUTOBIOGRAPHY 1936

OBSCENITY

10 More to the point, would you allow your
gamekeeper to read it?
*Anon. Of Mervyn Griffiths Jones' remark
during the Lady Chatterley trial*

11 A vocabulary that would take the feathers
off a hoody crow.
Lillian Beckwith, LIGHTLY POACHED

12 Obscenity is such a tiny kingdom that a
single tour covers it completely.
Heywood Brown. Quoted Bennett Cerf,
SHAKE WELL BEFORE USING 1948

13 I do not claim to be a literary critic, but I
know dirt when I smell it and here it is in
heaps — festering putrid heaps which smell
to high heaven.
W. Charles Pilley, John Bull, *review of*
WOMEN IN LOVE 17 *Sep* 1921

14 Obscenity is whatever happens to shock
some elderly and ignorant magistrate.
Bertrand Russell, Look magazine 23 *Feb*
1934

15 Obscenity can be found in every book
except the telephone directory.
George Bernard Shaw

OBSCURITY

16 I am afraid of losing my obscurity.
Genuineness only thrives in the dark. Like
celery.
Aldous Huxley, THOSE BARREN
LEAVES 1925

17 I'm never going to be famous. My name
will never be writ large on the roster of
Those Who Do Things. I don't do anything. Not a single thing. I used to bite my
nails, but I don't even do that now.
Dorothy Parker, THE LITTLE HOURS

OBVIOUSNESS

1 I deal with the obvious. I present, reiterate and glorify the obvious — because the obvious is what people need to be told.
Dale Carnegie. Speech, New York Luncheon Club

2 Never be afraid of the deafeningly obvious. It is always news to somebody.
P. J. Kavanagh, A SONG AND DANCE

3 It requires a very unusual mind to undertake the analysis of the obvious.
A. N. Whitehead. SCIENCE AND THE MODERN WORLD 1925

OLD AGE

4 Nobody hears old people complain because people think that's all old people do. And that's because old people are gnarled and sagged and twisted into the shape of a complaint.
Edward Albee, THE AMERICAN DREAM 1960

5 An old man looks permanent, as if he had been born an old man.
H. E. Bates, DEATH IN SPRING

6 Tidy the old into tall flats. Desolation at fourteen storeys becomes a view.
Alan Bennett, FORTY YEARS ON

7 While everything else physical and mental seems to diminish, the appreciation of beauty is on the increase. Landscapes, animals, men, women and children and all man-made things fascinate, delight and evoke my critical sense more and more.
Bernard Berenson (aged 85), SUNSET AND TWILIGHT 1960

8 Now all the world she knew is dead / In this small room she lives her days./ The wash-hand stand and single bed / Screened from the public gaze.
Sir John Betjeman, A FEW LATE CHRYSANTHEMUMS, *House of Rest*

9 Old age is . . . a lot of crossed off names in an address book.
Ronald Blythe, THE VIEW IN WINTER 1980

10 To be old is to be part of a huge and ordinary multitude . . . the reason why old age was venerated in the past was because it was extraordinary.
Id.

11 The robe of flesh wears thin, and with the years God shines through all things.
John Buchan, THE WISE YEARS

12 I smoke 10 to 15 cigars a day, at my age I have to hold on to something.
Comedian George Burns at 84

13 It is the misfortune of an old man that though he can put things out of his head he can't put them out of his feelings.
Joyce Cary, TO BE A PILGRIM 1942

14 Old age is the out-patients' department of purgatory.
Lord Hugh Cecil. Quoted David Cecil, THE CECILS OF HATFIELD HOUSE

15 Oh to be seventy again.
Georges Clemençeau on passing a pretty girl on the Champs Elysées on his eightieth birthday. Quoted James Agate, Ego 3, 19 *Apr* 1938

16 When Winston Churchill became Prime Minister he was over sixty-five years old, already qualified for an old age pension.
John Colville, THE CHURCHILLIANS

17 The dusky p.m. of our common existence.
Leon Edel, HENRY JAMES, THE MASTER 1901–1906

18 An old man in a dry month.
T. S. Eliot, GERONTION

19 Simply because I have no seniors / The literati will raise the cry / Ewart's a genius.
Gavin Ewart, THE COLLECTED EWART

20 It is not becoming to lay to virtue the weariness of old age.
André Gide, JOURNALS 25 *Jul* 1934

21 The first sign of his approaching end was when my old aunts, while undressing him, removed a toe with one of his socks.
Graham Greene, TRAVELS WITH MY AUNT 1969

22 With the approach of death I care less and less about religious truth. One hasn't long to wait for revelation and darkness.
Graham Greene, A SORT OF LIFE

23 For the ageing person it is a duty and a necessity to give serious attention to himself.
Carl Jung, MODERN MAN IN SEARCH OF A SOUL 1933

24 The afternoon of a human life must have a significance of its own, and cannot be merely a pitiful appendage to life's morning.
Carl Jung, PSYCHOLOGICAL REFLECTIONS 1953

1 The ultimate indignity is to be given a bedpan by a stranger who calls you by your first name.
Maggie Kuhn, Observer 20 *Aug* 1978

2 Presently, I shall be introduced as "this venerable old gentleman" and the axe will fall when they raise me to the degree of "grand old man". This means on our continent anyone with snow-white hair who has kept out of jail till eighty.
Stephen Leacock, THREE SCORE AND TEN

3 Will you still need me / Will you still feed me / When I'm sixty-four?
John Lennon and Paul McCartney, WHEN I'M SIXTY-FOUR *(song)*

4 You are beautiful and faded / Like an old opera tune / Played upon a harpsichord.
Amy Lowell, A LADY

5 They don't let me attend the board, but they allow me to come to lunch sometimes.
Harold Macmillan, at 85, *in a speech at Merton College, referring to his position as president of the firm*

6 Old Mr. Neave felt that he was too old for spring.
Katherine Mansfield, THE GARDEN PARTY 1922

7 When you have loved as she has loved you grow old beautifully.
W. Somerset Maugham, THE CIRCLE 1921

8 Growing old is a bad habit which a busy man has no time to form.
André Maurois, THE AGEING AMERICAN

9 A ready means of being cherished by the English is to adopt the simple expedient of living a long time. I have little doubt that if, say, Oscar Wilde had lived into his nineties, instead of dying in his forties, he would have been considered a benign, distinguished figure suitable to preside at a school prize-giving or to instruct and exhort scoutmasters at their jamborees. He might even have been knighted.
Malcolm Muggeridge, TREAD SOFTLY FOR YOU TREAD ON MY JOKES 1966

10 When one has reached 81 one likes to sit back and let the world turn by itself, without trying to push it.
Sean O'Casey, New York Times 25 *Sep* 1960

11 When you get to our age they miss out every other day.
Overheard. Quoted BBC Radio 4, *Quote Unquote* 28 *Oct* 1979

12 I'll dispose of my teeth as I think fit and after they've gone I'll get along. I started off living on gruel, and by God, I can always go back to it again.
S. J. Perelman, CRAZY LIKE A FOX 1944

13 One starts to get young at the age of sixty and then it is too late.
Pablo Picasso to Jean Cocteau. Quoted Derek Prouse, Sunday Times 20 *Oct* 1963

14 Growing old is like being increasingly penalised for a crime you haven't committed.
Anthony Powell, TEMPORARY KINGS

15 Old men are dangerous; it doesn't matter to them what is going to happen to the world.
George Bernard Shaw, HEARTBREAK HOUSE 1920

16 The greatest problem about old age is the fear that it may go on too long.
A. J. P. Taylor, Observer, *Sayings of the Week* 1 *Nov* 1981

17 Old age should burn and rave at close of day; / Rage, rage against the dying of the light.
Dylan Thomas, DO NOT GO GENTLE INTO THAT GOOD NIGHT 1952

18 Old age is the most unexpected of all things to happen to a man.
Leon Trotsky, DIARY IN EXILE

19 It is a terrible thing for an old woman to outlive her dogs.
Tennessee Williams, CAMINO REAL 1953

20 Your well beloved's hair has threads of grey / And little shadows come about her eyes.
W. B. Yeats, THE FOLLY OF BEING COMFORTED 1904

21 An aged man is but a paltry thing / A tattered coat upon a stick, unless / Soul clap its hands and sing.
W. B. Yeats, SAILING TO BYZANTIUM 1928

22 I pray — for fashion's word is out / And prayer comes round again — / That I may seem, though I die old, / A foolish passionate man.
W. B. Yeats, A PRAYER FOR OLD AGE

23 Withered old and skeleton-gaunt.
W. B. Yeats

OPERA

1 Opera is like a husband with a foreign title: expensive to support, hard to understand, and therefore a supreme social challenge.
Cleveland Amory, NBC TV 6 *Apr* 1960

2 I do not mind what language an opera is sung in so long as it is a language I do not understand.
Sir Edward Appleton. Quoted Observer 28 *Jul* 1955

3 No good opera plot can be sensible, for people do not sing when they are feeling sensible.
W. H. Auden, Time 29 *Dec* 1961

4 Wagner has done undeniably good work in humbling the singer.
Max Beerbohm. Quoted, THE FRANK MUIR BOOK

5 Opera has no business making money.
Sir Rudolf Bing, New York Times 15 *Nov* 1959

6 The absurdity of opera lies in the fact that rational elements are used and three-dimensional reality is aimed at while at the same time everything is neutralised by the music.
Berthold Brecht, THE MODERN THEATRE IS THE EPIC THEATRE 1930

7 Opera, next to Gothic architecture, is one of the strangest inventions of modern man. It could not have been foreseen by any logical process.
Kenneth, Lord Clark, CIVILISATION 1969

8 People are wrong when they say the opera isn't what it used to be. It is what it used to be. That's what's wrong with it.
Noël Coward, DESIGN FOR LIVING 1933

9 Blanche: (genially) I think we've slept together once.
Adrian: I don't remember.
Blanche: At the opera, during *Bérénice.*
Ronald Firbank, THE PRINCESS ZOUBAROFF

10 Nobody really sings in opera. They just make loud noises.
Amelia Galli-Curci. Quoted, THE FRANK MUIR BOOK

11 Opera is when a guy gets stabbed in the back and instead of bleeding he sings.
Ed Gardener on American radio show, Duffy's Tavern

12 God in his Almighty Wisdom and Fairness has not always given the greatest voices to the persons with the greatest intellect or the best education, or to the most beautiful of His Creatures.
Tyrone Guthrie, A LIFE IN THE THEATRE

13 Opera is like an oyster. It must be swallowed whole or not at all.
Spike Hughes and Barbara McFadgen, NIGHTS AT THE OPERA 1948

14 Opera in English is, in the main, just about as sensible as baseball in Italian.
H. L. Mencken. Quoted, THE FRANK MUIR BOOK

15 The opera is to music what a bawdy house is to a castle.
H. L. Mencken, letter to Isaac Goldberg 6 *May* 1925

16 Any subject is good for opera if the composer feels it so intensely that he must sing it out.
Gian-Carlo Menotti, Time 1 *May* 1950

17 Bel canto is to opera what pole vaulting is to ballet, the glorification of a performer's prowess and not a creator's imagination.
Ned Rorem, The New Republic 3 *Jun* 1972

18 His vocal cords were kissed by God.
Harold Schoenberg, of Luciano Pavarotti. Quoted John Heilpern, The Times 30 *Jun* 1981

19 Tenors are noble, pure and heroic and get the soprano. But baritones are born villains in opera. Always the heavy and never the hero.
Leonard Warren, New York World Telegram and Sun 13 *Feb* 1957

OPINION

20 A man's opinion on tramcars matters; his opinion on Botticelli matters; his opinion on all things does not matter.
G. K. Chesterton, HERETICS 1905

21 I suggest we worry less about the opinion that annoys, and more about those that remain unspoken.
William Hardcastle, Punch 12 *Jan* 1972

22 Opinions cannot survive if one has no chance to fight for them.
Thomas Mann, THE MAGIC MOUNTAIN 1924

23 It's not that I don't have opinions, rather that I'm paid not to think aloud.
President Yitzhak Navon of Israel. Quoted Observer, *Sayings of the Week* 9 *Jan* 1983

1 Refusing to have an opinion is a way of having one, isn't it?
Luigi Pirandello, EACH IN HIS OWN WAY

2 The average man's opinions are much less foolish than they would be if he thought for himself.
Bertrand Russell, AUTOBIOGRAPHY 1967

3 The fact that an opinion has been widely held is no evidence whatever that it is not utterly absurd.
Bertrand Russell, MARRIAGE AND MORALS 1929

4 It is difficult, if not impossible for most people to think otherwise than in the fashion of their own opinion.
George Bernard Shaw, SAINT JOAN, *Preface* 1927

5 The danger which faces so many people is to have no considered opinions on any subject . . . in most cases means an inability to distinguish between good and bad. There are still things which are worth fighting *against*.
Evelyn Waugh, A LITTLE ORDER

6 It is just when opinions universally prevail and we have added lip service to their authority that we become sometimes most keenly conscious that we do not believe a word that we are saying.
Virginia Woolf, THE COMMON READER 1925

7 People are responsible for their opinions but Providence is responsible for their morals.
W. B. Yeats. Quoted Christopher Hassall, EDWARD MARSH

OPPONENT

8 I respect only those who resist me; but I cannot tolerate them.
Gen. Charles de Gaulle. Quoted New York Times magazine 12 *May* 1966

OPPORTUNISM

9 The time to repair the roof is when the sun is shining.
John F. Kennedy, State of Union Message 11 *Jan* 1962

10 Just enjoy your ice-cream while it's on your plate — that's my philosophy.
Thornton Wilder, THE SKIN OF OUR TEETH 1942

OPPORTUNITY

11 Opportunities are usually disguised as hard work, so most people don't recognise them.
Ann Landers. Quoted Barbara Rowe, A BOOK OF QUOTES

12 One can present people with opportunities. One cannot make them equal to them.
Rosamond Lehmann, THE BALLAD AND THE SOURCE 1945

13 There is no security in this life. There is only opportunity.
Gen. Douglas MacArthur. Quoted Courtney Whitney, MACARTHUR, HIS RENDEZVOUS WITH HISTORY

14 Equality of opportunity means equal opportunity to be unequal.
Iain MacLeod. Quoted John Boyd Carpenter, WAY OF LIFE

15 Grab a chance and you won't be sorry for a might have been.
Arthur Ransome, WE DIDN'T MEAN TO GO TO SEA

OPPOSITION

16 One fifth of the people are against everything all the time.
Robert Kennedy. Quoted Punch 16 *Feb* 1972

OPTIMISM

17 The essence of optimism is that it takes no account of the present but it is a source of inspiration, of vitality and hope when others have resigned; it enables a man to hold his head high to claim the future for himself and not to abandon it to his enemy.
Dietrich Bonhoeffer, LETTERS AND PAPERS FROM PRISON, *After Ten Years*

18 The pessimist is the man who believes things couldn't possibly be worse, to which the optimist replies "Oh yes they could."
Vladimir Bukovsky, Guardian Weekly 10 *Jul* 1977

19 The optimist proclaims that we live in the best of all possible worlds; the pessimist fears that this is true.
J. B. Cabell, THE SILVER STALLION 1926

20 The place where optimism most flourishes is the lunatic asylum.
Havelock Ellis, THE DANCE OF LIFE 1923

21 Optimism is the content of small men in high places.
F. Scott Fitzgerald, THE CRACK-UP 1936

1 Optimism is a kind of heart stimulus — the digitalis of failure.
Elbert Hubbard, A THOUSAND AND ONE EPIGRAMS 1927

2 An optimist is a guy that never had much experience.
Don Marquis, ARCHY AND MEHITABEL 1926

3 I'm an optimist, but I'm an optimist who carries a raincoat.
Sir Harold Wilson. Quoted Nigel Rees, QUOTE UNQUOTE

ORATORIO

4 If I had the power I would insist on all oratorios being sung in the costume of the period — with a possible exception in the case of the *Creation*.
Sir Ernest Newman, New York Post 1924

ORATORY

5 In private conversation he tries on speeches like a man trying on ties in his bedroom to see how he would look in them.
Lionel Curtis of Winston Churchill in a letter to Nancy Astor 1912

6 The finest eloquence is that which gets things done; the worst is that which delays them.
David Lloyd George. Speech, Paris Peace Conference, Jan 1919

7 His speeches leave the impression of an army of pompous phrases moving over the landscape in search of an idea.
Senator William McAdoo. Quoted Leon Harris, THE FINE ART OF POLITICAL WIT

8 Oratory is just like prostitution; you must have little tricks.
Vittorio Emanuele Orlando, Time 8 *Dec* 1952

ORCHESTRA

9 You know why conductors live so long? Because we perspire so much.
Sir John Barbirolli. Quoted Nat Shapiro, ENCYCLOPEDIA OF QUOTATIONS ABOUT MUSIC

10 For a fine performance only two things are absolutely necessary; the maximum of virility coupled with the maximum of delicacy.
Sir Thomas Beecham. Quoted Humphrey Proctor-Gregg, BEECHAM REMEMBERED

11 We do not expect you to follow us all the time, but if you would have the goodness to keep in touch with us occasionally . . .
Sir Thomas Beecham. Quoted Harold C. Schonberg, THE GREAT CONDUCTORS 1967

12 I am not the greatest conductor in this country. On the other hand I am better than any damned foreigner.
Sir Thomas Beecham. Quoted Noël Goodwick, Daily Express 9 *Mar* 1961

13 Having an exaggerated sense of chivalry I am not over-fond of women in my orchestras because I find it embarassing to rebuke them.
Sir Thomas Beecham. Speech, the Savoy, on the re-forming of the Royal Philharmonic Orchestra, Aug 1948

14 The conductor has the advantage of not seeing the audience.
André Kostelanitz. Quoted Nat Shapiro, ENCYCLOPEDIA OF QUOTATIONS ABOUT MUSIC

15 A conductor should reconcile himself to the realisation that regardless of his approach or temperament the eventual result is the same. The orchestra will hate him.
Oscar Levant, A SMATTERING OF IGNORANCE 1940

16 Show me an orchestra that likes its conductor and I'll show you a lousy orchestra.
Goddard Lieberson. Quoted Hubert Kupferberg, THOSE FABULOUS PHILADELPHIANS 1969

17 I just don't think women should be in an orchestra. They become men. Men treat them as equals; they even change their pants in front of them. I think it is terrible.
Zubin Mehta, New York Times 18 *Oct* 1970

18 I never use a score when conducting my orchestra . . . Does a lion tamer enter a cage with a book on how to tame a lion?
Dimitri Mitropoulos. Quoted Nat Shapiro, ENCYCLOPEDIA OF QUOTATIONS ABOUT MUSIC

ORGY

19 An orgy looks particularly alluring when seen through the mists of righteous indignation.
Malcolm Muggeridge, TREAD SOFTLY FOR YOU TREAD ON MY JOKES 1966

1 Home is heaven and orgies are vile / But you need an orgy once in a while.
Ogden Nash, HOME 99.44/100% SWEET HOME

OXFORD

2 Not that I had any special reason for hating school. Strange as it may seem to my readers, I was not unpopular there. I was a modest, good-humoured boy. It is Oxford that has made me insufferable.
Max Beerbohm, GOING BACK TO SCHOOL

3 Americans have a perfect right to exist. But he did often find himself wishing Mr. Rhodes had not enabled them to exercise that right at Oxford.
Max Beerbohm, ZULEIKA DOBSON 1911

4 Balliol made me, Balliol fed me / Whatever I had she gave me again / And the best of Balliol loved and led me / God be with you, Balliol men.
Hilaire Belloc, TO THE BALLIOL MEN STILL IN AFRICA

5 There are few greater temptations on earth than to stay permanently in Oxford and read all the books in the Bodleian.
Hilaire Belloc. Quoted Robert Speaight, LIFE OF HILAIRE BELLOC 1957

6 Christchurch undergraduates give the impression of having dropped in at Oxford on their way to a seat in the House of Lords.
Sir John Betjeman, MY OXFORD

7 Noon strikes in England, noon on Oxford town / Beauty she was statue cold — there's blood upon her gown / Noon of my dreams, O noon! / Proud and godly kings had built her long ago / With her towers and tombs and statues all around / With her fair and floral air, and the love that lingers there / And the streets where the dead men go.
James Elroy Flecker, THE DYING PATRIOT

8 The clever men at Oxford / Know all that there is to be knowed / But the none of them know one half as much / As intelligent Mr. Toad.
Kenneth Grahame, WIND IN THE WILLOWS 1908

9 Oxford at least taught men to drink pint by pint with any man.
Graham Greene, A SORT OF LIFE

10 Cambridge sees Oxford as the Latin quarter of Cowley.
Marjorie Knight, letter to Daily Telegraph 15 *Aug* 1979

11 We think of Cambridge as a little town and Oxford as a hive of industry, but they aren't that different.
Katherine Whitehorn, Observer 14 *Jan* 1979

P

PACIFISM

1 My pacifism is not based on any intellectual theory but on a deep antipathy to every form of cruelty and hatred.
Albert Einstein on outbreak of 1914 *war*

PAIN

2 People will not readily bear pain unless there is hope.
Sir Michael Edwardes. Speech 2 Jul 1980

3 As painful as a grapestone under a dental plate.
George Orwell. Quoted from his notebooks by Bernard Crick, GEORGE ORWELL: A LIFE

PAINTING

4 *Painting, n.* The art of protecting flat surfaces from the weather and exposing them to the critic.
Ambrose Bierce, THE DEVIL'S DICTIONARY 1906

5 Once an object has been incorporated in a picture it accepts a new destiny.
Georges Braque. Quoted in his obituary The Times 21 *Sep* 1963

6 One needs a certain time to realise that the faces in the Italian primitives are those one meets daily on the streets. We have lost the habit of seeing what is really important in a face.
Albert Camus, NOTEBOOKS 1935–1942

7 The day is coming when a single carrot, freshly observed, will set off a revolution.
Paul Cézanne. Quoted Joachim Gasquet, PAUL CÉZANNE

8 Treat nature in terms of the cylinder, the sphere, the cone, all in perspective.
Paul Cézanne. Quoted Emile Bernard, PAUL CÉZANNE

9 The famous soft watches are nothing else than the tender, extravagant, solitary paranoiac-critical camembert of time and space.
Salvador Dali, CONQUEST OF THE IRRATIONAL

10 I do not paint a portrait to look like the subject, rather does the person grow to look like his portrait.
Salvador Dali. Quoted Evàn Esar, TREASURY OF HUMOROUS QUOTATIONS

11 The big artist does not sit down monkey-like and copy a coal scuttle or an ugly woman like some Dutch painters have done, nor a dung pile but he keeps a sharp eye on Nature and steals her roots.
Thomas Eakins. Quoted Gordon Hendricks, THE LIFE AND WORK OF THOMAS EAKINS

12 Never put more than two waves in a picture; it's fussy.
Winslow Homer. Quoted Lloyd Goodrich, WINSLOW HOMER

13 Every good painter invents a new way of painting.
Aldous Huxley, COLLECTED ESSAYS 1960

14 A seventeenth-century painting can be 'modern' because the living eye finds it fresh and new. A 'modern' painting can be outdated because it was a product of the moment and not of time.
Marya Mannes, MORE IN ANGER 1954

15 I try to apply colours like words that shape poems, like notes that shape music.
Joan Miró. Quoted John Gruen, CLOSE-UP

16 Everyone wants to understand painting. Why don't they try to understand the singing of birds? People love the night, a flower, everything which surrounds them without trying to understand them. But painting — that they *must* understand.
Pablo Picasso. Quoted Gerald Brenan, THOUGHTS IN A DRY SEASON 1979

1 I paint objects as I think them, not as I see them.
Pablo Picasso. Quoted John Golding, CUBISM

2 "How can you remember which paintings are yours?"
"If I like it, I say it's mine. If I don't I say it's a fake."
Pablo Picasso. Quoted Sunday Times 10 *Oct 1965*

3 Abstract painting is abstract. It confronts you. There was a reviewer a while back who wrote that my pictures didn't have any beginning or any end. He didn't mean it as a compliment but it was. It was a fine compliment.
Jackson Pollock. Quoted Francis V. O'Connor, JACKSON POLLOCK

4 A painter is not intellectual when, having painted a nude woman, he leaves in our minds the idea that she is going to get dressed again right away.
Odilon Rédon. Quoted R. Goldwater and M. Treves, ARTISTS ON ART

5 In a few generations you can breed a racehorse. The recipe for making a man like Delacroix is less well known.
Auguste Pierre Renoir. Quoted Jean Renoir, RENOIR, MY FATHER

6 I have a predilection for painting that lends joyousness to a wall.
Auguste Pierre Renoir. Quoted Ambrose Vollard, RENOIR

7 An Orpen or a Sargent can begin a portrait with a dab on the canvas which shall stand for the high light on the nose: but a tyro will find it safer to begin by drawing the outline of the head.
Frank Rutter, T.P.'s Weekly *17 Mar 1928*

8 Mr. Lewis's [(Percy) Wyndham Lewis] pictures appeared, as a very great painter said to me, to have been painted by a mailed fist in a cotton glove.
Edith Sitwell, TAKEN CARE OF

9 A painter should not paint what he sees, but what will be seen.
Paul Valéry, MAUVAISES PENSÉES ET AUTRES 1941

10 Give a painter money and see what he'll do. If he does not paint, his work is well lost to the world.
J. M. Whistler. Quoted Hesketh Pearson, THE MAN WHISTLER

PAKISTAN

11 We eat dust, breathe dust and think dust.
T. E. Lawrence, describing Karachi. Quoted Jean B. Villars, T. E. LAWRENCE: THE SEARCH FOR THE ABSOLUTE

PANTOMIME

12 Words can be deceitful, but pantomime necessarily is simple, clear and direct.
Marcel Marceau, Theatre Arts Magazine, *Mar 1958*

PARADISE

13 The longing for paradise is paradise itself.
Kahil Gibran, SPIRITUAL SAYINGS 1963

14 Even the paradise of fools is not an unpleasant abode while it is inhabitable.
W. R. Inge (Dean of St. Pauls)

PARADOX

15 Paradoxes are useful to attract attention to ideas.
Mandell Creighton, LIFE AND LETTERS 1904

16 He who confronts the paradoxical exposes himself to reality.
Friedrich Durrenmatt, THE PHYSICISTS 1962

PARANOIA

17 I wouldn't be paranoid if people didn't pick on me.
Graffito. Quoted Nigel Rees, GRAFFITI LIVES O.K.

PARENTS

18 I was born in 1896 and my parents were married in 1919.
J. R. Ackerley, opening words of MY FATHER AND MYSELF

19 Parents exist to teach the child, but also they must learn what the child has to teach them; and the child has a great deal to teach them.
Arnold Bennett, HOW TO MAKE THE BEST OF LIFE

20 If one is not going to take the necessary precautions to avoid having parents one must undertake to bring them up.
Quentin Crisp, THE NAKED CIVIL SERVANT

1 There are times when parenthood seems nothing but feeding the mouth that bites you.
Peter De Vries, TUNNEL OF LOVE 1954

2 Possessive parents rarely live long enough to see the fruits of their selfishness.
Alan Garner, epigraph to THE OWL SERVICE 1967

3 My father was frightened of his mother. I was frightened of my father, and I'm damned well going to make sure that my children are frightened of me.
George V. Quoted Randolph Churchill, LIFE OF THE EARL OF DERBY

4 You are the bows from which your children as living arrows are sent forth.
Kahil Gibran, THE PROPHET 1923

5 The real menace in dealing with a five-year-old is that in no time at all you begin to sound like a five-year-old.
Jean Kerr, PLEASE DON'T EAT THE DAISIES

6 The parent who could see his boy as he really is would shake his head and say "Willie is no good. I'll sell him."
Stephen Leacock, LITERARY LAPSES 1910

7 He is too experienced a parent ever to make positive promises.
Christopher Morley, THUNDER ON THE LEFT 1925

8 Children aren't happy with nothing to ignore / And that's what parents were created for.
Ogden Nash, THE PARENT

9 The worst misfortune that can happen to an ordinary man is to have an extraordinary father.
Austen O'Malley

10 What a relief it is when you find that you've actually brought up a reasonable and civilised human being.
Philip, Duke of Edinburgh. Quoted Peter Lane, OUR FUTURE KING

11 Parents are sometimes a bit of a disappointment to their children. They don't fulfil the promise of their early years.
Anthony Powell, A BUYER'S MARKET 1952

12 Parents lend children their experience and a vicarious memory; children endow their parents with a vicarious immortality.
George Santayana, THE LIFE OF REASON 1906

13 Parentage is a very important profession; but no test of fitness for it is ever imposed in the interest of the children.
George Bernard Shaw, EVERYBODY'S POLITICAL WHAT'S WHAT 1944

14 The natural term of the affection of the human animal for its offspring is six years.
George Bernard Shaw, HEARTBREAK HOUSE 1920

15 Parents learn a lot from their children about coping with life.
Muriel Spark, THE COMFORTERS 1957

16 The more people have studied different methods of bringing up children the more they have come to the conclusion that what good mothers and fathers instinctively feel like doing for their babies is best after all.
Dr. Benjamin Spock, THE COMMONSENSE BOOK OF BABY AND CHILD CARE 1946

17 I like children. I never gave them a second thought when I was making them, but I like them very much.
Jake Thackeray in an interview with Frank Kempe, North Devon Herald 6 *Sep* 1979

18 Maternity is a matter of fact; paternity is a matter of opinion.
Sir Miles Thomas. Speech, Association of Supervisory Electrical Engineers, Connaught Rooms, London 2 *Apr* 1953

19 Parents are the bones on which children sharpen their teeth.
Peter Ustinov, DEAR ME 1977

20 "Parents are strange," said Amy, "for their age."
Amanda Vail, LOVE ME LITTLE

21 Don't hold your parents up to contempt. After all, you are their son, and it is just possible that you may take after them.
Evelyn Waugh, Tablet 9 *May* 1951

22 Fatherhood ought to be emphasised as much as motherhood. The idea that women are solely responsible for deciding whether or not to have babies leads on to the idea that they are also responsible for bringing the children up.
Shirley Williams, Observer, *Interview with Miriam Gross* 22 *Mar* 1981

23 The thing that impresses me most about America is the way parents obey their children.
Duke of Windsor, Look magazine 5 *Mar* 1957

PARIS

1 The Eyefull Tower is devine.
Anita Loos, GENTLEMEN PREFER BLONDES 1925

2 Old crumbling walls and the pleasant sound of water running in the urinals.
Henry Miller, TROPIC OF CANCER 1934

3 When one has Paris around one for the first time, one must let it act more like a bath without trying to do too much about it oneself, save to feel and let it happen.
Rainer Maria Rilke, LETTERS 1892–1910

DOROTHY PARKER

4 She had the imagination of disaster, and she cultivated this form of imagination and made it flourish. Her knack for causing things to end badly amounted, in her friends' eyes, to genius.
Brendan Gill, Introduction to THE COLLECTED DOROTHY PARKER

5 A combination of Little Nell and Lady Macbeth.
Alexander Woollcott, WHILE ROME BURNS 1934

PARLIAMENT

6 The House of Lords is like a glass of champagne that has stood for five days.
Clement Attlee. Quoted Leon Harris, THE FINE ART OF POLITICAL WIT

7 The House of Lords is the British Outer Mongolia for retired politicians.
Tony Benn. Speech 11 Feb 1962

8 Like many other anachronisms in British public life, the House of Lords has one supreme merit. It works.
Lord Boothby. Quoted Leon Harris, THE FINE ART OF POLITICAL WIT

9 The House of Lords is a model of how to care for the elderly.
Frank Field MP. Quoted Observer 24 May 1981

10 The House of Lords is not the watchdog of the constitution; it is Mr. Balfour's poodle. It fetches and carries for him. It barks for him. It bites anyone that he sets it on to.
David Lloyd George. Speech, House of Commons 21 Dec 1908

11 The House of Lords must be the only institution in the world which is kept efficient by the persistent absenteeism of most of its members.
Viscount Samuel. Quoted News Review 5 Feb 1948

12 One does wish that there were a few more women in parliament. Then one could be less conspicuous oneself.
Margaret Thatcher. Quoted Observer 6 May 1979

PARTING

13 Goodbyes breed a sort of distaste for whomever you say goodbye to; this hurts, you feel; this must not happen again.
Elizabeth Bowen, THE HOUSE IN PARIS 1935

PARTY

14 I'd rather be a host than a guest. As Beerbohm wonderfully observed, a happy host makes a sad guest.
Harold Acton, The Times 18 Apr 1970

15 Elyot: Delightful parties Lady Bundle always gives, doesn't she?
Amanda: Entrancing. Such a dear old lady.
Elyot: And so gay. Did you notice her at supper blowing all those shrimps through her ear trumpet.
Noël Coward, PRIVATE LIVES 1930

16 The best number for a dinner party is two — myself and a dam' good head waiter.
Nubar Gulbenkian

17 At a dinner party one should eat wisely, but not too well, and talk well but not too wisely.
W. Somerset Maugham, A WRITER'S NOTEBOOK 1949

18 It was a fête worse than death.
Barbara Stanwyck. Quoted columnist Harrison Carroll

19 The final ritual for gentlemen before they rejoin the ladies is for their host to lead them outside to urinate in the garden. The resultant patches of dead grass on the lawn are put down to wireworm and the blighted roses are blamed on the damned greenfly.
Douglas Sutherland, THE ENGLISH GENTLEMAN 1978

20 "So like one's first parties," said Miss Runcible "being sick with other people singing."
Evelyn Waugh, VILE BODIES 1930

1 The main purpose of children's parties is to remind you that there are children more awful than your own.
Katherine Whitehorn, HOW TO SURVIVE CHILDREN

2 He would give them his every imitation from 'Eton and Oxford' to the flushing of the lavatory cistern, and so, perhaps, carry the evening through.
Angus Wilson, A BIT OFF THE MAP 1957

3 What with excellent browsing and sluicing and cheery conversation and what-not, the afternoon passed quite happily.
P. G. Wodehouse, JEEVES AND THE UNBIDDEN GUEST

PASSION

4 Bernard placed one arm tightly round her. When will you marry me Ethel he uttered you must be my wife it has come to that I love you so intensely that if you say no I shall perforce dash my body to the brink of yon muddy river he panted wildly.
O don't do that implored Ethel breathing rather hard.
Daisy Ashford (aged 9), THE YOUNG VISITERS 1919

5 Oh Bernard she sighed fervently I certainly love you madly you are to me like a Heathen god she cried, looking at his manly form and flashing face I will indeed marry you.
Id.

6 The man who is master of his passions is Reason's slave.
Cyril Connolly. Quoted V. S. Pritchett, TURNSTILE ONE

7 Violent physical passions do not, in themselves, separate men from each other, but rather tend to reduce them to the same state.
T. S. Eliot, AFTER STRANGE GODS

8 A madness of tender caressing seized her. She purred as a tiger might have done, while she undulated like a snake.
Elinor Glyn, THREE WEEKS 1907

9 A man who has not passed through the inferno of his passions has never overcome them.
Carl Jung, MEMORIES, DREAMS, REFLECTIONS

10 Mortal lovers must not try to remain at the first step; for lasting passion is the dream of a harlot and from it we can wake in despair.
C. S. Lewis, THE PILGRIM'S REGRESS

11 It is only with the passions of others that we are ever really familiar, and what we come to find out about our own can be no more than what other people have shown us.
Marcel Proust, REMEMBRANCE OF THINGS PAST 1913–1927

12 The worst sin — perhaps the only sin — passion can commit is to be joyless.
Dorothy L. Sayers, GAUDY NIGHT

13 "Mr. Little is certainly warm-hearted, sir."
"Warm-hearted! I should think he has to wear asbestos vests."
P. G. Wodehouse, BINGO AND THE LITTLE WOMAN

PAST

14 Man is a history-making creature who can neither repeat his past nor leave it behind.
W. H. Auden, THE DYER'S HAND 1963

15 It is unhealthy and undesirable to live so much in the past, and yet, God forgive me, how I do it. And one cannot bring it back and one would probably not like it, if one could.
Gamaliel Bradford, LETTERS

16 The world broke in two in 1922 or thereabouts and all that went before belongs with yesterday's seven thousand years.
Willa Cather, NOT UNDER FORTY, *Prefatory note*

17 I learnt to hate and fear the past because it threatened my future.
Christopher Isherwood, KATHLEEN AND FRANK

18 Why doesn't the past decently bury itself, instead of sitting and waiting to be admitted by the present?
D. H. Lawrence, ST. MAWR 1925

19 The earth is about five thousand million years old at least. Who can afford to live in the past?
Harold Pinter, THE HOMECOMING

20 Keep off your thoughts of things that are past and done / For thinking of the past wakes regret and pain.
Arthur Waley, RESIGNATION

21 We are tomorrow's past.
Mary Webb, PRECIOUS BANE 1925

22 Each has his past shut in him like the leaves of a book known to him by heart and his friends can only read the title.
Virginia Woolf, JACOB'S ROOM 1922

PASTIME

1 I say, let's banish bridge; let's find some pleasanter way of being miserable together.
Don Herold

2 Children make the most desirable opponents in Scrabble as they are both easy to beat and fun to cheat.
Fran Lebowitz. Quoted Frank Muir, ON CHILDREN

3 A man who wants to play billiards must have no other ambitions. Billiards is all.
E. V. Lucas, CHARACTER AND COMEDY

4 I hate people who play bridge as though they were at a funeral and knew their feet were getting wet.
W. Somerset Maugham, THE CIRCLE 1921

5 To play billiards well is a sign of a mis-spent youth.
Attr. Herbert Spencer

PATIENCE

6 Always remember that the future comes one day at a time.
Dean Acheson, SKETCHES FROM LIFE

7 A minor form of despair disguised as a virtue.
Ambrose Bierce, THE DEVIL'S DICTIONARY 1906

8 Suffer us not to mock ourselves with falsehood / Teach us to care and not to care / Teach us to sit still.
T. S. Eliot, ASH WEDNESDAY 1930

9 "Sir, you try my patience."
"I don't mind if I do. You must come over and try mine some time."
Groucho Marx, DUCK SOUP

PATRIOTISM

10 Patriotism is a lively sense of collective responsibility. Nationalism is a silly cock crowing on its own dung hill.
Richard Aldington, THE COLONEL'S DAUGHTER 1931

11 I regret that I have only one life to give for my country — I'd feel safer if I had two.
Anon. soldier at D-Day landings

12 I realise that patriotism is not enough. I must have no hatred or bitterness towards anyone.
Edith Cavell, last words, reported in The Times 23 *Oct* 1915

13 "My country right or wrong" is a thing that no patriot would think of saying except in a desperate case. It is like saying, "My mother, drunk or sober."
G. K. Chesterton, THE DEFENDANT 1911

14 A man who says that no patriot should attack the war until it is over is not worth answering intelligently; he is saying that no good son should warn his mother off a cliff until she has fallen over it.
G. K. Chesterton, ORTHODOXY 1908

15 Patriotism is easy to understand in America; it means looking out for yourself while looking out for your country.
Calvin Coolidge. Quoted Evan Esar, TREASURY OF HUMOROUS QUOTATIONS

16 The *Daily Mirror* does not believe that patriotism had to be proved in blood. Especially someone else's blood.
Daily Mirror *leader on the Falkland War, Apr* 1982

17 We prefer the less bad to the more bad and so become patriots, while keeping our brains and hearts intact.
E. M. Forster, TWO CHEERS FOR DEMOCRACY 1951

18 Originality and initiative are what I ask for my country.
Robert Frost, THE FIGURE A POEM MAKES

19 I have never understood why one's affections must be confined, as once with women, to a single country.
J. K. Galbraith, A LIFE IN OUR TIMES 1981

20 One of the great attractions of patriotism — it fulfils our worst wishes. In the person of our nation we are able, vicariously, to bully and to cheat. Bully and cheat, what's more, with a feeling that we are profoundly virtuous.
Aldous Huxley, EYELESS IN GAZA 1936

21 Those only can care intelligently for the future of England to whom the past is dear.
W. R. Inge (Dean of St. Pauls), ASSESSMENTS AND ANTICIPATIONS

22 Ask not what your country can do for you. Ask what you can do for your country.
John F. Kennedy. Inaugural address 20 *Jan* 1961

23 Is it an offence, is it a mistake, is it a crime to take a hopeful view of the prospects of your own country? Why should it be? Why should patriotism and pessimism be identical? Hope is the mainspring of patriotism.
David Lloyd George, House of Commons 30 *Oct* 1919

1 Duty and patriotism clad in glittering white; the great pinnacle of sacrifice pointing like a pinnacle to heaven.
David Lloyd George. Speech, Queens Hall, London 19 *Sep* 1914

2 Patriotism is often an arbitrary veneration of real estate above principles.
G. J. Nathan, TESTAMENT OF A CRITIC

3 Patriots always talk of dying for their country and never of killing for their country.
Bertrand Russell, AUTOBIOGRAPHY 1967

4 [Today] anyone standing to attention in a cinema during the playing of 'God Save the Queen' is either the producer of the little film of Her Majesty that goes with it or he has inadvertently tied his bootlaces together.
Harry Secombe, Punch 10 *May* 1972

5 The national anthem belongs to the eighteenth century. In it you find us ordering God about to do our dirty work.
George Bernard Shaw, THE ADVENTURES OF THE BLACK GIRL IN HER SEARCH FOR GOD

6 You'll never have a quiet world till you knock the patriotism out of the human race.
George Bernard Shaw, O'FLAHERTY V.C.

7 Patriotism is your conviction that this country is superior to all other countries because you were born in it.
George Bernard Shaw

8 To strike freedom of the mind with the fist of patriotism is an old and ugly subtlety.
Adlai Stevenson. Speech, American Legion Convention 30 *Aug* 1952

9 He was inordinately proud of England and he abused her incessantly.
H. G. Wells, MR. BRITLING SEES IT THROUGH 1916

10 Patriotism has become a mere national self assertion, a sentimentality of flag-cheering with no constructive duties.
H. G. Wells, THE FUTURE IN AMERICA

PATRONAGE

11 He liked to patronise coloured people and treated them as equals because he was quite sure they were not.
Bertrand Russell, AUTOBIOGRAPHY VOL 4 1967

12 Getting patronage is the whole art of life. A man cannot have a career without it.
George Bernard Shaw, CAPTAIN BRASSBOUND'S CONVERSION 1900

PEACE

13 In international affairs, a period of cheating between two periods of fighting.
Ambrose Bierce, THE DEVIL'S DICTIONARY 1906

14 What they could do with round here is a good war . . . You know what the trouble with peace is? No organisation.
Bertolt Brecht, MOTHER COURAGE AND HER CHILDREN 1939

15 Peace with honour. I believe it is peace in our time.
Neville Chamberlain after the Munich Agreement 30 *Sep* 1938

16 The Bomb brought peace but man alone can keep that peace.
Winston Churchill. Speech, House of Commons 16 *Aug* 1945

17 It is far easier to make war than to make peace.
Georges Clemençeau. Speech, Verdun 14 *Jul* 1919

18 Peace cannot be kept by force. It can only be achieved by understanding.
Albert Einstein, NOTES ON PACIFISM

19 The mere absence of war is not peace.
John F. Kennedy. State of the Union Message 14 *Jan* 1963

20 The peaceful two [John Lennon and Yoko] argued, reasonably enough, that if everyone stayed in bed, occupying themselves in growing their hair, there would be no wars.
Bernard Levin, THE PENDULUM YEARS 1976

21 Peace is indivisible.
Maxim Litvinov. Speech to League of Nations 1 *Jul* 1936

22 Peace is not only better than war, but infinitely more arduous.
George Bernard Shaw, HEARTBREAK HOUSE, *Preface* 1920

23 In the arts of peace, Man is a bungler.
George Bernard Shaw, MAN AND SUPERMAN 1905

PEDANTRY

24 Pedantry is the dotage of knowledge.
Holebrook Jackson, THE ANATOMY OF BIBLIOMANIA 1930

25 An artist may visit a museum, but only a pedant can live there.
George Santayana, THE LIFE OF REASON 1906

PEERAGE

1 I was obviously destined to go down and down when in 1958 my father and brother died within ten days of each other and I became an Earl . . . Life is much easier, being an Earl. It has changed me a lot. I'm much nastier now.
Earl of Arran [formerly Arthur Gore],
Sunday Times 15 *Jan* 1967

2 Accepting a peerage in 1916 was my greatest mistake.
Lord Beaverbrook quoted BBC 2 TV, *Reputations* 28 *Jun* 1981

3 I did have a coronet, until another duke borrowed the thing and lost it.
Duke of Bedford (John Robert Russell), on American TV

4 It was but a few weeks since he had taken his seat in the Lords; and this afternoon, for want of something better to do, he strayed in.
Max Beerbohm, ZULEIKA DOBSON 1906

5 The nobility of England, my lord, would have snored through the Sermon on the Mount.
Robert Bolt, A MAN FOR ALL SEASONS 1961

6 Who can fathom the mind of one suddenly raised to the peerage?
Edward Bond, RESTORATION

7 There are no credentials. They do not even need a medical certificate. They need not be sound either in body or mind. They only require a certificate of birth — just to prove that they are first of the litter. You would not choose a spaniel on these principles.
David Lloyd George. Budget speech 1909

8 When I want a peerage I shall buy one like an honest man.
Lord Northcliffe. Quoted Hannen Swaffer

9 A person seeking a quiet life is greatly helped by not having a title.
Captain Mark Phillips, explaining why he wished to remain a commoner

10 The hereditary system is the only method of selecting a body of people which is completely unbiased. Every other method, except perhaps lottery, must depend on someone's opinion.
Lord Saye and Sele. Maiden speech in House of Lords, reported in The Times

11 A life peer is like a mule — no pride of ancestry, no hope of posterity.
Lord Shackleton, himself a life peer

12 Only through the accident of being a hereditary peer can anyone, in these days of votes for Everybody, get into parliament if handicapped by serious modern cultural equipment.
George Bernard Shaw, HEARTBREAK HOUSE, *Preface* 1920

13 Titles distinguish the mediocre, embarrass the superior, and are disgraced by the inferior.
George Bernard Shaw, MAN AND SUPERMAN 1905

14 One way a peer can make a bit of extra money is by letting the public into his house. Another way is by letting the public into his head. Either way, the dottier the contents the better.
Sunday Times, *on the Earl of Arran's column in the* Evening News 15 *Jan* 1967

15 The House of Lords has lost, at the age of 91, one of its most picturesque personalities in the Earl of Morton. He had a great gift for silence, and during all the years that he attended at Westminster as a Scottish representative peer his voice was never heard in debate.
The Times *obituary*

16 I have heard it said of the 'backwoods' peer that he had three qualities. He knew how to kill a fox, he knew how to get rid of a bad tenant, and he knew how to discard an unwanted mistress. A man who possesses these three qualities would certainly have something to contribute to the work of the House.
Lord Winster. Speech, House of Lords

PELICAN

17 A wonderful bird is the pelican / His bill will hold more than his belican / He can take in his beak / Food enough for a week / But I'm damned if I see how the helican.
Dixon Lanier Merritt, THE PELICAN

PERFECTION

18 American women expect to find in their husbands a perfection that English women only hope to find in their butlers.
W. Somerset Maugham, A WRITER'S NOTEBOOK 1949

19 Perfection has one grave defect; it is apt to be dull.
W. Somerset Maugham, THE SUMMING UP 1938

1 People are willing to devise and praise Utopias but not to live in them.
David Pryce-Jones, The Times 20 *Mar* 1972

2 In anything at all, perfection is finally attained not when there is no longer anything to add, but when there is no longer anything to take away.
Antoine de Saint-Exupéry, WIND, SAND AND STARS 1939

PERMISSIVENESS

3 The terrible trouble nowadays is that they [youth] have lost the chance to disobey. That is what all children and all artists need. Today the rule is, do what you like.
Jean Cocteau in an interview with Derek Prouse, Sunday Times 20 *Oct* 1963

4 As he [Aldous Huxley] speaks a look of anxiety comes on the faces of the women present as though they would be unspeakably shocked if any thought they could possibly be shocked by anything.
William Gerhardie, MEMOIRS OF A POLYGLOT 1925

5 Take all the sexual pleasures you can but be very careful about the Pox.
Llewelyn Powys. Quoted Richard Perceval Graves, THE BROTHERS POWYS 1983

6 Love as a relation between men and women was ruined by the desire to make sure of the legitimacy of the children.
Bertrand Russell, MARRIAGE AND MORALS 1929

PERSEVERANCE

7 U-turn if you want to. The lady's not for turning.
Margaret Thatcher. Conservative Party Conference 11 *Oct* 1980

PESSIMISM

8 Pessimism does win us some great moments.
Max Beerbohm, AND EVEN NOW, *Hosts and Guests* 1920

9 Pessimism, when you get used to it, is just as agreeable as optimism.
Arnold Bennett, THINGS THAT HAVE INTERESTED ME

10 Scratch a pessimist and you find often a defender of privilege.
Lord Beveridge. Quoted Observer 17 *Oct* 1943

11 Only the man who finds everything wrong and expects it to get worse is thought to have a clear brain.
J. K. Galbraith, THE AGE OF UNCERTAINTY 1977

12 A bilious philosopher's opinion of the world can only be accepted with a pinch of salt, of Epsom salt for preference.
Aldous Huxley, PROPER STUDIES 1927

13 Nothing makes me more pessimistic than the obligation not to be pessimistic.
Eugene Ionesco. Quoted Martin Esslin, THE THEATRE OF THE ABSURD

14 If we see light at the end of the tunnel it is the light of an oncoming train.
Robert Lowell, DAY BY DAY. *Quoted* BBC Radio 4, *Quote Unquote* 21 *Jul* 1980

15 A pessimist is a man who looks both ways before crossing a one-way street.
Laurence J. Peter, PETER'S QUOTATIONS

PET

16 A British home is nothing without a pet.
Yvonne Arnaud, News Review 8 *Apr* 1948

17 The woman who is really kind to dogs is always one who has failed to inspire sympathy in men.
Max Beerbohm, ZULEIKA DOBSON 1911

18 I prefer cats to dogs because they are not so loud and clumsy, nor so overtly masculine. They have a feminine grace.
A. L. Rowse, THREE CORNISH CATS

19 If a dog jumps onto your lap it is because he is fond of you; but if a cat does the same thing it is because your lap is warmer.
A. N. Whitehead, DIALOGUES 1953

PHILANTHROPIST

20 Suspicion of one's own motives is especially necessary for the philanthropist.
Bertrand Russell, THE CONQUEST OF HAPPINESS 1930

PHILIP, DUKE OF EDINBURGH

21 A man attractive to women, envied by men, a bit vicious on the polo-field, autocratic, something of a ham actor — and in the red. He lives a good life but he has to pay for it. He has never been rich.
Andrew Duncan. Quoted Philip Howard, The Times, *Profile of the Duke of Edinburgh* 26 *Apr* 1982

1 The working girl's Adam Faith.
Bud Flanagan. Quoted Noël St. George,
ROYAL QUOTES

2 With his great (and carefully calculated) talent for putting his foot in it, we might consider Prince Philip to be the most eloquent, literate and classless member of the Royal Family.
Willie Hamilton. Quoted Philip Howard,
The Times, *Profile of the Duke of Edinburgh* 26 *Apr* 1982

3 No one has a kinder heart or takes more trouble to conceal it.
Michael Parker. Quoted Basil Boothroyd in his official biography of Prince Philip 1971

4 Whatever happens to him in his present capacity as royal poor relation can't do him much good in the long run. My advice to him would be — give up being a royal personage, stick to the sea, learn a trade and find an anchorage with an average good wife.
Daily Worker 12 *Dec* 1946

PHILOSOPHY

5 The dictionary definition of philosophical as meaning 'calm and temperate'. That is rubbish. I don't believe there is such a thing as a calm philosopher. Bertrand Russell, in my opinion the greatest, certainly isn't.
A. J. Ayer, The Times 28 *Aug* 1968

6 Truth is the object of philosophy, but not always of philosophers.
John Churton Collins. Quoted Logan Pearsall Smith, TREASURY OF ENGLISH APHORISMS

7 In philosophy it is not the attainment of the goal that matters, it is the things that are met with by the way.
Havelock Ellis, THE DANCE OF LIFE 1923

8 There is no such person as a philosopher; no one is detached; the observer, like the observed, is in chains.
E. M. Forster, TWO CHEERS FOR DEMOCRACY, *The Menace to Freedom* 1951

9 You can't do without philosophy, since everything has its hidden meaning which we must know.
Maxim Gorky, THE ZYKOS 1914

10 The object of studying philosophy is to know one's own mind, not other people's.
W. R. Inge (Dean of St. Pauls), OUTSPOKEN ESSAYS 1919

11 When philosophers try to be politicians they generally cease to be philosophers.
Walter Lippmann, A PREFACE TO POLITICS, *The Changing Focus* 1914

12 Most philosophical treatises show the human cerebrum loaded far beyond its Plimsoll mark.
H. L. Mencken, PREJUDICES 1924

13 Any genuine philosophy leads to action and from action back to wonder, to the enduring of mystery.
Henry Miller, THE WISDOM OF THE HEART 1941

14 Who could fathom Plato's mind? Unless one is a genius Philosophy is a mug's game.
Iris Murdoch, THE PHILOSOPHER'S PUPIL 1983

15 None can call himself a philosopher whose own days are not made more intense and dramatic by his philosophising. Even if his vision of things be bitter and grim, his world is made more interesting by his pondering on it, not more commonplace or tedious.
John Cowper Powys, THE MEANING OF CULTURE 1930

16 Nowadays there are no serious philosophers who are not looking forward to the pension to which their involvement with the subject entitles them.
Anthony Quinton, THOUGHTS AND THINKERS

17 To teach how to live without certainty and yet without being paralysed by hesitation is perhaps the chief thing that philosophy, in our age, can do for those who study it.
Bertrand Russell, HISTORY OF WESTERN PHILOSOPHY 1945

18 The point of philosophy is to start with something so simple as to seem not worth stating, and to end with something so paradoxical that no one will believe it.
Bertrand Russell, LOGIC AND KNOWLEDGE

19 For the learning of every virtue there is an appropriate discipline, and for this learning of suspended judgment the best discipline is philosophy.
Bertrand Russell, UNPOPULAR ESSAYS, *Philosophy for Laymen* 1950

20 My doctor said to me afterwards, "When you were ill you behaved like a true

philosopher. Every time you came to yourself you made a joke." I never had a compliment that pleased me more.
Bertrand Russell, after a bout of pneumonia, in a letter to Jean Nichol 2 *Oct* 1921

1 Philosophy is the replacement of category habits by category disciplines.
Gilbert Ryle, THE CONCEPT OF MIND

2 Philosophers are as jealous as women. Each wants a monopoly of praise.
George Santayana, DIALOGUES IN LIMBO

3 The philosopher is Nature's pilot. And there you have our difference; to be in hell is to drift; to be in heaven is to steer.
George Bernard Shaw, MAN AND SUPERMAN 1905

4 The greater the philosopher, the harder it is for him to answer the questions of the average man.
Henryk Sienkiewicz

5 A philosopher of imposing stature doesn't think in a vacuum. Even his most abstract ideas are, to some extent, conditioned by what is or what is not known in the time when he lives.
A. N. Whitehead, DIALOGUES 1953

6 Philosophy is the product of wonder.
A. N. Whitehead, NATURE AND LIFE

7 The safest general characterization of the European philosophical tradition is that it consists of a series of footnotes to Plato.
A. N. Whitehead, PROCESS AND REALITY 1929

PHOTOGRAPHY

8 Tony made my nose look wonderful, but everyone thought I'd had it fixed by plastic surgery.
Princess Alexandra, of a portrait by Lord Snowdon

9 The virtue of the camera is not the power it has to transform the photographer into an artist, but the impulse it gives him to keep on looking.
Brooks Anderson, ONCE AROUND THE SUN 1951

PHYSICS

10 The content of physics is the concern of physicists, its effect the concern of all men.
Friedrich Durrenmatt, THE PHYSICISTS, 21 *Points*

11 Physical concepts are free creations of the human mind and are not, however it may seem, uniquely determined by the external world.
Albert Einstein, EVOLUTION OF PHYSICS

12 We have no right to assume that any physical laws exist, or if they have existed up to now, that they will continue to exist in a similar manner in the future.
Max Planck, THE UNIVERSE IN THE LIGHT OF MODERN PHYSICS

PIANO

13 A pianist needs three things — muscles, a brain and a heart.
Bernard d'Ascoli, Observer 31 *Jan* 1982

14 They laughed when I sat down at the piano — but when I began to play!
John Caples, advertising slogan 1925

15 If there is time left over I fill in with a lot of runs up and down the keyboard.
Liberace. Quoted Stuart Hall and Paddy Whannel, THE POPULAR ARTS

16 Piano playing is more difficult than statesmanship. It is harder to waken emotions in ivory keys than it is in human beings.
Ignacy Paderewski. Quoted Nat Shapiro, ENCYCLOPEDIA OF QUOTATIONS ABOUT MUSIC

17 The notes I handle no better than many pianists. But the pauses between the notes — ah that is where the art resides.
Artur Schnabel. Quoted Chicago Daily News 11 *Jun* 1958

18 The kid that handles the music box was hitting a rag-time tune.
R. W. Service, THE SHOOTING OF DAN MAGRUE 1907

19 I wish the Government would put a tax on pianos for the incompetent.
Edith Sitwell, LETTERS 1916–1964

PABLO PICASSO

20 A Catalan wizard who fools with shapes.
Bernard Berenson. Quoted Sylvan Sprigge, BERENSON: A BIOGRAPHY

21 Nothing unites the English like war. Nothing divides them like Picasso.
Hugh Mills, PRUDENCE AND THE PILL

22 Many painters and writers have made beautiful works out of repulsive subjects:

Picasso enjoys making repulsive works out of beautiful subjects.
Raymond Mortimer, TRY ANYTHING ONCE

1 Picasso had a whim of iron.
John Richardson, PICASSO IN PRIVATE

PIETY

2 Bernard always had a few prayers in the hall and some whiskey afterwards as he was rather pious.
Daisy Ashford (aged 9), THE YOUNG VISITERS 1919

3 All great harlots become pious in their old age, as if faith could take the place of love.
Louis Bromfield, THE STRANGE CASE OF MISS ANNIE SPRAGG 1928

PIG

4 One disadvantage of being a hog is that at any moment some bleeding fool may try to make a silk purse out of your wife's ear.
Beachcomber (J. B. Morton), Daily Express, *By the Way*

PIGEON

5 Pigeons walking up and down the roof with their hands behind their backs.
Jean Cocteau. Quoted, Reader's Digest, *Dec* 1943

6 No bird sits a tree more proudly than a pigeon. It looks as though placed there by the Lord.
Katherine Mansfield, JOURNAL 1954

7 The lovesick woodpigeons mooning in bed.
Dylan Thomas, UNDER MILK WOOD 1954

PITY

8 We have only one thing to keep us sane, pity; and the man without pity is mad.
Edward Bond, LEAR

9 When Man evolved Pity, he did a queer thing — deprived himself of the power of living life as it is without wishing it to become something different.
John Galsworthy, letter to Thomas Hardy 27 Mar 1910

10 Pity is a corroding thing.
Martha Graham. Quoted Robin Stringer, Daily Telegraph 23 *Jul* 1979

11 Contempt for pain soon becomes a contempt for pity.
Francis Hackett, HENRY VIII 1929

12 The sparrow is sorry for the peacock at the burden of its tail.
Rabindranath Tagore, STRAY BIRDS 1916

PLAGIARISM

13 . . . the bubonic plagiarist.
Jonathan Miller of David Frost. Quoted, FROM FRINGE TO FLYING CIRCUS 1981

14 I would like to thank Beethoven, Brahms, Wagner, Strauss, Rimskykorsakov . . .
Dimitry Tiomkin. Speech accepting Academy Award for the best original dramatic score composed for THE HIGH AND THE MIGHTY 1955

PLATITUDE

15 The man who has the courage of his platitudes is always a successful man.
Van Wyck Brooks, A CHILMARK MISCELLANY

16 The banalities of a great man pass for wit.
Alexander Chase, PERSPECTIVES 1966

17 The Republicans stroke platitudes until they purr like epigrams.
Adlai Stevenson. Quoted Leon Harris, THE FINE ART OF POLITICAL WIT

18 His public utterances are sensible but never arresting. Even a platitude dropped from a sufficiently great height can sound like a brick.
Peregrine Worsthorne of Bernard Baruch, Daily Telegraph 14 *Apr* 1958

PLEASURE

19 Pleasure is by no means an infallible critical guide, but it is the least fallible.
W. H. Auden, THE DYER'S HAND 1963

20 I have finished my novel. What am I to do? There is pleasure, of course, but I like it only when it is stolen from my hours of work. When it is just a way of filling in leisure it no longer amuses me.
Julian Green, DIARY 1928–1957

21 Are creature comforts more demoralizing when consciously enjoyed or when taken for granted?
Ronald Knox, PENSÉE

22 There is no more lamentable pursuit than a life of pleasure.
W. Somerset Maugham, THE CIRCLE 1921

23 Surely a king who loves pleasure is less dangerous than one who loves glory.
Nancy Mitford, THE WATER BEETLE

1 A life of pleasure requires an aristocratic setting to make it interesting.
George Santayana, LIFE OF REASON, *Reason in Society* 1905

2 The most intolerable pain is produced by prolonging the keenest pleasures.
George Bernard Shaw, MAN AND SUPERMAN 1905

3 I take it as a prime cause of the present confusion of society that it is too sickly and too doubtful to use pleasure frankly as a test of value.
Rebecca West. Quoted Dr. Karl Menninger, A PSYCHIATRIST'S WORLD

POET AND POETRY

4 Poetry is the stuff in books that doesn't quite reach the margins.
Anonymous child's essay

5 When one thinks of the attention that a great poem demands there is something frivolous about the idea of spending every day with one. Masterpieces should be kept for High Days of the Spirit.
W. H. Auden, THE DYER'S HAND 1963

6 A verbal art like poetry is reflective. It stops to think. Music is immediate; it goes on to become.
W. H. Auden. Quoted Aaron Copland, MUSIC AND IMAGINATION 1952

7 Poetry makes nothing happen, it survives / In the valley of its saying.
W. H. Auden, ANOTHER TIME, *In Memory of W. B. Yeats* 1940

8 A poet is, before anything else, a person who is passionately in love with language.
W. H. Auden, New York Times 9 Oct 1960

9 It is not possible for a poet to be a professional. Poetry is essentially an amateur activity.
Viscount Barrington, House of Lords 23 Nov 1978

10 I agree with one of your reputable critics that a taste for drawing rooms has spoiled more poets than ever did a taste for gutters.
Thomas Beer, THE MAUVE DECADE 1926

11 Poetry is as much a part of the universe as mathematics and physics. It is not a cleverer device or recreation, unless the Eternal is clever.
Edmund Blunden on being elected Professor of Poetry at Oxford University 5 Feb 1966

12 I have nothing to say and I'm saying it and that is poetry.
John Cage, SILENCE 1961

13 Lyricism cannot exist without rules, and it is essential that they should be strict. Otherwise there is only a faculty for lyricism, and that exists everywhere.
Charles Albert Cingria. Quoted Igor Stravinsky, AN AUTOBIOGRAPHY 1936

14 A poet's technique is not something that should ever call attention to itself; technique can kill freshness.
Jean Cocteau in an interview with Derek Prouse, Sunday Times 20 Oct 1903

15 You don't make a poem with thoughts; you must make it with words.
Id.

16 Poetry does not necessarily have to be beautiful to stick in the depths of our memory.
Colette, EARTHLY PARADISE, *Under the Blue Lantern* 1960

17 Everyone writes so well nowadays that it is hardly worth while for any new poet to write well. All can raise the flower because all have got the seed.
Hubert Cornish. Quoted Maurice Baring, THE PUPPET SHOW OF MEMORY 1922

18 My mind has thunderstorms / That brood for heavy hours; / Until they rain me words / My thoughts are drooping flowers / And sucking silent birds.
W. H. Davies, COLLECTED POEMS 1943

19 A poet in history is divine, but a poet in the next room is a joke.
Max Eastman. Quoted Evan Esar, TREASURY OF HUMOROUS QUOTATIONS

20 Genuine poetry can communicate before it is understood.
T. S. Eliot, DANTE 1929

21 Immature poets imitate; mature poets steal.
T. S. Eliot, PHILIP MASSINGER 1920

22 The ordinary man falls in love, or reads Spinoza, and these two experiences have nothing to do with each other, or with the noise of the typewriter or the smell of cooking; in the mind of the poet these experiences are always forming new wholes.
T. S. Eliot, THE METAPHYSICAL POETS 1921

1 The majority of poems one outgrows and outlives, as one outgrows and outlives the majority of human passions.
T. S. Eliot, SELECTED ESSAYS

2 Poetry is not a turning loose of emotion but an escape from emotion; it is not the expression of personality, but an escape from personality. But of course, only those who have personality and emotions knows what it means to escape from these things.
T. S. Eliot, TRADITION AND THE INDIVIDUAL TALENT 1919

3 Poetry is not a career, but a mug's game. No honest poet can ever feel quite sure of the permanent value of what he has written, he may have wasted his time and messed up his life for nothing.
T. S. Eliot, THE USE OF POETRY AND THE USE OF CRITICISM 1932

4 I can understand you wanting to write poems. But I don't know what you mean by "being a poet".
T. S. Eliot. Quoted Stephen Spender, WORLD WITHIN WORLD

5 We all write poems; it is simply that poets are the ones who write in words.
John Fowles, THE FRENCH LIEUTENANT'S WOMAN

6 Like a piece of ice on a hot stove, the poem must ride on its own melting.
Robert Frost, COLLECTED WORKS, *Preface* 1951

7 No wonder poets sometimes have to *seem* more business-like than business men. Their wares are so much harder to get rid of.
Robert Frost, NEW HAMPSHIRE 1923

8 I have never started a poem yet whose end I knew. Writing a poem is discovering.
Robert Frost, New York Times 7 *Nov* 1955

9 Poetry is the language in which man explores his own amazement.
Christopher Fry, Time 3 *Apr* 1950

10 Poets should never marry. The world should thank me for not marrying you.
Maud Gonne to W. B. Yeats. Quoted Nancy Cardozo, MAUD GONNE

11 Most poets are dead by their late twenties.
Robert Graves. Quoted Observer 11 *Nov* 1962

12 It's hard to say why writing verse / Should terminate in drink or worse.
A. P. Herbert, Punch, *Lines For a Worldly Person*

13 Literature is a state of culture, poetry a state of grace, before and after culture.
Juan Ramon Jimenez, POETRY AND LITERATURE 1957

14 When power narrows the areas of man's concern, poetry reminds him of the richness and diversity of his existence. When power corrupts, poetry cleanses.
John F. Kennedy. Speech at dedication of Robert Frost Library, Nov 1962

15 A language not thoroughly recorded by poetry would become so discredited and stripped of meaning that a threat would arise to meaning itself.
Lord Kilmarnock, House of Lords 22 *Nov* 1978

16 I think more of a bird with broad wings flying and lapsing through the air, than anything when I think of metre.
D. H. Lawrence, letter to Edward Marsh, Nov 1913

17 Poetry can communicate the actual quality of experience with a subtlety and precision unapproachable by any other means.
F. R. Leavis, NEW BEARINGS IN ENGLISH POETRY 1932

18 A poem should not mean / But be.
Archibald MacLeish, STREETS IN THE MOON, *Ars Poetica* 1936

19 Verse libre; a device for making poetry easier to read and harder to write.
H. L. Mencken, A BOOK OF BURLESQUES 1916

20 When one hears of a poet past thirty-five he seems somehow unnatural and obscene.
H. L. Mencken, PREJUDICES 1919

21 Poetry is a comforting piece of fiction set to more or less lascivious music.
H. L. Mencken, PREJUDICES 1922 (3rd series)

22 The poem is the dream made flesh, in a two-fold sense as a work of art, and as life which is a work of art.
Henry Miller, THE WISDOM OF THE HEART, *Creative Death* 1941

23 The courage of the poet is to keep ajar the door that leads to madness.
Christopher Morley, INWARD HO 1923

24 A poet, any real poet, is simply an alchemist who transmutes his cynicism regarding human beings into an optimism regarding the moon, the stars, the heavens

and the flowers to say nothing of Spring, love, and dogs.
George Jean Nathan, MONKS ARE MONKS, *Poet* 1929

1 It is needful for a serious writer to try to measure his own limitations . . . Much verse . . . is deformed by the inability of its authors to harmonise what they intend to say with the way they are saying it, or to convince even the well-disposed reader that it is worth saying.
William Plomer, London Magazine, *Mar* 1956

2 I am at work on a cryselephantine poem of immeasurable length which will occupy one for the next four decades unless it becomes a bore.
Ezra Pound, of the CANTOS *in a letter to Milton Bronner* 21 *Sep* 1915

3 Poetry is a perfectly reasonable means of overcoming chaos.
I. A. Richards, SCIENCE AND POETRY

4 More often than prose or mathematics, poetry is received in a hostile spirit as if its publication were an affront to the reader.
Michael Roberts, Introduction to FABER BOOK OF MODERN VERSE

5 Poetry has too strong a tradition to acquire a vigorous modern life. With few exceptions nothing can be mentioned in poetry which was not known in the time of Shakespeare.
Bertrand Russell, FORTNIGHTLY REVIEW, *May* 1928

6 Poetry is the achievement of the synthesis of hyacinths and biscuits.
Carl Sandburg, Atlantic Monthly, *Poetry Considered, Mar* 1923

7 Poetry is the opening and closing of a door, leaving those who look through to guess about what is seen during a moment.
Carl Sandburg, TENTATIVE (FIRST MODEL), *Definitions of Poetry* 1950

8 Ordering a man to write a poem is like commanding a pregnant woman to give birth to a red-headed child. You can't do it — it's an act of God.
Carl Sandburg. Quoted Reader's Digest, *Dec* 1938

9 Popular poets are the parish priests of the Muse, retailing her ancient divinations to a long since converted public.
George Santayana, THE LIFE OF REASON, *Reason in Art* 1906

10 The truth, which is a standard for the naturalist, for the poet is only a stimulus.
George Santayana, SOLILOQUIES IN ENGLAND 1922

11 All poets' wives have rotten lives / Their husbands look at them like knives.
Delmore Schwartz. Quoted James Atlas in his biography, DELMORE SCHWARTZ: THE LIFE OF AN AMERICAN POET

12 It is as unseeing to ask what is the *use* of poetry as it would be to ask what is the use of religion.
Edith Sitwell, THE OUTCASTS, *Preface*

13 The poet speaks to all men of that other life of theirs that they have smothered and forgotten.
Edith Sitwell, RHYME AND REASON

14 One of the purposes of poetry is to show the dimensions of man that are, as Sir Arthur Eddington said "midway in scale between the atom and the star."
Id.

15 Poetry ennobles the heart and the eyes and unveils the meaning of things upon which the heart and the eyes dwell.
Id.

16 The poet is the priest of the invisible.
Wallace Stevens, OPUS POSTHUMOUS, *Adagio* 1957

17 Re-write the thrice re-written. Strive to say / Some older nothing in some newer way.
John St. Leo Strachey, THE POETASTER

18 A good poem is a contribution to reality. The world is never the same once a good poem has been added to it.
Dylan Thomas, QUITE EARLY ONE MORNING, *On Poetry* 1960

19 There is only one object: the removing of veils from your soul and scabs from your body.
Dylan Thomas. Quoted Andrew Sinclair, DYLAN THOMAS: POET OF HIS PEOPLE

20 To hell with everything except the inner necessity for expression and the medium of expression, everything except the great need of forever striving after this mystery and meaning I moan about.
Dylan Thomas at 18. *Quoted* Id.

21 I hold a beast, an angel and a madman in me, and my enquiry is as to their working, and my problem is their subjugation and

victory, downthrow and upheaval, and my effort is their self expression.
Dylan Thomas, letter to Henry Treece

1 The poet may be used as the barometer, but let us not forget he is also part of the weather.
Lionel Trilling, THE LIBERAL IMAGINATION, *The Sense of Past* 1950

2 There are no poetic ideas; only poetic utterances.
Evelyn Waugh, BOOKS ON TRIAL

3 The poet produces the beautiful by fixing his attention on something real.
Simone Weil, GRAVITY AND GRACE 1947

4 All poets who when reading from their own works experience a choking feeling are major. For that matter, all poets who read from their own works are major, whether they choke or not.
E. B. White, HOW TO TELL A MAJOR POET FROM A MINOR POET 1939

5 You cannot lecture on really pure poetry any more than you can talk about the ingredients of pure water — it is adulterated, methylated, sanded poetry that makes the best lectures.
Virginia Woolf of Christina G. Rossetti, SECOND COMMON READER 1932

6 "How are you?" / "Not very well. I can only write prose today."
W. B. Yeats in conversation

7 Too true, too sincere. The Muse prefers the liars, the gay and warty lads.
W. B. Yeats on the poetry of James Reed. Quoted Robert Graves and Alan Hodge, THE LONG WEEK END 1940

POLICE

8 I have never seen a situation so dismal that a policeman couldn't make it worse.
Brendan Behan. Quoted Barbara Rowe, A BOOK OF QUOTES

9 I like to see policemen about the place, preferably large ones who have been at it long enough not to look embarrassed by their hats.
H. F. Ellis, Punch 12 *Sep* 1962

10 I didn't like the police helmet. That's why I was hoping to get into the motor squad where I could have worn a flat cap.
Gilbert Harding to John Freeman, BBC TV, *Face to Face*

11 For the middle-class, the police protect property, give directions, and help old ladies. For the urban poor the police are those who arrest you.
Michael Harrington, THE OTHER AMERICA 1962

12 The general conclusion seems to be that police are not very popular but that they never have been. I suspect this is true and that the main difference between our times and Victorian times is that in Victorian times the classes that had most reasons for disliking the police had least facilities for expressing their opinions in print.
Christopher Hollis, Punch 1 *Aug* 1962

13 Why can't the police be equipped with fast-acting tranquilliser darts or pellets? If it works with rhinos, why not with robbers?
U. Light in a letter to Observer 21 *Jan* 1979

14 Policemen, like red squirrels, must be protected.
Joe Orton, LOOT

15 They stick people in dustbins and then ask us to sit on the lid.
A police constable in a TV *interview. Quoted Albert Hunt,* Radio Times 17 *Feb* 1979

16 The South African police would leave no stone unturned to see that nothing disturbed the even terror of their lives.
Tom Sharpe, INDECENT EXPOSURE

17 P. C. Attila Rees, ox-broad, barge-booted, stamping out of Handcuff House in a heavy, beef-red huff, blackbrowed under his damp helmet . . . and lumbering down towards the strand to see that the sea is still there.
Dylan Thomas, UNDER MILK WOOD 1954

18 The tragedy of the Police State is that it always regards all opposition as a crime, and there are no degrees.
Lord Vansittart, House of Lords, *Jun* 1947

POLITENESS

19 Being polite is when you eat sandwiches without looking inside first.
Caption to cartoon, TV Times, *Kidstuff* 5 *Mar* 1979

20 Politeness is only one half good manners and the other half good lying.
Mary Wilson Little. Quoted Evan Esar, TREASURY OF HUMOROUS QUOTATIONS

1 If we discarded the formal falsehoods which are the currency of conversation we should not be one step nearer the vital things of truth.
Agnes Repplier, AMERICANS AND OTHERS

2 If we treat people too long with that pretended liking called politeness, we shall find it hard not to like them in the end.
Logan Pearsall Smith, ALL TRIVIA, *Afterthoughts* 1931

3 Politeness is organised indifference.
Paul Valéry, TEL QUEL 1943

POLITICS

4 When the political columnists say 'Every thinking man' they mean themselves and when the candidates appeal to 'Every intelligent voter' they mean everybody who is going to vote for them.
Franklin P. Adams, NODS AND BECKS 1944

5 Politics, as a practice, whatever its professions, has always been the systematic organisation of hatreds.
Henry Brooks Adams, THE EDUCATION OF HENRY ADAMS 1907

6 Knowledge of human nature is the beginning and end of political education.
Id.

7 Practical politics consists in ignoring facts.
Id.

8 Political economy: two words that should be divorced on grounds of incompatibility.
Anon., Wall Street Journal. *Quoted* Reader's Digest, *Jul* 1981

9 As the intelligent are liberals, I am on the side of the idiots.
Maurice Baring, quoting his friend Brewster in THE PUPPET SHOW OF MEMORY 1922

10 Who — except a freakish intellectual — has ever been argued into giving up political power when he doesn't have to; and to give it up, moreover, for the sake of an abstraction, a principle? The idea is ludicrous!
Julian Barnes, Observer 6 *May* 1979

11 The connection between humbug and politics is too long established to be challenged.
Ronald Bell, MP *for Beaconsfield*, House of Commons 5 *Dec* 1979

12 Every Briton is at heart a Tory — especially every British Liberal.
Arnold Bennett, JOURNAL

13 We know what happens to people who stay in the middle of the road. They get run over.
Aneurin Bevan in a speech. Reported Observer 9 *Dec* 1953

14 I have never regarded politics as the arena of morals. It is the arena of interests.
Aneurin Bevan. Quoted Michael Foot, ANEURIN BEVAN 1897–1945

15 So far as I am concerned the Tory Party are lower than vermin.
Aneurin Bevan. Speech, Manchester 4 *Jul* 1949

16 Politics is a blood sport.
Aneurin Bevan. Quoted Jennie Lee, MY LIFE WITH NYE

17 Politics are not the task of a Christian.
Dietrich Bonhoeffer, NO RUSTY SWORDS

18 In politics it is immensely important to know what it *feels* like to be someone else . . . Human beings are not islands, least of all politicians.
Sir Edward Boyle. Quoted Susan Barnes, Sunday Express 25 *Aug* 1963

19 Politics, and the fate of mankind, are shaped by men without ideals and without greatness. Men who have greatness within them don't go in for politics.
Albert Camus, NOTEBOOKS 1935–1942

20 I am not made for politics because I am incapable of wishing for, or accepting the death of my adversary.
Albert Camus, THE REBEL 1951

21 No wonder Harold is back in form — every Labour politician feels more at home attacking his own party's politics.
Cartoon caption, Punch 31 *Jan* 1973

22 Every politician is emphatically a promising politician.
G. K. Chesterton, THE RED MOON OF MERU

23 It has been said that success in politics cannot be won without a conviction that one's opponents are not only wrong but damned.
Colin R. Coote, Daily Telegraph 7 *Mar* 1963

24 The only safe pleasure for a parliamentarian is a bag of boiled sweets.
Julian Critchley MP, Observer 13 *Jun* 1982

25 a politician is an arse upon / which everyone has sat except a man.
e. e. cummings, ONE TIMES ONE, *a politician* 1944

POLITICS

1 To sacrifice one's honour to one's party is so
unselfish an act that our most generous
statesmen have not hesitated to do it.
Charles John (Justice) Darling, SCINTIL-
LAE JURIS

2 My family would hardly approve of my
marrying a politician.
*Actress Joan Fontaine to Adlai Stevenson,
recorded in her autobiography*, NO BED OF
ROSES

3 You can't just read blue books. It's like
having straw for breakfast.
Michael Foot. Quoted John Mortimer,
Sunday Times, *Foot at Bay* 19 *Sep* 1982

4 Few things are as immutable as the
addiction of political groups to the ideas by
which they have once won office.
J. K. Galbraith, THE AFFLUENT SOCIETY
1958

5 Politics consists in choosing between the
disastrous and the unpalatable.
J. K. Galbraith, LIFE IN OUR TIMES 1981

6 There is just one rule for politicians all over
the world. Don't say in Power what you say
in Opposition: if you do you only have to
carry out what the other fellows have found
impossible.
John Galsworthy, MAID IN WAITING

7 Since a politician never believes what he
says, he is surprised when others believe
him.
Gen. Charles de Gaulle, Newsweek 1 *Oct*
1962

8 Politics is too serious a matter to be left to
the politicians.
Gen. Charles de Gaulle

9 Most British statesmen have either drunk
too much or womanised too much. I never
fell into the second category.
Lord George-Brown

10 There are too many men in politics and not
enough elsewhere.
Hermione Gingold. Quoted Observer
2 *Oct* 1958

11 One political party is very much like
another, especially in office.
Norman Ginsbury, VICEROY SARAH

12 If Labour is the answer it must have been a
bloody silly question.
Graffito, reported in the Daily Telegraph
25 *Jan* 1979

13 The thing about a politician is that you have
to take the smooth with the smooth.
Susan Hill, BBC Radio 4, *Quote Unquote*
29 *Aug* 1980

14 Never judge a country by its politics. After
all, we English are quite honest by nature,
aren't we?
Alfred Hitchcock, THE LADY VANISHES

15 You can't adopt politics as a profession and
remain honest.
*Louis McHenry Howe, F. D. Roosevelt's
secretary. Speech, Columbia University
School of Journalism* 17 *Jan* 1933

16 A politician rises on the backs of his
friends . . . but it is through his enemies he
will have to govern afterwards.
Richard Hughes, THE FOX IN THE ATTIC
1961

17 MPs are only human — give or take the
occasional vampire or Martian.
Frank Johnson, Daily Telegraph 20 *Mar*
1979

18 Mothers all want their sons to grow up to
become president, but they don't want
them to become politicians in the process.
John F. Kennedy. Quoted Barbara Rowe,
A BOOK OF QUOTES

19 Politicians are the same everywhere. They
promise to build bridges even where there
are no rivers.
*Nikita Khrushchev to American reporters,
Oct* 1960

20 We demand of our political life greater
certainty and greater perfection than we
demand of our personal life.
Max Lerner, ACTIONS AND PASSIONS 1946

21 The acting abilities of Mr. Wilson and Mr.
Macmillan were such that either could have
earned a substantial living and devoted
following on the stage of the theatre had he
not been called instead to the drama of
politics.
Bernard Levin, THE PENDULUM YEARS
1976

22 Politicians tend to live *in character* and
many a public figure has come to imitate the
journalism which describes him.
Walter Lippmann, A PREFACE TO POLI-
TICS 1914

23 The man who raises new issues has always
been distasteful to politicians. He messes
up what has been so tidily arranged.
Id.

1 What do you want to be a sailor for? There are greater storms in politics than you'll ever find at sea. Piracy, broadsides, blood on the deck—you'll find them all in politics.
David Lloyd George to Julian Amery. Quoted Observer, Buccaneer of the Right 2 Jan 1966

2 A politician is a person with whose politics you don't agree; if you agree with him he is a statesman.
David Lloyd George

3 When you're abroad you're a statesman. When you're at home you're just a politician.
Harold Macmillan. Speech 1958

4 A candidate for office can have no greater advantage than muddled syntax; no greater liability than a command of language.
Marya Mannes, MORE IN ANGER 1958

5 It is very unfair to expect a politician to live in private up to the statements he makes in public.
W. Somerset Maugham, THE CIRCLE 1921

6 Porteous: Shouldn't I have been Prime Minister, Clare?
Lady Kitty? Prime Minister? You haven't the brain, you haven't the character.
Champion-Cheny: Cheek, push and a gift of the gab will serve very well instead, you know.
Id.

7 One has to be a lowbrow, a bit of a murderer, to be a politician, ready and willing to see people sacrificed, slaughtered for the sake of an idea, whether a good one or a bad one.
Henry Miller, WRITERS AT WORK

8 The proper memory for a politician is one that knows when to remember and when to forget.
John Morley, RECOLLECTIONS 1917

9 Any party which takes credit for the rain must not be surprised if its opponents blame it for the drought.
Dwight W. Morrow. Campaign speech, Oct 1930

10 The misfortune of high-minded intellectuals [in politics] is that, until it is too late, they remain as unaware of the sudden waves of emotion by which the majority can be swayed as they do of the shabby secret stratagems of ambitious men.
Harold Nicolson, Observer 12 Oct 1958

11 I'll speak for the man, or against him, whichever will do him most good.
President Richard Nixon, when agreeing to support a politician

12 A politician is like quicksilver. If you try to put your finger on him you will find nothing under it.
Austin O'Malley

13 Political language — and with variations this is true of all political parties from Conservatives to Anarchists — is designed to make lies sound truthful, a murder respectable, and to give an appearance of solidity to pure wind.
George Orwell, SHOOTING AN ELEPHANT 1950

14 I gave up politics when I discovered that I would rather be a poet than a prime minister.
John Pardoe, BBC Radio 4 2 Apr 1980

15 Let us suppose that the post to be filled is that of Prime Minister. The modern method is to trust in various methods of election, with results that are almost invariably disastrous.
C. Northcote Parkinson, PARKINSON'S LAW 1957

16 All political lives, unless they are cut off in mid-stream at a happy juncture, end in failure.
Enoch Powell in a Sunday Times interview 6 Nov 1977

17 The amateur in politics is the person who is always sure he knows the result of the next General Election.
Enoch Powell. Speech 3 Feb 1981

18 The rule of practice for serious politicians is "Read, read, read". One can never read enough.
Enoch Powell. Quoted Observer, Sayings of the Week 9 Jan 1983

19 I used to say that politics was the second lowest profession and I have come to know that it bears a great similarity to the first.
Ronald Reagan. Quoted Observer 13 May 1979

20 Political campaigns are designedly made into emotional orgies which endeavour to distract attention from the real issues involved, and they actually paralyse what slight powers of cerebration man can normally master.
James Harvey Robinson, THE HUMAN COMEDY

1 The more you read about politics, you got to admit that each party is worse than the other.
Will Rogers, A ROGERS' THESAURUS

2 I am reminded of four definitions. A radical is a man with both feet firmly planted — in the air; a conservative is a man with two perfectly good legs who, however, has never learned to walk; a reactionary is a somnambulist walking backwards; a liberal is a man who uses his legs and his hands at the behest of his head.
Franklin D. Roosevelt. Radio broadcast 26 Oct 1939

3 I have seen too many people drop dead or become alcoholics because they can't get away from the glamour that seems to pervade being an MP.
Paul Rose MP for Manchester Blackley, explaining his reasons for giving up politics 22 Feb 1979

4 This evil-smelling bog.
Lord Roseberry. Quoted Winston Churchill, GREAT CONTEMPORARIES 1937

5 Revolutionary spirits of my father's generation waited for Lefty. Existentialist heroes of my youth waited for Godot. Neither showed up.
Theodore Roszak, UNFINISHED ANIMAL

6 Our great democracies still tend to think that a stupid man is more likely to be honest than a clever man, and our politicians take advantage of this prejudice by pretending to be even more stupid than nature has made them.
Bertrand Russell, NEW HOPES FOR A CHANGING WORLD 1951

7 An Englishman has to have a Party, just as he has to have trousers.
Bertrand Russell in a letter to Maurice Amos MP 16 Jun 1936

8 A remark once made to me by the late Philip Guedella was to the effect that voting papers should be made so complicated that only the most highly educated Liberals could understand them.
Mrs. Jean V. Saunders, letter to Daily Telegraph 21 *Mar* 1979

9 The politician who once had to learn how to flatter kings has now to learn how to fascinate, amuse, coax, humbug, frighten or otherwise strike the fancy of the electorate.
George Bernard Shaw, MAN AND SUPERMAN 1905

10 He knows nothing and thinks he knows everything. That points clearly to a political career.
George Bernard Shaw, MAJOR BARBARA 1905

11 A politician is a statesman who approaches every question with an open mouth.
Adlai Stevenson. Quoted L. Harris, THE FINE ART OF POLITICAL WIT

12 An independent is a guy who wants to take the politics out of politics.
Adlai Stevenson, THE ART OF POLITICS

13 A particular feature of British politics is 'the indispensable man'. He is the one who undertakes the awkward tasks that no one else wants to bother with. He gets down to work, solves most of the difficult problems and then trips up over one of them. On this he is cast out of office with a few words of regret.
A. J. P. Taylor, Observer, *Doing the donkey work, review* of *J. A. Cross's* LORD SWINTON 9 *Jan* 1983

14 Some of our best politicians are unable to form a grammatical sentence of more than ten words.
Daily Telegraph, *leader* 19 *Feb* 1983

15 In politics, if you want anything said, ask a man; if you want anything done, ask a woman.
Margaret Thatcher, in 1965. *Quoted Anthony Sampson,* THE CHANGING ANATOMY OF BRITAIN 1982

16 The Prime Minister is stealing our clothes but he is going to look pretty ridiculous walking around in mine.
Margaret Thatcher of James Callaghan 1973

17 I can trust my husband not to fall asleep on a public platform and he usually claps in the right places.
Margaret Thatcher, Observer 20 *Aug* 1978

18 You've got to accept it. Politicians can plait sawdust.
A trade union official. Quoted Sunday Times 2 *Jul* 1967

19 Politics is the art of preventing people from taking part in affairs which properly concern them.
Paul Valéry, TEL QUEL 1943

20 Politicians can forgive almost anything in the way of abuse; they can forgive subversion, revolution, being contradicted,

exposed as liars, even ridiculed, but they can never forgive being ignored.
Auberon Waugh, Observer, *How Wodehouse Had the Last Laugh* 11 *Oct* 1981

1 Margaret Thatcher's great strength seems to be the better people know her, the better they like her. But, of course, she has one great disadvantage — she is a daughter of the people and looks trim, as the daughters of the people desire to be. Shirley Williams has such an advantage over her because she's a member of the upper middle-class and can achieve that distraught kitchen-sink-revolutionary look that one cannot get unless one's been to a really good school.
Dame Rebecca West at age 83 in an interview with Jilly Cooper

2 A week is a long time in politics.
Sir Harold Wilson

3 A constant effort to keep his party together, without sacrificing either principle or the essentials of basic strategy, is the very stuff of political leadership. Macmillan was canonised for it.
Sir Harold Wilson, FINAL TERM: THE LABOUR GOVERNMENT 1974–76

4 The Labour party is like a stage-coach. If you rattle along at great speed everybody inside is too exhilarated or too seasick to cause any trouble. But if you stop everybody gets out and argues about where to go next.
Sir Harold Wilson. Quoted Leslie Smith, HAROLD WILSON, THE AUTHENTIC PORTRAIT

5 For socialists, going to bed with the Liberals is like having oral sex with a shark.
Larry Zolf

POLLUTION

6 The quality of Mersey is not strained.
Anon., Sunday Graphic 14 *Aug* 1932

7 The crowd has found the door into the secret garden. Now they will tear up the flowers by the roots, strip the borders and strew them with paper and broken bottles.
Alan Bennett, FORTY YEARS ON

8 Do no dishonour to the earth, lest you dishonour the spirit of man.
Henry Besson, THE OUTERMOST HOUSE

9 They [seaside resorts] improvidentially piped growing volumes of sewage into the

sea, the healing virtues of which were advertised on every railway station.
Robert Cecil, LIFE IN EDWARDIAN ENGLAND 1969

10 Our Georgian forerunners . . . ignored the natural smells of sweat and dung and dirt as we ignore the artificial smells of petrol fumes and industrial effluents.
John Gloag, GEORGIAN GRACE

11 Many people live in ugly wastelands but in the absence of imaginative standards most of them do not even know it.
C. Wright Mills, POWER POLITICS AND PEOPLE 1963

12 Unless man can make new and original adaptations to his environment as rapidly as his science can change the environment, our culture will perish.
Carl R. Rogers, ON BECOMING A PERSON

13 The emergence of intelligence, I am convinced, tends to unbalance the ecology. In other words, intelligence is the great polluter. It is not until a creature begins to manage its environment that nature is thrown into disorder.
Clifford D. Simax, SHAKESPEARE'S PLANET

POPULARITY

14 Everybody hates me because I'm so universally liked.
Peter De Vries, THE VALE OF LAUGHTER 1968

POPULATION

15 The command 'Be fruitful and multiply' was promulgated according to our authorities, when the population of the world consisted of two people.
W. R. Inge (Dean of St. Pauls), MORE LAY THOUGHTS OF A DEAN

16 The purpose of population is not ultimately peopling earth. It is to fill heaven.
Dr. Graham Leonard (Bishop of London), CHURCH OF ENGLAND SYNOD, *Church and Bomb debate* 10 *Feb* 1983

PORNOGRAPHY

17 Oh Calcutta is the sort of show that gives pornography a bad name.
Clive Barnes. Quoted, THE FRANK MUIR BOOK

18 It is not good enough to spend time and ink in describing the penultimate sensations

and physical movements of people getting into a state of rut, we all know them too well.
John Galsworthy of D. H. Lawrence's SONS AND LOVERS, *in a letter to Edward Garnett* 13 *Apr* 1914

1 It is just possible that those who are most vocally concerned about pornography are really pre-occupied with their own hang-ups.
William Hardcastle, Punch 1 *Dec* 1972

2 Pornography is the attempt to insult sex, to do dirt on it.
D. H. Lawrence, PHOENIX 1936

3 It is heartless and it is mindless and it is a lie.
John McGahern, THE PORNOGRAPHER

4 Inside every pornographer there is an infant screaming for the breast from which it has been torn. Pornography represents an endless and infinitely repeated effort to recapture that breast, and the bliss it offered.
Steven Marcus, THE OTHER VICTORIANS

5 Laughter serves to neutralise pornography and is therefore anathema to pornographers. A man I know was thrown out of a Marseilles brothel for laughing at a pornographic film which was being shown there to stimulate business.
Malcolm Muggeridge, TREAD SOFTLY FOR YOU TREAD ON MY JOKES 1966

6 Its avowed purpose is to excite sexual desire, which, I should have thought, is unnecessary in the case of the young, inconvenient in the case of the middle aged, and unseemly in the old.
Id.

7 Nine tenths of the appeal of pornography is due to the indecent feelings concerning sex which moralists inculcate in the young. The other tenth is physiological, and will occur in one way or another whatever the state of the law may be.
Bertrand Russell, MARRIAGE AND MORALS 1929

8 Don't be daft. You don't get pornography on there, not on the telly. You get filth, that's all. The only place you get pornography is in yer Sunday papers.
Johnny Speight, BBC 1 TV, *Till Death Us Do Part*

9 Dirty old men are incapable of being corrupted any further, and as long as they make up the majority of regular customers a bookseller does not break the law in selling dirty books to them, two High Court judges decided yesterday.
Daily Telegraph. *Quoted Alan Coren*, Punch 23 *Feb* 1972

10 I have never heard of a girl being seduced by a book.
James J. Walker, Mayor of New York. Quoted J. K. Galbraith, THE AGE OF UNCERTAINTY 1977

PORTRAIT

11 It's an outrage — but it's a masterpiece.
Lord Beaverbrook, on first seeing Graham Sutherland's portrait of him

12 It seems to be a law of nature that no man ever is loth to sit for his portrait.
Max Beerbohm, QUIA IMPERFECTUM

13 This portrait is a remarkable example of modern art. It certainly combines force with candour.
Winston Churchill on Graham Sutherland's portrait of him.

14 It makes me look as if I was straining at stool.
Id.

15 You have no idea what portrait painters suffer from the vanity of their sitters.
Kenneth, Lord Clark. Quoted Observer 29 *Mar* 1959

16 Mr. Fildes, to whom I am sitting for my portrait, is under the impression that I am a short, stout man.
Edward VII. Quoted L. V. Fildes, LUKE FILDES: A VICTORIAN PAINTER

17 The painter does not copy the expression a face may have shown, he divines and paints the expression the face must have shown had the man fully revealed himself.
Edward Howard Griggs, A BOOK OF MEDITATIONS

18 I think it's marvellous. I do so love sitting still while other people work.
Robert Morley, on having his portrait painted, The Times 21 *Dec* 1981

19 To have one's portrait painted is such good value for the ego in these troubled times. It is a pity the poor artist makes so little out of it. They have to buy all the paints, you know.
Id.

1 The person portrayed and the portrait are two entirely different things.
José Ortega y Gassett, THE DEHUMANISATION OF ART

2 Few persons who ever sat for a portrait can have felt anything but inferior while the process is going on.
Anthony Powell. Quoted Observer 9 Jan 1983

3 Every time I paint a portrait I lose a friend.
John Singer Sargent. Quoted Richard Ormond, JOHN SINGER SARGENT

4 More and more people are having their portraits painted. Once a company has set a precedent no chairman will miss his chance, whatever the cost, to hang on the boardroom wall with the rest of them, even though many regard the sittings in the same light as going to the dentist.
Carl De Winter, The Times 21 *Dec* 1981

POSSIBILITY

5 The only way of finding the limits of the possible is by going beyond them into the impossible.
Arthur C. Clarke, THE LOST WORLDS OF 2001

6 Knowledge of what is possible is the beginning of happiness.
George Santayana, LITTLE ESSAYS 1920

POSTERITY

7 Posterity is as likely to be wrong as anybody else.
Heywood Brown, SITTING ON THE WORLD

POTATO

8 Sir Walter Raleigh gripped his seat under the table. He had sailed half way round the world to find this root . . . and now Elizabeth of England was tasting it. Elizabeth of England spat. "Not, enough salt." she said.
Carl Brahms and S. J. Simon, NO BED FOR BACON 1963

9 What I say is that, if a fellow really likes potatoes, he must be a pretty decent sort of fellow.
A. A. Milne, NOT THAT IT MATTERS

EZRA POUND

10 I remember only one thing about Pound. He had a beard, and it looked false.
Anonymous critic in Times Literary Supplement. *Quoted Anthony Burgess*, Observer, *Mad About Writing* 13 *Mar* 1983

POVERTY

11 What fun it would be to be poor, as long as one was *excessively* poor. Anything in excess is most exhilarating.
Jean Anouilh, THE REHEARSAL 1950

12 Nothing is sadder than having worldly standards without worldly means.
Van Wyck Brooks, A CHILMARK MISCELLANY

13 When you have learnt all that Oxford can teach you, go and discover why, with so much wealth in Britain, there continues to be so much poverty, and how poverty can be cured.
Edward Caird, Master of Balliol to William, Lord Beveridge

14 People don't resent having nothing nearly as much as too little.
Ivy Compton-Burnett, A FAMILY AND A FORTUNE 1934

15 The very poor are unthinkable and only to be approached by the statistician and the poet.
E. M. Forster, HOWARDS END 1910

16 The arithmetic of modern politics makes it tempting to overlook the very poor, because they are an inarticulate minority.
J. K. Galbraith. Quoted Lyndon B. Johnson, THE VANTAGE POINT

17 For every talent that poverty has stimulated, it has blighted a hundred.
John W. Gardner, EXCELLENCE 1961

18 That is one of the bitter curses of poverty; it leaves no right to be generous.
George Gissing, THE PRIVATE PAPERS OF HENRY RYECROFT 1903

19 People who are much too sensitive to demand of cripples that they run races ask of the poor that they get up and act just like everyone else in society.
Michael Harrington, THE OTHER AMERICA 1962

20 If a free society cannot help the many who are poor it cannot save the few who are rich.
John F. Kennedy. Speech 20 *Jan* 1961

21 The trouble with being poor is that it takes up all your time.
William de Kooning. Quoted Barbara Rowe, A BOOK OF QUOTES

1 The poor insist on being buried. It's usually the only way they can ensure of getting a garden of their own.
Derek Marlowe, A DANDY IN ASPIC 1966

2 We shall never solve the paradox of want in the midst of plenty by doing away with plenty.
Ogden Mills. Speech, New York 21 Mar 1934

3 Poverty is the great reality. That is why the artist seeks it.
Anaïs Nin, DIARY, *Summer 1937*

4 Poverty keeps together more homes than it breaks up.
Saki, THE CHRONICLES OF CLOVIS, *Esme 1912*

5 I have been a common man and a poor man, and it has no romance for me.
George Bernard Shaw, MAJOR BARBARA 1905

6 It is very good, sometimes, to have nothing. I want society, not me, to have places to sit in and beds to lie in; and who wants a hatstand of his very own?
Dylan Thomas. Quoted Andrew Sinclair, DYLAN THOMAS: POET OF HIS PEOPLE

7 I have achieved poverty with distinction, but never poverty with dignity; the best I can manage is dignity with poverty.
Dylan Thomas, Letter to Henry Treece

8 A society of *poor* gentlemen, upon whose hands time lies heavy, is absolutely necessary to art and literature.
Jack B. Yeats in a letter. Quoted William Plomer, ELECTRIC DELIGHTS

POWER

9 A friend in power is a friend lost.
Henry Brooks Adams, THE EDUCATION OF HENRY ADAMS 1907

10 One man can change the world with a bullet in the right place.
Lindsay Anderson's 'IF . . .' *(film), script by David Sherwin 1968*

11 Power without responsibility has been the privilege of the harlot throughout the ages.
Stanley Baldwin, of Beaverbrook's newspapers, in a by-election speech 1931

12 If you are the summit of a volcano the least you can do is smoke.
Winston Churchill, GREAT CONTEMPORARIES, *The Ex-Kaiser 1937*

13 To be a great autocrat you must be a great barbarian.
Joseph Conrad, THE MIRROR OF THE SEA 1906

14 Men of power have not time to read; yet men who do not read are unfit for power.
Michael Foot, DEBTS OF HONOUR

15 Power is the ultimate aphrodisiac.
Henry Kissinger. Quoted Guardian 28 Nov 1976

16 Political power grows out of the barrel of a gun.
Mao Tse-Tung, THE THOUGHTS OF CHAIRMAN MAO

17 The men who really wield, retain and covet power are the kind who answer bedside telephones while making love.
Nicholas Pileggi. Quoted Barbara Rowe, A BOOK OF QUOTES

18 Religions, which condemn the pleasures of sense, drive men to seek the pleasures of power. Throughout history power has been the vice of the ascetic.
Bertrand Russell, New York Herald-Tribune Magazine 6 *May 1938*

19 The poor don't know that their function in life is to exercise our generosity.
Jean-Paul Sartre, THE WORDS 1964

20 The wrong sort of people are always in power because they would not be in power if they were not the wrong sort of people.
Jon Wynne Tyson, Times Literary Supplement

21 Cheerful, irresponsible people are rewarded for possessing some knack such as being able to hit a golf-ball accurately or play records on the wireless in a winning manner . . . It is all wrong. There is too much grit in the money-machine. When money is the key to power some of the power will get into the wrong hands.
John Wain, Punch 28 *Sep 1960*

PRACTICE

22 That practice makes perfect is not necessarily so. Practice makes permanent . . . Incorrect practice, bad practice, will eventually produce permanent bad habits.
Charles Hughes, THE F.A. COACHING BOOK OF SOCCER TACTICS AND SKILLS

23 If I go a week without practice the audience notices it. If I go a day without practice, I notice it.
Artur Rubenstein. Quoted Alistair Cooke BBC 4, *Letter From America 31 May 1974*

PRAGMATISM

1 The pragmatist knows that doubt is an art which has to be acquired with difficulty.
Charles Sanders Pierce, COLLECTED PAPERS

PRAISE

2 Praise out of season or tactlessly bestowed can freeze the heart as much as blame.
Pearl S. Buck, TO MY DAUGHTERS, WITH LOVE 1916

3 Watch how a man takes praise and there you have the measure of him.
Thomas Burke, T.P.'s Weekly, *Talks With Theodore Dreiser* 8 *Jun* 1928

4 From the moment I picked up your book until I laid it down, I was convulsed with laughter. Some day I intend reading it.
Groucho Marx to S. J. Perelman. Quoted Perelman, THE LAST LAUGH

5 People ask you for criticism, but they only want praise.
W. Somerset Maugham, OF HUMAN BONDAGE 1915

6 In recommending a book to a friend the less said the better. The moment you praise a book too highly you awaken resistance in your listener.
Henry Miller, THE BOOKS IN MY LIFE 1952

7 The highest term of praise that many English people ever use is "Not bad".
Bertrand Russell, Saturday Evening Post 3 *Jun* 1956

8 Praise shames me, for I secretly beg for it.
Rabindranath Tagore, STRAY BIRDS 1916

PRAYER

9 'Amen' is a special way of saying 'Over and out' to God.
Anonymous child

10 Even if there were no ear for them but the void our prayers would be the only things that sanctify our existence.
William Barrett, THE ILLUSION OF TECHNIQUE

11 The wish to pray is a prayer in itself.
George Bernanos, DIARY OF A COUNTRY PRIEST 1936

12 *Pray, v.* To ask that the rules of the universe be annulled on behalf of a single petitioner, confessedly unworthy.
Ambrose Bierce, THE DEVIL'S DICTIONARY 1906

13 "Does God always answer prayer?" the cardinal was asked. "Yes" he said. "And sometimes the answer is — 'No' "
Alistair Cooke, BBC Radio 4, *Letter from America* 8 *Mar* 1981

14 The most odious of concealed narcissisms — prayer.
John Fowles, THE ARISTOS

15 Lord forgive me all the little tricks I play on you and I'll forgive the great big one you played on me.
Robert Frost

16 Prayer is not an old woman's idle amusement. Properly understood and applied it is the most potent instrument of action.
Mahatma Gandhi, NON-VIOLENCE IN PEACE AND WAR 1948

17 You pray in your distress and in your need; would that you might pray also in the fullness of your joy and in your days of abundance.
Kahil Gibran, THE PROPHET 1926

18 Your cravings as a human animal do not become a prayer just because it is God whom you must ask to attend to them.
Dag Hammarskjöld, MARKINGS 1964

19 Work is prayer. Work is also stink. Therefore stink is prayer.
Aldous Huxley, JESTING PILATE 1926

20 Prayer is more than meditation. In meditation the source of strength is one's self. When one prays he goes to a source of strength greater than his own.
Mme Chiang Kai-shek, I CONFESS MY FAITH

21 Our dourest parsons, who followed the nonconformist fashion of long extemporary prayers, always seemed to me to be bent on bullying God. After a few 'beseech thees' as a mere politeness, they adopted a sterner tone and told Him what they expected from Him and more than hinted He must attend to His work.
J. B. Priestley, OUTCRIES AND ASIDES

22 Common people do not pray; they only beg.
George Bernard Shaw, MISALLIANCE 1910

23 And here's to you, Mrs. Robinson / Jesus loves you more than you will know. / God bless you please, Mrs. Robinson / Heaven holds a place for those who pray.
Paul Simon, MRS. ROBINSON

1 I don't want to bore God.
Orson Welles, explaining why he did not pray, Observer, *Sayings of the Week* 28 *Mar* 1982

2 Prayers for the condemned man will be offered on an adding machine. Numbers constitute the only universal language.
Nathanael West, MISS LONELY HEARTS 1933

PREACHING

3 Preaching to some people is like eating custard with a fork. It goes in one ear and out the other.
Anonymous curate. Quoted BBC Radio 4, *Quote Unquote* 2 *Feb* 1982

4 Ah, sir, you should have heard him throw down Jezebel.
Anthony C. Deane, quoting a verger, in TIME REMEMBERED

5 He [Adam Starkadder] paused and drew a long breath, then thundered at the top of his voice "Ye're all damned!"
An expression of lively interest and satisfaction passed over the faces of the Brethren, and there was a general rearranging of arms and legs as though they wanted to sit as comfortably as possible while listening to the bad news.
Stella Gibbons, COLD COMFORT FARM 1932

6 Only the sinner has the right to preach.
Robert Morley

7 The British churchgoer prefers a severe preacher because he thinks a few home truths will do his neighbours no harm.
George Bernard Shaw

PRECAUTION

8 I hate to depress you, but you'll hate the day you ever took this assignment. This is an ordeal by fire. Make sure you wear asbestos pants.
Hermann Mankiewicz, advice to S. J. Perelman on working for the Marx Brothers. Quoted S. J. Perelman, THE LAST LAUGH 1982

9 Reading and smoking in bed are the sort of faults of which wives complain, and they are the sort of things they could and should have found out before they got married.
Letter to Daily Mirror. *Quoted* News Review 15 *Apr* 1948

10 In baiting a mouse-trap with cheese always leave room for the mouse.
Saki, THE SQUARE EGG, *The Infernal Parliament* 1924

PREJUDICE

11 Mother is far too clever to understand anything she does not like.
Arnold Bennett, THE TITLE 1918

12 Prejudice is a vagrant opinion without visible means of support.
Ambrose Bierce, THE DEVIL'S DICTIONARY 1906

13 I am free of all prejudice. I hate everyone equally.
W. C. Fields. Quoted Jerome Beatty, Saturday Review 28 *Jan* 1967

14 Prejudices are the props of civilisation.
André Gide, THE COUNTERFEITERS 1926

15 Nobody outside of a baby carriage or a judge's chamber believes in an unprejudiced point of view.
Lillian Hellman. Quoted Barbara Rowe, A BOOK OF QUOTES

16 There is a tendency to judge a race, a nation, or a distinct group by its least worthy members.
Eric Hoffer, THE TRUE BELIEVER 1951

17 A great many people think they are thinking when they are merely rearranging their prejudices.
William James. Quoted A. A. Andrews, QUOTATIONS FOR SPEAKERS AND WRITERS. *Also attr. Ed Murrow,* AMERICAN BROADCASTER *and to Adlai Stevenson by Leon Harris in* THE FINE ART OF POLITICAL WIT

18 The tendency of the casual mind is to pick out or stumble upon a sample which supports or defines its prejudices, and then to make it representative of a whole class.
Walter Lippmann, PUBLIC OPINIONS 1929

19 One may no more live in the world without picking up the moral prejudice of the world than one will be able to go to hell without perspiring.
H. L. Mencken, PREJUDICES 1921

20 Everyone is a prisoner of his own experiences. No one can eliminate prejudices — just recognise them.
Ed Murrow, broadcast 31 *Dec* 1955

21 The collection of prejudices which is called political philosophy is useful provided it is not called philosophy.
Bertrand Russell, AUTOBIOGRAPHY 1967

PRESENT

1 The now, the here, through which all future plunges to the past.
James Joyce, ULYSSES 1922

2 The future will one day be the present and will seem as unimportant as the present does now.
W. Somerset Maugham, THE SUMMING UP 1938

3 The passing moment is all we can be sure of; it is only common sense to extract the utmost value from it.
Id.

4 The word 'now' is like a bomb through the window, and it ticks.
Arthur Miller, AFTER THE FALL 1964

5 The only living life is in the past and future — the present is an interlude — strange interlude in which we call on past and future to bear witness that we are living.
Eugene O'Neill, STRANGE INTERLUDE 1928

PRESTIGE

6 If the members of a tribal group are sufficiently conscious of the boundary that separates them from the rest of the world the tribe becomes *the* world to its members . . . This means in turn that the prestige system of the tribe is the only one that has meaning to a member and it is all important as everything within depends on the exclusion of what is without.
J. K. Galbraith, ECONOMICS, PEACE AND LAUGHTER 1971

PRETENTIOUSNESS

7 Last year the sanitary engineers suggested that they should be known as Public Health Officers. We should be lucky they did not want to call themselves Privy Counsellors.
Lord Mancroft. Speech to Auctioneers and Estate Agents, Dorchester Hotel 31 Oct 1957

8 [He] is always called a nerve specialist because it sounds better, but everyone knows he's a sort of janitor in a looney bin.
P. G. Wodehouse, THE INIMITABLE JEEVES 1924

PRIDE

9 Don't think yourself so pretty. Even if a man on a galloping horse did carry you off one dark night he would drop you off at the first lighted lamp post.
Sir Hugh Casson and Joyce Grenfell, NANNY SAYS 1972

10 The virtue of pride, which was once the beauty of mankind, has given place to that fount of all ugliness, Christian humility.
Max Ernst. Quoted John Russell, MAX ERNST

11 Many a man is praised for his reserve and so-called shyness when he is simply too proud to risk making a fool of himself. The vain man will cut capers in order to obtain notice and applause. The proud man asks for notice and applause without being willing to cut the capers, while the very proud man does not even want the applause.
J. B. Priestley, ALL ABOUT OURSELVES

12 A confessional passage has probably never been written that didn't stink a little of the writer's pride in having given up pride.
J. D. Salinger, SEYMOUR: AN INTRODUCTION 1963

13 Don't let that chip on your shoulder be your only reason for walking erect.
James Thurber, LANTERNS AND LANCES, *Midnight at Tim's Place* 1962

PRIEST

14 I always like to associate with a lot of priests because it makes me understand anti-clerical things so well.
Hilaire Belloc, letter to E.S.P. Haynes 9 Nov 1909

15 A priest is a man who is called Father by everyone except his own children who are obliged to call him Uncle.
Italian saying. Quoted Rupert Hart-Davis, THE LYTTELTON HART-DAVIS LETTERS 15 Jul 1956

PRINCIPLE

16 You can't learn too soon that the most useful thing about a principle is that it can always be sacrificed to an expediency.
W. Somerset Maugham, THE CIRCLE 1921

17 It is often easier to fight for principles than to live up to them.
Adlai Stevenson. Speech, New York 27 Aug 1952

PRISON

1 In prison they give you a green billiard ball and tell you it is an apple. If you try to eat it, they put you in the mailbag shop.
Anonymous prison inmate, BBC 1 TV, *Strangeways* 29 *Oct* 1980

2 All prisons are brimming over with innocence. It is those who cram their fellows into them, in the name of empty ideas, who are the only guilty ones.
Jean Anouilh, CATCH AS CATCH CAN 1960

3 The same skills needed to be a successful criminal are needed to survive in prison.
Robert Chesshyre, Observer, *This Is Your Life* 9 *Aug* 1981

4 In prison those things withheld from and denied the prisoner become precisely what he wants most of all.
Eldridge Cleaver, SOUL ON ICE, *On Becoming* 1968

5 The most efficient way for a man to survive in Britain is to be almost half-witted, completely irresponsible and spend a lot of time in prison, where his health is far better looked after than outside.
Charles Galton Darwin, THE NEXT MILLION YEARS

6 In the vocational training section prisoners were being taught the art of copper beating, and I saw some examples of excellent craftsmanship.
High Sheriff of Essex, letter to The Times. *Quoted*, Private Eye Bumper Book of Boobs

7 The only thing I really mind about going to prison is the thought of Lord Longford coming to visit me.
Richard Ingrams, editor of Private Eye

8 It feels like being in hospital without the fear of pain or in the army without fear of war.
Lord Kagan to reporters, on being released from prison 24 *Jun* 1981

9 It was better to be in a jail where you could bang the walls than in a jail you could not see.
Carson McCullers, THE MEMBER OF THE WEDDING 1946

10 We do not want our prisons to become dustbins.
Patrick Mayhew MP, House of Commons 26 *Nov* 1981

11 A prisoner has no sex. He is God's own eunuch.
Henry Miller, THE AIR-CONDITIONED NIGHTMARE 1945

12 There can be few places where false gods are more frequently found or more diligently followed than in the exercise yard of a large prison.
Sir Alexander Paterson, News Review 16 *Jan* 1947

13 Prison will not work until we start sending a better class of people there.
Laurence J. Peter

14 My fellow-prisoners seemed to me in no way morally inferior to the rest of the population though they were on the whole slightly below the usual level of intelligence, as was shown by their having been caught.
Bertrand Russell, AUTOBIOGRAPHY 1967

15 Here I have not a care in the world; the rest to nerves and will is heavenly. One is free from the torturing question: what more might I be doing? . . . Prison has some of the advantages of the Catholic Church.
Bertrand Russell, letter from prison to Frank Russell, May 1918

16 Prison is not a mere physical horror. It is using a pickaxe to no purpose that makes a prison.
Antoine de Saint-Exupéry, WIND SAND AND STARS 1939

17 The most anxious man in a prison is the warden.
George Bernard Shaw

18 Anyone who has been to an English public school will always feel comparatively at home in prison. It is the people brought up in the gay intimacy of the slums who find prison so soul-destroying.
Evelyn Waugh, DECLINE AND FALL 1928

PRIVACY

19 It is when we pass our own private gate, and open our own secret door, that we step into the land of the giants.
G. K. Chesterton, CHARLES DICKENS 1906

20 The human animal needs a privacy seldom mentioned, freedom from intrusion. He needs a little privacy quite as much as he wants understanding or vitamins or exercise or praise.
Phyllis McGinley, THE PROVINCE OF THE HEART, *A Lost Privilege* 1959

1 I might have been a goldfish in a glass bowl for all the privacy I got.
Saki, THE INNOCENCE OF REGINALD 1904

PRIVILEGE

2 People of privilege will always risk their complete destruction rather than surrender any material part of their advantage.
J. K. Galbraith. Quoted Barbara Rowe, A BOOK OF QUOTES

3 One of the privileges of the great is to witness catastrophes from a terrace.
Jean Giraudoux, TIGER AT THE GATES 1935

4 What men value in this world is not rights but privileges.
H. L. Mencken, MINORITY REPORT

5 Privilege is privilege, whether it is due to money or intellect or whether you have six toes.
Philip, Duke of Edinburgh. Quoted Noël St. George, ROYAL QUOTES

6 Privilege is not difficult to defend because even the most egalitarian societies have always recognised that it must be admitted to some extent.
John Wain, Punch 28 *Sep* 1960

PRIZE

7 The world continues to offer glittering prizes to those who have stout hearts and sharp swords.
Lord Birkenhead, COLLECTED SPEECHES

8 Not only should you not accept a prize. You should not try to deserve one either.
Jean Cocteau. Quoted Geoffrey Grigson, Sunday Times 23 *Jan* 1973

9 The real object of giving prizes in schools is to encourage the children to give as little trouble as possible.
George Bernard Shaw. Quoted Hesketh Pearson, BERNARD SHAW 1942

PROBLEM

10 I do not believe in final solutions. Even if you solve some problem the solution will always give rise to another problem.
Isaiah Berlin, CONCEPTS AND CATEGORIES

11 Few [problems] are difficult of solution. The difficulty, all but invariably, is in confronting them. We know what needs to be done; for reasons of inertia, pecuniary interest, passion or ignorance, we do not wish to say so.
J. K. Galbraith, THE AGE OF UNCERTAINTY 1977

12 The worst thing you can do to an important problem is discuss it.
Simon Gray, OTHERWISE ENGAGED *(play)*

13 You do not have to ignore problems in order to be happy, but you need to remind yourself constantly that the insurmountable difficulties of today are the solved problems of tomorrow.
Cardinal Heenan, THROUGH THE YEAR WITH CARDINAL HEENAN

14 Problems are only opportunities in work clothes.
Henry J. Kaiser. A favourite maxim, often quoted by him

15 Our problems are man-made, therefore they may be solved by man. And man can be as big as he wants. No problem of human destiny is beyond human beings.
John F. Kennedy. Speech, Washington University 10 *Jan* 1963

16 All progress is precarious, and the solution of one problem brings us face to face with another problem.
Martin Luther King, STRENGTH TO LIVE 1963

17 She probably laboured under the common delusion that you made things better by talking about them.
Rose Macaulay, CREWE TRAIN 1926

18 The man who is forever disturbed about the condition of humanity either has no problems of his own or has refused to face them.
Henry Miller, SUNDAY AFTER THE WAR 1944

19 The chief cause of problems is solutions.
Sevareid's Rule. Quoted Peter Dickson, THE OFFICIAL RULES

20 A problem left to itself dries up or goes rotten. But fertilise a problem with a solution — you'll hatch out a dozen others.
N. F. Simpson, A RESOUNDING TINKLE

21 No problem is insoluble given a big enough plastic bag.
Tom Stoppard, JUMPERS

PROCRASTINATION

22 Procrastination is the art of keeping up with yesterday.
Don Marquis, ARCHY AND MEHITABEL, *certain maxims of archy* 1927

1 Make me a beautiful word for doing things tomorrow, for that surely is a great and blessed invention.
George Bernard Shaw, BACK TO METHUSELAH 1922

2 In England we have come to rely upon a comfortable time lag of fifty years or a century intervening between the perception that something ought to be done and a serious attempt to do it.
H. G. Wells, THE WORK, WEALTH AND HAPPINESS OF MANKIND 1932

PRODIGY

3 *Prodigy:* A child who plays the piano when he ought to be asleep in bed.
Beachcomber (J. B. Morton)

PROFANITY

4 Pa's out and ma's out, let's talk dirt / Pee-poh-belly-bottom-drawers.
Children's rhyme. Quoted Robert Graves, OCCUPATION WRITER

5 How easy to swear if you're properly educated.
Christopher Fry, A PHOENIX TOO FREQUENT 1949

6 The word 'bloody' as we now use it is almost a term of affection.
Judge Rawlins, at Clerkenwell Court. Quoted News Review 20 *May* 1948

7 A foreign swear word is practically inoffensive except to the person who has learnt it early in life and knows its social limits.
Paul Theroux, THE GREAT RAILWAY BAZAAR

PROFESSION

8 All professions are conspiracies against the laity.
George Bernard Shaw, THE DOCTOR'S DILEMMA 1913

PROFESSOR

9 Our American professors like their literature clear, cold, pure and very dead.
Sinclair Lewis. Address, Swedish Academy 12 *Dec* 1930

PROFIT

10 It is a socialist idea that making profits is a vice. I consider the real vice is making losses.
Winston Churchill. Quoted Evan Esar, TREASURY OF HUMOROUS QUOTATIONS

11 The trouble with the profit system has always been that it was highly unprofitable to most people.
E. B. White, ONE MAN'S MEAT 1944

PROGRESS

12 All progress is based upon a universal innate desire on the part of every organism to live beyond its income.
Samuel Butler, NOTEBOOKS, *Life* 1912

13 Change is certain. Progress is not.
E. H. Carr, FROM NAPOLEON TO STALIN, AND OTHER ESSAYS

14 Unfortunately movement cannot be equated with progress.
Leslie Chapman, WASTE AWAY

15 Humanity has a naïve faith in progress. We are progressing, no doubt about that, but so were the Gadarene swine.
Bishop of Chelmsford, Courier Vol. 3 No. 2 1943

16 As enunciated today 'progress' is simply a comparative of which we have no settled superlative.
G. K. Chesterton, HERETICS 1905

17 Progress is merely a metaphor for walking along a road — very likely the wrong road.
G. K. Chesterton, ORTHODOXY 1908

18 pity this busy monster manunkind / not. Progress is a comfortable disease.
e. e. cummings, ONE TIMES ONE 1944

19 What we call progress is the exchange of one nuisance for another nuisance.
Havelock Ellis

20 What progress we are making. In the Middle Ages they would have burned me. Now they are content with burning my books.
Sigmund Freud, in a letter to Ernest Jones on the public burning of his books in Berlin 1933

21 They say you can't stop progress. But what is progress if it's just destroying everything?
Thor Heyerdahl, Radio Times, *interview with Tim Heald* 16 *Feb* 1979

1 The reason that men oppose progress is not that they hate progress but that they love inertia.
Elbert Hubbard, THE NOTEBOOK 1927

2 The world is moving so fast these days that the man who says it can't be done is generally interrupted by someone doing it.
Id.

3 Spiritual progress is our one ultimate aim. It may be towards the dateless and irrevocable, but it is inevitably dependent upon progress intellectual, moral and physical — progress in this changing, revolving world of dated events.
Julian Huxley, ESSAYS OF A BIOLOGIST 1923

4 The trouble with progress is that it can progress in any direction.
W. A. Ireland, Saturday Evening Post 26 *Apr* 1952

5 Progress is a nice word. But change is its motivator and change has its enemies.
Robert F. Kennedy, THE PURSUIT OF JUSTICE 1964

6 The notion of progress in a single line without goal or limit seems perhaps the most parochial notion of a very parochial century.
Lewis Mumford, TECHNICS AND CIVILISATION 1934

7 In every age the great human civilisations have depended far more upon emotional inspiration than upon the standard of plumbing.
Philip, Duke of Edinburgh, A QUESTION OF BALANCE

8 If anyone has a new idea in this country there are twice as many people who advocate putting a red flag in front of it.
Id.

9 To put it crudely, progress gives us better medical science, but it also gives us better bombs.
Philip, Duke of Edinburgh. Address to the Coal Industry Society

10 The test of our progress is not whether we add more to the abundance of those who have much; it is whether we provide enough for those who have too little.
F. D. Roosevelt. 2nd Inaugural Address 20 Jan 1937

11 Organic life has developed gradually from the protozoon to the philosopher and this development, we are assured, is indubitably an advancement. Unfortunately it is the philosopher not the protozoon, who gives this assurance.
Bertrand Russell, MYSTICISM AND LOGIC 1917

12 'Change' is scientific, 'progress' is ethical. Change is indubitable, whereas progress is a matter of controversy.
Bertrand Russell, UNPOPULAR ESSAYS 1950

13 Man's 'progress' is but a gradual discovery that his questions have no meaning.
Antoine Saint-Exupéry, THE WISDOM OF THE SANDS 1948

14 Three kinds of progress are significant; progress in knowledge and technology, progress in the socialisation of man, progress in spirituality. The last is the most important.
Albert Schweitzer, THE TEACHING OF REVERENCE FOR LIFE

15 In America getting on in the world means getting out of the world we have known before.
Ellery Sedgwick, THE HAPPY PROFESSION 1946

16 All progress means war with Society.
George Bernard Shaw, GETTING MARRIED 1911

17 When people shake their heads because we are living in a restless age, ask them how they would like to live in a stationary one and do without change.
George Bernard Shaw, INTELLIGENT WOMAN'S GUIDE TO SOCIALISM AND CAPITALISM 1928

18 The reasonable man adapts himself to the world; the unreasonable one persists in trying to adapt the world to himself. Therefore all progress depends on the unreasonable man.
George Bernard Shaw, MAN AND SUPERMAN 1905

19 Life means progress, and progress means suffering.
H. W. Van Loon, TOLERANCE

20 We are about to enter the age of flight before we've even developed a chair that a man can sit in comfortably.
Philip Wylie

PROHIBITION

1 Prohibition has made nothing but trouble.
Al Capone, gangster, in a newspaper interview

2 A great social and economic experiment, noble in motive and far-reaching in purpose.
President Herbert Hoover on the introduction of prohibition

3 Prohibition more than almost any human edict this century, proved that all extremes are wrong, and that bad extremes, pursued for ostensibly good ends, are worst of all.
Richard Last, Daily Telegraph 19 *Aug* 1981

4 Prohibition is going to be recorded as one of the results of the European War, foreseen by nobody.
Stephen Leacock, THE WOMAN QUESTION

5 The prohibition law, written for weaklings and derelicts, has divided the nation, like Gaul, into three parts — wets, drys and hypocrites.
Pauline Morton Sabu. Speech 9 *Mar* 1931

6 When by mere legislation, man can stop fruit from fermenting of its own accord after it falls to the ground he can talk about a law of prohibition. The very word destroys its meaning. You can't prohibit nature.
E. Temple Thurston, MR. BOTTLEBY DOES SOMETHING

PROMISCUITY

7 She thrived on advances — financial and sexual. She had four husbands and a regiment of lovers, and she could have had more if she hadn't been occupied with writing. She stopped being a *femme fatale* when she was 87 as the result of a series of strokes.
Paul Bailey, of Katherine Anne Porter, Observer, *Callie the Incredible* 13 *Mar* 1983

8 Like the bee its sting, the promiscuous leave behind in each encounter something of themselves by which they are made to suffer.
Cyril Connolly, THE UNQUIET GRAVE 1945

9 She's the original good time that was had by all.
Bette Davis of a rival actress. Quoted Leslie Halliwell, FILMGOER'S BOOK OF QUOTES

10 Elspeth had had so many men. Two of her sisters rode, so to speak, her discarded mounts.
F. Scott Fitzgerald, THE CRACK-UP 1936

11 If I'd been a ranch, they'd have named me the Bar Nothing.
Rita Hayworthe, lines spoken in the film GILDA

12 You were born with your legs apart. They'll send you to your grave in a Y-shaped coffin.
Joe Orton, WHAT THE BUTLER SAW *(play)*

13 That girl speaks eighteen languages and can't say no in any of them.
Dorothy Parker, of a film star. Quoted Leslie Halliwell, FILMGOER'S BOOK OF QUOTES

14 For Ian, women were like fishcakes. Mind you, he was very fond of fishcakes, but he never pretended that there was any great mystique about eating them.
John Pearson, quoting one of Ian Fleming's girl friends, LIFE OF IAN FLEMING 1966

15 I have been so misused by chaste men with one wife / That I would live with satyrs all my life.
Anna Wickham, SHIP NEAR SHOALS

PROMISE

16 If you won't give me your word of honour, will you give me your promise?
Sam Goldwyn. Quoted Alva Johnson, THE GREAT GOLDWYN

17 Since election promises are all the fashion, I challenge Mr. Gaitskell to meet this one; I promise you it'll rain on October 9th.
Harold Macmillan during election campaign, Sep 1959

18 A promise to men in grief is lightly broken.
John Masefield, THE WILD SWAN

19 A promise made is a debt unpaid.
Robert W. Service, THE SPELL OF THE YUKON 1907

PRONUNCIATION

20 "There's a moose loose."
"Are you English or Scots?"
Caption to cartoon, Punch

21 Everybody has the right to pronounce foreign names as he chooses.
Winston Churchill, Observer, *Sayings of the Week* 5 *Aug* 1951

1 Fine ear for the haspirate, that's what my darter Maria 'ave and what I, for one, 'ave not.
H. G. Hutchinson, Punch 29 *Jan* 1929

2 Elaine [Stritch] began to sing "When the tower of Babel fell" . . . and pronounced it to rhyme with scrabble.
Noël [Coward] stopped her and said "It's bayble Stritch."
"I've always said babble. Everyone says babble. It means mixed-up language, doesn't it? Gibberish. It's where we get babble from."
"That's a fabble," said Noël.
William Merchant, THE PRIVILEGE OF HIS COMPANY

3 To correct an Englishman's pronunciation is to imply that he is not quite a gentleman.
George Bernard Shaw, when chairman of the BBC's committee on standard pronunciation

4 While on the subject of voices — or verses as they would be called in Brooklyn . . .
P. G. Wodehouse, Punch 20 *Jul* 1960

PROPAGANDA

5 Propaganda is a soft weapon; hold it in your hands too long, and it will move about like a snake, and strike the other way.
Jean Anouilh, THE LARK 1953

6 The greater the lie, the greater the chance that it will be believed.
Adolf Hitler, MEIN KAMPF 1924

7 The greatest triumphs of propaganda have been accomplished, not by doing something, but by refraining from doing. Great is truth, but still greater from a practical point of view, is silence about truth.
Aldous Huxley, BRAVE NEW WORLD, *Foreword* 1932

8 The propagandist's purpose is to make one set of people forget that certain other sets of people are human.
Aldous Huxley, THE OLIVE TREE 1937

9 The first casualty when war comes is truth.
Hiram Johnson, US senator. Speech quoted Burton Stevenson, HOME BOOK OF QUOTATIONS

10 In our own day it would not be an unfair description of education to define it as the art which teaches men to be deceived by the printed word.
Prof. H. J. Laski, LIBERTY IN THE MODERN STATE

11 I give you bitter pills in sugar coating. The pills are harmless, the poison is in the sugar.
Stanislaw Lec, UNKEMPT THOUGHTS 1962

12 Your triumph as a propagandist will make you out of date. A great pamphlet perishes through lack of novelty, while a trivial drinking song may retain its freshness for centuries . . . few now read his [Swift's] Draper's Letters, compared with those who read Gulliver's Travels.
Robert Lynd, open letter to G. B. Shaw, John o'London's Weekly 16 *Dec* 1929

13 Nobody has ever succeeded in keeping nations at war except by lies.
Salvador de Madariaga. Quoted Burton Stevenson, THE HOME BOOK OF QUOTATIONS

14 Why is propaganda so much more successful when it stirs up hatred than when it tries to stir up friendly feeling?
Bertrand Russell, THE CONQUEST OF HAPPINESS 1936

PROPERTY

15 Property is necessary, but it is not necessary that it should remain for ever in the same hands.
Rémy de Gourmont

16 Property is organised robbery.
George Bernard Shaw, MAJOR BARBARA, *Preface* 1905

17 Gambling promises the poor what property performs for the rich — something for nothing.
George Bernard Shaw, MAJOR BARBARA 1905

PROPHECY

18 A hopeful disposition is not the sole qualification to be a prophet.
Winston Churchill, House of Commons 10 *Apr* 1927

19 There is no future, no present, in prophecy.
Alistair Cooke, BBC Radio 4, *Letter from America* 14 *Feb* 1982

20 The prophet himself stands under the judgment which he preaches. If he does not know that, he is a false prophet.
Reinhold Niebuhr, BEYOND TRAGEDY

21 It will be years — and not in my time — before a woman will lead the party or become Prime Minister.
Margaret Thatcher. Speech in 1974. *Quoted* Observer 8 *May* 1979

PROPRIETY

1 There can be no salacious or improper significance in applying the word 'Oomph' to women's footware.
Mr. Justice Evershed, giving judgment in the High Court 14 Oct 1946

PROSPERITY

2 Prosperity is only an instrument to be used, not a deity to be worshipped.
President Calvin Coolidge. Speech, Boston 11 Jun 1928

3 Armaments, universal debt and planned obsolescence — those are the three pillars of Western prosperity.
Aldous Huxley, ISLAND

4 The American economy is not going to be able to prosper unless Americans regard as necessities what other people look on as luxuries.
Wendell Wilkie, ONE WORLD

PROSTITUTION

5 Take the courtesan. It is inconceivable to Jack [J. B. Priestley] that a courtesan best expresses herself by being a courtesan. To him, an unfortunate is a woman who has been abused.
James Agate on J. B. Priestley's MUSIC AT NIGHT, Ego 4 11 Oct 1939

6 Even if you're a pro you've got to *look* like you're an amacher otherwise the kids are going to think you're doing something they couldn't do. That way you'd scare 'em.
Alex Atkinson, THE BIG CITY

7 If brothels were nationalised instead of merely legalised, prostitution would inevitably die out.
Brigit Batlow, letter to Daily Telegraph 19 Sep 1979

8 Men of good taste have complicated me on that carpet
Brendan Behan, THE HOSTAGE 1958

9 It is accepted by psychiatrists that prostitutes have a great therapeutic value in society and are practitioners of professional therapy.
Mrs Maureen Colquhoun, MP for Northants N., House of Commons 6 Mar 1979

10 Prostitution gives her an opportunity to meet people. It provides fresh air and wholesome exercise, and it keeps her out of trouble.
Joseph Heller, CATCH 22 1961

11 An epoch which is not an age of promiscuity is necessarily an age of prostitution.
James Laver, TASTE AND FASHION FROM THE FRENCH REVOLUTION UNTIL TODAY

12 If you want to buy my wares / Follow me and climb the stairs / Love for Sale.
Cole Porter, NEW YORKER (musical), Love For Sale

13 I am notorious. I will go down in history as another Lady Hamilton.
Mandy Rice-Davis in an interview after the Profumo affair

14 There is something utterly nauseating about a system of society which pays a harlot twenty-five times as much as it pays its Prime Minister.
Harold Wilson, referring to the Christine Keeler case in a speech, House of Commons 1963

PROTEST

15 The protest march has replaced the queue as Britain's favourite communal activity. It's lively, it's an outlet for aggressive instincts, and it gives one something to do on a rainy day. Not least, it's a good way of meeting the opposite sex. Hyde Park rallies, in particular, are noted for being a more than satisfactory substitute for the old *Palais de danse.*
William Davis, Punch 16 Feb 1972

16 Idealism is no excuse for irrational behaviour.
Sunday Telegraph of the anti-apartheid riots in New Zealand 26 Jul 1981

17 If you mean merely that noisiness and hysteria are proofs of unfitness for public life then every Parliament in the world should close, every election meeting be prohibited, every sex be disfranchised. Did Englishmen ever get their voting right save by noisiness and hysteria.
Israel Zangwill (on the suffragette movement), letter to The Times 29 Oct 1906

PROVERB

18 Proverbs are always platitudes until you have personally experienced the truth of them.
Aldous Huxley, JESTING PILATE 1926

1 Proverbs contradict each other. That is the wisdom of a nation.
Stanislaw Lec, UNKEMPT THOUGHTS 1962

PROVIDENCE

2 There is nothing more agreeable than to find providence dislikes the same people that we do. It adds to our good opinion of providence.
Frank Moore Colby, THE COLBY ESSAYS 1926

PRUDERY

3 Parsons always seem to be specially horrified about things like sunbathing and naked bodies. They don't mind poverty and misery and cruelty to animals nearly as much.
Susan Ertz, JULIAN PROBERT

PSYCHIATRY

4 Then there is goctophobia, or the fear of raising the hand too far and striking oneself in the face with the possibility of putting an eye out. These patients keep their hands in their pockets all the time and have to be fed by paid attendants. A nasty complication arises when they also have nictophobia, or fear of paid attendants.
Robert Benchley, MY TEN YEARS IN A QUANDARY 1936

5 There is, for example, kemophobia, or the fear of sitting too close to the edge of a chair and falling off. People with kemophobia are constantly hitching themselves back in their chairs until they tip themselves over backwards which gives the same general effect as falling off the chair forwards.
Id.

6 Psychiatry's chief contribution to philosophy is the discovery that the toilet is the seat of the soul.
Alexander Chase, PERSPECTIVES 1966

7 It might be said of psychoanalysis that if you give it your little finger it will soon have your whole hand.
Sigmund Freud, INTRODUCTORY LECTURES IN PSYCHOANALYSIS 1932

8 I do not think our successes can compete wih those at Lourdes. There are so many more people who believe in the miracles of the Blessed Virgin than in the existence of the unconscious.
Id.

9 Anyone who goes to a psychiatrist ought to have his head examined.
Sam Goldwyn. Quoted Alva Johnson, THE GREAT GOLDWYN

10 Fortunately psycho-analysis is not the only way to resolve inner conflicts. Life itself still remains a very effective therapist.
Karen Horney, OUR INNER CONFLICTS

11 So then Dr. Froyd said all I needed was to cultivate some inhibitions and get some sleep.
Anita Loos, GENTLEMEN PREFER BLONDES 1925

12 A psychiatrist is a man who goes to the Folies Bergères to look at the audience.
Mervyn Stockwood (Bishop of Southwark), Observer 15 *Jun* 1961

13 Psychiatrists classify a person as a neurotic if he suffers from his problems in living, and as psychotic if he makes others suffer.
Thomas Szasz, THE SECOND SIN, PSYCHIATRY

PSYCHOANALYSIS

14 Freud is the father of psychoanalysis. It has no mother.
Germaine Greer, THE FEMALE EUNUCH

15 Psychoanalysis has terrified educated parents with the fear of the harm they may unwittingly do their children.
Bertrand Russell, THE CONQUEST OF HAPPINESS 1930

16 Psychoanalysts believe that the only 'normal' people are those who cause no trouble either to themselves or anyone else.
A. J. P. Taylor, THE TROUBLE MAKERS 1957

PSYCHOLOGY

17 The subtle man is infinitely more easy to understand than the natural man.
G. K. Chesterton, ROBERT BROWNING 1903

18 Psychology has a long past, but only a short history.
Hermann Ebbinghaus, SUMMARY OF PSYCHOLOGY

19 The psychic development of the individual is a short repetition of the course of development of the race.
Sigmund Freud, LEONARDO DA VINCI

1 The British have never accepted the word psychology as relevant to their own lives . . . only in Britain do people need reminding that it is not just about rats, mental illness or Freud.
Beverley Hayne, Observer 25 *Feb* 1979

2 In certain persons, at least, the total possible consciousness may be split into parts which co-exist but mutually ignore each other, and share the objects of knowledge between them.
William James, THE PRINCIPLES OF PSYCHOLOGY

3 Freud was a hero. He descended to the 'Underworld' and met there stark terrors. He carried with him his theory as a Medusa's head which turned these terrors to stone.
R. D. Laing, THE DIVIDED SELF

4 Thousands of American women know far more about the subconscious than they do about sewing.
H. L. Mencken, PREJUDICES 1919

5 *Morgan:* Did you hear what the white rat said to the other white rat:
Analyst: What?
Morgan: I've got that psychologist so well trained that every time I ring the bell he brings me something to eat.
David Mercer, A SUITABLE CASE FOR TREATMENT (*TV play*)

6 Psychology which explains everything / Explains nothing / And we are still in doubt.
Marianne Moore, COLLECTED POEMS, *Marriage* 1951

7 The purpose of psychology is to give us a completely different idea of the things we know best.
Paul Valéry, TEL QUEL 1945

8 Psychology as the behaviourist views it is a purely objective experimental branch of natural science.
J. B. Watson. Quoted David Cohen, THE FOUNDER OF BEHAVIOURISM

PUBLICITY

9 All publicity is good, except an obituary notice.
Brendan Behan. Quoted Robert Pitman, Sunday Express 5 *Jan* 1964

10 Formerly a public man needed a *private* secretary for a barrier between himself and the public. Nowadays he has a *press* secretary to keep him properly in the public eye.
Daniel J. Boorstin, THE IMAGE 1962

11 It is a major story when an attractive young woman throws ink all over the Prime Minister or someone tries to blow up the Post Office Tower. The very fact that such acts guarantee vast publicity is a powerful incentive to commit them.
William Davis, Punch 9 *Feb* 1972

12 I want it so that you can't wipe your ass on a piece of paper that hasn't got my picture on it.
Lyndon B. Johnson to his press agents. Quoted Robert A. Caro, THE PATH TO POWER 1983

13 To have news value is to have a tin can tied to one's tail.
T. E. Lawrence, letter to Sir Evelyn Wrench, Mar 1935

14 All publicity is disturbing to the nervous system, total publicity totally disturbing.
Anthony Powell, THE STRANGERS ALL GONE

15 Reviews matter very little in the case of a novel. The important thing is to make people talk about it. You can do this by forcing yourself into the newspaper in some other way. Attempt to swim the Channel, get unjustly arrested in a public park, disappear. There are innumerable means of attracting public notice.
Evelyn Waugh, Passing Show 2 *Feb 1929*

PUBLIC OPINION

16 Public opinion, a vulgar, impertinent, anonymous tyrant who deliberately makes life unpleasant for anyone who is not content to be the average man.
W. R. Inge (Dean of St. Pauls), OUTSPOKEN ESSAYS, *Our Present Discontents* 1919

PUBLIC SCHOOL

17 They had the Eton something or the Harrow something. I felt I was nearer to grasping what the something is than ever before. It is a sleek happiness that comes of a shininess which only Eton — or Harrow — can import. The nearest thing to it must be boot polish.
J. M. Barrie, letter to Lady Cynthia Asquith 10 Jul 1920

1 A public schoolboy must be acceptable at a dance, and invaluable in a shipwreck.
Alan Bennett, FORTY YEARS ON

2 His English education at one of the great public schools had preserved his intellect perfectly and permanently at the stage of boyhood.
G. K. Chesterton, THE MAN WHO KNEW TOO MUCH 1922

3 The ape-like virtues without which no one can enjoy a public school.
Cyril Connolly, ENEMIES OF PROMISE 1938

4 A mildewy scriptural odour pervaded the institution — it reeked of Jeroboam and Jesus; the masters struck me as supercilious humbugs; the food was so vile that for the first day or two after returning from holidays I could not get it down. The only good which ever came out of the place was cheese from the neighbouring Stilton, and that of course, they never gave us.
Norman Douglas, LOOKING BACK 1933

5 It is not that the Englishman can't feel, it is that he is afraid to feel. He has been taught at his public school that feeling is bad form.
E. M. Forster, ABINGER HARVEST 1936

6 It is hardly surprising if judges who have been to Eton or Winchester have few qualms about sending lower-class young men to Parkhurst or Wormwood Scrubs.
David Frost and Anthony Jay, TO ENGLAND WITH LOVE

7 By virtue of his [Public School] training he kept his pores open and his mouth shut.
Rudyard Kipling, THE BRUSHWOOD BOY

8 There's nothing like a public school for hiding your true feelings; it must have been a wonderful training ground for a spy.
Julian Mitchell in an interview with Sheridan Morley, The Times 29 *Oct* 1981

9 You can't expect a boy to be depraved until he has been to a good school.
Saki, A BAKER'S DOZEN

10 "Which do you consider to be public schools?"
"Well, Eton — and Harrow."
"Rugby?"
"No, that's a railway junction."
Dorothy L. Sayers, MURDER MUST ADVERTISE 1933

11 Having been to Westminster is like being able to waggle your ears. It's a facility you will have all your life, but the value of it isn't quite clear.
A pupil named Simon Target, BBC 1 TV, *Public School* 14 *Sep* 1979

12 There at Westminster School I was given the clothes of an undertaker, together with a furled umbrella, in order, we were told, to distinguish the boys from City of London bank messengers.
Peter Ustinov, DEAR ME 1977

13 Anyone who has been to an English public school will feel comparatively at home in prison.
Evelyn Waugh, DECLINE AND FALL 1928

14 You send a boy to school in order to make friends — the right sort.
Virginia Woolf, in her diary. Quoting Countess of Cromer

PUBLIC SPEAKING

15 It's not the way people in my audience start looking at their watch that worries me — it's when they keep tapping them to see if they have stopped.
Lady Barnett in a radio interview

16 I do not object to people looking at their watches when I am speaking — but I strongly object when they start shaking them to make certain they are still going.
Lord Birkett, New York Times 13 *Nov* 1960

17 An after-dinner speech should be like a lady's dress — long enough to cover the subject and short enough to be interesting.
R. A. Butler, Anglo-Jewish Association dinner, Dorchester Hotel 1 *Jun* 1957

18 Oratory is the art of making a loud noise sound like a deep thought.
Bennett Cerf, LAUGHING STOCK 1952

19 Haven't you learned yet that I put something more than whisky into my speeches.
Winston Churchill to his son Randolph

20 He is one of those orators of whom it was well said "Before they get up they do not know what they are going to say; when they are speaking they do not know what they are saying; and when they sit down they do not know what they have said."
Winston Churchill of Lord Charles Beresford, House of Commons 20 *Dec* 1912

21 A good rule is to resist the temptation to say ". . . and finally" unless you have actually reached your penultimate sentence.
Paul Johnson, Daily Telegraph, Sending for a Phrase 21 *Jul* 1979

1 I have heard, on Xmas Day, in the First Lesson, "Wonderful, Counsellor, Prince of Peace" etc. read as if they were the names of stations on the Underground. The truth, of course, is that the path between too little expression and too much is a very narrow one.
G. W. Lyttelton, THE LYTTELTON HART-DAVIS LETTERS 2 *May* 1956

2 I listen to my own speeches with keen interest and extreme pleasure. I have seldom listened to a speech of mine without learning something.
Bonar Thompson, Hyde Park orator, THE BLACK HAT

3 If you want me to talk for ten minutes I'll come next week. If you want me to talk for an hour I'll come tonight.
Woodrow Wilson, answering an invitation to make a speech. Quoted Adlai Stevenson to Leon Harris, THE FINE ART OF POLITICAL WIT

PUBLISHING

4 There is probably no hell for authors in the next world — they suffer too much from critics and publishers in this.
Christian Nastell Boyce, SUMMARIES OF THOUGHT

5 As repressed sadists are said to become policemen or butchers so those with an irrational fear of life become publishers.
Cyril Connolly, ENEMIES OF PROMISE 1938

6 Great editors do not discover nor produce great authors, great authors create and produce great publishers.
John Farrar, WHAT HAPPENS IN BOOK PUBLISHING 1957

7 I have never been rich in anything but unsold books and of them I have warehouses full.
Rupert Hart-Davis, THE LYTTELTON HART-DAVIS LETTERS 20 *Nov* 1955

8 Some say the reason for these [misprints] is the increasingly liberal attitude of the Church of England. Not enough parsons are unfrocked these days. The unfortunates of earlier days were often happy to find themselves employment in printing houses, correcting proofs.
David Holloway, Daily Telegraph 21 *Apr* 1979

9 Curse the blasted, jelly-boned swines, the slimy, the belly-wriggling invertebrates, the miserable sodding rutters, the flaming sods, the snivelling, dribbling, dithering, palsied, pulse-less lot that make up England today. They've got white of egg in their veins and their spunk is that watery it's a marvel they can breed.
D. H. Lawrence to Edward Garnet on Heinemann's rejection of SONS AND LOVERS

10 The unpublished manuscript is like an unconfessed sin that festers in the soul, corrupting and contaminating it.
Antonio Machado, JUAN DE MAIRENA 1943

11 Publishing a volume of poetry is like dropping a rose petal down the Grand Canyon and waiting for the echo.
Don Marquis, THE SUN DIAL

12 A person who publishes a book wilfully appears before the public with his pants down.
Edna St. Vincent Millay, LETTERS 1952

13 They [publishers] are like Methodists. They love to keep the Sabbath and everything else they can lay their hands on.
Amanda Ross, letter to Lord Ponsonby 1910

14 The trouble with you, my dear Rupert, is that you will persist in seeing me "in book form."
G. M. Young to Rupert Hart-Davis. Quoted THE LYTTELTON HART-DAVIS LETTERS 20 *Nov* 1955

15 Being published by the O.U.P. is rather like being married to a duchess; the honour is almost greater than the pleasure.
Id. 29 *Nov* 1956

PUNCTUALITY

16 We are not saints but we have kept our appointment. How many people can boast as much?
Samuel Beckett, WAITING FOR GODOT 1952

17 Gioacchimo Rossini was born in 1792, five months after his parents got married, and it taught him a lesson. He was never early for another appointment in his whole life.
Victor Borge, MY FAVOURITE INTERVALS

18 He was so punctual you could regulate the sun by him.
Christopher Fry, A PHOENIX TOO FREQUENT 1959

1 I am a believer in punctuality, though it makes me lonely.
E. V. Lucas, READING, WRITING AND REMEMBERING

2 I have noticed that the people who are late are often so much jollier than the people who have to wait for them.
Id.

3 "Twenty-three and a quarter minutes past", Uncle Matthew was saying furiously, "in precisely six and three-quarter minutes the damned fella will be late."
Nancy Mitford, LOVE IN A COLD CLIMATE

4 I make unpunctuality an art. The only time I am conscious of the time is when I am on time. Then I am frankly astonished.
George Sava, TWICE THE CLOCK ROUND

5 A gentleman is punctual to a fault. He sits down to his meals exactly at the appointed hour and expects to be served even if there has been a power cut or the cook has run off with the second footman.
Douglas Sutherland, THE ENGLISH GENTLEMAN 1978

6 If you're there before it's over, you're on time.
James J. Walker, Mayor of New York

7 Punctuality is the virtue of the bored.
Evelyn Waugh, DIARIES 26 *Mar* 1962

PUNCTUATION

8 Cut out all those exclamation marks. An exclamation mark is like laughing at your own joke.
F. Scott Fitzgerald. Quoted Sheila Graham and Gerald Frank, BELOVED INFIDEL

PUNISHMENT

9 Guilt always hurries towards its complement, punishment; only there does its satisfaction lie.
Lawrence Durrell, JUSTINE 1957

10 The use of the birch is not to be deplored. All the best men in the country have been beaten, archbishops, bishops and even deans. Without sensible correction they could not be the men they are today.
Dean Ely, reported in the Manchester Guardian

11 The refined punishments of the spiritual minds are usually much more indecent and dangerous than a good smack.
D. H. Lawrence, FANTASIA OF THE UNCONSCIOUS 1922

12 My father believed in smiting sin wherever he found it; what I complained of was that he always seemed to find it in the same place.
Saki and Charles Maude, THE WATCHED POT

13 If you strike a child take care that you strike it in anger, even at the risk of maiming it for life. A blow in cold blood neither can nor should be forgiven.
George Bernard Shaw, MAN AND SUPERMAN 1905

14 Every child should have an occasional pat on the back, as long as it is applied low enough, and hard enough.
Bishop Fulton J. Sheen. Quoted Frank Muir, ON CHILDREN

PUPIL

15 He was his pupil, so now he is his enemy.
Bertolt Brecht, GALILEO 1939

PURITY

16 To the puritan all things are impure.
D. H. Lawrence, ETRUSCAN PLACES 1927

17 I was surprised when I learnt that Mrs. Hicks had a mother — she was so pure I thought she had come to life out of the house-dress section of the Sears Roebuck catalogue.
Betty MacDonald, THE EGG AND I 1946

18 The impurity of those to whom all things pertaining to themselves are pure.
Muriel Spark, THE GO-AWAY BIRD

19 Purity is the ability to contemplate defilement.
Simone Weil, GRAVITY AND GRACE 1914

PURPOSE

20 If after all, men cannot always make history have a meaning, they can always act so that their own lives have one.
Albert Camus, RESISTANCE, REBELLION AND DEATH 1961

1 Modern man . . . is living in a world in which he is a means, and the end is not his business.
Alberto Moravia, MAN IS AN END 1964

2 There must be more to life than having everything.
Maurice Sendak, HIGGLETY PIGGLETY POP

Q

QUESTION

1 To ask the hard question is simple.
W. H. Auden, THE QUESTION

2 We have found all the questions that can be found. It is time we gave up looking for questions and began looking for answers.
G. K. Chesterton, ORTHODOXY 1908

QUOTATION

3 The surest way of making a monkey out of a man is to quote him.
Robert Benchley, QUICK QUOTATIONS

4 Some men have a mania for Greek and Latin quotations. This is to be avoided. It is like pulling up the stones from a tomb to kill the living.
Michael Brett, THINGS A GENTLEMAN WOULD LIKE TO KNOW CONCERNING THE SOCIAL GRACES

5 It is a good thing for an uneducated man to read books of quotations.
Winston Churchill, MY EARLY LIFE 1930

6 It would be nice if sometimes the kind things I say were considered worthy of quotation. It isn't difficult, you know, to be witty or amusing when one has something to say that is destructive, but damned hard to be clever and quotable when you are singing someone's praises.
Noël Coward. Quoted William Marchant, THE PLEASURE OF HIS COMPANY 1981

7 Sometimes it seems the only accomplishment my education ever bestowed on me was the ability to think in quotations.
Margaret Drabble, A SUMMER BIRDCAGE

8 Everything I've ever said will be credited to Dorothy Parker.
George S. Kaufman. Quoted BBC Radio 4, Quote Unquote 28 Jun 1979

9 In England only uneducated people show off their knowledge; nobody quotes Latin or Greek authors in the course of conversation, unless he has never read them.
George Mikes, HOW TO BE AN ALIEN 1946

10 To be amused by what you read — that is the great spring of happy quotations.
C. E. Montague, A WRITER'S NOTES ON HIS TRADE 1930

11 I might repeat to myself, slowly and soothingly, a list of quotations beautiful from minds profound; if I can remember any of the damn things.
Dorothy Parker, THE LITTLE HOUR

12 If with the literate I am / Impelled to try an epigram / I never seek to take the credit / We all assume that Oscar said it.
Dorothy Parker, OSCAR WILDE

13 Misquotation is the pride and privilege of the learned.
Hesketh Pearson. Quoted BBC Radio 4, Quote Unquote 24 Apr 1980

14 A man can be forgiven a lot if he can quote Shakespeare in an economic crisis.
Philip, Duke of Edinburgh, of Karl Marx

15 The quotation of two or three lines of a stanza from Spenser's *Faery Queen* is probably as good an all-round silencer as anything.
Stephen Potter, LIFEMANSHIP 1950

16 To say that anything was a quotation was an excellent method, in Eleanor's eyes, for withdrawing it from discussion.
Saki, THE JESTING OF ARLINGTON STRINGHAM

17 I often quote myself. It adds spice to my conversation.
George Bernard Shaw. Quoted Reader's Digest, Jun 1943

18 Famous remarks are seldom quoted correctly.
Simeon Strunksy, NO MEAN CITY

19 In the dying world I come from, quotation is a national vice. It used to be the classics, now it's lyric verse.
Evelyn Waugh, THE LOVED ONE 1948

1 One has to secrete a jelly in which to slip
  quotations down people's throats and one
  always secretes too much jelly.
  Virginia Woolf, LEAVE THE LETTERS TILL
  WE ARE DEAD 1981

R

RACE RELATIONS

1 It is a great shock at the age of five or six to find that in a world of Gary Coopers you are the Indian.
James Baldwin. Speech, Cambridge Union 17 Feb 1965

2 to like an individual because he's black is just as insulting as to dislike him because he isn't white.
e. e. cummings. Quoted Barbara Rowe, A BOOK OF QUOTES

3 When people like me, they tell me it is in spite of my colour. When they dislike me they point out it is not because of my colour.
Frantz Fanon, BLACK SKIN WHITE MASKS

4 What we need is hatred. From it are our ideas born.
Jean Genet, THE NEGROES

5 My heart is as black as yours.
Malcolm Gluck. Quoting white politician to Harlem audience, Punch 18 *Aug* 1976

6 Racial Prejudice is a pigment of the imagination.
Graffito. Quoted Nigel Rees, GRAFFITI LIVES O.K.

7 An English anti-semitic seeing a Jew in his club does not throw him out. He leaves the club himself.
Lord Kagan. Quoted Observer 24 *Dec* 1979

8 There are no 'white' or 'coloured' signs on the fox holes or graveyards of battles.
John F. Kennedy. Message to Congress on Civil Rights 19 Jan 1963

9 I wouldn't trust an Aryan with my great-grandmother.
V. S. Naipaul, A HOUSE FOR MR. BISWAS 1961

10 If you want to make beautiful music you must play the black and the white notes together.
Richard Nixon. Quoted Barbara Rowe, A BOOK OF QUOTES, *but probably not original*

11 He's really awfully fond of coloured people. Well, he says himself, he wouldn't have white servants.
Dorothy Parker, ARRANGEMENTS IN BLACK AND WHITE

RAILWAY

12 Rumbling under blackened girders Midland bound for Cricklewood / Puffed its sulphur to the sunset where that land of laundries stood.
Sir John Betjeman, PARLIAMENT HILL FIELDS

13 People's back yards are much more interesting than their front gardens, and houses that back on to railways are public benefactors.
Sir John Betjeman. Quoted Janet Watts, Observer magazine, *The Time of His Life* 13 *Mar* 1983

14 A third-class carriage is a community, while a first-class carriage is a place of wild hermits.
G. K. Chesterton, HERETICS 1905

15 God set a limit to man's locomotive ambition in the construction of his body. Man immediately proceeded to discover means of over-riding the limit . . . Railways are a most dangerous institution.
Mahatma Gandhi. Quoted This and That magazine 25 *Jan* 1930

16 Here at the wayside station, as many a morning / I watch the smoke torn from the fumy engine / Crawling across the fields in serpent sorrow.
Edwin Muir, THE WAYSIDE STATION

17 We like a tidy station and passengers make it untidy.
Official explanation for not providing seats at Euston station. Quoted Bernard Levin, THE PENDULUM YEARS 1976

RAIN

18 I love the rain. I want the feeling of it on my face.
Katherine Mansfield, last words

291

1 Still falls the Rain / Dark as the world of man, black as our loss — / Blind as the nineteen hundred and forty nails / Upon the Cross.
Edith Sitwell, STILL FALLS THE RAIN

READING

2 The middle brows like [John Henry] O'Hara because his books remind them of the lives they imagine themselves to be leading.
John W. Aldridge, TIME TO MURDER AND CREATE

3 He has only half learned the art of reading who has not added to it the even more refined accomplishments of skipping and skimming.
A. J. Balfour. Quoted E. T. Raymond, MR. BALFOUR

4 The test of a first-rate work, and a test of your sincerity in calling it a first-rate work, is that you finish it.
Arnold Bennett, THINGS THAT HAVE INTERESTED ME

5 It is impossible to read properly without using all one's engine power. If we are not tired after reading, commonsense is not in us.
Id.

6 Of all odd crazes, the craze to be forever reading new books in one of the oddest.
Augustine Birrell, ESSAYS, *Books Old and New* 1922

7 I read books like mad, but I am careful not to let anything I read influence me.
Michael Caine, Woman's Own Magazine

8 When one can read, can penetrate the enchanting world of books, why write?
Colette, EARTHLY PARADISE 1966

9 Reading after a certain age diverts the mind too much from its creative pursuits. Any man who reads too much and uses his own brain too little falls into lazy habits of thinking.
Albert Einstein. Quoted Edwin Muller, EINSTEIN: A STUDY IN SIMPLICITY

10 One always tends to overpraise a long book because one has got through it.
E. M. Forster, ASPECTS OF THE NOVEL 1927

11 We can never know that a piece of writing is bad unless we have begun by trying to read it as if it was very good and ended by discovering that we were paying the author an undeserved compliment.
C. S. Lewis, AN EXPERIMENT IN CRITICISM 1961

12 The pleasure of all reading is doubled when one lives with another who shares the same books.
Katherine Mansfield, LETTERS 1928

13 I would sooner read a time-table or a catalogue than nothing at all. They are much more entertaining than half the novels that are written.
W. Somerset Maugham, THE SUMMING UP 1938

14 All my good reading, you might say, was done in the toilet.
Henry Miller, BLACK SPRING 1936

15 I have only read one book in my life and that is *White Fang*. It's so frightfully good I've never bothered to read another.
Nancy Mitford, THE PURSUIT OF LOVE 1945

16 Have you read any good books lately?
Catch phrase used by Richard Murdoch in BBC radio series, Much Binding in the Marsh

17 I'm quite illiterate, but I read a lot.
J. D. Salinger, THE CATCHER IN THE RYE 1951

18 We shouldn't teach great books; we should teach a love of reading.
B. F. Skinner. Quoted R. Evans, B. F. SKINNER: THE MAN AND HIS IDEALS

19 People say that life is the thing, but I prefer reading.
Logan Pearsall Smith, AFTERTHOUGHTS 1931

20 I read a good deal of criticism, but only as a vice, not so good as reading science fiction, rather better than reading mystery stories.
Gore Vidal, BEHIND THE SCENES

21 As in the sexual experience, there are never more than two persons present in the act of reading — the writer who is the impregnator and the reader who is the respondent.
E. B. White, THE SECOND TREE FROM THE CORNER 1954

RONALD REAGAN

22 That youthful sparkle in his eye is caused by his contact lenses, which he keeps highly polished.
Sheila Graham, The Times 22 *Aug* 1981

1 I have a strange feeling that he will wake up one day and ask "What movie am I in?"
Id.

2 He is the first man for twenty years to make the Presidency a part-time job, a means of filling up a few of the otherwise blank days of retirement.
Simon Hoggart, Observer 21 *Jun* 1981

3 In a disastrous fire in President Reagan's library both books were destroyed. And the real tragedy is that he hadn't finished colouring one.
Jonathan Hunt, Observer, *Public Eye* 30 *Aug* 1981

4 As the age of television progresses the Reagans will be the rule, not the exception. To be perfect for television is all a President has to be these days.
Gore Vidal. Quoted Martin Amis, Observer 7 *Feb* 1982

5 A triumph of the embalmer's art.
Gore Vidal. Quoted John Heilpern, Observer 26 .*Apr* 1981

6 Ask him the time and he'll tell you how the watch was made.
Jane Wyman (Ronald Reagan's first wife). Quoted Sheila Graham The Times 22 *Aug* 1981

REALITY

7 I like reality. It tastes of bread.
Jean Anouilh, CATCH AS CATCH CAN 1960

8 An independent reality in the ordinary physical sense can neither be ascribed to the phenomenon nor to the agencies of observation.
Niels Bohr 1927

9 Reality only reveals itself when it is illuminated by a ray of poetry.
Georges Braques. Quoted in his obituary, The Times 2 *Sep* 1963

10 Everything is a dangerous drug except reality, which is unendurable.
Cyril Connolly, THE UNQUIET GRAVE 1945

11 I am afraid of this word Reality, not connoting an ordinary definable characteristic of the things it is applied to, but used as though it were some kind of celestial halo.
Sir Arthur Eddington, THE NATURE OF THE PHYSICAL WORLD 1928

12 Human kind / Cannot bear much reality.
T. S. Eliot, BURNT NORTON 1935

13 There is no reality except the one contained within us. That is why so many people live such an unreal life. They take the images outside them for reality and never allow the world within to assert itself.
Hermann Hesse, DAMIAN 1919

14 The horror, no less than the charm of real life, consists precisely in the recurrent actualisation of the inconceivable.
Aldous Huxley, THEME AND VARIATIONS 1930

15 We live in a fantasy world, a world of illusion. The great task in life is to find reality.
Iris Murdoch. Quoted Rachel Billington, The Times, *Profile: Iris Murdoch* 15 *Apr* 1983

16 Reality is a staircase going neither up nor down, we don't move, today is today, always is today.
Octavio Paz, MODERN EUROPEAN POETRY, *The Endless Instant* 1966

17 Reality is pretty brutal, pretty filthy, when you come to grips with it. Yet it's glorious all the same. It's so real and satisfactory.
George Bernard Shaw, FANNY'S FIRST PLAY 1912

18 A test of what is real is that it is hard and rough. Joys are found in it, not pleasures. What is pleasant belongs to dreams.
Simone Weil, GRAVITY AND GRACE 1947

REASON

19 Men do not live by reason, but are merely controlled by it. Otherwise why do they fall in love and practise the arts.
Gerald Brenan, THOUGHTS IN A DRY SEASON 1979

20 Human reason needs only to will more strongly than fate, and she *is* fate.
Thomas Mann, THE MAGIC MOUNTAIN 1924

21 The man who listens to Reason is lost; Reason enslaves all whose minds are not strong enough to master her.
George Bernard Shaw, MAN AND SUPERMAN, *Maxims for Revolutionists* 1905

REBELLION

22 Every act of rebelling expresses a nostalgia for innocence and an appeal to the essence of being.
Albert Camus, THE REBEL 1951

1 No one can go on being a rebel too long without turning into an autocrat.
Laurence Durrell, BALTHAZAR 1958

REFORM

2 It is simply impertinence for any man, or any body of men, to begin, or contemplate reform of the whole world. To attempt to do so by means of highly artificial and speedy locomotion is to attempt the impossible.
Mahatma Gandhi. Quoted in his obituary, News Chronicle 31 *Jan* 1948

3 Reform must come from within, not from without. You cannot legislate for virtue.
Cardinal Gibbons. Speech, Baltimore 13 *Sep* 1909

4 Unless the reformer can invent something which substitutes attractive virtues for attractive vices he will fail.
Walter Lippmann, A PREFACE TO POLITICS, *The Taboo* 1914

5 Every reform movement has a lunatic fringe.
Theodore Roosevelt. Speech 1913

6 There are too many people trying to change this world who could not change a fuse.
Nicholas Shakespeare, The Times, *Critic's Choice* 4 *Dec* 1982

7 A reformer is a guy who rides through a sewer in a glass-bottomed boat.
James J. Walker, Mayor of New York, in a speech 1928

REGRET

8 What I regret, on behalf of myself of long ago, is not the overweeningness, but the playing it safe.
Elizabeth Bowen. Quoted Reader's Digest, *Nov* 1946

9 *Victor:* It's easy enough to be sorry.
Elyot: On the contrary. I find it exceedingly difficult. I seldom regret anything. This is a very rare and notable exception, a sort of red letter day. We must all make the most of it.
Noël Coward, PRIVATE LIVES 1930

10 Only with beauty wake wild memories — / Sorrow for where you are, for where you would be.
Walter De La Mare, THE CAGE

11 Never regret and never look back. Regret is an appalling waste of energy; you can't build on it; it is only good for wallowing in.
Katherine Mansfield, BLISS 1920

12 Miss Otis regrets she is unable to lunch today.
Cole Porter, first line of lyric

13 Regrets are idle, yet history is one long regret. Everything might have turned out so differently.
Charles Dudley Warner, MY SUMMER IN A GARDEN

REINCARNATION

14 I hold that when a person dies / His soul returns again to earth; / Arrayed in some new flesh-disguise / Another mother gives him birth / With sturdier limbs and brighter brain / The old soul takes the roads again.
John Masefield, A CREED

15 Sex is one of the nine reasons for reincarnation — the other eight are unimportant.
Henry Miller. Quoted Barbara Rowe, A BOOK OF QUOTES

SIR JOHN REITH

16 Dante without the poetry, Irving without the mystery, Mephistopheles without the fun.
Alan Dent's characterisation. Quoted James Agate, Ego 4 17 *Apr* 1939

REJECTION

17 "It's not twenty-four hours since she turned me down."
"Turned you down?"
"Like a bedspread. In this very garden."
P. G. Wodehouse, RIGHT HO JEEVES

REJUVENATION

18 In Vienna you can see whole rows of decrepit old rats carrying on like Tiller girls.
Noël Coward, PRIVATE LIVES 1930

RELATIVITY

19 When you are courting a nice girl an hour seems like a second. When you sit on a red-hot cinder a second seems like an hour. That's relativity.
Albert Einstein. Quoted Ritchie Calder, News Chronicle 14 *Mar* 1949

20 I believe my theory of relativity to be true. But it will only be proved for certain in 1981, when I am dead.
Albert Einstein. Quoted Edwin Miller, EINSTEIN: A STUDY IN SIMPLICITY 1938

1 Going to work for a large company is like getting on a train. Are you going sixty miles an hour or is the train going sixty miles an hour or you're just sitting still?
J. Paul Getty. Quoted Barbara Rowe, A BOOK OF QUOTES

RELEVANCE

2 What does my hair-do have to do with my husband's ability to be president?
Jacqueline Kennedy. Quoted BARBARA ROWE, BOOK OF QUOTES

RELIGION

3 He was of the faith chiefly in the sense that the church he currently did not attend was Catholic.
Kingsley Amis, ONE FAT ENGLISHMAN 1963

4 Religion is not proficiency in the fine art of mystical knowledge, but just the love of God and our neighbour.
Father Andrew, LIFE AND LETTERS

5 An American girl who spoke scoldingly of the Ten Commandments said 'They don't tell you what you ought to do and only put ideas into your head.'
Herbert Henry Asquith Earl of Oxford

6 I'm a Communist by day and a Catholic as soon as it gets dark.
Brendan Behan

7 The children of dogmatic atheists tend to become Wesleyan missionaries.
Gerald Brenan, THOUGHTS IN A DRY SEASON 1979

8 Every day people are straying away from the church and going back to God.
Lenny Bruce, THE ESSENTIAL LENNY BRUCE

9 A cosmic philosophy is not constructed to fit a man, a cosmic philosophy is constructed to fit a cosmos. A man can no more possess a private religion than he can possess a private sun or moon.
G. K. Chesterton, THE BOOK OF JOB 1929

10 In my religion there would be no exclusive doctrine; all would be love, poetry and doubt.
Cyril Connolly, THE UNQUIET GRAVE 1945

11 Science without religion is lame; religion without science is blind.
Albert Einstein. Quoted Reader's Digest, *Nov* 1973

12 If one purges Judaism of the Prophets and Christianity as Jesus Christ taught it of all subsequent additions, especially those of priests, one is left with a teaching which is capable of curing all the social ills of humanity.
Albert Einstein, THE WORLD AS I SEE IT 1934

13 To know that what is impenetrable to us really exists . . . is at the centre of true religiousness. In this sense, and in this sense only, I belong to the ranks of the devoutly religious men.
Albert Einstein, WHAT I BELIEVE

14 The whole religious complexion of the modern world is due to the absence from Jerusalem of a lunatic asylum.
Havelock Ellis, IMPRESSIONS AND COMMENTS

15 A refusal to come to an unjustified conclusion is an element of an honest man's religion.
Bergen Evans, THE NATURAL HISTORY OF NONSENSE

16 Religion is far more acute than science, and if it only added judgment to insight, would be the greatest thing in the world.
E. M. Forster, MAURICE

17 Ronnie approved of religion as long as it endorsed the National Anthem, but he objected when it attempted to influence his life.
E. M. Forster, A PASSAGE TO INDIA 1924

18 Religion is an attempt to get control over the sensory world . . . by means of the wish world which we have developed inside us as a result of biological and psychological necessities.
Sigmund Freud, LECTURES IN PSYCHO-ANALYSIS, *A Philosophy of Life* 1932

19 Religion is an illusion and it derives its strength from the fact that it falls in with our instinctual desires.
Id.

20 If the truth of religious doctrines is dependent on an inner experience that bears witness to that truth, what is one to make of the many people who do not have that experience?
Sigmund Freud, THE FUTURE OF AN ILLUSION

21 Religion is comparable to a childhood neurosis.
Id.

1 Religions revolve madly round sexual questions.
Rémy de Gourmont

2 Formal religion was organised for slaves; it offered them consolation which earth did not provide.
Elbert Hubbard, Philistine Vol. 25

3 [My father] considered a walk among the mountains as the equivalent of church-going.
Aldous Huxley, BARREN LEAVES 1925

4 You never see animals going through the absurd and often horrible fooleries of magic and religion . . . It is the price [man] has to pay for being intelligent, but not, as yet, intelligent enough.
Aldous Huxley, BRIEF CANDLES

5 For English Catholics, sacraments are the psychological equivalent of tractors in Russia.
Aldous Huxley, EYELESS IN GAZA 1936

6 Nobody can have the consolations of religion or philosophy unless he has first experienced their desolations.
Aldous Huxley, THEME AND VARIATIONS, *Variations on a Baroque Tomb* 1950

7 Religion is caught, not taught.
W. R. Inge (Dean of St. Pauls)

8 Religion is what the individual does with his own solitude. If you are never solitary you are never religious.
Id.

9 It is difficult to accept a position that gives only atheism the right of citizenship in public and social life while believers are, as though by principle, barely tolerated or are treated as second-class citizens.
Pope John Paul II, ENCYCLICAL: THE REDEEMER OF MAN

10 The idea of Christ as a political figure, a revolutionary, as the subversive man from Nazareth does not tally with the Church's catechesis.
Pope John Paul II during a visit to Mexico 1 Feb 1979

11 Among all my patients in the second half of life — that is to say over thirty-five — there has not been one whose problem in the last resort was not that of finding a religious outlook on life.
Carl Jung, MODERN MAN IN SEARCH OF HIS SOUL

12 Religion is the tendency to prefer God to the government, most commonly found in Communist countries.
Miles Kington, The Times, *A Guide to Real Meanings* 2 Jul 1982

13 Religion is the frozen thought of men, out of which they build temples.
Krishnamurti, Observer, *Sayings of the Week* 22 Apr 1928

14 Jehovah's Witnesses, awaiting the Last Day with the quiet kind of satisfaction that a man gets in a dry season when he knows his neighbour's house is not insured against fire.
Bernard Levin, THE PENDULUM YEARS 1976

15 "You must never forget, Laurie, that dissenters are often excellent Christian people. You must never be narrow minded."
I promised that I never would.
"Though of course" my aunt added, "you must always remember that *we* are always *right*."
I promised that I always would.
Rose Macaulay, THE TOWERS OF TREBIZOND 1956

16 What mean and cruel things men do for the love of God.
W. Somerset Maugham, A WRITER'S NOTEBOOK 1945

17 Religion is always revolutionary, far more revolutionary than bread-and-butter philosophies.
Henry Miller, THE AIR CONDITIONED NIGHTMARE 1943

18 Of course Low Churches are very holy, but they do so treat God like their first cousin.
Nancy Mitford quoting her grandmother in a letter to Mark Ogilvie-Grant 30 Dec 1929

19 I want nothing to do with any religion concerned with keeping the masses satisfied to live in hunger, filth and ignorance. I want nothing to do with any order, religious or otherwise, which does not teach people that they are capable of becoming happier and more civlised.
Jawaharlal Nehru. Quoted Edgar Snow, JOURNEY TO THE BEGINNING

20 I've taken up the Bible again somewhat in the spirit of W. C. Fields — looking for loopholes.
David Niven. Quoted Observer 24 Dec 1978

1 You are not an agnostic, Paddy. You are just a fat slob who is too lazy to go to Mass.
Conor Cruise O'Brien, quoting an Irish parish priest, Observer 4 *Feb* 1979

2 We ought to have as great a regard for religion as we can, so as to keep it out of as many things as possible.
Sean O'Casey, THE PLOUGH AND THE STARS 1926

3 One cannot really be a Catholic and grown-up.
George Orwell, COLLECTED ESSAYS, *Manuscript Notebook* 1965

4 The truth of religion is in its ritual and the truth of dogma is in its poetry.
John Cowper Powys, THE COMPLEX VISION

5 A church which starves itself and its members in the contemplative life deserves whatever spiritual leanness it may experience.
Michael Ramsey, CANTERBURY PILGRIM

6 Religious terms towards the end of the book have been rearranged so that dissenters and nonconformists are no longer grouped with idolaters, fire-worshippers and other heathens.
Introduction to Everyman edition of ROGET'S THESAURUS

7 I think the most important quality in a person concerned with religion is absolute devotion to truth.
Albert Schweitzer, OUT OF MY LIFE AND THOUGHT 1932

8 Good-natured unambitious men are cowards when they have no religion.
George Bernard Shaw, BACK TO METHUSELAH, *Preface* 1921

9 I am a sort of collector of religions, and the curious thing is I find I can believe in them all.
George Bernard Shaw, MAJOR BARBARA 1905

10 I judge the character of a man of the Church not by the reason they find for things, but by the things they find reasons for.
George Bernard Shaw, letter to William Temple, Archbishop of Canterbury

11 We must disentangle what is Christian from what is middle class.
Rev. Chris Smith. Quoted Alan Road, Observer magazine 8 *Mar* 1974

12 Extreme happiness invites religion almost as much as extreme misery.
Dodie Smith, I CAPTURE THE CASTLE 1948

13 The one certain way for a woman to hold a man is to leave him for religion.
Muriel Spark, THE COMFORTERS 1957

14 I know that a community of God-seekers is a great shelter for man. But directly this grows into an Institution it is apt to give ready access to the Devil by its back door.
Rabindranath Tagore, LETTERS TO A FRIEND

15 I haven't been to mass for years. I've got every mortal sin on my conscience, but I know when I'm doing wrong. I'm still a Catholic.
Angus Wilson, THE WRONG SET

16 I would rather think of my religion as a gamble than think of it as an insurance policy.
Stephen Samuel Wise. Quoted Justin Wintle and Richard Kenin, DICTIONARY OF BIOGRAPHICAL QUOTATIONS.

REMEDY

17 Stimulate the phagocytes
George Bernard Shaw, THE DOCTOR'S DILEMMA 1906

18 There is no doubt that Jeeves' pick-me-up will produce immediate results in anything short of an Egyptian mummy.
P. G. Wodehouse, THE INIMITABLE JEEVES 1924

REMEMBRANCE

19 At the going down of the sun and in the morning we will remember them.
Laurence Binyon, FOR THE FALLEN

20 Rejoice ye dead, where'er your spirits dwell / Rejoice that yet on earth your fame is bright / And that your names, remembered day and night / Live on the lips of those who love you well.
Robert Bridges, ODE TO MUSIC

21 Who will remember, passing through this gate / The unheroic dead who fed the guns? / Who shall absolve the foulness of their fate — / Those doomed, conscripted, unvictorious ones?
Siegfried Sassoon, ON PASSING THE NEW MENIN GATE 1918

REMORSE

22 Sighs for follys said and done / Twist our narrow days
W. H. Auden, FISH IN THE UNRUFFLED LAKE 1936

1 Chronic remorse is a most undesirable sentiment . . . Rolling in the muck is not the best way of getting clean.
Aldous Huxley, BRAVE NEW WORLD 1932

2 Remorse is pride's *ersatz* for repentance.
Aldous Huxley, TIME MUST HAVE A STOP 1944

3 Remorse is impotence, it will sin again. Only repentance is strong, it can end everything.
Henry Miller, THE WISDOM OF THE HEART 1941

4 There are people who are very resourceful / At being remorseful / And who apparently feel the best way to make friends / Is to do something terrible and then make amends.
Ogden Nash, MAN LONG YEARS AGO, Hearts of Gold 1945

REPENTANCE

5 American people like to have you repent, then they are generous.
Will Rogers, THE ILLITERATE DIGEST, *One Oil Lawyer per Barrel* 1924

REPETITION

6 Repetition does not transform a lie into a truth.
Franklin D. Roosevelt, Radio Fireside Chat 26 Oct 1939

7 Repetition is the only form of permanence that nature can achieve.
George Santayana, SOLILOQUIES IN ENGLAND, *A version From Platonism* 1922

8 After people have repeated a phrase a great many times they begin to realise it has meaning and may even be true.
H. G. Wells, THE HAPPY JOURNEY 1946

9 Repetition is the death of art.
A. N. Whitehead, DIALOGUES 1953

REPRESSION

10 Stalin when he killed off his egg-heads like Bukharin, was only establishing a sound and stable government. In this country the victims would have been given the O.M. and sent to the House of Lords, but the end result would have been the same.
Malcolm Muggeridge, TREAD SOFTLY FOR YOU TREAD ON MY JOKES 1966

REPRISAL

11 When Lady Cunard was displeased by a horse introduced into a picture she had commissioned, Marie Laurencin painted her on a camel.
René Gimpel, DIARY OF AN ART DEALER

12 I'll hit you over the head with my diamond necklace.
Paulette Goddard, to someone who called her a Communist. Quoted News Review 2 Oct 1947

REPUTATION

13 The reputation through a thousand years may depend upon the conduct through a single moment.
Ernest Bramah, KAI LUNG UNROLLS HIS MAT 1928

14 The easiest way to get a reputation is to go outside the fold, shout around for a few years as a violent atheist or a dangerous radical and then crawl back to shelter.
F. Scott Fitzgerald, NOTEBOOKS

15 Worldly wisdom teaches us that it is better for the reputation that one should fail conventionally than to succeed unconventionally.
J. M. Keynes, GENERAL THEORY OF EMPLOYMENT 1936

16 The Englishman wants to be recognised as a gentleman, or as some other suitable species of human being; the American wants to be considered a good guy.
Louis Kronenberger, COMPANY MANNERS 1954

17 My reputation grew with every failure.
George Bernard Shaw of his unsuccessful early novels. Quoted Hesketh Pearson, BERNARD SHAW 1942

RESEARCH

18 . . . curse those clever scientists who dissect away the wings and the haggard heart from the dove.
Dannie Abse, letter to Alex Comfort

19 Basic research is what I am doing when I don't know what I am doing.
Wernher van Braun. Quoted Barbara Rowe, BOOK OF QUOTES

20 Behavioural psychology is the science of pulling habits out of rats.
Dr. Douglas Busch

1 There is only one proved method of assisting the advancement of pure science — that of picking men of genius, backing them heavily, and leaving them to direct themselves.
J. B. Conant, letter to New York Times 13 *Aug* 1945

2 In science the credit goes to the man who convinces the world not to the man to whom the idea first occurred.
Sir Francis Darwin. Galton Lecture to Eugenics Society 1914

3 When Dr. Watson watches rats in mazes, what he knows, apart from difficult inferences, are certain events in himself.
Sir Arthur Eddington, SCIENCE AND THE UNSEEN WORLD

4 It is a very great mistake to think that the enjoyment of seeing and searching can be promoted by means of coercion and a sense of duty.
Albert Einstein, AUTOBIOGRAPHY

5 I want to know how God created the world. I'm not interested in this or that phenomenon. I want to know his thoughts, the rest are details.
Albert Einstein. Quoted Ronald W. Clark, EINSTEIN: HIS LIFE AND TIMES

6 The cosmic religious experience is the strongest and noblest driving force behind scientific research.
Albert Einstein. Quoted in an obituary 19 *Apr* 1955

7 It is a good morning exercise for a research scientist to discard a pet hypothesis every day before breakfast. It keeps him young.
Konrad Lorenz, ON AGGRESSION

8 What economic history needs at present is not more documents but a pair of stout boots.
R. H. Tawney. Quoted A. L. Rowse, THE USE OF HISTORY

RESIGNATION

9 Resignation, open-eyed, conscious, and informed by love, is the only one of our feelings for which it is impossible to become a sham.
Joseph Conrad, SOME REMINISCENCES 1912

10 Teach us to care and not to care / Teach us to sit still.
T. S. Eliot, ASH WEDNESDAY 1930

RESPECT

11 His indolence was qualified with enough basic bad temper to ensure the respect of those about him.
Evelyn Waugh, PUT OUT MORE FLAGS 1942

RESPECTABILITY

12 A respectable girl is one who doesn't want to go to bed with anyone.
Mervyn Griffith-Jones during the Stephen Ward trial

13 Men have to do some awfully mean things to keep up their respectability.
George Bernard Shaw, FANNY'S FIRST PLAY 1912

14 The more things a man is ashamed of, the more respectable he is.
George Bernard Shaw, MAN AND SUPERMAN 1905

RESPONSIBILITY

15 We take no responsibility, like the owners of umbrella stands in hotels.
Malcolm Bradbury, STEPPING WESTWARD

16 A wrong decision can make me very miserable. But I have trust in God. If you have this trust you don't have to worry, as you don't have sole responsibility.
Lord Denning, longest serving judge, on retiring at the age of 83, *Sep* 1982

17 Man's responsibility increases as that of God's decreases.
André Gide, JOURNALS 27 *Sep* 1940

18 No snowflake in an avalanche ever feels responsible.
Stanislaw Lec, MORE UNKEMPT THOUGHTS 1962

19 Life has no meaning except in terms of responsibility.
Reinhold Neibuhr, FAITH AND HISTORY

20 To be a man is, precisely, to be responsible.
Antoine de Saint-Exupéry, WIND, SAND AND STARS 1939

21 The buck stops here.
Harry S Truman, sign on his presidential desk

22 Every man who takes office in Washington either grows or swells, and when I give a man office I watch him carefully to see whether he is growing or swelling.
Woodrow Wilson. Speech 15 *May* 1916

RESURRECTION

1 . . . those coming out of church / Spread all over the churchyard. They scan / The crowd, recognise, smile and shake hands / By each tombstone a well-dressed person stands / It looks just like the / Resurrection.
Patricia Beer, CONCERT AT LONG MELFORD CHURCH

2 I think the resurrection of the body, unless much improved in construction, a mistake.
Evelyn Underhill, LETTERS

RETALIATION

3 If you kick a man he kicks you back again. Therefore never be too eager to engage in combat.
Bertolt Brecht, THE THREEPENNY OPERA 1928

4 If you start throwing hedgehogs under me I shall throw two porcupines under you.
Nikita Khrushchev. Quoted Observer 10 *Nov* 1963

RETICENCE

5 He [Alexander of Tunis] believed that reticence increases a soldier's authority. It was his nature. A gentleman does not utter everything he thinks.
Harold Nicolson, ALEX: THE LIFE OF FIELD MARSHAL EARL ALEXANDER OF TUNIS

RETIREMENT

6 I must adjust myself to private life and try to grow old gracefully without being a nuisance to anyone.
Stanley Baldwin. Speech to Federation of British Industries 13 *Apr* 1937

7 Lady Bancroft and I have eighty thousand golden reasons for retiring and every one lodged in the bank.
Squire Bancroft, AUTOBIOGRAPHY

8 Retirement at sixty-five is ridiculous. When I was sixty-five I still had pimples.
George Burns. Quoted Barbara Rowe, A BOOK OF QUOTES

9 To forge a fixed and arbitrary rule in terms of years as the limit of a man's usefulness of human service would only be to behead a large portion of the world's intellectual and moral leadership and thereby impoverish mankind.
Dr. Nicholas Murray Butler. Address to Columbia University 1 *Jun* 1937

10 Queen Victoria in her eighties was more known, more revered and a more important part of the life of the country than she had ever been. Retirement, for a monarch, is not a good idea.
Charles, Prince of Wales. Speech 1974

11 I want to retire at 50. I want to play cricket in the summer and geriatric football in the winter, and sing in the choir.
Neil Kinnock MP, The Times 28 *Jul* 1980

12 Have you ever been out for a late autumn walk in the closing part of the afternoon and suddenly looked up to realise that the leaves have practically all gone? And the sun has set and the day gone before you knew it — and with that a cold wind blows across the landscape? That's retirement.
Stephen Leacock, TOO MUCH COLLEGE

13 Few men of action have been able to make a graceful exit at the appropriate time.
Malcolm Muggeridge, CHRONICLES OF WASTED TIME 1972

14 We know how to make our predecessors retire. When it comes to forcing us to retire our successors must find some method of their own.
C. Northcote Parkinson, PARKINSON'S LAW 1957

RETRIBUTION

15 Don't wait for the Last Judgement. It takes place every day.
Albert Camus, THE FALL 1956

REVENGE

16 She wrote a polite refusal to the wedding to which she had not been asked on the grounds that she had a prior engagement, and sent a richly wrapped parcel bearing the name of a top people's shop. When opened it was found to contain a can of a well-known deodorant.
Douglas Sutherland, THE ENGLISH GENTLEMAN'S WIFE 1979

REVOLUTION

17 All modern revolutions have ended in a reinforcement of the power of the State.
Albert Camus, THE REBEL 1951

1 The slave begins by demanding justice and ends by wanting to wear a crown. He must be dominated in his turn.
Id.

2 The overwhelming pressure of mediocrity, sluggish and indomitable as a glacier, will mitigate the most violent, and depress the most exalted revolution.
T. S. Eliot, THE IDEA OF A CHRISTIAN SOCIETY 1939

3 I bid you to a one-man revolution — / The only revolution that is coming.
Robert Frost, BUILD SOIL — A POLITICAL PASTORAL 1932

4 The violence of revolution is the violence of men who charge into a vacuum.
J. K. Galbraith, THE AGE OF UNCERTAINTY 1977

5 All successful revolutions are the kicking in of a rotten door.
Id.

6 A non-violent revolution is not a programme of seizure of power. It is a programme of transformation of relationships, ending in a peaceful transfer of power.
Mahatma Gandhi, NON-VIOLENCE IN PEACE AND WAR 1948

7 It wasn't a revolution that would have led anywhere. Kerensky's rather than Lenin's.
Bamber Gascoigne, FROM FRINGE TO FLYING CIRCUS, *Preface* 1980

8 Though a revolution may call itself *national* it always works the victory of a single party.
André Gide, JOURNALS 17 *Oct* 1941

9 Revolution is the festival of the oppressed.
Germaine Greer, THE FEMALE EUNUCH

10 We used to think that revolutions are the cause of change. Actually it is the other way round; change prepares the ground for revolution.
Eric Hoffer, THE TEMPER OF OUR TIME, *A Time of Juveniles* 1967

11 Revolution is delightful in the preliminary stages. So long as it's a question of getting rid of the people at the top.
Aldous Huxley, EYELESS IN GAZA 1936

12 Every revolution evaporates, leaving behind only the slime of a new bureaucracy.
Franz Kafka

13 It has all been tried before. The older Puritans took away the maypoles and the mince pies, but they did not bring in the millennium, they only brought in the Restoration.
C. S. Lewis, A PREFACE TO PARADISE LOST, *being the Ballard Matthews Lectures, delivered at University College, North Wales* 1941

14 "There won't be any revolution in America," said Isodore. "The people are too clean. They spend all their time changing their shirts and washing themselves. You can't feel fierce and revolutionary in a bathroom."
Eric Linklater, JUAN IN AMERICA 1931

15 A revolution only remains victorious through methods which are alien to those who made it.
André Malraux. Quoted Fitzroy McLean, BACK TO BOKHARA

16 Revolution is the proper occupation of the masses.
Mao Tse Tung. Quoted Dennis Bloodworth, THE MESSIAH AND THE MANDARINS 1983

17 It was not Napoleon who made the French Revolution; but Rousseau, a crazy Swiss who took to knitting and dressing up in Armenian costume, had a lot to do with it.
Malcolm Muggeridge, TREAD SOFTLY FOR YOU TREAD ON MY JOKES 1966

18 Those countries which choose tyrannies for themselves must be left to get on with it. They created their revolutions.
V. S. Naipaul, Radio Times 24 *Mar* 1979

19 A revolution only lasts fifteen years, a period which coincides with the effectiveness of a generation.
José Ortega y Gasset, THE REVOLT OF THE MASSES 1930

20 The revolution eats its own. Capitalism re-creates itself.
Mordecai Richter, COCKSURE

21 You can jail a revolutionary but you cannot jail the revolution.
Bobby Seale, Chairman of the Black Panthers

22 Hot water is the revolutionist's element. You clean men as you clean milk-pans, by scalding them.
George Bernard Shaw, MAN AND SUPERMAN 1905

23 The export of revolution is nonsense. Every country makes its own revolution if

it wants to, and if it does not want to there will be no revolution.
Joseph Stalin, in an interview 1936

1 Revolution is a trivial shift in the emphasis of suffering.
Tom Stoppard, Quoted Barbara Rowe, A BOOK OF QUOTES

2 Insurrection is an art, and like all arts it has its laws.
Leon Trotsky, HISTORY OF THE RUSSIAN REVOLUTION

3 Power fell into the street.
Leon Trotsky, MY LIFE

RHYME

4 "I have spent uncomfortable week-ends looking for a rhyme for Balenciaga."
I looked a question.
"Forsyte Saga" he [Noël Coward] said.
William Marchant, THE PRIVILEGE OF HIS COMPANY 1981

5 I can think of no rhyme to Stella but umbrella.
George Bernard Shaw, letter to Mrs. Pat Campbell

RISK

6 Take calculated risks. That is quite different from being rash.
Gen. George Smith Patton, letter to Cadet G. S. Patton IV 6 *Jun* 1944

7 The only way to be absolutely safe is never to try anything for the first time.
Dr. Magnus Pyke, BBC Radio 17 *Mar* 1979

RIVER

8 I do not know much about gods, but I / Think that the river / Is a strong brown god.
T. S. Eliot, FOUR QUARTETS, *The Dry Salvages* 1941

9 Ol' man river, dat ol' man river / He must know sumpen but don't say nothin' / He just keeps rollin', he just keeps on rollin' along.
Oscar Hammerstein II, OL' MAN RIVER 1927

10 Riveruns, past Eve and Adam's, from swerve of shore to bend of bay, brings us by a commodius vicus of recirculation back to Howth Castle and Environs.
James Joyce, FINNEGANS WAKE, *opening words* 1939

ROMANCE

11 Do I remember when I first met your mother, you ask? Ah, as if I could ever forget. A beautiful June night, a garden party, a full moon, Japanese lanterns glimmering softly in the trees, a Strauss waltz playing. Then, to make the evening complete, this sublime creature appeared — no wait a minute, that was the night I met Alice Fletcher. Let me see, where did I first meet your mother?
Father to child, cartoon caption by Follette, Saturday Evening Post 9 *Feb* 1950

12 Is not this the true romantic feeling — not to desire to escape life, but to prevent life from escaping you?
Thomas Wolfe. Quoted Andrew Turnbull, THOMAS WOLFE

ROOM

13 A room is a place where you hide from the wolves outside and that's all any room is.
Jean Rhys, GOOD MORNING, MIDNIGHT 1939

ELEANOR ROOSEVELT

14 No woman has ever so comforted the distressed or so distressed the comfortable.
Clare Boothe Luce, ANNA ELEANOR ROOSEVELT

15 She would rather light candles than curse the darkness, and her glow has warmed the world.
Adlai Stevenson. Speech, United Nations Assembly 9 *Nov* 1962

FRANKLIN D. ROOSEVELT

16 The best newspaperman who has ever been President of the United States.
Heywood Brown. Quoted D. Boorstin, THE IMAGE

17 Restless and mercurial in his thinking, a connoisseur of theories but impatient with people who took theories seriously, he trusted no system except the system of endless experimentation.
Earl Goldman, RENDEZVOUS WITH DESTINY

18 A chameleon on plaid.
Herbert Hoover. Quoted James MacGregor Burns, ROOSEVELT: THE LION AND THE FOX

1 He [Roosevelt] would rather follow public opinion than lead it.
Harry Hopkins. Quoted G. Wolfskill and J. A. Hudson, ALL BUT THE PEOPLE: F. D. ROOSEVELT AND HIS CRITICS

2 The man who started more creations than were ever begun since Genesis — and finished none.
Hugh Johnson. Id.

3 If he became convinced tomorrow that coming out for cannibalism would get him the votes he so sorely needs, he would begin fattening a missionary on the White House backyard come Wednesday.
H. L. Mencken, FRANKLIN D. ROOSEVELT, A PROFILE *(ed. W. E. Leuchtenburg)*

THEODORE ROOSEVELT

4 He contained within him the best and worst of America, the whole spectrum from practical enlightenment and sound moral judgement to sentimentalism and braggadocio.
John M. Blum, THE REPUBLICAN ROOSEVELT

5 Theodore Roosevelt is affectionately recalled today as a half heroic, half comic figure, a bespectacled barrel of a man, choking with teeth and jingoism.
Alistair Cooke, AMERICA

ROYALTY

6 The Royal Family are as complicated a thesis as only a sophisticated nation like Great Britain could invent. They are as full of paradoxes as cricket. Only the British really understand them and then more by instinct than by rule of law.
Anon. Topic Magazine. Quoted Noël St. George, ROYAL QUOTES

7 The British Royal Family is an adman's dream, a unique selling proposition with a pliable market strongly predisposed towards the product.
Andrew Duncan, THE REALITY OF MONARCHY

8 Royalty must think the whole country always smells of fresh paint.
Elizabeth Dunn, Sunday Times

RUDENESS

9 "You are extremely rude, young man." "As a matter of fact, we both are; the only difference being that I am trying to be, and you can't help it."
Lord Birkenhead (F. E. Smith) to Judge Willis. Quoted by his son and biographer, The Second Lord Birkenhead

10 It's not a slam at *you* when people are rude — it's a slam at the people they've met before.
F. Scott Fitzgerald, THE LAST TYCOON 1941

BERTRAND RUSSELL

11 I told D. H. Lawrence how enchanted I had been by the lucidity, the suppleness and pliability of Bertrand Russell's mind. He sniffed. "Have you ever seen him in a bathing dress?" he asked "Poor Bertie Russell! He is all Disembodied Mind."
William Gerhardie, MEMOIRS OF A POLYGLOT

RUSSIA

12 Don't you forget what's divine in the Russian soul — and that's resignation.
Joseph Conrad, UNDER WESTERN EYES 1911

13 One Russian is an anarchist / Two Russians are a chess game / Three Russians are a revolution / Four Russians are the Budapest String Quartet.
Jascha Heifetz. Quoted Nat Shapiro, ENCYCLOPEDIA OF QUOTATIONS ABOUT MUSIC

14 I have been there. It's a paradise. No ladies and gentlemen.
George Bernard Shaw, letter to Alfred Douglas

RUTHLESSNESS

15 You can only help one of your luckless brothers / By trampling down a dozen others.
Bertolt Brecht, THE GOOD WOMAN OF SETZUAN 1940

16 Never fight fair with a stranger, boy. You'll never get out the jungle that way.
Arthur Miller, DEATH OF A SALESMAN 1947

S

SACRIFICE

1 Sacrificers are not the ones to pity, the ones to pity are those they sacrifice.
Elizabeth Bowen, THE DEATH OF THE HEART 1938

2 No sacrifice is worth the name unless it is a joy. Sacrifice and a long face go ill together.
Mahatma Gandhi

3 If a man hasn't discovered something that he would die for, he isn't fit to live.
Martin Luther King. Speech, Detroit 23 *Jun* 1963

4 Too long a sacrifice / Can make a stone of the heart.
W. B. Yeats, EASTER 1916

SADNESS

5 Sadness is almost never anything but a form of fatigue.
André Gide, JOURNALS 1922

6 Sadness is a communicable disease.
Martha Graham. Quoted Robin Stringer, Daily Telegraph 23 *Jul* 1979

SAINT

7 Saintliness is also a temptation.
Jean Anouilh, BECKET 1959

8 *Saint, n.* a dead sinner, revised and edited.
Ambrose Bierce, THE DEVIL'S DICTIONARY 1906

9 *More:* You are either idiots or children.
Chapuys: Or saints, my lord.
Robert Bolt, A MAN FOR ALL SEASONS 1961

10 Can one be a saint if God does not exist? That is the only concrete problem I know of today.
Albert Camus, THE PLAGUE 1947

11 It is easier to make a saint out of a libertine than out of a prig.
George Santayana, THE LIFE OF REASON 1905

12 I don't believe in God, but I do believe in his saints.
Edith Wharton. Quoted Percy Lubbock, PORTRAIT OF EDITH WHARTON

SALESMANSHIP

13 He's a man way out there in the blue, riding on a smile and a shoeshine.
Arthur Miller, THE SALESMAN 1949

14 A salesman is got to dream, boy. It comes with the territory.
Id.

SALVATION

15 Human salvation lies in the hands of the creatively maladjusted.
Martin Luther King, STRENGTH TO LOVE 1963

16 I always claim the mission workers came out too early to catch any sinners on this part of Broadway. At such an hour the sinners are in bed resting up from their sinning of the night before, so they will be in good shape for more sinning a little later on.
Damon Runyon, GUYS AND DOLLS 1932

17 Mrs. Ape, as was her invariable rule, took round the hat and collected nearly two pounds. "Salvation doesn't do them the same good if they think it's free" was her favourite axiom.
Evelyn Waugh, VILE BODIES 1930

SANCTIMONIOUSNESS

18 Sophia wished that Florence would not talk about the Almighty as if his real name was Godfrey, and God was just Florence's nickname for him.
Nancy Mitford, PIGEON PIE

DOROTHY L. SAYERS

19 An enormously definite person.
John Gielgud. Quoted BBC Radio 4 31 *Jan* 1982

SCEPTICISM

1 She believed in nothing; only her scepticism kept her from being an atheist.
Jean-Paul Sartre, WORDS

SCHIZOPHRENIA

2 Schizophrenic behaviour is a special strategy that a person invents in order to live in an unlivable situation.
R. D. Laing, THE POLITICS OF EXPERIENCE

SCHOOL

3 The dread of beatings, / Dread of Being Late / And greatest dread of all, the dread of games.
Sir John Betjeman, SUMMONED BY BELLS 1960

4 Headmasters have powers at their disposal with which Prime Ministers have never yet been invested.
Winston Churchill, MY EARLY LIFE 1930

5 When I was a boy at school I never minded the lessons. I just resented having to work terribly hard at playing.
John Mortimer, A VOYAGE ROUND MY FATHER

6 There is nothing on earth intended for innocent people so horrible as a school. It is in some respects more cruel than a prison. In a prison, for example, you are not forced to read books written by the warders and the governor.
George Bernard Shaw, PARENTS AND CHILDREN

7 School is where you go between when your parents can't take you and industry can't take you.
John Updike, THE CENTAUR 1963

8 We class schools, you see, into four grades; Leading School, First-Rate School, Good School, and School.
Evelyn Waugh, DECLINE AND FALL 1928

SCHOOLTEACHER

9 Whenever I look in the glass or see a photograph of myself, I am reminded of Petrarch's simple statement "Nothing is more hideous than an old schoolmaster"!
G. W. Lyttelton, THE LYTTELTON HART-DAVIS LETTERS 11 *Apr* 1956

10 Every schoolmaster after the age of 49 is inclined to flatulence, is apt to swallow frequently, and to puff.
Harold Nicolson, THE OLD SCHOOL

11 I expect you'll be becoming a schoolmaster, sir. That's what most of the young gentlemen does, sir, that gets sent down for indecent behaviour.
Evelyn Waugh, DECLINE AND FALL 1928

12 Assistant masters came and went. Some liked little boys too little and some too much.
Evelyn Waugh, A LITTLE LEARNING

SCIENCE

13 When I find myself in the company of scientists I feel like a shabby curate who has strayed by mistake into a drawing-room full of dukes.
W. H. Auden, THE DYER'S HAND 1962

14 And the continuity of our science has not been affected by all these turbulent happenings, as the older theories have always been included as limiting cases in the new ones.
Max Born, PHYSICS IN THE LAST FIFTY YEARS 1951

15 That is the essence of science; ask an impertinent question and you are on the way to a pertinent answer.
J. Bronowski, THE ASCENT OF MAN 1973

16 When a distinguished elderly scientist says something is possible, he is probably right; when he says something is impossible he is probably wrong.
Arthur C. Clarke

17 Man is slightly nearer to the atom than the stars. From his central position he can survey the grandest works of Nature with the astronomer, or the minutest works with the physicist.
Sir Arthur Eddington, STARS AND ATOMS

18 The whole of science is nothing more than a refinement of everyday thinking.
Albert Einstein, OUT OF MY LATER YEARS

19 Science has 'explained' nothing; the more we know the more fantastic the world becomes and the profounder the surrounding darkness.
Aldous Huxley, VIEWS OF HOLLAND

20 The wallpaper with which the men of science have covered the world of reality is falling to tatters.
Henry Miller, TROPIC OF CANCER 1934

1 Science may be described as the art of systematic over-simplificatiaon.
Karl Popper, Observer, *Sayings of the Week* 1 *Aug* 1982

2 Science may well be converging ultimately to a unique truth.
H. R. Post, Stud. Hist. Phil. Sci. 2 (1971)

3 A good scientific theory should be explicable to a barmaid.
Ernest Rutherford. Quoted Ronald W. Clark, THE GREATEST POWER ON EARTH

4 Classical physics has been superseded by quantum theory: quantum theory is verified by experiments. Experiments must be described in terms of classical physics.
C. F. von Weizsäcker

5 If we could all agree where science was going, everything would be solved and we would have no recourse but to be engineers or doctors.
Maurice Wilkins. Quoted James D. Watson, THE DOUBLE HELIX

SCOT

6 Join a Highland regiment, me boy. The kilt is an unrivalled garment for fornication and diarrhoea.
John Masters, BUGLES AND A TIGER

7 Is anything worn beneath the kilt?
No, it's all in perfect working order.
Spike Milligan, THE GREAT MCGONAGALL SCRAPBOOK

8 It is never difficult to distinguish between a Scotsman with a grievance and a ray of sunshine.
P. G. Wodehouse. Quoted R. Usborne, WODEHOUSE AT WORK 1961

SCULPTURE

9 A lot was lost when colour was abandoned in sculpture. It's a lovely sensation painting on terra-cotta and no one has done it for 600 years.
Quentin Bell in an interview with Sarah Howell, Observer magazine 18 *Mar* 1979

10 I always liked big women. I suppose I was meant to be a sculptor.
Joyce Cary, THE HORSE'S MOUTH 1944

11 I'm having a bust made of my wife's hands.
Sam Goldwyn. Quoted Alva Johnson, THE GREAT GOLDWYN

SEA

12 I've never seen the point of the sea, except where it meets the land. The shore has point. The sea has none.
Alan Bennett, THE OLD COUNTRY

13 There is nothing more enticing, disenchanting and enslaving, than the life of the sea.
Joseph Conrad, LORD JIM 1900

14 The sea has never been friendly to man. At most it has been the accomplice of human restlessness.
Joseph Conrad, THE MIRROR OF THE SEA 1906

15 The sea never changes and its works, for all the talk of men, are wrapped in mystery.
Joseph Conrad, TYPHOON 1903

16 It tosses up our losses, the torn seine, / The shattered lobster pot, the broken oar / And the gear of foreign dead men. The sea has many voices.
T. S. Eliot, FOUR QUARTETS, *The Dry Salvages* 1941

17 The snotgreen sea. The scrotumtightening sea.
James Joyce, ULYSSES

18 The sea hates a coward.
Eugene O'Neill, MOURNING BECOMES ELECTRA 1931

19 A man who is not afraid of the sea will soon be drowned.
J. M. Synge, THE ARAN ISLANDS 1907

20 The sloe-black, slow black, crow black, fishing-boat bobbing sea.
Dylan Thomas, UNDER MILK WOOD 1954

SEASIDE

21 There's sand in the porridge and sand in the bed / And if this is pleasure we'd rather be dead.
Noël Coward, THE ENGLISH LIDO

SECRET

22 There are no secrets except the secrets that keep themselves.
George Bernard Shaw, BACK TO METHUSELAH 1922

SEDUCTION

23 Older women are best because they always think they may be doing it for the last time.
Ian Fleming, from his private notebooks. Quoted John Pearson, LIFE OF IAN FLEMING 1966

1 Candy / Is dandy / But liquor / Is quicker.
Ogden Nash, VERSUS, *Reflections on Ice-Breaking* 1949

2 Men seldom make passes / At girls who wear glasses / But a girl on a sofa / Is easily won ofa.
Dorothy Parker, ENOUGH ROPE 1927

SEDUCTIVENESS

3 When she raises her eyelids it's as if she were taking off all her clothes.
Colette, CLAUDINE AND ANNIE

SELF-INDULGENCE

4 My problem lies in reconciling my gross habits with my net income.
Errol Flynn. Quoted Jane Mercer, GREAT LOVERS OF THE MOVIES

SELF-PITY

5 I never saw a wild thing / Sorry for itself. / A small bird will drop frozen dead / From a bough / Without ever having felt sorry for itself.
D. H. Lawrence, SELF-PITY

SELF-RESPECT

6 Self-respect — the secure feeling that no one, as yet, is suspicious.
H. L. Mencken, A MENCKEN CHRESTO-MATHY 1949

SELF-SACRIFICE

7 Self-sacrifice enables us to sacrifice / Other people without blushing.
George Bernard Shaw, MAN AND SUPER-MAN 1905

SENTIMENTALITY

8 Sentimentality is the emotional promiscuity of those who have no sentiment.
Norman Mailer, CANNIBALS AND CHRISTIANS, *Lambs* 1966

SERVANT

9 There are only two kinds of people in the world. Those who are nice to their servants and those who aren't.
Duke of Argyll. Quoted Art Buchwald, I CHOSE CAVIAR

10 His lordship may compel us to be equal upstairs, but there will never be equality in the servants' hall.
J. M. Barrie, THE ADMIRABLE CRICHTON 1902

11 Servants should not be ill. We have quite enough illnesses of our own without them adding to the symptoms.
Lady Diana Cooper. Quoted Philip Ziegler, DIANA COOPER

12 I am aware of the damp souls of housemaids / Sprouting despondently at area gates.
T. S. Eliot, MORNING AT THE WINDOW 1917

13 He was caught / Red-handed with the silver and his Grace / Being short of staff at the time asked him to stay / And clean it.
Christopher Fry, VENUS OBSERVED 1950

14 Servants must not be spoiled.
Aldous Huxley, VULGARITY IN LITERATURE

15 On a raw Wednesday morning, in a few ill-chosen words, she told the cook that she drank. She remembered the scene afterwards as vividly as though it had been painted in her mind by Abbey. The cook was a good cook, as cooks go; and as cooks go she went.
Saki, REGINALD ON BESETTING SINS 1901

16 Nannies never retire but continue to live, long after their charges have married and had children of their own, in 'nanny's room'. There they sit all day long, surrounded by eyeless teddy bears and broken toys, knitting endless socks and sewing on trouser buttons.
Douglas Sutherland, THE ENGLISH GENTLEMAN 1978

SEX

17 Is sex dirty? Only when it is being done right.
Woody Allen, ALL YOU'VE EVER WANTED TO KNOW ABOUT SEX *(film)*

18 In the old days a lot of people, men as well as women, didn't quite know what to expect from sex so they didn't worry when it didn't work too well.
Kingsley Amis, JAKE'S THING

19 It isn't the ecstatic leap across that I deplore, it's the weary trudge home.
Anon, comment on single beds

1 He said it was artificial respiration but now I find I'm to have his child.
Anthony Burgess, INSIDE MR. ENDERBY 1966

2 There is more difference within the sexes than between them.
Ivy Compton-Burnett, MOTHER AND SON 1955

3 It would take a far more concentrated woman than Amanda to be unfaithful every five minutes.
Noël Coward, PRIVATE LIVES 1930

4 What happens is that, as with drugs, one needs a stronger shot each time, and women are just women. The consumption of one woman is the consumption of all. You can't double the dose.
Ian Fleming. Quoted John Pearson, LIFE OF IAN FLEMING 1960

5 Life to him was identified with the intimate charm of the feminine form in its greatest variety: and so he spent his days in quest of the red light.
William Gerhardie, THE POLYGLOTS 1925

6 Sex is bad for one — but it's good for two.
Graffito. Quoted BBC Radio 4, *Quote Unquote*

7 To succeed with the opposite sex, tell her you're impotent. She can't wait to disprove it.
Cary Grant, at the age of 72

8 Mr. Mercaptan went on to preach a brilliant sermon on that melancholy sexual perversion known as continence.
Aldous Huxley, ANTIC HAY 1923

9 I don't see so much of Alfred any more since he got so interested in sex.
Mrs. Alfred Kinsey, wife of the author of THE KINSEY REPORT ON SEXUAL BEHAVIOUR

10 No sex without responsibility.
Lord Longford, Observer 3 *May* 1964

11 How alike are the groans of love to those of the dying.
Malcolm Lowry, UNDER THE VOLCANO 1947

12 Continental people have sex-life; the English have hot-water bottles.
George Mikes, HOW TO BE AN ALIEN 1946

13 Sex is one of the nine reasons for reincarnation. The other eight aren't important.
Henry Miller, BIG SIR AND THE ORANGES OF HIERONYMUS BOSCH 1957

14 When she saw the sign 'Members Only' she thought of him.
Spike Milligan, PUCKOON

15 I thought oral contraception was when you talked your way out of it.
Overheard. Quoted Peterborough, Daily Telegraph 12 *Feb* 1970

16 I've been the whole hog plenty of times. Sometimes you can be happy and not go the whole hog. Now and again you can be happy without going any hog.
Harold Pinter, HOMECOMING 1965

17 On a sofa upholstered in panther skin / Mona did researches in original sin.
William Plomer, MEWS FLAT MONA

18 There is nothing like desire for preventing the thing one says from bearing any resemblance to what one has in mind.
Marcel Proust, REMEMBRANCE OF THINGS PAST 1913–1927

19 The Christian view of sex is that it is, indeed, a form of holy communion.
John Robinson (Bishop of Woolwich), giving evidence for the defence in the LADY CHATTERLY'S LOVER *case* 1960

20 Even people who think themselves quite advanced believe that only the sexually starved can exert a wholesome moral influence.
Bertrand Russell in a letter to A. S. Neill 31 *Jan* 1931

21 I keep making up these sex rules for myself and then I break them right away.
J. D. Salinger, THE CATCHER IN THE RYE 1951

22 All this fuss about sleeping together. For physical pleasure I'd sooner go to my dentist any day.
Evelyn Waugh, VILE BODIES 1930

23 Being a sex symbol is rather like being a convict.
Raquel Welch. Quoted Observer 25 *Feb* 1979

24 It's not the men in my life that count; it's the life in my men.
Mae West

SHARK

25 Oh the shark has pretty teeth dear / And he shows them pearly white.
Bertolt Brecht, THE THREEPENNY OPERA, *The Ballad of Mack the Knife* 1928

GEORGE BERNARD SHAW

1 Shaw was charming with one person, fidgety with two, and stood on his head with four.
Stanley Baldwin. Quoted G. W. Lyttelton, THE LYTTELTON HART-DAVIS LETTERS 18 *Jul* 1956

2 I really enjoy only his stage directions; the dialogue is vortical, and, I find, fatiguing. It is like being harangued . . . He uses the English language like a truncheon.
Max Beerbohm. Quoted S. N. Behrens, CONVERSATION WITH MAX 1960

3 This astonishing Mr. Shaw has been greater than anything even he has ever written.
John Mason Brown

4 Shaw, one day you will eat a pork chop and then God help all women.
Mrs. Pat Campbell

5 Mr. Shaw is (I suspect) the only man on earth who has never written any poetry.
G. K. Chesterton, ORTHODOXY 1908

6 Shaw's works make me admire the magnificent tolerance and broadmindedness of the English.
James Joyce. Quoted Gerald Griffin, THE WILD GEESE

7 He is a good man fallen among Fabians.
V. I. Lenin

8 He writes like a Pakistani who has learned English when he was twelve years old in order to become a chartered accountant.
John Osborne

9 Shaw is the most fraudulent, inept writer of Victorian melodramas ever to gull a timid critic or fool a dull public.
Id.

10 I remember coming across him at the Grand Canyon and finding him peevish, refusing to admire it or even look at it properly. He was jealous of it.
J. B. Priestley, THOUGHTS IN THE WILDERNESS

11 The absence of fine shades and atmosphere explains why repertory companies in a hurry so often choose a Shaw play. You have only to learn the lines, slam them across, and the piece comes to life.
Id.

12 I am a disciple of Bernard Shaw.
George Bernard Shaw, THE DOCTOR'S DILEMMA 1906

13 He is an idiot child screaming in a hospital.
H. G. Wells, Daily Chronicle 1914

14 At 83 Shaw's mind was perhaps not quite as good as it used to be. It was still better than anyone else's.
Alexander Woollcott, WHILE ROME BURNS 1934

SHIP

15 First Mate: There are four stowaways in the forward hatch.
Captain: How do you know there are four?
First Mate: They keep singing 'Sweet Adeline'.
Marx Brothers, MONKEY BUSINESS

16 Women are jealous of ships. They always suspect the sea. They know they're three of a kind when it comes to a man.
Eugene O'Neill, MOURNING BECOMES ELECTRA 1931

SHOCK

17 I can still remember the day when I encountered my first Conservative, a shock all the greater in that it coincided with the crisis of puberty.
Prof. Gwyn Williams, Observer, *Sayings of the Week* 30 *Aug* 1981

SHOOTING

18 He [Godfrey Webb] went out duck shooting. He was asked afterwards whether he had shot many. "Not even a Mallard imaginaire" was his answer.
Maurice Baring, THE PUPPET SHOW OF MEMORY 1922

SHOP

19 Pile it high, sell it cheap.
Motto of Sir John Cohen, founder of Tesco supermarkets

20 All English shop assistants are Miltonists. All Miltonists firmly believe that 'they also serve who only stand and wait.'
George Mikes, HOW TO BE INIMITABLE 1960

SHYNESS

21 I have all the shyness of the very vain.
V. S. Naipaul, Radio Times 24 *Mar* 1979

SILENCE

1 Silence is the best substitute for brains ever invented.
Senator Henry F. Ashurst. Quoted Leon Harris, THE FINE ART OF POLITICAL WIT

2 Silences have a climax, when you have to speak.
Elizabeth Bowen, THE HOUSE IN PARIS 1935

3 Silence is the most perfect expression of scorn.
George Bernard Shaw, BACK TO METH-USELAH 1922

4 My personal hobbies are reading, listening to music, and silence.
Edith Sitwell

5 God is the friend of silence. Trees, flowers, grass grow in silence. See the stars, moon and sun, how they move in silence.
Mother Teresa, FOR THE BROTHERHOOD OF MAN 1981

SIR JOHN SIMON

6 The Right Honourable and Learned gentleman has twice crossed the floor of this House, each time leaving behind him a trail of slime.
David Lloyd George, House of Commons 1931

SIMPLICITY

7 The ability to simplify means to eliminate the unnecessary so that the necessary may speak.
Hans Hofmann, SEARCH FOR THE REAL 1967

SIN

8 All sins are attempts to fill voids.
W. H. Auden, A CERTAIN WORLD

9 There are different kinds of wrong. The people sinned against are not always the best.
Ivy Compton-Burnett, THE MIGHTY AND THEIR FALL 1962

10 It is right to hate sin, but not to hate the sinner.
Giovanni Guareschi, THE LITTLE WORLD OF DON CAMILLO

11 There is but one thing more dangerous than sin — the murder of a man's sense of sin.
Pope John Paul II. Quoted Observer 8 *Apr* 1979

12 The only people who should really sin / Are the people who can sin with a grin.
Ogden Nash, I'M A STRANGER HERE MYSELF, *Inter-Office Memorandum* 1938

13 Sin cannot be undone, only forgiven.
Igor Stravinsky, CONVERSATIONS WITH STRAVINSKY 1959

SINCERITY

14 Sincerity is all that counts. It's a widespread modern heresy. Think again. Bolsheviks are sincere. Fascists are sincere. Lunatics are sincere. People who believe the earth is flat are sincere. They can't all be right. Better make certain first you've got something to be sincere about and with.
Tom Driberg, Daily Express 1937

15 It is dangerous to be sincere unless you are also stupid.
George Bernard Shaw, MAN AND SUPERMAN 1905

SINGING

16 Her singing reminds me of a cart coming downhill with the brake on.
Sir Thomas Beecham of a soprano in DIE WALKÜRE. *Quoted Harold Atkins and Archie Newman*, BEECHAM STORIES

17 Most sopranos sound as if they live on seaweed.
Sir Thomas Beecham, Newsweek 3 *Apr* 1956

18 He made a mistake — he thinks he's the bull instead of the toreador.
Sir Thomas Beecham, auditioning a baritone for CARMEN. *Quoted Harold Atkin and Archie Newman*, BEECHAM STORIES

19 To be a great singer you need a big chest, a big mouth, 90 per cent memory, 10 per cent intelligence, lots of hard work and something in the heart.
Enrico Caruso. Quoted Dorothy Caruso, ENRICO CARUSO

20 All the intelligence and talent in the world can't make a singer. The voice is a wild thing. It can't be bred in captivity.
Willa Cather, THE SONG OF THE LARK 1915

21 She was a singer who had to take any note above A with her eyebrows.
Montague Glass. Quoted Frank Muir, THE FRANK MUIR BOOK

1 I can't stand to sing the same song the same way two nights in succession. If you can, then it ain't music, it's close order drill, or exercise or yodelling or something, not music.
Billy Holliday, LADY SINGS THE BLUES 1956

2 There are few moments during her [Margaret Truman's] recital when one can relax and feel confident that she will make her goal, which is the end of the song.
Paul Hume, Washington Post

3 The Italian language is peculiarly suitable for singing, having no awkward diphthongs and virtually no final consonants.
Frank Muir, THE FRANK MUIR BOOK

4 My own objection to the prima donna is that, as a rule, she represents merely tone and technique without intelligence.
Sir Ernest Newman, A MUSICAL MOTLEY 1919

5 My arias made me take off as if I was on a trampoline.
Jessye Norman, Radio Times 24 Oct 1931

6 A prima donna, you know, should always sing with her vowels open.
Arthur Wimperis to Luella Paikin. Quoted Reginald Pound, THEIR MOODS AND MINE 1935

EDITH SITWELL

7 Then Edith Sitwell appeared, her nose longer than an anteater's, and read some of her absurd stuff.
Lytton Strachey, of an evening with Arnold Bennett, in a letter to Dora Carrington 28 Jun 1921

8 So you've been reviewing Edith Sitwell's latest piece of virgin dung, have you? Isn't she a poisonous thing of a woman, lying, concealing, flipping, plagiarising, misquoting, and being as clever a literary publicist as ever.
Dylan Thomas, letter to Glyn Jones 1934

9 I am as appreciatively indifferent to Edith Sitwell as I am to the quaint patterns of old chintzes, the designs on dinner plates, or the charm of nursery rhymes.
H. G. Wells, EXPERIMENT IN AUTOBIOGRAPHY

SKY

10 For rich people, the sky is just an extra, a gift of nature. The poor, on the other hand, can see it as it is, a gift of infinite grace.
Albert Camus, NOTEBOOKS 1935–1942

SLANG

11 I know only two words of American slang, 'swell' and 'lousy'. I think 'swell' is lousy, but 'lousy' is swell.
J. B. Priestley when interviewed on American radio

SLAVERY

12 Death is a slave's freedom.
Nikki Giovanni at the funeral of Martin Luther King 1968

SLEEP

13 I like heat without weight. Henry likes weight without heat. I sleep under a couple of Shetland shawls. Henry would be happy stark naked under a grand piano.
Margot Asquith, AUTOBIOGRAPHY 1936

14 By day she never looked old. She grew up in sleep. Then a map of unwilling adult-awareness lines, tensions and hollows — appeared in her exposed face.
Elizabeth Bowen, A LOVE STORY

15 Laugh and the world laughs with you; snore and you sleep alone.
Anthony Burgess, INSIDE MR. ENDERBY 1966

16 Sleep is when all the unsorted stuff comes flying out as from a dustbin upset in a high wind.
William Golding, PINCHER MARTIN 1956

17 That we are not much sicker and much madder than we are is due exclusively to that most blessed and blessing of natural graces, sleep.
Aldous Huxley, THEME AND VARIATIONS 1950

18 Sleep, whom the old writers called the brother of Death.
Louis MacNeice, NOW THAT THE SHAPES OF MIST

19 Just begin a story with such a phrase as 'I remember Disraeli — poor old Dizzy! — once saying to me, in answer to my poke in

the eye," and you will find me and Morpheus off in a corner, necking.
Dorothy Parker (Constant Reader) of Margot Asquith's autobiography, The New Yorker 22 *Oct* 1927

1 I can't be expected to drop everything and start counting sheep at my age. I hate sheep.
Dorothy Parker, THE LITTLE HOURS

2 Those no-sooner-have-I-touched-the-pillow people are past my comprehension. There is something bovine about them.
J. B. Priestley, ALL ABOUT OURSELVES

3 I have come to the borders of sleep / The unfathomable deep / Forest where all must lose / Their way, however straight / Or winding, soon or late; / They cannot choose.
Edward Thomas, LIGHTS OUT

4 I haven't been to sleep for over a year. That's why I go to bed early. One needs more rest if one doesn't sleep.
Evelyn Waugh, DECLINE AND FALL 1928

SLOUGH

5 Come friendly bombs and fall on Slough / It isn't fit for humans now / There isn't grass to graze on now / Swarm over, Death.
Sir John Betjeman, SLOUGH

SMELL

6 To me, smells are like music; they have an aching familiar power to evoke the past. A good strong whiff can stab you to the heart with longing and remembrance.
Ray Bolitho, Daily Telegraph 20 *Dec* 1978

7 I love the people with their straightforward minds. It's just that their smell brings on my migraine.
Bertolt Brecht, THE CAUCASIAN CHALK CIRCLE 1945

8 A police officer could have confused the smell of cannabis with that of smelly feet, a defendant claimed at Beaconsfield on Tuesday.
Bucks Free Press. Quoted Punch 16 *May* 1973

9 "The lotuses smell like pineapples."
"Everything smells like something else. It's so dreadfully confusing."
Noël Coward, SHADOW PLAY

SMILE

10 She gave me a smile I could feel in my hip pocket.
Raymond Chandler, FAREWELL MY LOVELY 1940

11 A smile that snapped back after using, like a stretched rubber band.
Sinclair Lewis. Quoted Reader's Digest, *Aug* 1941

12 Smiling encouragement like a clumsy dentist.
Katherine Mansfield, BANK HOLIDAY

13 A smile that floated without support, in the air.
Marcel Proust, REMEMBRANCE OF THINGS PAST, *Cities of the Plain* 1921–2

14 He had a smile like a razor-blade.
Anthony Sampson, of Moss Evans, THE CHANGING ANATOMY OF BRITAIN 1982

15 He smiled, bunching his fat cheeks like twin rolls of smooth pink toilet paper.
Nathanael West, MISS LONELYHEARTS 1933

SMOKING

16 "You won't object if I smoke?"
"Certainly not — if you don't object if I'm sick."
Sir Thomas Beecham replying to a woman in a non-smoking railway compartment

17 Men have always smoked. With women it's just a habit.
Letter to Bradford Telegraph and Argus. *Quoted Michael Bateman,* THIS ENGLAND

18 Smokers, male and female, inject and excuse idleness in their lives every time they light a cigarette.
Colette, EARTHLY PARADISE, *Freedom* 1966

DAME ETHEL SMYTHE

19 Nobody ever managed to kiss Ethel.
Sir Thomas Beecham

20 She would be like Richard Wagner, if only she looked a bit more feminine.
Osbert Sitwell. Quoted Elizabeth Lutyens, A GOLDFISH BOWL

SNOBBERY

21 In our way we were both snobs, and no snob welcomes another who has risen with him.
Sir Cecil Beaton of Evelyn Waugh

1 One of those refined people who go out to sew for the rich because they cannot bear contact with the poor.
Colette, THE OTHER ONE

2 Marie Laurencin loves princes. She lunched with the King and Queen of the Belgians but was disillusioned on learning that Belgium was so small.
René Gimpel, DIARY OF AN ART DEALER

3 Dukes and dustmen are generally not snobs as both are devoid of social pretension.
Neil Mackwood, IN AND OUT

4 His hatred of snobs was a derivative of his snobbishness, but made the simpletons (in other words, everyone) believe that he was immune from snobbishness.
Marcel Proust, REMEMBRANCE OF THINGS PAST 1913–1927

5 The English have no respect for their language. It is impossible for an Englishman to open his mouth without making some other Englishman despise him.
George Bernard Shaw, PYGMALION 1913

6 I mustn't go on singling out names. One must not be a name-dropper, as Her Majesty remarked to me yesterday.
Norman St. John Stevas. Speech at Museum of the Year luncheon 20 Jun 1979

SNOW

7 His soul swooned slowly as he heard the snow falling faintly through the universe and faintly falling, like the descent of their last end, upon all the living and the dead.
James Joyce, DUBLINERS, *The Dead* 1914

8 The first fall of snow is not only an event, it is a magical event. You go to bed in one kind of world and wake up in another quite different, and if this is not enchantment then where is it to be found?
J. B. Priestley, APES AND ANGELS

SOCIALISM

9 What a genius the Labour Party has for cutting itself in half and letting the two parts writhe in public.
Cassandra (Sir William Connor), Daily Mirror

10 The disastrous element in the Labour party is its intellectuals.
G. N. Clark. Quoted A. L. Rowse, A MAN OF THE THIRTIES

11 We need less *egalité* and more *fraternité*.
John Fowles, THE ARISTOS

12 As with the Christian religion, the worst advertisement for Socialism is its adherents.
George Orwell, THE ROAD TO WIGAN PIER 1937

13 I am a socialist — and I only wish the Labour Party was.
Rev. Donald Soper, BBC Radio 4, *Any Questions* 11 *May* 1979

SOCIETY

14 There are two classes in good society in England. The equestrian classes and the neurotic classes.
George Bernard Shaw, HEARTBREAK HOUSE 1920

SOCIOLOGY

15 Sociology is the science with the greatest number of methods and the least results.
J. H. Poincaré. Quoted Bertrand Russell, SCIENCE AND METHOD

16 Those terrible sociologists who are the astrologers and alchemists of our twentieth century.
Miguel de Unamuno, FANATICAL SCEPTICISM

SOLDIER

17 O what is that sound which so thrills the ear / Down in the valley, drumming, drumming? / Only the scarlet soldiers, dear / The soldiers coming.
W. H. Auden, O WHAT IS THAT SOUND?

18 It must have been a little trying to the colonel who came up to him [Osbert Sitwell] and asked him if he was fond of horses to be told "No but I adore giraffes."
Beverley Nichols, TWENTY FIVE 1926

19 Today we have naming of parts. Yesterday / We had daily cleaning. And tomorrow morning / We shall have what to do after firing. But today, / Today we have naming of parts.
Henry Reed, LESSONS OF WAR 1946

20 The soldier's body becomes a stock of accessories that are not his property.
Antoine de Saint-Exupéry, FLIGHT TO ARRAS 1942

1 Soldiers are citizens of death's grey land /
Drawing no dividend from time's tomorrow.
Siegfried Sassoon, DREAMER 1918

2 The British soldier can stand up to anything
except the British War Office.
George Bernard Shaw, THE DEVIL'S DISCIPLE 1900

3 I never expect a soldier to think.
Id.

4 He [the recruiting officer] asked me "Why
tanks?" I replied that I preferred to go into
battle sitting down.
Peter Ustinov, DEAR ME 1977

SOLITUDE

5 Bold gnats that revel round my solitude.
Edmund Blunden, POEMS 1911–1930

6 Solitude, a luxury of the rich.
Albert Camus, NOTEBOOKS 1935–1942

7 Only solitary men know the full joys of
friendship. Others have their family — but
to a solitary and an exile his friends are
everything.
Willa Cather, SHADOWS ON THE ROCK 1931

8 There are days when solitude is a heady
wine that intoxicates you with freedom,
others when it is a bitter tonic, and still
others when it is a poison that makes you
beat your head against the wall.
Colette, EARTHLY PARADISE, *Freedom* 1966

9 I want to be alone.
*Popularly attr. to Greta Garbo, although
she frequently denied ever having said it*

10 The more powerful and original a mind, the
more it will incline towards the religion of
solitude.
Aldous Huxley, PROPER STUDIES 1927

11 People could with advantage be compelled
to remain alone for several hours a day; and
a week's solitary confinement would be an
excellent provision.
(Percy) Wyndham Lewis, TIME AND WESTERN MAN 1927

12 Solitude gives birth to the original in us: to
beauty unfamiliar and perilous — to poetry.
But also it gives birth to the opposite, to the
perverse, the illicit, the absurd.
Thomas Mann, DEATH IN VENICE 1913

13 Solitude is the playfield of Satan.
Vladimir Nabokov, PALE FIRE 1962

14 Life is for each man a solitary cell whose
walls are mirrors.
Eugene O'Neill, LAZARUS LAUGHED 1927

SONG

15 It is the best of all trades to make songs, and
the second best to sing them.
Hilaire Belloc, ON EVERYTHING, *On
Song* 1909

16 Song: the licensed medium for bawling in
public things too silly or too sacred to be
uttered in ordinary speech.
Oliver Herford. Quoted Nat Shapiro,
ENCYCLOPEDIA OF QUOTATIONS ABOUT
MUSIC

17 Why 'words for music' are almost invariably trash now, though the words of
Elizabethan songs are better than any
music, is a gloomy and difficult question.
Andrew Lang, ESSAY ON T. H. BAYLY

18 Cheap music set to noble words exposes
the cheapness of the music; beautiful and
profound music set to insignificant words
still communicates the beauty of the music.
Artur Schnabel, MUSIC AND THE LINE OF
MOST RESISTANCE 1947

19 Some of the songs making the rounds now
will be popular when Bach, Beethoven and
Wagner are forgotten — but not before.
Louis Sobel. Quoted Nat Shapiro, ENCYCLOPEDIA OF QUOTATIONS ABOUT MUSIC

20 Having verse set to music is like looking at
a painting through a stained glass window.
Paul Valéry. Ibid.

SORROW

21 Sorrow is tranquillity remembered in emotion.
Dorothy Parker, SENTIMENT

SOUND

22 The church clock chimed like a cat in a
well.
George Barker, RESOLUTION OF DEPENDENCE

SOUVENIR

23 I don't have a photograph, but you can
have my footprints. They are upstairs in my
socks.
Groucho Marx, A NIGHT AT THE OPERA

24 Over the chimney-piece . . . hangs an
entrenching tool with which, in 1915, Uncle
Matthew had whacked to death eight

Germans one by one as they crawled out of a dug-out. It is still covered in blood and hairs, an object of fascination to us children.
Nancy Mitford, THE PURSUIT OF LOVE 1945

SPACE-RESEARCH

1 One small step for man, one giant leap for mankind.
Neil Armstrong, first man on the moon 21 *Jul* 1969

2 Outer space is no place for a person of breeding.
Lady Violet Bonham Carter. Quoted B. G., New Yorker 11 *Jun* 1979

3 Today we can no more predict what use mankind may make of the Moon than could Columbus have imagined the future of the continent he had discovered.
Arthur C. Clarke, THE EXPLORATION OF SPACE

4 Space isn't remote at all. It's only an hour's drive away if your car could go straight upwards.
Sir Fred Hoyle, Observer 9 *Sep* 1979

5 Treading the soil of the moon, palpitating its pebbles, tasting the panic and splendour of the event, feeling in the pit of one's stomach the separation from terra — these form the most romantic sensation an explorer has ever known.
Vladimir Nabokov, New York Times 21 *Jul* 1969

6 This is the greatest week in the history of the world since the creation.
Richard Nixon of the moon landing 24 *Jul* 1969

7 Because of what you have done the heavens have become part of man's world. And as you talk to us from the Sea of Tranquillity it inspires us to redouble our efforts to bring peace and tranquillity to earth.
Richard Nixon, Radio message to astronauts on the moon 20 *Jul* 1969

8 For years politicians have promised the moon. I'm the first one to be able to deliver it.
Id.

9 According to information received from Cape Canaveral a rocket with a man on board was launched. After fifteen minutes the capsule with the pilot, Alan Shepard, fell into the Atlantic Ocean.
Tass, *Russian news agency* 5 *May* 1961

10 The astronauts . . . Rotarians in outer space.
Gore Vidal, TWO SISTERS 1970

SPEECH

11 Words fluttered from him like swallows leaving a barn at daylight.
O. Henry

12 Speech is civilisation itself. The word, even the most contradictory word, preserves contact — it is silence which isolates.
Thomas Mann, THE MAGIC MOUNTAIN 1924

13 I don't want to talk grammar. I want to talk like a lady.
George Bernard Shaw, PYGMALION 1913

14 Remember that you are a human being with the divine gift of articulate speech; that your native language is the language of Shakespeare and Milton and the Bible; and don't sit there crooning like a bilious pigeon.
Id.

SPEED

15 Speed provides the one genuinely modern pleasure.
Aldous Huxley, MUSIC AT NIGHT, *Wanted, a New Pleasure* 1931

16 In the past human life was lived in a bullock cart, in the future it will be lived in an aeroplane, and the change in speed amounts to a difference in quality.
A. N. Whitehead, SCIENCE AND THE MODERN WORLD 1925

SPINSTER

17 Being an old maid is like death by drowning, a really delightful sensation after you cease to struggle.
Edna Ferber, A PECULIAR TREASURE 1939

SPIRITUALISM

18 Miss Erickson looked more peculiar than ever this morning. Is her spiritualism getting worse?
Noël Coward, PRESENT LAUGHTER 1943

SPORT

1 I went skiing and broke a leg. Fortunately it wasn't mine.
Anon. Quoted Daily Telegraph

2 It is international sport that helps to kick the world downhill. Started by foolish athletes, who thought it would promote 'understanding' it is supported today by the desire for political prestige and by the interests involved in gate monies. It is completely harmful.
E. M. Forster, TWO CHEERS FOR DEMOCRACY 1957

SPRING

3 Every year, back Spring comes, with nasty little birds, yapping their fool heads off, and the ground all mucked up with arbutus.
Dorothy Parker. Quoted Robert N. Linscott, AN OMNIBUS OF AMERICAN HUMOUR

4 In the spring your lovely Chloe lightly turns one mass of spots.
Ronald Searle and Timothy Sly, THE TERROR OF ST. TRINIANS

5 Spring makes everything look filthy.
Katherine Whitehorn, Observer, *Wonder Shirkers* 24 Feb 1980

SPY

6 The members of our secret service have apparently spent so much time looking under the beds for Communists, they haven't had time to look in the bed.
Michael Foot, at the time of the Profumo affair

JOSEPH STALIN

7 My father died a difficult and terrible death . . . God grants an easy death only to the just.
Svetlana Alliluyeva, Stalin's daughter, TWENTY LETTERS TO A FRIEND

8 I like old Joe Stalin. He's a good fellow but he's a prisoner of the Politburo. He would make certain agreements but they won't let him keep them.
Harry S Truman. Speech. Quoted News Review 24 *Jun* 1948

STATELY HOME

9 An extraordinary aspect of running a stately home is that much of its success depends, not on how many Van Dycks you have, but how many loos. No amount of beautiful objects can compensate a visitor who is kept queuing in the cold.
Duchess of Bedford, NICOLE NOBODY

10 These comfortably padded lunatic asylums which are known, euphemistically, as the stately homes of England.
Virginia Woolf, THE COMMON READER 1925

STATESMAN

11 He therefore was at strenuous pains / To atrophy his puny brains / And registered success in this / Beyond the dreams of avarice / Till when he had at last become / Blind, paralytic, deaf and dumb / Insensible and cretinous / He was admitted ONE OF US.
Hilaire Belloc, THE STATESMAN

12 When statesmen forsake their own private conscience for the sake of their public duties they lead their country by a short route to chaos.
Robert Bolt, A MAN FOR ALL SEASONS 1961

13 The difference between being an elder statesman / And posing successfully as an elder statesman / Is practically negligible.
T. S. Eliot, THE ELDER STATESMAN

14 A statesman is a politician when he has been dead ten years.
Harry S Truman, interview, New York World Telegram 12 *Apr* 1958

STATISTICS

15 Nearly half of Northern Ireland's sub-postmistresses are women.
Journal of the Federation of Sub-Postmasters

16 He uses statistics as a drunken man uses lamp-posts — for support rather than illumination.
Andrew Lang. Quoted A. L. Mackay, HARVEST OF A QUIET EYE

17 Statistical figures referring to economic events are historical data. They tell us what happened in a non-repeatable historical case.
Ludwig Elder von Mises, HUMAN ACTION

18 Statistics will prove anything, even the truth.
Lord Moynihan. Quoted Lore and Maurice Cowen, THE WIT OF MEDICINE

1 A single death is a tragedy; a million is a statistic.
Joseph Stalin. Quoted John Bartlett, FAMILIAR QUOTATIONS

2 Statistics are mendacious truths.
Lionel Strachey

STATUE

3 A garden without its statue is like a sentence without its verb.
Joseph W. Beach, MEEK AMERICANS

STATUS

4 There is a lot to be said in schools and in communities generally for seeing that nobody is below the rank of lance-corporal.
Rhodes Boyson, Observer 23 *Nov* 1980

5 A man's name, title and rank are artificial and impermanent; they do nothing to reveal what he really is, even to himself.
Jean Giraudoux, SIEGFRIED 1928

6 A society person who is enthusiastic about modern painting or Truman Capote is already half a traitor to his class. It is only middle-class people who, quite mistakenly, imagine that a lively pursuit of the latest in reading or painting will advance their status in the world.
Mary McCarthy, ON THE CONTRARY 1961

GERTRUDE STEIN

7 Reading Gertrude Stein at length is not unlike making one's way through an interminable and badly printed game book.
Richard Bridgeman, GERTRUDE STEIN IN PIECES

8 While she believed that most writers failed to allow writing to express all that it could, in her own practice she scrupulously saw to it that writing expressed less than it would.
John Malcolm Brinnin, THE THIRD ROSE 1959

9 Gertrude Stein is the mama of dada.
Clifton Fadiman

10 Gertrude Stein's prose song is a cold, black suet-pudding. We can represent it as a cold suet roll of fabulously reptilian length. Cut it at any point, it is the same thing; the same heavy, sticky, opaque mass all through, and all along . . . it is mournful and monstrous, composed of dead and inanimate material.
(Percy) Wyndham Lewis.

NORMAN ST. JOHN STEVAS

11 A Catholic layman who has never been averse to giving advice to the Pope, or indeed anybody else who he thought might be in need of it.
Bernard Levin, THE PENDULUM YEARS 1976

LYTTON STRACHEY

12 Strachey had recently published *Eminent Victorians*, and *Queen Victoria*. Someone incautiously asked him who would be the subject of his next biography. At the top of his small, weak, but piercing voice he shouted 'God.'
Jacques-Emile Blanche, MORE PORTRAITS OF A LIFETIME 1918–1938

IGOR STRAVINSKY

13 His music used to be original. Now it is aboriginal.
Sir Ernest Newman, Musical Times, *Jul* 1921

STRENGTH

14 The awareness of our own strength makes us modest.
Paul Cézanne, LETTERS 1937

STRIKE

15 It is difficult to go on strike if there is no work in the first place.
Lord George-Brown, Observer 24 *Feb* 1980

STUPIDITY

16 Just as the results of inebriety are most painful with the habitually sober, and just as the greatest saints have often been the greatest sinners, so, when the first class brain does something stupid, the stupidity of that occasion is colossal.
Stanley Baldwin, House of Commons 13 *May* 1924

17 Nothing in the world is more dangerous than sincere ignorance and conscientious stupidity.
Martin Luther King, STRENGTH TO LOVE 1963

18 "How can you be so stupid?"
"I can do anything if I apply my mind to it."
Simon Moss, COCK UPS *(Play. First presented at Edinburgh Festival, Aug* 1981)

1 "I simply cannot *bear* fools."
"Apparently your mother did not have the same difficulty."
Dorothy Parker. Quoted Bennett Cerf, TRY AND STOP ME 1947

2 A routine of port and a fall on his head once a week kept him in that state of chronic, numbing confusion which was then the aim of every cavalry officer.
Osbert Sitwell, GREAT MORNING 1947

3 "Dyall, you're a perfect idiot."
"Oh no, sir. I wouldn't say that. No one is perfect."
Hal Wilton, ROCKFIST ROGAN

4 He was in many ways one of the most pronounced fatheads that ever pulled on a suit of gent's underwear.
P. G. Wodehouse, MY MAN JEEVES 1919

STYLE

5 Swinburne mastered his technique, which is a great deal, but he did not make it to the extent of being able to take liberties with it, which is everything.
T. S. Eliot, REFLECTIONS ON VERS LIBRE

6 Properly understood style is not a seductive decoration added to a functional structure; it is of the essence of a work of art.
Evelyn Waugh, BOOKS ON TRIAL

7 Bruce Cabot and Myrna Loy make a crash landing in the jungle and crawl out of the wreckage in their Abercrombie & Fitch white safari blouses and tan gabardine jodhpurs and stagger into a clearing.
Tom Wolfe, FROM BAUHAUS TO OUR HOUSE

SUCCESS

8 The penalty of success is to be bored by people who used to snub you.
Lady Astor. Quoted Geoffrey Bocca, Sunday Express 12 *Jan* 1956 *(also attr. to Mary Wilson Little)*

9 The toughest thing about success is that you've got to keep on being a success. Talent is only a starting point in this business.
Irving Berlin, Theatre Arts, *Feb* 1958

10 Success is like knowledge; where is the fun if everybody's got it?
Basil Boothroyd, Punch 10 *May* 1972

11 Success is relative. It is what we can make of the mess we have made of things.
T. S. Eliot, THE FAMILY REUNION 1939

12 The compensation of very early success is a conviction that life is a romantic matter. In the best sense one stays young.
F. Scott Fitzgerald, THE CRACK-UP 1945

13 Gentleman, I have invented a new slogan — Goldwyn pictures griddle the earth.
Sam Goldwyn. Quoted Alva Johnson, THE GREAT GOLDWYN

14 There are two reasons why I am successful in show business and I am standing on both of them.
Betty Grable

15 Success is always temporary; success is only delayed failure.
Graham Greene, A SORT OF LIFE 1971

16 I've never consciously striven for success. But once I was aware I had it I must say I was terrified of losing it.
Gilbert Harding to John Freeman on BBC TV, *Face to Face*

17 Success — "the bitch-goddess Success" in William James' phrase — demands strange sacrifices from those who worship her.
Aldous Huxley, PROPER STUDIES 1927

18 Unless a man has been taught what to do with success after getting it, the achievement of it must inevitably leave him prey to boredom.
Bertrand Russell, THE CONQUEST OF HAPPINESS 1930

19 The only way to succeed is to make people hate you. That way, they remember you.
Joseph von Sternberg, AUTOBIOGRAPHY

20 There are no gains without pains.
Adlai Stevenson. Nomination address 1952

21 Success to me is having ten honeydew melons and eating only the top half of each one.
Barbra Streisand, Life 20 *Sep* 1963

22 To succeed in life it is not enough to be stupid. One must be well mannered as well.
Bonar Thompson (Hyde Park orator), THE BLACK HAT

23 The best thing that can come with success is the knowledge that it is nothing to long for.
Liv Ullmann, CHANGING MASKS

1 Whenever a friend succeeds, a little something in me dies.
Gore Vidal. Quoted Susan Barnes,
BEHIND THE IMAGE

2 It is not enough to succeed. Others must fail.
Gore Vidal, BBC Radio 4, *Quote Unquote 5 Jun 1980. Also attr. to David Merrick in Barbara Rowe*, A BOOK OF QUOTES

SUFFERING

3 [Suffering is] a form of gratitude to experience or an opportunity to experience evil and change it into good.
Saul Bellow, HERZOG 1964

4 A cause is like champagne and high heels — one must be prepared to suffer for it.
Arnold Bennett, THE TITLE 1918

5 If you are convinced of your despair, you must either act as if you did hope after all — or kill yourself. Suffering gives no rights.
Albert Camus, NOTEBOOKS 1935–1942

6 Every now and then people have preferred sorrow to joy and asserted that wisdom and creation can only result from suffering.
E. M. Forster, TWO CHEERS FOR DEMOCRACY

7 Few can believe that suffering, especially by others, is in vain. Anything that is disagreeable must surely have beneficial economic effects.
J. K. Galbraith, THE AGE OF UNCERTAINTY 1977

8 We are healed of a suffering only by experiencing it to the full.
Marcel Proust, REMEMBRANCE OF THINGS PAST, *The Fugitive* 1925

9 There is also a cup of pain for you to drink all up / Or setting it aside for sweeter drink / Thirst ever more.
Stevie Smith, AND SO TO FATNESS COME

10 He groaned slightly, and winced, like Prometheus watching his vulture dropping in for lunch.
P. G. Wodehouse. Quoted Richard Usborne, WODEHOUSE AT WORK 1961

SUICIDE

11 If I had the use of my body I would throw it out of the window.
Samuel Beckett, MALONE DIES 1956

12 There is but one truly serious philosophical problem, and that is suicide. Judging whether life is, or is not worth living amounts to answering the fundamental question of philosophy.
Albert Camus, THE MYTH OF SISYPHUS

13 Not only is suicide a sin, it is the sin. It is the ultimate and absolute evil, the refusal to take the oath of loyalty to life. The man who kills a man, kills a man. The man who kills himself kills all men; as far as he is concerned he wipes out the world.
G. K. Chesterton, ORTHODOXY 1908

14 There are many who dare not kill themselves for fear of what the neighbours might say.
Cyril Connolly, THE UNQUIET GRAVE 1945

15 My work is done. Why wait.
George Eastman. Suicide note

16 Doesn't it seem a little like going where you haven't been invited.
Richard Eberhart, HOW IT IS

17 No neurotic harbours thoughts of suicide which are not murderous impulses against others redirected upon himself.
Sigmund Freud, TOTEM AND TABOO 1918

18 Razors pain you / Rivers are damp / Acids stain you / And drugs cause cramp / Guns aren't lawful / Nooses give / Gas smells awful, / You might as well live.
Dorothy Parker, ENOUGH ROPE, *Résumé* 1927

19 When you're between any sort of devil and the deep blue sea, the deep blue sea sometimes looks very inviting.
Terence Rattigan, THE DEEP BLUE SEA 1952

20 "It is against the law to commit suicide in this man's town" I say, "although what the law can do to a guy who commits suicide I am never able to figure out."
Damon Runyon, GUYS AND DOLLS 1932

21 Suicide . . . is about life, being in fact the sincerest criticism life gets.
Wilfrid Sheed, THE GOOD WORD

22 The body of Pipkin lay spreadeagled on the roof of an Austin Princess, the owner of which was surveying it with the weary distaste he normally reserved for pigeon droppings.
E. S. Turner, Punch 10 *May* 1973

1 I am the only man in the world who cannot commit suicide.
Rev. Chad Varah (founder of the Samaritans)

SUMMER

2 Summer has filled her veins with light / And her warm heart is washed with noon.
C. Day Lewis, FROM FEATHERS TO IRON

3 The dynamo hum of summer running down.
Reginald Pound, THEIR MOODS AND MINE 1937

4 Summer makes a silence after spring.
Vita Sackville-West, THE LAND 1926

5 In this noble country of ours there is no such thing as summer weather or summer clothing. There are simply different kinds of temperature and different kinds of garments appropriate to them. As a guide the calendar is a monstrous fraud.
Times leader. *Quoted* News Review 17 *Jul* 1947

SUN

6 O praise / With lion-music such as that heard in the air / When the roaring golden lion that roams the heavens / Devours the dark, and multitudes and magnitudes respond.
Edith Sitwell, THE OUTCASTS, *Praise We Great Men*

7 Thank heavens the sun has gone in and I don't have to go out and enjoy it.
Logan Pearsall Smith, last words

SUNDAY

8 The boredom of Sunday afternoon, which drove De Quincey to opium also gave birth to surrealism; hours propitious to making bombs.
Cyril Connolly, THE UNQUIET GRAVE 1945

9 The feeling of Sunday is the same everywhere, heavy, melancholy, standing still. Like when they say "As it was in the beginning, is now, and ever shall be, world without end."
Jean Rhys, VOYAGE IN THE DARK 1934

10 Do not take a bath in Jordan / Gordon / On the Holy Sabbath, on the peaceful day!
Edith Sitwell, SCOTCH RHAPSODY

11 And the sabbath rang slowly / In the pebbles of the holy streams.
Dylan Thomas, FERN HILL 1952

SUNSET

12 Shipwrecked, the sun sinks down harbours / of a sky, unloads its liquid cargo / of marigolds.
Dannie Abse, WALKING UNDER WATER, *Epithalamion*

13 There is nothing more musical than a sunset.
Claude Debussy. Quoted Nat Shapiro, ENCYCLOPEDIA OF QUOTATIONS ABOUT MUSIC

14 Or autumn sunsets exquisitely dying.
Aldous Huxley, THE NORTH PHILOSOPHER'S SONG

15 I have a horror of sunsets. They are so romantic, so operatic.
Marcel Proust, REMEMBRANCE OF THINGS PAST, *Cities of the Plain* 1921–2

SUPERFLUITY

16 When struck by a thunderbolt it is unnecessary to consult the Book of Rules as to the precise meaning of the omen.
Ernest Bramah, THE WALLET OF KAI LUNG 1920

17 Life is too short to stuff a mushroom.
Shirley Conran, SUPERWOMAN

18 As superfluous as a Gideon Bible in the Ritz.
F. Scott Fitzgerald, THE CRACK-UP 1936

SUPERIORITY

19 He was not brought by the stork; he was delivered by a man from the Audubon Society personally.
Fred Allen, American radio comedian

20 He lies below, correct in cypress wood / And entertains the most exclusive worms.
Dorothy Parker, EPITAPH FOR A VERY RICH MAN

SUPERNATURAL

21 Religion / Has made an honest woman of the supernatural.
Christopher Fry, THE LADY'S NOT FOR BURNING 1949

SUPERSTITITION

1 I miss my daily Mass, and have a superstitious feeling that anything may happen on the days I don't go. However, nothing in particular has.
Rose Macaulay, LETTERS TO A FRIEND 1961

SURGERY

2 A man will bleed to death from a severed carotid artery in three minutes. You can tie his artery in two minutes *if you are not in a hurry*.
Anon. Variously attrib.

3 The greatest discoveries of surgery are anaesthesia, asepsis and roentonology — and none was discovered by a surgeon.
Martin Henry Fisher

SURPRISE

4 The thing startled poor old Bully considerably. He rose from his seat like a rocketing pheasant.
P. G. Wodehouse, JEEVES AND THE HARD BOILED EGG

5 Captain Biggar's strong jaw fell like an unsupported stick of asparagus.
P. G. Wodehouse, THE RETURN OF JEEVES

SURREALISM

6 To them, chaos is the shape and order. This seems to me to be exceedingly presumptuous; the Surrealists imagine that whatever they dredge up from their sub-conscious selves and put down in paint or words must essentially be of some value. I deny this.
Dylan Thomas. Quoted Andrew Sinclair, DYLAN THOMAS, POET OF HIS PEOPLE

SURVIVAL

7 It isn't important to come out on top; what matters is to come out alive.
Bertolt Brecht, JUNGLE OF CITIES 1924

8 People are inexterminable — like flies and bed-bugs. There will always be some that survive in cracks and crevices — that's us.
Robert Frost. Quoted Observer 29 Mar 1959

9 He was as fitted to survival in this modern world as a tapeworm in an intestine.
William Golding, FREE FALL 1959

10 We can survive if we dig enough holes.
T. K. Jones, a Reagan aide. Quoted BBC Radio 4, *World Tonight, Nov* 1982

11 The supreme reality of our time is . . . the vulnerability of this planet.
John F. Kennedy. Speech, Dublin 28 *Jun* 1963

12 Building up arms is not a substitute for diplomacy.
Samuel Pisar, OF BLOOD AND HOPE

13 When you get to the end of your rope, tie a knot and hang on.
Franklin D. Roosevelt

SUSPICION

14 Suspicion is a thing very few people can entertain without letting the hypothesis turn, in their minds, to fact.
David Cort, SOCIAL ASTONISHMENTS

15 He had the sort of convoluted mind that could attribute evil and devious motives to a bee-keeper offering him a pot of honey as a gift.
Hugh Cudlipp, of H. G. Bartholomew, editor of the Daily Mirror; WALKING ON THE WATER

16 I found a long grey hair on Kevin's jacket last night — If it's another woman's I'll kill him. If it's mine I'll kill myself.
Neil Simon, IT HURTS ONLY WHEN I LAUGH *(play)*

17 We have to distrust each other. It is our only defence against betrayal.
Tennessee Williams, CAMINO REAL 1953

SWEARING

18 Ordinary men . . . / Put up a barrage of common sense to baulk / Intimacy, but by mistake interpolate / Swear-words like roses in their talk.
Louis MacNeice, CONVERSATION 1929

SWITZERLAND

19 The Swiss are not a people so much as a neat, clean, quite solvent business.
William Faulkner, INTRUDER IN THE DUST 1948

20 In Italy for thirty years under the Borgias they had warfare, terror, murder, bloodshed and they produced Michelangelo, Leonardo da Vinci and the Renaissance. In Switzerland they had brotherly

love, five hundred years of democracy and peace and what did they produce? The cuckoo clock.
Orson Welles, added by him to the script of his film The Third Man

SYCOPHANCY

1 I see her as one great stampede of lips directed at the nearest derrière.
Noël Coward of a newspaper columnist. Quoted William Marchant, THE PRIVILEGE OF HIS COMPANY 1980

2 Don't say "Yes" until I finish talking.
Attrib. Darryl F. Zanuck. Quoted in his obituary, Daily Telegraph 24 *Dec* 1979

SYMBOLISM

3 In so far as a symbol is a living thing, it is the expression of a thing not to be characterised in any other way. The symbol is alive in so far as it is pregnant with meaning.
Carl Jung

SYMPATHY

4 To be sympathetic without discrimination is so very debilitating.
Ronald Firbank, PRANCING NIGGER 1924

5 She was a machine gun, riddling her hostess with sympathy.
Aldous Huxley, THE GIACONDA SMILE

T

TACT

1 My advice was delicately poised between the cliché and the indiscretion.
Robert Runcie (Archbishop of Canterbury) to the press concerning his advice to the Prince of Wales and Lady Diana Spencer on their approaching wedding 13 *Jul* 1981

TACTLESSNESS

2 Although there exist many thousand subjects for elegant conversation, there are persons who cannot meet a cripple without talking about feet.
Ernest Bramah, THE WALLET OF KAI LUNG 1920

3 Never speak of rope in the house of a man who has been hanged.
Franklin D. Roosevelt. Campaign speech, Washington 23 *Sep* 1944

TALENT

4 In this world people have to pay an extortionate price for any exceptional gift whatever.
Willa Cather, THE OLD BEAUTY AND OTHERS 1948

5 Middle age snuffs out more talent than ever wars or sudden deaths do.
Richard Hughes, THE FOX IN THE ATTIC 1961

TASTE

6 Between friends differences in taste or opinions are irritating in direct proportion to their triviality.
W. H. Auden, THE DYER'S HAND 1962

7 People care more about being thought to have taste than about being thought either good, clever or amiable.
Samuel Butler, NOTEBOOKS 1912

8 The kind of people who always go on about whether a thing is in good taste invariably have very bad taste.
Joe Orton, BEHIND THE SCENES *(edited by Joseph F. McCrindle)*

9 We talk of acquired taste, but all tastes are really acquired, and it is doubtful whether we are any better off for having acquired them, better in the sense that through them our enjoyment of life is rendered any more intense.
Alec Waugh, ON DOING WHAT ONE LIKES

TAXATION

10 When they fire a rocket at Cape Canaveral, I feel as if I own it.
William Holden. Quoted Robert Ottaway, TV Times 24 *Aug* 1972

11 The taxpayer is someone who works for the federal government but doesn't have to take a civil service examination.
Ronald Reagan. Quoted Barbara Rowe, A BOOK OF QUOTES

ELIZABETH TAYLOR

12 Miss Taylor lists about, her hands fluttering idly like a wind-up doll in need of a new mainspring.
New York Times, *of her performance in* PRIVATE LIVES 9 *May* 1983

13 Just how garish her commonplace accent, her squeakily shrill voice, and the childish petulance with which she delivers her lines are, my pen is neither scratchy nor leaky enough to convey.
John Simon, of Elizabeth Taylor's performance in THE TAMING OF THE SHREW

TEA

14 If I had known there was no Latin word for tea I would have let the vulgar stuff alone.
Hilaire Belloc. Quoted Frank Muir, THE FRANK MUIR BOOK

1 The best thing to do when you've got a dead body and it's your husband's, on the kitchen floor, and you don't know what to do about it, is to make a cup of tea.
Anthony Burgess, ONE HAND CLAPPING

2 I like a nice cup of tea in the morning / For to start the day you see / And at half-past eleven / Well my idea of Heaven / Is a nice cup of tea / I like a nice cup of tea with my dinner / And a nice cup of tea with my tea / And when it's time for bed / There's a lot to be said / For a nice cup of tea.
A. P. Herbert, the Cochran revue, HOME AND BEAUTY

3 When I makes tea I makes tea as old mother Grogan said. And when I makes water I makes water.
James Joyce, ULYSSES 1922

TEACHING

4 It is nothing short of a miracle that the modern methods of instruction have not entirely strangled the holy curiosity of enquiry.
Albert Einstein. Quoted George B. Leonard, EDUCATION AND ECSTASY

5 You sought the last resort of feeble minds with classical educations. You became a schoolmaster.
Aldous Huxley, ANTIC HAY 1923

TECHNOLOGY

6 Any sufficiently advanced technology is indistinguishable from magic.
Arthur C. Clarke, THE LOST WORLDS OF 2001

TEETH

7 Now Albert's coming back, make yourself a bit smart / He'll want to know what you done with that money he gave you / To get yourself some teeth. He did, I was there / You have them all out, Lil, and get a nice set / He said, I swear, I can't bear to look at you.
T. S. Eliot, THE WASTE LAND 1922

TELEPHONE

8 I never pass an empty telephone box without pressing Button B. Button B has often been kind to me.
Joyce Cary, THE HORSE'S MOUTH 1942

9 *Witness:* I went to the Elephant to make a telephone call.
Lord Darling: A trunk call, no doubt.
Lord Darling. Quoted Edward Bell, THESE MEDDLESOME ATTORNEYS

TELEVISION

10 Three quarters of television is for half-wits. The boxing's all right.
Sir Thomas Beecham. Quoted Harold Atkins and Archie Newman, BEECHAM STORIES

11 All the music I have ever seen on television looks grotesque . . . You see right down the larynx, almost into the tummy, the eyes go this way, the nose goes that way, and the mouth is twisted round. The whole thing is revolting. That's television, so far as music is concerned.
Sir Thomas Beecham. Quoted Lord Boothby, MY YESTERDAY YOUR TOMORROW

12 Why should people go out and pay to see bad films when they can stay at home and see bad television for nothing?
Sam Goldwyn. Quoted Observer *9 Sep 1956*

13 I'll believe in colour television when I see it in black and white.
Sam Goldwyn. Quoted Benny Green, Radio Times *17 Feb 1979*

14 He doesn't suit daylight does he?
Elderly lady's comment on Michael Parkinson. Quoted Russell Harty, Observer *4 Nov 1979*

15 Television won't matter in your lifetime or mine.
Rex Lambert, The Listener *1936*

16 Television brought the brutality of war into the comfort of the living room. Vietnam was lost in the living rooms of America, not on the battlefields of Vietnam.
Marshall McLuhan, Montreal Gazette *16 May 1975*

17 Television? No good will come of this new device. The word is half Greek and half Latin.
C. P. Scott, Manchester Guardian

18 I'm still big. It's the pictures that got small.
Gloria Swanson, SWANSON ON SWANSON 1981

19 Marietta . . . knows all the right questions. Unfortunately she is driven to give wrong

answers. She is very effective on television panel programmes.
Gore Vidal, TWO SISTERS

1 The television screen is the finest medium ever devised for showing old films.
Keith Waterhouse, Radio Times 17 *Mar* 1979

2 The camera brings out exhibitionist streaks in the quietest people.
Viscount Weymouth, BBC 2 TV, A Year in the Life of 1 *Oct* 1981

3 Chewing-gum for the eyes.
Attr. Frank Lloyd Wright and, by J. B. Simpson, to John Mason Brown

TEMPTATION

4 The Devil, having nothing else to do / Went off to tempt my Lady Poltagrue / My Lady, tempted by a private whim / To his annoyance tempted him.
Hilaire Belloc, EPIGRAMS

5 She's not so pretty anyone would want to ruin her.
Bertolt Brecht, MOTHER COURAGE AND HER CHILDREN 1939

6 No temptation can ever be measured by the value of its object.
Colette, EARTHLY PARADISE, *Human Nature* 1966

7 In this new experience you may find temptations both in wine and women. You must entirely resist both temptations, and while treating all women with perfect courtesy, you should avoid any intimacy.
Lord Kitchener. Message in soldier's pay books 1914–18 war

8 Better to enjoy and suffer than sit around with folded arms. You know the only true prayer? Please God, lead me into temptation.
Jennie Lee, MY LIFE WITH NYE

9 We cannot go about, unfortunately, telling everybody about the temptations we have resisted. As a result people judge us exclusively by the temptations to which we yield.
Robert Lynd, THE PEAL OF BELLS

10 I never resist temptation because I have found that things that are bad for me never tempt me.
George Bernard Shaw, THE APPLE CART 1929

11 I have always despised Adam because he had to be tempted by the woman, as she was by the serpent, before he could be induced to pluck the apple from the tree of knowledge. I should have swallowed every apple on the tree the moment the owner's back was turned.
George Bernard Shaw. Quoted Hesketh Pearson, BERNARD SHAW 1942

12 She had no use for morals and always omitted "Lead us not into temptation" from the Lord's Prayer. "It's no business of His" she proclaimed.
Philip Ziegler, DIANA COOPER

TENNIS

13 Pam, I adore you, Pam, you great big mountainous sports girl, / Whizzing them over the net, full of the strength of five.
Sir John Betjeman, POT POURRI FROM A SURREY GARDEN

14 "If you can't volley, wear velvet socks" one Old Gamesman used to say.
Stephen Potter, GAMESMANSHIP 1947

15 Players must provide their own rackets and must wear shoes without heels. Balls for practice may be obtained on application to the gardener.
Rules for the first tennis competition at Wimbledon. Quoted A. Wallis Myers, MEMORY'S PARADE

TERRORISM

16 It's too bad that blood is involved, otherwise one might almost say that terrorism is a good thing.
Ken Glass, BBC Radio 3, *Terror* 19 *Aug* 1981

TESTIMONIAL

17 He coxed his college boat at Oxford — and I'm told he sings Gilbert and Sullivan in his bath, which immediately makes us take him to our hearts.
Alec Douglas-Home, of the Pakistan Prime Minister, Evening Standard. *Quoted Michael Bateman*, THIS ENGLAND

THAMES

18 Sweet Thames run softly till I end my song.
T. S. Eliot, THE WASTE LAND 1922

MARGARET THATCHER

1 She is trying to wear the trousers of Winston Churchill.
Leonid Brezhnev. Speech 1979

2 She is clearly the best man among them.
Barbara Castle, DIARIES

3 Politicians are either warriors or healers. Margaret Thatcher is a healer.
Patrick Cosgrave, BIOGRAPHY OF MARGARET THATCHER

4 She has been beastly to the Bank of England, has demanded that the BBC "set its house in order", and tends to believe the worst of the Foreign and Commonwealth Office. She cannot see an institution without hitting it with her handbag.
Julian Critchley, The Times profile, *Margaret Thatcher* 21 *Jun* 1982

5 She has no imagination, and that means no compassion.
Michael Foot. Quoted John Mortimer, Sunday Times, *Foot at Bay* 19 *Sep* 1982

6 Attila the Hen.
Clement Freud, BBC Radio 4, *News Quiz* 26 *Oct* 1979

7 She approaches the problem of our country with all the one-dimensional subtlety of a comic strip.
Denis Healey, House of Commons 22 *May* 1979

8 Mrs. Thatcher is doing for monetarism what the Boston Strangler did for door-to-door salesmen.
Id. 15 *Dec* 1977

9 For the past few months she has been charging about like some bargain-basement Boadicea.
Denis Healey, Observer, *Sayings of the Week* 7 *Nov* 1982

10 She is the Enid Blyton of economics. Nothing must be allowed to spoil her simple plots.
Richard Holme. Speech, Liberal Party Conference 10 *Sep* 1980

11 She sounded like the book of Revelations read out over a railway station public address system by a headmistress of a certain age wearing calico knickers.
Clive James, of Margaret Thatcher on television, Observer 1979

12 I am a great admirer of Mrs. Thatcher — one of the most splendid headmistresses there has ever been.
Arthur Marshall, BBC Radio 4, *Any Questions* 22 *Jan* 1982

13 I think I'm thoroughly in favour of Mrs. Thatcher's visit to the Falklands. I find a bit of hesitation, though, about her coming back.
John Mortimer, BBC Radio 4, *Any Questions?* 1983

14 Mrs. Thatcher has taken to power the way others take to the air of Colwyn Bay. It braces her. She is invigorated. She knocks people down.
Edward Pearce, Daily Telegraph 27 *Jun* 1979

15 She is the best man in England.
Ronald Reagan to reporters 7 *Jan* 1983

16 This woman is headstrong, obstinate and dangerously self-opinionated.
Report on Margaret Thatcher by personnel officer at ICI when rejecting her for a job in 1948

17 Margaret Thatcher is David Owen in drag.
Rhodesia Herald 8 *Aug* 1979

18 I am extraordinarily patient, provided I get my own way in the end.
Margaret Thatcher. Quoted Observer, *Sayings of the Year* 2 *Jan* 1983

19 Don't forget Denis (her husband) when you're considering the influences on her. He sees her every morning at breakfast — far more often than any of us.
A Tory MP on Mrs. Thatcher becoming Prime Minister. Quoted Laurence Marks, Observer 6 *May* 1979

20 Plunder Woman.
Harry Unwin. Trades Union Congress, Brighton 6 *Sep* 1980

THEATRE

21 The reason why Absurdist plays take place in No Man's Land with only two characters is mainly financial.
Arthur Adamov. Speech, Edinburgh 13 *Sep* 1962

22 Some of my plays peter out, and some pan out.
J. M. Barrie. Quoted Leonard Rossiter, LOWEST FORM OF WIT

1 It was one of those plays in which all the actors unfortunately enunciated very clearly.
Robert Benchley, CHIPS OFF THE OLD BENCHLEY 1949

2 My companion had a point when, listening to one of the bursts of noise off stage from time to time, she remarked that there was obviously a better play going on back stage.
Katherine Brisbane of a performance of OTHELLO, Australian 10 *Oct* 1967

3 I go to the theatre to be entertained. I don't want to see plays about rape, sodomy and drug addiction — I can get all that at home.
Cartoon caption in Observer 8 *Jul* 1962

4 The play was a success but the audience was a failure.
William Collier. Quoted Bennett Cerf, TRY AND STOP ME 1947

5 Don't put your daughter on the stage, Mrs. Worthington.
Noël Coward, song title

6 Don't whatever you do, be nervous on the opening night. It's *such* a waste of time and spoils most of the fun.
Noël Coward. Quoted William Marchant, THE PRIVILEGE OF HIS COMPANY 1980

7 Generally speaking, the American theatre is the aspirin of the middle classes.
Wolcott Gibbs, MORE IN SORROW, *Shakespeare, Here's Your Hat*

8 No good play is a success; fine writing and high morals are useless on the stage. I have been scribbling twaddle for thirty-five years to suit the public taste, and I should know.
W. S. Gilbert. Quoted Isaac Goldberg, THE STORY OF GILBERT AND SULLIVAN

9 The Twenties did indeed temporarily raise the mental age of the average theatre-goer from fourteen to seventeen.
Robert Graves and Alan Hodge, THE LONG WEEK-END 1940

10 All that Russian gloom and doom, and people shooting themselves from loneliness and depression and that sort of thing. But then, mother says I don't understand comedy. I expect she's right.
Simon Gray, QUARTERMAINE'S TERMS *(play)*

11 I have knocked everything except the knees of the chorus girls. Nature anticipated us there.
Percy Hammond. Quoted Frank Muir, THE FRANK MUIR BOOK

12 Characters in a play don't always have to be bigger fools than in everyday life.
Eugene Ionesco, FOURSOME

13 I thought the play was frightful but I saw it under particularly unfortunate circumstances. The curtain was up.
George Kaufman. Quoted Bennett Cerf, SATURDAY REVIEW OF LITERATURE

14 Coughing in the theatre is not a respiratory ailment. It is a criticism.
Alan Jay Lerner, THE STREET WHERE I LIVE

15 When I go to the theatre I like the curtain to rise to reveal a smart maid at the telephone saying "I am afraid her ladyship isn't back yet!" And through the window a view of Sloane Square may be seen.
Arthur Marshall, Radio Times 23 *Jul* 1977

16 How can you write a play of which the ideas are so significant that they will make the critic of *The Times* get up in his stall and at the same time induce the shop girl in the gallery to forget the young man who is holding her hand?
W. Somerset Maugham, CAKES AND ALE 1930

17 I hate harrowing plays. *Love on the Dole* made me cry with rage — to think that one of the greatest of the arts had been used to upset people so.
Evelyn Millard, THE ERA

18 *The House Beautiful* is the play lousy.
Dorothy Parker, Life magazine

19 Depending upon shock tactics is easy, whereas writing a good play is difficult. Pubic hair is no substitute for wit.
J. B. Priestley, OUTCRIES AND ASIDES

20 A novelist may lose his readers for a few pages; a playwright never dares lose his audience for a minute.
Terence Rattigan, New York Journal American 29 *Oct* 1956

21 *Peter Pan* is a charming play for children. It is not a rule of conduct for a great nation.
Edith Shackleton. Quoted James Agate, Ego 3, 4 *Dec* 1936

22 A novel is a static thing that one moves through: a play is a dynamic thing that moves past one.
Kenneth Tynan, CURTAINS

23 A good many inconveniences attend playgoing in any large city, but the greatest of them is usually the play itself.
Kenneth Tynan, New York Herald Tribune 17 *Feb* 1957

1 What a pity it is that there are so few of you and so many of me.
Orson Welles, when facing a tiny audience in Wisconsin

2 One of the best tips for writing a play is 'Never let them sit down'. Keep the characters buzzing about without a pause.
P. G. Wodehouse, PERFORMING FLEA 1953

3 The play left a taste of lukewarm parsnip juice.
Alexander Woollcott. Quoted Howard Techmann, SMART ALEX 1976

THEOLOGY

4 Only a minority of the religions of the world have a theology. There was no systematic series of statements which the Greeks agreed in believing about Zeus.
C. S. Lewis, IS THEOLOGY POETRY?

5 All your Western theologies, the whole mythology of them are based on the concept of God as a senile delinquent.
Tennessee Williams, THE NIGHT OF THE IGUANA 1961

THEORY

6 Factual evidence can never 'prove' a hypothesis; it can only fail to disprove it, which is what we generally mean when we say, somewhat inexactly, that the hypothesis is 'confirmed' by experience.
Milton Friedman, ESSAYS IN POSITIVE ECONOMICS

7 No theory is good except on condition that one uses it to go beyond.
André Gide, JOURNALS 1918

8 A first rate theory predicts; a second rate theory forbids, and a third rate theory explains after the event.
A. I. Kitaigorodskii. Quoted A. L. Mackay, HARVEST OF A QUIET EYE

9 Theory, glamorous mother of the drudge experiment.
Harlan Mayer Jr. Quoted Eric M. Rogers, PHYSICS FOR THE INQUIRING MIND 1949

DYLAN THOMAS

10 The fear of being unable to write was nearer the root of his troubles than the fear of not being able to pay the grocer.
Anon. New Yorker 21 *Nov* 1977

11 The crabbed and dark-eyed Welshman, Dylan Thomas, whose poems were strewn with wild, organic, telescoped images underneath which, perhaps, ran a submerged stream of poetic thought.
Robert Graves and Alan Hodge, THE LONG WEEK-END 1940

12 He was a detestable man. Men pressed money on him, and women their bodies. Dylan took both with equal contempt. His great pleasure was to humiliate people.
A. J. P. Taylor, A PERSONAL HISTORY 1983

JEREMY THORPE

13 He was looking more than usual like a super-brilliant monkey with astonishing sex appeal.
Jean Rook, Daily Express 6 *Mar* 1975

THOUGHT

14 As soon as you can say what you think and not what some other person has thought for you, you are on your way to being a remarkable man.
J. M. Barrie, TOMMY AND GRIZEL 1900

15 He can't think without his hat.
Samuel Beckett, WAITING FOR GODOT 1952

16 What was once thought can never be unthought.
Friedrich Durrenmatt, THE PHYSICISTS 1960

17 Thinking is a momentary dismissal of irrelevances.
R. Buckminster Fuller, UTOPIA OR OBLIVION

18 Thinking does not bring knowledge as do the sciences.
Martin Heidegger. Quoted Hannah Arendt, New Yorker 21 *Nov* 1977

19 A thing in itself never expresses anything. It is the relation between things that gives meaning to them and that formulates a thought. A thought functions only as a fragmentary part in the formulation of an idea.
Hans Hoffman, SEARCH FOR THE REAL

20 How can I know what I think until I have heard what I have said?
Christopher Hollis (Conservative MP for Devizes). Quoted News Review 12 *Dec* 1946

1 Most of one's life is a prolonged effort to avoid thinking.
Aldous Huxley, GREEN TUNNELS

2 Sooner or later false thinking brings wrong conduct.
Julian Huxley, ESSAYS OF A BIOLOGIST 1923

3 One has to multiply thoughts to the point where there aren't enough policemen to control them.
Stanislaw Lec, UNKEMPT THOUGHTS 1962

4 If you make people think they're thinking, they'll love you: but if you really make them think, they'll hate you.
Don Marquis, ARCHY AND MEHITABEL 1927

5 My thought is *one*. That is why I cannot stop. I exist by what I think.
Jean-Paul Sartre, NAUSEA 1938

6 As soon as man does not take his existence for granted, but beholds it as something unfathomably mysterious, thought begins.
Albert Schweitzer, THE TEACHING OF REVERENCE FOR LIFE

7 You can't think of nothing.
Subtitle of THE AVIATOR'S WIFE *(film)*

THRIFT

8 The man who tips a shilling every time he stops for petrol is giving away annually the cost of lubricating his car.
J. Paul Getty. Quoted Barbara Rowe, A BOOK OF QUOTES

9 Whenever you save five shillings you put a man out of work for a day.
J. M. Keynes, TREATISE ON MONEY 1931

10 The woman who can sacrifice a clean unspoiled penny stamp is probably unborn.
Saki, THE UNBEARABLE BASSINGTON 1912

THUNDER

11 Dry sterile thunder without rain.
T. S. Eliot, THE WASTE LAND 1922

TIDINESS

12 Keep London tidy — eat a pigeon a day.
Graffito. Quoted BBC Radio 4, *Quote Unquote* 7 *Jun* 1979

TIME

13 "Well, that's passed the time"
"It would have passed in any case."
Samuel Beckett, WAITING FOR GODOT 1952

14 I have not found out why we humans think of time as a line going from backwards, forwards, whilst it must be in all directions like everything else in the system of the world.
Ferruccio Busoni, BUSONI'S LETTERS TO HIS WIFE

15 It is so interminable and exasperating to watch the hand turn for five minutes on a clock that it is almost impossible to do so.
Albert Camus, NOTEBOOKS 1935–1942

16 Time present and time past / Are both perhaps present in time future / And time future contained in time past.
T. S. Eliot, FOUR QUARTETS, *Burnt Norton* 1936

17 We have all passed a lot of water since then.
Sam Goldwyn

18 In theory one is aware that the earth revolves but in practice one does not perceive it, the ground upon which one treads seems not to move, and one can live undisturbed. So it is with Time in one's life.
Marcel Proust, REMEMBRANCE OF THINGS PAST, *Within a Budding Grove* 1919

19 The necessity of not missing a train has taught us to account for minutes whereas among ancient Romans . . . the notion not of minutes but even of fixed hours barely existed.
Marcel Proust, REMEMBRANCE OF THINGS PAST, *Cities of the Plain* 1921–2

20 They do that to pass the time, nothing more. But Time is too large, it refuses to let itself be filled up.
Jean-Paul Sartre, NAUSEA 1938

21 Three o'clock is always too late or too early for anything you want to do.
Id.

22 Ah! The clock is always slow; / It is later than you think.
Robert W. Service, SONGS OF A SOURDOUGH 1907

23 The last years of his life had become so precious to him that, as he said, he would willingly stand at street corners hat in hand,

begging passers-by to drop their unused minutes into it.
John Walker, of Bernard Berenson, THE BERNARD BERENSON TREASURY

TIMIDITY

1 I'm really a timid person — I was beaten up by Quakers.
Woody Allen and Marshall Brickman, SLEEPER *(film)*

2 People wish to learn to swim and at the same time to keep one foot on the ground.
Marcel Proust, REMEMBRANCE OF THINGS PAST, *The Fugitive* 1925

TOLERANCE

3 More and more people care about religious tolerance as fewer and fewer care about religion.
Alexander Chase, PERSPECTIVES 1966

4 Tolerance is a very dull virtue. It is boring. Unlike love, it has always had a bad press. It is negative. It merely means putting up with people, being able to stand things.
E. M. Forster, TWO CHEERS FOR DEMOCRACY, *Tolerance* 1951

5 If you don't like people, put up with them as well as you can. Don't try to love them; you can't, you'll only strain yourself.
Id.

6 We tolerate shapes in human beings that would horrify us if we saw them in a horse.
W. R. Inge (Dean of St. Pauls). Quoted J. M. and M. J. Cohen, PENGUIN DICTIONARY OF MODERN QUOTATIONS

7 Once lead this people into war and they'll forget there ever was such a thing as tolerance.
President Woodrow Wilson. Quoted Jon Dos Passos, MR. WILSON'S WAR

TOWN

8 Parks are but pavements disguised with a growth of grass.
George Gissing, THE PRIVATE PAPERS OF HENRY RYECROFT 1903

TRADE UNION

9 I thought the miners' leaders were the stupidest body of men in the world — until I met the mine owners.
Lord Birkenhead on the General Strike 1926

10 There are those who collect the refuse of the public streets, but in order to be received into the band it is necessary to have been born one of the Hereditary Confederacy of Superfluity Removers and Abandoned Oddment Gatherers.
Ernest Bramah, KAI LUNG UNROLLS HIS MAT 1928

11 There are only two good unions. The Mothers Union and Rugby Union.
Graffito. Quoted Daily Telegraph 3 *Feb* 1979

12 We are very good at stopping what we do not like, but not at starting anything.
Len Murray, in 1976. *Quoted Robert Taylor*, THE FIFTH ESTATE 1978

TRADITION

13 Tradition becomes our security, and when the mind is secure it is in decay.
Krishnamurti, THE PENGUIN KRISHNAMURTI READER

TRAFFIC

14 *Rush hour:* that hour when traffic is almost at a standstill.
Beachcomber (J. B. Morton), MORTON'S FOLLY

15 Horsedrawn carriages used to average 11½ miles an hour in New York's midtown traffic; the average speed of automobiles is a bare six miles an hour.
Norman B. Geddes, MAGIC MOTORWAYS

TRAGEDY

16 Tragedy is restful and the reason is that hope, that foul, deceitful thing, has no part in it.
Jean Anouilh, ANTIGONE 1942

17 The bad end unhappily, the good unluckily. That is what tragedy means.
Tom Stoppard, ROSENCRANTZ AND GUILDENSTERN ARE DEAD 1966

18 We begin to live when we have conceived life as a tragedy.
W. B. Yeats, AUTOBIOGRAPHY 1926

TRANSLATION

19 The best translation is not that which is most like the original, but that which is the most different from it.
Gamaliel Bradford, LETTERS

1 There are a number of mistranslations of that famous motto '*Honi Soit Qui Mal Y Pense*', the latest I have heard is 'I honestly think I am going to be sick'.
Philip, Duke of Edinburgh. Speech to French Chamber of Commerce in Great Britain 1963

2 She has ideas above her station. How could you say that in French? You can't say au-dessus de sa gare. It isn't the same station.
Terence Rattigan, FRENCH WITHOUT TEARS 1936

3 A translation is no translation unless it will give you the music of a poem along with the words of it.
J. M. Synge, THE ARAN ISLANDS 1902

╌4 An idea does not pass from one language to another without change.
Miguel de Unamuno, TRAGIC SENSE OF LIFE 1913

5 Humour is the first of the gifts to perish in a foreign tongue.
Virginia Woolf, THE COMMON READER 1925

TRAVEL

6 The time to enjoy a European tour is about three weeks after you unpack.
George Ade, FORTY MODERN FABLES, *The Hungry Man From the Bird Centre* 1901

7 You'd think, with all these tourists about, they would build an elevator.
American lady climbing the Parthenon

8 I have recently been all round the world and have formed a very poor opinion of it.
Sir Thomas Beecham. Speech at the Savoy. Quoted News Review 22 *Aug* 1946

9 The longer the cruise the older the passengers.
Peg Bracken, BUT I WOULDN'T HAVE MISSED IT FOR THE WORLD

10 It is easier to find a travelling companion than to get rid of one.
Id.

11 One of the main troubles about going to Europe is that no one wants to hear about your trip when you get back home. Your friends and relatives are rife with jealousy, and are not only sorry that you went to Europe, but deeply regret that you came back.
Art Buchwald, Vogue 1 *Apr* 1954

12 There is no pleasure in travelling and I look upon it more as an occasion for spiritual testing.
Albert Camus, NOTEBOOKS 1939–1942

13 Henry wants me to take a trip around the world, but I'd rather go somewhere else.
Cartoon caption in New Yorker 1938

14 Men travel faster now, but I do not know if they go to better things.
Willa Cather, DEATH COMES FOR THE ARCHBISHOP 1927

15 It is a pity that people travel in foreign countries; it narrows their minds so much.
G. K. Chesterton

16 [Railway stations] are our gates to the glorious and the unknown. Through them we pass out into adventure and sunshine, and to them, alas, we return.
E. M. Forster, HOWARDS END 1910

17 If you put to sea in a wooden raft, with a parrot and five companions, it is inevitable that sooner or later you will wake up one morning out at sea, perhaps a little better rested than ordinarily, and begin to think about it.
Thor Heyerdahl, THE KON-TIKI EXPEDITION

18 Americans are people who prefer the Continent to their own country but refuse to learn its languages.
E. V. Lucas, WANDERINGS AND DIVERSIONS

19 The great and recurrent question about abroad is, is it worth getting there?
Rose Macaulay. Quoted J. M. and M. J. Cohen, PENGUIN DICTIONARY OF MODERN QUOTATIONS

20 [Everyone] hoped silently that the sense of being imprisoned in a decaying hotwater bottle would pass away in the fresh Atlantic breezes.
Compton Mackenzie, POOR RELATIONS

21 Whenever I prepare for a journey I prepare as though for death. Should I never return, all is in order. That is what life has taught me.
Katherine Mansfield, JOURNAL 1922

22 The only places John likes on the continent are those in which it is only by an effort of the imagination that you can tell you're not in England.
W. Somerset Maugham, THE CONSTANT WIFE 1926

1 *Seagoon:* I want you to accompany me on the safari.
Bloodnock: Gad sir, I'm sorry, I've never played one.
Spike Milligan, BBC Radio, *The Goon Show*

2 Only on the third class tourist class passengers' deck was it a sultry overcast morning, but then if you do things on the cheap you must expect these things.
Spike Milligan, A DUSTBIN OF MILLIGAN

3 There are only two rules. One is E. M. Forster's guide to Alexandria; the best way to know Alexandria is to wander aimlessly. The second is from the Psalms; grin like a dog and run about through the city.
Jan Morris, DESTINATIONS

4 Travel is glamorous only in retrospect.
Paul Theroux. Quoted Observer 7 *Oct* 1979

5 He travelled in order to come home.
William Trevor, MATILDA'S ENGLAND (BBC *play*)

6 I have travelled so much because travel has enabled me to arrive at unknown places within my clouded self.
Laurens Van Der Post

7 One of the great things about travelling is you find out how many good, kind people there are.
William Wharton, DAD 1981

TREE

8 The boughs of the oak are roaring / inside the acorn shell.
Charles Tomlinson, A SENSE OF DISTANCE

TROUBLE

9 I see the President of Romania's mother is dead — there's always trouble for somebody.
Alan Bennett. Quoted Roger Wilmot, FROM FRINGE TO FLYING CIRCUS 1980

10 A trouble shared is a trouble dragged out till bedtime.
Victoria Wood, HAPPY SINCE I MET YOU, Granada TV play 8 *Aug* 1981

TRUTH

11 — three fundamental truths without a recognition of which there can be no effective liberty; that what we believe is not necessarily true; that what we like is not necessarily good; and that all questions are open.
Clive Bell, CIVILISATIONS 1928

12 Truth is so precious that it must be protected by a bodyguard of lies.
Winston Churchill. Quoted Leo Rosten, THE POWER OF POSITIVE NONSENSE

13 "I am wedded to the truth My Lord"
"How long have you been a widower?"
Lord Darling to a witness. Quoted Derek Walker-Smith, LIFE OF LORD DARLING

14 Ethical axioms are found and tested not very differently from the axioms of science. Truth is what stands the test of experience.
Albert Einstein, OUT OF MY LATER YEARS 1950

15 A truth is something that everyone can be shown to know and to have known, as people say, all along.
Mary McCarthy, ON THE CONTRARY 1961

16 It is hard to believe that a man is telling the truth when you know that you would lie if you were in his place.
H. L. Mencken, PREJUDICES 1919

17 We find so many who think truth is on their side but precious few who are "on the side of truth".
Sir William Oder. Quoted Lore and Maurice Cowan, THE WIT OF MEDICINE

18 Truths that become old become decrepit and unreliable and sometimes they may be kept going for a certain length of time but there is no life in them.
P. D. Ouspensky, A NEW MODEL OF THE UNIVERSE

19 Truth is stranger than fiction; fiction has to make sense.
Leo Rosten, THE POWER OF POSITIVE NONSENSE

20 Truth is not that which is demonstrable, but that which is ineluctable.
Antoine de Saint-Exupéry, WIND, SAND AND STARS 1939

21 Truth has no special time of its own. Its hour is now — always.
Albert Schweitzer, OUT OF MY LIFE AND THOUGHT

22 Truth telling is not compatible with the defence of the realm.
George Bernard Shaw, HEARTBREAK HOUSE 1920

1 Mr. Mencken talks about truth as if she were his mistress, but he handles her like an iceman.
Stuart P. Sherman

2 When truth is discovered by someone else it loses some of its attractiveness.
Alexander Solzhenitsyn, CANDLE IN THE WIND

3 I never give them hell. I just tell the truth and they think it is hell.
Harry S Truman, Look magazine 3 *Apr* 1956

4 The only truths which are universal are those gross enough to be thought so.
Paul Valéry, MAUVAISE PENSÉES 1942

TYRANNY

5 Under conditions of tyranny it is easier to act than to think.
Hannah Arendt. Quoted W. H. Auden, A CERTAIN WORLD

6 The slave begins by demanding justice and ends by wanting to wear a crown. He must dominate in his turn.
Albert Camus, THE REBEL, *Metaphysical Rebellion* 1951

7 Tyranny is always better organised than freedom.
Charles Péguy, BASIC VIRTUES, *War and Peace*

8 People will endure their tyrants for years but they tear their deliverers to pieces if a millennium is not created immediately.
President Woodrow Wilson. Quoted John Dos Passos, MR. WILSON'S WAR 1963

U

UGLINESS

1 It's nothing to be born ugly. Sensibly, the ugly woman comes to terms with her ugliness and exploits it as a grace of nature.
Colette, JOURNEY FOR MYSELF

2 The secret of my success is that no woman has ever been jealous of me.
Elsa Maxwell. Quoted Noël Barber, THE NATIVES WERE FRIENDLY

UNCERTAINTY

3 We are not certain, we are never certain. If we were we could reach some conclusions, and we could, at last, make others take us seriously.
Albert Camus, THE FALL 1956

4 Without measureless and perpetual uncertainty the drama of human life would be destroyed.
Winston Churchill, THE GATHERING STORM 1948

UNDERSTANDING

5 Between / Our birth and death we may touch understanding / As a moth brushes a window with its wing.
Christopher Fry, THE BOY WITH A CART 1925

6 Understanding is the beginning of approving.
André Gide, JOURNALS 1902

UNDERTAKER

7 Evan the Death presses hard with black gloves on the coffin of his breast in case his heart jumps out.
Dylan Thomas, UNDER MILK WOOD 1957

UNEMPLOYMENT

8 Giz a job.
Yosser Hughes in Alan Bleasdale's BOYS FROM THE BLACKSTUFF, BBC TV 1982

9 When a great many people are unable to find work, unemployment results.
Calvin Coolidge, in a syndicated newspaper column. Quoted Stanley Walker, CITY EDITOR

10 A lot of fellows nowadays have a B.A., M.D. or Ph.D. Unfortunately they don't have a J.O.B.
Fats Domino. Quoted Barbara Rowe, A BOOK OF QUOTES

UNHAPPINESS

11 I have the true feeling of myself only when I am unbearably unhappy.
Franz Kafka, DIARIES 1914–1923

12 He has simply got the instinct for being unhappy highly developed.
Saki, THE CHRONICLES OF CLOVIS 1912

13 Those who are unhappy have no need for anything in this world but people capable of giving them their attention.
Simone Weil, WAITING FOR GOD 1950

UNITED STATES OF AMERICA

14 Americans have a perfect right to exist.
Max Beerbohm, ZULEIKA DOBSON 1911

15 America is the only nation in history which, miraculously, has gone directly from barbarism to degeneration without the usual interval of civilisation.
Georges Clemençeau

16 The business of America is business.
Calvin Coolidge. Speech 17 *Jan* 1923

17 When I was a boy I was told that anybody could become President of the United States. I am beginning to believe it.
Clarence Darrow

18 I went to Philadelphia one Sunday. The place was closed.
W. C. Fields

1 The Americans cannot build aeroplanes. They are very good at refrigerators and razor blades.
Hermann Goering's assurances to Hitler. Quoted Alistair Cooke, AMERICA

2 Everything about the behaviour of American society reveals that it is half judaised and half negrified. How can one expect a state like that to hold together.
Adolf Hitler at a secret conference

3 The American character looks always as if it had just had a rather bad haircut, which gives it, in our eyes at least, a greater humanity than the European, which even among its beggars gives it an all too professional air.
Mary McCarthy, ON THE CONTRARY 1961

4 American women expect to find in their husbands the perfection that English women only hope to find in their butlers.
W. Somerset Maugham

5 When you become used to never being alone you may consider yourself Americanised.
André Maurois

6 A nation which does not appreciate that the simple elocution exercise 'Merry Mary married hairy Harry' contains not one but *three* vowel sounds.
Jessica Mitford. Quoted Sue Arnold, Observer magazine 25 *Feb* 1979

7 America . . . where law and customs alike are based on the dreams of spinsters.
Bertrand Russell, MARRIAGE AND MORALS 1929

8 The reason American cities are prosperous is that there is no place to sit down.
Alfred J. Talley (American lawyer), on returning from a visit to Europe. Quoted Burton Stevenson, HOME BOOK OF QUOTATIONS

9 America is a large, friendly dog in a very small room. Every time it wags its tail it knocks over a chair.
Arnold Toynbee. Broadcast 14 *Jul* 1954

10 The thing that impresses me most about America is the way parents obey their children.
Duke of Windsor

UNIVERSE

11 There is no reason to assume that the universe has the slightest interest in intelligence — or even in life. Both may be random accidental by-products of its operations like the beautiful patterns on a butterfly's wings. The insect would fly just as well without them.
Arthur C. Clarke, THE LOST WORLDS OF 2001

12 listen; there's a hell of a good universe next door: let's go.
e.e. cummings, PITY THIS BUSY MONSTER, MANKIND

13 Universe is the aggregate of all humanity's consciously apprehended and communicated non-simultaneous and only partially overlapping experiences.
R. Buckminster Fuller, SYNERGETICS

14 The universe begins to look more like a great thought than like a great machine.
Sir James Jeans, THE MYSTERIOUS UNIVERSE 1930

15 In my youth I regarded the universe as an open book, printed in the language of physical equations, whereas now it appears to me as a text written in invisible ink, of which in our rare moments of grace we are able to decipher a small fragment.
Arthur Koestler, BRICKS TO BABEL, Epilogue 1983

16 Out of all possible universes, the only one which can exist, in the sense that it can be known, is simply the one which satisfies the narrow conditions necessary for the development of intelligent life.
Sir Bernard Lovell, IN THE CENTRE OF IMMENSITIES

17 If at that moment [one second after beginning to expand] the rate of expansion had been reduced by only a part in a thousand billion then the universe would have collapsed after a few million years.
Id.

18 I do not pretend to understand the universe. It is a great deal bigger than I am.
Tom Stoppard, LORD MALQUIST AND MR. MOON

UNIVERSITY

19 If you feel that you have both feet planted on the ground then the university has failed you.
Robert Coheen, Time 23 *Jun* 1961

1 There are as many fools at university as elsewhere, but their folly has a certain stamp — the stamp of university training. It is a trained folly.
William Gerhardie, THE POLYGLOTS 1925

2 I find that the three major administrative problems on a campus are sex for the students, athletics for the alumni and parking for the faculty.
Clark Kerr (President of the University of California), Time 17 *Nov* 1958

3 Finals, the very name of which implies that nothing of importance can happen after it. The British postgraduate student is a lonely forlorn soul.
David Lodge, CHANGING PLACES

UNSELFISHNESS

4 There is nothing in Christianity or Buddhism that quite matches the sympathetic unselfishness of an oyster.
Saki, CHRONICLES OF CLOVIS 1912

V

VALUE

1 Nothing is intrinsically valuable; the value of everything is attributed to it, assigned to it from outside the thing itself, by people.
John Barth, THE FLOATING OPERA 1956

2 What we must decide is perhaps how we are valuable, rather than how valuable we are.
F. Scott Fitzgerald, THE CRACK-UP 1945

VANITY

3 Vanity is a great toughener.
Brendan Bracken, to Lord Beaverbrook, during the Suez crisis. Quoted David Carlton, ANTHONY EDEN

4 Vanity plays lurid tricks with our memory.
Joseph Conrad, LORD JIM 1900

5 Half of the harm that is done in this world / Is due to people who want to feel important.
T. S. Eliot, THE COCKTAIL PARTY 1949

6 It's always our touches of vanity / That manage to betray us.
Christopher Fry, THE LADY'S NOT FOR BURNING 1949

7 I have all the shyness of the very vain.
V. S. Naipaul, Radio Times 24 *Mar* 1979

8 Self-love seems so often unrequited.
Anthony Powell, THE ACCEPTANCE WORLD 1955

9 Whatever talents I possess may suddenly diminish or suddenly increase. I can with ease become an ordinary fool. I may be one now. But it doesn't do to upset one's own vanity.
Dylan Thomas, NOTEBOOKS

10 She keeps on being queenly in her own room with the door shut.
Edith Wharton, THE HOUSE OF MIRTH 1905

11 Vanity is so intimately associated with our spiritual identity that whatever hurts it, above all if it came from it, is more painful in the memory than serious sin.
W. B. Yeats, DRAMATIS PERSONAE

VASECTOMY

12 Vasectomy means never ever having to say 'Sorry'.
Larry Adler, BBC Radio 4, *Interview*

VEGETARIAN

13 Vegetarians have wicked, shifty eyes and laugh in a cold calculating manner. They pinch little children, steal stamps, drink water, favour beards.
Beachcomber (J.B. Morton), Daily Express, *By the Way*

14 I have known many meat-eaters to be far more non-violent than vegetarians.
Mahatma Gandhi, NON-VIOLENCE IN PEACE AND WAR 1948

15 Vegetarianism is harmless enough, though it is apt to fill a man with wind and self righteousness.
Sir Robert Hutchinson (President, Royal College of Physicians). Quoted Lore and Maurice Cowan, THE WIT OF MEDICINE

16 A man of my spiritual intensity does not eat corpses.
George Bernard Shaw. Quoted Hesketh Pearson, BERNARD SHAW 1942

17 There are millions of vegetarians in the world but only one Bernard Shaw. You do not obtain eminence quite so cheaply as by eating macaroni instead of mutton chops.
George Bernard Shaw, when, during the meat shortage of the 1914–18, war, it was suggested he should be cited as an example of the advantages of vegetarianism

VICE

18 It is the function of vice to keep virtue within reasonable bounds.
Samuel Butler, NOTEBOOKS 1912

19 Half the vices which the world condemns most loudly have seeds of good in them and

require moderate use rather than total abstinence.
Samuel Butler, THE WAY OF ALL FLESH 1903

1 It is the restrictions placed on vice by our social code which makes its pursuit so peculiarly agreeable.
Kenneth Grahame, PAGAN PAPERS

2 Vice is waste of life. Poverty, obedience and celibacy are the canonical vices.
George Bernard Shaw, MAN AND SUPERMAN 1905

3 Never support two weaknesses at the same time. It's your combination sinners — your lecherous liars and your miserly drunkards — who dishonour the vices and bring them into disrepute.
Thornton Wilder, THE MATCHMAKER 1955

VICTIM

4 It takes two to make a murder. There are born victims, born to have their throats cut.
Aldous Huxley, POINT COUNTER POINT 1934

5 Every reformation must have its victims. You can't expect the fatted calf to show the enthusiasm of the angels over the prodigal's return.
Saki, REGINALD AND THE ACADEMY

VICTORY

6 Victory at all costs, victory in spite of all terror, victory however long and hard the road may be; for without victory there is no survival.
Winston Churchill. Speech, House of Commons 13 *May* 1940

7 The earth is still bursting with the dead bodies of the victors.
George Bernard Shaw, HEARTBREAK HOUSE, *Preface* 1920

VIETNAM WAR

8 To win in Vietnam we will have to exterminate a nation.
Dr. Benjamin Spock, ON VIETNAM

VIEWPOINT

9 The loveliest face in all the world will not please you if you see it suddenly eye to eye, at a distance of half an inch from your own.
Max Beerbohm, ZULEIKA DOBSON 1911

10 Part of the reason for the ugliness of adults, in a child's eyes, is that the child is usually looking upwards, and few faces are at their best when seen from below.
George Orwell, ESSAYS 1946

11 What critics call dirty in our movies they call lusty in foreign films.
Billy Wilder. Quoted Leslie Halliwell, A FILMGOER'S BOOK OF QUOTES 1973

VIOLENCE

12 Keep violence in the mind where it belongs.
Brian Aldiss, BAREFOOT IN THE HEAD

13 A bit of shooting takes your mind off your troubles — it makes you forget the cost of living.
Brendan Behan, THE HOSTAGE 1958

14 Violence is the repartee of the illiterate.
Alan Brien, Punch 7 *Feb* 1973

15 It is better to be violent, if there is violence in our hearts, than to put on the cloak of non-violence to cover impotence.
Mahatma Gandhi, NON-VIOLENCE IN PEACE AND WAR 1948

16 It is possible to disagree with someone about the ethics of non-violence without wanting to kick his teeth in.
Christopher Hampton, TREATS *(play)*

17 I went out and caught that boy and shook him until his freckles rattled.
O. Henry, THE RANSOM OF RED CHIEF

18 In violence we forget who we are.
Mary McCarthy, ON THE CONTRARY 1961

19 If someone puts his hand on you, send him to the cemetery.
Malcolm X, MALCOLM X SPEAKS 1965

20 Remove your pants before resorting to violence.
Yoko Ono. Quoted Bernard Levin, THE PENDULUM YEARS 1976

21 Today violence is the rhetoric of the period.
José Ortega y Gasset, THE REVOLT OF THE MASSES 1930

22 The argument of the broken pane of glass is the most valuable argument in modern politics.
Emmeline Pankhurst, VOTES FOR WOMEN 23 *Feb* 1912

23 I distrust the incommunicable. It is the source of all violence.
Jean-Paul Sartre, WHAT IS LITERATURE?

VIOLIN

1 *Fiddle, n.* An instrument to tickle human ears by function of a horse's tail on the entrails of a cat.
Ambrose Bierce, THE DEVIL'S DICTIONARY 1906

2 In respect to violins, I am polygamous.
Fritz Kreisler

VIRTUE

3 Righteous people terrify me . . . Virtue is its own punishment.
Aneurin Bevan. Quoted *Michael Foot,* ANEURIN BEVAN 1897–1945

4 Wolfgang Amadeus Mozart honoured his parents, loved his sister and adored his wife. In fact he was such a nice fellow it's a wonder he ever amounted to anything at all.
Victor Borge, MY FAVOURITE INTERVALS

5 Whenever there are tremendous virtues it's a sure sign something's wrong.
Bertolt Brecht, MOTHER COURAGE 1939

6 A virtue to be serviceable must, like gold, be alloyed with some commoner but more durable metal.
Samuel Butler, THE WAY OF ALL FLESH 1903

7 Virtue consisted in avoiding scandal and venereal disease.
Robert Cecil, LIFE IN EDWARDIAN ENGLAND 1969

8 My virtue's still far too small, I don't trot it out and about yet.
Colette, CLAUDINE AT SCHOOL

9 Our age is an age of moderate virtue.
T. S. Eliot

10 The absence of vices adds so little to the sum of one's virtues.
Antonio Machado, JUAN DE MAIRENO 1943

11 I am not impressed by external devices for the preservation of virtue in men or women. Marriage laws, the police, armies and navies are the mark of human incompetence.
Dora Russell, THE RIGHT TO BE HAPPY

VOCABULARY

12 William Nicholson, noticing that J. M. Barrie always ordered Brussels sprouts and never ate them, one day asked him why. J.

M. B. replied "I cannot resist ordering them. The words are so lovely to say."
Anon. Sunday Referee 5 *Dec* 1927

13 All the artistic words have changed their meaning in California. *Book* means magazine, *music* means jazz, *act* means behaving, *picture* means a snapshot.
Stella Benson, THE POOR MAN 1922

14 The monstrous word 'electrocute' for kill by electricity is now of regular occurrence, and bids fair to become part of our language. When we have the legitimately formed word 'electrocide' at our service why should it not be adopted and so detestable a solecism as the word referred to be repudiated.
J. Churton Collins, letter to The Times 29 *Mar* 1906

15 It comes in three sizes, Large, Giant and Super. I gave you the small size — Large.
Shop assistant. Quoted by correspondent to Competitor's Journal

16 The four-letter words in *Lady Chatterley* are not likely to be included in the Oxford Dictionary as a result of the case. "The legal judgment is irrelevant to our purpose" said Oxford University Press. "We don't take into account anything but common usage."
Daily Express. *Quoted Michael Bateman,* THIS ENGLAND

17 "Well" said the Owl, "the customary procedure in such cases is as follows."
"What does Crustimoney Proseedcake mean?" said Pooh. "For I am a bear of Very Little Brain, and long words bother me."
A. A. Milne, WINNIE THE POOH 1927

18 One forgets words as one forgets names. One's vocabulary needs constant fertilisation or it will die.
Evelyn Waugh, DIARIES

VOICE

19 A voice of plum-coloured velvet.
James Agate, of Ellen Terry

20 There was nothing wrong with her that a vasectomy of her vocal cords wouldn't fix.
Lisa Alther, KINFLICKS 1976

21 . . . a young man with so superior a voice that he might have been to Oxford twice.
Vernon Bartlett, AND NOW, TOMORROW

22 That voice! She sounds as if she thinks a crèche is something that happens on the M1.
Jeananne Crowley, Sunday Times

1 There was always something in her voice that made you think of lorgnettes.
O. Henry, THE DEFEAT OF THE CITY

2 A good voice has ruined more actors than whiskey.
Actor Joseph Jefferson. Quoted Gary Cooper, WELL, IT WAS THIS WAY 1956

3 The most remarkable thing about her was her voice, high, metallic . . . irritating to the nerves like the pitiless clamour of the pneumatic drill.
W. Somerset Maugham, RAIN 1922

4 The unique quality of his voice was the fact that it could reach higher and lower notes than have ever been reached by any other human being, some of which were so high that only bats, others so low that only horses, could hear them.
Nancy Mitford, PIGEON PIE 1940

5 His [André Gide] voice so clear and true, like the bells of those little Swiss churches sounding out on a Sunday morning in the chill mountain air.
Malcolm Muggeridge, CHRONICLES OF WASTED TIME 1972

6 His voice was intimate as the rustle of sheets.
Dorothy Parker, DUSK BEFORE FIREWORKS

7 She possessed a voice that, like a mill, ground silence into its component parts.
Sir Osbert Sitwell, THE SCARLET TREE 1945

8 Mr. [Michael] Foot sounded like an affronted peke.
Honor Tracy, Daily Telegraph 12 *May* 1979

9 He spoke with a certain what-is-it in his voice, and I could tell that, if not actually disgruntled, he was far from being gruntled.
P. G. Wodehouse, CODE OF THE WOOSTERS 1938

VOLUNTEER

10 To qualify as a member of the Women's Royal Voluntary Service you need to be able to wear a cardigan and jumper and a rope of pearls and to have had a hysterectomy.
Stella, Lady Reading, chairman of WRVS, *in an address to members*

VOTE

11 What's the point of having a vote if there is nobody worth voting for.
Sheila MacLeod, Sunday Times, *Look* 26 *Jul* 1981

12 Actually I vote Labour, but my butler's a Tory.
Lord Mountbatten, to a Tory canvasser during the 1945 *election*

13 It's not the voting that's democracy; it's the counting.
Tom Stoppard, JUMPERS

14 I shall not vote because I do not aspire to advise my sovereign on the choice of her servants.
Evelyn Waugh, A LITTLE ORDER

VULGARITY

15 The need to be right — the sign of a vulgar mind.
Albert Camus, NOTEBOOKS 1935–42

16 It is disgusting to pick your teeth. What is vulgar is to use a gold toothpick.
Louis Kronenberger, THE CAT AND THE HORSE

W

WALES

1 The land of my fathers. And my fathers can
have it.
*Dylan Thomas. Quoted in the biography of
him by John Ackerman*

2 There are still parts of Wales where the
only concession to gaiety is a striped
shroud.
Gwyn Thomas, Punch 18 *Jan* 1958

3 The girls of Blaenau Ffestiniog / Can be
had for a penny (Welsh: *ceiniog*) / This I
know for a fact / I was caught in the act / By
Lord Hailsham (formerly Mr. Quintiniog)
*Wynford Vaughan Thomas. Quoted Alan
Watkins*, Observer 13 *May* 1979

4 We can trace almost all the disasters of
English history to the influence of Wales.
Evelyn Waugh, DECLINE AND FALL 1928

WALKING

5 It is a fact that not once in all my life have I
gone out for a walk. I have been taken out
for walks; but that is another matter.
Sir Max Beerbohm, GOING OUT FOR A
WALK 1918

6 I enjoy my legs crunching the pebbles
under my feet — the way I used to enjoy
crunching a crust of bread when I had teeth.
Bernard Berenson (at 90), SUNSET AND
TWILIGHT

7 He walks as if balancing the family tree on
his nose.
Raymond Morley

8 Walking is the favourite sport of the good
and the wise.
A. L. Rowse, THE USE OF HISTORY

WILLIAM WALTON

9 Walton wrote 'Balshazzar's Feast' in that
barn out there. He made such a frightful din
on the piano we had to banish him from the
house.
*Sacheverell Sitwell. Quoted Alan Hamil-
ton*, The Times, *profile* 16 *Nov* 1982

WAR

10 What price Glory?
Maxwell Anderson, title of play 1924

11 The only defence is offence, which means
that you have to kill more women and
children more quickly than the enemy if
you wish to save yourselves.
Stanley Baldwin, House of Commons, Nov
1932

12 It takes twenty years or more of peace to
make a man, it takes only twenty seconds of
war to destroy him.
*King Baudouin of the Belgians, addressing
US Congress* 12 *May* 1959

13 I have never understood this liking for war.
It panders to instincts already catered for
within the scope of any respectable domestic establishment.
Alan Bennett, FORTY YEARS ON

14 I was not anxious to go.
Edmund Blunden, opening words of
UNDERTONES OF WAR 1928

15 War is like love. It always finds a way.
Bertolt Brecht, MOTHER COURAGE AND
HER CHILDREN 1939

16 Nothing on this earth is perfect — a war of
which we could say it left nothing to be
desired will probably never exist.
Id.

17 I wanted the experience of war. I thought
there would be no more wars.
*Joyce Cary, on being asked why he had
gone to the Balkan War in* 1912

18 Wars, conflict, it's all business. One
murder makes a villain. Millions a hero.
Numbers sanctify.
Charles Chaplin, MONSIEUR VERDOUX
(film)

19 We must be careful not to assign to this
deliverance (at Dunkirk) the attributes of a
victory. Wars are not won by evacuations.
Winston Churchill, THEIR FINEST HOUR
1949

1 Be calm! Nobody is ever wounded twice on the same day.
Winston Churchill, shortly before his capture by Boers

2 The only time in his life he [Marshal Joffre] ever put up a fight was when we asked him for his resignation.
Georges Clemençeau. Quoted A. M. Thomson, HERE I LIE 1937

3 War is too important to be left to the generals.
Georges Clemençeau. Quoted J. M. Keynes, ESSAYS IN BIOGRAPHY

4 We are not at war with Egypt. We are in a state of armed conflict.
Anthony Eden, House of Commons 4 Nov 1956

5 There is nothing that war has ever achieved that we could not better achieve without it.
Havelock Ellis, THE PHILOSOPHY OF CONFLICT

6 Men love war because it allows them to look serious. Because it is the one thing that stops women laughing at them.
John Fowles, THE MAGUS 1965

7 Either man is obsolete, or war is.
R. Buckminster Fuller, I SEEM TO BE A VERB

8 The English do not treat very kindly the men who conduct their wars for them.
Joseph Goebbels, DIARIES

9 I'd like to see the government get out of war altogether and leave the whole feud to private industry.
Joseph Heller, CATCH 22

10 In starting and waging a war it is not right that matters but victory.
Adolf Hitler. Quoted W. L. Sherer, THE RISE AND FALL OF THE THIRD REICH

11 Old men declare war. But it is the youth that must fight and die.
Herbert C. Hoover. Speech 27 Jun 1944

12 The statistics of suicide show that, for non-combatants at least, life is more interesting in war than in peace.
W. R. Inge (Dean of St. Pauls), THE END OF AN AGE 1918

13 War should belong to the tragic past, to history: it should find no place on humanity's agenda for the future.
Pope John Paul II, Coventry 1982

14 War alone brings up to their highest tension all human energies and imposes the stamp of nobility upon the peoples who have the courage to make it.
Benito Mussolini, ENCYCLOPEDIA ITALIANE 1932

15 The only alternative to co-existence is co-destruction.
Pandit Nehru. Quoted Observer 29 Aug 1954

16 The shrill demented choirs of wailing shells / And buglers calling for them from sad shires.
Wilfred Owen, ANTHEM FOR DOOMED YOUTH 1920

17 What passing bells for those who die as cattle? / Only the monstrous anger of the guns / Only the stuttering rifle's rapid rattle / Can patter out their hasty orisons.
Id.

18 Red lips are not so red / As the stained stones kissed by the English dead.
Wilfred Owen, GREATER LOVE 1920

19 All wars are planned by old men / In council rooms apart.
Grantland Rice, TWO SIDES OF WAR

20 I discovered to my amazement that average men and women were delighted at the prospect of war. I had fondly imagined what most pacifists contended, that wars were forced upon a reluctant population by despotic and Machiavellian governments.
Bertrand Russell, AUTOBIOGRAPHY 1967

21 War is not an adventure. It is a disease. It is like typhus.
Antoine de Saint-Exupéry, FLIGHT TO ARRAS 1942

22 Sometime they'll give a war and no one will come.
Carl Sandburg, THE PEOPLE, *Yes* 1936

23 When the rich wage war it is the poor who die.
Jean-Paul Sartre, THE DEVIL AND THE GOOD LORD 1951

24 All wars are popular for the first thirty days.
Arthur Schlesinger Jr. Quoted Barbara Rowe, A BOOK OF QUOTES

25 Wars come because not enough people are sufficiently afraid.
Hugh Schonfield, Peace News. Quoted News Review 26 Feb 1948

1 Nothing is ever done in this world until men are prepared to kill each other if it is not done.
George Bernard Shaw, MAJOR BARBARA 1905

2 They start bloody wars they can't afford. Chamberlain . . . didn't give a thought to the cost of it — didn't enter his head to get an estimate — soppy old sod.
Johnny Speight, BBC TV, *Till Death Us Do Part*

3 War is capitalism with the gloves off.
Tom Stoppard, TRAVESTIES

4 The military don't start wars. The politicians start wars.
Gen. William Westmorland. Quoted Barbara Rowe, A BOOK OF QUOTES

5 Bombs are unbelievable until they actually fall.
Patrick White, RIDERS IN THE CHARIOT

6 For Hon. Members opposite the deterrent is a phallic symbol. It convinces them that they are men.
George Wigg MP, House of Commons 1964

7 It takes only one gramme of explosive to kill a man, so why waste five tons?
Solly Zuckermann, FROM APES TO WARLORDS

WASTE

8 Nature is as wasteful of promising young men as she is of fish spawn.
Richard Hughes, THE FOX IN THE ATTIC 1961

9 Nothing is surely a waste of time when one enjoys the day.
Arthur Koestler. Quoted Observer, *Sayings of the Week* 8 Oct 1972

10 The biggest waste of water in the country by far is when you spend half a pint and flush two gallons.
Philip, Duke of Edinburgh in a speech 1965

EVELYN WAUGH

11 He had the sharp eye of a Hogarth alternating with that of the ancient mariner.
Harold Acton, ADAM

12 He drank port and put on weight, and attempted to behave in the manner of an Edwardian aristocrat . . . In fact Evelyn's abiding complex and the source of much of his misery was that he was not a six-foot tall extremely handsome and rich duke.
Cecil Beaton, THE STRENUOUS YEARS

13 The satire of Evelyn Waugh in his early books was derived from his ignorance of life. He found cruel things funny because he did not understand them and he was able to communicate that fun.
Cyril Connolly, ENEMIES OF PROMISE 1938

WEALTH

14 A rich man is one who isn't afraid to ask the salesman to show him something cheaper.
Anon. Ladies Home Journal, *Jan* 1946

15 Lord Finchley tried to mend the electric light / It struck him dead and serve him right. / It is the business of the wealthy man / To give employment to the artisan.
Hilaire Belloc, CAUTIONARY TALES 1907

16 The confidence inspired by the possession of a well-filled vault of silver will last an ordinary person a lifetime.
Ernest Bramah, KAI LUNG UNROLLS HIS MAT 1928

17 The rich have fallen into bleak disapproval. In the age of egalitarianism it is assumed that no one should have very much more than anyone else, unless he wins it in a football pool.
William Davis, NO SIN TO BE RICH 1976

18 Wealth is not without its advantages and the case to the contrary, although it has often been made, has never proved widely persuasive.
J. K. Galbraith, THE AFFLUENT SOCIETY 1958

19 I don't know how many millions I am worth. If you can actually count your money you are not a really rich man.
Paul Getty. Quoted Bernard Levin, THE PENDULUM YEARS 1976

20 The rich hate signing cheques. Hence the success of credit cards.
Graham Greene, DR. FISCHER OF GENEVA

21 I have a prejudice against people with money. I have known so many, and none have escaped the corruption of power. In this I am a purist. I love people motivated by love and not by power. If you have money and power, and are motivated by love, you give it all away.
Anaïs Nin, DIARIES, VOL 4 1970

1 God shows his contempt for wealth by the kind of person he selects to receive it.
Austin O'Malley

2 You can tell how wealthy they are. They even have fruit on the sideboard when no one is poorly.
Contestant describing her employers to Wilfred Pickles in radio show Have a Go

3 I believe the power to make money is a gift of God.
J. D. Rockefeller. Quoted Matthew Josephson, THE ROBBER BARONS

4 I am a millionaire. That is my religion.
George Bernard Shaw, MAJOR BARBARA 1905

5 If all the rich people in the world divided up their money among themselves there wouldn't be enough to go round.
Christina Stead, HOUSE OF ALL NATIONS

6 There is nothing sinful about being rich. My fortune is as large as my credit rating is limitless.
Lord Thomson of Fleet

7 Until the age of twelve I sincerely believed that everybody had a house on Fifth Avenue, a villa in Newport and a steam-driven, ocean-going yacht.
Cornelius Vanderbilt Jr., FAREWELL TO FIFTH AVENUE

8 People are seldom so harmlessly engaged as when they are working to become rich. It is a far less damaging occupation than the pursuit of political power. The rich tend to be ashamed of their riches, but politicians are never ashamed of themselves, though they should be.
Woodrow Wyatt, Observer 17 Oct 1976

WEAPON

9 Our scientific power has outrun our spiritual power. We have guided missiles and misguided men.
Martin Luther King, STRENGTH TO LOVE 1963

10 A bayonet is a weapon with a worker at both ends.
Pacifist slogan between the world wars

11 And this you can see is the bolt. The purpose of this / Is to open the breech, as you can see. We can slide it / Rapidly backwards and forwards; we call this / Easing the spring.
Herbert Reed, LESSONS OF THE WAR, *Naming of Parts* 1946

WEATHER

12 We regret we are unable to give you the weather. We rely on weather reports from the airport, which is closed because of the weather. Whether we are able to give you the weather tomorrow depends on the weather.
Arab News, Jan 1979. Quoted Stephen Pile, THE BOOK OF HEROIC FAILURES

WELFARE STATE

13 There is the fundamental paradox of the welfare state; that it is not built for the desperate, but for those who are already capable of helping themselves.
Michael Harrington, THE OTHER AMERICA

H. G. WELLS

14 All Wells' characters are as flat as a photograph and agitated with such vigour that we forget their complexities lie on the surface and would disappear if it was scratched or curled up.
E. M. Forster, ASPECTS OF THE NOVEL 1927

15 A history of humanity to the present time in which Shakespeare is not mentioned and Jesus is dismissed in a page carelessly, as if not worth contempt, shocks me.
Frank Harris, MY LIFE AND LOVES 1927

16 Whatever Wells writes is not only alive, but kicking.
Henry James. Quoted G. K. Chesterton, AUTOBIOGRAPHY

17 He is the old maid among novelists; even the sex obsession that lay clotted on Anne Veronica and the New Machiavelli like cold white sauce was merely old maid's mania, the reaction towards the flesh of a mind too long absorbed in airships and colloids.
Rebecca West. Quoted Jill Craigie, The Times 6 Dec 1982

MAE WEST

18 I've been in *Who's Who*, and I know what's what, but this is the first time I ever made the dictionary.
Mae West, on having a World War II life jacket named after her

19 She stole everything but the camera.
George Raft, after co-starring with her

WICKEDNESS

1 It takes a certain courage and a certain greatness even to be truly base.
Jean Anouilh, ARDELE 1948

2 The belief in a supernatural source of evil is not necessary, men alone are quite capable of every sort of wickedness.
Joseph Conrad, UNDER WESTERN EYES 1911

3 A good man can be stupid and still be good. But a bad man must have brains.
Maxim Gorky, THE LOWER DEPTHS

WIFE

4 Obviously a wife is worth something because she has attracted another man. Therefore she has some value, and must have had some value in the eyes of her husband.
Judge Essenhigh, in a divorce action. Quoted News Review 13 Feb 1947

5 Always see a fellow's weak point in his wife.
James Joyce, ULYSSES 1922

6 A loving wife will do anything for her husband except stop criticising and trying to improve him.
J. B. Priestley, RAIN ON GODSHILL

7 Marriage is for women the commonest mode of livelihood, and the total amount of undesired sex endured by women is probably greater in marriage than in prostitution.
Bertrand Russell, MARRIAGE AND MORALS, Prostitution 1929

HAROLD WILSON

8 If Harold has a fault it is that he will smother everything with H.P. sauce
Mrs. Harold Wilson in an interview 1962

WOODROW WILSON

9 A slim bespectacled man with a long jaw and the contained self-assurance of a bishop.
Alistair Cooke, AMERICA

10 Like Odysseus, he looked wiser when seated.
J. M. Keynes. Quoted Robert L. Heilbroner, THE WORLDLY PHILOSOPHERS

11 The air currents of the world never ventilated his mind.
Walter Hines Page. Quoted Patrick Devlin, TOO PROUD TO FIGHT, WOODROW WILSON'S NEUTRALITY

WIND

12 Wind moving through grass so that the grass quivers. This moves me with an emotion I don't even understand.
Katherine Mansfield, JOURNALS 1928

DUCHESS OF WINDSOR

13 Wallis is a very vulgar woman in gesture, she sticks her beautifully scented face within two inches and just asks to be kissed, only of course you don't do it.
Lord Eccles, BY SAFE HAND, LETTERS OF DAVID AND SYBIL ECCLES 1939–42, 1983

WINE

14 This wine is too good for toast-drinking, my dear. You don't want to mix emotions up with a wine like that. You lose the taste.
Ernest Hemingway, THE SUN ALSO RISES 1926

15 It's a Naive Domestic Burgundy, Without Any Breeding. But I think you'll be Amused by its Presumption.
James Thurber, cartoon caption, MEN, WOMEN AND DOGS 1943

WISDOM

16 *Judge:* I have read your case, Mr. Smith and am no wiser now than I was when I started.
F. E. Smith: Possibly not my Lord; but far better informed.
Lord Birkenhead. Quoted Second Earl of Birkenhead, LIFE OF F. E. SMITH

17 If one is too lazy to think, too vain to do a thing badly, too cowardly to admit it, one will never attain wisdom.
Cyril Connolly, THE UNQUIET GRAVE 1945

18 Knowledge can be communicated but not wisdom.
Hermann Hesse, SIDDHARTHA 1923

19 God grant me the serenity to accept the things I cannnot change, courage to change the things I can, and wisdom always to tell the difference.
Kurt Vonnegut, SLAUGHTERHOUSE-FIVE 1969

1 He was gifted with the sly, sharp instinct for self-preservation that passes for wisdom among the rich.
Evelyn Waugh, SCOOP 1938

WIT

2 There's a hell of a distance between wisecracking and wit. Wit has truth in it; wisecracking is simply callisthenics with words.
Dorothy Parker, WRITERS AT WORK *(ed. Malcolm Cowley)* 1958

P. G. WODEHOUSE

3 Literature's performing flea.
Sean O'Casey

4 There is no suggestion that either club man or girl would recognise a double bed except as so much extra sweat to make an apple pie of.
Richard Usborne, WODEHOUSE AT WORK 1961

5 For Mr. Wodehouse there has been no fall of man, no 'aboriginal calamity'. His characters have never tasted the forbidden fruit. They are still in Eden. The gardens of Blandings Castle are the original gardens from which we are all exiled.
Evelyn Waugh in a broadcast tribute to P. G. Wodehouse on his 80th birthday 1961

WOMAN

6 The sort of woman who, if accidentally locked in alone in the National Gallery, would start rearranging the pictures.
Anon.

7 One is not born a woman. One becomes one.
Simone de Beauvoir, THE SECOND SEX 1949

8 Intimacies between women often go backwards, beginning in revelations and ending in small talk without loss of esteem.
Elizabeth Bowen, THE DEATH OF THE HEART 1938

9 Certain women should be struck regularly, like gongs.
Noël Coward, PRIVATE LIVES 1930

10 Women never have young minds. They are born three thousand years old.
Shelagh Delaney, A TASTE OF HONEY 1958

11 Women are most fascinating between the ages of thirty-five and forty, after they have won a few races and know how to pace themselves. Since few women ever pass forty, maximum fascination can continue indefinitely.
Christian Dior, Colliers Magazine 10 *Jun* 1955

12 There are only three things to be done with a woman. You can love her, you can suffer for her, or you can turn her into literature.
Lawrence Durrell, JUSTINE 1957

13 All Berkshire women are very silly. I don't know why women in Berkshire are more silly than anywhere else.
Judge Claude Duveen, Reading County Court. Quoted Observer, *Sayings of the Week* 9 *Jul* 1972

14 As long as a woman's flesh is clean and healthy what does it matter what shape she is?
Ian Fleming, from his private notebooks

15 When a woman behaves like a man, why doesn't she behave like a nice man?
Dame Edith Evans. Quoted Observer 30 *Sep* 1956

16 A woman should be an illusion.
Ian Fleming. Quoted John Pearson, LIFE OF IAN FLEMING 1966

17 Women are equal because they are not different any more.
Eric Fromm, THE ART OF LOVING 1956

18 If men knew how women pass their time when they are alone, they'd never marry.
O. Henry, THE FOUR MILLION MEMOIRS OF A YELLOW DOG 1906

19 The female of the species is more deadly than the male.
Rudyard Kipling, THE FEMALE OF THE SPECIES 1921

20 A woman should open everything to a man except her mouth.
Derek Marlowe, A DANDY IN ASPIC 1966

21 The Professor of Gynaecology began his course of lectures as follows: Gentlemen, woman is an animal that micturates once a day, defecates once a week, menstruates once a month, parturates once a year and copulates whenever she has the opportunity.
W. Somerset Maugham, A WRITER'S NOTE-BOOK 1949

1 There are two kinds of women; those who want power in the world, and those who want power in bed.
Jacqueline Kennedy Onassis. Quoted Barbara Rowe, A BOOK OF QUOTES

2 Most good women are hidden treasures who are only safe because nobody looks for them.
Dorothy Parker. Quoted in her obituary, New York Times 8 *Jun* 1967

3 There are two kinds of women — goddesses and doormats.
Pablo Picasso. Quoted Barbara Rowe, A BOOK OF QUOTES

4 Women are like dreams — they are never the way you would like to have them.
Luigi Pirandello, EACH IN HIS OWN WAY

5 A woman is like a tea bag. Only when in hot water do you realise how strong she is.
Nancy Reagan, Observer, *Sayings of the Week* 29 *Mar* 1981

6 The doctors said at the time that she couldn't live more than a fortnight, and she's been trying ever since to see if she could. Women are so opinionated.
Saki, REGINALD ON WOMEN

7 Women are not so completely enslaved as farm stock.
George Bernard Shaw, GETTING MARRIED 1908

8 This Englishwoman is so refined / She has no bosom and no behind.
Stevie Smith, THIS ENGLISHWOMAN

9 The great and almost only comfort about being a woman is that one can always pretend to be more stupid than one is, and no one is surprised.
Freya Stark, THE VALLEY OF THE ASSASSINS 1934

WOMEN'S LIBERATION

10 We don't want revenge. We want promotion.
Sadie Roberts, Thames TV. *Quoted Elkan Allan*, The Times 21 *Aug* 1981

WONDER

11 To be surprised, to wonder, is to begin to understand.
José Ortega y Gasset, THE REVOLT OF THE MASSES 1930

VIRGINIA WOOLF

12 One of my *fears* — I don't think I was quite alone in this — was that one day she would speak to me (but she never did).
Hugo Dyson. Quoted Humphrey Carpenter, THE INKLINGS

13 I enjoyed talking to her, but thought *nothing* of her writing. I considered her "a beautiful little knitter".
Edith Sitwell, letter to G. Singleton 11 *Jul* 1955

WORD

14 Words, as is well known, are great foes of reality.
Joseph Conrad, UNDER WESTERN EYES, *Prologue* 1911

15 It's strange that words are so inadequate / Yet, like the asthmatic struggling for breath, / so the lover must struggle for words.
T. S. Eliot, THE ELDER STATESMAN 1958

16 You can stroke people with words.
F. Scott Fitzgerald, THE CRACK-UP 1945

17 Words build bridges into unexplored regions.
Adolf Hitler. Quoted Alan Bullock, HITLER, A STUDY IN TYRANNY

18 Isn't everyone consoled when faced with a trouble or fact he doesn't understand, by a word, some simple word, which tells us nothing and yet calms us.
Luigi Pirandello, SIX CHARACTERS IN SEARCH OF AN AUTHOR 1921

WORK

19 *Rich:* Do you know how much I have to show for seven months' work?
More: Work?
Rich: Work! Waiting is work when you wait as I wait, Lord!
Robert Bolt, A MAN FOR ALL SEASONS 1961

20 Whether our work is art or science or the daily work of society, it is only the form in which we explore our experience that is different.
Jacob Bronowski, SCIENCE AND HUMAN VALUES, *The Sense of Human Dignity* 1956

21 There is dignity in work only when it is work freely accepted.
Albert Camus, NOTEBOOKS 1935–1942

1 Work is more fun than fun.
Noël Coward. Quoted Cole Leslie, NOËL COWARD AND HIS FRIENDS

2 One of the saddest things is that the only thing a man can do for eight hours a day, day after day, is work. You can't eat eight hours a day, nor drink for eight hours a day, nor make love for eight hours.
William Faulkner, WRITERS AT WORK 1958

3 The idea that to make a man work you've got to hold gold in front of his eyes is a growth, not an axiom. We've done that for so long that we've forgotten there's any other way.
F. Scott Fitzgerald, THIS SIDE OF PARADISE 1920

4 When work is a pleasure, life is a joy! When work is a duty, life is slavery.
Maxim Gorky, THE LOWER DEPTHS 1903

5 Work is the greatest thing in the world, so we should always save some for tomorrow.
Don Herold. Quoted Frank Muir, ON CHILDREN

6 I haven't had time to work in weeks.
Jack Kerouac, ON THE ROAD 1957

7 Why should I let the toad *work* / Squat on my life? / Can't I use my wit as a pitchfork / And drive the brute off?
Philip Larkin, TOADS

8 Work is the province of cattle.
Dorothy Parker

9 Work expands to fill the time available for its completion. General recognition of this fact is shown in the proverbial phrase 'It is the busiest man who has time to spare.'
C. Northcote Parkinson, PARKINSON'S LAW 1962

10 Work is necessary for man. Man invented the alarm clock.
Pablo Picasso. Quoted Barbara Rowe, A BOOK OF QUOTES

11 I should have worked just long enough to discover that I didn't like it.
Paul Theroux. Quoted Alan Road, Observer magazine 1 *Apr* 1979

WORLD

12 The world is the mirror of myself dying.
Henry Miller, BLACK SPRING 1936

WORRY

13 He lives on a diet of fingernails and coffee.
May Livingstone of Jack Benny. Quoted Frederick Van Ryn, Redbook, *May* 1943

WRESTLING

14 Professional wrestling's most mystifying hold is on its audience.
Luke Neely, Saturday Evening Post 27 *Nov* 1953

WRITING

15 Writing comes more easily if you have something to say.
Sholem Asch, New York Herald Tribune 6 *Nov* 1955

16 As a rule, the sign that a beginner has genuine original talent is that he is more interested in playing with words than in saying something original.
W. H. Auden, THE DYER'S HAND AND OTHER ESSAYS 1962

17 Like the man who was complimented on the shortness of a speech and who remarked that he would have made it shorter if he'd had more time, I am a believer in economy of words.
Armiger Barclay (Countess Barcynska), T. P.'s Weekly 15 *Sep* 1938

18 To give an accurate and exhaustive account of that period would need a far less brilliant pen than mine.
Max Beerbohm, DIMINUENDO

19 If you cannot say what you have to say in twenty minutes go away and write a book about it.
Lord Brabazon. Speech 1956

20 To write is to become disinterested. There is a certain renunciation in art.
Albert Camus, NOTEBOOKS 1935–1942

21 Writing has laws of perspective, of light and shade, just as painting does, or music. If you are born knowing them, fine. If not, learn them. Then rearrange the rules to suit yourself.
Truman Capote, WRITERS AT WORK 1958

22 When I split an infinitive, God damn it, I split it so that it will stay split, and when I interrupt the velvety smoothness of my more or less literate syntax with a few sudden words of bar-room vernacular that

is done with the eyes wide open and the mind relaxed.
Raymond Chandler in a letter to his publisher. Quoted, RAYMOND CHANDLER SPEAKING

1 The health of a writer should not be too good, and perfect only in those periods of convalescence when he is not writing.
Cyril Connolly, ENEMIES OF PROMISE 1938

2 If, as Dr. Johnson said, a man who is not married is only half a man, so a man who is very much married is only half a writer.
Id.

3 I feel his books are all written in hotels with the bed unmade at the back of the chair.
Ronald Firbank, THE FLOWER BENEATH THE FOOT 1923

4 Writers aren't exactly people, or, if they're any good, they're a whole lot of people trying so hard to be one person.
F. Scott Fitzgerald, THE LAST TYCOON 1941

5 All good writing is *swimming under water* and holding your breath.
F. Scott Fitzgerald, in a letter

6 If I had to give young writers advice I would say don't listen to writers talking about writing or themselves.
Lillian Hellman, New York Times 21 *Feb* 1960

7 Writing, at its best, is a lonely life. Organisations for writers palliate his loneliness but I doubt if they improve his writing.
Ernest Hemingway, Nobel Prize Speech 10 *Dec* 1954

8 The fact that many people should be shocked by what he writes practically imposes it as a duty on a writer to go on shocking them.
Aldous Huxley, MUSIC AT NIGHT

9 A bad book is as much of a labour to write as a good one; it comes as sincerely from the author's soul.
Aldous Huxley, POINT COUNTER POINT 1928

10 So far as good writing goes, the use of the exclamation mark is a sign of failure. It is the literary equivalent of a man holding up a card reading LAUGHTER to a studio audience.
Miles Kington, Punch 18 *Aug* 1976

11 I like to write when I feel spiteful; it's like having a good sneeze.
D. H. Lawrence, letter to Cynthia Asquith, Nov 1913

12 All human activity to me is a way of avoiding writing. Thus, I sleep as much as possible or spend a hard day lying on the sofa.
Fran Lebowitz. Quoted in an interview with John Heilpern, Observer 21 *Jan* 1979

13 I stumbled on a form of writing that sets off recollections.
Laurie Lee in an interview with Philip Radcliffe, Observer 8 *Jan* 1979

14 It has been said that good prose should resemble the conversation of a well-bred man.
W. Somerset Maugham, THE SUMMING UP 1938

15 A writer is essentially a man who does not resign himself to loneliness.
François Mauriac, DIEU ET MAMMON 1929

16 Sin is the writer's element.
François Mauriac, SECOND THOUGHTS, *Literature and Sin* 1961

17 No man would set a word down on paper if he had the courage to live out what he believed in.
Henry Miller, SUNDAY AFTER THE WAR 1944

18 A writer is unfair to himself when he is unable to be hard on himself.
Marianne Moore, WRITERS AT WORK 1963

19 The writer is the Faust of modern society, the only surviving individualist in a mass age. To his orthodox contemporaries he seems a semi-madman.
Boris Pasternak, Observer 20 *Dec* 1959

20 "I do want you to meet Miss Leighton-Buzzard" said Mrs. Bovey-Tracey, asking me to dinner the other day. "She's such an interesting woman, and most unusual. She *doesn't write* you know."
William Plomer, ELECTRIC DELIGHTS

21 Our passions shape our books, repose writes them in the intervals.
Marcel Proust, REMEMBRANCE OF THINGS PAST, *Time Regained* 1927

22 He [Laurie Lee] writes, as he has always done, in pencil. Not just any pencil, but a 3B. "It doesn't make any noise", he says.
Philip Radcliffe, Observer 8 *Jan* 1979

1 Writing is not a profession but a vocation of unhappiness.
Georges Simenon, WRITERS AT WORK 1958

2 A born writer is born scrofulous; his career is an accident dictated by physical or circumstantial disabilities.
Dylan Thomas, letter to Pamela Hansford Johnson

3 You have to spend half your leisure in writing articles for the papers; the editors buy these because people buy your books, and people buy your books because they see your articles in the papers.
Evelyn Waugh, LABELS

4 I regard writing not as investigation of character but as an exercise in the use of language, and with this I am obsessed. I have no technical psychological interest. It is drama, speech and events that interest me.
Evelyn Waugh, PARIS REVIEW 1962

5 The fact that — these books — two novels, a book of travel, a biography, a work of contemporary history — never got beyond the first ten thousand words was testimony to the resilience of his character.
Evelyn Waugh, PUT OUT MORE FLAGS 1942

6 I constantly rewrite — an incinerator is a writer's best friend.
Thornton Wilder, New York Times 6 *Nov* 1961

7 Literature is strewn with the wreckage of men who have minded beyond reason the opinion of others.
Virginia Woolf, A ROOM OF ONE'S OWN 1929

350

Y

W. B. YEATS

1 Earth, receive an honoured guest / William Yeats is laid to rest / Let the Irish vessel lie / Emptied of its poetry.
W. H. Auden, IN MEMORY OF W. B. YEATS 1940

2 I left him in my room to himself and at lunch time he told me he had done an excellent morning's work having written four lines and destroyed them.
John Drinkwater, DISCOVERY

3 I am too old for Yeats, just as I am too old to hear the cry of a bat.
G. W. Lyttelton, THE LYTTELTON HART-DAVIS LETTERS 20 *Nov* 1955

YOUTH

4 All evil comes from the old. They grow fat on ideas and young men die of them.
Jean Anouilh, CATCH AS CATCH CAN 1960

5 If age, which is certainly / As wicked as youth, looks any wiser / It is only that youth is still able to believe / It will get away with anything, while age / Knows only too well that it has got away with nothing.
W. H. Auden, THE SEA AND THE MIRROR 1945

6 The only thing I regret about my past life is the length of it. If I had my past life over again I'd make all the same mistakes — only sooner.
Talullah Bankhead. Quoted, The Times 28 *Jul* 1981

7 Americans began by loving youth and now, out of self-pity, they worship it.
Jacques Barzun, THE HOUSE OF INTELLECT 1959

8 Youth is like spring, an overpraised season.
Samuel Butler, THE WAY OF ALL FLESH 1903

9 It is typically the most sensitive and intelligent of the young who become revolutionaries, destroyers.
Joyce Cary, ART AND REALITY

10 If youth did not matter so much to itself it would never have the heart to go on.
Willa Cather, SONG OF THE LARK 1915

11 "And youth is cruel, and has no remorse / And smiles at situations which it cannot see." / I smile of course, / And go on drinking tea.
T. S. Eliot, PORTRAIT OF A LADY 1917

12 Everybody's youth is a dream, a form of chemical madness.
F. Scott Fitzgerald, THE DIAMOND AS BIG AS THE RITZ

13 I never dared be radical when young, for fear it would make me conservative when old.
Robert Frost, PRECAUTION

14 The American ideal is youth — handsome, empty youth.
Henry Miller, THE WISDOM OF THE HEART, Raimu 1941

15 Youth is a malady of which one becomes cured a little every day.
Benito Mussolini, on his 50th birthday

16 Youth does not require reasons for living, only pretexts.
José Ortega y Gasset, THE REVOLT OF THE MASSES 1930

17 All that the young can do for the old [is] to shock them and keep them up to date.
George Bernard Shaw, FANNIE'S FIRST PLAY 1912

18 All youth is bound to be misspent, there is something in its very nature that makes it so, and that is why all men regret it.
Thomas Wolfe, OF TIME AND THE RIVER 1935

Z

ZEST

1 What hunger is in relation to food, zest is in relation to life.
Bertrand Russell, THE CONQUEST OF HAPPINESS 1930

ZOO

2 The sort of man who likes to spend his time watching a cage of monkeys chase one another, or a lizard catch flies, or a lion gnaw its tail, is precisely the sort of man whose mental weakness should be combatted at the public expense, and not fostered.
H. L. Mencken, New York Evening Mail 2 *Feb* 1918

Index

Quotation references are given by page, followed by the number of the quotation on that page. The latter appears in italics where the person indexed is being referred to in the quotation rather than quoting.

357

359